Journeys Through Philosophy

A Classical Introduction
Revised Edition

Edited by Nicholas Capaldi,
Eugene Kelly,
and Luis E. Navia

PB Prometheus Books
Buffalo, N.Y. 14215

Published 1982 by Prometheus Books
700 East Amherst Street, Buffalo, New York 14215

Library of Congress Card Number 81-85574
ISBN 0-87975-171-1

Printed in the United States of America

Contents

Journeys Through Philosophy

Chapter I—Introduction

What is Philosophy?

In the study of any discipline, the first question that should be kept in mind is the definition of its name. It is, therefore, wise to begin by attempting to give a clear, concise definition of philosophy, as a guide for our subsequent questions. Unfortunately, in the case of philosophy, there are certain initial problems which make the task of arriving at a satisfactory definition somewhat difficult. Different philosophers have given different definitions of their discipline, and in different historical times diverse understandings of its meaning have been entertained. The situation is otherwise with the sciences, which have generally accepted definitions. When, for example, we undertake the study of astronomy, we know perfectly well what it entails, what its limitations are, and what its general objectives should be. We know that the astronomer studies and investigates the positions, movements, structure, and origin of such bodies as the moon, the planets, the sun, and stars, and nebulae, and the galaxies. The methods of the astronomer are clearly understood, and the relationship between astronomy and the other physical sciences can be grasped from the very beginning, even though in the elaboration of its principles and in the organization of its data, changes may have to be introduced from time to time.

In trying to define philosophy, however, we often find ourselves in a predicament. To begin with, practically everybody has used the term "philosophy" at one time or another, as when we speak of the "philosophy of an educational institution," "the philosophy of the democratic party," "a philosophical attitude toward life," and so on. In this context, we probably have in mind the general principles on which an educational institution operates, the ideological basis of the democratic party, and the certain unemotional attitude with which this or that person faces the vicissitudes of life.

We are also aware that some of the most influential historical people of Western Civilization have been "philosophers," and although we may not be quite sure of what this means, we do not hesitate to refer to Plato, Aristotle, Descartes, and Einstein as "philosophers." The same can be said about many eminent individuals who belong to non-Western traditions. Buddha is said to have been a "great philosopher," and the moralistic sayings of Confucius are classified as "philosophical."

Lastly, we know that practically every major university has a "philosophy department" which offers courses in philosophy, and in which students study strange sounding subjects like epistemology, metaphysics, ontology, logic, ethics, cosmology, aesthetics, political philosophy, and the like. The instructors of these courses refer to themselves as "professional philosophers," which simply means that they have received a degree in philosophy which allows them to make a living by "teaching philosophy." Their degrees are usually doctoral degrees which permit them to add to their names the letters "Ph.D."

But we also know other instructors who use the same letters, and who are in no way related to philosophy. A person with a degree in economics, psychology, sociology, mathematics, or astronomy, also holds a Ph.D., which means literally *doctor philosophiae* or "doctor of philosophy." Why should other instructors have the same degree as the professional philosophers? Is economics, perhaps, a part of philosophy? In what sense can the astronomer call himself a philosopher?

In order to understand this curious circumstance in the academic world, we must briefly review some aspects of the history of the term "philosophy." Until the beginning of the twentieth century, any human activity which sought to shed light on the nature of the universe in general and man in particular was deemed to be a part of philosophy. All the theoretical sciences were seen as integral parts of one and the same human endeavor, to gain knowledge; and regardless of the specific interest of each human being involved, it was an established practice to classify them as philosophic. Philosophy was then regarded as a common name that applied to all the sciences. One example will illustrate this custom.

The name of Isaac Newton (1642-1727) is familiar to those who study the physical sciences. Indeed, Newton made so profound an impact on the development of the sciences that we can safely look upon him as one of the most decisive influences in Western Civilization. He was, above all, a mathematician, and to him we owe one of the earliest and most revealing formulations of the principles of calculus. He also was a physicist, and as such, he left us the first coherent statement of the law of gravitation. But he was an astronomer too, whose main concern was the structure of the universe, the principles of celestial mechanics, the nature of the sun, and other crucially important astronomical problems. He dealt extensively with astrology and magic through which he attempted to gain a better understanding of reality. He was concerned with the nature of time and space, and formulated an impressive system of cosmology which exercised a tremendous influence for more than a century. And yet, he regarded himself above all as a "philosopher." To him, all his varied interests were truly "philosophic," and he would have found it difficult to answer questions such as, "Are you a philosopher *or* an astronomer?" In fact, the very title of his masterpiece gave ample testimony of this. He entitled it *Mathematical Principles of Natural Philosophy,* where the term *natural philosophy* signified the investigation of the physical world.

We find a similar situation in the cases of most philosophers and men of science until the beginning of the twentieth century. The currently accepted distinction between philosophy on the one hand, and the sciences on the other, simply did not exist. Philosophy was regarded as the matrix out of which the sciences developed. This is, therefore, the origin of the custom of conferring upon economists, psychologists, sociologists, mathematicians, astronomers, and other theoretical scientists, the degree of "doctor of philosophy."

Today, however, we find ourselves in a different situation. With the overwhelming development of the sciences in the nineteenth century, scientists saw themselves compelled to become highly specialized in some limited realm of theoretical knowledge, and specialization, among other things, forced the sciences to grow increasingly apart from one another, and from what began to be known as "academic philosophy." In the twentieth century, the scientist does not refer to himself as a "philosopher," his Ph.D. notwithstanding, but neither does the academic philosopher generally call himself a scientist. As we will see later, this virtual divorce between philosophy and the sciences is both fortunate and unfortunate, as its effects are both good and bad.

It is fortunate inasmuch as it has given rise to a group of people among us who devote themselves almost exclusively to examining certain general problems of man's experience of the universe and of himself, from which some advantages have been derived. Much attention has been paid on the part of academic philosophers to issues related to the analysis of language, the overall methodology of the sciences, the nature and limits of human knowledge, the grounds for belief and disbelief in the existence of God, the general structure of the human self, the basis of moral values, the fundamental character of the universe, and other problems that are today considered to be the specific domain of philosophy. Furthermore, the separation of the sciences from philosophy has permitted scientists to become immersed in the more immediate issues of their disciplines, leaving for others the investigation of more comprehensive questions.

But, indeed, it is unfortunate, insofar as it has given birth to many academic philosophers among us who know little or nothing of what is going on in the sciences. It is possible to complete a doctoral degree in philosophy without ever having studied anything about the structure of the physical universe or about the basis of Darwinian evolution, so that often the statements made by contemporary philosophers about the universe are grounded on the most precarious foundations. Moreover, our scientists have become so preoccupied with the specific branches of their respective disciplines that they overlook the fact that all things are related. They lack, accordingly, the comprehensive vision which characterized Newton, Kant, Schopenhauer, Hume, and other earlier philosophers and scientists. They have become myopic and see the world only from the limited perspective of their limited interests, and eventually they develop into scientific technicians who think that a statistical table, a stuffed monkey, or the gadgets of a laboratory reveal at once this world in which, as St. Paul said, "we live, move, and have our being."

In order to avoid as much as possible the limited character which is inherent in many manifestations of contemporary philosophy and science, we have decided to expose students to readings of classical philosophers, that is to say, philosophers whose vision was comprehensive and penetrating. From these great thinkers we still have much to learn. It is undeniable that our technological and scientific progress has no counterpart in what pertains to man's understanding of himself and the universe. And yet, in many ways, we have not advanced one inch beyond the ancient Greeks, and the grave questions which they faced more than two thousand years ago are still unanswered. We have gone endlessly around the very same point around which they moved, but our real progress has been minimal. Perhaps this is the unavoidable predicament of human beings who find themselves in the midst of an immense universe, immense in terms of both time and space, while they are allotted only a very small time on an insignificant planet called the earth. Human reason, as Immanuel Kant (1724-1804) once said, is condemned to a most peculiar fate inasmuch as it is constantly beset with questions which it cannot avoid but which it cannot answer. The confrontation with these unavoidable and yet perhaps unanswerable questions; the perennial search for adequate and satisfying answers; the titanic struggle of the mind to reach a reasonable plateau of understanding; the necessity to introduce sense and order into the wilderness of existence; the hope that beneath the mantle of disorder and confusion, the universe is still rational and logical—this is what traditionally has been called philosophy. It is in a literal sense a collection of journeys through the strange land of ideas and speculations. It always begins, as Aristotle observed, with a disquieting feeling of wonder about the meaning of things.

This innate sense of wonder which appears to be an essential quality of every healthy human being is often crushed under the weight of dogmatism. Moved by an understandable urge to appease its questioning, the mind takes refuge in solutions that introduce supernatural explanations, acts of faith, traditional commitments, or ritualistic practices, with the support of which the mind no longer has to cope with the enigma of existence. Indeed, it is apparently better to stifle within us our tendency to question the multitude of experiences that flow daily into our consciousness. God, soul, death, time, space, moral values—all these become reduced to impertinent issues, as soon as we have accepted categorical statements and pontifical truths that others have uttered and defended.

The philosopher, however, is never at home among such statements. The very term *philosophy* clearly conveys the nature of his quest. This term appears to have been coined by the Greek mathematician Pythagoras of Samos (572-497 B.C.). It comes from two Greek words, *philos,* which means "yearning," and *sophia,* which means "wisdom." Philosophy is, then, a yearning after wisdom. The Greeks of Pythagoras' time distinguished those who claimed to know from those who were merely seeking to know. The former were called "sophists," which means simply "wise people." The latter became known as "philosophers." The former had at their disposal a finished body of knowledge which was available in the form of wise sayings, traditional beliefs, and superstitious ideas about practically everything. They *knew* or thought they knew, and in this proud conviction, they imparted their knowledge to others. For them, all human questions were answerable in terms of gods, mythological accounts, magical incantations, socially acceptable practices, and authoritarian pronouncements.

The birth of philosophy took place when the first human being decided to liberate himself from the sages or sophists. When the first thinking-individual chose not to dance, so to speak, around the tribal fire where the others sat submissively to hear the sterile wisdom of the sophists, the initial journey of philosophy began. This must have taken place countless times among all sorts of people of antiquity, perhaps long before written records began to be made. But our knowledge of the history of mankind is so limited that we cannot speak meaningfully about these forgotten births of philosophy. This is why we must turn our attention to ancient Greece; we have sufficient historical records, and there is a direct line of intellectual continuity between the Greeks and us.

The first Greek thinker whose philosophical ideas have come down to us was a man named Thales (sixth century B.C.). We know little about his life, and none of his writings has withstood the passage of time. We do know, however, that he predicted successfully and explained correctly an eclipse of the sun that took place in the year 585 B.C. He was born in Miletus, a city on the coast of Turkey founded by the Athenians some two hundred years before his birth. He traveled extensively, and had a long sojourn in Egypt. As in the case of other Greek philosophers who visited Egypt (Pythagoras, Plato, and others), it is practically impossible to tell how much Thales learned from the Egyptians.

The importance of Thales in the history of philosophy cannot be exaggerated. In the few fragments concerning his philosophy that have survived (fragments that are really later quotations from other writers), we discern at once a powerful mind dominated by a yearning after wisdom. The principles of his philosophy constitute a clear example of what a philosophical attitude toward the world should be. In the first place, he made every attempt to explain the universe in strictly rational and human terms, thereby avoiding any appeal to supernatural entities such as gods or invisible forces. He was convinced that nature was thoroughly explainable, that is to say, completely rational, and that its apparently mysterious character was the result of human limitations and prejudices. This led him to postulate the reality of certain inflexible laws according to which events take place. Nothing in nature happens by mere chance;

nothing in nature is the work of whimsical gods and demons who play with human beings as a child plays with worthless toys. There is, then, a universal regularity in all that happens. An eclipse of the sun, for example, is a natural event brought about by natural causes, and as such, it is both predictable and explainable. The understanding of nature is, therefore, possible if we are able to grasp the *principles* of its operation.

Here we can see how the philosophical mind is not satisfied with the apparently senseless concatenation of events and accidents that surround us daily. The philosopher goes beyond the mantle of sense impressions and experiences, and asks, What is it that underlies all events? Are there any universal principles, in compliance with which all things take place? Even if there are gods who watch over the affairs of human beings, these gods have to operate within the frame of universal principles.

Thales attempted to formulate these principles by postulating a universal substance of which all things are the manifestations. Beneath the multiplicity of things, he thought, there had to exist a primordial *element*, something basic, which gave rise to them. He arrived at the conclusion that this element was *water*. Water, he believed, turns into ice, vapor, air, earth, or fire, depending on the changes of temperature which it undergoes; but regardless of its deceptive appearance, it remains water, no more, no less. Moreover, he reasoned that if in reality the gods of religious beliefs exist, they too are made of water.

It is obvious that the philosophy of Thales presents to us a system of mechanistic materialism in which matter, or rather water, constitutes everything. We will see, in subsequent chapters, how this was revised and challenged by Thales' successors, and how within two hundred years it was fully transformed. It is important to bear in mind that in the history of philosophy there are no inflexible dogmas and no infallible masters. A text like the Bible does not have a counterpart in the world of philosophy. Accordingly, those who inherited Thales' teachings felt perfectly free to question not only his conclusions about water and his astronomical ideas, but the very principles on which his thought stood. Anaximander of Miletus (sixth century B.C.) spoke of the evolution of the species and of the multiplicity of earths in space, and rejected Thales' preference for water as the basic element. According to Anaximander, the basic element was a nameless substance, much too subtle to be observed, which he named "the boundless." Anaximenes of Miletus, a contemporary of Anaximander, replaced the boundless with ordinary air. Pythagoras, of whom we spoke earlier, maintained that numbers were the fundamental elements of things, and introduced a spiritual realm of being which would have been totally foreign to Thales. Heraclitus of Ephesus (536-470 B.C.) became convinced that the primordial substance was fire, and that the universal law was eternal change. Empedocles of Sicily (490-430 B.C.) spoke of the basic element as being fourfold: air, water, earth, and fire, and Anaxagoras (about 430 B.C.) conceived of an infinite number of elements. By the time of Socrates (469-399 B.C.), the original ideas of Thales were practically unrecognizable. They had been subjected to the merciless questioning of philosophers.

But let us return for a moment to these ideas. Indeed, to say that "everything is water" does appear to be a most unsophisticated utterance, something which only a fool could say. Don't we see many things around us that are evidently not water? How could Thales have believed that earth, fire, air, and other things are really water? It is curious to observe, however, that if our present understanding of the universe is correct, Thales' contention is almost correct. We believe that ninety percent of the observable universe is hydrogen, and that the other ten percent (helium, oxygen, nitrogen, and the rest of the elements) is the result of transformations undergone by primitive hydrogen. Our understanding of the physical processes that go on in the stars has led us to this conclusion. Now then, water itself is mostly hydrogen (two atoms of hydrogen and one atom of oxygen). Hence we must conclude that the most prevailing constituent of water is also the most prevailing constituent of the universe. Thales' mistake, if one can talk here about "mistakes," was due to his inadequate knowledge concerning the chemical composition of water. In spite of this, however, he was practically correct in his choosing water as the fundamental substance that underlies all things.

The appearance of Thales and the other early Greek philosophers constitutes an extraordinary event in the history of Western Civilization. It signals the birth of a new epoch for mankind, in which nature and the universe are approached from a rational point of view. The superstitions of darker times begin to give way to the outlook of the philosopher who searches, amid the variety of daily experiences, for basic principles, inflexible laws, and understandable patterns according to which things exist. The miracles and surprises of our ancestors, the randomness of their world, the dazzlement and fear with which they perceived the world, the mythological and religious accounts with which they attempted to make sense of the universe—all these begin to move into the background of speculation in the minds of those who call themselves "the lovers of wisdom."

Naturally, among the early Greeks it would have been unreasonable to expect to find a clear distinction between philosophy and the sciences on the one hand, and between one science and another on the other. The body of data which made up their knowledge was relatively limited, and the principles according to which they grasped their experiences were few. A philosopher in those days was what we might call a "universal scientist." We have seen how Thales was an astronomer *and* a physicist *and* a political man *and* a cartographer *and* many other things. The same can be said of Pythagoras for whom mathematics *and* physics *and* music were manifestations of philosophy. Plato, too, combined in his fabulous writings (more than twenty-four dialogues) a vast variety of subjects. He wrote on the meaning of reality, the nature of perception, the purpose of life, the significance of death, the organization of the political state, the complexity of language, the reality of the gods, the basis of moral values, the origin of mankind, and many other themes, some of which we would call today philosophical, while others would be relegated to the sciences. The example of Aristotle is indeed extraordinary. He investigated a tremendous variety of fields: the nature of the stars, the shape of the earth, the structure of the universe, the nature of man, the meaning of dreams, the political constitutions of Greek states, the birth of tragedy, and so on. He saw all these fields as the specific realms in which one and the same philosophical activity is at work. In Aristotle, however, we do find the first attempt to classify the sciences, and the first indication that the name "philosophy" should be reserved for that endeavor in which we seek to grasp the principles or general laws that prevail in nature.

Hence, it is not altogether inappropriate to define philosophy, following Aristotle's suggestion, as the intellectual activity in which the human mind attempts to gain some understanding of the principles, laws, concepts, and patterns that govern existence. In this sense, then, philosophy can be distinguished from the sciences insofar as it deals with the ideas that underlie the specific sciences. For example, concepts such as time, space, being, existence, reality, meaning, value, purpose, causality, are either taken for granted in the sciences, or are examined from a narrow point of view. These concepts constitute the very essence of the philosophical enterprise.

It is to be expected that with the great accumulation of scientific data and with the proliferation of sciences, philosophy has been compelled to separate itself from the sciences, not in the sense that it does something entirely different from what they do, but in the sense that it is called upon to do something they cannot do, namely, to examine the foundations of science in general, and thereby to shed light on human experience. Furthermore, there are many questions that contemporary scientists do not usually examine, but which, on account of their importance, must be examined. Among these problems, there is, for example, the question of the existence of God. The philosopher cannot avoid turning his attention to it.

Throughout the introductions and selections of this text, the student will find a variety of examples of philosophical activity. They represent intelligent attempts to deal with problems that now, as much as in antiquity, are regarded as the special province of the philosopher. There are few solutions, and the problems of the past remain problems for us. But before we plunge ourselves into the subject matter itself, it is important to spend some time on a preliminary issue, namely, how to read and study philosophy.

How to Read Philosophy

Every discipline, no matter whether it is mathematics, poetry, history, or philosophy, has both a subject matter or content and an approach to that content which is unique. In fact, it is probably easier to understand a discipline by grasping its special techniques than it is by trying to isolate its subject matter. Philosophy is no exception. Philosophers have their own special ways of handling their subject matter, special ways of thinking about it as well as special ways of trying to communicate their thoughts to others. With increasing specialization in the academic world, these techniques have become more and more refined, and consequently require more effort on the part of novices to grasp. This is true of all fields of endeavor.

There is a special set of circumstances that makes philosophy appear formidable to the beginner. Whereas all students come to college having studied mathematics and history, or having read poetry at least in high school, very few students have had any exposure at all to philosophy. Regretably and unjustifiably, philosophy is not part of the standard high school curriculum. The language of philosophy therefore appears strange, mysterious, and even frightening to some. It would be the same if students were required to count for the first time when they entered college as freshmen, and it undoubtedly appears that way to some who study a foreign langauge for the first time. But once the student grasps and masters the techniques of a discipline, it is the content that presents the challenge and not the techniques. We believe that the content of philosophy is so important and so interesting that it is a great shame to turn readers off by inadequate preparation and mystery-mongering. In short, philosophy is too important to be left to an élite or to be ignored, and that is why it must be properly introduced. We have found that there are ways of giving beginners the basic skills necessary for reading philosophy. When you finish this book, we earnestly expect that you will be able to read most philosophical works and all of the classics, and you will probably wonder at your earlier reluctance in a way similar to trying to imagine what it was like before you read at all.

There are, of course, different styles and formats for philosophers presenting their ideas to the public. In the history of philosophy, two stand out: the dialogue and the essay. Since the essay is the most common, we shall begin with it and leave the discussion of reading the dialogue for the next chapter.

Our guide to reading philosophy is in three parts. First, we shall present a brief outline for future reference. Second, we shall discuss each part of the outline. Third, we shall exemplify how the outline actually works by using it to read one of the great philosophical classics, John Stuart Mill's essay *On Liberty,* Chapter One.

I. What is the *problem?*
  A. How is the problem formulated?
  B. Why is this problem an important one?
  C. What is the history of this problem?
  D. Which prominent personalities have been interested in this problem?
II. What *solutions* to this problem are there?
  A. What conclusion is reached?
  B. By what argument(s) is the conclusion reached?
  C. What facts and assumptions serve as premises?
  D. Does the author raise objections to alternative solutions? Does he consider potential objections to his own solution?
III. *Evaluation*
  A. What are the advantages and disadvantages of the alternative formulations to the problem?
  B. Has the importance or history of the problem been misrepresented?
  C. Are the "facts" really facts? Are the assumptions acceptable? Are the objections answerable?

I. What is the *Problem?*

Every philosophical work is concerned with a particular problem, issue, or controversy. The choice of a word is not important here as long as the readers ask themselves what is the particular issue or set of issues about which the work is written. Until the reader uncovers this issue his reading is either pointless or undirected. Sometimes that issue is stated explicitly, and sometimes it is only implicit. Sometimes that issue is stated in the first paragraph and sometimes it is buried deep within the work. When the latter prevails, the reader must search for it, and perhaps even reread the work once it is found. But until you can state exactly what problem is being dealt with, your reading is merely tentative, hypothetical, and should be pursued cautiously.

Not every philosopher would win the Nobel prize for literature, anymore than every freshman essay belongs in the literary hall of fame. Some philosophers are notoriously poor writers, and this should be kept in mind so that readers do not feel that all of the problem is theirs. However, every essay in this volume has been carefully chosen for its readability.

A. *How is the problem formulated?* Law students are familiar with the old joke of the attorney who, while cross-examining a witness, asked: "Have you stopped beating your wife? Answer 'yes' or 'no.'" Either way the witness would be admitting that he had beaten his wife in the past. This, of course, may not be true, but the clever attorney will have tried to embarrass the witness by asking his question in a particular way. The moral of this story is that *how a question is asked determines the kind of answer you can expect*. When you read about Socrates you will see just how true this is. More important, you will discover that what distinguishes one philosopher from another, one philosophical style from another, is the manner in which questions are asked.

This is largely what is meant by saying that in philosophy the question is more important than the answer. It does not mean that philosophers are uninterested in the answer; on the contrary, most philosophers are passionately involved with answers. It means that the answer is implicitly structured by the question and how it is asked.

It also means that the sophisticated reader must be aware of the fact that there are alternative ways of asking a question, and the alternatives have momentous consequences. In the beginning when you have read only one or even a few philosophers, it will be difficult to think about alternatives, but after you have become familiar with several alternatives it will be easy to conceive of others. For example, after you have read Plato and Aristotle, you may read Descartes. While reading Descartes and noting how he asks questions you will automatically ask yourself, "How would Plato have viewed that question? How would Aristotle handle that issue?" and so on. The more background knowledge you accumulate, both in philosophy and in other fields, the more possibilities will occur. After a while, the only limitation will be your own imagination. By the time you are doing this, you will, in a manner of speaking be "doing philosophy."

B. *Why is this problem an important one?* Questions do not arise in a vacuum. There is a reason why, when, where, and how they occur. We say that the problem exists in a certain context, and that the context structures the problem, which is another way of saying that how the question is asked determines the answer. Knowing the background to a question is essential to understanding it. That is why we have provided sufficient background information for each essay to ensure that the reader will understand the context. It is interesting that even professional philosophers disagree with each other because they approach the same essay with different background assumptions, and that there have been major shifts in the interpretation of classical works with the discovery of more background information.

In addition to the background, there is the all-important element of how the author or philosopher sees his own problem. A clear writer will not only state the problem but he will also try to indicate just why he thinks that the problem is important enough to deserve his energies as an author, and to be worthy of the reader's attention. Spotting this element helps you to comprehend the issue and its solution. Problems are important for many reasons in philosophy, all the way from the survival of the human race (and you will be surprised at how many philosophers have this foremost in mind) to seemingly technical issues that might appear to be of interest only to specialists. Even in the latter case, these technical issues are usually related to very practical concerns. Finally, it will be interesting to see how what looks like the same problem takes on an interesting history, because in different ages the same problem may be important but for different reasons.

C. *What is the history of this problem?* Not only will the careful writer state his personal reasons for believing the problem to be important, but he will also indicate the history of the problem. Usually the same problem has appeared before, or at least has been treated by other authors. Some reference to this history or previous treatment is usually made. For the moment we are not concerned with how accurately the history of the problem has been portrayed. Rather, we are concerned with how the author "sees" the history of the problem. In some cases you might want to point out that the author "does not see." We may even grant that philosophers, especially the greatest, are frequently unfair to their predecessors and colleagues. We grant all this for the moment because what is of interest here is how the *author's personal preconceptions help structure the way in which he has asked his question.* We must always try to understand the author first from his own interior point of view. Even if we later criticize that point of view, our criticism will be fair if we have the first made a sincere attempt to see from that point of view.

D. *What prominent personalities have been interested in this problem?* Everything said above applies to this question as well. Authors will often mention other authors either explicitly or implicitly, and when they do we shall notify the reader. Knowing those other works helps to understand the work you are reading at the moment. In the beginning this is impossible, so we have provided more background information. After you have read the first few works you will be able to do this for the remaining works in this anthology.

Given the foregoing, it should be clear why in part we have chosen a historical perspective. You may address posterity but you can only answer the past. Moreover, philosophers not only read other philosophers but they react to general intellectual climates as well. You will be surprised by how much of philosophy is a response to developments in the sciences, so that not knowing the history of science is a disadvantage in trying to understand a philosophical work. The same can be said for artistic, political, social, and religious developments.

II. What *solutions* to the problem are there?

After you have identified the problem or set of problems about which the author is writing, you will be in a position to look for the answer or answers he provides. When looking for the solution, the following should be kept in mind.

A. *What are the conclusions reached?* Although we have stated matters in the form of questions and answers we should bear in mind that there are at least three possibilities.

(1) *A direct answer:* An author may have a direct answer to give to a specific problem. If so, you should look for it and state it.

(2) *Dissolving the problem:* Another possibility is the case where the author declares the problem to be a pseudo-problem; that is, no problem at all. For example, an old standby in philosophy is the question, What came first—the chicken or the egg? This question is exemplary of the Aristotelian problem of the cause of motion. In Aristotle's physics, rest is the natural state and motion is what has to be explained. The very beginning of motion, or of anything, is what an Aristotelian philosopher concerns himself with. To him, the question is important. On the contrary, in Newtonian physics, motion is a natural state, so that one can never meaningfully ask what causes motion. The very beginning of anything is not a serious issue if we take Newton's physics as our standard, and this is just exactly what Hume did. Hence, in Hume the question of most concern to an Aristotelian would be dismissed as meaningless.

It is not our purpose here to decide on the relative merits of competing theories of physics, or whether Aristotle or Hume is correct. We are concerned with pointing out how a question can seem vital to a philosopher who looks out on the world from one point of view, and how that same question can appear to be no question at all to a philosopher with another point of view. If we have prepared our ground in asking the right question about what the problem is, then we shall be able to anticipate the maneuvering that goes on in finding the solution.

(3) *Plea for recognition:* Sometimes a philosopher will not have a solution to a particular problem. Rather, it will be his purpose to point out that the problem exists. In itself this can be a great contribution since we cannot solve problems if we do not know that they exist, and even then we must be able to recognize them in time. The philosopher's penchant for seeing the forest and not just the trees gives him a unique advantage in spotting issues before others do. In a time of increasing specialization, this penchant is all the more precious.

B. *By what argument(s) is the conclusion reached?* In many ways this is the most interesting question for the philosopher. While most people think it sufficient to simply know the conclusions of this or that particular philosopher, it is much more vital to know the reasons behind the conclusion. By *reasons* here we do not mean motives, but those logical considerations which lead to the adoption of the conclusion. Why is this so?

First, we may agree with the conclusion but not with the argument behind it. A bad argument may lose support for an otherwise acceptable conclusion.

Second, we may disagree with the conclusion but find the argument powerful or useful for other purposes. Finally, by understanding the arguments we may be able to extend them to other contexts that the original author never considered. In short, we can learn from the argument more than we can from the conclusion.

Moreover, if we are to be rational men and women, then presumably we will want to defend our conclusions as rational and not merely accepted as a matter of blind faith. It is not enough to complain about the irrationality of others and then refuse to make the effort to be rational oneself.

An argument will be said to have the following structure: one or more premises and one conclusion. The *conclusion* is that which the author is trying to prove. The *premises* are those beliefs which the author gives as reason for accepting the conclusion. For our purposes it is not necessary to go into greater detail about the complexities of logic. Suffice it to say that the great philosophers, at the very least in the selections we have chosen, do not make logical mistakes. Hence, if you accept the premises you "must" accept the conclusion. If you disagree with the conclusion, then you must reject one or more of the premises.

C. *What facts or assumptions serve as the premises?* The premises are those reasons offered in support of the conclusion. Authors usually appeal to those beliefs which they think that their audience already accepts and then try to show that the favored conclusion also follows from those beliefs or is at least consistent with those beliefs.

In different historical periods and places different beliefs prevail. Many arguments are thus "dated" in the sense that what is acceptable in one time or place is not necessarily acceptable in another. Presumably, this holds for some of our own favorite beliefs as well.

There is another distinction worth making, as long as it is not made too sharply. We may distinguish between facts and assumptions. Facts are those alleged beliefs which we feel can be easily checked against experience, such as the color of an object, the temperature of a liquid, or the date of someone's birth. Assumptions are those beliefs which either cannot be checked directly, or are in principle not the sorts of things that can be checked. For example, the temperature in the center of the sun is not checkable, at least now, because no thermometer could withstand the heat. More interestingly, the belief that the future will resemble the past or the belief that mankind will one day understand everything, are not really checkable at all. Such assumptions guide our thinking about other things. Philosophers are very much concerned with the status of such *ultimate* premises. For our purposes at this stage it is only important to try to recognize when an author is stating a fact that he believes can be checked, and when he is appealing to an ultimate premise.

D. *What alternatives are considered?* Philosophers not only present arguments for their own solutions but also raise objections against alternative solutions. Frequently the case for one's conclusion is not so much its own strength but the weakness of alternative views. In line with this, the reader must learn to ask: does the author argue for or against the solutions of other authors? Does he raise objections to those solutions, and if so what are they? Does he consider objections to his own solution? A wise writer anticipates the kinds of responses he will receive and tries to meet these objections before they can ever be articulated.

A good deal of philosophical reading involves the laying out of both the author's own position and his consideration of alternative positions. Here it is important to keep asking yourself as you read, "Is the author speaking for himself or is he reporting the viewpoint of the opposition?" This is part of the dialectic of philosophical argument, and mastering it is the key to successful comprehension.

III. *Evaluation*

Students frequently ask, "Do you want us to summarize the author or do you want our opinion?" Putting the question this way presupposes that the two activities are distinct. It also presupposes a rather naive view of presenting one's own opinion. I would point out that it is impossible to "summarize" another philosopher without raising some evaluative questions. In fact, without evaluation you cannot really be said to comprehend. Then again, it is impossible to evaluate without fully comprehending. I think that if the reader makes an attempt to comprehend an author in the manner suggested by Parts I and II of the outline, then he will already have been engaged in an evaluative process. Let us spell this out.

A. Look at IA. *What are the advantages or disadvantages of the alternative formulations of the problem?* Once you have become aware of the alternative formulations, that is, once you have read at least two selections, you can at the very least use one against the other. You might even want to use each against the other in order to suggest a third possibility.

B. Look at IB and IC. *Has the importance or history of the problem been misrepresented?* Maybe the problem is no longer important, or maybe it is important for totally new reasons. Maybe a better knowledge of the history of the problem leads to a different solution. It is not only in Orwell's *1984* that history is systematically distorted. It is even possible that what a classical philosopher said many years ago caused or influenced the problem to change in the meantime. Finally, we risk pointing out that the way one interprets the history of anything is symptomatic of a particular philosophical point of view.

C. Look at IIC. *Do you agree with the facts appealed to?* As we have already pointed out, the conclusions follow from the premises. If you do not like the conclusion, then you must reject either one or more of the facts alleged or the assumptions made. Here, expressing a dissenting opinion can be a philosophically sophisticated response on your part, and not just an emotional reaction.

D. Look at IID. *Are the objections answerable?* Here there are several possibilities. If author A attacks author B, and you agree with author B, then why not try to show how author B would respond? That is, respond on his behalf. The fact that an author is attacked does not imply that the attack is a good one, and you can show how it has failed. Moreover, the fact that an author considers objections in advance of his solution does not mean that he has successfully answered them. If you feel that the reply is insufficient, offer a rebuttal of your own. Finally, if you agree with an author, you may want to present additional arguments in support of his case, for he may not have been in a position to consider them. By the time you have done all this, your philosophical reading will not be a mere summary or a simple-minded personal opinion but a kind of philosophy in its own right.

John Stuart Mill: On Liberty—Text and Analysis

Paragraph 1: "The subject of this essay is . . . civil, or social liberty: the nature and limits of the power which can be legitimately exercised by society over the individual." Mill immediately informs his readers of the *problem* with which he will be dealing. This corresponds to (I) in the reading guide outline. (IA) *How is the problem formulated?* The formulation of the problem involves a contrast: *society* on the one hand and the *individual* on the other. Mill thus makes a sharp distinction between the individual and society. As we shall discover later, other philosophers will not agree with this separation. As a reader of English you probably take this distinction as obvious, but that is a result of the fact that Mill represents the mainstream of Anglo-Saxon thought. It should also be noted that Mill is not asking about the present limits (a sociological question) but what *ought* to be the limits, legitimately; that is a moral question. Finally, we note that Mill does not mention the government, rather, he mentions society.

(IB) *Why is this problem an important one?* Mill notes that this problem has a long history which he will discuss shortly. But he claims that there are "new conditions" which "require a different and more fundamental treatment." What these circumstances are he does not discuss in this paragraph. See paragraphs 3, 4, and 15.

> The subject of this Essay is not the so-called Liberty of the Will, so unfortunately opposed to the misnamed doctrine of Philosophical Necessity; but Civil, or Social Liberty: the nature and limits of the power which can be legitimately exercised by

> society over the individual, a question seldom stated, and hardly ever discussed, in general terms, but which profoundly influences the practical controversies of the age by its latent presence, and is likely soon to make itself recognised as the vital question of the future. It is so far from being new, that in a certain sense, it has divided mankind, almost from the remotest ages; but in the stage of progress into which the more civilized portions of the species have now entered, it presents itself under new conditions, and requires a different and more fundamental treatment.

Paragraph 2: In this paragraph, Mill gives his version of the *history of the problem* (IC). His history refers to three countries: *Greece, Rome* (of the Republican period, not the Empire), and *England*. His history is limited to those times and places relevant to the history of modern England (and the U.S. by extension) since he is writing for a specific audience. Obviously, referring to other times and places would produce a different history. In these examples, the *problems* of the individual versus society was understood in terms of an adversary relationship: "The rulers were conceived . . . as in a necessarily antagonistic position to the people whom they ruled." Some of our contemporary talk of the government as the "they" in "Washington" preserves the flavor of this history. In short, rulers were necessary evils. The individual was protected in two ways: (1) a doctrine of "rights" and (2) "constitutional checks." The U.S. Constitution with its Bill of Rights, as well as the doctrine of checks and balances, is a perfect example of this. The U.S. Constitution was the product of the eighteenth century and the previous influence upon the founding fathers of Hobbes, Locke, Hume, and Montesquieu. Mill was writing in the nineteenth century, and was an heir of that tradition. (ID)

> The struggle between Liberty and Authority is the most conspicuous feature in the portions of history with which we are earliest familiar, particularly in that of Greece, Rome, and England. But in old times this contest was between subjects, or some classes of subjects, and the government. By liberty was meant protection against the tyranny of the political rulers. The rulers were conceived (except in some of the popular governments of Greece) as in a necessarily antagonistic position to the people whom they ruled. They consisted of a governing One, or a governing tribe or caste, who derived their authority from inheritance or conquest, who, at all costs, did not hold it at the pleasure of the governed, and whose supremacy men did not venture, perhaps did not desire to contest, whatever precautions might be taken against its oppressive exercise. Their power was regarded as necessary, but also as highly dangerous; as a weapon which they would attempt to use against their subjects, no less than against external enemies. To prevent the weaker members of the community from being preyed upon by innumerable vultures, it was needful that there should be an animal of prey stronger than the rest, commissioned to keep them down. But as the king of the vultures would be no less bent upon preying on the flock, than any of the minor harpies, it was indispensable to be in a perpetual attitude of defence against his beak and claws. The aim, therefore, of patriots, was to set limits to the power which the ruler should be suffered to exercise over the community; and this limitation was what they meant by liberty. It was attempted in two ways. First, by obtaining a recognition of certain immunities, called political liberties or rights, which it was to be regarded as a breach of duty in

the ruler to infringe, and which if he did infringe, specific resistance, or general rebellion, was held to be justifiable. A second, and generally a later expedient, was the establishment of constitutional checks; by which the consent of the community or of a body of some sort, supposed to represent its interests, was made a necessary condition to some of the more important acts of the governing power. To the first of these modes of limitation, the ruling power, in most European countries, was compelled, more or less, to submit. It was not so with the second; and to attain this, or when already in some degree possessed, to attain it more completely, became everywhere the principle object of the lovers of liberty. And so long as mankind were content to combat one enemy by another, and to be ruled by a master, on condition of being guaranteed more or less efficaciously against his tyranny, they did not carry their aspirations beyond this point.

Paragraph 3: Here Mill returns to the importance of the problem (IB). What are the new circumstances that require our problem to be re-thought? As some governments became more representative, the old adversary relationship disappeared. Now instead of limiting the government's power, there grew the idea of increasing it. "The nation did not need to be protected against its own will."

The reader should compare the difference between the "old" liberal who seeks to curb government power and the "new" liberal who seeks to increase it. Which people today ask for the government to control social security, Medicare, welfare, wages and prices? Can the same government avoid fraud in public programs without resort to illegal wiretaps for example? Are we making contradictory demands?

A time, however, came, in the progress of human affairs, when men ceased to think it a necessity of nature that their governors should be an independent power, opposed in interest to themselves. It appeared to them much better that the various magistrates of the State should be their tenants or, delegates, revocable at their pleasure. In that way alone, it seemed, could they have complete security that the powers of government would never be abused to their disadvantage. By degrees, this new demand for elective and temporary rulers became the prominent object of the exertions of the popular party, wherever any such party existed; and superseded, to a considerable extent, the previous efforts to limit the power of rulers. As the struggle proceeded for making the ruling power emanate from the periodical choice of the ruled, some persons began to think that too much importance had been attached to the limitation of the power itself. *That* (it might seem) was a resource against rulers whose interests were habitually opposed to those of the people. What was now wanted was, that the rulers should be identified with the people; that their interest and will should be the interest and will of the nation. The nation did not need to be protected against it own will. There was no fear of its tyrannizing over itself. Let the rulers be effectually responsible to it, promptly removable by it, and it could afford to trust them with power of which it could itself dictate the use to be made. Their power was but the nation's own power, concentrated, and in a form convenient for exercise. This mode of thought, or rather perhaps of feeling, was common among the last generation of European liberalism, in the Continental section of which, it still apparently predominates.

> Those who admit any limit to what a government may do, except in the case of such governments as they think ought not to exist, stand out as brilliant exceptions among the political thinkers of the Continent. A similar tone of sentiment might by this time have been prevalent in our own country, if the circumstances which for a time encouraged it, had continued unaltered.

Paragraph 4: Mill continues to discuss IB. The concept he introduces to explain the new circumstances for the old problem is "the tyranny of the majority." ***What is the tyranny of the majority?***

(1) the oppression of the minority or minorities by the majority;
(2) the oppression of minorities by a minority which is the "most active part of the people," that is, an active minority that speaks or claims to speak on behalf of the "people."

Does the tyranny of the majority exist? What is the position of blacks in a predominantly white society? What will the position of whites be when Rhodesia and South Africa become countries ruled by a majority of blacks? What is the position of Catholics in Protestant Northern Ireland? What is the position of Jews in a Moslem country such as Iraq, or vice versa? Do these tyrannies exist because some groups are more immoral than others, or because they are majorities? Mill borrowed the expression "tyranny of the majority" from Alexis de Tocqueville (1805-59), a French liberal politician and writer, who used it in his classic work *Democracy in America* (1835). The original meaning of the term *democracy* in Greek was mob rule.

> But, in political and philosophical theories, as well as in persons, success discloses faults and infirmities which failure might have concealed from observation. The notion, that the people have no need to limit their power over themselves, might seem axiomatic, when popular government was a thing only dreamed about, or read of as having existed at some distant period of the past. Neither was that notion necessarily disturbed by such temporary aberrations as those of the French Revolution, the worst of which were the work of an usurping few, and which, in any case, belonged, not to the permanent working of popular institutions, but to a sudden and convulsive outbreak against monarchical and aristocratic despotism. In time, however, a democratic republic came to occupy a large portion of the earth's surface, and made itself felt as one of the most powerful members of the community of nations; and elective and responsible government became subject to the observations and criticisms which wait upon a great existing fact. It was now perceived that such phrases as 'self-government,' and 'the power of the people over themselves,' do not express the true state of the case. The 'people' who exercise the power, are not always the same people with those over whom it is exercised; and the 'self-government' spoken of, is not the government of each by himself, but of each by all the rest. The will of the people, moreover, practically means, the will of the most numerous or the most active *part* of the people; the majority, or those who succeed in making themselves accepted as the majority: the people, consequently, *may* desire to oppress a part of their number; and precautions are as much needed against this, as against any other abuse of power. The limitation,

therefore, of the power of government over individuals, loses none of its importance when the holders of power are regularly accountable to the community, that is, to the strongest party therein. This view of things, recommending itself equally to the intelligence of thinkers and to the inclination of those important classes in European society to whose real or supposed interests democracy is adverse, has had no difficulty in establishing itself; and in political speculations 'the tyranny of the majority' is now generally included among the evils against which society requires to be on its guard.

Paragraph 5: Mill further defines the problem. The real culprit is not the government but society. "Social tyranny" is "more formidable than many kinds of political oppression." Why? Can you think of a serious social problem recently solved through political means?

Mill begins to approach the solution of his problem by formulating the question (IA) more clearly; notice the importance of "society" as opposed to government in Mill's formulation. "There is a limit to the legitimate interference of collective opinion with individual independence: and to find that limit, and maintain it against encroachment, is as indispensable to a good condition of human affairs as protection against political despotism."

Like other tyrannies, the tyranny of the majority was at first, and is still vulgarly, held in dread, chiefly as operating through the acts of the public authorities. But reflecting persons perceived that when society is itself the tyrant—society collectively, over the separate individuals who compose it—its means of tyrannizing are not restricted to the acts which it may do by the hands of its political functionaries. Society can and does execute its own mandates: and if it issues wrong mandates instead of right, or any mandates at all in things with which it ought not to meddle, it practises a social tyranny more formidable than many kinds of political oppression, since, though not usually upheld by such extreme penalties, it leaves fewer means of escape, penetrating much more deeply into the details of life, and enslaving the soul itself. Protection, therefore, against the tyranny of the magistrate is not enough: there needs protection also against the tyranny of the prevailing opinion and feeling; against the tendency of society to impose, by other means than civil penalties, its own ideas and practices as rules of conduct on those who dissent from them; to fetter the development, and, if possible, prevent the formation, of any individuality not in harmony with its ways, and compel all characters to fashion themselves upon the model of its own. There is a limit to the legitimate interference of collective opinion with individual independence: and to find that limit, and maintain it against encroachment, is as indispensable to a good condition of human affairs, as protection against political despotism.

Paragraph 6: Before offering his own answer, Mill considers the answers we already have or have operated with. These (IID) include:

(a) custom
(b) personal feelings
(c) self-interest
(d) religious prejudice.

Note Mill's mention of women and their subservient position to men in most societies. This is another instance of tyranny. Mill was one of the first to champion the liberation of women. His work *On the Subjection of Women* (written in 1861 and published in 1869) is still a classic. Mrs. Harriet Taylor undoubtedly influenced him on this issue, both before and after their marriage. Women are now fifty-two percent of the U.S. population. Will women's liberation eventually become a kind of tyranny?

> But though this proposition is not likely to be contested in general terms, the practical question, where to place the limit—how to make the fitting adjustment between individual independence and social control—is a subject on which nearly everything remains to be done. All that makes existence valuable to any one, depends on the enforcement of restraints upon the actions of other people. Some rules of conduct, therefore, must be imposed, by law in the first place, and by opinion on many things which are not fit subjects for the operation of law. What these rules should be, is the principal question in human affairs; but if we except a few of the most obvious cases, it is one of those which least progress has been made in resolving. No two ages, and scarcely any two countries, have decided it alike; and the decision of one age or country is a wonder to another. Yet the people of any given age and country no more suspect any difficulty in it, than if it were a subject on which mankind had always been agreed. The rules which obtain among themselves appear to them self-evident and self-justifying. This all but universal illusion is one of the examples of the magical influence of custom, which is not only, as the proverb says, a second nature, but is continually mistaken for the first. The effect of custom, in preventing any misgiving respecting the rules of conduct which mankind impose on one another, is all the more complete because the subject is one on which it is not generally considered necessary that reasons should be given, either by one person to others, or by each to himself. People are accustomed to believe, and have been encouraged in the belief by some who aspire to the character of philosophers, that their feelings, on subjects of this nature, are better than reasons, and render reasons unnecessary. The practical principle which guides them to their opinions on the regulation of human conduct, is the feeling in each person's mind that everybody should be required to act as he, and those with whom he sympathizes, would like them to act. No one, indeed, acknowledges to himself that his standard of judgment is his own liking; but an opinion on a point of conduct, not supported by reasons, can only count as one person's preference; and if the reasons, when given, are a mere appeal to a similar preference felt by other people, it is still only many people's liking instead of one. To an ordinary man, however, his own preference, thus supported, is not only a perfectly satisfactory reason, but the only one he generally has for any of his notions of morality, taste, or propriety, which are not expressly written in his religious creed; and his chief guide in the interpretation even of that. Men's opinions, accordingly, on what is laudable or blameable, are affected by all the multifarious causes which influence their wishes in regard to the conduct of others, and which are as numerous as those which determine their wishes on any other subject. Sometimes their reason—at other times their prejudices or superstitions; often their social affections, not seldom their antisocial ones, their envy or jealousy, their arrogance or contemptuousness: but most commonly, their desires or fears for themselves—their legitimate or illegitimate self-interest. Wherever there is an ascendant class, a large portion of the morality of the country emanates from its class interests, and

its feelings of class superiority. The morality between Spartans and Helots, between planters and negroes, between princes and subjects, between nobles and roturiers, between men and women, has been for the most part the creation of these class interests and feelings; and the sentiments thus generated, react in turn upon the moral feelings of the members of the ascendant class, in their relations among themselves. Where, on the other hand, a class, formerly ascendant, has lost its ascendancy, or where its ascendancy is unpopular, the prevailing moral sentiments frequently bear the impress of an impatient dislike of superiority. Another grand determining principle of the rules of conduct, both in act and forebearance, which have been enforced by law or opinion, has been the servility of mankind towards the supposed preferences or aversions of their temporal masters, or of their gods. This servility, though essentially selfish, is not hyprocrisy; it gives rise to perfectly genuine sentiments of abhorrence; it made men burn magicians and heretics. Among so many baser influences, the general and obvious interests of society have of course had a share, and a large one, in the direction of the moral sentiments: less, however, as a matter of reason, and on their own account, than as a consequence of the sympathies and antipathies which grew out of them: and sympathies and antipathies which had little or nothing to do with the interests of society, have made themselves felt in the establishment of moralities with quite as great force.

Paragraph 7 & 8: (IID): Mill has two objections to previous answers. First, (paragraph 7) past reformers have concentrated on substituting new dogma for old. Second, there has been (paragraph 8) a total "absence of rule or principle." That is, there has not been a consistent policy. Can you think of cases where our society has been too oppressive? Can you think of cases where our society has been too permissive? If a society can be both at the same time, how would you account for this possibility?

The likings and dislikings of society, or of some powerful portion of it, are thus the main thing which has practically determined the rules laid down for general observance, under the penalities of law or opinion. And in general, those who have been in advance of society in thought and feeling, have left this condition of things unassailed in principle, however they may have come into conflict with it in some of its details. They have occupied themselves rather in inquiring what things society ought to like or dislike, than in questioning whether its likings or dislikings should be a law to individuals. They preferred endeavouring to alter the feelings of mankind on the particular points on which they were themselves heretical, rather than make common cause in defence of freedom, with heretics generally. The only case in which the higher ground has been taken on principle and maintained with consistency, by any but an individual here and there, is that of religious belief: a case instructive in many ways, and not least so as forming a most striking instance of the fallibility of what is called the moral sense: for the *odium theologicum*, in a sincere bigot, is one of the most unequivocal cases of moral feeling. Those who first broke the yoke of what called itself the Universal Church, were in general as little willing to permit difference of religious opinion as that Church itself. But when the heat of the conflict was over, without giving a complete victory to any party, and each church or sect was reduced to limit its hopes to retaining possession of the ground it already occupied; minorities, seeing that they had no chance of becoming majorities, were under the necessity of pleading to those whom they could not convert, for permission to differ. It is accordingly on this battlefield, almost solely, that the rights of the individual against society have been asserted on broad grounds of principle, and the claim of society to exercise authority over dissentients, openly controverted. The great writers to whom the world owes what religious liberty it possesses, have mostly asserted freedom of conscience as an indefeasible right, and denied absolutely that a human being is accountable to others for his religious belief. Yet so natural to mankind is intolerance in whatever they really care about, that religious freedom has hardly anywhere been practically realized, except where religious indifference, which dislikes to have its peace disturbed by theological quarrels, has added its weight to the scale. In the minds of almost all religious persons, even in the most tolerant countries, the duty of toleration is admitted with tacit reserves. One person will bear with dissent in matters of church government, but not of dogma; another can tolerate everybody, short of a Papist or an Unitarian, another, every one who believes in revealed religion; a few extend their charity a little further, but stop at the belief in a God and in a future state. Wherever the sentiment of the majority is still genuine and intense, it is found to have abated little of its claim to be obeyed.

In England, from the peculiar circumstances of our political history, though the yoke of opinion is perhaps heavier, that of law is lighter, than in most other countries of Europe; and there is considerable jealousy of direct interference, by the legislative or the executive power, with private conduct; not so much from any just regard for the independence of the individual, as from the still subsisting habit of looking on the government as representing an opposite interest to the public. The majority have not yet learnt to feel the power of the government their power, or its opinions their opinions. When they do so, individual liberty will probably be as much exposed to invasion from the government, as it already is from public opinion. But, as yet, there is a considerable amount of feeling ready to be called forth against any attempt of the law to control individuals in things in which they have not hitherto been accustomed to be controlled by it; and this with very little discrimination as to whether the matter is, or is not, within the legitimate sphere of legal control; insomuch that the feeling, highly salutary on the whole, is perhaps quite as often misplaced as well grounded in the particular instances of its application. There is, in fact, no recognised principle by which the propriety or impropriety of government interference is customarily tested. People decide according to their personal preferences. Some, whenever they see any good to be done, or evil to be remedied, would willingly instigate the government to undertake the business; while others prefer to bear almost any amount of social evil, rather than add one to the departments of human interests amenable to governmental control. And men range themselves on one or the other side in any particular case, according to this general direction of their sentiments; or according to the degree of interest which they feel in the particular thing which it is proposed that the government should do, or according to the belief they entertain that the government would, or would not, do it in the manner they prefer; but very rarely on account of any opinion to which they consistently adhere, as to what things are fit to be done by a government. And it seems to me that in consequence of this absence of rule or principle, one side is at present as often wrong as the other; the interference of government is, with about equal frequency improperly invoked and improperly condemned.

Paragraph 9: Mill gives his answer (IIA): "The sole end for which mankind are warranted . . . in interfering with the liberty of action of any of their number is self-protection. . . . to prevent harm to others." The private area is defined by Mill as "the body and mind." Mill specifically excludes interfering when the private person's "own good, either physical or moral," is involved. This does not imply that we may not interfere with another's body when harm to others is at stake. Sufferers of contagious diseases are not at liberty to disregard their bodies.

Note as well that Mill does not advocate indifference to others in the private zone: "There are good reasons for remonstrating with him, or reasoning with him, or persuading him, or entreating him, but not for compelling him or visiting him with any evil in case he do otherwise."

> The object of this Essay is to assert one very simple principle, as entitled to govern absolutely the dealings of society with the individual in the way of compulsion and control, whether the means used be physical force in the form of legal penalties, or the moral coercion of public opinion. That principle is, that the sole end for which mankind are warranted, individually or collectively, in interfering with the liberty of action of any of their number, is self-protection. That the only purpose for which power can be rightfully exercised over any member of a civilized community, against his will, is to prevent harm to others. His own good, either physical or moral, is not a sufficient warrant. He cannot rightfully be compelled to do or forbear because it will be better for him to do so, because it will make him happier, because, in the opinions of others, to do so would be wise, or even right. These are good reasons for remonstrating with him, or reasoning with him, or persuading him, or entreating him, but not for compelling him, or visiting him with any evil in case he do otherwise. To justify that, the conduct from which it is desired to deter him, must be calculated to produce evil to some one else. The only part of the conduct of any one, for which he is amenable to society, is that which concerns others. In the part which merely concerns himself, his independence or right, is absolute. Over himself, over his own body and mind, the individual is sovereign.

Paragraph 10: Mill adds some qualifications to his answer (IIA). His theory only applies to *rational individuals.* Such individuals are defined as those with "the capacity of being guided to their own improvement by conviction or persuasion," that is, those who are "capable of being improved by free and equal discussion." According to Mill this excludes: (1) children and (2) backward states of society. It follows that "despotism is a legitimate mode of government in dealing with barbarians, provided the end be their improvement and the means justified by actually effecting that end."

It should be clear that Mill views both of these states as temporary, not permanent or inherent. Mill was very much concerned with the problems of colonialism. He and his father, by their employment in the East India Company, had great experience with the ruling of India. For J. S. Mill's views on this subject consult his *Considerations on Representative Government* (1861), chapter eighteen. There Mill debunks the economic interpretation of empires, points out that in "the subject community also there are oppressors and oppressed," and claims that no one really knows yet how to establish a benevolent and temporary despotism. Those who are concerned with introducing democracy into other countries may well ponder this difficulty.

> It is, perhaps, hardly necessary to say that this doctrine is meant to apply only to human beings in the maturity of their faculties. We are not speaking of children or of young persons below the age which the law may fix as that of manhood or womanhood. Those who are still in a state to require being taken care of by others, must be protected against their own actions as well as against external injury. For the same reason, we may leave out of consideration those backward states of society in which the race itself may be considered as in its nonage. The early difficulties in the way of spontaneous progress are so great, that there is seldom any choice of means for overcoming them; and a ruler full of the spirit of improvement is warranted in the use of any expedients that will attain an end, perhaps otherwise unattainable. Despotism is a legitimate mode of government in dealing with barbarians, provided the end be their improvement, and the means justified by actually effecting that end. Liberty, as a principle has no application to any state of things anterior to the time when mankind have become capable of being improved by free and equal discussion. Until then, there is nothing for them but implicit obedience to an Akbar or a Charlemagne, if they are so fortunate as to find one. But as soon as mankind have attained the capacity of being guided to their own improvement by conviction or persuasion (a period long since reached in all nations with whom we need here concern ourselves), compulsion, either in the direct form or in that of pains and penalties for non-compliance, is no longer admissible as a means to their own good, and justifiable only for the security of others.

Paragraph 11: Mill turns now to the defense of his answer (IIB). First, Mill avoids appealing to "rights." Why? To begin with, since there are so many rights, many of which come into conflict in specific cases, we would be left without a guiding principle in cases of conflict. Second, the theory of rights presupposes a clear conception of an unchanging and fixed human nature. Against this, Mill argues for the notion of man "as a progressive being." This will become clearer in other chapters of the essay, but Mill does not believe in a fixed human nature. His perspective is evolutionary (man grows) but not teleological; that is, we are not growing in a predetermined direction.

Let us return to the first argument, namely that rights are inadequate. Mill suggests that we need a system in which we have a principle of ultimate appeal in case of conflict. This he proposes to find in the appeal to *utility*. Mill is known as a utilitarian, and he wrote a famous work, entitled *Utilitarianism* (1863). We cannot go into that complex work here, but it is only necessary to point out that Mill defended the principle of utility because it could resolve disputes when lower level principles conflicted. His example in *On Liberty* for the application of his answer is two-tiered: First we ask, "Is an act hurtful to others?" Next we ask, "Would preventing that hurtful act produce other evils, greater than those which it would prevent?" Consider the case of Prohibition.

It is proper to state that I forgo any advantage which could be derived to my argument from the idea of abstract right, as a thing independent of utility. I regard utility as the ultimate appeal on all ethical questions; but it must be utility in the largest sense, grounded on the permanent interests of man as a progressive being. Those interests, I contend, authorize the subjection of individual spontaneity to external control, only in respect to those actions of each, which concern the interest of other people. If any one does an act hurtful to others, there is a *primâ facie* case for punishing him, by law, or, where legal penalities are not safely applicable, by general disapprobation. There are also many positive acts for the benefit of others, which he may rightfully be compelled to perform; such as, to give evidence in a court of justice; to bear his fair share in the common defence, or in any other joint work necessary to the interest of the society of which he enjoys the protection; and to perform certain acts of individual beneficence, such as saving a fellow creature's life, or interposing to protect the defenceless against ill-usage, things which whenever it is obviously a man's duty to do, he may rightfully be made responsible to society for not doing. A person may cause evil to others not only by his actions but by his inaction, and in either case he is justly accountable to them for the injury. The latter case, it is true, requires a much more cautious exercise of compulsion than the former. To make any one answerable for doing evil to others, is the rule; to make him answerable for not preventing evil, is, comparatively speaking, the exception. Yet there are many cases clear enough and grave enough to justify that exception. In all things which regard the external relations of the individual, he is *de jure* amenable to those whose interests are concerned, and if need be, to society as their protector. There are often good reasons for not holding him to the responsibility; but these reasons must arise from the special expediencies of the case: either because it is a kind of case in which he is on the whole likely to act better, when left to his own discretion, than when controlled in any way in which society have it in their power to control him; or because the attempt to exercise control would produce other evils, greater than those which it would prevent. When such reasons as these preclude the enforcement of responsibility, the conscience of the agent himself should step into the vacant judgment seat, and protect those interests of others which have no external protection; judging himself all the more rigidly, because the case does not admit of his being made accountable to the judgment of his fellow-creatures.

Paragraph 12: in this paragraph Mill does two things. First, he further clarifies what his answer implies. Second, he considers objections to his theory.

The zone of privacy has already been established in paragraph 9 as the mind and body. This means specifically: (1) freedom of thought and expression (further elaborated in Chapter Two); (2) freedom to choose one's life style (further elaborated in Chapter Three); and (3) freedom for "combination among individuals" to do the same again with the provision that it not "harm others."

The reader should note how carefully Mill's first chapter sets the stage for his later chapters. He was apparently always asking himself how his reader would respond to what he had just said. He must have also worked with an outline and asked himself, "Why write this rather than that; why put this paragraph here rather than there?"

We come now to IID. What objection against his theory does Mill consider?

He considers something that has become the standard reply: ***Is there any such thing as an action which only concerns the individual?*** He readily admits that "whatever affects himself may affect others through himself." His reply is to postpone a direct answer to this objection. He takes it up at length in Chapter Four. See the next paragraph.

> But there is a sphere of action in which society, as distinguised from the individual, has, if any, only an indirect interest; comprehending all that portion of a person's life and conduct which affects only himself, or if it also affects others, only with their free, voluntary, and undeceived consent and participation. When I say only himself, I mean directly, and in the first instance: for whatever affects himself, may affect others *through* himself; and the objection which may be grounded on this contingency, will receive consideration in the sequel. This, then, is the appropriate region of human liberty. It comprises, first, the inward domain of consciousness; demanding liberty of conscience, in the most comprehensive sense; liberty of thought and feeling; absolute freedom of opinion and sentiment on all subjects, practical or speculative, scientific, moral, or theological. The liberty of expressing and publishing opinions may seem to fall under a different principle, since it belongs to that part of the conduct of an individual which concerns other people; but, being almost of as much importance as the liberty of thought, itself, and resting in great part on the same reasons, is practically inseparable from it. Secondly, the principle requires liberty of tastes and pursuits; of framing the plan of our life to suit our own character; of doing as we like, subject to such consequences as may follow: without impediment from our fellow-creatures, so long as what we do does not harm them, even though they should think our conduct foolish, perverse, or wrong. Thirdly, from this liberty of each individual, follows the liberty, within the same limits, of combination among individuals; freedom to unite, for any purpose not involving harm to others; the persons combining being supposed to be of full age, and not forced or deceived.

Paragraph 13: In this paragraph Mill does indicate what his ultimate answer will be and in so doing reveals more clearly what his facts and assumptions are (IIC). He says, "Mankind are greater gainers by suffering each other to live as seems good to themselves than by compelling each to live as seems good to the rest." He goes no further here, but in Chapter Three he tries to show, through *factual historical examples,* that societies have always progressed because some individuals were courageous enough to be different.

The *assumption* behind his argument, as seen in paragraph 11, is that man does not have a fixed nature. There will always be new conditions to be faced requiring new responses, and as long as the race is free to develop alternatives, it is likely to survive. To assume that man has a fixed nature, or that no new conditions will have to be faced, are assumptions of infallible knowledge on the part of Mill's opponents. He will demolish the assumption of infallibility in Chapter Two.

> No society is which these liberties are not, on the whole, respected, is free, whatever may be its form of government; and none is completely free in which they do not exist absolute and unqualified. The only freedom which deserves the name,

is that of pursuing our own good in our own way, so long as we do not attempt to deprive others of theirs, or impede their efforts to obtain it. Each is the proper guardian of his own health, whether bodily, or mental and spiritual. Mankind are greater gainers by suffering each other to live as seems good to themselves, than by compelling each to live as seems good to the rest.

Paragraph 14: In this paragraph Mill considers the objection (IID) which would be raised by those who would formulate the problem differently (IIIA) and (IID). There are those who would argue that "the State" has "a deep interest in the whole bodily and mental discipline of every one of its citizens." Mill thinks of the individual as related to society the way a person may or may not be a member of a club. Presumably, individuals may choose and be chosen. His opponents have an *organic* conception of the individual and society. That is, they would argue that an individual is like a part of the body, a limb for example, and cannot survive or have a separate identity apart from social function. The reader must decide which of these alternatives is more plausible.

Mill attributes his opponents' views to the insecure conditions of ancient life, which no longer existed for him. Is this a correct account of why others have the organic view (IIIB)? Mill cites as an example the French thinker Comte (ID). Other examples not mentioned would be Marx, Hegel, and in England, T. H. Green.

Though this doctrine is anything but new, and, to some persons, may have the air of a truism, there is no doctrine which stands more directly opposed to the general tendency of existing opinion and practice. Society has expended fully as much effort in the attempt (according to its lights) to compel people to conform to its notions of personal, as of social excellence. The ancient commonwealths thought themselves entitled to practice, and the ancient philosophers countenanced, the regulation of every part of private conduct by public authority, on the ground that the State had a deep interest in the whole bodily and mental discipline of every one of its citizens; a mode of thinking which may have been admissible in small republics surrounded by powerful enemies, in constant peril of being subverted to foreign attack or internal commotion, and to which even a short interval of relaxed energy and self-command might so easily be fatal, that they could not afford to wait for the salutary permanent effects of freedom. In the modern world, the greater size of political communities, and above all, the separation between spiritual and temporal authority (which placed the direction of men's consciences in other hands than those which controlled their worldly affairs), prevented so great an interference by law in the details of private life; but the engines of moral repression have been wielded more strenuously against divergence from the reigning opinion in self-regarding, than even in social matters; religion, the most powerful of the elements which have entered into the formation of moral feeling, having almost always been governed either by the ambition of a hierarchy, seeking control over every department of human conduct, or by the spirit of Puritanism. And some of those modern reformers who have placed themselves in strongest opposition to the religions of the past, have been noway behind either churches or sects in their assertion of the right of spiritual domination: M. Comte, in particular, whose social system, as unfolded in his *Traité de Politique Positive*, aims at establishing (though by moral more than by legal appliances) a despotism of society over the individual, surpassing anything contemplated in the political ideal of the most rigid disciplinarian among the ancient philosophers.

Apart from the peculiar tenets of individual thinkers, there is also, in the world at large an increasing inclination to stretch unduly the powers of society over the individual, both by the force of opinion and even by that of legislation: and as the tendency of all the changes taking place in the world is to strengthen society, and diminish the power of the individual, this encroachment is not one of the evils which tend spontaneously to disappear, but, on the contrary, to grow more and more formidable. The disposition of mankind, whether as rulers or as fellow-citizens, to impose their own opinions and inclinations as a rule of conduct on others, is so energetically supported by some of the best and by some of the worst feelings incident to human nature, that it is hardly ever kept under restraint by anything but want of power; and as the power is not declining, but growing, unless a strong barrier of moral conviction can be raised against the mischief, we must expect, in the present circumstances of the world, to see it increase.

It will be convenient for the argument, if, instead of at once entering upon the general thesis, we confine ourselves in the first instance to a single branch of it, on which the principle here stated, is, if not fully, yet to a certain point, recognised by the current opinions. This one branch is the Liberty of Thought: from which it is impossible to separate the cognate liberty of speaking and of writing. Although these liberties, to some considerable amount, form part of the political morality of all countries which profess religious toleration and free institutions, the grounds, both philosophical and practical, on which they rest, are perhaps not so familiar to the general mind, nor so thoroughly appreciated by many even of the leaders of opinion, as might have been expected. Those grounds, when rightly understood, are of much wider application than to only one division of the subject, and a thorough consideration of this part of the question will be found the best introduction to the remainder. Those to whom nothing which I am about to say will be new, may therefore, I hope, excuse me, if on a subject which for now three centuries has been so often discussed, I venture on one discussion more.

Paragraph 15: Mill repeats why the problem is important for his own time. Is it important for our time?

Paragraph 16: Mill ends this chapter by indicating what he will do in the next chapter. He claims that he will take up the issue of censorship and use it as an example; if you agree with what he says about censorship, then he thinks you will agree with his argument as a whole. "Those grounds, when rightly understood, are of much wider application."

Chapter II — Socrates and Plato

Introduction

Among all the philosophers of Western Civilization, Plato and Aristotle occupy a special position. Their influence has been so profound in the development of ideas that it can be said that they constitute the sources out of which most of our intellectual heritage has emerged. Even today, almost twenty-five centuries after their historical presence, Plato and Aristotle are indispensable elements in any study of philosophy. As we will see in this and the subsequent chapter, Platonism and Aristotelianism represent the two most powerful philosophical currents that have dominated our development since the time of the ancient Greeks. These two currents have, of course, much in common: after all, they both grew out of the same historical context, and they are both manifestations of the experiences of the same people. Yet, curiously enough, they disclose before our eyes two profoundly different concepts of reality, and the fundamental ideas on which they rest are distinctly opposed.

Plato was born in Athens in 427 B.C., during the time when the Spartan armies were challenging the supremacy of the Athenians. He came from a wealthy, aristocratic family, some of whose members held considerable power over the affairs of the city. Plato himself appears to have desired at first to devote his life to political activities. It was customary in Athens at that time for aristocratic young men to enter the political sphere, which was dominated by a long tradition of democratic practices instituted by Solon. Undoubtedly, Plato would have reached much prominence in government inasmuch as his extraordinary intelligence, his wealth, and his distinguished family would have lent him ample support.

During his lifetime, Plato witnessed many political upheavals. He was born only two years after the death of the great statesman Pericles (461-429 B.C.), the man who ruled the affairs of Athens for more than thirty years, and brought the city to its peak of cultural, military, and political power. The death of Pericles plunged the Athenian world into disarray, especially since the Spartans took advantage of his disappearance in order to devastate the whole Attic peninsula, where Athens was the chief town. Plato lived, then, through the most difficult years of the Peloponnesian War, in which Athens and Sparta fought each other with an unprecedented degree of savagery. When he was only twelve years old, he witnessed the catastrophic defeat of the Athenian fleet at the hands of the Syracuseans, and during his twenty-third year, he saw the Spartan armies march triumphantly into Athens. After the year 404 B.C., he lived in an Athens which was only a vestige of what it had been during his youth.

Sometime around the year 409 B.C., he made the acquaintance of a man about whom we will have much to say presently. His meeting Socrates became indeed the turning point of Plato's life. He abandoned all political ambitions, and devoted himself exclusively to the study of philosophy, first in a constant dialogue with Socrates, and then, after Socrates' execution in 399 B.C., in the company of a wide variety of philosophers both in Greece and elsewhere. The tribulations and trial of Socrates compelled Plato to abandon Athens for a number of years. He travelled accordingly to other neighboring Greek towns where he studied mathematics and physics, and found himself living in Italy where he made the acquaintance of the Pythagoreans. From them he learned, we will see later, a number of fundamental ideas, such as the belief in the immortality of the soul, in reincarnation, and in a spiritual world of nonphysical realities which coexists with the physical world of ordinary sense-perception. We are also told by his biographers that he spent some time in Egypt, probably in the city of Thebes, where he became an initiate of some of the mystery cults practiced by the Egyptians since the remotest times.

Sometime before 390 B.C. he returned to Athens. The political atmosphere created by Socrates' execution had already given way to a climate of tolerance and intellectual openness. He proceeded to establish an academic institution where people from all over the world could devote themselves to the study of philosophy. Its name was simply "the Academy." Here hundreds of scholars pursued mathematical, physical, and philosophical investigations. Plato, a single man throughout his life, was able to dedicate himself to his institution, and with the exception of two or three periods of absence during which he returned to Italy, he remained faithful to his post as head of the Academy.

His philosophical writings were all produced while at the Academy. These comprised about twenty-four dialogues and a few lengthy letters. The *Dialogues* of Plato cover a variety of subjects and can be divided into three groups: (1) The Socratic Dialogues, in which we are given what appears to be a rather accurate description of Socrates' philosophical activity, together with an account of Socrates' trial and death. In them, Socrates is always the main speaker, and it is safe to assume that the words of Socrates are a faithful statement of his actual ideas. The *Apology*, the *Crito*, and the *Euthyphro*, belong to this first group. (2) The *Middle Dialogues*, which were written during Plato's middle years. These include dialogues such as the *Republic*, Plato's most famous work, and in them one notices immediately that Socrates, who still remains the chief speaker, advances ideas which cannot be associated with the historical Socrates. It seems that with the passage of time, Plato outgrew the overwhelming influence of Socrates on his life. He became accordingly more independent and felt free to move far beyond the teaching of his great friend. In philosophy, unlike in religion, there is no master-disciple relationship. In the search for wisdom, the disciple, or rather the student, has to be prepared to revise, expand, or even reject some or all the ideas of the person who has introduced him to philosophy. This was precisely the case with Plato, and we should not be misguided by his *literary* practice of using the name of Socrates in his *Middle Dialogues*. When Socrates speaks in them, it is actually Plato, who is presenting his own ideas. Finally, (3) there are the *Late Dialogues*, written in Plato's last years. In them, the name of Socrates does not always appear, and when it does, the statements put into Socrates' mouth bear little relationship with Socrates' thoughts in actuality. The late dialogues reflect Plato's tendency towards mysticism. They deal with enigmatic themes, as for example when he introduces the much debated subject of a lost continent called Atlantis.

It is impossible, and indeed unwise, to insist on identifying Plato with any one of the characters of the dialogues or with any specific group of dialogues. In a sense, he is all of them and none of them. In his Seventh Letter, for example, he explicitly maintains that his philosophy is not to be found in his writings. These, he says, are mere preparatory exercises which may be of some assistance to those who, like himself, are engaged in the business of looking for the truth. It is possible that the very fact that they are *dialogues*, that is to say, conversations and discussions on human experiences, may stem from his conviction that truth has to be found by each person by himself.

And yet, it is customary to attribute some of the basic ideas expressed by the Platonic Socrates to Plato himself, especially in the context of the *Middle Dialogues*. Tradition, at any rate, has sanctioned this perhaps unfortunate practice, and the development of Platonism is precisely the outgrowth of this. For example, Plato is said to have believed in a certain type of government in which all decisions are made by "philosopher-kings," a government that is far-removed from the democratic egalitarianism in which most of us have been brought up. It is also maintained that Plato believed in the immortality of the soul, in the doctrine of reincarnation, in the existence of a world of divine realities, in the evil character of the human body, in punishments and rewards after death, in the fallibility of sense-perception, in the universal power of mathematics, and in a dualistic conception of reality. It is true that all these ideas can be found in the *Dialogues*, but it is also true that other, perhaps less acceptable notions are encountered everywhere in them. For example, in Plato's writings we are presented with countless myths, tales, and legends concerning the origin of mankind; with ideas about the magical power of numbers; with strange superstitions; with political convictions which were, even during Plato's own time, entirely out of place. Thus, the question is, What was in the mind of this extraordinary man who has determined to so great an extent the fate of Western Civilization?

The most appropriate answer is that all those ideas, indeed many others as well, were in his mind. A man of his spiritual and intellectual stature has to live, as he surely did, with a constant state of change and turmoil in his mind. It is for this reason that we look upon him as a "seminal mind." This is a mind in which there is always something new to be found, a mind that can give itself the rare luxury of contradiction with perfect impunity, a mind out of which countless schools of thought can emerge. Plato had in fact such a mind. Friedrich Nietzsche (1844-1900) once said that the gap that separates Plato from the average man is far wider than the gap that separates the average man from the chimpanzee. Whatever truth there may be in this somewhat unkind comment, we still have to admit that behind the *Dialogues* there must have lived a writer of unusual intelligence, spirituality, and dedication.

Plato died in the year 347 B.C. at the age of eighty, and his biographers tell us that he died in the midst of a wedding festivity given in honor of a student of the Academy. It is curious to observe in this context, that having a superior mind does not always prevent a man from participating in the frolicking feasts of the average human being.

Now that we talk about frolicking activities of the masses, we should introduce the person of Socrates, who was constantly engaged in the affairs of the common man. There are few historical characters as colorful, interesting, and overpowering, as Socrates. Born in the year 469 B.C., he came into this world as the son of an ordinary midwife and an ordinary Athenian citizen. He belonged to an ordinary social class, and for several years practiced a perfectly ordinary vocation: he was a brick layer. He was married to an ordinary woman named Xantippe, with whom he had two children. There was nothing in Socrates' origin, family, social position, or physical appearance, which disclosed the enormity of his intellect and the earnestness with which he viewed human existence. His biographers tell us that he disliked physical work (a common characteristic of most philosophers), and that he enjoyed simple activities such as dancing, drinking, walking, and talking.

We are told by Plato in the *Apology* and by an Athenian general named Xenophon, who wrote extensively on Socrates' life, that when he was still a young man, Socrates underwent a profound conversion as the result of an incident involving the Delphic Oracle. The Greeks of antiquity, a devotedly religious nation, placed great trust in the statements of the priests and priestesses who spoke on behalf of the gods in shrines called "oracles." In the ancient town of Delphi, one of these oracles was found: it was dedicated to Apollo, the magnificent god who "could never speak untruth." It seems that a man named Chaerophon went to Delphi to inquire from Apollo's priestess, "Who among all human beings is the wisest." The priestess replied in unmistakable terms: "Socrates of Athens is the wisest man." When given the disturbing news, Socrates was plunged into a sea of perplexities, for he was aware of his ignorance but was also conscious of the fact that Apollo could not speak except the truth.

From this point on, he felt called to follow a divinely appointed vocation, namely, that of resolving the predicament created by the priestess' utterance. In fact, he spent more than fifty years in search of anyone whose knowledge would surpass his. He questioned many Athenian workers who, like himself, knew practically nothing, politicians who claimed to know what was good for the people, wise men who spoke with authority about the world, poets who described the nature and the affairs of the gods, and philosophers who were in search of wisdom. In the process of so doing, he gained the animosity of many whose sense of security was threatened by the questioning Socrates, and whose feelings of pride were challenged by a humble brick layer who claimed to know nothing, but who consistently unveiled the inauthentic character of their assumed knowledge. At the end of his life, Socrates found himself surrounded by enemies who saw in him a busybody, an impertinent fellow and a public danger.

At the age of seventy, charges were brought against him before an Athenian court, and after a legally suicidal defense, he was convicted of high crimes and condemned to death by drinking poison. He stood before the jury as a man who had fulfilled his destiny; he knew that the only thing that he knew was that he knew nothing, and that, therefore, he knew more than his fellow citizens who only *thought* that they knew, but who in reality did not know anything either. In this sense, he knew more than they; he was, after all, the wisest man, and Apollo, always true to his divine nature, had indeed spoken the truth.

The story is itself a simple one, but beneath this mantle of simplicity there is a whole world of profound philosophical significance. Socrates, the ordinary brick layer, was able to alter the course of Western Civilization. He teaches us that the first duty of a human being is to search for the truth, and that in this sense we should all be philosophers. Pleasures, wealth, money, power, fame—all the common ambitions of human beings—are secondary in life. The search for truth should dominate a person's entire life, even if it entails the renunciation of what ordinary people cherish as indispensable. The only hope that death offers Socrates is that, if there should be another life, he may be able to spend eternity asking questions.

Truth, for Socrates, is not to be found in the external, objective world. The early philosophers like Thales and Anaximander had turned their eyes to the universe in the expectation of finding truth there. But physical investigation, according to Socrates, can only reveal the surface of reality and can only create further confusion in the questioner. Truth, he maintains, can only be found within oneself. "Know thyself" were the words engraved at the entrance of Apollo's shrine in Delphi, and they became the motivating force behind Socrates' search. This search for an understanding of the meaning of one's life is often guided by an inner voice that each one of us can hear within himself if the distractions of the external world have not entirely made him deaf. This voice, either the manifestation of one's subjective conscience, or perhaps the living link between the human self and some superior reality, constitutes the highest tribunal of personal behavior, before which human customs, traditions, beliefs, and accomplishments are of little value. It is because of this that Socrates always assumed an air of arrogance and superiority over the masses of people who acted only by reference to an external source of authority.

In the Socratic dialogues which we will read in this chapter, we will find three different examples of Socrates' activity, and his personality and philosophical significance will become abundantly clear. We will be able to understand Plato's fascination with him and with his search for knowledge. But it is important to observe at this point that Socrates was not, as it may appear at first, a man convinced of the impossibility of attaining truth. The fact that *he* was unsuccessful in his quest, the fact that he stressed his ignorance and his persistent perplexities, and the fact that he went to his death without having come to any firm conclusions about what death is, should not obscure the undeniable fact that he always remained convinced that knowledge was attainable. This conviction was inherited by Plato who, if we take some of the statements of his late dialogues literally, believed that he finally attained truth, but again an inner truth which has little to do with the revelations of the senses.

This explains the change from the Socratic uncertainty of the early dialogues (*Apology* and *Euthyphro*) to the Platonic dogmatism of some sections of the *Phaedo* which will be given in this chapter. In the development of the Platonic tradition, the presence of an even more dogmatic philosophical outlook is easily discernible. Platonism, as this tradition became known, took only certain elements of Socrates' philosophy, and extended its frontier far beyond.

Plato: Euthyphro

Persons of the Dialogue: Socrates; Euthyphro.
Scene: The Porch of the King Archon

[*2*] *Euthyphro.* Why have you left the Lyceum, Socrates? and what are you doing in the Porch of the King Archon? Surely you cannot be concerned in a suit before the King, like myself?

Socrates. Not in a suit, Euthyphro; impeachment is the word which the Athenians use.

Euth. What! I suppose that some one has been prosecuting you, for I cannot believe that you are the prosecutor of another.

Soc. Certainly not.

Euth. Then some one else has been prosecuting you?

Soc. Yes.

Euth. And who is he?

Soc. A young man who is little known, Euthyphro; and I hardly know him: his name is Meletus, and he is of the deme of Pitthis. Perhaps you may remember his appearance; he has a beak, and long straight hair, and a beard which is ill grown.

Euth. No, I do not remember him, Socrates. But what is the charge which he brings against you?

Soc. What is the charge? Well, a very serious charge, which shows a good deal of character in the young man, and for which he is certainly not to be despised. He says he knows how the youth are corrupted and who are their corruptors. I fancy that he must be a wise man, and seeing that I am the reverse of a wise man, he has found me out, and is going to accuse me of corrupting his young friends. And of this our mother the state is to be the judge. Of all our political men he is the only one who seems to me to begin in the right way, with the cultivation of virtue in youth; like a good husbandman, he makes the young shoots his first care, and [*3*] clears away us who are the destroyers of them. This is only the first step; he will afterwards attend to the elder branches; and if he goes on as he has begun, he will be a very great public benefactor.

Euth. I hope that he may; but I rather fear, Socrates, that the opposite will turn out to be the truth. My opinion is that in attacking you he is simply aiming a blow at the foundation of the state. But in what way does he say that you corrupt the young?

Soc. He brings a wonderful accusation against me, which at first hearing excites surprise: he says that I am a poet or maker of gods, and that I invent new gods and deny the existence of old ones; this is the ground of his indictment.

Euth. I understand, Socrates; he means to attack you about the familiar sign which occasionally, as you say, comes to you. He thinks that you are a neologian, and he is going to have you up before the court for this. He knows that such a charge is readily received by the world, as I myself know too well; for when I speak in the assembly about divine things, and foretell the future to them, they laugh at me and think me a madman. Yet every word that I say is true. But they are jealous of us all; and we must be brave and go at them.

Soc. Their laughter, friend Euthyphro, is not a matter of much consequence. For a man may be thought wise; but the Athenians, I suspect, do not much trouble themselves about him until he begins to impart his wisdom to others; and then for some reason or other, perhaps, as you say, from jealousy, they are angry.

Translated by B. Jowett, 1892.

Euth. I am never likely to try their temper in this way.

Soc. I dare say not, for you are reserved in your behaviour, and seldom impart your wisdom. But I have a benevolent habit of pouring out myself to everybody, and would even pay for a listener, and I am afraid that the Athenians may think me too talkative. Now if, as I was saying, they would only laugh at me, as you say that they laugh at you, the time might pass gaily enough in the court; but perhaps they may be in earnest, and then what the end will be you soothsayers only can predict.

Euth. I dare say that the affair will end in nothing, Socrates, and that you will win your cause; and I think that I shall win my own.

Soc. And what is your suit, Euthyphro? are you the pursuer or the defendant?

Euth. I am the pursuer.

Soc. Of whom?

[*4*] *Euth.* You will think me mad when I tell you.

Soc. Why, has the fugitive wings?

Euth. Nay, he is not very volatile at his time of life.

Soc. Who is he?

Euth. My father.

Soc. Your father! my good man?

Euth. Yes.

Soc. And of what is he accused?

Euth. Of murder, Socrates.

Soc. By the powers, Euthyphro! how little does the common herd know of the nature of right and truth. A man must be an extraordinary man, and have made great strides in wisdom, before he could have seen his way to bring such an action.

Euth. Indeed, Socrates, he must.

Soc. I suppose that the man whom your father murdered was one of your relatives—clearly he was; for if he had been a stranger you would never have thought of prosecuting him.

Euth. I am amused, Socrates, at your making a distinction between one who is a relation and one who is not a relation; for surely the pollution is the same in either case, if you knowingly associate with the murderer when you ought to clear yourself and him by proceeding against him. The real question is whether the murdered man has been justly slain. If justly, then your duty is to let the matter alone; but if unjustly, then even if the murderer lives under the same roof with you and eats at the same table, proceed against him. Now the man who is dead was a poor dependant of mine who worked for us as a field labourer on our farm in Naxos, and one day in a fit of drunken passion he got into a quarrel with one of our domestic servants and slew him. My father bound him hand and foot and threw him into a ditch, and then sent to Athens to ask of a diviner what he should do with him. Meanwhile he never attended to him and took no care about him, for he regarded him as a murderer; and thought that no great harm would be done even if he did die. Now this was just what happened. For such was the effect of cold and hunger and chains upom him, that before the messenger returned from the diviner, he was dead. And my father and family are angry with me for taking the part of the murderer and prosecuting my father. They say that he did not kill him and that if he did, the dead man was but a murderer, and I ought not to take any notice, for that a son is impious who prosecutes a father. Which shows, Socrates, how little they know what the gods think about piety and impiety.

Soc. Good heavens, Euthyphro! and is your knowledge of religion and things pious and impious so very exact, that, supposing the circumstances to be as you state them, you are not afraid lest you too may be doing an impious thing in bringing an action against your father?

Euth. The best of Euthyphro, and that which distinguishes him, Socrates, [*5*] from other men, is his exact knowledge of all such matters. What should I be good for without it?

Soc. Rare friend! I think that I cannot do better than be your disciple. Then before the trial with Meletus comes on I shall challenge him, and say that I have always had a great interest in religious questions, and now, as he charges me with rash imaginations and innovations in religion, I have become your disciple. You, Meletus, as I shall say to him, acknowledge Euthyphro to be a great theologian, and sound in his opinions; and if you approve of him you ought to approve of me, and not have me into court; but if you disapprove, you should begin by indicting him who is my teacher, and who will be the ruin, not of the young, but of the old; that is to say, of myself whom he instructs, and of his old father whom he admonishes and chastises. And if Meletus refuses to listen to me, but will go on, and will not shift the indictment from me to you, I cannot do better than repeat this challenge in the court.

Euth. Yes, indeed, Socrates; and if he attempts to indict me, I am mistaken if I do not find a flaw in him; the court shall have a great deal more to say to him than to me.

Soc. And I, my dear friend, knowing this, am desirous of becoming your disciple. For I observe that no one appears to notice you—not even this Meletus; but his sharp eyes have found me out at once, and he has indicted me for impiety. And therefore, I adjure you to tell me the nature of piety and impiety, which you said that you knew so well, and of murder, and of other offences against the gods. What are they? Is not piety in every action always the same? and impiety, and—is it not always the opposite of piety, and also the same with itself, having, as impiety, one notion which includes whatever is impious?

Euth. To be sure, Socrates.

Soc. And what is piety, and what is impiety?

Euth. Piety is doing as I am doing; that is to say, prosecuting any one who is guilty of murder, sacrilege, or of any similar crime—whether he be your father or mother, or whoever he may be—that makes no difference; and not to prosecute them is impiety. And please to consider, Socrates, what a notable proof I will give you of the truth of my words, a proof which I have already given to others:—of the principle, I mean, that the impious, whoever he may be, ought not to go unpunished. For do not men regard Zeus as the best and most righteous of the gods? *[6]*—and yet they admit that he bound his father (Cronos) because he wickedly devoured his sons, and that he too had punished his own father (Uranus) for a similar reason, in a nameless manner. And yet when I proceed against my father, they are angry with me. So inconsistent are they in their way of talking when the gods are concerned, and when I am concerned.

Soc. May not this be the reason, Euthyphro, why I am charged with impiety—that I cannot [accept] these stories about the gods? and therefore I suppose that people think me wrong. But, as you who are well informed about them approve of them, I cannot do better than assent to your superior wisdom. What else can I say, confessing as I do, that I know nothing about them? Tell me, for the love of Zeus, whether you really believe that they are true.

Euth. Yes, Socrates; and things more wonderful still, of which the world is in ignorance.

Soc. And do you really believe that the gods fought with one another, and had dire quarrels, battles, and the like, as the poets say, and as you may see represented in the works of great artists? The temples are full of them; and notably the robe of Athene, which is carried up to the Acropolis at the great Panathenaea, is embroidered with them. Are all these tales of the gods true, Euthyphro?

Euth. Yes, Socrates; and, as I was saying, I can tell you, if you would like to hear them, many other things about the gods which would quite amaze you.

Soc. I dare say; and you shall tell me them at some other time when I have leisure. But just at present I would rather hear from you a more precise answer, which you have not as yet given, my friend, to the question, What is "piety"? When asked, you only replied, Doing as you do, charging your father with murder.

Eith. And what I said was true, Socrates.

Soc. No doubt, Euthyphro; but you would admit that there are many other pious acts?

Euth. There are.

Soc. Remember that I did not ask you to give me two or three examples of piety, but to explain the general idea which makes all pious things to be pious. Do you not recollect that there was one idea which made the impious impious, and the pious pious?

Euth. I remember.

Soc. Tell me what is the nature of this idea, and then I shall have a standard to which I may look, and by which I may measure actions, whether yours or those of any one else, and then I shall be able to say that such and such an action is pious, such another impious.

Euth. I will tell you, if you like.

Soc. I should very much like.

Euth. Piety, then, is that which is dear to the gods, and impiety is that which is not dear to them.

[7] Soc. Very good. Euthyphro; you have now given me the sort of answer which I wanted. But whether what you say is true or not I cannot as yet tell, although I make no doubt that you will prove the truth of your words.

Euth. Of course.

Soc. Come, then, and let us examine what we are saying. That thing or person which is dear to the gods is pious, and that thing or person which is hateful to the gods is impious, these two being the extreme opposites of one another. Was not that said?

Euth. It was.

Soc. And well said?

Euth. Yes, Socrates, I thought so; it was certainly said.

Soc. And further, Euthyphro, the gods were admitted to have enmities and hatreds and differences?

Euth. Yes, that was also said.

Soc. And what sort of difference creates enmity and anger? Suppose for example that you and I, my good friend, differ about a number; do differences of this sort make us enemies and set us at variance with one another? Do we not go at once to arithemtic, and put an end to them by a sum?

Euth. True.

Soc. Or suppose that we differ about magnitudes, do we not quickly end the differences by measuring?

Euth. Very true.

Soc. And we end a controversy about heavy and light by resorting to a weighing machine?

Euth. To be sure.

Soc. But what differences are there which cannot be thus decided, and which therefore make us angry and set us at enmity with one another? I dare say the answer does not occur to you at the moment, and therefore I will suggest that these enmities arise when the matters of difference are the just and unjust, good and evil, honourable and dishonourable. Are not these the points about which men differ, and about which when we are unable satisfactorily to decide our differences, you and I and all of us quarrel, when we do quarrel?

Euth. Yes, Socrates, the nature of the differences about which we quarrel is such as you describe.

Soc. And the quarrels of the gods, noble Euthyphro, when they occur, are of a like nature?

Euth. Certainly they are.

Soc. They have differences of opinion, as you say, about good and evil, just and unjust, honourable and dishonourable: there would have been no quarrels among them, if there had been no such differences—would there now?

Euth. You are quite right.

Soc. Does not every man love that which he deems noble and just and good, and hate the opposite of them?

Euth. Very true.

Soc. But, as you say, people regard the same things, some as just and others as unjust,—about these they dispute; and so there arise wars and fightings among them. [*8*]

Euth. Very true.

Soc. Then the same things are hated by the gods and loved by the gods, and are both hateful and dear to them?

Euth. True.

Soc. And upon this view the same things, Euthyphro, will be pious and also impious?

Euth. So I should suppose.

Soc. Then, my friend, I remark with surprise that you have not answered the question which I asked. For I certainly did not ask you to tell me what action is both pious and impious: but now it would seem that what is loved by the gods is also hated by them. And therefore, Euthyphro, in thus chastising your father you may very likely be doing what is agreeable to Zeus but disagreeable to Cronos or Uranus, and what is acceptable to Hephaestus but unacceptable to Here, and there may be other gods who have similar differences of opinion.

Euth. But I believe, Socrates, that all the gods would be agreed as to the propriety of punishing a murderer: there would be no difference of opinion about that.

Soc. Well, but speaking of men, Euthyphro, did you ever hear any one arguing that a murderer or any sort of evil-doer ought to be let off?

Euth. I should rather say that these are the questions which they are always arguing, especially in courts of law: they commit all sorts of crimes, and there is nothing which they will not do or say in their own defence.

Soc. But do they admit their guilt, Euthyphro, and yet say that they ought not to be punished?

Euth. No; they do not.

Soc. Then there are some things which they do not venture to say and do: for they do not venture to argue that the guilty are to be unpunished, but they deny their guilt, do they not?

Euth. Yes.

Soc. Then they do not argue that the evil-doer should not be punished, but they argue about the fact of who the evil-doer is, and what he did and when?

Euth. True.

Soc. And the gods are in the same case, if, as you assert, they quarrel about just and unjust, and some of them say while others deny that injustice is done among them. For surely neither God nor man will ever venture to say that the doer of injustice is not to be punished?

Euth. That is true, Socrates, in the main.

Soc. But they join issue about the particulars —gods and men alike; and, if they dispute at all, they dispute about some act which is called in question, and which by some is affirmed to be just, by others to be unjust. Is not that true?

Euth. Quite true.

[*9*] *Soc.* Well then, my dear friend Euthyphro, do tell me, for my better instruction and information, what proof have you that in the opinion of all the gods a servant who is guilty of murder, and is put in chains by the master of the dead man, and dies because he is put in chains before he who bound him can learn from the interpreters of the gods what he ought to do with him, dies unjustly; and that on behalf of such an one a son ought to proceed against his father and accuse him of murder. How would you show that all the gods absolutely agree in approving of his act? Prove to me that they do, and I will applaud your wisdom as long as I live.

Euth. It will be a difficult task; but I could make the matter very clear indeed to you.

Soc. I understand; you mean to say that I am not so quick of apprehension as the judges: for to them you will be sure to prove that the act is unjust, and hateful to the gods.

Euth. Yes indeed, Socrates; at least if they will listen to me.

Soc. But they will be sure to listen if they find that you are a good speaker. There was a notion that came into my mind while you were speaking; I said to myself: "Well, and what if Euthyphro does prove to me that all the gods regarded the death of the serf as unjust, how do I know anything more of the nature of piety and impiety? for granting that this action may be hateful to the gods, still piety and impiety are not adequately defined by these distinctions, for that which is hateful to the gods has been shown to be also pleasing and dear to them." And therefore, Euthyphro, I do not ask you to prove this; I will suppose, if you like, that all the gods condemn and abominate such an action. But I will amend the definition so far as to say that what all the gods hate is impious, and what they love pious or holy; and what some of them love and others hate is both or neither. Shall this be our definition of piety and impiety?

Euth. Why not, Socrates?

Soc. Why not! certainly, as far as I am concerned, Euthyphro, there is no reason why not. But whether this admission will greatly assist you in the task of instructing me as you promised, is a matter for you to consider.

Euth. Yes, I should say that what all the gods love is pious and holy, and the opposite which they all hate, impious.

Soc. Ought we to enquire into the truth of this, Euthyphro, or simply to accept the mere statement on our own authority and that of others? What do you say?

Euth. We should enquire; and I believe that the statement will stand the test of enquiry.

Soc. We shall know better, my good friend, in a little while. The point which I should first wish to understand is whether the pious or holy is beloved by the gods because it is holy, [*10*] or holy because it is beloved of the gods.

Euth. I do not understand your meaning, Socrates.

Soc. I will endeavour to explain: we speak of carrying and we speak of being carried, of leading and being led, seeing and being seen. You know that in all such cases there is a difference, and you know also in what the difference lies?

Euth. I think that I understand.

Soc. And is not that which is beloved distinct from that which loves?

Euth. Certainly.

Soc. Well; and now tell me, is that which is carried in this state of carrying because it is carried, or for some other reason?

Euth. No; that is the reason.

Soc. And the same is true of what is led and of what is seen?

Euth. True.

Soc. And a thing is not seen because it is visible, but conversely, visible because it is seen; nor is a thing led because it is in the state of being led, or carried because it is in the state of being carried, but the converse of this. And now I think, Euthyphro, that my meaning will be intelligible; and my meaning is, that any state of action or passion implies previous action or passion. It does not become because it is becoming, but it is in a state of becoming because it becomes; neither does it suffer because it is in a state of suffering, but it is in a state of suffering because it suffers. Do you not agree?

Euth. Yes.

Soc. Is not that which is loved in some state either of becoming or suffering?

Euth. Yes.

Soc. And the same holds as in the previous instances; the state of being loved follows the act of being loved, and not the act the state.

Euth. Certainly.

Soc. And what do you say of piety, Euthyphro: is not piety, according to your definition, loved by all the gods?

Euth. Yes.

Soc. Because it is pious or holy, or for some other reason?

Euth. No, that is the reason.

Soc. It is loved because it is holy, not holy because it is loved?

Euth. Yes.

Soc. And that which is dear to the gods is loved by them, and is in a state to be loved of them because it is loved of them?

Euth. Certainly.

Soc. Then that which is dear to the gods, Euthyphro, is not holy, nor is that which is holy loved of God, as you affirm; but they are two different things.

Euth. How do you mean, Socrates?

Soc. I mean to say that the holy has been acknowledged by us to be loved of God because it is holy, not to be holy because it is loved.

Euth. Yes.

Soc. But that which is dear to the gods is dear to them because it is loved by them, not loved by them because it is dear to them.

Euth. True.

Soc. But, friend Euthyphro, if that which is holy is the same with that which is dear to God, and is loved because it is holy, then that which is dear to God would have been loved as being [*11*] dear to God; but if that which is dear to God is dear to him because loved by him, then that which is holy would have been holy becauses loved by him. But now you see that the reverse is the case, and that they are quite different from one another. For one is of a kind to be loved because it is loved, and the other is loved because it is of a kind to be loved. Thus you appear to me, Euthyphro, when I ask you what is the essence of holiness, to offer an attribute of being loved by all the gods. But you still refuse to explain to me the nature of holiness. And therefore, if you please, I will ask you not to hide your treasure, but to tell me once more what holiness or piety really is, whether dear to the gods or not (for that is a matter about which we will not quarrel); and what is impiety?

Euth. I really do not know, Socrates, how to express what I mean. For somehow or other our arguments, on whatever ground we rest them, seem to turn round and walk away from us.

Soc. Your words, Euthyphro, are like the handiwork of my ancestor Daedalus; and if I were the sayer or propounder of them, you might say that my arguments walk away and will not remain fixed where they are placed because I am a descendant of his. But now, since these notions are your own, you must find some other gibe, for they certainly, as you yourself allow, show an inclination to be on the move.

Euth. Nay, Socrates, I shall still say that you are the Daedalus who sets arguments in motion; not I, certainly, but you make them move or go round, for they would never have stirred, as far as I am concerned.

Soc. Then I must be greater than Daedalus; for whereas he only made his own inventions to move, I move those of other people as well. And the beauty of it is, that I would rather not. For I would give the wisdom of Daedalus, and the wealth of Tantalus, to be able to detain them and keep them fixed. But enough of this. As I perceive that you are lazy, I will myself endeavor to show you how you might instruct me in the nature of piety; and I hope that you will not grudge your labour. Tell me, then,—Is not that which is pious necessarily just?

Euth. Yes.

Soc. And is, then, all which is just pious? or, is that which is pious all just, [*12*] but that which is just, only in part and not all, pious?

Euth. I do not understand you, Socrates.

Soc. And yet I know that you are as much wiser than I am, as you are younger. But, as I was saying, revered friend, the abundance of your wisdom makes you lazy. Please to exert yourself, for there is no real difficulty in understanding me. What I mean I may explain by an illustration of what I do not mean. The poet (Stasinus) sings—

> *Of Zeus, the author and creator of all these things, You will not tell: for where there is fear there is also reverence.*

Now I disagree with this poet. Shall I tell you in what respect?

Euth. By all means.

Soc. I shall not say that where there is fear there is also reverence; for I am sure that many persons fear poverty and disease, and the like evils, but I do not perceive that they reverence the objects of their fear.

Euth. Very true.

Soc. But where reverence is, there is fear; for he who has a feeling of reverence and shame about the commission of any action, fears and is afraid of an ill reputation.

Euth. No doubt.

Soc. Then we are wrong in saying that where there is fear there is also reverence; and we should say, where there is reverence there is also fear. But there is not always reverence where there is fear; for fear is a more extended notion, and reverence is a part of fear, just as the odd is a part of number, and number is a more extended notion than the odd. I suppose that you follow me now?

Euth. Quite well.

Soc. That was the sort of question which I meant to raise when I asked whether the just is always the pious, or the pious always the just; and whether there may not be justice where there is not piety; for justice is the more extended notion of which piety is only a part. Do you dissent?

Euth. No, I think that you are quite right.

Soc. Then, if piety is a part of justice, I suppose that we should enquire what part. If you had pursued the enquiry in the previous cases; for instance, if you had asked me what is an even number, and what part of number the even is, I should have had no difficulty in replying, a number which represents a figure having two equal sides. Do you not agree?

Euth. Yes, I quite agree.

Soc. In like manner, I want you to tell me what part of justice is piety or holiness, that I may be able to tell Meletus not to do me injustice, or indict me for impiety, as I am now adequately instructed by you in the nature of piety or holiness and their opposites.

Euth. Piety or holiness, Socrates, appears to me to be that part of justice which attends to the gods, as there is the other part of justice which attends to men.

[*13*] *Soc.* That is good, Euthyphro; yet still there is a little point about which I should like to have further information, What is the meaning of "attention"? For attention can hardly be used in the same sense when applied to the gods as when applied to other things. For instance, horses are said to require attention, and not every person is able to attend to them; but only a person skilled in horsemanship. Is it not so?

Euth. Certainly.

Soc. I should suppose that the art of horsemanship is the art of attending to horses?

Euth. Yes.

Soc. Nor is every one qualified to attend to dogs, but only the huntsman?

Euth. True.

Soc. And I should also conceive that the art of attending to oxen?

Euth. Very true.

Soc. In like manner holiness or piety is the art of attending to the gods—that would be your meaning, Euthyphro?

Euth. Yes.

Soc. And is not attention always designed for the good or benefit of that to which the attention is given? As in the case of horses, you may observe that when attended to by the horseman's art they are benefited and improved, are they not?

Euth. True.

Soc. As the dogs are benefited by the huntsman's art, and the oxen by the art of the oxherd, and all other things are tended or attended for their good and not for their hurt?

Euth. Certainly, not for their hurt.

Soc. But for their good?

Euth. Of course.

Soc. And does piety or holiness, which has been defined to be the art of attending to the gods, benefit or improve them? Would you say that when you do a holy act you make any of the gods better?

Euth. No, no; that was certainly not what I meant.

Soc. And I, Euthyphro, never supposed that you did. I asked you the question about the nature of the attention, because I thought that you did not.

Euth. You do me justice, Socrates; that is not

the sort of attention which I mean.

Soc. Good: but I must still ask what is this attention to the gods which is called piety?

Euth. It is such, Socrates, as servants show to their masters.

Soc. I understand—a sort of ministration to the gods.

Euth. Exactly.

Soc. Medicine is also a sort of ministration or service, having in view the attainment of some object—would you say of health?

Euth. I should.

Soc. Again, there is an art which ministers to the ship-builder with a view to the attainment of some result?

Euth. Yes, Socrates, with a view to the building of a ship.

Soc. As there is an art which ministers to the housebuilder with a view to the building of a house?

Euth. Yes.

Soc. And now tell me, my good friend, about the art which ministers to the gods: what work does that help to accomplish? For you must surely know if, as you say, you are of all men living the one who is best instructed in religion.

Euth. And I speak the truth, Socrates.

Soc. Tell me then, oh tell me—what is that fair work which the gods do by the help of our ministrations?

Euth. Many and fair, Socrates, are the works which they do.

[*14*] *Soc.* Why, my friend, and so are those of a general. But the chief of them is easily told. Would you not say that victory in war is the chief of them?

Euth. Certainly.

Soc. Many and fair, too, are the works of the husbandman, if I am not mistaken; but his chief work is the production of food from the earth?

Euth. Exactly.

Soc. And of the many and fair things done by the gods, which is the chief or principal one?

Euth. I have told you already, Socrates, that to learn all these things accurately will be very tiresome. Let me simply say that piety or holiness is learning how to please the gods in word and deed, by prayers and sacrifices. Such piety is the salvation of families and states, just as the impious, which is unpleasing to the gods, is their ruin and destruction.

Soc. I think that you could have answered in much fewer words the chief question which I asked, Euthyphro, if you had chosen. But I see plainly that you are not disposed to instruct me—clearly not: else why, when we reached the point, did you turn aside? Had you only answered me I should have truly learned of you by this time the nature of piety. Now, as the asker of a question is necessarily dependent on the answerer, whither he leads I must follow; and can only ask again, what is the pious, and what is piety? Do you mean that they are a sort of science of praying and sacrificing?

Euth. Yes, I do.

Soc. And sacrificing is giving to the gods, and prayer is asking of the gods?

Euth. Yes, Socrates.

Soc. Upon this view, then, piety is a science of asking and giving?

Euth. You understand me capitally, Socrates.

Soc. Yes, my friend; the reason is that I am a votary of your science, and give my mind to it, and therefore nothing which you say will be thrown away upon me. Please then to tell me, what is the nature of this service to the gods? Do you mean that we prefer requests and give gifts to them?

Euth. Yes, I do.

Soc. Is not the right way of asking to ask of them what we want?

Euth. Certainly.

Soc. And the right way of giving is to give to them in return what they want of us. There would be no meaning in an art which gives to any one that which he does not want.

Euth. Very true, Socrates.

Soc. Then piety, Euthyphro, is an art which gods and men have of doing business with one another?

Euth. That is an expression which you may use, if you like.

Soc. But I have no particular liking for anything but the truth. I wish, however, that you would tell me what benefit accrues to the gods from our gifts. There is no doubt about what they give to us; [*15*] for there is no good thing which they do not give; but how we can give any good thing to them in return is far from being equally clear. If they give everything and we give nothing, that must be an affair of business in which we have very greatly the advantage of them.

Euth. And do you imagine, Socrates, that any benefit accrues to the gods from our gifts?

Soc. But if not, Euthyphro, what is the meaning of gifts which are conferred by us upon the gods?

Euth. What else, but tributes of honour; and, as I was just now saying, what pleases them?

Soc. Piety, then, is pleasing to the gods, but not beneficial or dear to them?

Euth. I should say that nothing could be dearer.

Soc. Then once more the assertion is repeated that piety is dear to the gods?

Euth. Certainly.

Soc. And when you say this, can you wonder at your words not standing firm, but walking away? Will you accuse me of being the Daedalus who makes them walk away, not perceiving that there is another and far greater artist than Daedalus who makes them go round in a circle, and he is yourself; for the argument, as you will perceive, comes round to the same point. Were we not saying that the holy or pious was not the same with that which is loved of the gods? Have you forgotten?

Euth. I quite remember.

Soc. And are you not saying that what is loved of the gods is holy and, is not this the same as what is dear to them—do you see?

Euth. True.

Soc. Then either we were wrong in our former assertion; or, if we were right then, we are wrong now.

Euth. One of the two must be true.

Soc. Then we must begin again and ask, What is piety? That is an enquiry which I shall never be weary of pursuing as far as in me lies; and I entreat you not to scorn me, but to apply your mind to the utmost, and tell me the truth. For, if any man knows, you are he; and therefore I must detain you, like Proteus, until you tell. If you had not certainly known the nature of piety and impiety, I am confident that you would never, on behalf of a serf, have charged your aged father with murder. You would not have run such a risk of doing wrong in the sight of the gods, and you would have had too much respect for the opinions of men. I am sure, therefore, that you know the nature of piety and impiety. Speak out then, my dear Euthyphro, and do not hide your knowledge.

Euth. Another time, Socrates; for I am in a hurry, and must go now.

Soc. Alas! my companion, and will you leave me in despair? I was hoping that you would instruct me in the nature of piety and impiety; and then I might have cleared myself of Meletus and his indictment. [*16*] I would have told him that I had been enlightened by Euthyphro, and had given up rash innovations and speculations, in which I indulged only through ignorance, and that now I am about to lead a better life.

Plato: Apology

[17] How you, O Athenians, have been affected by my accusers, I cannot tell; but I know that they almost made me forget who I was—so persuasively did they speak; and yet they have hardly uttered a word of truth. But of the many falsehoods told by them, there was one which quite amazed me;—I mean when they said that you should be upon your guard and not allow yourselves to be deceived by the force of my eloquence. To say this, when they were certain to be detected as soon as I opened my lips and proved myself to be anything but a great speaker, did indeed appear to me most shameless—unless by the force of eloquence they mean the force of truth; for if such is their meaning, I admit that I am eloquent. But in how different a way from theirs! Well, as I was saying, they have scarcely spoken the truth at all; but from me you shall hear the whole truth: not, however, delivered after their manner in a set oration duly ornamented with words and phrases. No, by heaven! but I shall use the words and arguments which occur to me at the moment; for I am confident in the justice of my cause: at my time of life I ought not to be appearing before you, O men of Athens, in the character of a juvenile orator—let no one expect it of me. And I must beg of you to grant me a favour:—If I defend myself in my accustomed manner, and you hear me using the words which I have been in the habit of using in the agora, at the tables of the money-changers, or anywhere else, I would ask you not to be surprised, and not to interrupt me on this account. For I am more than seventy years of age, and appearing now for the first time in a court of law, I am quite a stranger to the language of the place; and therefore I would have you regard me as if I were really a stranger, [18] whom you would excuse if he spoke in his native tongue, and after the fashion of his country:—Am I making an unfair request of you? Never mind the manner, which may or may not be good; but think only of the truth of my words, and give heed to that: let the speaker speak truly and the judge decide justly.

Translated by B. Jowett, 1892.

And first, I have to reply to the older charges and to my first accusers, and then I will go on to the later ones. For of old I have had many accusers, who have accused me falsely to you during many years; and I am more afraid of them than of Anytus and his associates, who are dangerous, too, in their own way. But far more dangerous are the others, who began when you were children, and took possession of your minds with their falsehoods, telling of one Socrates, a wise man, who speculated about the heaven above, and searched into the earth beneath, and made the worse appear the better cause. The disseminators of this tale are the accusers whom I dread; for their hearers are apt to fancy that such enquirers do not believe in the existence of the gods. And they are many, and their charges against me are of ancient date, and they were made by them in the days when you were more impressible than you are now—in childhood, or it may have been in youth—and the cause when heard went by default, for there was none to answer. And hardest of all, I do not know and cannot tell the names of my accusers; unless in the chance case of a Comic poet. All who from envy and malice have persuaded you—some of them having first convinced themselves—all this class of men are most difficult to deal with; for I cannot have them up here, and cross-examine them, and therefore I must simply fight with shadows in my own defence, and argue when there is no one who answers. I will ask you then to assume with me, as I was saying, that my opponents are of two kinds, one recent, the other ancient; and I hope that you will see the propriety of my answering the latter first, for these accusations you heard long before the others, and much oftener.

[*19*] Well, then, I must make my defence, and endeavor to clear away in a short time a slander which has lasted a long time. May I succeed, if to succeed be for my good and yours, or likely to avail me in my cause! The task is not an easy one; I quite understand the nature of it. And so leaving the event with God, in obedience to the law I will now make my defence

I will begin at the beginning and ask what is the accusation which has given rise to the slander of me, and in fact has encourged Meletus to prefer this charge against me. Well, what do the slanderers say? They shall be my prosecutors, and I will sum up their words in an affidavit: "Socrates is an evil-doer, and a curious person, who searches into things under the earth and in heaven, and he makes the worse appear the better cause; and he teaches the aforesaid doctrines to others." Such is the nature of the accusation: it is just what you have yourselves seen in the comedy of Aristophanes, who has introduced a man whom he calls Socrates, going about and saying that he walks in air, and talking a deal of nonsense concerning matters of which I do not pretend to know either much or little—not that I mean to speak disparagingly of any one who is a student of natural philosophy. I should be very sorry if Meletus could bring so grave a charge against me. But the simple truth is, O Athenians, that I have nothing to do with physical speculations. Very many of those here present are witnesses to the truth of this, and to them I appeal. Speak then, you who have heard me, and tell your neighbours whether any of you have ever known me to hold forth in few words or in many upon such matters. . . . You hear their answer. And from what they say of this part of the charge you will be able to judge of the truth of the rest.

As little foundation is there for the report that I am a teacher, and take money; this accusation has no more truth in it than the other. Although, if a man were really able to instruct mankind, to receive money for giving instruction would, in my opinion, be an honour to him. There is Gorgias of Leontium, and Prodicus of Ceos, and Hippias of Elis, who go the round of the cities, and are able to persuade the young men to leave their own citizens by whom they might be taught for nothing, [*20*] and come to them whom they not only pay, but are thankful if they may be allowed to pay them. There is at this time a Parian philosopher residing in Athens, of whom I have heard; and I came to hear of him in this way:—I came across a man who has spent a world of money on the Sophists, Callias, the son of Hipponicus, and knowing that he had sons, I asked him: "Callias," I said, "if your two sons were foals or calves, there would be no difficulty in finding some one to put over them; we should hire a trainer of horses, or a farmer probably, who would improve and perfect them in their own proper virtue and excellence; but as they are human beings, whom are you thinking of placing over them? Is there any one who understands human and political virtue? You must have thought about the matter, for you have sons; is there any one?" "There is," he said. "Who is he?" said I; "and of what country? and what does he charge?" "Evenus the Parian," he replied; "he is the man, and his charge is five minae." Happy is Evenus, I said to myself, if he really has this wisdom, and teaches at such a moderate charge. Had I the same, I should have been very proud and conceited; but the truth is that I have no knowledge of the kind.

I dare say, Athenians, that some one among you will reply, "Yes, Socrates, but what is the origin of these accusations which are brought against you; there must have been something strange which you have been doing? All these rumours and this talk about you would never have arisen if you had been like other men: tell us, then, what is the cause of them, for we should be sorry to judge hastily of you." Now I regard this as a fair challenge, and I will endeavour to explain to you the reason why I am called wise and have such an evil fame. Please to attend then. And although some of you may think that I am joking, I declare that I will tell you the entire truth. Men of Athens, this reputation of mine has come to a certain sort of wisdom which I possess. If you ask me what kind of wisdom, I reply, wisdom such as may perhaps be attained by man, for to that extent I am inclined to believe that I am wise; whereas the persons of whom I was speaking have a superhuman wisdom, which I may fail to describe, because I have it not myself; and he who says that I have, speaks falsely, and is taking away my character. And here, O men of Athens, I must beg you not to interrupt me, even if I seem to say something extravagant. For the word which I will speak is not mine. I will refer you to a witness who is worthy of credit; that witness shall be the God of Delphi —he will tell you about my wisdom, if I have any, and of what sort it is. You must have known Chaerephon; he was early a friend of mine, and also a friend of yours, [*21*] for he shared in the recent exile of the people, and returned with you. Well, Chaerephon, as you know, was very impetuous in all his doings, and he went to Delphi and boldly asked the oracle to tell him whether—as I was saying, I must beg you not to interrupt—he asked the oracle to tell him whether any one was wiser than I was, and the Pythian prophetess answered, that there was no man wiser. Chaerephon is dead himself; but his brother, who is in court, will confirm the truth of what I am saying.

Why do I mention this? Because I am going to explain to you why I have such an evil name. When I heard the answer, I said to myself, What can the god mean? and what is the interpretation of his riddle? for I know that I have no wisdom, small or great. What then can he mean when he says that I am the wisest of men? And yet he is a god, and cannot lie; that would be against his nature. After long consideration, I thought of a method of trying the question. I reflected that if I could only find a man wiser than myself, then I might go to the god with a refutation in my hand. I should say to him, "Here is a man who is wiser than I am; but you said that I was the wisest." Accordingly I went to one who had the reputation of wisdom, and observed him—his name I need not mention; he was a politician whom I selected for examination—and the result was as follows: When I began to talk with him, I could not help thinking that he was not really wise, although he was thought wise by many, and still wiser by himself; and thereupon I tried to explain to him that he thought himself wise, but was not really wise; and the consequence was that he hated me, and his enmity was shared by several who were present and heard me. So I left him, saying to myself, as I went away: Well, though I do not suppose that either of us knows anything really beautiful and good, I am better off than he is,—for he knows nothing, and thinks that he knows: I neither know nor think that I know. In this latter particular, then, I seem to have slightly the advantage of him. Then I went to another who had still higher pretensions to wisdom, and my conclusion was exactly the same. Whereupon I made another enemy of him, and of many others besides him.

Then I went to one man after another, being not unconscious of the enmity which I provoked, and I lamented and feared this: But necessity was laid upon me,—the word of God, I thought, ought to be considered first. And I said to myself, Go I must to all who appear to know, [*22*] and find out the meaning of the oracle. And I swear to you, Athenians, by the dog I swear!—for I must tell you the truth—the result of my mission was just this: I found that the men most in repute were all but the most foolish; and that others less esteemed were really wiser and better. I will tell you the tale of my wanderings and of the "Herculean" labours, as I may call them, which I endured only to find at last the oracle irrefutable. After the politicians, I went to the poets; tragic, dithyrambic, and all sorts. And there, I said to myself, you will be instantly detected; now you will find out that you are more ignorant than they are. Accordingly, I took them some of the most elaborate passages in their own writings, and asked what was the meaning of them—thinking that they would teach me something. Will you believe me? I am almost ashamed to confess the truth, but I must say that there is hardly a person present who would not have talked better about their poetry than they did themselves. Then I knew that not by wisdom do poets write poetry, but by a sort of genius and inspiration; they are like diviners or soothsayers who also say many fine things, but do not understand the meaning of them. The poets appeared to me to be much in the same case; and I further observed that upon the strength of their poetry they believed themselves to be the wisest of men in other things in which they were not wise. So I departed, conceiving myself to be superior to them for the same reason that I was superior to the politicians.

At last I went to the artisans, for I was conscious that I knew nothing at all, as I may say, and I was sure that they knew many fine things; and here I was not mistaken, for they did know many things of which I was ignorant, and in this they certainly were wiser than I was. But I observed that even the good artisans fell into the same error as the poets;—because they were good workmen, they thought that they also knew all sorts of high matters, and this defect in them overshadowed their wisdom; and therefore I asked myself on behalf of the oracle, whether I would like to be as I was, neither having their knowledge nor their ignorance, or like them in both; and I made answer to myself and to the oracle that I was better off as I was.

This inquisition has led to my having many enemies of the worst and most dangerous kind, [*23*] and has given occasion also to many calumnies. And I am called wise, for my hearers always imagine that I myself possess the wisdom which I find wanting in others: but the truth is, O men of Athens, that God only is wise; and by his answer he intends to show that the wisdom of men is worth little or nothing; he is not speaking of Socrates; he is only using my name by way of illustration, as if he said, He, O men, is the wisest, who, like Socrates, knows that his wisdom is in truth worth nothing. And so I go about the world, obedient to the god, and search and make enquiry into the wisdom of any one, whether citizen or stranger, who appears to be wise; and if he is not wise, then in vindication of the oracle I show him that he is not wise; and my occupation quite absorbs me, and I have no time to give either to any public matter of interest or to any concern of my own, but I am in utter poverty by reason of my devotion to the god.

There is another thing:—young men of the richer classes, who have not much to do, come about me of their own accord; they like to hear the pretenders examined, and they often imitate me, and proceed to examine others; there are plenty of persons, as they quickly discover, who think that they know something, but really know little or nothing; and then those who are examined by them instead of being angry with themselves are angry with me: This confounded Socrates, they say; this villainous misleader of youth!—and then if somebody asks them, Why, what evil does he practise or teach? they do not know, and cannot tell; but in order that they may not appear to be at a loss, they repeat the ready-made charges which are used against all philosophers about teaching things up in the clouds and under the earth, and having no gods, and making the worse appear the better cause; for they do not like to confess that their pretence of knowledge has been detected—which is the truth; and as they are numerous and ambitious and energetic, and are drawn up in battle array and have persuasive tongues, they have filled your ears with their loud and inveterate calumnies. And this is the reason why my three accusers, Meletus and Anytus and Lycon, have set upon me; Meletus, who has a quarrel with me on behalf of the poets; Anytus, on behalf of the craftsmen and politicians; [*24*] Lycon, on behalf of the rhetoricians: and as I said at the beginning, I cannot expect to get rid of such a mass of calumny all in a moment. And this, O men of Athens, is the truth and the whole truth; I have concealed nothing, I have dissembled nothing. And yet, I know that my plainness of speech makes them hate me, and what is their hatred but a proof that I am speaking the truth?—Hence has arisen the prejudice against me; and this is the reason of it, as you will find out either in this or in any future enquiry.

I have said enough in my defence against the first class of my accusers; I turn to the second class. They are headed by Meletus, that good man and true lover of this country, as he calls himself. Against these, too, I must try to make a defence:—Let their affidavit be read: it contains something of this kind: It says that Socrates is a doer of evil, who corrupts the youth; and who does not believe in the gods of the state, but has other new divinities of his own. Such is the charge; and now let us examine the particular counts. He says that I am a doer of evil, and corrupt the youth; but I say, O men of Athens that Meletus is a doer of evil, in that he pretends to be in earnest when he is only in jest, and is so eager to bring men to trial from a pretended zeal and interest about matters in which he really never had the smallest interest. And the truth of this I will endeavour to prove to you.

Come hither, Meletus, and let me ask a question of you. You think a great deal about the improvement of youth?

Yes, I do.

Tell the judges, then, who is their improver;

for you must know, as you have taken the pains to discover their corrupter, and are citing and accusing me before them. Speak, then, and tell the judges who their improver is.—Observe, Meletus, that you are silent, and have nothing to say. But is not this rather disgraceful, and a very considerable proof of what I was saying, that you have no interest in the matter? Speak up, friend, and tell us who their improver is.

The laws.

But that, my good sir, is not my meaning. I want to know who the person is, who, in the first place, knows the laws.

The judges, Socrates, who are present in court.

What, do you mean to say, Meletus, that they are able to instruct and improve youth?

Certainly they are.

What, all of them, or some only and not others?

All of them.

By the goddess Here, that is good news! There are plenty of improvers, [*25*] then. And what do you say of the audience,—do they improve them?

Yes, they do.

And the senators?

Yes, the senators improve them.

But perhaps the members of the assembly corrupt them?—or do they too improve them?

They improve them.

Then every Athenian improves and elevates them; all with the exception of myself; and I alone am their corrupter? Is that what you affirm?

That is what I stoutly affirm.

I am very unfortunate if you are right. But suppose I ask you a question: How about horses? Does one man do them harm and all the world good? Is not the exact opposite the truth? One man is able to do them good, or at least not many;—the trainer of horses, that is to say, does them good, and others who have to do with them rather injure them? Is not that true, Meletus, of horses, or of any other animals? Most assuredly it is; whether you and Anytus say yes or no. Happy indeed would be the condition of youth if they had one corrupter only, and all the rest of the world were their improvers. But you, Meletus, have sufficiently shown that you never had a thought about the young: your carelessness is seen in your not caring about the very things which you bring against me.

And now, Meletus, I will ask you another question—by Zeus I will: Which is better, to live among bad citizens, or among good ones? Answer, friend, I say; the question is one which may be easily answered. Do not the good do their neighbours good, and the bad do them evil?

Certainly.

And is there any one who would rather be injured than benefited by those who live with him? Answer, my good friend, the law requires you to answer—does any one like to be injured?

Certainly not.

And when you accuse me of corrupting and deteriorating the youth, do you allege that I corrupt them intentionally or unintentionally?

Intentionally, I say.

But you have just admitted that the good do their neighbours good, and evil do them evil. Now, is that a truth which your superior wisdom has recognized thus early in life, and am I, at my age, in such darkness and ignorance as not to know that if a man with whom I have to live is corrupted by me, I am very likely to be harmed by him; and yet I corrupt him, and intentionally, too—so you say, although neither I nor any other human being is ever likely to be convinced by you. [*26*] But either I do not corrupt them, or I corrupt them unintentionally and on either view of the case you lie. If my offense is unintentional, the law has no cognizance of unintentional offences: you ought to have taken me privately, and warned and admonished me; for if I had been better advised, I should have left off doing what I only did unintentionally—no doubt I should; but you would have nothing to say to me and refused to teach me. And now you bring me up in this court, which is a place not of instruction, but of punishment.

It will be very clear to you, Athenians, as I was saying, that Meletus has no care at all, great or small, about the matter. But still I should like to know, Meletus, in what I am affirmed to corrupt the young. I suppose you mean, as I infer from your indictment, that I teach them not to acknowledge the gods which the state acknowledges, but some other new divinities or spiritual agencies in their stead. These are the lessons by which I corrupt the youth, as you say.

Yes, that I say emphatically.

Then, by the gods, Meletus, of whom we are

speaking, tell me and the court, in somewhat plainer terms, what you mean! For I do not as yet understand whether you affirm that I teach other men to acknowledge some gods, and therefore that I do believe in gods, and am not an entire atheist—this you do not lay to my charge,—but only you say that they are not the same gods which the city recognizes—the charge is that they are different gods. Or, do you mean that I am an atheist simply, and a teacher of atheism?

I mean the latter—that you are a complete atheist.

What an extraordinary statement! Why do you think so, Meletus? Do you mean that I do not believe in the godhead of the sun or moon, like other men?

I assure you, judges, that he does not: for he says that the sun is stone, and the moon earth.

Friend Meletus, you think that you are accusing Anaxagoras: and you have but a bad opinion of the judges, if you fancy them illiterate to such a degree as not to know that these doctrines are found in the books of Anaxagoras the Clazomenian, which are full of them. And so, forsooth, the youth are said to be taught them by Socrates, when there are not unfrequently exhibitions of them at the theatre (price of admission one drachma at the most); and they might pay their money, and laugh at Socrates if he pretends to father these extraordinary views. And so, Meletus, you really think that I do not believe in any god?

I swear by Zeus that you believe absolutely in none at all.

Nobody will believe you, Meletus, and I am pretty sure that you do not believe yourself. I cannot help thinking, men of Athens, that Meletus is reckless and impudent, and that he has written this indictment in a spirit of mere wantonness and youthful bravado. [*27*] Has he not compounded a riddle, thinking to try me? He said to himself:—I shall see whether the wise Socrates will discover my facetious contradiction, or whether I shall be able to deceive him and the rest of them. For he certainly does appear to me to contradict himself in the indictment as much as if he said that Socrates is guilty of not believing in the gods, and yet of believing in them—but this is not like a person who is in earnest.

I should like you, O men of Athens, to join me in examining what I conceive to be his inconsistency; and do you, Meletus, answer. And I must remind the audience of my request that they would not make a disturbance if I speak in my accustomed manner:

Did ever man, Meletus, believe in the existence of human things, and not of human beings? . . . I wish, men of Athens, that he would answer, and not be always trying to get up an interruption. Did ever any man believe in horsemanship, and not in horses? or in flute-playing, and not in flute-players? No, my friend; I will answer to you and to the court, as you refuse to answer for yourself. There is no man who ever did. But now please to answer the next question: Can a man believe in spiritual and divine agencies, and not in spirits or demigods?

He cannot.

How lucky I am to have extracted that answer, by the assistance of the court! But then you swear in the indictment that I teach and believe in divine or spiritual agencies (new or old, no matter for that); at any rate, I believe in spiritual agencies,—so you say and swear in the affidavit; and yet if I believe in divine beings, how can I help believing in spirits or demigods; —must I not? To be sure I must; and therefore I may assume that your silence gives consent. Now what are spirits or demigods? are they not either gods or the sons of gods?

Certainly they are.

But this is what I call the facetious riddle invented by you:The demigods or spirits are gods, and you say first that I do not believe in gods, and then again that I do believe in gods; that is, if I believe in demigods. For if the demigods are the illegitimate sons of gods—whether by the nymphs or by any other mothers, of whom they are said to be the sons—what human being will ever believe that there are no gods if they are the sons of gods? You might as well affirm the existence of mules, and deny that of horses and asses. Such nonsense, Meletus, could only have been intended by you to make trial of me. You have put this into the indictment because you had nothing real of which to accuse me. But no one who has a particle of understanding will ever be convinced by you that the same men can believe in divine and superhuman things, and yet not believe that there are gods and demigods and heroes. [*28*]

I have said enough in answer to the charge of Meletus; any elaborate defence is unnecessary;

but I know only too well how many are the enmities which I have incurred, and this is what will be my destruction if I am destroyed;—not Meletus, nor yet Anytus, but the envy and detraction of the world, which has been the death of many good men, and will probably be the death of many more; there is no danger of my being the last of them.

Some one will say: And are you not ashamed, Socrates, of a course of life which is likely to bring you to an untimely end? To him I may fairly answer: There you are mistaken: a man who is good for anything ought not to calculate the chance of living or dying; he ought only to consider whether in doing anything he is doing right or wrong—acting the part of a good man or of a bad. Whereas, upon your view, the heroes who fell at Troy were not good for much, and the son of Thetis above all, who altogether despised danger in comparison with disgrace; and when he was so eager to slay Hector, his goddess mother said to him that, if he avenged his companion Patroclus and slew Hector, he would die himself—"Fate," she said, in these or the like words, "waits for you next after Hector"; he, receiving this warning, utterly despised danger and death, and instead of fearing them, feared rather to live in dishonour, and not to avenge his friend. "Let me die forthwith," he replies, "and be avenged of my enemy, rather than abide here by the beaked ships, a laughing-stock and a burden of the earth." Had Achilles any thought of death and danger? For wherever a man's place is, whether the place which he has chosen or that in which he has been placed by a commander, there he ought to remain in the hour of danger; he should not think of death or of anything but of disgrace. And this, O men of Athens, is a true saying.

Strange, indeed, would be my conduct, O men of Athens, if I who, when I was ordered by the generals whom you chose to command me at Potidaea and Amphipolis and Delium, remained where they placed me, like any other man, facing death—if now, when, as I conceive and imagine, God orders me to fulfil the philosopher's mission of searching into myself and other men, I were to desert my post through fear of death, [*29*] or any other fear; that would indeed be strange, and I might justly be arraigned in court for denying the existence of the gods, if I disobeyed the oracle because I was afraid of death, fancying that I was wise when I was not wise. For the fear of death is indeed the pretence of wisdom, and not real wisdom, being a pretence of knowing the unknown; and no one knows whether death, which men in their fear apprehend to be the greatest evil, may not be the greatest good. Is not this ignorance of a disgraceful sort, the ignorance which is the conceit that man knows what he does not know? And in this respect only I believe myself to differ from men in general, and may perhaps claim to be wiser than they are:—that whereas I know but little of the world below, I do not suppose that I know: but I do know that injustice and disobedience to a better, whether God or man, is evil and dishonourable, and I will never fear or avoid a possible good rather than a certain evil. And therefore if you let me go now, and are not convinced by Anytus, who said that since I had been prosecuted I must be put to death (or if not that I ought never to have been prosecuted at all); and that if I escape now, your sons will all be utterly ruined by listening to my words—if you say to me, Socrates, this time we will not mind Anytus, and you shall be let off, but upon one condition, that you are not to enquire and speculate in this way any more, and that if you are caught doing so again you shall die—if this was the condition on which you let me go, I should reply: Men of Athens, I honour and love you; but I shall obey God rather than you, and while I have life and strength I shall never cease from the practice and teaching of philosophy, exhorting any one whom I meet and saying to him after my manner: You, my friend,—a citizen of the great and mighty and wise city of Athens—are you not ashamed of heaping up the greatest amount of money and honour and reputation, and caring so little about wisdom and truth and the greatest improvement of the soul, which you never regard or heed at all? And if the person with whom I am arguing, says: Yes, but I do care; then I do not leave him or let him go at once; but I proceed to interrogate and examine and cross-examine him, and if I think that he has no virtue in him, but only says that he has, I reproach him with undervaluing the greater, and overvaluing the less. [*30*] And I shall repeat the same words to every one whom I meet, young and old, citizen and alien, but especially to the citizens, inasmuch as they are my brethren. For know that this is the command of

God, and I believe that no greater good has ever happened in the state than my service to the God. For I do nothing but go about persuading you all, old and young alike, not to take thought for your persons or your properties, but first and chiefly to care about the greatest improvement of the soul. I tell you that virtue is not given by money, but that from virtue comes money and every other good of man, public as well as private. This is my teaching, and if this is the doctrine which corrupts the youth, I am a mischievous person. But if any one says that this is not my teaching, he is speaking an untruth. Wherefore, O men of Athens, I say to you, do as Anytus bids or not as Anytus bids, and either acquit me or not; but whichever you do, understand that I shall never alter my ways, not even if I have to die many times.

Men of Athens, do not interrupt, but hear me; there was an understanding between us that you should hear me to the end: I have something more to say, at which you may be inclined to cry out; but I believe that to hear me will be good for you, and therefore I beg that you will not cry out. I would have you know, that if you kill such an one as I am, you will injure yourselves more than you will injure me. Nothing will injure me, not Meletus nor yet Anytus—they cannot, for a bad man is not permitted to injure a better than himself. I do not deny that Anytus may, perhaps, kill him, or drive him into exile, or deprive him of civil rights; and he may imagine, and others may imagine, that he is inflicting a great injury upon him: but there I do not agree. For the evil of doing as he is doing—the evil of unjustly taking away the life of another—is greater far.

And now, Athenians, I am not going to argue for my own sake, as you may think, but for yours, that you may not sin against the God by condemning me, who am his gift to you. For if you kill me you will not easily find a successor to me, who, if I may use such a ludicrous figure of speech, am a sort of gadfly, given to the state by God; and the state is a great and noble steed who is tardy in his motions owing to his very size, and requires to be stirred into life. [*31*] I am that gadfly which God has attached to the state, and all day long and in all places am always fastening upon you, arousing and persuading and reproaching you. You will not easily find another like me, and therefore I would advise you to spare me. I dare say that you may feel out of temper (like a person who is suddenly awakened from sleep), and you think that you might easily strike me dead as Anytus advises, and then you would sleep on for the remainder of your lives, unless God in his care of you sent you another gadfly. When I say that I am given to you by God, the proof of my mission is this:—if I had been like other men, I should not have neglected all my own concerns or patiently seen the neglect of them during all these years, and have been doing yours, coming to you individually like a father or elder brother, exhorting you to regard virtue; such conduct, I say, would be unlike human nature. If I had gained anything, or if my exhortations had been paid, there would have been some sense in my doing so; but now, as you will perceive, not even the impudence of my accusers dares to say that I have ever exacted or sought pay of any one; of that they have no witness. And I have a sufficient witness to the truth of what I say—my poverty.

Some one may wonder why I go about in private giving advice and busying myself with the concerns of others, but do not venture to come forward in public and advise the state. I will tell you why. You have heard me speak at sundry times and in divers places of an oracle or sign which comes to me, and is the divinity which Meletus ridicules in the indictment. This sign, which is a kind of voice, first began to come to me when I was a child; it always forbids but never commands me to do anything which I am going to do. This is what deters me from being a politician. And rightly, as I think. For I am certain, O men of Athens, that if I had engaged in politics, I should have perished long ago, and done no good either to you or to myself. And do not be offended at my telling you the truth: for the truth is, that no man who goes to war with you or any other multitude, honestly striving against the many lawless and unrighteous deeds which are done in a state, [*32*] will save his life; he who will fight for the right, if he would live even for a brief space, must have a private station and not a public one.

I can give you convincing evidence of what I say, not words only, but what you value far more—actions. Let me relate to you a passage of my own life which will prove to you that I should never have yielded to injustice from any fear of death, and that "as I should have refused to yield," I must have died at once. I will tell you a tale of the courts, not very interesting perhaps, but nevertheless true. The only office of state which I ever held, O men of Athens, was that of senator: the tribe Antiochis, which is my tribe, had the presidency at the trial of the generals who had not taken up the bodies of the slain after the battle of Arginusae; and you proposed to try them in a body, contrary to law, as you all thought afterwards; but at the time I was the only one of the Prytanes who was opposed to the illegality, and I gave my vote against you; and when the orators threatened to impeach and arrest me, and you called and shouted, I made up my mind that I would run the risk, having law and justice with me, rather than take part in your injustice because I feared imprisonment and death. This happened in the days of the democracy. But when the oligarchy of the Thirty was in power, they sent for me and four others into the rotunda, and bade us bring Leon the Salaminian from Salamis, as they wanted to put him to death. This was a specimen of the sort of commands which they were always giving with the view of implicating as many as possible in their crimes; and then I showed, not in word only but in deed, that, if I may be allowed to use such an expression, I cared not a straw for death, and that my great and only care was lest I should do an unrighteous or unholy thing. For the strong arm of that oppressive power did not frighten me into doing wrong; and when we came out of the rotunda the other four went to Salamis and fetched Leon, but I went quietly home. For which I might have lost my life, had not the power of the Thirty shortly afterwards come to an end. And many will witness to my words.

Now do you really imagine that I could have survived all these years, if I had led a public life, supposing that like a good man I had always maintained the right and had made justice, as I ought, the first thing? No indeed, men of Athens, neither I nor any other man. [*33*] But I have been always the same in all my actions, public as well as private, and never have I yielded any base compliance to those who are slanderously termed my disciples, or to any other. Not that I have any regular disciples. But if any one likes to come and hear me while I am pursuing my mission, whether he be young or old, he is not excluded. Nor do I converse only with those who pay; but any one, whether he be rich or poor, may ask and answer me and listen to my words; and whether he turns out to be a bad man or a good one, neither result can be justly imputed to me; for I never taught or professed to teach him anything. And if any one says that he has ever learned or heard anything from me in private which all the world has not heard, let me tell you that he is lying.

But I shall be asked, Why do people delight in continually conversing with you? I have told you already, Athenians, the whole truth about this matter: they like to hear the cross-examination of the pretenders to wisdom; there is amusement in it. Now this duty of cross-examining other men has been imposed upon me by God; and has been signified to me by oracles, visions, and in every way in which the will of divine power was ever intimated to any one. This is true, O Athenians; or, if not true, would be soon refuted. If I am or have been corrupting the youth, those of them who are now grown up and become sensible that I gave them bad advice in the days of their youth should come forward as accusers, and take their revenge; or if they do not like to come themselves, some of their relatives, fathers, brothers, or other kinsmen, should say what evil their families have suffered at my hands. Now is their time. Many of them I see in the court. There is Crito, who is of the same age and of the same deme with myself, and there is Critobulus his son, whom I also see. Then again there is Lysanias of Sphettus, who is the father of Aeschines—he is present, and also there is Antiphon of Cephisus, who is the father of Epigenes; and there are the brothers of several who have associated with me. There is Nicostratus, the son of Theosdotides, and the brother of Theodotus (now Theodotus himself is dead, and therefore he, at any rate, will not seek to stop him); and there is Paralus, the son of Demodocus, who had a brother Theages; and Adeimantus the son of Ariston [*34*] whose brother Plato is present; and Aeantodorus, who is the brother of Apollodorus, whom I also see. I might mention a great many others, some of whom Meletus should have produced as witnesses in the course of his speech; and let him still produce them, if he has forgotten—I will make way for him. And let him say, if he has any testimony of the sort which he can produce. Nay, Athenians, the very opposite is the truth.

For all these are ready to witness on behalf of the corrupter, of the injurer of their kindred, as Meletus and Anytus call me; not the corrupted youth only—there might have been a motive for that—but their uncorrupted elder relatives. Why should they too support me with their testimony? Why, indeed, except for the sake of truth and justice, and because they know that I am speaking the truth, and that Meletus is a liar.

Well, Athenians, this and the like of this is all the defence which I have to offer. Yet a word more. Perhaps there may be some one who is offended at me, when he calls to mind how he himself on a similar, or even a less serious occasion, prayed and entreated the judges with many tears, and how he produced his children in court, which was a moving spectacle, together with a host of relations and friends; whereas I, who am probably in danger of my life, will do none of these things. The contrast may occur to his mind, and he may be set against me, and vote in anger because he is displeased at me on this account. Now if there be such a person among you,—mind, I do not say that there is,—to him I may fairly reply: My friend, I am a man, and like other men, a creature of flesh and blood, and not "of wood or stone," as Homer says; and I have a family, yes, and sons, O Athenians, three in number, one almost a man, and two others who are still young; and yet I will not bring any of them hither in order to petition you for an acquittal. And why not? Not from any self-assertion or want of respect for you. Whether I am or am not afraid of death is another question, of which I will not now speak. But, having regard to public opinion, I feel that such conduct would be discreditable to myself, and to you, and to the whole state. One who has reached my years, and who has a name for wisdom, ought not to demean himself. Whether this opinion of me be deserved or not, at any rate the world has decided that Socrates is in some way superior to other men. [*35*] And if those among you who are said to be superior in wisdom and courage, and any other virtue, demean themselves in this way, how shameful is their conduct! I have seen men of reputation, when they have been condemned, behaving in the strangest manner: they seemed to fancy that they were going to suffer something dreadful if they died, and that they could be immortal if you only allowed them to live; and I think that such are a dishonor to the state, and that any stranger coming in would have said of them that the most eminent men of Athens, to whom the Athenians themselves give honour and command, are no better than women. And I say that these things ought not to be done by those of us who have a reputation; and if they are done, you ought not to permit them; you ought rather to show that you are far more disposed to condemn the man who gets up a doleful scene and makes the city ridiculous, than him who holds his peace.

But, setting aside the question of public opinion, there seems to be something wrong in asking a favour of a judge, and thus procuring an acquittal, instead of informing and convincing him. For his duty is, not to make a present of justice, but to give judgment; and he has sworn that he will judge according to the laws, and not according to his own good pleasure; and we ought not to encourage you, nor should you allow yourself to be encouraged, in this habit of perjury—there can be no piety in that. Do not then require me to do what I consider dishonourable and impious and wrong, especially now, when I am being tried for impiety on the indictment of Meletus. For if, O men of Athens, by force of persuasion and entreaty I could overpower your oaths, then I should be teaching you to believe that there are no gods, and in defending should simply convict myself of the charge of not believing in them. But that is not so—far otherwise. For I do believe that there are gods, and in a sense higher than that in which any of my accusers believe in them. And to you and to God I commit my cause, to be determined by you as best for you and me.

There are many reasons why I am not grieved, O men of Athens, at the vote of condemnation. [*36*] I expected it, and am only surprised that the votes are so nearly equal; for I had thought that the majority against me would have been far larger; but now, had thirty votes gone over to the other side, I should have been acquitted. And I may say, I think, that I have escaped Meletus. I may say more; for without the assistance of Anytus and Lycon, any one may see that he would not have had a fifth part of the votes, as the law required; in which case he would have incurred a fine of a thousand drachmae.

And so he proposes death as the penalty. And what shall I propose on my part, O men of Athens? Clearly that which is my due. And what is my due? What return shall be made to the man who has never had the wit to be idle during his whole life; but has been careless of what the many care for—wealth, and family interests, and military offices, and speaking in the assembly, and magistracies, and plots, and parties. Reflecting that I was really too honest a man to be a politician and live, I did not go where I could do no good to you or to myself; but where I could do the greatest good privately to every one and to you; thither I went, and sought to persuade every man among you that he must look to himself, and seek virtue and wisdom before he looks to his private interests, and look to the state before he looks to the interests of the state; and that this should be the order which he observes in all his actions. What shall be done to such an one? Doubtless some good thing, O men of Athens, if he has his reward; and the good should be of a kind suitable to him. What would be a reward suitable to a poor man who is your benefactor, and who desires leisure that he may instruct you? There can be no reward so fitting as maintenance in the Prytaneum, O men of Athens, a reward which he deserves far more than the citizen who has won the prize at Olympia in the horse or chariot race, whether the chariots were drawn by two horses or by many. For I am in want, and he has enough; and he only gives you the appearance of happiness, and I give you the reality. And if I am to estimate the penalty fairly, I should say that maintenance in the Prytaneum is the just return. [*37*]

Perhaps you think that I am braving you in what I am saying now, as in what I said before about the tears and prayers. But this is not so. I speak rather because I am convinced that I never intentionally wronged any one, although I cannot convince you—the time has been too short; if there were a law at Athens, as there is in other cities, that a capital cause should not be decided in one day, then I believe that I should have convinced you. But I cannot in a moment refute great slanders; and, as I am convinced that I never wronged another, I will assuredly not wrong myself. I will not say of myself that I deserve any evil, or propose any penalty. Why should I? Because I am afraid of the penalty of death which Meletus proposes? When I do not know whether death is a good or an evil, why should I propose a penalty which would certainly be an evil? Shall I say imprisonment? And why should I live in prison, and be the slave of the magistrates of the year—of the Eleven? Or shall the penalty be a fine, and imprisonment until the fine is paid? There is the same objection. I should have to lie in prison, for money I have none, and cannot pay. And if I say exile (and this may possibly be the penalty which you will affix), I must indeed be blinded by the love of life, if I am so irrational as to expect that when you, who are my own citizens, cannot endure my discourses and words, and have found them so grievous and odious that you will have no more of them, others are likely to endure me. No indeed, men of Athens, that is not very likely. And what a life should I lead, at my age, wandering from city to city, ever changing my place of exile, and always being driven out! For I am quite sure that wherever I go, there, as here, the young men will flock to me; and if I drive them away, their elders will drive me out at their request, and if I let them come, their fathers and friends will drive me out for their sakes.

Some one will say: Yes, Socrates, but cannot you hold your tongue, and then you may go into a foreign city, and no one will interfere with you? Now I have great difficulty in making you understand my answer to this. For if I tell you that to do as you say would be a disobedience to the God, and therefore that I cannot hold my tongue, [*38*] you will not believe that I am serious; and if I say again that daily to discourse about virtue, and of those other things about which you hear me examining myself and others, is the greatest good of man, and that the unexamined life is not worth living, you are still less likely to believe me. Yet I say what is true, although a thing of which it is hard for me to persuade you. Also, I have never been accustomed to think that I deserve to suffer any harm. Had I money I might have estimated the offence at what I was able to pay, and not have been much the worse. But I have none, and therefore I must ask you to proportion the fine to my means. Well, perhaps I could afford a mina, and therefore I propose that penalty: Plato, Crito, Critobulus, and Apolodorus, my friends here, bid me say thirty minae, and they will be the sureties. Let thirty minae be the penalty; for which sum they will be ample security to you.

Not much time will be gained, O Athenians, in return for the evil name which you will get from the detractors of the city, who will say that you killed Socrates, a wise man; for they will call me wise, even although I am not wise, when they want to reproach you. If you had waited a little while, your desire would have been fulfilled in the course of nature. For I am far advanced in years, as you may perceive, and not far from death. I am speaking now not to all of you, but only to those who have condemned me to death. And I have another thing to say to them: You think that I was convicted because I had no words of the sort which would have procured my acquittal—I mean, if I had thought fit to leave nothing undone or unsaid. Not so: the deficiency which led to my conviction was not of words—certainly not. But I had not the boldness or impudence or inclination to address you as you would have liked me to do, weeping and wailing and lamenting, and saying and doing many things which you have been accustomed to hear from others, and which, as I maintain, are unworthy of me. I thought at the time that I ought not to do anything common or mean when in danger: nor do I now repent of the style of my defence; I would rather die having spoken after my manner, than speak in your manner and live. For neither in war nor yet at law ought I or any man to use every way of escaping death. [*39*] Often in battle there can be no doubt that if a man will throw away his arms, and fall on his knees before his pursuers, he may escape death; and in other dangers there are other ways of escaping death, if a man is willing to say and do anything. The difficulty, my friends, is not to avoid death, but to avoid unrighteousness; for that runs faster than death. I am old and move slowly, and my accusers are keen and quick, and the faster runner, who is unrighteousness, has overtaken them. And now I depart hence condemned by you to suffer the penalty of death,—they too go their ways condemned by the truth to suffer the penalty of villainy and wrong; and I must abide by my award—let them abide by theirs. I suppose that these things may be regarded as fated,—and I think that they are well.

And now, O men who have condemned me, I would fain prophesy to you; for I am about to die, and in the hour of death men are gifted with prophetic power. And I prophesy to you who are my murderers, that immediately after my departure punishment far heavier than you have inflicted on me will surely await you. Me you have killed because you wanted to escape the accuser, and not to give an account of your lives. But that will not be as you suppose: far otherwise. For I say that there will be more accusers of you than there are now; accusers whom hitherto I have restrained: and as they are younger they will be more inconsiderate with you, and you will be more offended at them. If you think that by killing men you can prevent some one from censuring your evil lives, you are mistaken; that is not a way of escape which is either possible or honourable; the easiest and the noblest way is not to be disabling others, but to be improving yourselves. This is the prophecy which I utter before my departure to the judges who have condemned me.

Friends, who would have acquitted me, I would like also to talk with you about the thing which has come to pass, while the magistrates are busy, and before I go to the place at which I must die. Stay then a little, for we may as well talk with one another while there is time. [*40*] You are my friends, and I should like to show you the meaning of this event which has happened to me. O my judges—for you I may truly call judges—I should like to tell you of a wonderful circumstance. Hitherto the divine faculty of which the internal oracle is the source has constantly been in the habit of opposing me even about trifles, if I were going to make a slip or error in any matter; and now as you see there has come upon me that which may be thought, and is generally believed to be, the last and worst evil. But the oracle made no sign of opposition, either when I was leaving my house in the morning, or when I was on my way to the court, or while I was speaking, at anything which I was going to say; and yet I have often been stopped in the middle of a speech, but now in nothing I either said or did touching the matter in hand has the oracle opposed me. What do I take to be the explanation of this silence? I will tell you. It is an intimation that what has happened to me is a good, and that those of us who think that death is an evil are in error. For the customary sign would surely have opposed me had I been going to evil and not to good.

Let us reflect in another way, and we shall see that there is great reason to hope that death is a good; for one of two things—either death is a state of nothingness and utter unconsciousness, or, as men say, there is a change and migration of the soul from this world to another. Now if you suppose that there is no consciousness, but a sleep like the sleep of him who is undisturbed even by dreams, death will be an unspeakable gain. For if a person were to select the night in which his sleep was undisturbed even by dreams, and were to compare with this the other days and nights of his life, and then were to tell us how many days and nights he had passed in the course of his life better and more pleasantly than this one, I think that any man, I will not say a private man, but even the great king will not find many such days or nights, when compared with the others. Now if death be of such a nature, I say that to die is gain; for eternity is then only a single night. But if death is the journey to another place, and there, as men say, all the dead abide, what good, O my friends and judges, can be greater than this? If indeed when the pilgram arrives in the world below, [*41*] he is delivered from the professors of justice in this world, and finds the true judges who are said to give judgment there, Minos and Rhadamanthus and Aeacus and Triptolemus, and other sons of God who were righteous in their own life, that pilgrimage will be worth making. What would not a man give if he might converse with Orpheus and Musaeus and Hesiod and Homer? Nay, if this be true, let me die again and again. I myself, too, shall have a wonderful interest in there meeting and conversing with Palamedes and Ajax, the son of Telamon, and any other ancient hero who has suffered death through an unjust judgment; and there will be no small pleasure, as I think, in comparing my own sufferings with theirs. Above all, I shall then be able to continue my search into true and false knowledge; as in this world, so also in the next; and I shall find out who is wise, and who pretends to be wise, and is not. What would not a man give, O judges, to be able to examine the leader of the great Trojan expedition; or Odysseus or Sisyphus, or numberless others, men and women too! What infinite delight would there be in conversing with them and asking them questions! In another world they do not put a man to death for asking questions: assuredly not. For besides being happier than we are, they will be immortal, if what is said is true.

Therefore, O judges, be of good cheer about death, and know of a certainty, that no evil can happen to a good man, either in life or after death. He and his are not neglected by the gods; nor has my own approaching end happened by mere chance. But I see clearly that the time had arrived when it was better for me to die and be released from trouble; wherefore the oracle gave no sign. For which reason, also, I am not angry with my condemners, or with my accusers; they have done me no harm, although they did not mean to do me any good; and for this I may gently blame them.

Still I have a favour to ask of them. When my sons are grown up, I would ask you, O my friends, to punish them; and I would have you trouble them, as I have troubled you, if they seem to care about riches, or anything, more than about virtue; or if they pretend to be something when they are really nothing—then reprove them, as I have reproved you, for not caring about that for which they ought to care, and thinking that they are something when they are really nothing. [*42*] And if you do this, both I and my sons will have received justice at your hands.

The hour of departure has arrived, and we go our ways—I to die, and you to live. Which is better God only knows.

Plato: Crito

Persons of the Dialogue: Socrates; Crito.
Scene: The Prison of Socrates

[*43*] *Socrates.* Why have you come at this hour, Crito? It must be quite early?

Crito. Yes, certainly.

Soc. What is the exact time?

Cr. The dawn is breaking.

Soc. I wonder that the keeper of the prison would let you in.

Cr. He knows me, because I often come, Socrates; moreover, I have done him a kindness.

Soc. And are you only just arrived?

Cr. No, I came some time ago.

Soc. Then why did you sit and say nothing, instead of at once awakening me?

Cr. I should not have liked myself, Socrates, to be in such great trouble and unrest as you are—indeed I should not: I have been watching with amazement your peaceful slumbers; and for that reason, I did not awake you, because I wished to minimize the pain. I have always thought you to be of a happy disposition; but never did I see anything like the easy, tranquil manner in which you bear this calamity.

Soc. Why, Crito, when a man has reached my age he ought not to be repining at the approach of death.

Cr. And yet other old men find themselves in similar misfortunes, and age does not prevent them from repining.

Soc. That is true. But you have not told me why you come at this early hour.

Cr. I come to bring you a message which is sad and painful; not, as I believe, to yourself, but to all of us who are your friends, and saddest of all to me.

Soc. What? Has the ship come from Delos, on the arrival of which I am to die?

Cr. No, the ship has not actually arrived, but she will probably be here to-day, as persons who have come from Sunium tell me that they left her there; and therefore to-morrow, Socrates, will be the last day of your life.

Soc. Very well, Crito; if such is the will of God, I am willing; but my belief is that there will be a delay of a day.

[*44*] *Cr.* Why do you think so?

Soc. I will tell you. I am to die on the day after the arrival of the ship.

Cr. Yes; that is what the authorities say.

Soc. But I do not think that the ship will be here until to-morrow; this I infer from a vision which I had last night, or rather only just now, when you fortunately allowed me to sleep.

Cr. And what was the nature of the vision?

Soc. There appeared to me the likeness of a woman, fair and comely, clothed in bright raiment, who called to me and said: O Socrates,

> The third day hence to fertile Phthia, shalt thou go.

Cr. What a singular dream, Socrates!

Soc. There can be no doubt about the meaning, Crito, I think.

Cr. Yes; the meaning is only too clear. But, oh! my beloved Socrates, let me entreat you once more to take my advice and escape. For if you die I shall not only lose a friend who can never be replaced, but there is another evil: people who do not know you and me will believe that I might have saved you if I had been willing to give money, but that I did not care. Now, can there be a worse disgrace than this—that I should be thought to value money more than the life of a friend? For the many will not be persuaded that I wanted you to escape, and

Translated by B. Jowett, 1892.

that you refused.

Soc. But why, my dear Crito, should we care about the opinion of the many? Good men, and they are the only persons who are worth considering, will think of these things truly as they occurred.

Cr. But you see, Socrates, that the opinion of the many must be regarded, for what is now happening shows that they can do the greatest evil to any one who has lost their good opinion.

Soc. I only wish it were so, Crito; and that the many could do the greatest evil; for then they would also be able to do the greatest good—and what a fine thing this would be! But in reality they can do neither; for they cannot make a man either wise or foolish; and whatever they do is the result of chance.

Cr. Well, I will not dispute with you; but please to tell me, Socrates, whether you are not acting out of regard to me and your other friends: are you not afraid that if you escape from prison we may get into trouble with the informers for having stolen you away, and lose either the whole or a great part of our property; or that even a worse evil may happen to us? [*45*] Now, if you fear on our account, be at ease; for in order ot save you, we ought surely to run this, or even a greater risk; be persuaded, then, and do as I say.

Soc. Yes, Crito, that is one fear which you mention, but by no means the only one.

Cr. Fear not—there are persons who are willing to get you out of prison at no great cost; and as for the informers, they are far from being exorbitant in their demands—a little money will satisfy them. My means, which are certainly ample, are at your service, and if you have a scruple about spending all mine, here are strangers who will give your the use of theirs; and one of them, Simmias the Theban, has brought a large sum of money for this very purpose; and Cebes and many others are prepared to spend their money in helping you to escape. I say, therefore, do not hestitate on our account, and do not say, as you did in the court, that you will have a difficulty in knowing what to do with yourself anywhere else. For men will love you in other places to which you may go, and not in Athens only; there are friends of mine in Thessaly, if you like to go to them, who will value and protect you, and no Thessalian will give you any trouble. Nor can I think that you are at all justified, Socrates, in betraying your own life when you might be saved; in acting thus you are playing into the hands of your enemies, who are hurrying on your destruction. And further I should say that you are deserting your own children; for you might bring them up and educate them; instead of which you go away and leave them, and they will have to take their chance; and if they do not meet with the usual fate of orphans, there will be small thanks to you. No man should bring children into the world who is unwilling to perserve to the end in their nurture and education. But you appear to be choosing the easier part, but the better and manlier, which would have been more becoming in one who professes to care for virtue in all his actions, like yourself. And indeed, I am ashamed not only of you, but of us who are your friends, when I reflect that the whole business will be attributed entirely to our want of courage. The trial need never have come on, or might have been managed differently; and this last act, or crowning folly, will seem to have occurred through our negligence and cowardice, who might have saved you, [*46*] if we had been good for anything; and you might have saved yourself, for there was no difficulty at all. See now, Socrates, how sad and discreditable are the consequences, both to us and you. Make up your mind then, or rather have your mind already made up, for the time of deliberation is over, and there is only one thing to be done, which must be done this very night, and if we delay at all will be no longer practicable or possible; I beseech you therefore, Socrates, be persuaded by me, and do as I say.

Soc. Dear Crito, your zeal is invaluable, if a right one; but if wrong, the greater the zeal the greater the danger; and therefore we ought to consider whether I shall or shall not do as you say. For I am and always have been one of those natures who must be guided by reason, whatever the reason may be which upon reflection appears to me to be the best; and now that this chance has befallen me, I cannot repudiate my own words: the principles which I have hitherto honoured and revered I still honour, and unless we can at once find other and better principles, I am certain not to agree with you; no, not even if the power of the multitude could inflict many more imprisonments, confiscations, deaths, frightening us like children with hobgoblin terrors. What will be the fairest way of considering the question? Shall I return to your old argument about the opinions of men?—we were saying that some of them are to be regarded, and others not. Now were we right in maintaining this before I was condemned? And has the argument which was once good now proved to be talk for the sake of talking—mere childish nonsense? That is what I want to consider with your help, Crito:—whether, under my present circumstances, the argument appears to be in any way different or not; and is to be allowed by me or disallowed. That argument, which, as I believe, is maintained by many persons of authority, was to the effect, as I was saying, that the opinions of some men are to be regarded, and of other men not to be regarded. Now you, Crito, are not going to die to-morrow—at least, [*47*] there is no human probability of this—and therefore you are disinterested and not liable to be deceived by the circumstances in which you are placed. Tell me then, whether I am right in saying that some opinions, and the opinions of some men only, are to be valued, and that other opinions, and the opinions of other men, are not to be valued. I ask you whether I was right in maintaining this?

Cr. Certainly.

Soc. The good are to be regarded, and not the bad?

Cr. Yes.

Soc. And the opinions of the wise are good, and the opinions of the unwise are evil?

Cr. Certainly.

Soc. And what was said about another matter? Is the pupil who devotes himself to the practice of gymnastics supposed to attend to the praise and blame and opinion of every man, or of one man only—his physician or trainer, whoever he may be?

Cr. Of one man only.

Soc. And he ought to fear the censure and welcome the praise of that one only, and not of the many?

Cr. Clearly so.

Soc. And he ought to act and train, and eat and drink in the way which seems good to his single master who has understanding, rather than according to the opinion of all other men put together?

Cr. True.

Soc. And if he disobeys and disregards the opinion and approval of the one, and regards the opinion of the many who have no understanding, will he not suffer evil?

Cr. Certainly he will.

Soc. And what will the evil be, whither tending and what affecting, in the disobedient person?

Cr. Clearly, affecting the body; that is what is destroyed by the evil.

Soc. Very good; and is not this true, Crito, of other things which we need not separately enumerate? In questions of just and unjust, fair and foul, good and evil, which are the subjects of our present consultation, ought we to follow the opinion of the many and to fear them; or the opinion of the one man who has understanding? ought we not to fear and reverence him more than all the rest of the world: and if we desert him shall we not destroy and injure that principle in us which may be assumed to be improved by justice and deteriorated by injustice;—there is such a principle?

Cr. Certainly there is, Socrates.

Soc. Take a parallel instance:—if, acting under the advice of those who have no understanding, we destroy that which is improved by health and is deteriorated by disease, would life be worth having? And that which has been destroyed is—the body?

Cr. Yes.

Soc. Could we live, having an evil and corrupted body?

Cr. Certainly not.

Soc. And will life be worth having, if that higher part of man be destroyed, which is improved by justice and depraved by injustice? Do we suppose that principle, [*48*] whatever it may be in man, which has to do with justice and injustice, to be inferior to the body?

Cr. Certainly not.

Soc. More honourable than the body?

Cr. Far more.

Soc. Then, my friend, we must not regard what the many say of us: but what he, the one man who has understanding of just and unjust, will say, and what the truth will say. And therefore you begin in error when you advise that we would regard the opinion of the many about just and unjust, good and evil, honourable and dishonourable.—"Well," some one will say, "but the many can kill us."

Cr. Yes, Socrates; that will clearly be the answer.

Soc. And it is true: but still I find with surprise that the old argument is unshaken as ever. And I should like to know whether I may say the same of another proposition—that not life, but a good life, is to be chiefly valued?

Cr. Yes, that also remains unshaken.

Soc. And a good life is equivalent to a just and honourable one—that holds also?

Cr. Yes, it does.

Soc. From these premises I proceed to argue the question whether I ought or ought not to try and escape without the consent of the Athenians: and if I am clearly right in escaping, then I will make the attempt; but if not, I will abstain. The other considerations which you mention, of money and loss of character and the duty of educating one's children, are, I fear, only the doctrines of the multitude, who would be as ready to restore people to life, if they were able, as they are to put them to death—and with as little reason. But now, since the argument has thus far prevailed, the only question which remains to be considered is, whether we shall do rightly either in escaping or in suffering others to aid to our escape and paying them in money and thanks, or whether in reality we shall not do rightly; and if the latter, then death or any other calamity which may ensure on my remaining here must not be allowed to enter into the calculation.

Cr. I think that you are right, Socrates; how then shall we proceed?

Soc. Let us consider the matter together, and do you either refute me if you can, and I will be convinced; or else cease, my dear friend, from repeating to me that I ought to escape against the wishes of the Athenians: for I highly value your attempts to persuade me to do so, but I may not be persuaded against my own better judgment. [*49*] And now please to consider my first position, and try how you can best answer me.

Cr. I will.

Soc. Are we to say that we are never intentionally to do wrong, or that in one way we ought and in another we ought not to do wrong, or is doing wrong always evil and dishonourable, as I was just now saying, and as has been already acknowledged by us? Are all our former admissions which were made within a few days to be thrown away? And have we, at our age, been earnestly discoursing with one another all our life long only to discover that we are no better than children? Or, in spite of the opinion of the many, and in spite of consequences whether better or worse, shall we insist on the truth of what was then said, that injustice is always an evil and dishonour to him who acts unjustly? Shall we say so or not?

Cr. Yes.

Soc. Then we must do no wrong?

Cr. Certainly not.

Soc. Nor when injured injure in return, as the many imagine; for we must injure no one at all?

Cr. Clearly not.

Soc. Again, Crito, may we do evil?

Cr. Surely not, Socrates.

Soc. And what of doing evil in return for evil, which is the morality of the many—is that just or not?

Cr. Not just.

Soc. For doing evil to another is the same as injuring him?

Cr. Very true.

Soc. Then we ought not to retaliate or render evil for evil to any one, whatever evil we may have suffered from him. But I would have you consider, Crito, whether you really mean what you are saying. For this opinion has never been held, and never will be held, by any considerable number or persons; and those who are agreed and those who are not agreed upon this point have no common ground, and can only despise one another when they see how widely they differ. Tell me, then, whether you agree with and assent to my first principle, that neither injury nor retaliation nor warding off evil by evil is ever right. And shall that be the premiss of our argument? Or do you decline and dissent from this? For so I have ever thought, and continue to think; but, if you are of another opinion, let me hear what you have to say. If, however, you remain of the same mind as formerly, I will proceed to the next step.

Cr. You may proceed, for I have not changed my mind.

Soc. Then I will go on the next point, which may be put in the form of a question:—Ought a man to do what he admits to be right, or ought he to betray the right?

Cr. He ought to do what he thinks right.

Soc. But if this is true, what is the application? In leaving the prison against the will of the Athenians, [*50*] do I wrong any? or rather do I not wrong those whom I ought least to wrong? Do I not desert the principles which were acknowledged by us to be just—what do you say?

Cr. I cannot tell, Socrates; for I do not know.

Soc. Then consider the matter is this way:—Imagine that I am about to play truant (you may call the proceeding by any name which you like), and the laws and the government come and interrogate me: "Tell us, Socrates," they say; "what are you about? are you not going by an act of yours to overturn us—the laws, and the whole state, as far as in you lies? Do you imagine that a state can subsist and not be overthrown, in which the decisions of law have no power, but are set aside and trampled upon by individuals?" What will be our answer, Crito, to these and the like words? Any one, and especially a rhetorician, will have a good deal to say on behalf of the law which requires a sentence to be carried out. He will argue that this law should not be set aside; and shall we reply, "Yes; but the state has injured us and given an unjust sentence." Suppose I say that?

Cr. Very good, Socrates.

Soc. "And was that our agreement with you?" the law would answer; "or were you to abide by the sentence of the state?" And if I were to express my astonishment at their words, the law would probably add: "Answer, Socrates instead of opening your eyes—you are in the habit of asking and answering questions. Tell us,—What complaint have you to make against us which justifies you in attempting to destroy us and the state? In the first place did we not bring you into existence? Your father married your mother by our aid and begat you. Say whether you have any objection to urge against those of us who regulate marriage?" None, I shall reply. "Or against those of us who after birth regulate the nurture and education of children, in which you also were trained? Were not the laws, which have the charge of education, right in commanding your father to train you in music and gymnastic?" Right, I should reply. "Well then, since you were brought into the world and nurtured and educated by us, can you deny in the first place that you are our child and slave, as your fathers were before you? And if this is true you are not on equal terms with us; nor can you think that you have a right to do to us what we are doing to you. Would you have any right to strike or revile or do any other evil to your father or your master, if you had one, because you have been struck or reviled by him, or received some other evil at his hands?—you would not say this? [*51*] And because we think right to destroy you, do you think that you have any right to destroy us in return, and your country as far as in you lies? Will you, O professor of true virtue, pretend that you are justified in this? Has a philosopher like you failed to discover that our country is more to be valued and higher and holier far than mother or father or any ancestor, and more to be regarded in the eyes of the gods and of men of understanding? also to be soothed, and gently and reverently entreated when angry, even more than a father, and either to be persuaded, or if not persuaded, to be obeyed? And when we are punished by her, whether with imprisonment or stripes, the punishment is to be endured in silence: and if she leads us to wounds or death in battle, thither we follow as is right; neither may any one yield or retreat or leave his rank, but whether in battle or in a court of law, or in any other place, he must do what his city and his country order him; or he must change their view of what is just: and if he may do no violence to his father or mother, much less may he do violence to his country." What answer shall we make to this, Crito? Do the laws speak truly, or do they not?

Cr. I think that they do.

Soc. Then the laws will say, "Consider, Socrates, if we are speaking truly that in your present attempt you are going to do us an injury. For, having brought you into the world, and nurtured and educated you, and given you and every other citizen a share in every good which we had to give, we further proclaim to any Athenian by the liberty which we allow him, that if he does not like us when he has become of age and has seen the ways of the city, and made our acquaintance, he may go where he pleases and take his goods with him. None of us laws will forbid him or interfere with him. Any one who does not like us and the city, and who wants to emigrate to a colony or to any other city, may go where he likes, retaining his property. But he who has experience of the manner in which we order justice and administer the state, and still remains, has entered into an implied contract that he will do as we command him. And he who disobeys us is, as we maintain, thrice wrong; first, because in disobeying us he is disobeying his parents; secondly, because we are the authors of his education; thirdly, because he has made an agreement with us that he will duly obey our commands; [*52*] and he neither obeys them nor convinces us that our commands are unjust; and we do not rudely impose them, but give him the alternative of obeying or convincing us;—that is what we offer, and he does neither.

"These are the sort of accusations to which, as we were saying, you, Socrates, will be exposed if you accomplish your intentions; you above all other Atheniams." Suppose now I ask, why I rather than anybody else? they will justly retort upon me that I above all other men have acknowledged the agreement. "There is clear proof," they will say, "Socrates, that we and the city were not displeasing to you. Of all Athenians you have been the most constant resident in the city, which, as you never leave, you may be supposed to love. For you never went out of the city either to see the games, except once when you went to the Isthmus, or to any other place unless when you were on military service; nor did you travel as other men do. Nor had you any curiosity to know other states or their laws: your affections did not go beyond us and our state; we were your special favourites, and you acquiesced in our government of you; and here in this city you begat your children, which is a proof of your satisfaction. Moreover, you might in the course of the trial, if you had liked, have fixed the penalty at banishment; the state which refuses to let you go now would have let you go then. But you pretended that you preferred death to exile, and that you were not unwilling to die. And now you have forgotten these fine sentiments, and pay no respect to us the laws, of whom you are the destroyer; and are doing what only a miserable slave would do, running away and turning your back upon the compacts and agreements which you made as a citizen. And first of all answer this very question: Are we right in saying that you agreed to be governed according to us in deed, and not in word only? Is that true or not?" How shall we answer, Crito? Must we not assent?

Cr. We cannot help it, Socrates.

Soc. Then will they not say: "You, Socrates, are breaking the covenants and agreements which you made with us at your leisure, not in any haste or under any compulsion or deception, but after you have had seventy years to think of them, during which time you were at liberty to leave the city, if we were not to your mind, or if our covenants appeared to you to be unfair. You had your choice, and might have gone either to Lacedaemon or Crete, both which states are often praised by you for their good government, [*53*] or to some other Hellenic or foreign state. Whereas you, above all other Athenians, seemed to be so fond of the state, or, in other words, of us her laws (and who would care about a state which has no laws?), that you never stirred out of her; the halt, the blind, the maimed were not more stationary in her than you were. And now you run away and forsake your agreements. Not so, Socrates, if you will take our advice; do not make yourself ridiculous by escaping out of the city.

"For just consider, if you transgress and err in this sort of way, what good will you do either to yourself or to your friends? That your friends will be driven into exile and deprived of citizenship, or will lose their property, is tolerably certain; and you yourself, if you fly to one of the neighbouring cities, as, for example, Thebes or Megara, both of which are well governed, will come to them as an enemy, Socrates, and their government will be against you, and all patriotic citizens will cast an evil eye upon you as a subverter of the laws, and you will confirm in the minds of the judges the justice of their own condemnation of you. For he who is a corrupter of the laws is more than likely to be a corrupter of the young and foolish portion of mankind. Will you then flee from well-ordered cities and virtuous men? and its existence worth having on these terms? Or will you go to them without shame, and talk to them, Socrates? And what will you say to them? What you say here about virtue and justice and institutions and laws being the best things among men? Would that be decent of you? Surely not. But if you go away from well-governed states to Crito's friends in Thessaly, where there is a great disorder and licence, they will be charmed to hear the tale of your escape from prison, set off with ludicruous particulars of the manner in which you were wrapped in a goatskin or some other disguise, and metamorphosed as the manner is of runaways; but will there be no one to remind you that in your old age you were not ashamed to violate the most sacred laws from a miserable desire of a little more life? Perhaps not, if you keep them in a good temper; but if they are out of temper you will hear many degrading things; you will live, but how?—as the flatterer of all men, and the servant of all men; and doing what?—eating and drinking in Thessaly, having gone abroad in order that you may get a dinner. And where will be your fine sentiments about justice and virtue? [*54*] Say that you wish to live for the sake of your children—you want to bring them up and educate them—will you take them into Thessaly, and deprive them of Athenian citizenship? Is this the benefit which you will confer upon them? Or are you under the impression that they will be better cared for and educated here if you are still alive, although absent from them; for your friends will take care of them? Do you fancy that if you are an inhabitant of Thessaly they will take care of them, and if you are an inhabitant of the other world that they will not take care of them? Nay; but if they who call themselves friends are good for anything, they will—to be sure they will.

"Listen, then, Socrates, to us who have brought you up. Think not of life and children first, and of justice afterwards, but of justice first, that you may be justified before the princes of the world below. For neither will you nor any that belong to you be happier or holier or juster in this life, or happier in another, if you do as Crito bids. Now you depart in innocence, a sufferer and not a doer of evil; a victim, not of the laws but of men. But if you go forth, returning evil for evil, and injury for injury, breaking the convenants and agreements which you have made with us, and wronging those whom you ought least of all to wrong, that is to say, yourself, your friends, your country, and us, we shall be angry with you while you live, and our brethren, the laws in the world below, will receive you as an enemy; for they will know that you have done your best to destroy us. Listen, then, to us and not to Crito."

This, dear Crito, is the voice which I seem to hear murmuring in my ears, like the sound of the flute in the ears of the mystic; that voice, I say, is humming in my ears, and prevents me from hearing any other. And I know that anything more which you may say will be vain. Yet speak, if you have anything to say.

Cr. I have nothing to say, Socrates.

Soc. Leave me then, Crito, to fulfil the will of God, and to follow whither he leads.

Plato: Phaedo

In matters of this sort philosophers, above all other men, may be observed in every sort of way to separate the soul from the communion [*65*] of the body.

Very true.

Whereas, Simmias, the rest of the world are of opinion that to him who has no sense of pleasure and no part in bodily pleasure, life is not worth having; and that he who is indifferent about them is as good as dead.

That is also true.

What again shall we say of the actual acquirement of knowledge?—is the body, if invited to share in the enquiry, a hinderer or a helper? I mean to say, have sight and hearing any truth in them? Are they not as the poets are always telling us, inaccurate witnesses? and yet, if even they are inaccurate and indistinct, what is to be said of the other senses?—for you will allow that they are the best of them?

Certainly, he replied.

Then when does the soul attain truth?—for in attempting to consider anything in company with the body she is obviously deceived.

True.

Then must not true existence be revealed to her in thought, if at all?

Yes.

And thought is best when the mind is gathered into herself and none of these things trouble her—neither sounds nor sights nor pain nor any pleasure,—when she takes leave of the body, and has as little as possible to do with it, when she has no bodily sense or desire, but is aspiring after true being?

Certainly.

And in this the philosopher dishonours the body; his soul runs away from his body and desires to be alone and by herself?

That is true.

Well, but there is another thing, Simmias: Is there or is there not an absolute justice?

Assuredly there is.

And an absolute beauty and absolute good?

Of course.

But did you ever behold any of them with your eyes?

Certainly not.

Or did you ever reach them with any other bodily sense?—and I speak not of these alone, but of absolute greatness, and health, and strength, and of the essence or true nature of everything. Has the reality of them ever been perceived by you through the bodily organs? or rather, is not the nearest approach to the knowledge of their several natures made by him who so orders his intellectual vision as to have the most exact conception of the essence of each thing which he considers?

Certainly.

And he attains to the purest knowledge of them who goes to each with the mind alone, not introducing or intruding in the act of thought sight or any other sense together with reason, but with the very light of the mind in her own clearness searches into the very [*66*] truth of each; he who has got rid, as far as he can, of eyes and ears and, so to speak, of the whole body, these being in his opinion distracting elements which when they infect the soul hinder her from acquiring truth and knowledge—who, if not he, is likely to attain to the knowledge of true being?

What you say has a wonderful truth in it, Socrates, replied Simmias.

And when real philosophers consider all

Translated by B. Jowett, 1892. (selections).

these things, will they not be led to make a reflection which they will express in words something like the following? "Have we not found," they will say, "a path of thought which seems to bring us and our argument to the conclusion, that while we are in the body, and while the soul is infected with the evils of the body, our desire will not be satisfied? and our desire is of the truth. For the body is a source of endless trouble to us by reason of the mere requirement of food; and is liable also in the search after true being: it fills us full of lies, and lusts, and fears, and fancies of all kinds, and endless foolery, and in fact, as men say, takes away from us the power of thinking at all. Whence come wars, and fightings, and factions? whence but from the body and the lusts of the body? Wars are occasioned by the love of money, and money has to be acquired for the sake and in the service of the body; and by reason of all these impediments we have no time to give to philosophy; and, last and worst of all, even if we are at leisure and betake ourselves to some speculation, the body is always breaking in upon us causing turmoil and confusion in our enquiries, and so amazing us that we are prevented from seeing the truth. It has been proved to us by experience that if we would have pure knowledge of anything we must be quit of the body—the soul in herself must behold things in themselves: and then we shall attain the wisdom which we desire, and of which we say that we are lovers; not while we live, but after death; for if while in company with the body, the soul cannot have pure knowledge, one of two things follows—either knowledge is not to be attained at all, or, if at all, [*67*] after death. For then, and not till then, the soul will be parted from the body and exist in herself alone. In this present life, I reckon that we make the nearest approach to knowledge when we have the least possible intercourse or communion with the body, and are not surfeited with the bodily nature, but keep ourselves pure until the hour when God himself is pleased to release us. And thus having got rid of the foolishness of the body we shall be pure and hold converse with the pure, and know of ourselves the clear light everywhere, which is no other than the light of truth." For the impure are not permitted to approach the pure. These are the sort of words, Simmias, which the true lovers of knowledge cannot help saying to one another, and thinking. You would agree; would you not?

Undoubedly, Socrates.

But, O my friend, if this be true, there is great reason to hope that, going whither I go when I have come to the end of my journey, I shall attain that which has been the pursuit of my life. And therefore I go on my way rejoicing, and not I only, but every other man who believes that his mind has been made ready and that he is in a manner purified.

Certainly, replied Simmias.

And what is purification but the separation of the soul from the body, as I was saying before; the habit of the soul gathering and collecting herself into herself from all sides out of the body; the dwelling in her own place alone, as in another life, so also in this, as far as she can;—the release of the soul from the chains of the body?

Very true, he said.

And this separation and release of the soul from the body is termed death?

To be sure, he said.

And the true philosophers, and they only, are ever seeking to release the soul. Is not the separation and release of the soul from the body their special study?

That is true.

And, as I was saying at first, there would be a ridiculous contradiction in men studying to live as nearly as they can in a state of death, and yet repining when it comes upon them.

Clearly.

And the true philosophers, Simmias, are always occupied in the practice of dying, wherefore also to them least of all men is death terrible. Look at the matter thus:—if they have been in every way the enemies of the body, and are wanting to be alone with the soul, when this desire of theirs is granted, how inconsistent would they be if they trembled and repined, instead of rejoicing at their departure to that place where, when they arrive, they hope to gain that which in life they desired—and this was wisdom—and at the [*68*] same time to be rid of the company of their enemy. Many a man has been willing to go to the world below animated by the hope of seeing there an earthly love, or wife, or son, and conversing with them. And will he who is a true lover of wisdom, and is strongly persuaded in like manner that only in the world below he can worthily enjoy her, still repine at death? Will he not depart with joy? Surely he will, O my friend, if he be a true philosopher. For he will have a firm conviction that there, and there only, he can find wisdom in her purity. And if this be true, he would be very absurd, as I was saying, if he were afraid of death.

He would indeed, replied Simmias.

And when you see a man who is repining at the approach of death, is not his reluctance a sufficient proof that he is not a lover of wisdom, but a lover of the body, and probably at the same time a lover of either money or power, or both?

Quite so, he replied.

When I was young, Cebes, I had a prodigious desire to know that department of philosophy which is called the investigation of nature; to know the causes of things, and why a thing is and is created or destroyed appeared to me to be a lofty profession; and I was always agitating myself with the consideration of questions such as these:—Is the growth of animals the result of some decay which the hot and cold principle contracts, as some have said? Is the blood the element with which we think, or the air, or the fire? or perhaps nothing of the kind—but the brain may be the originating power of the perceptions of hearing and sight and smell, and memory and opinion may come from them and science may be based on memory and opinion when they have attained fixity. And then I went on to examine the corruption of them, and then to the things of heaven and earth, and at last I concluded myself to be utterly and absolutely incapable of these enquiries, as I will satisfactorily prove to you. For I was fascinated by them to such a degree that my eyes grew blind to things which I had seemed to myself, and also to others, to know quite well; I forgot what I had before thought self-evident truths; e.g. such a fact as that the growth of man is the result of eating and drinking; for when by the digestion of food flesh is added to flesh and bone to bone, and whenever there is an aggregation of congenial elements, the lesser bulk becomes larger and the small man great. Was not that a reasonable notion?

Yes, said Cebes, I think so.

Well; but let me tell you something more. There was a time when I thought that I understood the meaning of greater and less pretty well; and when I saw a great man standing by a little one, I fancied that one was taller than the other by a head; or one horse would appear to be greater than another horse: and still more clearly did I seem to perceive that ten is two more than eight, and that two cubits are more than one, because two is the double of one.

And what is now your notion of such matters? said Cebes.

I should be far enough from imagining, he replied, that I knew the cause of any of them, by heaven I should; for I cannot satisfy myself that, [*97*] when one is added to one, the one to which the addition is made becomes two, or that the two units added together make two by reason of the addition. I cannot understand how, when separated from the other, each of them was one and not two, and now, when they are brought together, the mere juxtaposition or meeting of them should be the cause of their becoming two: neither can I understand how the vision of one is the way to make two; for then a different cause would produce the same effect,—as in the former instance the addition and juxtaposition of one to one was the cause of two, in this the separation and subtraction of one from the other would be the cause. Nor am I any longer satisfied that I understand the reason why one or anything else is either generated or destroyed or is at all, but I have in my mind some confused notion of a new method, and can never admit the other.

Then I heard some one reading, as he said, from a book of Anaxagoras, that mind was the disposer and cause of all, and I was delighted at this notion, which appeared quite admirable, and I said to myself: If mind is the disposer, mind will dispose all for the best, and put each particular in the best place; and I argued that if any one desired to find out the cause of the generation or destruction or existence of anything, he must find out what state of being or doing or suffering was best for that thing, and therefore a man had only to consider the best for himself and others, and then he would also know the worse, since the same science comprehended both. And I rejoiced to think that I had found in Anaxagoras a teacher of the causes of existence such as I desired, and I imagined that he would tell me first whether the earth is flat or round; and whichever was true, he would proceed to explain the cause and the necessity of this being so, and then he would teach me the nature of the best and show that this was best; and if he said that the earth was in the centre, he would further explain that this position was the best, and I should be satisfied with the explanation given, and not want any other sort of cause. [*98*] And I thought that I would then go on and ask him about the sun and moon and stars, and that he would explain to me their comparative swiftness, and their returnings and various states, active and passive, and how all of them were for the best. For I could not imagine that when he spoke of mind as the disposer of them, he would give any other account of their being as they are, except that this was best; and I thought that when he had explained to me in detail the cause of each and the cause of all, he would go on to explain to me what was best for each and what was good for all. These hopes I would not have sold for a large sum of money, and I seized the books and read them as fast as I could in my eagerness to know the better and the worse.

What expectations I had formed, and how grievously was I disappointed! As I proceeded, I found my philosopher altogether forsaking mind or any other principle of order, but having recourse to air, and ether, and water, and other eccentricities. I might compare him to a person who began by maintaining generally that mind is the cause of the actions of Socrates, but who, when he endeavoured to explain the causes of my several actions in detail, went on to show that I sit here because my body is made up of bones and muscles; and the bones as he would say, are hard and have joints which divide them, and the muscles are elastic, and they cover the bones, which have also a covering or environment of flesh and skin which contains them; and as the bones are lifted at their joints by the contraction or relaxation of the muscles, I am able to bend my limbs, and this is why I am sitting here in a curved posture —that is what he would say; and he would have a similar explanation of my talking to you, which he would attribute to sound, and air, and hearing, and he would assign ten thousand other causes of the same sort, forgetting to mention the true cause, which is, that the Athenians have thought fit to condemn me, and accordingly I have thought it better and more right to remain here and undergo my sentence; [*99*] for I am inclined to think that these muscles and bones of mine would have gone off long ago to Megara or Boeotia—by the dog, they would, if they had been moved only by their own idea of what was best, and if I had not chosen the better and nobler part, instead of playing truant and running away, of enduring any punishment which the state inflicts. There is surely a strange confusion of causes and conditions in all this. It may be said, indeed, that without bones and muscles and the other parts of the body I cannot execute my purposes. But to say that I do as I do because of them, and that this is the way in which mind acts, and not from the choice of the best, is a very careless and idle mode of speaking. I wonder that they cannot distinguish the cause from the condition, which the many, feeling about in the dark, are always mistaking and misnaming. And thus one man makes a vortex all round and steadies the earth by the heaven; another gives the air as a support to the earth, which is a sort of broad trough. Any power which in arranging them as they are arranges them for the best never enters into their minds; and instead of finding any superior strength in it, they rather expect to discover another Atlas of the world who is stronger and more everlasting and more containing than the good;—of the obligatory and containing power of the good they think nothing; and yet this is the principle which I would fain learn if any one would teach me. But as I have failed either to discover myself, or to learn of any one else, the nature of the best, I will exhibit to you, if you like, what I have found to be the second best mode of enquiring into the cause.

I should very much like to hear, he replied.

Socrates proceeded: I thought that as I had failed in the contemplation of true existence, I ought to be careful that I did not lose the eye of my soul; as people may injure their bodily eye by observing and gazing on the sun during an eclipse, unless they take the precaution of only looking at the image reflected in the water, or in some medium. So in my own case, I was afraid that my soul might be blinded altogether if I looked at things with my eyes or tried to apprehend them by the help of the senses. And I thought that I had better have recourse to the world of mind and seek there the truth of existence. [*100*] I dare say that the simile is not perfect—for I am very far from admitting that he who contemplates existences through the medium of thought, sees them only "through a glass darkly," any more than he who considers them in action and operation. However, this was the method which I adopted: I first assumed some principle which I judged to be the strongest, and then I affirmed as true whatever seemed to agree with this, whether relating to the cause or to anything else; and that which disagreed I regarded as untrue. But I should like to explain my meaning more clearly, as I do not think that you as yet understand me.

No indeed, replied Cebes, not very well.

There is nothing new, he said, in what I am about to tell you; but only what I have been always and everywhere repeating in the previous discussion and on other occasions: I want to show you the nature of that cause which has occupied my thoughts. I shall have to go back to those familiar words which are in the mouth of every one, and first of all assume that there is an absolute beauty and goodness and greatness, and the like; grant me this, and I hope to be able to show you the nature of the cause, and to prove the immortality of the soul.

Cebes said: You may proceed at once with the proof, for I grant you this.

Well, he said, then I should like to know whether you agree with me in the next step: for I cannot help thinking, if there be anything beautiful other than absolute beauty should there be such, that it can be beautiful only in so far as it partakes of absolute beauty—and I should say the same of everything. Do you agree in this notion of the cause?

Yes, he said, I agree.

He proceeded: I know nothing and can understand nothing of any other of those wise causes which are alleged; and if a person says to me that the bloom of colour, or form, or any such thing is a source of beauty, I leave all that, which is only confusing to me, and simply and singly, and perhaps foolishly, hold and am assured in my own mind that nothing makes a thing beautiful but the presence and participation of beauty in whatever way or manner obtained; for as to the manner I am uncertain, but I stoutly contend that by beauty all beautiful things become beautiful. This appears to me to be the safest answer which I can give, either to myself or to another, and to this I cling, in the persuasion that this principle will never be overthrown, and that to myself or to any one who asks the question, I may safely reply, That by beauty beautiful things become beautiful. Do you not agree with me?

I do.

And that by greatness only great things become great and greater, and by smallness the less become less?

True.

Then if a person were to remark that A is taller by a head than B, [*101*] and B less by a head than A, you would refuse to admit his statement, and would stoutly contend that what you mean is only that the greater is greater by, and by reason of, greatness, and the less is less only by, and by reason of, smallness; and thus you would avoid the danger of saying that the greater is greater and the less less by the measure of the head, which is the same in both, and would also avoid the monstrous absurdity of supposing that the greater man is greater by reason of the head, which is small. You would be afraid to draw such an inference, would you not?

Indeed, I should, said Cebes, laughing.

In like manner you would be afraid to say that ten exceeded eight by, and by reason of, two; but would say by, and by reason of, number; or you would say that two cubits exceed one cubit not by a half, but by magnitude?—for there is the same liability to error in all these cases.

Very true, he said.

Again, would you not be cautious of affirming that the addition of one to one, or the division of one, is the cause of two? And you would loudly asseverate that you know of no ways in which anything comes into existence except by participation in duality—this is the way to make two, and the participation in one is the way to make one. You would say: I will let alone puzzles of division and addition—wiser heads than mine may answer them; inexperienced as I am, and ready to start, as the proverb says, at my own shadow, I cannot afford to give up the sure ground of a principle. And if any one assails you there, you would not mind him, or answer him until you had seen whether the consequences which follow agree with one another or not, and when you are further required to give an explanation of this principle, you would go on to assume a higher principle, and a higher, until you found a resting-place in the best of the higher; but you would not confuse the principle and the consequences in your reasoning, like the Eristics—at least if you wanted to discover real existence. Not that this confusion signifies to them, who never care or think about the matter at all, for they have the wit to be well pleased with themselves however great may be the turmoil of their ideals. [*102*] But you, if you are a philosopher, will certainly do as I say.

What you say is most true, said Simmias and Cebes, both speaking at once.

But then, O my friends, he said, if the soul is really immortal, what care should be taken of her, not only in respect of the portion of time which is called life, but of eternity! And the danger of neglecting her from this point of view does indeed appear to be awful. If death had only been the end of all, the wicked would have had a good bargain in dying, for they would have been happily quit not only of their body, but of their own evil together with their souls. But now, inasmuch as the soul is manifestly immortal, there is no release or salvation from evil except the attainment of the highest virtue and wisdom. For the soul when on her progress to the world below takes nothing with her but nurture and education; and these are said greatly to benefit or greatly to injure the departed, at the very beginning of his journey thither.

For after death, as they say, the genius of each individual, to whom he belonged in life, leads him to a certain place in which the dead are gathered together, whence after judgment has been given they pass into the world below, following the guide, who is appointed to conduct them from this world to the other: and when they have there received their due and remained their time, another guide brings them back again after many revolutions of ages. Now this way to the other world is not, [*108*] as Aeschylus says in the *Telephus,* a single and straight path—if that were so no guide would be needed, for no one could miss it; but there are many partings of the road, and windings, as I infer from the rites and sacrifices which are offered to the gods below in places where three ways meet on earth. The wise and orderly soul follows in the straight path and is conscious of her surroundings; but the soul which desires the body, and which, as I was relating before, has long been fluttering about the lifeless frame and the world of sight, is after many struggles and many sufferings hardly and with violence carried away by her attendant genius; and when she arrives at the place where the other souls are gathered, if she be impure and have done impure deeds, whether foul murders or other crimes which are the brothers of these, and the works of brothers in crime—from that soul every one flees and turns away; no one will be her companion, no one her guide, but alone she wanders in extremity of evil until certain times are fulfilled, and when they are fulfilled, she is borne irresistibly to her own fitting habitation; as every pure and just soul which has passed through life in the company and under the guidance of the gods has also her own proper home.

A man of sense ought not to say, nor will I be very confident, that the description which I have given to the soul and her mansions is exactly true. But I do say that, inasmuch as the soul is shown to be immortal, he may venture to think, not improperly or unworthily, that something of the kind is true. The venture is a glorious one, and he ought to comfort himself with words like these, which is the reason why I lengthen out the tale. Wherefore, I say, let a man be of good cheer about his soul, who having cast away the pleasures and ornaments of the body as alien to him and working harm rather than good, has sought after the pleasures of knowledge; and has arrayed the soul, not in some foreign attire, but in her own proper jewels, temperance, and justice, and courage, and nobility, [*115*] and truth—in these adorned she is ready to go on her journey to the world below, when her hour comes. You Simmias and Cebes, and all other men, will depart at some time or other. Me already, as a tragic poet would say, the voice of fate calls. Soon I must drink the poison; and I think that I had better repair to the bath first, in order that the women may not have the trouble of washing my body after I am dead....

When he had done speaking, Crito said: And have you any commands for us, Socrates—anything to say about your children, or any other matter in which we can serve you?

Nothing particular, Crito, he replied: only, as I have always told you, take care of yourselves; that is a service which you may be ever rendering to me and mine and to all of us, whether you promise to do so or not. But if you have no thought for yourselves, and care not to walk according to the rule which I have prescribed for you, not now for the first time, however much you may profess or promise at the moment, it will be of no avail.

We will do our best, said Crito: And in what way shall we bury you?

In any way that you like; but you must get hold of me, and take care that I do not run away from you. Then he turned to us and added with a smile:—I cannot make Crito believe that I am the same Socrates who have been talking and conducting the argument; he fancies that I am the other Socrates whom he will soon see, a dead body—and he asks, How shall he bury me? And though I have spoken many words in the endeavour to show that when I have drunk the poison I shall leave you and go to the joys of the blessed,—these words of mine, with which I was comforting you and myself, have had, as I perceive, no effect upon Crito. And therefore I want you to be surety for me to him now, as at the trial he was surety to the judges for me: but let the promise be of another sort; for he was surety for me to the judges that I would remain, and you must be my surety to him that I shall not remain, but go away and depart; and not be grieved when he sees my body being burned or buried. I would not have him sorrow at my hard lot, or say at the burial, Thus we lay out Socrates, or, Thus we follow him to the grave or bury him; for false words are not only evil in themselves, but they infect the soul with evil. Be of good cheer then, my dear Crito, and say that you are burying my body only, [*116*] and do with that whatever is usual, and what you think best.

When he had spoken these words, he arose and went into a chamber to bathe; Crito followed him and told us to wait. So we remained behind, talking and thinking of the subject of discourse, and also of the greatness of our sorrow; he was like a father of whom we were being bereaved, and we were about to pass the rest of our lives as orphans. When he had taken the bath his children were brought to him—(he had two young sons and an elder one); and the women of his family also came, and he talked to them and gave them a few directions in the presence of Crito; then he dismissed them and returned to us.

Now the hour of sunset was near, for a good deal of time had passed while he was within. When he came out, he sat down with us again after his bath, but not much was said. Soon the jailer, who was the servant of the Eleven, entered and stood by him, saying:—To you, Socrates, whom I know to be the noblest and gentlest and best of all who ever came to this place, I will not impute the angry feelings of other men, who rage and swear at me, when, in obedience to the authorities, I bid them drink the poison—indeed, I am sure that you will not be angry with me; for others, as you are aware, and not I, are to blame. And so fare you well, and try to bear lightly what must needs be—you know my errand. Then bursting into tears he turned away and went out.

Socrates looked at him and said: I return your good wishes, and will do as you bid. Then turning to us, he said, How charming the man is: since I have been in prison he has always been coming to see me, and at times he would talk to me, and was as good to me as could be, and now see how generously he sorrows on my account. We must do as he says, Crito; and therefore let the cup be brought, if the poison is prepared: if not, let the attendant prepare some.

Yet, said Crito, the sun is still upon the hill-tops, and I know that many a one has taken the draught late, and after the announcement has been made to him, he has eaten and drunk, and enjoyed the society of his beloved; do not hurry—there is time enough.

Socrates said: Yes, Crito, and they of whom you speak are right in so acting, for they think that they will be gainers by the delay; but I am right in not following their example, for I do not think that I should gain anything by drinking the poison a little later; [*117*] I should only be ridiculous in my own eyes for sparing and saving a life which is already forfeit. Please then to do as I say, and not to refuse me.

Crito made a sign to the servant, who was standing by; and he went out, and having been absent for some time, returned with the jailer carrying the cup of poison. Socrates said: You, my good friend, who are experienced in these matters, shall give me directions how I am to proceed. The man answered: You have only to walk about until your legs are heavy, and then to lie down, and the poison will act. At the same time he handed the cup to Socrates, who in the easiest and gentlest manner, without the least fear or change of colour or feature, looking at the man with all his eyes, Echecrates, as his manner was, took the cup and said: What do you say about making a libation out of this cup to any god? May I, or not? The man answered:

We only prepare, Socrates, just so much as we deem enough. I understand, he said: but I may and must ask the gods to prosper my journey from this to the other world—even so—and so be it according to my prayer. Then raising the cup to his lips, quite readily and cheerfully he drank off the poison. And hitherto most of us had been able to control our sorrow; but now when we saw him drinking, and saw too that he had finished the draught, we could no longer forbear, and in spite of myself my own tears were flowing fast; so that I covered my face and wept, not for him, but at the thought of my own calamity in having to part from such a friend. Nor was I the first; for Crito, when he found himself unable to restrain his tears, had got up, and I followed; and at that moment, Apollodorus, who had been weeping all the time, broke out in a loud and passionate cry which made cowards of us all. Socrates alone remained his calmness: What is this strange outcry? he said. I sent away the women mainly in order that they might not misbehave in this way, for I have been told that a man should die in peace. Be quiet then, and have patience. When we heard his words we were ashamed, and refrained our tears; and he walked about until, as he said, his legs began to fail, and then he lay on his back, according to the directions, and the man who gave him the poison now and then looked at his feet and legs; and after a while he pressed his foot hard, and asked him if he could feel; and he said, [*118*] No; and then his leg, and so upwards and upwards, and showed us that he was cold and stiff. And he felt them himself, and said: When the poison reaches the heart, that will be the end. He was beginning to grow cold about the groin, when he uncovered his face, for he had covered himself up, and said—they were his last words—he said: Crito, I owe a cock to Asclepius; will you remember to pay the debt? The debt shall be paid, said Crito; is there anything else? There was no answer to this question; but in a minute or two a movement was heard, and the attendents uncovered him; his eyes were set, and Crito closed his eyes and mouth.

Such was the end, Echecrates, of our friend; concerning whom I may truly say, that of all the men of his time whom I have known, he was the wisest and justest and best.

Plato: The Republic

But still I must say, Socrates, that if you are allowed to go on in this way you will entirely forget the other question which at the commencement of this discussion you thrust aside: —Is such an order of things possible, and how, if at all? For I am quite ready to acknowledge that the plan which you propose, if only feasible, would do all sorts of good to the State. I will add, what you have omitted, that your citizens will be the bravest of warriors, and will never leave their ranks, for they will all know one another, and each will call the other father, brother, son; and if you suppose the women to join their armies, whether in the same rank or in the rear, either as a terror to the enemy, or as auxiliaries in case of need, I know that they will then be absolutely invincible; and there are many domestic advantages which might also be mentioned and which I also fully acknowledge: but, as I admit all these advantages and as many more as you please, if only this State of yours were to come into existence, we need say no more about them; assuming then the existence of the State, let us now turn to the question of possibility and ways and means—the rest may be left.

[*472*] If I loiter for a moment, you instantly make a raid upon me, I said, and have no mercy; I have hardly escaped the first and second waves, and you seem not to be aware that you are now bringing upon me the third, which is the greatest and heaviest. When you have seen and heard the third wave, I think you will be more considerate and will acknowledge that some fear and hesitation was natural respecting a proposal so extraordinary as that which I have now to state and investigate.

Translated by B. Jowett, 1892. (selections).

The more appeals of this sort which you make, he said, the more determined are we that you shall tell us how such a State is possible: speak out and at once.

Let me begin by reminding you that we found our way hither in the search after justice and injustice.

True, he replied; but what of that?

I was only going to ask whether, if we have discovered them, we are to require that the just man should in nothing fail of absolute justice; or may we be satisfied with an approximation, and the attainment in him of a higher degree of justice than is to be found in other men?

The approximation will be enough.

We are enquiring into the nature of absolute justice and into the character of the perfectly just, and into injustice and the perfectly unjust, that we might have an ideal. We were to look at these in order that we might judge of our own happiness and unhappiness according to the standard which they exhibited and the degree in which we resembled them, but not with any view of showing that they could exist in fact.

True, he said.

Would a painter be any the worse because, after having delineated with consummate art an ideal of a perfectly beautiful man, he was unable to show that any such man could ever have existed?

He would be none the worse.

Well, and were we not creating an ideal of a perfect State?

To be sure.

And is our theory a worse theory because we are unable to prove the possibility of a city being ordered in the manner described?

Surely not, he replied.

That is the truth, I said. But if, at your request, I am to try and show how and under what conditions the possibility is highest, I must ask you, having this in view, to repeat your former admissions.

What admissions?

[*473*] I want to know whether ideals are ever fully realized in language? Does not the word express more than the fact, and must not the actual, whatever a man may think, always, in the nature of things, fall short of the truth? What do you say?

I agree.

Then you must not insist on my proving that the actual State will in every respect coincide with the ideal: if we are only able to discover how a city may be governed nearly as we proposed, you will admit that we have discovered the possibility which you demand; and will be contended. I am sure that I should be contented—will not you?

Yes, I will.

Let me next endeavour to show what is that fault in States which is the cause of their present maladministration, and what is the least change which will enable a State to pass into the truer form; and let the change, if possible, be of one thing only, or, if not, of two; at any rate, let the changes be as few and slight as possible.

Certainly, he replied.

I think, I said, that there might be a reform of the State if only one change were made, which is not a slight or easy though still a possible one.

What is it? he said.

Now then, I said, I go to meet that which I liken to the greatest of the waves; yet shall the word be spoken, even though the wave break and drown me in laughter and dishonour; and do you mark my words.

Proceed:

I said: *Until philosophers are kings, or the kings and princes of this world have the spirit and power of philosophy, and political greatness and wisdom meet in one, and those commoner natures who pursue either to the exclusion of the other are compelled to stand aside, cities will never have rest from their evils—no, nor the human race, as I believe—and then only will this our State have a possibility of life and behold the light of day.* Such was the thought, my dear Glaucon, which I would fain have uttered if it had not seemed too extravagant; for to be convinced that in no other State can there be happiness private or public is indeed a hard thing.

Socrates, what do you mean? I would have you consider that the word which you have uttered is one at which numerous persons, and very respectable persons too, [*474*] in a figure pulling off their coats all in a moment, and seizing any weapon that comes to hand, will run at you might and main, before you know where you are, intending to do heaven knows what; and if you don't prepare an answer, and put yourself in motion, you will be "pared by their fine wits," and no mistake.

You got me into the scrape, I said.

And I was quite right; however, I will do all I can to get you out of it; but I can only give you good-will and good advice, and, perhaps, I may be able to fit answers to your questions better than another—that is all. And now, having such an auxiliary, you must do your best to show the unbelievers that you are right.

I ought to try, I said, since you offer me such invaluable assistance. And I think that, if there is to be a chance of our escaping, we must explain to them whom we mean when we say that philosophers are to rule in the State; then we shall be able to defend ourselves: There will be discovered to be some natures who ought to study philosophy and to be leaders in the State; and others who are not born to be philosophers, and are meant to be followers rather than leaders.

Then now for a definition, he said.

Follow me, I said, and I hope that I may in some way or other be able to give you a satisfactory explanation.

Proceed.

I dare say that you remember, and therefore I need not remind you, that a lover, if he is worthy of the name, ought to show his love, not to some one part of that which he loves, but to the whole.

I really do not understand, and therefore beg of you to assist my memory.

Another person, I said, might fairly reply as you do; but a man of pleasure like yourself ought to know that all who are in the flower of youth do somehow or other raise a pang or emotion in a lover's breast, and are thought by him to be worthy of his affectionate regards. Is not this a way which you have with the fair: one has a snub nose, and you praise his charming face; the hook-nose of another has, you say, a royal look; while he who is neither snub nor hooked has the grace of regularity: the dark visage is manly, the fair are children of the gods; and as to the sweet "honey pale," as they are called, what is the very name but the invention of a lover who talks in diminutives, and is not adverse to paleness if appearing on the cheek of youth? *[475]* In a word, there is no excuse which you will not make, and nothing which you will not say, in order not to lose a single flower that blooms in the spring-time of youth.

If you make me an authority in matters of love, for the sake of the argument, I assent.

And what do you say of lovers of wine? Do you see them doing the same? They are glad of any pretext of drinking any wine.

Very good.

And the same is true of ambitious men; if they cannot command an army, they are willing to command a file; and if they cannot be honoured by really great and important persons, they are glad to be honoured by lesser and meaner people—but honour of some kind they must have.

Exactly.

Once more let me ask: Does he who desires any class of goods, desire the whole class or a part only?

The whole.

And may we not say of the philosopher that he is a lover, not of a part of wisdom only, but of the whole?

Yes, of the whole.

And he who dislikes learning, especially in youth, when he has no power of judging what is good and what is not, such an one we maintain not to be a philosopher or a lover of knowledge, just as he who refuses his food is not hungry, and may be said to have a bad appetite and not a good one?

Very true, he said.

Whereas he who has a taste for every sort of knowledge and who is curious to learn and is never satisfied, may be justly termed a philosopher? Am I not right?

Glaucon said: If curiosity makes a philosopher, you will find many a strange being will have a title to the name. All the lovers of sights have a delight in learning, and must therefore be included. Musical amateurs, too, are a folk strangely out of place among philosophers, for they are the last persons in the world who would come to anything like a philosophical discussion, if they could help, while they run about at the Dionysiac festivals as if they had let out their ears to hear every chorus; whether the performance is in town or country—that makes no difference—they are there. Now are we to maintain that all these and any who have similar tastes, as well as the professors of quite minor acts, are philosophers?

Certainly not, I replied; they are only an imitation.

He said: Who then are the true philosophers?

Those, I said, who are lovers of the vision of truth.

That is also good, he said; but I should like to know what you mean?

To another, I replied, I might have a difficulty in explaining; but I am sure that you will admit a proposition which I am about to make.

What is the proposition?

That since beauty is the opposite of ugliness, they are two?

Certainly.

[476] And inasmuch as they are two, each of them is one?

True Again.

And of just and unjust, good and evil, and of every other class, the same remark holds: taken singly, each of them is one; but from the various combinations of them with actions and things and with one another, they are seen in all sorts of lights and appear many?

Very true.

And this is the distinction which I draw between the sight-loving, art-loving, practical class and those of whom I am speaking, and who are alone worthy of the name of philosophers.

How do you distinguish them? he said.

KNOWLEDGE AND OPINION

The lovers of sounds and sights, I replied, are, as I conceive, fond of fine tones and colors and forms and all the artificial products that are made out of them, but their mind is incapable of seeing or loving absolute beauty.

True, he replied.

Few are they who are able to attain to the sight of this.

Very true.

And he who, having a sense of beautiful things has no sense of absolute beauty, or who, if another lead him to a knowledge of that beauty is unable to follow—of such an one I ask, Is he awake or in a dream only? Reflect: is not the dreamer, sleeping or waking, one who likens dissimilar things, who puts the copy in the place of the real object?

I should certainly say that such an one was dreaming.

But take the case of the other, who recognises the existence of absolute beauty and is able to distinguish the idea from the objects which participate in the idea, neither putting the objects in the place of the idea nor the idea in the place of the objects—is he a dreamer, or is he awake?

He is wide awake.

And may we not say that the mind of the one who knows has knowledge, and that the mind of the other, who opines only, has opinion?

Certainly.

But suppose that the latter should quarrel with us and dispute our statement, can we administer any soothing cordial or advice to him, without revealing to him that there is sad disorder in his wits?

We must certainly offer him some good advice, he replied.

Come, then, and let us think of something to say to him. Shall we begin by assuring him that he is welcome to any knowledge which he may have, and that we are rejoiced at his having it? But we should like to ask him a question: Does he who has knowledge know something or nothing? (You must answer for him.)

I answer that he knows something.

Something that is or is not?

Something that is; for how can that which is not ever be known?

[*477*] And we are assured, after looking at the matter from many points of view, that absolute being is or may be absolutely known, but that the utterly non-existent is utterly unknown?

Nothing can be more certain.

Good. But if there be anything which is of such a nature as to be and not to be, that will have a place intermediate between pure being and the absolute negation of being?

Yes, between them.

And, as knowledge corresponded to being and ignorance of necessity to not-being, for that intermediate between being and not-being there has to be discovered a corresponding intermediate between ignorance and knowledge, if there be such?

Certainly.

Do we admit the existence of opinion?

Undoubtedly.

As being the same with knowledge, or another faculty?

Another faculty.

Then opinion and knowledge have to do with different kinds of matter corresponding to this difference of faculties?

Yes.

And knowledge is relative to being and knows being. But before I proceed further I will make a division.

What division?

I will begin by placing faculties in a class by themselves: they are powers in us, and in all other things, by which we do as we do. Sight and hearing, for example, I should call faculties. Have I clearly explained the class which I mean?

Yes, I quite understand.

Then let me tell you my view about them. I do not see them, and therefore the distinctions of figure, colour, and the like, which enable me to discern the differences of some things, do not apply to them. In speaking of a faculty I think only of its sphere and its result; and that which has the same sphere and the same result I call the same faculty, but that which has another sphere and another result I call different. Would that be your way of speaking?

Yes.

And will you be so very good as to answer one more question? Would you say that knowledge is a faculty, or in what class would you place it?

Certainly knowledge is a faculty, and the mightiest of all faculties.

And is opinion also a faculty?

Certainly, he said: for opinion is that with which we are able to form an opinion.

And yet you were acknowledging a little while ago that knowledge is not the same as opinion?

[*478*] Why, yes, he said: how can any reasonable being ever identify that which is infallible with that which errs?

An excellent answer, proving, I said, that we are quite conscious of a distinction between them.

Yes.

Then knowledge and opinion having distinct powers have also distinct spheres or subject-matters?

That is certain.

Being is the sphere or subject-matter of knowledge, and knowledge is to know the nature of being?

Yes.

And opinion is to have an opinion?

Yes.

And do we know what we opine? or is the subject-matter of opinion the same as the subject-matter of knowledge?

Nay, he replied, that has been already disproven; if difference in faculty implies difference in the sphere or subject-matter, and if, as we were saying, opinion and knowledge are distinct faculties, then the sphere of knowledge and of opinion cannot be the same.

Then if being is the subject-matter of knowledge, something else must be the subject-matter of opinion?

Yes, something else.

Well, then, is not-being the subject-matter of opinion? or, rather, how can there be an opinion at all about not-being? Reflect: when a man has an opinion, has he not an opinion about something? Can he have an opinion which is an opinion about nothing?

Impossible.

He who has an opinion has an opinion about some one thing?

Yes.

And not-being is not one thing but, properly speaking, nothing?

True.

Of not-being, ignorance was assumed to be the necessary correlative; of being, knowledge?

True, he said.

Then opinion is not concerned either with being or with not-being?

Not with either.

And can therefore neither be ignorance nor knowledge?

That seems to be true.

But is opinion to be sought without and beyond either of them, in a greater clearness than knowledge, or in a greater darkness than ignorance?

In neither.

Then I suppose that opinion appears to you to be darker than knowledge, but lighter than ignorance?

Both; and in no small degree.

And also to be within and between them?

Yes.

Then you would infer that opinion is intermediate?

No question.

But were we not saying before, that if anything appeared to be of a sort which is and is not at the same time, that sort of thing would appear also to lie in the interval between pure being and absolute not-being; and that the corresponding faculty is neither knowledge nor ignorance, but will be found in the interval between them?

True.

And in that interval there has now been discovered something which we call opinion?

There has.

Then what remains to be discovered is the object which partakes equally of the nature of being and not-being, and cannot rightly be termed either, pure and simple; this unknown term, when discovered, we may truly call the subject of opinion, and assign each to their proper faculty—the extremes to the faculties of the extremes and the mean to the faculty of the mean.

True.

[*479*] This being premised, I would ask the gentleman who is of opinion that there is no absolute or unchangeable idea of beauty—in whose opinion the beautiful is the manifold—he, I say, your lover of beautiful sights, who cannot bear to be told that the beautiful is one, and the just is one, or that anything is one—to him I would appeal, saying, Will you be so very kind, sir, as to tell us whether, of all these beautiful things, there is one which will not be found ugly; or of the just, which will not be found unjust; or of the holy, which will not also be unholy?

No, he replied; the beautiful will in some point of view be found ugly; and the same is true of the rest.

And may not the many which are doubles be also halves?—doubles, that is, of one thing, and halves of another?

Quite true.

And things great and small, heavy and light, as they are termed, will not be denoted by these any more than by the opposite names?

True; both these and the opposite names will

always attach to all of them.

And can any one of those many things which are called by particular names be said to be this rather than not to be this?

He replied: They are like the punning riddles which are asked at feasts or the children's puzzle about the eunuch aiming at the bat, with what he hit him, as they say in the puzzle, and upon what the bat was sitting. The individual objects of which I am speaking are also a riddle, and have a double sense: nor can you fix them in your mind, either as being or not-being, or both, or neither.

Then what will you do with them? I said. Can they have a better place than between being and not-being? For they are clearly not in greater darkness or negation than not-being, or more full of light and existence than being.

That is quite true, he said.

Thus then we seem to have discovered that the many ideas which the multitude entertain about the beautiful and about all other things are tossing about in some region which is half-way between pure being and pure not-being?

We have.

Yes: and we had before agreed that anything of this kind which we might find was to be described as matter of opinion, and not as matter of knowledge; being the intermediate flux which is caught and detained by the intermediate faculty.

Quite true.

Then those who see the many beautiful, and who yet neither see absolute beauty, nor can follow any guide who points the way thither; who see the many just, and not absolute justice, and the like— such persons may be said to have opinion but not knowledge?

That is certain.

But those who see the absolute and eternal and immutable may be said to know, and not to have opinion only?

Neither can that be denied.

The one love and embrace the subjects of knowledge, the other those of opinion? The latter are the same, as I dare say you will remember, [*480*] who listened to sweet sounds and gazed upon fair colours, but would not tolerate the existence of absolute beauty.

Yes, I remember.

Shall we then be guilty of any impropriety in calling them lovers of opinion rather than lovers of wisdom, and will they be very angry with us for thus describing them?

I shall tell them not to be angry; no man should be angry at what is true.

But those who love the truth in each thing are to be called lovers of wisdom and not lovers of opinion.

Assuredly. . . .

THE PHILOSOPHER, THE STATE, AND THE CROWD

[*484*] And thus, Glaucon, after the argument has gone a weary way, the true and the false philosophers have at length appeared in view.

I do not think, he said, that the way could have been shortened.

I suppose not, I said; and yet I believe that we might have had a better view of both of them if the discussion could have been confined to this one subject and if there were not many other questions awaiting us, which he who desires to see in what respect the life of the just differs from that of the unjust must consider.

And what is the next question? he asked.

Surely, I said, the one which follows next in order. Inasmuch as philosophers only are able to grasp the eternal and unchangeable, and those who wander in the region of the many and variable are not philosophers, I must ask you which of the two classes should be the rulers of our State?

And how can we rightly answer that question?

Whichever of the two are best able to guard the laws and institutions of our State—let them be our guardians.

Very good.

Neither, I said, can there be any question that the guardian who is to keep anything should have eyes rather than no eyes?

There can be no question of that.

And are not those who are verily and indeed wanting in the knowledge of the true being of each thing, and who have in their souls no clear pattern, and are unable as with a painter's eye to look at the absolute truth and to that original to repair, and having perfect vision of the other world to order the laws about beauty, goodness, justice in this . . . are not such persons, I ask, simply blind?

Truly. . . .

And again, if he is forgetful and retains nothing of what he learns, will he not be an empty vessel?

That is certain.

Labouring in vain, he must end in hating himself and his fruitless occupation?

Yes.

Then a soul which forgets cannot be ranked among genuine philosophic natures; we must insist that the philosopher should have a good memory?

Certainly.

And once more, the inharmonious and unseemly nature can only tend to disproportion?

Undoubtedly.

And do you consider truth to be akin to proportion or to disproportion?

To proportion.

Then, besides other qualities, we must try to find a naturally well-proportioned and gracious mind, which will move spontaneously towards the true being of everything.

Certainly.

Well, and do not all these qualities, which we have been enumerating, go together, and are they not, in a manner, necessary to a soul, which is to have a full and perfect participation of being?

[*487*] They are absolutely necessary, he replied.

And must not that be a blameless study which he only can pursue who has the gift of a good memory, and is quick to learn—noble, gracious, the friend of truth, justice, courage, temperance, who are his kindred?

The god of jealousy himself, he said, could find no fault with such a study.

And to men like him, I said, when perfected by years and education, and to these only you will entrust the State.

Here Adeimantus interposed and said: To these statements, Socrates, no one can offer a reply; but when you talk in this way, a strange feeling passes over the minds of your hearers: They fancy that they are led astray a little at each step in the argument, owing to their own want of skill in asking and answering questions; these littles accumulate, and at the end of the discussion they are found to have sustained a mighty overthrow and all their former notions appear to be turned upside down. And as unskilful players of draughts are at last shut up by their more skilful adversaries and have no piece to move, so they too find themselves shut up at last; for they have nothing to say in this new game of which words are the counters; and yet all the time they are in the right. The observation is suggested to me by what is now occurring. For any one of us might say, that although in words he is not able to meet you at each step of the argument, he sees as a fact that the votaries of philosophy, when they carry on the study, not only in youth as a part of education, but as the pursuit of their maturer years, most of them become strange monsters, not to say utter rogues, and that those who may be considered the best of them are made useless to the world by the very study which you extol.

Well, and do you think that those who say so are wrong?

I cannot tell, he replied; but I should like to know what is your opinion.

Hear my answer; I am of opinion that they are quite right.

Then how can you be justified in saying that cities will not cease from evil until philosophers rule in them, when philosophers are acknowledged by us to be of no use to them?

You ask a question, I said, to which a reply can only be given in a parable.

Yes, Socrates; and that is a way of speaking to which you are not at all accustomed, I suppose.

I perceive, I said, that you are vastly amused at having plunged me into such a hopeless discussion; but now hear the parable, [*488*] and then you will be still more amused at the meagreness of my imagination: for the manner in which the best men are treated in their own States is so grievous that no single thing on earth is comparable to it; and therefore, if I am to plead their cause, I must have recourse to fiction, and put together a figure made up of many things, like the fabulous unions of goats and stags which are found in pictures. Imagine then a fleet or a ship in which there is a captain who is taller and stronger than any of the crew, but he is a little deaf and has a similar infirmity in sight, and his knowledge of navigation is not much better. The sailors are quarreling with one another about the steering—every one is of opinion that he has a right to steer, though he has never learned the art of navigation and cannot tell who taught him or when he learned, and will further assert that it cannot be taught, and they are ready to cut in pieces any one who says the contrary. They throng about the captain, begging and praying him to commit the helm to them; and if at any time they do not prevail, but others are preferred to them, they kill the others or throw them overboard, and having first chained up the noble captain's sense with drink or some narcotic drug, they mutiny and take possession of the ship and make free with the stores; thus, eating and drinking, they proceed on their voyage in such a manner as might be expected of them. Him who is their partisan and cleverly aids them in their plot for getting the ship out of the captain's hands into their own whether by force or persuasion, they compliment with the name of sailor, pilot, able seaman, and abuse the other sort of man, whom they call a good-for-nothing; but that the true pilot must pay attention to the year and seasons and sky and stars and winds, and whatever else belongs to his art, if he intends to be really qualified for the command of a ship, and that he must and will be the steerer, whether other people like or not—the possibility of this union of authority with the steerer's art has never seriously entered into their thoughts or been made part of their calling. [*489*] Now in vessels which are in a state of mutiny and by sailors who are mutineers, how will the true pilot be regarded? Will he not be called by them a prater, a star-gazer, a good-for-nothing?

Of course, said Adeimantus.

Then you will hardly need, I said, to hear the interpretation of the figure, which describes the true philosopher in his relation to the State; for you understand already.

Certainly.

Then suppose you now take this parable to the gentleman who is surprised at finding that philosophers have no honour in their cities; explain it to him and try to convince him that their having honour would be far more extraordinary.

I will.

Say to him, that, in deeming the best votaries of philosophy to be useless to the rest of the world, he is right; but also tell him to attribute their uselessness to the fault of those who will not use them, and not to themselves. The pilot should not humbly beg the sailors to be commanded by him—that is not the order of nature; neither are "the wise to go to the doors of the rich"—the ingenious author of this saying told a lie—but the truth is, that, when a man is ill, whether he be rich or poor, to the physician he must go, and he who wants to be governed, to him who is able to govern. The ruler who is good for anything ought not to beg his subjects to be ruled by him; although the present governors of mankind are of a different stamp; they may be justly compared to the mutinous sailors, and the true helmsmen to those who are called by them good-for-nothings; and star-gazers.

Precisely so, he said.

For these reasons, and among men like these, philosophy, the noblest pursuit of all, is not likely to be much esteemed by those of the opposite faction; not that the greatest and most lasting injury is done to her by her opponents but by her own professing followers, the same of whom you suppose the accuser to say, that the greatest number of them are arrant rogues, and the best are useless; in which opinion I agreed.

Yes.

And the reason why the good are useless has now been explained?

True.

Then shall we proceed to show that the corruption of the majority is also unavoidable, and that this is not to be laid to the charge of philosophy any more than the other?

By all means.

And let us ask and answer in turn, first going back to the description of the gentle and noble nature. [*490*] Truth, as you will remember, was his leader, whom he followed always and in all things; failing in this, he was an impostor, and had no part or lot in true philosophy.

Yes, that was said.

Well, and is not this one quality, to mention no others, greatly at variance with present notions of him?

Certainly, he said.

And have we not a right to say in his defence that the true lover of knowledge is always striving after being—that is his nature; he will not rest in the multiplicity of individuals which is an appearance only, but will go on—the keen edge will not be blunted, nor the force of his desire abate until he have attained the knowledge of the true nature of every essence by a sympathetic and kindred power in the soul, and by that power drawing near and mingling and becoming incorporate with very being, having begotten mind and truth, he will have knowledge and will live and grow truly, and then and not till then, will he cease from his travel.

Nothing, he said, can be more just than such a description of him.

And will the love of a lie be any part of a philosopher's nature? Will he not utterly hate a lie?

He will.

And when truth is the captain, we cannot suspect any evil of the band which he leads?

Impossible.

Justice and health of mind will be of the company, and temperance will follow after?

True, he replied.

Neither is there any reason why I should again set in array the philosopher's virtues, as you will doubtless remember that courage, magnificence, apprehension, memory, were his natural gifts. And you objected that, although no one could deny what I then said, still, if you leave words and look at facts, the persons who are thus described are some of them manifestly useless, and the greater number utterly depraved; we were then led to enquire into the grounds of these accusations, and have now arrived at the point of asking why are the majority bad, which question of necessity brought us back to the examination and definition of the true philosopher.

Exactly.

And we have next to consider the corruptions of the philosophic nature, why so many are spoiled and so few escape spoiling—I am speaking of those who were said to be useless but not wicked—and, [*491*] when we have done with them, we will speak of the imitators of philosophy, what manner of men are they who aspire after a profession which is above them and of which they are unworthy, and then, by their manifold inconsistencies, bring upon philosophy, and upon all philosophers, that universal reprobation of which we speak.

What are these corruptions? he said.

I will see if I can explain them to you. Every one will admit that a nature having in perfection all the qualities which we required in a philosopher, is a rare plant which is seldom seen among men.

Rare indeed.

And what numberless and powerful causes tend to destroy these rare natures!

What causes?

In the first place there are their own virtues, their courage, temperance, and the rest of them, every one of which praiseworthy qualities (and this is a most singular circumstance) destroys and distracts from philosophy the soul which is the possessor of them.

That is very singular, he replied.

Then there are all the ordinary goods of life—beauty, wealth, strength, rank, and great connections in the State—you understand the sort of things—these also have a corrupting and distracting effect.

I understand; but I should like to know more precisely what you mean about them.

Grasp the truth as a whole, I said, in the right way; you will then have no difficulty in apprehending the preceding remarks, and they will no longer appear strange to you.

And how am I to do so? he asked.

Why, I said, we know that all germs or seeds, whether vegetable or animal, when they fail to meet with proper nutriment or climate or soil, in proportion to their vigour, are all the more sensitive to the want of a suitable environment, for evil is a greater enemy to what is good than what is not.

Very true.

There is reason in supposing that the finest natures, when under alien conditions, receive more injury than the inferior, because the contrast is greater.

Certainly.

And may we not say, Adeimantus, that the most gifted minds, when they are ill-educated, become pre-eminently bad? Do not great crimes and the spirit of pure evil spring out of a fullness of nature ruined by education rather than from any inferiority, whereas weak natures are scarcely capable of any very great good or very great evil?

There I think that you are right.

[*492*] And our philosopher follows the same analogy—he is like a plant which, having proper nurture, must necessarily grow and mature into all virtue, but, if sown and planted in an alien soil, becomes the most noxious of all weeds, unless he be preserved by some divine power. Do you really think, as people so often say, that our youth are corrupted by Sophists, or that private teachers of the art corrupt them in any degree worth speaking of? Are not the public who say these things the greatest of all Sophists? And do they not educate to perfection young and old, men and women alike, and fashion them after their own hearts?

When is this accomplished? he said.

When they meet together, and the world sits down at an assembly, or in a court of law, or a theatre, or a camp, or in any other popular resort, and there is a great uproar, and they praise some things which are being said or done, and blame other things, equally exaggerating both, shouting and clapping their hands, and the echo of the rocks and the place in which they are assembled redoubles the sound of the praise or blame—at such a time will not a young man's heart, as they say, leap within him? Will any private training enable him to stand firm against the overwhelming flood of popular opinion? or will he be carried away by the stream? Will he not have the notions of good and evil which the public in general have—he will do as they do, and as they are, such will he be?

Yes, Socrates; necessity will compel him.

And yet, I said, there is a still greater necessity, which has not been mentioned.

What is that?

The gentle force of attainder or confiscation or death, which, as you are aware, these new Sophists and educators, who are the public, apply when their words are powerless.

Indeed they do; and in right good earnest.

Now what opinion of any other Sophist, or of any private person, can be expected to overcome in such an unequal contest?

None, he replied.

No, indeed, I said, even to make the attempt is a great piece of folly; there neither is, nor has been, nor is ever likely to be, any different type of character which has had no other training in virtue but that which is supplied by public opinion—I speak, my friend, of human virtue only; what is more than human, as the proverb says, is not included: for I would not have you ignorant, whatever is saved and comes to good is saved by the power of God, [*493*] as we may truly say.

I quite assent, he replied.

Then let me crave your assent also to a further observation.

What are you going to say?

Why, that all those mercenary individuals, whom the many call Sophists and whom they deem to be their adversaries, do, in fact, teach nothing but the opinion of the many, that is to say, the opinions of their assemblies; and this is their wisdom. I might compare them to a man who should study the tempers and desires of a mighty strong beast who is fed by him—he would learn how to approach and handle him, also at what times and from what causes he is dangerous or the reverse, and what is the meaning of his several cries, and by what sounds, when another utters them, he is soothed or infuriated; and you may suppose further, that when, by continually attending upon him, he has become perfect in all this, he calls his knowledge wisdom, and makes of it a system or art, which he proceeds to teach, although he has no real notion of what he means by the principles or passions of which he is speaking, but calls this honourable and that dishonourable, or good or evil, or just or unjust, all in accordance with the tastes and tempers of the great brute. Good he pronounces to be that in which the beast delights and evil to be that which he dislikes; and he can give no other account of them except that the just and noble are the necessary, having never himself seen, and having no power of explaining to others the nature of either, or the difference between them, which is immense. By heaven, would not such an one be a rare educator?

Indeed he would.

And in what way does he who thinks that wisdom is the discernment of the tempers and tastes of the motley multitude, whether in painting or music, or, finally, in politics, differ from him whom I have been describing? For when a man consorts with the many, and exhibits to them his poem or other work of art or the service which he has done the State, making them his judges when he is not obliged, the so-called necessity of Diomede will oblige him to produce whatever they praise. And yet the reasons are utterly ludicrous which they give in confirmation of their own notions about the honourable and good. Did you ever hear any of them which were not?

No, nor am I likely to hear.

You recognise the truth of what I have been saying? Then let me ask you to consider further whether the world will ever be induced to believe in the existence of absolute beauty rather than of the many beautiful, [*494*] or of the absolute in each kind rather than of the many in each kind?

Certainly not.

Then the world cannot possibly be a philosopher?

Impossible.

And therefore philosophers inevitably fall under the censure of the world?

They must.

And of individuals who consort with the mob and seek to please them?

That is evident.

Then, do you see any way in which the philosopher, can be preserved in his calling to the end? and remember what we were saying of him, that he was to have quickness and memory and courage and magnificence—these were admitted by us to be the true philosopher's gifts.

Yes.

Will not such an one from his early childhood be in all things first among all, especially if his bodily endowments are like his mental ones?

Certainly, he said.

And his friends and fellow-citizens will want to use him as he gets older for their own purposes?

No question.

Falling at his feet, they will make requests to him and do him honour and flatter him, because they want to get into their hands now, the power which he will one day possess.

That often happens, he said.

And what will a man such as he is be likely to do under such circumstances, especially if he be a citizen of a great city, rich and noble, and a tall proper youth? Will he not be full of boundless aspirations, and fancy himself able to manage the affairs of Hellenes and barbarians, and having got such notions into his head will he both dilate and elevate himself in the fulness of vain pomp and senseless pride?

To be sure he will.

Now, when he is in this state of mind, if some one gently comes to him and tells him that he is a fool and must get understanding, which can only be got by slaving for it, do you think that, under such adverse circumstances, he will be easily induced to listen?

Far otherwise.

And even if there be some one who through inherent goodness or natural reasonableness has had his eyes opened a little and is humbled and taken captive by philosophy, how will his friends behave when they think that they are likely to lose the advantage which they were hoping to reap from his companionship? Will they not do and say anything to prevent him from yielding to his better nature and to render his teacher powerless, using to this end private intrigues as well as public prosecutions?

[*495*] There can be no doubt of it.

And how can one who is thus circumstanced ever become a philosopher?

Impossible.

Then were we not right in saying that even the very qualities which make a man a philosopher may, if he be ill-educated, divert him from philosophy, no less than riches and their accompaniments and the other so-called goods of life?

We were quite right.

Thus, my excellent friend, is brought about all that ruin and failure which I have been describing of the natures best adapted to the best of all pursuits; they are natures which we maintain to be rare at any time; this being the class out of which come the men who are the authors of the greatest evil to States and individuals; and also the greatest good when the tide carries them in that direction; but a small man never was the doer of any great thing either to individuals or to States.

That is most true, he said.

And so philosophy is left desolate, with her marriage rite incomplete: for her own have fallen away and forsaken her, and while they are leading a false and unbecoming life, other unworthy persons, seeing that she has no kinsmen to be her protectors, enter in and dishonour her; and fasten upon her the reproaches which, as you say, her reprovers utter, who affirm of her votaries that some are good for nothing, and that the greater number deserve the severest punishment.

That is certainly what people say.

Yes; and what else would you expect, I said, when you think of the puny creatures who, seeing this land open to them—a land well stocked with fair names and showy titles—like prisoners running out of prison into a sanctuary, take a leap out of their trades into philosophy; those who do so being probably the cleverest hands at their own miserable crafts? For, although philosophy be in this evil case, still there remains a dignity about her which is not to be found in the arts. And many are thus attracted by her whose natures are imperfect and whose souls are maimed and disfigured by their meannesses, as their bodies are by their trades and crafts. Is not this unavoidable?

Yes.

Are they not exactly like a bald little tinker who has just got out of durance and come into a fortune; he takes a bath and puts on a new coat, and is decked out as a bridegroom going to marry his daughter, who is left poor and desolate?

[*496*] A most exact parallel.

What will be the issue of such marriages? Will they not be vile and bastard?

There can be no question of it.

And when persons who are unworthy of education approach philosophy and make an alliance with her who is a rank above them what sort of ideas and opinions are likely to be generated? Will they not be sophisms captivating to the ear, having nothing in them genuine, or worthy of or akin to true wisdom?

No doubt, he said.

Then, Adeimantus, I said, the worthy disciples of philosophy will be but a small remnant: perchance some noble and well educated person, detained by exile in her service, who in the absence of corrupting influences remains devoted to her; or some lofty soul born in a mean city, the politics of which he contemns and neglects; and there may be a gifted few who leave the arts, which they justly despise, and come to her—or peradventure there are some who are restrained by our friend Theages' bridle; for everything in the life of Theages conspired to divert him from philosophy; but ill-health kept him away from politics. My own case of the internal sign is hardly worth mentioning, for rarely, if ever, has such a monitor been given to any other man. Those who belong to this small class have tasted how sweet and blessed a possession philosophy is, and have also seen enough of the madness of the multitude; and they know that no politician is honest, nor is there any champion of justice at whose side they may fight and be saved. Such an one may be compared to a man who has fallen among wild beasts—he will not join in the wickedness of his fellows, but neither is he able singly to resist all their fierce natures, and therefore seeing that he would be of no use to the State or to his friends, and reflecting that he would have to throw away his life without doing any good either to himself or others, he holds his peace, and goes his own way. He is like one who, in the storm of dust and sleet which the driving wind hurries along, retires under the shelter of a wall; and seeing the rest of mankind full of wickedness, he is content, if only he can live his own life and be pure from evil or unrighteousness, and depart in peace and good-will, with bright hopes.

Yes, he said, and he will have done a great work before he departs.

A great work—yes; but not the greatest, unless he find a State suitable to him; [*497*] for in a State which is suitable to him, he will have a larger growth and be the saviour of his country, as well as of himself.

The causes why philosophy is in such an evil name have now been sufficiently explained: the injustice of the charges against her has been shown—is there anything more which you wish to say?

Nothing more on that subject, he replied; but I should like to know which of the governments now existing is in your opinion the one adapted to her.

Not any of them, I said; and that is precisely the accusation which I bring against them—not one of them is worthy of the philosophic nature . . . what I would have you term the idea of good, and this you will deem to be the cause of science, and of truth in so far as the latter becomes the subject of knowledge; beautiful too, as are both truth and knowledge, you will be right in esteeming this other nature as more beautiful than either; [*509*] and, as in the previous instance, light and sight may be truly said to be like the sun, and yet not to the sun, so in this other sphere, science and truth may be deemed to be like the good, but not the good; the good has a place of honour yet higher.

What a wonder of beauty that must be, he said, which is the author of science and truth, and yet surpasses them in beauty; for you surely cannot mean to say that pleasure is the good?

God forbid, I replied; but may I ask you to consider the image in another point of view?

In what point of view?

You would say, would you not, that the sun is not only the author of visibility in all visible things, but of generation and nourishment and growth, though he himself is not generation?

Certainly.

In like manner the good may be said to be not only the author of knowledge to all things known, but of their being and essence, and yet the good is not essence, but far exceeds essence in dignity and power.

Glaucon said, with a ludicrous earnestness: By the light of heaven, how amazing!

Yes, I said, and the exaggeration may be set down to you; for you made me utter my fancies.

And pray continue to utter them; at any rate let us hear if there is anything more to be said about the similitude of the sun.

Yes, I said, there is a great deal more.

Then omit nothing, however slight.

I will do my best, I said; but I should think that a great deal will have to be omitted.

THE DIVIDED LINE OF KNOWLEDGE

You have to imagine, then, that there are two ruling powers, and that one of them is set over the intellectual world, the other over the visible. I do not say heaven, lest you should fancy that I am playing upon the name (*ovpavos, oparos*). May I suppose that you have this distinction of the visible and intelligible fixed in your mind.

I have.

Now take a line which has been cut into two unequal parts, and divide each of them again in the same proportion, and suppose the two main divisions to answer, one to the visible and the other to the intelligible, and then compare the subdivisions in respect of their clearness and want of clearness, and you will find that the first section in the sphere of the visible consists of images. [*510*] And by images I mean, in the first place, shadows, and in the second place reflections in water and in solid, smooth and polished bodies and the like: Do you understand?

Yes, I understand.

Imagine, now, the other section, of which this is only the resemblance, to include the animals which we see, and everything that grows or is made.

Very good.

Would you not admit that both the sections of this division have different degrees of truth, and that the copy is to the original as the sphere of opinion is to the sphere of knowledge?

Most undoubtedly.

Next proceed to consider the manner in which the sphere of the intellectual is to be divided.

In what manner?

Thus:—There are two subdivisions, in the lower of which the soul uses the figures given by the former division as images: the enquiry can only be hypothetical, and instead of going upwards to a principle descends to the other end; in the higher of the two, the soul passes out of hypotheses, and goes up to a principle which is above hypotheses, making no use of images as in the former case, but proceeding only in and through the ideas themselves.

I do not quite understand your meaning, he said.

Then I will try again; you will understand me better when I have made some preliminary remarks. You are aware that students of geometry, arithmetic, and the kindred sciences assume the odd and the even and the figures and three kinds of angles and the like in their several branches of science; these are their hypotheses, which they and everybody are supposed to know, and therefore they do not deign to give any account of them either to themselves or others; but they begin with them, and go on until they arrive at last, and in a consistent manner, at their conclusion?

Yes, he said, I know.

And do you not know also that although they make use of the visible forms and reason about them, they are thinking not of these, but of the ideals which they resemble; not of the figures which they draw, but of the absolute square and the absolute diameter, and so on—the forms which they draw or make, and which have shadows and reflections in water of their own, are converted by them into images, but they are really seeking to behold the things themselves, which can only be seen with the eye of the mind?

[*511*] That is true.

And of this kind I spoke as the intelligible, although in the search after it the soul is compelled to use hypotheses; not ascending to a first principle, because she is unable to rise above the region of hypothesis, but employing the objects of which the shadows below are resemblances in their turn as images, they having in relation to the shadows and reflections of them a greater distinctness, and therefore a higher value.

I understand, he said, that you are speaking of the province of geometry and the sister arts.

And when I speak of the other division of the intelligible, you will understand me to speak of that other sort of knowledge which reason herself attains by the power of dialectic, using the hypotheses not as first principles, but only as hypotheses—that is to say, as steps and points of departure into a world which is above hypotheses, in order that she may soar beyond them to the first principle of the whole; and clinging to this and then to that which depends on this, by successive steps she descends again without the aid of any sensible object, from ideas, through ideas, and in ideas she ends.

I understand you, he replied; not perfectly, for you seem to me to be describing a task which is really tremendous; but, at any rate, I understand you to say that knowledge and being, which the science of dialetic contemplates, are clearer than the notions of the arts, as they are termed, which proceed from hypotheses only: these are also contemplated by the understanding, and not by the senses: yet, because they start from hypotheses and do not ascend to a principle, those who contemplate them appear to you not to exercise the higher reason upon them, although when a first principle is added to them they are cognizable by the higher reason. And the habit which is concerned with geometry and the cognate sciences I suppose that you would term understanding and not reason, as being intermediate between opinion and reason.

You have quite conceived my meaning, I said; and now, corresponding to these four divisions, let there be four faculties in the soul—reason answering to the highest, understanding to the second, faith (or conviction) to the third, and perception of shadows to the last—and let there be a scale of them, and let us suppose that the several faculties have clearness in the same degree that their objects have truth.

I understand, he replied, and give my assent, and accept your arrangement.

THE CAVE

[*514*] And now, I said, let me show in a figure how far our nature is enlightened or unenlightened:—Behold! human beings living in an underground den, which has a mouth open towards the light and reaching all along the den; here they have been from their childhood, and have their legs and necks chained so that they cannot move, and can only see before them, being prevented by the chains from turning round their heads. Above and behind them a fire is blazing at a distance, and between the fire and the prisoners there is a raised way; and you will see, if you look, a low wall built along the way, like the screen which marionette players have in front of them, over which they show the puppets.

I see.

And do you see, I said, men passing along the wall carrying all sorts of vessels, [*515*] and statues and figures of animals made of wood and stone and various materials, which appear over the wall? Some of them are talking, others silent.

You have shown me a strange image, and they are strange prisoners.

Like ourselves, I replied; and they see only their own shadows, or the shadows of one another, which the fire throws on the opposite wall of the cave?

True, he said: how could they see anything but the shadows if they were never allowed to move their heads?

And of the objects which are being carried in like manner they would only see the shadows?

Yes, he said.

And if they were able to converse with one another, would they not suppose that they were naming what was actually before them?

Very true.

And suppose further that the prison had an echo which came from the other side, would they not be sure to fancy when one of the passers-by spoke that the voice which they heard came from the passing shadow?

No question, he replied.

To them, I said, the truth would be literally nothing but the shadows of the images.

That is certain.

And now look again, and see what will naturally follow if the prisoners are released and disabused of their error. At first, when any of them is liberated and compelled suddenly to stand up and turn his neck round and walk and look towards the light, he will suffer sharp pains; the glare will distress him, and he will be unable to see the realities of which in his former state he had seen the shadows; and then conceive some one saying to him, that what he saw before was an illusion, but that now, when he is approaching nearer to being and his eye is turned towards more real existence, he has a clearer vision—what will be his reply? And you may further imagine that his instructor is pointing to the objects as they pass and requiring him to name them—will he not be perplexed? Will he not fancy that the shadows which he formerly saw are truer than the objects which are now shown to him?

Far truer.

And if he is compelled to look straight at the light, will he not have a pain in his eyes which will make him turn away to take refuge in the objects of vision which he can see, and which he will conceive to be in reality clearer than the things which are now being shown to him?

True, he said.

And suppose once more, that he is reluctantly dragged up a steep and rugged ascent, and held fast until he is forced into the presence of the sun himself, [*516*] is he not likely to be pained and irritated? When he approaches the light his eyes will be dazzled, and he will not be able to see anything at all of what are now called realities.

Not all in a moment, he said.

He will require to grow accustomed to the sight of the upper world. And first he will see the shadows best, next the reflections of men and other objects in the water, and then the objects themselves; then he will gaze upon the light of the moon and the stars and the spangled heaven; and he will see the sky and the stars by night better than the sun or the light of the sun by day?

Certainly.

Last of all he will be able to see the sun, and not mere reflections of him in the water, but he will see him in his own proper place, and not in another; and he will contemplate him as he is.

Certainly.

He will then proceed to argue that this is he who gives the season and the years, and is the guardian of all that is in the visible world, and in a certain way the cause of all things which he and his fellows have been accustomed to behold?

Clearly, he said, he would first see the sun and then reason about him.

And when he remembered his old habitation, and the wisdom of the den and his fellow-prisoners, do you not suppose that he would felicitate himself on the change, and pity them?

Certainly, he would.

And if they were in the habit of conferring honours among themselves on those who were quickest to observe the passing shadows and to remark which of them went before, and which followed after, and which were together; and who were therefore best able to draw conclusions as to the future, do you think that he would care for such honours and glories, or envy the possessors of them? Would he not say with Homer,

> *Better to be the poor servant of a poor master,*

and to endure anything, rather than think as they do and live after their manner?

Yes, he said, I think that he would rather suffer anything than entertain these false notions and live in this miserable manner.

Imagine once more, I said, such an one coming suddenly out of the sun to be replaced in his old situation; would he not be certain to have his eyes full of darkness?

To be sure, he said.

And if there were a contest, and he had to compete in measuring the shadows with the prisoners who had never moved out of the [*517*] den, while his sight was still weak, and before his eyes had become steady (and the time which would be needed to acquire this new habit of sight might be very considerable), would he not be ridiculous? Men would say of him that up he went and down he came without his eyes; and that it was better not even to think of ascending; and if any one tried to loose another and lead him up to the light, let them only catch the offender, and they would put him to death.

No question, he said.

This entire allegory, I said, you may now append, dear Glaucon, to the previous argument; the prison-house is the world of sight, the light of the fire is the sun, and you will not misapprehend me if you interpret the journey upwards to be the ascent of the soul into the intellectual world according to my poor belief, which, at your desire, I have expressed—whether rightly or wrongly God knows. But, whether true or false, my opinion is that in the world of knowledge the idea of good appears last of all, and is seen only with an effort; and, when seen, is also inferred to be the universal author of all things beautiful and right, parent of light and of the lord of light in this visible world, and the immediate source of reason and truth in the intellectual; and that this is the power upon which he who would act rationally either in public or private life must have his eye fixed.

I agree, he said, as far as I am able to understand you.

Moreover, I said, you must not wonder that those who attain to this beatific vision are unwilling to descend to human affairs; for their souls are ever hastening into the upper world where they desire to dwell; which desire of theirs is very natural, if our allegory may be trusted.

Yes, very natural.

And is there anything surprising in one who passes from divine contemplations to the evil state of man, misbehaving himself in a ridiculous manner; if, while his eyes are blinking and before he has become accustomed to the surrounding darkness, he is compelled to fight in courts of law, or in other places, about the images or the shadows of images of justice, and is endeavouring to meet the conceptions of those who have never yet seen absolute justice?

Anything but surprising, he replied.

[*518*] Any one who has common sense will remember that the bewilderments of the eyes are of two kinds, and arise from two causes, either from coming out of the light or from going into the light, which is true of the mind's eye, quite as much as the bodily eye; and he who remembers this when he sees any one whose vision is perplexed and weak, will not be too ready to laugh; he will first ask whether that soul of man has come out of the brighter life, and is unable to see because unaccustomed to the dark, or having turned from darkness to the day is dazzled by excess of light. And he will count the one happy in his condition and state of being, and he will pity the other; so, if he have a mind to laugh at the soul which comes from below into the light, there will be more reason in this than in the laugh which greets him who returns from above out of the light into the den.

That, he said, is a very just distinction.

But then, if I am right, certain professors of education must be wrong when they say that they can put a knowledge into the soul which was not there before, like sight into blind eyes.

They undoubtedly say this, he replied.

Whereas, our argument shows that the power and capacity of learning exists in the soul already; and that just as the eye was unable to turn from darkness to light without the whole body, so too the instrument of knowledge can only by the movement of the whole soul be turned from the world of becoming into that of being, and learn by degrees to endure the sight of being, and of the brightest and best of being, or in other words, of the good.

Very true.

And must there not be some art which will effect conversion in the easiest and quickest manner; not implanting the faculty of sight, for that exists already, but has been turned in the wrong direction, and is looking away from the truth?

Yes, he said, such an art may be presumed.

And whereas the other so-called virtues of the soul seem to be akin to bodily qualities, for even when they are not originally innate they can be implanted later by habit and exercise, the virtue of wisdom more than anything else contains a divine element which always remains, and by this conversion is rendered useful and profitable; [*519*] or, on the other hand, hurtful and useless. Did you never observe the narrow intelligence flashing from the keen eye of a clever rogue—how eager he is, how clearly his paltry soul sees the way to his end; he is the reverse of blind, but his keen eye-sight is forced into the service of evil, and he is mischievous in proportion to his cleverness?

Very true, he said.

But what if there had been a circumcision of such natures in the days of their youth; and they had been severed from those sensual pleasures, such as eating and drinking, which, like leaden weights, were attached to them at their birth, and which drag them down and turn the vision of their souls upon the things that are below—if, I say, they had been released from these impediments and turned in the opposite direction, the very same faculty in them would have seen the truth as keenly as they see what their eyes are turned to now.

Very likely.

Yes, I said; and there is another thing which is likely, or rather a necessary inference from what has preceded, that neither the uneducated and uninformed of the truth, nor yet those who never make an end of their education, will be able ministers of State; not the former, because they have no single aim of duty which is the rule of all their actions, private as well as public; nor the latter, because they will not act at all except upon compulsion, fancying that they are already dwelling apart in the islands of the blest.

Very true, he replied.

Then, I said, the business of us who are the founders of the State will be to compel the best minds to attain that knowledge which we have already shown to be the greatest of all—they must continue to ascend until they arrive at the good; but when they have ascended and seen enough we must not allow them to do as they do now.

What do you mean?

I mean that they remain in the upper world: but this must not be allowed; they must be made to descend again among the prisoners in the den, and partake of their labours and honours, whether they are worth having or not.

But is not this unjust? he said; ought we to give them a worse life, when they might have a better?

You have again forgotten, my friend, I said, the intention of the legislator, who did not aim at making any one class in the State happy above the rest; the happiness was to be in the whole State, and he held the citizens together by persuasion and necessity, making them benefactors of the State, [*520*] and therefore benefactors of one another; to this end he created them, not to please themselves, but to be his instruments in binding up the State.

True, he said, I had forgotten.

Observe, Glaucon, that there will be no injustice in compelling our philosophers to have a care and providence of others; we shall explain to them that in other States, men of their class are not obliged to share in the toils of politics and this is reasonable, for they grow up at their own sweet will, and the government would rather not have them. Being self-taught, they cannot be expected to show any gratitude for a culture which they have never received. But we have brought you into the world to be rulers of the hive, kings of yourselves and of the other citizens, and have educated you far better and more perfectly than they have been educated and you are better able to share in the double duty. Wherefore each of you, when his turn comes, must go down to the general under ground abode, and get the habit of seeing in the dark. When you have acquired the habit, you will see ten thousand times better than the inhabitants of the den, and you will know what the several images are, and what they represent because you have seen the beautiful and just and good in their truth. And thus our State which is also yours will be a reality, and not a dream only, and will be administered in a spirit unlike that of other States, in which men fight with one another about shadows only and are distracted in the struggle for power, which in their eyes is a great good. Whereas the truth is that the State in which the rulers are most reluctant to govern is always the best and most quietly governed, and the State in which they are most eager, the worst.

Quite true, he replied.

And will our pupils, when they hear this, refuse to take their turn at the toils of State, when they are allowed to spend the greater part of their time with one another in the heavenly light?

Impossible, he answered; for they are just men, and the commands which we impose upon them are just; there can be no doubt that every one of them will take office as a stern necessity, and not after the fashion of our present rulers of State.

Yes, my friend, I said; and there lies the point. You must contrive for your future rulers another and a better life than that of [*521*] a ruler, and then you may have a well-ordered State; for only in the State which offers this, will they rule who are truly rich, not in silver and gold, but in virtue and wisdom, which are the true blessings of life. Whereas if they go to the administration of public affairs, poor and hungering after their own private advantage, thinking that hence they are to snatch the chief good, order there can never be: for they will be fighting about office, and the civil and domestic broils which thus arise will be the ruin of the rulers themselves and of the whole State.

Most true, he replied.

And the only life which looks down upon the life of political ambition is that of true philosophy. Do you know of any other?

Indeed, I do not, he said.

And those who govern ought not to be lovers of the task? For, if they are, there will be rival lovers, and they will fight.

No question.

Who then are those whom we shall compel to be guardians? Surely they will be the men who are wisest about affairs of State, and by whom the State is best administered, and who at the same time have other honours and another and a better life than that of politics?

They are the men, and I will choose them, he replied. . . .

Chapter III — Aristotle

Introduction

With the exception of Plato, no philosopher has exercised a greater influence on the development of Western Civilization than Aristotle. His ideas have managed to survive among us for more than two thousand years, and his immense contributions to philosophy and science are still regarded as paradigms of human achievement. Like Plato, Aristotle was a seminal thinker. He has served as a source of inspiration to countless human beings who have dedicated their lives to the pursuit of wisdom. During medieval times, for example, Aristotle was referred to as "the philosopher," and his writings constituted the firm basis on which much of medieval philosophy rested. Today, even though many of his ideas and insights into the nature of the universe and man have been replaced by perhaps more adequate notions, he still remains one of the foundations of our thinking.

Aristotle was born in 384 B.C. Like many other Greek philosophers of his time, he was not an Athenian. His home was the small town of Stagira in northern Greece, and his family appears to have been devoted to the service of the Macedonian King Philip, the father of Alexander the Great. Aristotle's father, a man named Nicomachus, was the king's personal physician. The philosopher's early training was in the medical and biological sciences, and we are told by his biographers that by the age of seventeen he was already an accomplished physician.

Around the year 367 B.C., he travelled to Athens for the purpose of completing his education. Athens was the cultural capital of the Greek world, and

Plato's Academy was the place where many prominent scholars congregated. Aristotle, accordingly, entered Plato's Academy, where he remained for close to twenty years. There he functioned in the capacity of student and teacher, and it appears that the philosophy of Plato exercised a profound influence on him. We know, for example, that like Plato, he wrote philosophical dialogues, and that during his first years at the Academy he developed a system of philosophy along the lines suggested by Plato's thought. In later years, however, his relationship with Plato became somewhat strained due to the ideological differences between the two philosophers. Eventually, this led to Aristotle's leaving the Academy several years before Plato's death in 347 B.C.

Subsequently, Aristotle travelled extensively throughout the ancient Greek world, and settled down in a province of Asia Minor (Turkey) called Mycia. In 341 B.C. he was summoned by King Philip of Macedonia to serve as Alexander's tutor, and in compliance with the ancient ties of his family with the Macedonian crown, Aristotle remained close to Alexander for five years. Afterwards, he moved back to Athens, probably in the company of the invading Macedonian armies which eventually came to conquer most of the Greek world. In Athens, with the political and financial support of the Macedonians, he founded an institution of higher learning which became known as the Lyceum. Here, Aristotle taught and engaged in scientific research for thirteen years. Upon the untimely death of Alexander, who had become emperor, Aristotle was accused of impiety and treason. We can surmise, of course, that these accusations, not unlike those brought up against Socrates, were the legalistic mantle beneath which there lurked a political conspiracy against the philosopher. Unlike Socrates, however, Aristotle chose to escape from Athens even before the trial. He took refuge in the neighboring town of Chalcis, where he died one year later of natural causes.

Aristotle's writings are many and varied. Unfortunately, almost half of them perished during the Roman occupation of Greece, and there is little hope of ever finding them. But what survived is probably a sufficient basis for forming an idea of Aristotle's philosophy. Among the surviving writings, there are treatises on logic and scientific methodology, on cosmology and astronomy, on physics and biology, on dreams and psychology, on the nature of political institutions and the Athenian constitution, on poetry and drama, on ethics and history, on metaphysics, and on many other philosophical subjects. Unlike the *Dialogues* of Plato, the writings of Aristotle are designed to serve as the basis for lectures and therefore have a strictly didactic texture.

It can be safely said that no philosopher in the history of Western Civilization has made a greater attempt to systematize knowledge and to reach a more comprehensive understanding of the universe and man, than Aristotle. This is, among other things, one of the reasons for his enormous influence among us. He gave us, for the very first time, the elements for an organization of the sciences.

Aristotle held a number of ideas about the universe which are no longer accepted by the scientific orthodoxy. He believed, for example, that the earth occupied the center of the universe, and that the moon, the planets, the sun, and the stars were attached to invisible spheres which rotated daily around the earth.

The earth, of which Aristotle gave us the first recorded spherical dimensions, rested motionless at the very center of the universe. There is no reference in Aristotle's writings to the idea of development in the universe. It appears as if he thought that the universe at large was changeless.

These geocentric notions have little adequacy in the present world of astronomy. Today we are accustomed to take for granted the insignificance of our planet in the context of the Solar System, the insignificance of the sun and its system in the context of the Milky Way, and the insignificance of the Milky Way in the context of the billions of galaxies which constitute the observable universe. We are far removed from the limitations of Aristotle's geocentric cosmology. But what is curious is that this cosmology dominated the minds of human beings until the time of Copernicus (1473-1543). In medieval times, the authority of Aristotle was regarded as sufficient proof that the earth did not move in space, and even in the sixteenth century, when Galileo was prosecuted by the Catholic Inquisition, the Aristotelian ideas were quoted in the inquisitional indictment.

What the medievals and the inquisitors forgot however was, that Aristotle himself had said on repeated occasions that "experience, not authority, should be taken as the ultimate standard of judgment." If one day, said Aristotle, my ideas are found to be contrary to experience, let my ideas be forgotten. Human beings, however, feel more at ease when they can quote a distinguished authority, instead of examining their own experiences. This explains the unjustified use of Aristotle's name in order to settle controversies. As we saw in Chapter One, philosophy should have no dogmas, no final authority, no sanctified belief. In philosophy, the mind is free to explore for itself all possible regions of human experience, and to form its own judgments accordingly. All that is required is a large dose of Socratic honesty and a great deal of perseverance.

Honesty and perseverance—these are the unmistakable characteristics of Aristotle's writings, even when, from our present point of view, we are unable to agree with some of their contentions. Before examining any issue, Aristotle always begins by reviewing, in a spirit of compassion and thoroughness, most of the views held by his predecessors on the same issue. This Aristotelian habit, something which should be emulated by all philosophers and scientists, constitutes one of the major merits of his writings. In all of them, we are allowed to examine, albeit briefly, the ideas of ancient philosophers whose writings have never come to us. There are many passages in Aristotle's writings devoted to the analysis of Plato's ideas, and reading them, one becomes immediately aware of the gap that separated the two philosophers. But even when Aristotle expresses his dissatisfaction with one or another Platonic idea, he invariably displays a profound sense of respect and humility. Aristotle knew perfectly well that above the names of philosophers and their systems of ideas, the ultimate court of judgment is human experience.

His philosophy, therefore, makes a constant appeal to experience. Knowledge, he says in the *Metaphysics,* is inevitably rooted in sense experience, and ultimate knowledge has to do with individual objects of experience. In the few selections from his writings to which the student will be introduced, this will become abundantly clear.

Aristotle's Philosophy

The Problem of Change

We have identified Thales as the first philosopher, since he was the first of a long line of Greek thinkers who were concerned with defining the nature of reality. Despite giving divergent answers to the question, all of these thinkers agreed that some definitive statement could be given about the permanent nature of the real. One of the consequences of this assumption is that *change* becomes something of a problem. In our talk about things that change, we seem to be assuming that something remains permanent during the process of change. Moreover, if there is change, then there must be some permanent principles according to which change takes place. In short, Greek philosophers assumed that what was permanent was real, and they either denied the reality of what appears to change, or they interpreted change as a manifestation of what was unchanging.

Aristotle took change seriously and sought to explain it better than his predecessors had. At the same time, he never challenged their assumption that basic to this process was the existence of something unchanging.

Biology as a Guide

Since biology was the field he understood best, Aristotle sought to extend his understanding from that field to nature or to reality as a whole. In this there is nothing unusual, since if we believe that the world is intelligible there is nothing to prevent us from extending the principles of intelligibility from one discipline to another (properly qualified, of course). In fact, the demands of a total philosophical vision would seem to require this step.

There are certain principles which appear almost inescapable, or so men have thought, if we are to properly understand *life*. Life at every level seems to be characterized by growth, development, and decay—in short, by change. Moreover, that change seems to be designed to achieve certain purposes. Nutrition, growth, and reproduction seem to be fundamental to all organic activity. These functions are true of all living things, plants as well as animals. Beyond this, animals exhibit sensation, desire, and locomotion (change of place or position). And some animals exhibit the additional function or capacity for deliberate behavior (for example, beavers build dams). Beyond this, there is the purely theoretical thought of human beings. In fact, we seem to find a hierarchy wherein each level contains all that we find on the lower levels, plus something additional and peculiar to that level. Another remarkable principle discovered from the observation of animals is the persistence of the form, the species, through a changing succession of individuals. This is clear in oak trees producing acorns, which grow into other oak trees; and it is present in human reproduction, wherein certain genetic traits are preserved through the successive generations of a family.

The Causes of Change

Equipped with his knowledge of biological change, Aristotle turns to change in general. Previous thinkers had distinguished in varying and confused degrees two principles: the material constituents and the formal structure or *essence* which makes the constituent the determinate kind of thing it is. We say that the matter has the *potential* for embodying that form. Moreover, the form exists only in the succession of material objects in which it is embodied. On this crucial issue Aristotle disagrees with Plato, who had held that the forms (universals common to many objects) exist independently of the objects, which manifest the forms imperfectly. As opposed to the materialists, Aristotle insists upon the need for actual forms, because otherwise matter cannot be conceived of as actualizing its potential.

As with the animal kingdom, Aristotle conceives of the material world in general as comprising a system or hierarchy of graded existences. The simplest matter comprises the traditional four elements of earth, air, fire, and water. From these the more complex manifestations of inorganic bodies and the world of organic beings (living things) emerges. All this occurs because of the existence of more complex forms. Within this process of increasing complexity Aristotle distinguishes three kinds of change: alteration (qualitative change), quantitative change, and locomotion (change of place).

Locomotion is the most basic kind of change, but it involves more than impact. The locomotion of the four elements or primary bodies depends upon the assumption (traditional to Greek philosophy and shared by Aristotle) that each has a natural place in which it finally comes to rest. Since rest is natural, every movement requires the existence of a mover. Moreover, if the world is rational, there cannot be an infinite chain or series of movers. Hence, there must be a self-sufficient, self-explanatory, unmoved mover. In short, there must be a *first mover* or first movers. Finally, since motion is eternal, the first mover or movers must be eternal.

Unlike later Christian thought, which employs his thought, Aristotle spoke of *movers,* not one mover. Moreover, motion is eternal, otherwise a beginning to time (creation) would be needed, and such a concept would be unexplainable rationally. We also note that the need for a supreme form (unmoved mover) is part of Aristotle's biology, for the hierarchy in nature implies increasing consciousness. Even the reason by which mankind grasps the intelligibility of the world requires for its actualization a higher reason. This supreme form of intelligence is thought thinking about itself.

The Four Causes

The aim of rational inquiry is to discover the causes of a phenomenon. Aristotle finds that there are four kinds of causes: (1) material cause, (2) efficient cause, (3) formal cause, and (4) final cause. The material cause is that of which a thing is made; the efficient cause is that by which it comes into existence; the formal cause is its essence or essential nature; and the final cause is that end for which it exists. In the case of natural objects, as opposed to the products of human art, the last three causes coincide. That is, the efficient, formal, and final causes are the same.

What does this mean? Let us distinguish between the products of human art, like a statue or a house, and a natural object, like an acorn. We are concerned with natural objects. To explain an acorn we might describe the organic material of which it is made, but this is relatively unimportant. What is important are the other three causes. Where does an acorn come from? It comes from an oak tree. What happens to an acorn? It grows into an oak tree. Why does this all happen? It happens because the essence or form of an acorn is just that, namely, to become an oak tree. If we really understood or grasped the nature of the acorn, we could see that it must have come from an oak tree and that it is destined itself to become an oak tree. Such biological facts are generalized by Aristotle into a full-blown theory about how the universe works.

In Aristotelian language, the end or final cause of an object in nature is to realize its essence or formal cause. It also means that this formal cause or essence is embodied in another entity, which possesses an identical form or essence and serves as the efficient cause of its production. It is this coincidence of formal and efficient causes which permits us to infer unerringly what a cause must *necessarily* be, from mere acquaintance with the effect. The formal cause becomes in practice the basic explanatory principle, since what a thing is essentially is built into it.

The Place of Man

There is an element of Aristotle's philosophy which is difficult for some readers to grasp. As we know, most acorns do not grow into oak trees. Hence, we would say that under perfect or ideal conditions acorns grow into oaks. But note that these ideal conditions do sometimes exist in experience, unlike the Platonic ideal which need never be actualized in experience. This sense of something having an end which it does not always achieve is important for understanding Aristotle's views on man and society.

The good or end for man must be the full development of *human nature.* Human nature is understood in terms of those faculties which are distinctive of man, that separate or distinguish him from other entities. What is distinctive of us is our rational faculty, not our appetites. Our reason operates in two ways, first in the habitual subordination of appetite or passion to rational control, and second in the contemplation of truth. The first way is described as the set of moral virtues and involves the doctrine of the mean. Most moral virtues are means between extremes, as courage is the mean between being a coward and acting rashly.

In his discussion of politics, Aristotle makes it clear that a civilized community is a necessary prerequitisite for the full development of human nature. Again, for Aristotle the natural state is social life, for he finds nature only in the fully developed case. Aristotle would be appalled by the modern notion that what is natural is either what is primitive or what is usual in the statistical sense. Most acorns do not develop into oaks; but that, nevertheless, is their nature if only they get a chance to develop properly. Likewise, the highest good for man is contemplation, even though most individuals do not have the opportunity to become professional philosophers. Finally, we note that the ultimate end is not practical but theoretical.

The Metaphysics

All men by nature desire to know[1] and an indication of this is the love of the senses; for even, irrespective of their utility, are they loved for their own sakes, and pre-eminently above the rest, the sense of sight. For not only for practical purposes, but also when not intent on doing anything; we choose the power of vision in preference, so to say, to all the rest of the senses. And a cause of this is the following,—that this one of the senses particularly enables us to apprehend whatever knowledge it is the inlet of, and that it makes many distinctive qualities manifest.

By nature then, indeed, are animals formed endowed with sense; but in some of them memory is not innate from sense, and in others it is. And for this reason are these possessed of more foresight, as well as a greater aptitude for discipline, than those which are wanting in this faculty of memory. Those furnished with foresight, indeed, are yet without the capability of receiving instruction, whatever amongst them are unable to understand the sounds they hear; as, for instance, bees, and other similar tribes of animals; but those are capable of receiving instruction as many as, in addition to memory, are provided with this sense also.

The rest, indeed, subsist then through impressions and the operations of memory, but share experience in a slight degree; whereas the human race exists by means of art also and the powers of reasoning.

Now, experience accrues to men from memory; for repeated acts of memory about the same thing done constitute the force of a single experience: and experience seems to be a thing almost similar to science and art.

Aristotle, *The Metaphysics*.
Translated by John H. McMahon.

But science and art result unto men by means of experience; for experience, indeed, as Polus saith, and correctly so, has produced art, but inexperience, chance. But an art comes into being when, out of many conceptions of experience, one universal opinion is evolved with respect to similar cases. For, indeed, to entertain the opinion that this particular remedy has been of service to Callias, while labouring under this particular disease, as well as to Socrates, and so individually to many, this is an inference of experience; but that it has been conducive to the health of all,—such as have been defined according to one species,—while labouring under this disease, as, for instance, to the phlegmatic, or the choleric, or those sick of a burning fever, this belongs to the province of art.

As regards, indeed, practical purposes,[2] therefore, experience seems in no wise to differ from art; . . . experience, indeed, is a knowledge of singulars, whereas art, of universals; but all things in the doing, and all generations, are concerned about the singular: for he whose profession it is to practise medicine, does not restore man to health save by accident, but Callias, or Socrates, or any of the rest so designated, to whom it happens to be a man. If, therefore, any one without the experience is furnished with the principle, and is acquainted with the universal, but is ignorant of the singular that is involved therein, he will frequently fall into error in the case of his medical treatment; for that which is capable of cure is rather the singular.

But, nevertheless, we are of opinion that, at least, knowledge and understanding appertain to art rather than experience; and we reckon artists more wise than the experienced, inasmuch as wisdom is the concomitant of all philosophers rather in proportion to their knowledge.

But this is so because some, indeed, are aware of the cause, and some are not. For the experienced, indeed, know that a thing is so, but they do not know why it is so; but others —I mean the scientific—are acquainted with the why and the cause. Therefore, also we reckon the chief artificers in each case to be entitled to more dignity, and to the reputation of superior knowledge, and to be more wise than the handicraftsmen, because the former are acquainted with the causes of the things that are being constructed; whereas the latter produce things, as certain inanimate things do, indeed; yet these perform their functions unconsciously,—as the fire when it burns. Things indeed, therefore, that are inanimate, by a certain constitution of nature, perform each of these their functions, but the handicraftsmen through habit; inasmuch as it is not according as men are practical that they are more wise, but according as they possess the reason of a thing, and understand causes.

And, upon the whole, a proof of a person's having knowledge is even the ability to teach; and for this reason we consider art, rather than experience, to be a science; for artists can, whereas the handicraftsmen cannot, convey instruction.

And further, we regard none of the senses to be wisdom, although, at least, these are the most decisive sources of knowledge about singulars; but they make no affirmation of the why in regard of anything,—as, for example, why fire is hot, but only the fact that it is hot.

Therefore,[3] indeed, is it natural for the person who first discovers any art whatsoever, beyond the ordinary power of the senses, to be the object of human admiration, not only on account of something of the things that have been discovered being useful, but as one that is wise and superior to the rest of men. But when more arts are being discovered—both some, indeed, in relation to things that are necessary, and others for pastime—we invariably regard such more wise than those,[4] on account of their sciences not being for bare utility. Whence all things of such a sort having been already procured, those sciences have been invented which were pursued neither for purposes of pleasure nor necessity, and first in those places where the inhabitants enjoyed leisure: wherefore, in the neighborhood of Egypt the mathematical arts were first established; for there leisure was spared unto the priestly caste. It has then, indeed, been declared in the Ethics[5] what is the difference between an art and a science, and the rest of the things of the same description.

But, at present, the reason of our producing this treatise is the fact, that all consider what is termed wisdom to be conversant about first causes and principles; so that—as has been said on a former occasion—the experienced seem to be more wise than those possessing any sense whatsoever, and the artificer than the experienced, and the master-artist than the handicraftsman, and the speculative rather than those that are productive. That, indeed, wisdom, therefore, is a science conversant about certain causes and first principles is obvious.

Now, since we are engaged in investigating this science, the following must form a subject for our consideration; namely, about what kind of causes, and what kind of first principles, is this science—I mean wisdom—conversant. If, doubtless, one would receive the opinions which we entertain concerning the wise man, perhaps from this our proposed inquiry would be evident the more.

Now, in the first place, indeed, we go on the supposition that the wise man, especially is acquainted with all things scientifically, as far as this is possible, not, however, having a scientific knowledge of them singly. In the next place, a person who is capable of knowing things that are difficult, and not easy for a man to understand, such as one we deem wise (for perception by the senses is common to all, wherefore it is a thing that is easy, and by no means wise). Further, one who is more accurate, and more competent to give instruction in the causes of things, we regard more wise about every science. And of the sciences, also, that which is desirable for its own account, and for the sake of knowledge, we consider to be wisdom in preference to that which is eligible on account of its probable results, and that which is more qualified for preeminence we regard as wisdom, rather than that which is subordinate, —for that, the wise man ought not to be dictated to, but should dictate unto others; and that this person ought not to be swayed in his opinions by another, but one less wise by this man. Respecting this wisdom and wise men[6] do we entertain such and so many suppositions.

But of these characteristics the scientific knowlege of all things must needs be found in him most especially who possesses the universal science;[7] for this person, in a manner, knows all things that are the subjects of it. But, also, the most difficult nearly for men to know are the things that are especially universal, for they are most remote from the senses. But the most accurate of the sciences are those respecting things that are primary, in the most eminent sense of the word; for those from fewer principles are more accurate than those said to be from addition, as arithmetic than geometry. But, also, that science, without doubt, is more adapted towards giving instruction, at least, which speculates about causes; for those do afford instruction who assign the causes in regard of each individual thing. Now, understanding and scientific knowledge, for their own sakes, most especially reside in the science of that which is most particularly fitted for being scientifically known. For he who selects scientific knowledge, for its own sake, will especially choose that which is preeminently science; but such is that which is the science of that which is particularly fitting as an object of scientific knowledge, and particularly fitting as objects of scientific knowledge are the first principles and causes; for on account of these, and by means of these, are the other objects of knowledge capable of being made known: but not these by means of those things that are subordinate to them. Most fit for preeminence likewise amongst the sciences, and fit for preeminence in preference to that which is subservient, is the science which communicates the knowledge of that on account of which each thing is to be done; but this constitutes the good in each particular, but, in general, that which is the best in every nature.

From all, therefore, that has been stated, the sought-for appellation lights upon the same science; for it is necessary that this be a science speculative of first principles and of causes, for the good, also, viewed as a final cause, is one from amongst our classified list of causes.

But that the science under investigation is not a science employed in producing,[8] is evident from the case of those who formed systems of philosophy in the earliest ages. For from wonder men, both now and at the first, began to philosophize, having felt astonishment originally at the things which were more obvious, indeed, amongst those that were doubtful; then, by degrees, in this way having advanced onwards, and, in process of time, having stated difficulties about more important subjects,—as, for example, respecting the passive conditions of the moon, and those brought to pass about the sun and stars, and respecting the generation of the universe. But he that labours under perplexity and wonder thinks that he is involved in ignorance. Therefore, also, the philosopher—that is, the lover of wisdom—is somehow a lover of fables, for the fable is made up of the things that are marvellous. Wherefore, if, for the avoidance of ignorance, men from time to time have been induced to form systems of philosophy, it is manifest that they went in pursuit of scientific knowledge for the sake of understanding it, and not on account of any utility that it might possess. But the event itself also bears witness to the truth of this statement; for on the supposition of almost all those things being in existence that are requisite towards both cause and the management of life, prudence of such a sort as this began to be in requisition. Therefore is it evident that we seek scientific knowledge from no other actual ground of utility save what springs from itself.

But as we say a free man exists who is such for his own sake, and not for the sake of another, so, also, this alone of the sciences is free, for this alone subsists for its own sake.

Wherefore, also, the acquisition of this science may be justly regarded as not human, for, in many instances, human nature is servile.

So that, according to Simonides, the Deity only should, enjoy this prerogative; yet that it is unworthy for a man not to investigate the knowledge that is in conformity with his condition. But if, in reality, the poets make any such assertion, and if the Godhead is in its nature constituted so as to envy, in this respect it is especially natural that it should happen, and that all those that are over-subtle should be unfortunate: but neither does the Divine essence admit of being affected by envy, but—according to the proverb—the bards utter many falsehoods.

Nor ought we to consider any other science more entitled to honour than such as that under investigation at present. For that which is most divine is also most worthy of honour.

But such will be so in only two ways; for that which the Deity would especially possess is a divine one amongst the sciences; and if there is any such science, this would be the case with the science of things divine. But this science, such as we have described it, alone is possessed of both of these characteristics; for to all speculators the Deity appears as a cause and a certain first principle;[9] and such a science as this, either God alone, or he principally, would possess. Therefore, indeed, may all sciences else be more requisite than this one; but none is more excellent.

It is, indeed, necessary, in a manner, to establish the order[10] of this science, in its development, in a direction contrary to the speculations that have been carried on from the beginning. For, indeed—as we have remarked—all men commence their inquiries from wonder whether a thing be so, as in the case of the spontaneous movements of jugglers' figures to those who have not as yet speculated into their cause; or respecting the solstices, or the incommensurability of the diameter; for it seems to be a thing astonishing to all, if any quantity of those that are the smallest is not capable of being measured. But it is necessary to draw our inquiry to a close in a direction the contrary to this, and towards what is better, according to the proverb. As also happens in the case of these, when they succeed in learning those points; for nothing would a geometrician so wonder at, as if the diameter of a square should be commensurable with its side. What, therefore, is the nature of the science under investigation has been declared; as, also, what the aim should be which the present inquiry and the entire treatise should strive and attain.[11]

But since it is manifest that one ought to be in possession of a science of primary causes (for then we say that we know each individual thing when we think that we are acquainted with the first cause); and since causes are denominated under four different heads,[12] the first of which we assert to be the substance and the essence of a thing (for the inquiry of the wherefore, in the first instance of a thing, is referred to the last reason,[13] but the first wherefore of a thing is a cause and first principle); and the second cause we affirm to be the matter and the subject; and the third is the source of the first principle of motion; and the fourth, the cause that is in opposition to this,—namely, both the final cause and the good; for such is an end of every generation.[14]

But they who put forward ideas as causes, in their early investigations, indeed, to acquire the causes of these entities, in the first place have adduced other things equal in number to these;[15] as if one, desiring to have reckoned certain things, when these were less numerous, would consider this impossible, but, by creating a greater number, should succeed in counting them; for almost equal, or not less numerous, are the forms than those things respecting which, in investigating their causes, they have advanced from these to those: for, according to each individual thing, there is a certain homonymous form, and, in addition to the substances, also, of other things, there is the unity involved in the notion of plurality, both in the case of these and of things that are eternal.

Moreover,[16] in the ways in which it is demonstrated that there are forms, according to none of these the subsistence of forms becomes apparent; for, indeed, from some there is no necessity, in the sequence of the reasoning, that a syllogism arise: but from other things, also,—not of such as we should expect to find forms,—of these are there forms generated. For according to the rational principles deducible from the sciences will there be forms of all things, of as many as there are sciences; and in accordance with the argument for ideas founded on the notion of unity involved in plurality, will there also be forms or ideas of negations: and according to the ability to understand something of what has been destroyed of things liable to decay will there also be forms, for of these there is a certain phantasm. . . .

But most of all would one feel perplexed as to what at all[17] the forms contribute, either to those things that are eternal amongst sensibles, or to things that are being produced and being corrupted. For neither are they to them a cause of any motion or change whatever. But, truly, neither are they of any assistance towards the science of other things (for neither are those the substance of these, for in such a case they would be in these), nor do they contribute towards the existence of other things, inasmuch as they are not inherent in things that are their participants, at least; for so, indeed, they would perhaps be supposed as causes, just as if the white were mixed with the white it might be called the cause of a white body. But, indeed, this theory is very easily overthrown, which Anaxagoras, indeed, first and Endoxus subsequently, and certain others, advanced; for it would be easy to collect together, also, many impossibilities in reference to such an opinion; but, truly, neither do other things subsist from forms in accordance with any mode of existence of those that are wont to be mentioned.

But the assertion that these forms are exemplars, and that the rest of entities participate in them, is to speak vain words, and to utter poetic metaphors. For in what respect, may I ask does that which operates look towards the ideas as a model? for it is possible that anything whatever that is similar both should exist and be produced, and yet that it be not made like in reference to that to which it is similar. Wherefore, also, on the supposition of the existence and non-existence of Socrates, just such another one as Socrates it would be produced. And, in like manner, is it evident that this would follow, even though Socrates were eternal; and, besides, there will be many exemplars of the same thing; wherefore, also the forms—for instance, of man, such as animal and biped, and at the same time, also, ideal man—will have a subsistence. Further, not only of things sensible are forms the exemplars, but also of forms themselves; as, for example, the genus as a genus will be an exemplar of species; wherefore, an exemplar and an image will be the same thing.

Further, it would seem impossible for the substance to be separate from that of which it is the substance; therefore, in what way can the ideas, when they are substances of things, exist separately from them?

But in the *Phaedo* an assertion is made to this effect,—that the forms are causes of existence and of production. On the supposition, however, of the existence of forms, nevertheless, those things that are participants will not be produced, if there be not in existence that which is likely to be the origin of motion; and many other things are produced, such as a house and a ring, of which we do not say that there are forms. Wherefore, it is evident that it is possible, also, for other things both to exist and be produced from such causes, likewise, on account of which, also, arise those entities mentioned just now. . . .

And upon the whole,[18] seeing that wisdom investigates into the cause, in respect of things that are manifest, this consideration, indeed, have we omitted; for we say nothing regarding the cause of the origin of the principle of change: but thinking to mention the substance of these, we say that there are different substances; but in what manner those may be substances of these we ineffectually describe, for as to such being accomplished by participation—as also we have stated on a former occasion—there is no advantage gained in saying this. Neither, truly, are ideas such causes as we see to be a cause to the sciences, on account of which both every mind and every nature operate; nor that cause which we affirm to be one of the first principles do forms in any wise touch upon; but to men, in the present age, mathematics have become *the* philosophy; although they say that persons ought to cultivate these sciences for the sake of other sciences.

But, further, one may suppose the subject-substance to be as matter that is more mathematical, and rather to be converted into a predicable, and to constitute a difference of substance and of matter,—as, for instance, the great and the small,—just as, also, the natural philosophers mention the rare and the dense, saying that there are these primary differences of the subject, for these are a certain excess and defect. And respecting motion, if, indeed, these will constitute motion, it is evident that the forms will be moved; but if they are not, whence has motion originated? for thereby the entire investigation about Nature has been abolished.

And what seems to be easy—namely, the demonstration that all things are one—does not turn out to be so; for, according to the interpretation, all things do not become one, but a certain thing itself is one, if any one would grant that all things are so: and neither would he allow this, unless one would admit the existence of a universal as a genus; but this, in some cases, is impossible. . . .

But how can any one learn the elements of all things? for it is evident that it is not possible that he should be previously a person having prior knowledge thereof. For, as to one learning geometry, it is, indeed, possible to see beforehand other things; but of such things as the science consists of, and concerning which he is about to receive instruction, he can have no prior knowledge so, also, is it in the case of other things. Wherefore, if there is a certain science of all things, as some affirm, nothing could this person know beforehand. Every system of learning, however, subsists, or is attainable by means of previous knowledge, either of all things, or of certain particular things: and either by demonstration is this accomplished, or by definitions; for those things whereof the definition consists it is requisite to understand beforehand, and that they be known. In like manner is it the case with knowledge by induction. But, truly, if also it happens that there is in our possession a congenital knowledge of things, it is astonishing how we, in possession of the most excellent of the sciences, are unconscious of such a treasure.

Further, how will any one know from what particulars all things consist, and how will this be manifest? for this also involves perplexity; for one would feel a doubt, just as also concerning some syllable: for certain affirm that SMA is composed of S and M and A, but others say that it possesses a different sound from its components, and none of those that are known.

Moreover, those things of which there is perception by sense, how could any one know if he were not furnished with the capacity of perceiving by sense? although one ought, if these are the elements of all things whereof they consist, just as the compound sounds arise from their own proper elements.

That, therefore, all seem to seek the causes mentioned in our Physics, and, besides these, that we have no other to adduce, is likewise from the foregoing statements evident. But the early philosophers, I admit have treated of these causes,—obscurely, however; and, indeed, in a certain manner, all such four causes have been enumerated by speculators of an age prior to ours: and, in a certain manner, by no means has this been the case; for the earliest system of philosophy concerning all things was like unto one articulating with a stammer, inasmuch as it was new as regards, first principles, and a thing the first in its kind. For Empedocles says that a bone exists from form by the principle of composition; but this is the essence and the substance of that thing. But, truly, if this be admitted, in like manner, also, is it necessary that of both flesh, and everything else of the other things, there should subsist this principle of concretion, or that it should not subsist as a principle of anything at all; for on account of this are both flesh and bone, and each of the other things, in existence, and not on account of the matter, which he says is fire, and earth, and water, and air. But, also, with any other indeed, who would make these assertions, he would by necessity concur; but he has not expressed himself with clearness respecting them. The case regarding such points, therefore, has been made evident on a former occasion; but as many doubts as any one might indulge in respecting these same, we will a second time enumerate; for perhaps we shall thereby acquire a facility for having our difficulties resolved in reference to subsequent questions of doubt.

Since, however, that which is produced is produced[19] both by something (now, I mean that whence also originates the first principle of generation, that is, its efficient cause) and from something, (but let this be not privation, but matter, for already has it been defined in what manner we have denominated this,) also must there be that which is produced; and this is either a sphere or a circle, or whatever else of the other things that may chance to present itself; as neither the efficient cause produces the subject, (I mean, the brass,) so neither does it make the sphere, unless by accident, because a brazen sphere is a sphere; but it does not produce the sphere itself. For the production of a certain thing of this kind is the production of this particular thing from the entire subject. Now, I say, that to make the brass round is not to make the round or the sphere, but something different, such as this form in another thing. For, if the artist produces it, he would produce this from something else; for this would be the subject: as, for example, to make a brazen sphere; and this the artist makes in this manner because from this particular thing which is brass he forms this which is a sphere. If, therefore, also, he produces this very thing, it is evident that in like manner he will produce another; and the productions will go on in a process *ad infinitum*.

It is palpable, then, that neither form (or by whatever name we must needs term form, as it subsists in that which is cognisable to sense) is produced, nor is there a generation thereof, nor is this the essence or very nature of a thing; for this is that which is produced in another subject either from Art, or from Nature, or potentiality, and the efficient cause it is which produces the existence of a brazen sphere; for it produces it from brass and a sphere: for into this particular thing, which is the form, the efficient cause moulds the brass, and this constitutes a brazen sphere. And if, in short, of the being or existence of sphere there exists a generation, it will be a something that is a generation from a certain thing: for it will be necessary that what is produced always be divisible, and that this should be this particular thing, and that should be something else: now, I mean that this should be matter, and that form. Therefore, if a sphere be a figure equal from the centre to all points of its periphery, of this one part will be that in which that which produces will be inherent, and the other part that which resides in this part; but the whole is that which has been produced or generated; as, for instance, the brazen sphere. It is evident, therefore, from the statements that have been made, that what is denominated as form or as substance is not generated, but that the union which is said to take place according to this is generated, and that in everything which is being produced matter is inherent, and that one part is matter, but the other form. . . .

After these inquiries there remains for us to make our readers aware that neither matter nor form is generated. Now, I speak thus of the extremities of things; for everything that undergoes any change is changed both by something and into something—by something, of course, I mean that which is the first imparter of motion, and of something, that is, matter, and that into which the thing is changed; this is the form. Therefore, they go on in a progression to infinity, if not only the brass becomes spherical, but also the spherical or the brass is generated: therefore, must we sooner or later come to a standstill in the series.

After these inquiries we must show how each substance is generated from one synonymous with itself; for those things that are being generated by Nature, as well as other things, are substances. For things are produced either by Art, or Nature, or Chance, or Spontaneity. Art, indeed, therefore, constitutes a first principle which subsists in another subject, whereas Nature constitutes a first principle which subsists in the thing itself; for man begets man: and the remaining causes are the privations of these. Substances likewise are three in number, and one of these is matter; which is this certain particular thing in consequence of its appearance as certain particular things in consequence of its appearance as such; for as many things as are one by contact, and not by cohesion, constitute matter and a subject: but another of these substances is Nature, which likewise is this certain particular thing, and into Nature is there the transition of a certain habit. Further, the third substance is that which subsists from these, and is ranked as a singular; for example, Socrates or Callias.

As regards some things, therefore, this certain particular thing involves no subsistence independent of a composite substance, as the form of a house, unless art constitutes this form. Neither is there any generation and corruption of these, but after a different manner they are, and are not, both the house itself, which is unconnected with matter, and health, and everything that is produced according to art; but if forms subsist, they subsist in the case of those things that are generated by Nature. Wherefore, doubtless, not injudiciously affirmed Plato that forms belong to those things as many as involve a natural subsistence, on the supposition of the existence of forms different from, or independent of, these; as, for example, fire, flesh, the head, and so forth. For all these things are matter, and belong to substance especially—I mean, such a description of matter as is ultimate.

Some causes, therefore that impart motion subsist as entities that have been previously generated, whereas other causes which subsist as the formed principle are simultaneously generated with their results; for when a man is in sound health then also is there present with him sound health, and the form of the brazen sphere subsists simultaneously with the brazen sphere.

And whether, also, there remains anything subsequently to the separation of form from the subject of form, we must examine; for in the case of some forms there is no hindrance to this taking place; as if soul were a thing of this description: not, to be sure, every soul, but the understanding; for that this should be so with every soul is not, perhaps, a thing that is possible. It is evident, therefore, that there is no necessity that on account of these, at least, ideas should have an existence; for man begets man, the singular begets a certain individual. And in like manner does the case stand with the arts; for the medicinal art is the formal principle of health.

And as regards causes and first principles in a manner are they different according as they belong to different things, and in a manner this is not the case. Supposing one to express himself universally, and according to analogy the causes and first principles of all things will be the same. For one might raise the question as to whether the first principles and elements of substances, and of things which subsist as relatives, are different or the same? and, therefore, in like manner is it the case with each of the categories. But it would be absurd if there were the same principles and elements of all things, for from the same things will relatives derive their subsistence as well as substance. What, therefore, will this be? for besides substance and the rest of the things that are predicated there is nothing that is in common. Prior, however, is the element to those things of which it is an element; but, assuredly, neither is substance an element of relatives, nor is any of these an element of substance. Further, how is it admissible that there should be the same elements of all things? for none of the elements can be the same with that which is a composite nature of the elements; as, for instance, neither B nor A can be the same with BA. Neither, therefore, is it possible that any one element of those natures that are intelligible—as, for example, unity or entity—can be the element of all things; for these are present with each of the compound natures likewise. No one of them, therefore, will have a subsistence either as substance or relation; but it will be a thing expedient, however, that they should subsist in some form or other. The elements, then, of all things are not the same.

Or, shall we say—just as we have already affirmed—that in one way this is the case, and in another that it is not? as, perhaps, in regard of sensible bodies that which is hot subsists in one way as form, and after another mode that which is cold subsists as the privation thereof; but matter subsists as that which primarily and essentially constitutes both of these in capacity; substances, however, are both these and such as consist of those things of which these are the first principles. Or, if any one thing is generated from what is hot and from what is cold, as flesh or bone, stiil that which is produced from thence must needs be different from these. The first principle and elements of these, I admit, then, are the same, yet there are different elements of different things; and, without doubt, we cannot say that the case stands in this way with all things; but analogically are the elements and first principles of all things the same; just as if one should say that there are three first principles in existence—namely, form, and privation, and matter; each of these, however, is different according as it is conversant about every genus, as in colour, white, black, surface, light, darkness, air; and from these emerge forth day and night.

Since, however, not only things that are inherent are causes, but also causes of things that are external—as, for example, in the case of what imparts motion—it is evident that a first principle is a different thing from an element; yet both are causes, and into these is a first principle divided: but what subsists as that which imparts motion or rest constitutes a certain first principle and substance.

Wherefore, there are in existence three elements, indeed, according to analogy, but four causes and first principles; and a different cause subsists where the subject is different, and the first cause constitutes, as it were, that which imparts motion, and is different according as the subject is different. Thus, health is as form, disease as privation, body as matter: that which imparts motion is the medicinal art. Again, a house is as form, this certain sort of confusion[20] as privation; the bricks are as matter, and that which imparts motion, or the efficient cause, is the builder's art. And into these, therefore, is a first principle divided.

But since that which imparts motion in physical or natural things is a man, and in things springing from the understanding form, or the contrary, in one respect would there be three causes, and in another four; for the medicinal art constitutes in a manner health, and the building art the form of the house, and man begets man; further, beside these—as that which is the first of all things—is that which imparts motion, or is the efficient cause, to all things.

NOTES

1. The assertion, however, that all men desire knowledge has been objected to, on the ground that in some this desire is wholly absent; but this absence merely amounts to a suppression of the natural desire from various causes; *e.g.* want of leisure for intellectual pursuits, constitutional laziness, voluptuous habits.

2. Aristotle demonstrates that knowledge is a thing more honourable than action, in order to show that wisdom, being involved in knowledge, and not in practice, is likewise itself, on that account, more worthy of respect.

3. Aristotle here shows the paths through which men must travel into this "wisdom," or first philosophy; and for this purpose adduces the example of the Egyptian priests, who were enabled to construct the speculative sciences of geometry and mathematics by having enjoyed leisure from the laborious employments of life. They were thus allowed an opportunity of contemplating the heavenly phenomena, and, from such observations of experiences, of deducing the abstract sciences.

4. That is, that those who knew the reason of things were more wise than the artificers.

5. The objection which Aristotle imagines is tacitly implied in the foregoing remarks amounts to this,—that such are tantamount to destroying the distinction between art, science, and wisdom. Aristotle, however, repels the imputation that he is using these words in the same sense by a reference to his Ethics, book VI. chap. iii, where distinctions between them are carefully drawn.

6. Aristotle having shown, in the first chapter, that the science under investigation—which he here calls wisdom, though elsewhere by a different denomination—is conversant about causes, proceeds now to lay down what sort these causes are, their nature, and number.

7. During the first age of Greek philosophy it was styled "wisdom," and its cultivators, "wise men"; and the term philosopher was first applied to Pythagoras. This change, no doubt, betokened a corresponding change in men's mode of thought; for thereby an element hitherto undiscovered was brought into notice,—namely, the relation of our emotions to scientific investigations.

8. Aristotle shows that the science under investigation is speculative, not active, from the fact that the earliest philosophy sprang from wonder,—that wonder flows from ignorance,—that the removal of ignorance amounts to knowledge,—that this was accomplished by speculation and not practice; and that therefore wisdom, the source of the highest knowledge, was speculative and not active.

9. This is a remarkable passage to occur in the writings of Aristotle, about whose deism or atheism so much has been said and written.

10. That whereas the old philosophy originated from wonder,—that is, ignorance,—and attained unto a sort of knowledge, yet that when men reached this knowledge, knowledge, as such, became the great actuating motive in speculation. This present science under investigation, however, would set out from an opposite point in this progress, because it started from the consideration of that which is the highest object of speculative knowledge.

11. Aristotle now proceeds to examine into the labours of his predecessors; and the course he pursues is first to enumerate the opinions thereupon of the early schools of philosophy, and of individual speculators; and next, to set down arguments for or against these theories, and show how far they are true, and how far false.

12. This fourfold enumeration of causes is taken from the Physics, books I. and II. We have the same division laid down in the Posterior Analytics, book II. chap. xi.

13. "The last reason." This refers to the method of demonstration adopted by the mathematicians in their problems. . . .

14. Aristotle now proceeds to examine into another system of the supranaturalists,—namely, that of Plato: first, in respect of his theory regarding the substance of things; and secondly, respecting the first principles of things.

15. Aristotle first complains of the inconsistency of Plato; for he contends that, in proposing to assign the causes of sensibles, he should have kept the phenomena of sensibles before his eyes, and not have devised, as he has done, a theory applicable to anything else save sensibles.

16. Aristotle here details his objections against the ideal system of Plato, which he strives to overthrow by turning the reasoning of Plato against himself.

17. Aristotle now proceeds to prove the utter irrelevancy of ideas as accounting for sensible phenomena.

18. Aristotle now proceeds to argue against Plato in his theory concerning the first principles of things.

19. What Aristotle aims to establish is this, that it is not strictly true to say that naked form is generated, but that matter, in combination with a certain invariable form is. This dogma may be regarded as a necessary sequence to the reasoning that has gone before.

20. That is, the materials of the house before they are reduced by the builder to the form and shape of a house.

The Nicomachean Ethics

BOOK I.

Every art and every scientific inquiry, and similarly every action and purpose, may be said to aim at some good. Hence the good has been well defined as that at which all things aim. But it is clear that there is a difference in the ends; for the ends are sometimes activities, and sometimes results beyond the mere activities. Also, where there are certain ends beyond the actions, the results are naturally superior to the activities.

As there are various actions, arts, and sciences, it follows that the ends are also various. Thus health is the end of medicine, a vessel of shipbuilding, victory of strategy, and wealth of domestic economy. It often happens that there are a number of such arts or sciences which fall under a single faculty, as the art of making bridles, and all such other arts as make the instruments of horsemanship, under horsemanship, and this again as well as every military action under strategy, and in the same way other arts or sciences under other faculties. But in all these cases the ends of the architectonic arts or sciences, whatever they may be, are more desirable than those of the subordinate arts or sciences, as it is for the sake of the former that the latter are themselves sought after. It makes no difference to the argument whether the activities themselves are the ends of the actions, or something else beyond the activities as in the above mentioned sciences.

If it is true that in the sphere of action there is an end which we wish for its own sake, and for the sake of which we wish everything else, and that we do not desire all things for the sake of something else (for, if that is so, the process will go on *ad infinitum,* and our desire will be idle and futile) it is clear that this will be the good or the supreme good. Does it not follow then that the knowledge of this supreme good is of great importance for the conduct of life, and that, *if we know it,* we shall be like archers who have a mark at which to aim, we shall have a better chance of attaining what we want? But, if this is the case, we must endeavour to comprehend, at least in outline, its nature, and the science or faculty to which it belongs.

It would seem that this is the most authoritative or architectonic science or faculty, and such is evidently the political; for it is the political science or faculty which determines what sciences are necessary in states, and what kind of sciences should be learnt, and how far they should be learnt by particular people. We perceive too that the faculties which are held in the highest esteem, e.g. strategy, domestic economy, and rhetoric, are subordinate to it. But as it makes use of the other practical sciences, and also legislates upon the things to be done and the things to be left undone, it follows that its end will comprehend the ends of all the other sciences, and will therefore be the true good of mankind. For although the good of an individual is identical with the good of a state, yet the good of the state, whether in

---

Aristotle, *The Nicomachean Ethics.* Translated by J. E. C. Weldon, 1892.

attainment or in preservation, is evidently greater and more perfect. For while in an individual by himself it is something to be thankful for, it is nobler and more divine in a nation or state.

These then are the objects at which the present inquiry aims, and it is in a sense a political inquiry. But our statement of the case will be adequate, if it be made with all such clearness as the subject-matter admits; for it would be as wrong to expect the same degree of accuracy in all reasonings as in all manufactures. Things noble and just, which are the subjects of investigation in political science, exhibit so great a diversity and uncertainty that they are sometimes thought to have only a conventional, and not a natural, existence. There is the same sort of uncertainty in regard to good things, as it often happens that injuries result from them; thus there have been cases in which people were ruined by wealth, or again by courage. As our subjects then and our premisses are of this nature, we must be content to indicate the truth roughly and in outline; and as our subjects and premisses are true generally *but not universally,* we must be content to arrive at conclusions which are only generally true. It is right to receive the particular statements which are made in the same spirit; for an educated person will expect accuracy in each subject only so far as the nature of the subject allows; he might as well accept probable reasoning from a mathematician as require demonstrative proofs from a rhetorician. But everybody is competent to judge the subjects which he understands, and is a good judge of them. It follows that in particular subjects it is a person of *special* education, and in general a person of universal education, who is a good judge. Hence the young are not proper students of political science, as they have no experience of the actions of life which form the premisses and subjects of the reasonings. Also it may be added that from their tendency to follow their emotions they will not study the subject to any purpose or profit, as its end is not knowledge but action. It makes no difference whether a person is young in years or youthful in character; for the defect *of which I speak* is not one of time but is due to the emotional character of his life and pursuits. Knowledge is as useless to such a person as it is to an intemperate person. But where the desires and actions of people are regulated by reason the knowledge of these subjects will be extremely valuable.

But having said so much by way of preface as to the students of political science, the spirit in which it should be studied, and the object which we set before ourselves, let us resume our argument as follows:

As every knowledge and moral purpose aspires to some good, what is in our view the good at which the political science aims, and what is the highest of all practical goods? As to its name there is, I may say, a general agreement. The masses and the cultured classes agree in calling it happiness, and conceive that "to live well" or "to do well" is the same thing as "to be happy." But as to the nature of happiness they do not agree, nor do the masses give the same account of it as the philosophers. The former define it as something visible and palpable, e.g. pleasure, wealth, or honour; different people give different definitions of it, and often the same person gives different definitions at different times; for when a person has been ill, it is health, when he is poor, it is wealth, and, if he is conscious of his own ignorance, he envies people who use grand language above his own comprehension. Some *philosophers* on the other hand have held that, besides these various goods, there is an absolute good which is the cause of goodness in them all. It would perhaps be a waste of time to examine all these opinions, it will be enough to examine such as are most popular or as seem to be more or less reasonable.

But we must not fail to observe the distinction between the reasonings which proceed from first principles and the reasonings which lead up to first principles. For Plato was right in raising the difficult question whether the *true* way was from first principles or to first principles, as in the race-course from the judges to the goal, or *vice versa.* We must begin then with such facts as are known. But facts may be known in two ways, i.e. either relatively to ourselves or absolutely. It is probable then that *we* must begin with such facts as are known to us, *i.e. relatively.* It is necessary therefore, if a person is to be a competent student of what is noble and just and of politics in general, that he should have received a good moral training. For the fact that a thing is so is a first principle or starting-point, and, if the fact is sufficiently clear, it will not be necessary to go on to ask the reason of it. But a person who has received a good moral training either possesses first principles, or will have no difficulty in acquiring them. But if he does not possess them, and cannot acquire them, he had better lay to heart Hesiod's lines:

"Far best is he who is himself all-wise,
And he, too, good who listens to wise words;
But whoso is not wise nor lays to heart
Another's wisdom is a useless man."

But to return from our digression: It seems not unreasonable that people should derive their conception of the good or of happiness from men's lives. Thus ordinary or vulgar people conceive it to be pleasure, and accordingly approve a life of enjoyment. For there are practically three prominent lives, the sensual, the political, and, thirdly, the speculative. Now the mass of men present an absolutely slavish appearance, as choosing the life of brute beasts, but they meet with consideration because so many persons in authority share the tastes of Sardanapalus. Cultivated and practical people, on the other hand, identify happiness with honour, as honour is the general end of political life. But this appears too superficial for our present purpose; for honour seems to depend more upon the people who pay it than upon the person to whom it is paid, and we have an intuitive feeling that the good is something which is proper to a man himself and cannot easily be taken away from him. It seems too that the reason why men seek honour is that they may be confident of their own goodness. Accordingly they seek it at the hands of the wise and of those who know them well, and they seek it on the ground of virtue; hence it is clear that in their judgment at any rate virtue is superior to honour. It would perhaps be right then to look upon virtue rather than honour as being the end of the political life. Yet virtue again, it appears, lacks completeness; for it seems that a man may possess virtue and yet be asleep or inactive throughout life, and, not only so but he may experience the greatest calamities and misfortunes. But nobody would call such a life a life of happiness, unless he were maintaining a paradox. It is not necessary to dwell further on this subject, as it is sufficiently discussed in the popular philosophical treatises. The third life is the speculative which we will investigate hereafter.

The life of money-making is in a sense a life of constraint, and it is clear that wealth is not the good of which we are in quest; for it is useful in part as a means to something else. It would be a more reasonable view therefore that the things mentioned before, viz. *sensual pleasure, honour and virtue,* are ends than that wealth is, as they are things which are desired on their own account. Yet these too are apparently not ends, although much argument has been employed to show that they are.

We may now dismiss this subject; but it will perhaps be best to consider the universal *good,* and to discuss the meaning in which the phrase is used, although there is this difficulty in such an enquiry, that the *doctrine of* ideas has been introduced by our friends. Yet it will perhaps seem the best, and indeed the right course, at least when the truth is at stake, to go so far as to sacrifice what is near and dear to us, especially as we are philosophers. For friends and truth are both dear to us, but it is a sacred duty to prefer the truth.

Now the authors of this theory did not make ideas of things in which they predicated priority and posteriority. Hence they did not constitute an idea of numbers. But good is predicated equally of substance, quality and relation, and the absolute or essential, *i.e. substance,* is in its nature prior to the relative, as relativity is like an offshoot or accident of existence; hence there cannot be an idea which is common to them both. Again, there are as many ways of predicating good as of predicating existence; for it is predicated of substance as e.g. of God or the mind, or of quality as of the virtues, or of quantity as of the mean, or of relativity as of the useful, or of time as of opportunity, or of place as of a habitation, and so on. It is clear then that it cannot be a common universal idea or a unity; otherwise it would not be predicated in all the categories but only in one. Thirdly, as there is a single science of all such things as fall under a single idea, there would have been a single science of all good things, *if the idea of "good" were single*; but in fact there are many sciences even of such good things as fall under a single category, strategy, e.g. being the science of opportunity in war, and medicine the science of opportunity in disease, medicine again being the science of the mean in respect of food, and gymnastic the science of the mean in respect of exercise. It would be difficult, too, to say what is meant by the "absolute" in anything, if in "absolute man" and in "man" there is one and the same conception of man. For there will be no difference between them in respect of manhood, and, if so, neither will there be any difference between "absolute good" and "good" in respect of goodness. Nor again will good be more good if it is eternal, since a white thing which lasts for a long time is not whiter than that which lasts for a single day. There seems to be more plausibility in the doctrine of the Pythagoreans who place unity in the catalogue of goods, and Speusippus apparently agrees with them. However these are questions which may be deferred to another occasion; but there is an objection to my arguments which suggests itself, viz. that the *Platonic* theory does not apply to every good, that the things which in themselves are sought after and welcomed are reckoned as one species and the things which tend to produce or in any sense preserve these or to prevent their opposites are reckoned as goods in a secondary sense as being means to these. It is clear then that there will be two kinds of goods, some being absolute goods, and others secondary. Let us then separate goods which are merely serviceable from absolute goods and consider if they are conceived as falling under a single idea. But what kind of things is it that may be defined as absolute goods? Will it be all such as are sought after independently of their consequences, e.g. wisdom, sight, and certain pleasures and honours? For granting that we seek after these sometimes as means to something else, still we may define them as absolute goods. Or is none of these things an absolute good, nor anything else except the idea? But then the type *or idea* will be purposeless, *i.e. it will not comprise any particulars.* If, on the other hand, these things too are absolute goods, the conception of the good will necessarily appear the same in them all, as the conception of whiteness appears the same in snow and in white lead. But the conception of honour, wisdom and pleasure, are distinct and different in respect of goodness. "Good" then is not a common term falling under one idea. But in what sense is the term used? For it does not seem to be an accidental homonymy. Is it because all goods issue from one source or all tend to one end; or is it rather a case of analogy? for as the sight is to the body, so is the mind to the soul, *i.e. the mind may be called the eye of the soul, and so on.* But it will perhaps be well to leave this subject for the present, as an exact discussion of it would belong rather to a different branch of philosophy. But the same is true of the idea; for even if there is some one good which is predicated of all these things, or some abstract and absolute good, it will plainly not be such as a man finds practicable and attainable, and therefore will not be such a good as we are in search of. It will possibly be held, however, that it is worth while to apprehend this *universal good,* as having a relation to the goods which are attainable and practicable; for if we have this as a model, we shall be better able to know the things which are good relatively to ourselves, and, knowing them, to acquire them. Now although there is a certain plausibility in this theory, it seems not to harmonize with scientific experience; for while all sciences aim at a certain good and seek to supply a deficiency, they omit the knowledge of the universal good. Yet it is not reasonable to suppose that what would be so extremely helpful is ignored, and not sought at all by artists generally. But it is difficult to see what benefit a cobbler or carpenter will get in reference to his art by knowing the absolute good, or how the contemplation of the absolute idea will make a person a better physician or general. For it appears that a physician does not regard health abstractedly, but regards the health of man or rather perhaps of a particular man, as he gives his medicine to individuals.

But leaving this subject for the present let us revert to the good of which we are in quest and consider what its nature may be. For it is clearly different in different actions or arts; it is one thing in medicine, another in strategy, and so on. What then is the good in each of these instances? It is presumably that for the sake of which all else is done. This in medicine is health, in strategy, victory, in domestic architecture, a house, and so on. But in every action and purpose it is the end, as it is for the sake of the end that people all do everything else. If then there is a certain end of all action, it will be this which is the practicable good, and if there are several such ends it will be these.

Our argument has arrived by a different

path at the same conclusion as before; but we must endeavour to elucidate it still further. As it appears that there are more ends than one and some of these, e.g. wealth, flutes, and instruments generally we desire as means to something else, it is evident that they are not all final ends. But the highest good is clearly something final. Hence if there is only one final end, this will be the object of which we are in search, and if there are more than one, it will be the most final of them. We speak of that which is sought after for its own sake as more final than that which is sought after as a means to something else; we speak of that which is never desired as a means to something else as more final than the things which are desired both in themselves and as a means to something else; and we speak of a thing as absolutely final, if it is always desired in itself and never as a means to something else.

It seems that happiness preeminently answers to this description, as we always desire happiness for its own sake and never as a means to something else, whereas we desire honour, pleasure, intellect, and every virtue, partly for their own sakes (for we should desire them independently of what might result from them) but partly also as being means to happiness, because we suppose they will prove the instruments of happiness. Happiness, on the other hand, nobody desires for the sake of these things, nor indeed as a means to anything else at all.

We come to the same conclusion if we start from the consideration of self-sufficiency, if it may be assumed that the final good is self-sufficient. But when we speak of self-sufficiency, we do not mean that a person leads a solitary life all by himself, but that he has parents, children, wife, and friends, and fellow-citizens in general, as man is naturally a social being. But here it is necessary to prescribe some limit; for if the circle be extended so as to include parents, descendants, and friends' friends, it will go on indefinitely. Leaving this point, however, for future investigation, we define the self-sufficient as that which, taken by itself, makes life desirable, and wholly free from want, and this is our conception of happiness.

Again, we conceive happiness to be the most desirable of all things, and that not merely as one among other good things. If it were one among other good things, the addition of the smallest good would increase its desirableness; for the accession makes a superiority of goods, and the greater of two goods is always the more desirable. It appears then that happiness is something final and self-sufficient, being the end of all action.

Perhaps, however, it seems a truth which is generally admitted, that happiness is the supreme good; what is wanted is to define its nature a little more clearly. The best way of arriving at such a definition will probably be to ascertain the function of Man. For, as with a flute-player, a statuary, or any artisan, or in fact anybody who has a definite function and action, his goodness, or excellence seems to lie in his function, so it would seem to be with Man, if indeed he has a definite function. Can it be said then that, while a carpenter and a cobbler have definite functions and actions, Man, unlike them, is naturally functionless? The reasonable view is that, as the eye, the hand, the foot, and similarly each several part of the body has a definite function, so Man may be regarded as having a definite function apart from all these. What then, can this function be? It is not life; for life is apparently something which man shares with the plants; and it is something peculiar to him that we are looking for. We must exclude therefore the life of nutrition and increase. There is next what may be called the life of sensation. But this too, is apparently shared by Man with horses, cattle, and all other animals. There remains what I may call the practical life of the rational part *of Man's being*. But the rational part is twofold; it is rational partly in the sense of being obedient to reason, and partly in the sense of possessing reason and intelligence. The practical life too may be conceived of in two ways, *viz., either as a moral state, or as a moral activity:* but we must understand by it the life of activity, as this seems to be the truer form of the conception.

The function of Man then is an activity of soul in accordance with reason, or not independently of reason. Again the functions of a person of a certain kind, and of such a person who is good of his kind, e.g. of a harpist and a good harpist, are in our view generically the same, and this view is true of people of all kinds without exception, the superior excellence being only an addition to the function;

for it is the function of a harpist to play the harp, and of a good harpist to play the harp well. This being so, if we define the function of Man as a kind of life, and this life as an activity of soul, or a course of action in conformity with reason, if the function of a good man is such activity or action of a good and noble kind, and if everything is successfully performed when it is performed in accordance with its proper excellence, it follows that the good of Man is an activity of soul in accordance with virtue or, if there are more virtues than one, in accordance with the best and most complete virtue. But it is necessary to add the words "in a complete life." For as one swallow or one day does not make a spring, so one day or a short time does not make a fortunate or happy man.

This may be taken as a sufficiently accurate sketch of the good; for it is right, I think, to draw the outlines first and afterwards to fill in the details. it would seem that anybody can carry on and complete what has been satisfactorily sketched in outline, and that time is a good inventor or cooperator in so doing. This is the way in which the arts have made their advances, as anybody can supply a deficiency.

But bearing in mind what has been already said, we must not look for the same degree of accuracy in all subjects; we must be content in each class of subjects with accuracy of such a kind as the subject-matter allows, and to such an extent as is proper to the inquiry. For while a carpenter and a geometrician both want to find a right angle, they do not want to find it in the same sense; the one wants only such an approximation to it as will serve his practical purpose, the other, as being concerned with truth, wants to know its nature or character. We must follow the same course in other subjects, or we shall sacrifice the main points to such as are subordinate. Again, we must not insist with equal emphasis in all subjects upon ascertaining the reason of things. We must sometimes e.g. in dealing with first principles be content with the proper evidence of a fact; the fact itself is a first point or principle. But there are various ways of discovering first principles; some are discovered by induction, others by perception, others by what may be called habituation, and so on. We must try to apprehend them all in the natural *or appropriate* way, and must take pains to define them satisfactorily, as they have a vital influence upon all that follows from them. For it seems that the first principle or beginning is more than half the whole, and is the means of arriving at a clear conception of many points which are under investigation.

In considering the first principle we must pay regard not only to the conclusion and the premisses of our argument, but also to such views as are popularly held about it. For while all experience harmonizes with the truth, it is never long before truth clashes with falsehood.

Goods have been divided into three classes, viz. external goods as they are called, goods of the soul and goods of the body. Of these three classes we consider the goods of the soul to be goods in the strictest or most literal sense. But it is to the soul that we ascribe psychical actions and activities. Thus our definition is a good one, at least according to this theory, which is not only ancient but is accepted by students of philosophy at the present time. It is right too, inasmuch as certain actions and activities are said to be the end; for thus it appears that the end is some good of the soul and not an external good. It is in harmony with this definition that the happy man should live well and do well, as happiness, it has been said, is in fact a kind of living and doing well.

It appears too that the requisite characteristics of happiness are all contained in the definition; for some people hold that happiness is virtue, others that it is prudence, others that it is wisdom of some kind, others that it is these things or one of them conjoined with pleasure or not dissociated from pleasure, others again include external prosperity. Some of these views are held by many ancient thinkers, others by a few thinkers of high repute. It is probable that neither side is altogether wrong, but that in some one point, if not in most points, they are both right.

Now the definition is in harmony with the view of those who hold that happiness is virtue or excellence of some sort; for activity in accordance with virtue implies virtue. But it would seem that there is a considerable difference between taking the supreme good to consist in acquisition or in use, in a moral state or in an activity. For a moral state, although it exists, may produce nothing good, e.g. if a person is asleep, or has in any other way become inactive. But this cannot be the case with an activity, as activity implies action and good action. As in the Olympian games it is not the most beautiful and strongest persons who receive the crown but they who actually enter the lists as combatants—for it is some of these who become victors—so it is they who act rightly that attain to what is noble and good in life. Again, their life is pleasant in itself. For pleasure is a psychical fact, and whatever a man is said to be fond of is pleasant to him, e.g. a horse to one who is fond of horses, a spectacle to one who is fond of spectacles, and similarly just actions to a lover of justice, and virtuous actions in general to a lover of virtue. Now most men find a sense of discord in their pleasures, because their pleasures are not such as are naturally pleasant. But to the lovers of nobleness natural pleasures are pleasant. It is actions in accordance with virtue that are naturally pleasant. Such actions then are pleasant both relatively to these persons and in themselves. Nor does their life need that pleasure should be attached to it as a sort of amulet; it possesses pleasure in itself. For it may be added that a person is not good, if he does not take delight in noble actions, as nobody would call a person just if he did not take delight in just actions, or liberal if he did not take delight in liberal actions, and so on. But if this is so, it follows that actions in accordance with virtue are pleasant in themselves. But they are also good and noble, and good and noble in the highest degree, if the judgment of the virtuous man upon them is right, his judgment being such as we have described. Happiness then is the best and noblest and pleasantest thing in the world, nor is there any such distinction between goodness, nobleness, and pleasure as the epigram at Delos suggests:

> "Justice is noblest, Health is best,
> To gain one's end is pleasantest."

For these are all essential characteristics of the best activities, and we hold that happiness consists in these or in one and the noblest of these. Still it is clear that happiness requires the addition of external goods, as we said; for it is impossible, or at least difficult for a person to do what is noble unless he is furnished with external means. For there are many things which can only be done through the instrumentality of friends or wealth or political power, and there are some things the lack of which must mar felicity, e.g. noble birth, a prosperous family, and personal beauty. For a person is incapable of happiness if he is absolutely ugly in appearance, or low born, or solitary and childless, and perhaps still more so, if he has exceedingly bad children or friends, or has had good children or friends and has lost them by death. As we said, then, it seems that prosperity of this kind is an indispensable addition to virtue. It is for this reason that some persons identify good fortune, and others virtue, with happiness.

The question is consequently raised whether happiness is something that can be learnt or acquired by habit or discipline of any other kind, or whether it comes by some divine dispensation or even by chance.

Now if there is anything in the world that is a gift of the Gods to men, it is reasonable to suppose that happiness is a divine gift, especially as it is the best of human things. This however is perhaps a point which is more appropriate to another investigation than the present. But even if happiness is not sent by the Gods but is the result of virtue and of learning or discipline of some kind, it is apparently one of the most divine things in the world; for it would appear that that which is the prize and end of virtue is the supreme good and is in its nature divine and blessed. It will also be widely extended; for it will be capable of being produced in all persons, except such as are morally deformed, by a process of study or care. And if it is better that happiness should be produced in this way than by chance, it may reasonably be supposed that it is so produced, as the order of things is the best possible in Nature and so too in art, and in causation generally, and most of all in the highest kind of causation. But it would be altogether inconsistent to leave what is greatest and noblest to chance. But the definition *of happiness* itself helps to clear up the question; for happiness has been defined as a certain kind of activity of the soul in accordance with virtue. Of the other goods, *i.e. of goods besides those of the soul,* some are necessary as antecedent conditions of happiness, others are in their nature co-operative and serviceable as instruments of happiness.

The conclusion at which we have arrived agrees with our original position. For we laid it down that the end of political science is the supreme good; and political science is concerned with nothing so much as with producing a certain character in the citizens, or in other words with making them good, and capable of performing noble actions. It is reasonable then not to speak of an ox, or a horse, or any other animal as happy; for none of them is capable of participating in activity as so defined. For the same reason no child can be happy, as the age of a child makes it impossible for him to display this activity at present, and if a child is ever said to be happy, the ground of the felicitation is his promise, *rather than his actual performance.* For happiness demands, as we said, a complete virtue and a complete life. For there are all sorts of changes and chances in life, and it is possible that the most prosperous of men will, in his old age, fall into extreme calamities as is told of Priam in the heroic legends. But if a person has experienced such chances, and has died a miserable death, nobody calls him happy.

Is it the case then that nobody in the world may be called happy so long as he is alive? Must we adopt Solon's rule of looking to the end? and, if we follow Solon, can it be said that a man is really happy after his death? Surely such a view is wholly absurd, especially for us who define happiness as a species of activity. But if we do not speak of one who is dead as happy, and if Solon's meaning is not this but rather that it is only when a man is dead that it is safe to call him fortunate as being extempt at last from evils and calamities, this again is a view which is open to some objection. For it seems that one who is dead is capable of being affected both by good and by evil in the same way as one who is living but unconscious, e.g. by honours and dishonours and by the successes or reverses of his children and his descendants generally. But here again a difficulty occurs. For if a person has lived a fortunate life up to old age, and has died a fortunate death, it is possible that he may experience many vicissitudes of fortune in the persons of his descendants. Some of them may be good and may enjoy such a life as they deserve; others may be bad and may have a bad life. It is clear, too, that descendants may stand in all sorts of different degrees of relationship to their ancestor. It would be an extraordinary result, if the dead man were to share the vicissitudes of their fortune and to become happy at one time and miserable at another, *as they became either happy or miserable.* But it would be equally extraordinary, if the future of descendants should not affect their parents at all or for a certain time. It will be best, however, to revert to the difficulty which was raised before, as it will perhaps afford an answer to the present question. If it is right to look to the end, and when the end comes to felicitate a person not as being fortunate but as having been so before, surely it is an extraordinary thing that at the time when he is happy we should not speak the truth about him, because we do not wish to call the living happy in view of the vicissitudes to which they are liable and because we have formed a conception of happiness as something that is permanent and exempt from the possibility of change and because the same persons are liable to many revolutions of fortune. For it is clear that, if we follow the changes of fortune, we shall often call the same person happy at one time, and miserable at another, representing the happy man as "a sort of chameleon without any stability of position." It cannot be right to follow the changes of fortune. It is not upon these that good or evil depends; they are necessary accessories of human life, as we said; but it is a man's activities in accordance with virtue that constitute his happiness and the opposite activities that constitute his misery. The difficulty which has now been discussed is itself a witness that this is the true view. For there is no human function so constant as the activities in accordance with virtue; they seem to be more permanent than the sciences themselves. Among these activities, too, it is the most honourable which are the most permanent, as it is in them that the life of the fortunate chiefly and most continuously consists. For this is apparently the reason why such activities are not liable to be forgotten.

The element of permanency which is required will be found in the happy man, and he will preserve his character throughout life; for he will constantly or in a preeminent degree pursue such actions and speculations as accord with virtue; nor is there anybody who will bear the chances of life so nobly, with such a perfect and complete harmony, as he who is truly good and "foursquare without a flaw." Now the events of chance are numerous and of different magnitudes. It is clear then that small incidents of good fortune, or the reverse, do not turn the scale of life, but that such incidents as are great and numerous augment the felicity of life, if they are fortunate, as they tend naturally to embellish it and the use of them is noble and virtuous, and on the other hand, if they are of a contrary character, mar and mutilate its felicity by causing pains and hindrances to various activities. Still even in these circumstances nobility shines out, when a person bears the weight of accumulated misfortunes with calmness, not from insensibility but from innate dignity and magnanimity.

But if it is the activities which determine the life, as we said, nobody who is fortunate can become miserable; for he will never do what is hateful and mean. For our conception of the truly good and sensible man is that he bears all the chances of life with decorum and always does what is noblest in the circumstances, as a good general uses the forces at his command to the best advantage in war, a good cobbler makes the best shoe with the leather that is given him, and so on through the whole series of the arts. If this is so, it follows that the happy man can never become miserable; I do not say that he will be fortunate, if he meets such chances of life as Priam. Yet he will not be variable or liable to frequent change, as he will not be moved from his happiness easily or by ordinary misfortunes but only by such misfortunes as are great and numerous; and after them it will not be soon that he will regain his happiness, but, if he regains it at all, it will be only in a long and complete period of time and after attaining in it to great and noble results.

We may safely then define a happy man as one whose activity accords with perfect virtue and who is adequately furnished with external goods, not for a casual period of time but for a complete or perfect lifetime. But perhaps we ought to add, that he will always live so, and will die as he lives; for it is not given us to foresee the future, but we take happiness to be an end, and to be altogether perfect and complete, and, this being so, we shall call people fortunate during their lifetime, if they possess and will possess these characteristics, but fortunate only so far as men may be fortunate.

But to leave the discussion of this subject: The idea that the fortunes of one's descendants and of one's friends generally have no influence at all upon oneself seems exceedingly harsh, and contrary to received opinions. But as the events of life are numerous and present all sorts of differences, and some are of more concern to us than others, it would be clearly a long, if not an infinite task, to define them individually; we must, I think, be content to describe them generally and in outline. Now, as in personal misfortunes some have a certain weight and influence upon our life, and others, it seems, are comparatively light, so it is with such misfortunes as affect our friends generally. But as the difference between the experiences of the living or the dead is far greater than the difference between terrible crimes when enacted upon the stage in tragedies and the same crimes when merely assumed to have already occurred, it is necessary to take account of this difference also, and still more perhaps of the serious doubt which has been raised as to the participation of the dead in any good or evil. For it is probable in this view that if anything, whether good or evil, reaches the dead at all, it is feeble and insignificant, either absolutely, or in relation to them, or if not, is of such a magnitude and character as to be incapable of making people happy if they are not happy or of depriving them of their felicity, if they are.

It would seem then that the dead are affected or influenced in some way by the prosperity and the adversity of their friends, but that the influence is of such a kind and degree as not to make people happy, if they are not happy, nor to have any similar effect.

Having determined these points, let us consider whether happiness belongs rather to such things as are objects of praise or to such things as are objects of honour. For it is clearly not a mere potential good.

It appears that whatever is an object of praise is praised as possessing a certain character, and standing in a certain relation to something. For we praise one who is just and manly and good in any way, or we praise virtue, because of their actions and productions. We praise one who is strong and swift and so on, as naturally possessing a certain character and standing in a certain relation to something that is itself good and estimable. The truth of this statement becomes clear, if we take the case of praises bestowed upon the Gods. Such praise appears ridiculous as implying a reference to ourselves, and there must be such a reference, because, as we said, praise invariably implies a reference *to a higher standard.* But if this is the nature of praise, it is clear that it is not praise but something greater and better which is appropriate to all that is best, as indeed is evident; for we speak of the Gods as "blessed" and "happy" *rather than as "praiseworthy"* and we speak of the most godlike men as "blessed." It is the same with goods; for nobody praises happiness as he praises justice, but he calls it blessed, as being in its nature better and more divine. It is sometimes held on these grounds that Eudoxus was right in advocating the supremacy of pleasure; for the fact that pleasure is a good and yet is not praised, indicates, as he thought, that it is higher than the objects of praise, as God and the good are higher, these being the standards to which everything else is referred. For praises are appropriate to virtue, as it is virtue which makes us capable of noble deeds; but panegyrics to accomplished results, whether they be results of the body or of the soul. But it may be said that an exact discussion of these points belongs more properly to the special study of panegyrics. We see clearly, however, from what has been said, that happiness is something honourable and final. And that it is so seems to follow also from the fact that it is a first principle; for it is for the sake of happiness that we all do everything else, and the first principle or the cause of all that is good we regard as something honourable and divine.

Inasmuch as happiness is an activity of soul in accordance with complete or perfect virtue, it is necessary to consider virtue, as this will perhaps be the best way of studying happiness.

It appears that virtue is the object upon which the true statesman has expended the largest amount of trouble, as it is his wish to make the citizens virtuous and obedient to the laws. We have instances of such statesmen in the legislators of Crete and Lacedaemon and such other legislators as have resembled them. But if this inquiry is proper to political science, it will clearly accord with our original purpose to pursue it. But it is clear that it is human virtue which we have to consider; for the good of which we are in search is, as we said, human good, and the happiness, human happiness. By human virtue or excellence we mean not that of the body, but that of the soul, and by happiness we mean an activity of the soul.

If this is so, it is clearly necessary for statesmen to have some knowledge of the nature of the soul in the same way as it is necessary for one who is to treat the eye or any part of the body, to have some knowledge of it, and all the more as political science is better and more honourable than medical science. Clever doctors take a great deal of trouble to understand the body, and similarly the statesman must make a study of the soul. But he must study it with a view to his particular object and so far only as his object requires; for to elaborate the study of it further would, I think, be to aggravate unduly the labour of our present undertaking.

There are some facts concerning the soul which are adequately stated in the popular or exoterical discourses, and these we may rightly adopt. It is stated e.g. that the soul has two parts, one irrational and the other possessing reason. But whether these parts are distinguished like the parts of the body and like everything that is itself divisible, or whether they are theoretically distinct, but in fact inseparable, as convex and concave in the circumference of a circle, is of no importance to the present inquiry.

Again, it seems that of the irrational part of the soul one part is common, *i.e. shared by man with all living things,* and vegetative; I mean the part which is the cause of nutrition and increase. For we may assume such a faculty of the soul to exist in all things that receive nutrition, even in embryos, and the same faculty to exist in things that are full grown, as it is more reasonable to suppose that it is the same faculty than that it is different. It is clear then that the virtue or excellence of this faculty is not distinctively human but is shared by man with all living things; for it seems that this part and this faculty are especially active in sleep, whereas good and bad people are never so little distinguishable as in sleep—whence the saying that there is no difference between the happy and the miserable during half their lifetime. And this is only natural; for sleep is an inactivity of the soul in respect of its virtue or vice, except in so far as certain impulses affect it to a slight extent, and make the visions of the virtuous better than those of ordinary people. But enough has been said on this point, and we must now leave the principle of nutrition, as it possesses no natural share in human virtue.

It seems that there is another natural principle of the soul which is irrational and yet in a sense partakes of reason. For in a continent or incontinent person we praise the reason, and that part of the soul which possesses reason, as it exhorts men rightly and exhorts them to the best conduct. But it is clear that there is in them another principle which is naturally different from reason and fights and contends against reason. For just as the paralysed parts of the body, when we intend to move them to the right, are drawn away in a contrary direction to the left, so it is with the soul; the impulses of incontinent people run counter to reason. But there is this difference, however, that while in the body we see the part which is drawn astray, in the soul we do not see it. But it is probably right to suppose with equal certainty that there is in the soul too something different from reason, which opposes and thwarts it, although the sense in which it is distinct from reason is immaterial. But it appears that this part too partakes of reason, as we said; at all events in a continent person it obeys reason, while in a temperate or courageous person it is probably still more obedient, as being absolutely harmonious with reason.

It appears then that the irrational part of the soul is itself twofold; for the vegetative faculty does not participate at all in reason, but the faculty of desire or general concupiscence participates in it more or less, in so far as it is submissive and obedient to reason. But *it is obedient* in the sense in which we speak of "paying attention to a father" or "to friends," but not in the sense in which we speak of "paying attention to mathematics." All correction, rebuke and exhortation is a witness that the irrational part of the soul is in a sense subject to the influence of reason. But if we are to say that this part too possesses reason, then the part which possesses reason will have two divisions, one possessing reason absolutely and in itself, the other listening to it as a child listens to its father.

Virtue or excellence again, admits of a distinction which depends on this difference. For we speak of some virtues as intellectual and of others as moral, wisdom, intelligence and prudence, being intellectual, liberality and temperance being moral, virtues. For when we describe a person's character, we do not say that he is wise or intelligent but that he is gentle or temperate. Yet we praise a wise man too in respect of his mental state, and such mental states as deserve to be praised we call virtuous.

BOOK II.

Virtue or excellence being twofold, partly intellectual and partly moral, intellectual virtue is both originated and fostered mainly by teaching; it therefore demands experience and time. Moral virtue on the other hand is the outcome of habit, and accordingly its name is derived by a slight deflexion from habit. From this fact it is clear that no moral virtue is implanted in us by nature; a law of nature cannot be altered by habituation. Thus a stone naturally tends to fall downwards, and it cannot be habituated or trained to rise upwards, even if we were to habituate it by throwing it upwards ten thousand times; nor again can fire be trained to sink downwards, nor anything else that follows one natural law be habituated or trained to follow another. It is neither by nature then nor in defiance of nature that virtues are implanted in us. Nature gives us the capacity of receiving them, and that capacity is perfected by habit.

Again, if we take the various natural powers which belong to us, we first acquire the proper faculties and afterwards display the activities. It is clearly so with the senses. It was not by seeing frequently or hearing frequently that we acquired the senses of seeing or hearing; on the contrary it was because we possessed the senses that we made use of them, not by making use of them that we obtained them. But the virtues we acquire by first exercising them, as is the case with all the arts, for it is by doing what we ought to do when we have learnt the arts that we learn the arts themselves; we become e.g. builders by building and harpists by playing the harp. Similarly it is by doing just acts that we become just, by doing temperate acts that we become temperate, by doing courageous acts that we become courageous. The experience of states is a witness to this truth, for it is by training the habits that legislators make the citizens good. This is the object which all legislators have at heart; if a legislator does not succeed in it, he fails of his purpose, and it constitutes the distinction between a good polity and a bad one.

Again, the causes and means by which any virtue is produced and by which it is destroyed are the same; and it is equally so with any art; for it is by playing the harp that both good and bad harpists are produced and the case of builders and all other *artisans* is similar, as it is by building well that they will be good builders and by building badly that they will be bad builders. If it were not so, there would be no need of anybody to teach them; they would all be born good or bad *in their several trades.* The case of the virtues is the same. It is by acting in such transactions as take place between man and man that we become either just or unjust. It is by acting in the face of danger and by habituating ourselves to fear or courage that we become either cowardly or courageous. It is much the same with our desires and angry passions. Some people become temperate and gentle, others become licentious and passionate, according as they conduct themselves in one way or another way in particular circumstances. In a word, moral states are the results of activities corresponding to the moral states themselves. It is our duty therefore to give a certain character to the activities, as the moral states depend upon the differences of the activities. Accordingly the difference between one training of the habits and another from early days is not a light matter, but is serious or rather all-important.

Our present study is not, like other studies, purely speculative in its intention; for the object of our enquiry is not to know the nature of virtue but to become ourselves virtuous, as that is the sole benefit which it conveys. It is necessary therefore to consider the right way of performing actions, for it is actions as we have said that determine the character of the resulting moral states.

That we should act in accordance with right reason is a common general principle, which may here be taken for granted. The nature of right reason, and its relation to the virtues generally, will be subjects of discussion hereafter. But it must be admitted at the outset that all reasoning upon practical matters must be like a sketch in outline, it cannot be scientifically exact. We began by laying down the principle that the kind of reasoning demanded in any subject must be such as the subject-matter itself allows; and questions of practice and expediency no more admit of invariable rules than questions of health.

But if this is true of general reasoning *upon Ethics,* still more true is it that scientific exactitude is impossible in reasoning upon particular *ethical* cases. They do not fall under any art or any law, but the agents themselves are always bound to pay regard to the circumstances of the moment as much as in medicine or navigation.

Still, although such is the nature of the present argument, we must try to make the best of it.

The first point to be observed then is that in such matters as we are considering deficiency and excess are equally fatal. It is so, as we observe, in regard to health and strength; for we must judge of what we cannot see by the evidence of what we do see. Excess or deficiency of gymnastic exercise is fatal to strength. Similarly an excess or deficiency of meat and drink is fatal to health, whereas a suitable amount produces, augments and sustains it. It is the same then with temperance, courage, and the other virtues. A person who avoids and is afraid of everything and faces nothing becomes a coward; a person who is not afraid of anything but is ready to face everything becomes foolhardy. Similarly he who enjoys every pleasure and never abstains from any pleasure is licentious; he who eschews all pleasures like a boor is an insensible sort of person. For temperance and courage are destroyed by excess and deficiency but preserved by the mean state.

Again, not only are the causes and the agencies of production, increase and destruction in the moral states the same, but the sphere of their activity will be proved to be the same also. It is so in other instances which are more conspicuous, e.g. in strength; for strength is produced by taking a great deal of food and undergoing a great deal of labour, and it is the strong man who is able to take most food and to undergo most labour. The same is the case with the virtues. It is by abstinence from pleasures that we become temperate, and, when we have become temperate, we are best able to abstain from them. So too with courage; it is by habituating ourselves to despise and face alarms that we become courageous, and, when we have become courageous, we shall be best able to face them.

The pleasure or pain which follows upon

actions may be regarded as a test of a person's moral state. He who abstains from physical pleasures and feels delight in so doing is temperate; but he who feels pain at so doing is licentious. He who faces dangers with pleasure, or at least without pain, is courageous; but he who feels pain at facing them is a coward. For moral virtue is concerned with pleasures and pains. It is pleasure which makes us do what is base, and pain which makes us abstain from doing what is noble. Hence the importance of having had a certain training from very early days, as Plato says, such a training as produces pleasure and pain at the right objects; for this is the true education.

Again, if the virtues are concerned with actions and emotions, and every action and every emotion is attended by pleasure and pain, this will be another reason why virtue should be concerned with pleasures and pains. There is also a proof of this fact in the use of pleasure and pain as means of punishment; for punishments are in a sense remedial measures, and the means employed as remedies are naturally the opposites of the diseases to which they are applied. Again, as we said before, every moral state of the soul is in its nature relative to, and concerned with, the thing by which it is naturally made better or worse. But pleasures and pains are the causes of vicious moral states, if we pursue and avoid such pleasures and pains as are wrong, or pursue and avoid them at the wrong time or in the wrong manner, or in any other of the various ways in which it is logically possible to do wrong. Hence it is that people actually define the virtues as certain apathetic or quiescent states; but they are wrong in using this absolute language, and not qualifying it by the addition of the right or wrong manner, time and so on.

It may be assumed then that moral virtue tends to produce the best action in respect of pleasures and pains, and that vice is its opposite. But there is another way in which we may see the same truth. There are three things which influence us to desire them, viz. the noble, the expedient, and the pleasant; and three opposite things which influence us to eschew them, viz. the shameful, the injurious, and the painful. The good man then will be likely to take a right line, and the bad man to take a wrong one, in respect of all these, but especially in respect of pleasure; for pleasure is felt not by Man only but by the lower animals, and is associated with all things that are matters of desire, as the noble and the expedient alike appear pleasant. Pleasure too is fostered in us all from early childhood, so that it is difficult to get rid of the emotion of pleasure, as it is deeply ingrained in our life. Again, we make pleasure and pain in a greater or less degree the standard of our actions. It is inevitable therefore that our present study should be concerned from first to last with pleasures and pains; for right or wrong feelings of pleasure or pain have a material influence upon actions. Again, it is more difficult to contend against pleasure than against anger, as Heraclitus says, and it is *not what is easy but* what is comparatively difficult that is in all cases the sphere of art or virtue, as the value of success is proportionate to the difficulty. This then is another reason why moral virtue and political science should be exclusively occupied with pleasures and pains; for to make a good use of pleasures and pains is to be a good man, and to make a bad use of them is to be a bad man.

We may regard it then as established that virtue is concerned with pleasures and pains, that the causes which produce it are also the means by which it is augmented, or, if they assume a different character, is destroyed, and that the sphere of its activity is the things which were themselves the causes of its production.

But it may be asked what we mean by saying that people must become just by doing what is just and temperate by doing what is temperate. For if they do what is just and temperate, they are *ipso facto* proved, it will be said, to be just and temperate in the same way as, if they practise grammar and music, they are proved to be grammarians and musicians.

But is not the answer that the case of the arts is not the same? For a person may do something that is grammatical either by chance or at the suggestion of somebody else; hence he will not be a grammarian unless he not only does what is grammatical but does it in a grammatical manner, i.e. in virtue of the grammatical knowledge which he possesses.

There is another point too of difference between the arts and the virtues. The productions of art have their excellence in themselves. It is enough therefore that, when they are produced, they should be of a certain character. But actions in accordance with virtue are not e.g. justly or temperately performed because they are in themselves just or temperate. It is necessary that the agent at the time of performing them should satisfy certain conditions, i.e. in the first place that he should know what he is doing, secondly that he should deliberately choose to do it and to do it for its own sake, and thirdly that he should do it as an instance of a settled and immutable moral state. If it be a question whether a person possesses any art, these conditions, except indeed the condition of knowledge, are not taken into account; but if it be a question of possessing the virtues, the mere knowledge is of little or no avail, and it is the other conditions, which are the results of frequently performing just and temperate actions, that are not of slight but of absolute importance. Accordingly deeds are said to be just and temperate, when they are such as a just or temperate person would do, and a just and temperate person is not merely one who does these deeds but one who does them in the spirit of the just and the temperate.

It may fairly be said then that a just man becomes just by doing what is just and a temperate man becomes temperate by doing what is temperate, and if a man did not so act, he would not have so much as a chance of becoming good. But most people, instead of doing such actions, take refuge in theorizing; they imagine that they are philosophers and that philosophy will make them virtuous; in fact they behave like people who listen attentively to their doctors but never do anything that their doctors tell them. But it is as improbable that a healthy state of the soul will be produced by this kind of philosophizing as that a healthy state of the body will be produced by this kind of medical treatment.

We have next to consider the nature of virtue.

Now, as the qualities of the soul are three, viz. emotions, faculties and moral states, it follows that virtue must be one of the three. By the emotions I mean desire, anger, fear, courage, envy, joy, love, hatred, regret, emulation, pity, in a word whatever is attended by pleasure or pain. I call those faculties in respect of which we are said to be capable of experiencing these emotions, e.g. capable of getting angry or being pained or feeling pity. And I call those moral states in respect of which we are well or ill disposed towards the emotions, ill-disposed e.g. towards the passion of anger, if our anger be too violent or too feeble, and well-disposed, if it be duly moderated, and similarly towards the other emotions.

Now neither the virtues nor the vices are emotions; for we are not called good or evil in respect of our emotions but in respect of our virtues or vices. Again, we are not praised or blamed in respect of our emotions; a person is not praised for being afraid or being angry, nor blamed for being angry in an absolute sense, but only for being angry in a certain way; but we are praised or blamed in respect of our virtues or vices. Again, whereas we are angry or afraid without deliberate purpose, the virtues are in some sense deliberate purposes, or do not exist in the absence of deliberate purpose. It may be added that while we are said to be moved in respect of our emotions, in respect of our virtues or vices we are not said to be moved but to have a certain disposition.

These reasons also prove that the virtues are not faculties. For we are not called either good or bad, nor are we praised or blamed, as having an abstract capacity for emotion. Also while Nature gives us our faculties, it is not Nature that makes us good or bad, but this is a point which we have already discussed. If then the virtues are neither emotions nor faculties, it remains that they must be moral states.

The nature of virtue has been now generically described. But it is not enough to state merely that virtue is a moral state, we must also describe the character of that moral state.

It must be laid down then that every virtue or excellence has the effect of producing a good condition of that of which it is a virtue or excellence, and of enabling it to perform its function well. Thus the excellence of the eye makes the eye good and its function good, as it is by the excellence of the eye that we see well. Similarly, the excellence of the horse makes a horse excellent and good at racing, at carrying its rider and at facing the enemy.

If then this is universally true, the virtue or excellence of man will be such a moral state as makes a man good and able to perform his proper function well. We have already explained how this will be the case, but another way of making it clear will be to study the nature or character of this virtue.

Now in everything, whether it be continuous

or discrete, it is possible to take a greater, a smaller, or an equal amount, and this either absolutely or in relation to ourselves, the equal being a mean between excess and deficiency. By the mean in respect of the thing itself, or the absolute mean, I understand that which is equally distinct from both extremes; and this is one and the same thing for everybody. By the mean considered relatively to ourselves I understand that which is neither too much nor too little; but this is not one thing, nor is it the same for everybody. Thus if 10 be too much and 2 too little we take 6 as a mean in respect of the thing itself; for 6 is as much greater than 2 as it is less than 10, and this is a mean in arithmetical proportion. But the mean considered relatively to ourselves must not be ascertained in this way. It does not follow that if 10 pounds *of meat* be too much and 2 be too little for a man to eat, a trainer will order him 6 pounds, as this may itself be too much or too little for the person who is to take it; it will be too little e.g. for Milo, but too much for a beginner in gymnastics. It will be the same with running and wrestling; *the right amount will vary with the individual.* This being so, everybody who understands his business avoids alike excess and deficiency; he seeks and chooses the mean, not the absolute mean, but the mean considered relatively to ourselves.

Every science then performs its function well, if it regards the mean and refers the works which it produces to the mean. This is the reason why it is usually said of successful works that it is impossible to take anything from them or to add anything to them, which implies that excess or deficiency is fatal to excellence but that the mean state ensures it. Good artists too, as we say, have an eye to the mean in their works. But virtue, like Nature herself, is more accurate and better than any art; virtue therefore will aim at the mean;—I speak of moral virtue, as it is moral virtue which is concerned with emotions and actions, and it is these which admit of excess and deficiency and the mean. Thus it is possible to go too far, or not to go far enough, in respect of fear, courage, desire, anger, pity, and pleasure and pain generally, and the excess and the deficiency are alike wrong; but to experience these emotions at the right times and on the right occasions and towards the right persons and for the right causes and in the right manner is the mean or the supreme good, which is characteristic of virtue. Similarly there may be excess, deficiency, or the mean, in regard to actions. But virtue is concerned with emotions and actions, and here excess is an error and deficiency a fault, whereas the mean is successful and laudable, and success and merit are both characteristics of virtue.

It appears then that virtue is a mean state, so far at least as it aims at the mean.

Again, there are many different ways of going wrong; for evil is in its nature infinite, to use the Pythagorean figure, but good is finite. But there is only one possible way of going right. Accordingly the former is easy and the latter difficult; it is easy to miss the mark but difficult to hit it. This again is a reason why excess and deficiency are characteristics of vice and the mean state a characteristic of virtue.

"For good is simple, evil manifold."

Virtue then is a state of deliberate moral purpose consisting in a mean that is relative to ourselves, the mean being determined by reason, or as a prudent man would determine it.

It is a mean state *firstly as lying* between two vices, the vice of excess on the one hand, and the vice of deficiency on the other, and secondly because, whereas the vices either fall short of or go beyond what is proper in the emotions and actions, virtue not only discovers but embraces the mean.

Accordingly, virtue, if regarded in its essence or theoretical conception, is a mean state, but, if regarded from the point of view of the highest good, or of excellence, it is an extreme.

But it is not every action or every emotion that admits of a mean state. There are some whose very name implies wickedness, as e.g. malice, shamelessness, and envy, among emotions, or adultery, theft, and murder, among actions. All these, and others like them, are censured as being intrinsically wicked, not merely the excesses or deficiencies of them. It is never possible then to be right in respect of them; they are always sinful. Right or wrong in such actions as adultery does not depend on our committing them with the right person, at the right time or in the right manner; on the contrary it is sinful to do anything of the kind at all. It would be equally wrong then to suppose that there can be a mean state or an excess or deficiency in unjust, cowardly or licentious conduct; for, if it were so, there would be a mean state of an excess or of a deficiency, an excess of an excess and a deficiency of a deficiency. But as in temperance and courage there can be no excess or deficiency because the mean is, in a sense, an extreme, so too in these cases there cannot be a mean or an excess or deficiency, but, however the acts may be done, they are wrong. For it is a general rule that an excess or deficiency does not admit of a mean state, nor a mean state of an excess or deficiency.

But it is not enough to lay down this as a general rule; it is necessary to apply it to particular cases, as in reasonings upon actions general statements, although they are broader, are less exact than particular statements. For all action refers to particulars, and it is essential that our theories should harmonize with the particular cases to which they apply.

We must take particular virtues then from the catalogue *of virtues*.

In regard to feelings of fear and confidence, courage is a mean state. On the side of excess, he whose fearlessness is excessive has no name, as often happens, but he whose confidence is excessive is foolhardy, while he whose timidity is excessive and whose confidence is deficient is a coward.

In respect of pleasures and pains, although not indeed of all pleasures and pains, and to a less extent in respect of pains than of pleasures, the mean state is temperance, the excess is licentiousness. We never find people who are deficient in regard to pleasures; accordingly such people again have not received a name, but we may call them insensible.

As regards the giving and taking of money, the mean state is liberality, the excess and deficiency are prodigality and illiberality. Here the excess and deficiency take opposite forms; for while the prodigal man is excessive in spending and deficient in taking, the illiberal man is excessive in taking and deficient in spending.

(For the present we are giving only a rough and summary account *of the virtues*, and that is sufficient for our purpose; we will hereafter determine their character more exactly.)

In respect of money there are other dispositions as well. There is the mean state which is magnificence; for the magnificent man, as having to do with large sums of money, differs from the liberal man who has to do only with small sums; and the excess *corresponding to it* is bad taste or vulgarity, the deficiency is meanness. These are different from the excess and deficiency of liberality; what the difference is will be explained hereafter.

In respect of honour and dishonour the mean state is highmindedness, the excess is what is called vanity, the deficiency littlemindedness. Corresponding to liberality, which, as we said, differs from magnificence as having to do *not with great but* with small sums of money, there is a moral state which has to do with petty honour and is related to highmindedness which has to do with great honour; for it is possible to aspire to honour in the right way, or in a way which is excessive or insufficient, and if a person's aspirations are excessive, he is called ambitious, if they are deficient, he is called unambitious, while if they are between the two, he has no name. The dispositions too are nameless, except that the disposition of the ambitious person is called ambition. The consequence is that the extremes lay claim to the mean or intermediate place. We ourselves speak of one who observes the mean sometimes as ambitious, and at other times as unambitious; we sometimes praise an ambitious, and at other times an unambitious person. The reason for our doing so will be stated in due course, but let us now discuss the other virtues in accordance with the method which we have followed hitherto.

Anger, like other emotions, has its excess, its deficiency, and its mean state. It may be said that they have no names, but as we call one who observes the mean gentle, we will call the mean state gentleness. Among the extremes, if a person errs on the side of excess, he may be called passionate and his vice passionateness, if on that of deficiency, he may be called impassive and his deficiency impassivity.

There are also three other mean states with a certain resemblance to each other, and yet with a difference. For while they are all concerned with intercourse in speech and action, they are different in that one of them is concerned with truth in such intercourse, and the others with pleasantness, one with pleasantness in amusement and the other with pleasantness in the various circumstances of life. We must therefore discuss these states in order to make it clear that in all cases it is the mean state which is an object of praise, and the extremes are neither right nor laudable but censurable. It is true that these mean and extreme states are generally nameless, but we must do our best here as elsewhere to give them a name, so that our argument may be clear and easy to follow.

In the matter of truth then, he who observes the mean may be called truthful, and the mean state truthfulness. Pretence, if it takes the form of exaggeration, is boastfulness, and one who is guilty of pretence is a boaster; but if it takes the form of depreciation it is irony, and he who is guilty of it is ironical.

As regards pleasantness in amusement, he who observes the mean is witty, and his disposition wittiness; the excess is buffoonery, and he who is guilty of it a buffoon, whereas he who is deficient in wit may be called a boor and his moral state boorishness.

As to the other kind of pleasantness, viz. pleasantness in life, he who is pleasant in a proper way is friendly, and his mean state friendliness; but he who goes too far, if he has no ulterior object in view, is obsequious, while if his object is self interest, he is a flatterer, and he who does not go far enough and always makes himself unpleasant is a quarrelsome and morose sort of person.

There are also mean states in the emotions and in the expression of the emotions. For although modesty is not a virtue, yet a modest person is praised as if he were virtuous; for here too one person is said to observe the mean and another to exceed it, as e.g. the bashful man who is never anything but modest, whereas a person who has insufficient modesty or no modesty at all is called shameless, and one who observes the mean modest.

Righteous indignation, again, is a mean state between envy and malice. They are all concerned with the pain and pleasure which we feel at the fortunes of our neighbours. A person who is righteously indignant is pained at the prosperity of the undeserving; but the envious person goes further and is pained at anybody's prosperity, and the malicious person is so far from being pained that he actually rejoices *at misfortunes*.

We shall have another opportunity however of discussing these matters. But in regard to justice, as the word is used in various senses, we will afterwards define those senses and explain how each of them is a mean state. And we will follow the same course with the intellectual virtues.

There are then three dispositions, two being vices, viz. one the vice of excess and the other that of deficiency, and one virtue, which is the mean state between them; and they are all in a sense mutually opposed. For the extremes are opposed both to the mean and to each other, and the mean is opposed to the extremes. For as the equal if compared with the less is greater but if compared with the greater is less, so the mean states, whether in the emotions or in actions, if compared with the deficiencies, are excessive, but if compared with the excesses are deficient. Thus the courageous man appears foolhardy as compared with the coward, but cowardly as compared with the foolhardy. Similarly, the temperate man appears licentious as compared with the insensible but insensible as compared with the licentious, and the liberal man appears prodigal as compared with the illiberal, but illiberal as compared with the prodigal. The result is that the extremes mutually repel and reject the mean; the coward calls the courageous man foolhardy, but the foolhardy man calls him cowardly, and so on in the other cases.

But while there is this mutual opposition between the extremes and the mean, there is greater opposition between the two extremes than between either extreme and the mean; for they are further removed from each other than from the mean, as the great from the small and the small from the great than both from the equal. Again, while some extremes exhibit more or less similarity to the mean, as foolhardiness to courage and prodigality to liberality, there is the greatest possible dissimilarity between the extremes. But things which are furthest removed from each other are defined to be opposites; hence the further things are removed, the greater is the opposition between them.

It is in some cases the deficiency and in others the excess which is the more opposed to the mean. Thus it is not foolhardiness the excess, but cowardice the deficiency which is the more opposed to courage, nor is it insensibility the deficiency, but licentiousness the excess which is the more opposed to temperance. There are two reasons why this should be so. One lies in the nature of the thing itself; for as one of the two extremes is the nearer and more similar to the mean, it is not this extreme, but its opposite, that we chiefly set against the mean. For instance, as it appears that foolhardiness is more similar and nearer to courage than cowardice, it is cowardice that we chiefly set against courage: for things which are further removed from the mean seem to be more opposite to it. This being one reason which lies in the nature of the thing itself, there is a second which lies in our own nature. It is the things to which we ourselves are naturally more inclined that appear more opposed to the mean. Thus we are ourselves naturally more inclined to pleasures *than to their opposites,* and are more prone therefore to licentiousness than to decorum. Accordingly we speak of those things, in which we are more likely to run to great lengths, as being more opposed to the mean. Hence it follows that licentiousness which is an excess is more opposed to temperance than insensibility.

It has now been sufficiently shown that moral virtue is a mean state, and in what sense it is a mean state; it is a mean state as lying between two vices, a vice of excess on the one side and a vice of deficiency on the other, and as aiming at the mean in the emotions and actions.

That is the reason why it is so hard to be virtuous; for it is always hard work to find the mean in anything, e.g. it is not everybody, but only a man of science, who can find the mean or centre of a circle. So too anybody can get angry—that is an easy matter—and anybody can give or spend money, but to give it to the right persons, to give the right amount of it and to give it at the right time and for the right cause and in the right way, this is not what anybody can do, nor is it easy. That is the reason why it is rare and laudable and noble to do well. Accordingly one who aims at the mean must begin by departing from that extreme which is the more contrary to the mean; he must act in the spirit of Calypso's advice,

"Far from this smoke and swell keep thou thy bark,"

for of the two extremes one is more sinful than the other. As it is difficult then to hit the mean exactly, we must take the second best course, as the saying is, and choose the lesser of two evils, and this we shall best do in the way that we have described, *i.e. by steering clear of the evil which is further from the mean.* We must also observe the things to which we are ourselves particularly prone, as different natures have different inclinations, and we may ascertain what these are by a consideration of our feelings of pleasure and pain. And then we must drag ourselves in the direction opposite to them; for it is by removing ourselves as far as possible from what is wrong that we shall arrive at the mean, as we do when we pull a crooked stick straight.

But in all cases we must especially be on our guard against what is pleasant and against pleasure, as we are not impartial judges of pleasure. Hence our attitude towards pleasure must be like that of the elders of the people in the *Iliad* towards Helen, and we must never be afraid of applying the words they use; for if we dismiss pleasure as they dismissed Helen, we shall be less likely to go wrong. It is by action of this kind, to put it summarily, that we shall best succeed in hitting the mean.

It may be admitted that this is a difficult task, especially in particular cases. It is not easy to determine e.g. the right manner, objects, occasions, and duration of anger. There are times when we ourselves praise people who are deficient in anger, and call them gentle, and there are other times when we speak of people who exhibit a savage temper as spirited. It is not however one who deviates a little from what is right, but one who deviates a great deal, whether on the side of excess or of deficiency, that is censured; for he is sure to be found out. Again, it is not easy to decide theoretically how far and to what extent a man may go before he becomes censurable, but neither is it easy to define theoretically anything else within the region of perception; such things fall under the head of particulars, and our judgment of them depends upon our perception.

So much then is plain, that the mean state is everywhere laudable, but that we ought to incline at one time towards the excess and at another towards the deficiency; for this will be our easiest manner of hitting the mean, or in other words of attaining excellence.

The Politics

1 Every state is a community of some kind, and every community is established with a view to some good; for mankind always act in order to obtain that which they think good. But, if all communities aim at some good, the state or political community, which is the highest of all, and which embraces all the rest, aims at good in a greater degree than any other, and at the highest good.

Some people think that the qualifications of a statesman, king, householder, and master are the same, and that they differ, not in kind, but only in the number of their subjects. For example, the ruler over a few is called a master; over more, the manager of a household; over a still larger number, a statesman or king, as if there were no difference between a great household and a small state. The distinction which is made between the king and the statesman is as follows: When the government is personal, the ruler is a king; when, according to the rules of the political science, the citizens rule and are ruled in turn, then he is called a statesman.

But all this is a mistake; for governments differ in kind, as will be evident to any one who considers the matter according to the method which has hitherto guided us. As in other departments of science, so in politics, the compound should always be resolved into the simple elements or least parts of the whole. We must therefore look at the elements of which the state is composed, in order that we may see in what the different kinds of rule differ from one another, and whether any scientific result can be attained about each one of them.

Translated by B. Jowett (selections)

2 He who thus considers things in their first growth and origin, whether a state or anything else, will obtain the clearest view of them. In the first place there must be a union of those who cannot exist without each other; namely, of male and female, that the race may continue (and this is a union which is formed, not of deliberate purpose, but because, in common with other animals and with plants, mankind have a natural desire to leave behind them an image of themselves), and of natural ruler and subject, that both may be preserved. For that which can foresee by the exercise of mind is by nature intended to be lord and master, and that which can with its body give effect to such foresight is a subject, and by nature a slave, hence master and slave have the same interest. Now nature has distinguished between the female and the slave. For nature is not niggardly, like the smith who fashions the Delphian knife for many uses; she makes each thing for a single use, and every instrument is best made when intended for one and not for many uses. But among barbarians no distinction is made between women and slaves, because there is no natural ruler among them: they are a community of slaves, male and female. Wherefore the poets say—

> 'It is meet that Hellenes should rule
> over barbarians';

as if they thought that the barbarian and the slave were by nature one.

Out of these two relationships between man

and woman, master and slave, the first thing to arise is the family, and Hesiod is right when he says—

> 'First house and wife and an ox
> for the plough',

for the ox is the poor man's slave. The family is the association established by nature for the supply of men's everyday wants, and the members of it are called by Charondas 'companions of the cupboard', and by Epimenides the Cretan, 'companions of the manger.' But when several families are united, and the association aims at something more than the supply of daily needs, the first society to be formed is the village. And the most natural form of the village appears to be that of a colony from the family, composed of the children and grandchildren, who are said to be 'suckled with the same milk'. And this is the reason why Hellenic states were originally governed by kings; because the Hellenes were under royal rule before they came together, as the barbarians still are. Every family is ruled by the eldest, and therefore in the colonies of the family the kingly form of government prevailed because they were of the same blood. As Homer says:

> 'Each one gives law to his children and
> to his wives.'

For they lived dispersedly, as was the manner in ancient times. Wherefore men say that the Gods have a king, because they themselves either are or were in ancient times under the rule of a king. For they imagine, not only the forms of the Gods, but their ways of life to be like their own.

When several villages are united in a single complete community, large enough to be nearly or quite self-sufficing, the state comes into existence, originating in the bare needs of life, and continuing in existence for the sake of a good life. And therefore, if the earlier forms of society are natural, so is the state, for it is the end of them, and the nature of a thing is its end. For what each thing is when fully developed, we call its nature, whether we are speaking of a man, a horse, or a family. Besides, the final cause and end of a thing is the best, and to be self-sufficing is the end and the best.

Hence it is evident that the state is a creation of nature, and that man is by nature a political animal. And he who by nature and not by mere accident is without a state, is either a bad man or above humanity; he is like the

> 'Tribeless, lawless, hearthless one,'

whom Homer denounces—the natural outcast is forthwith a lover of war; he may be compared to an isolated piece at draughts.

Now, that man is more of a political animal than bees or any other gregarious animals is evident. Nature, as we often say, makes nothing in vain, and man is the only animal whom she has endowed with the gift of speech. And whereas mere voice is but an indication of pleasure or pain, and is therefore found in other animals (for their nature attains to the perception of pleasure and pain and the intimation of them to one another, and no further), the power of speech is intended to set forth the expedient and inexpedient, and therefore likewise the just and the unjust. And it is a characteristic of man that he alone has any sense of good and evil, of just and unjust, and the like, and the association of living beings who have this sense makes a family and a state.

Further, the state is by nature clearly prior to the family and to the individual, since the whole is of necessity prior to the part; for example, if the whole body be destroyed, there will be no foot or hand, except in an equivocal sense, as we might speak of a stone hand; for when destroyed the hand will be no better than that. But things are defined by their working and power; and we ought not to say that they are the same when they no longer have their proper quality, but only that they have the same name. The proof that the state is a creation of nature and prior to the individual is that the individual, when isolated, is not self-sufficing; and therefore he is like a part in relation to the whole. But he who is unable to live in society, or who has no need because he is sufficient for himself, must be either a beast or a god: he is no part of a state. A social instinct is implanted in all men by nature, and yet he who first founded the state was the greatest of benefactors. For man, when perfected, is the best of animals, but, when separated from law and justice, he is the worst of all; since armed injustice is the more dangerous, and he is equipped at birth with arms, meant to be used by intelligence and virtue, which he may use for the worst ends. Wherefore, if he has no virtue, he is the most unholy and the most savage of animals, and the most full of lust and gluttony. But justice is the bond of men in states, for the administration of justice, which is the determination of what is just, is the principle of order in political society. . . .

BOOK III

1 He who would inquire into the essence and attributes of various kinds of governments must first of all determine 'What is a state?' At present this is a disputed question. Some say that the state has done a certain act; others, no, not the state, but the oligarchy or the tyrant. And the legislator or statesman is concerned entirely with the state; a constitution or government being an arrangement of the inhabitants of a state. But a state is composite, like any other whole made up of many parts;—these are the citizens, who compose it. It is evident, therefore, that we must begin by asking, Who is the citizen, and what is the meaning of the term? For here again there may be a difference of opinion. He who is a citizen in a democracy will often not be a citizen in an oligarchy. Leaving out of consideration those who have been made citizens, or who have obtained the name of citizen in any other accidental manner, we may say, first, that a citizen is not a citizen because he lives in a certain place, for resident aliens and slaves share in the place; nor is he a citizen who has no legal right except that of suing and being sued; for this right may be enjoyed under the provisions of a treaty. Nay, resident aliens in many places do not possess even such rights completely, for they are obliged to have a patron, so that they do but imperfectly participate in citizenship, and we call them citizens only in a qualified sense, as we might apply the term to children who are too young to be on the register, or to old men who have been relieved from state duties. Of these we do not say quite simply that they are citizens, but add in the one case that they are not of age, and in the other, that they are past the age, or something of that sort; the precise expression is immaterial, for our meaning is clear. Similar difficulties to those which I have mentioned may be raised and answered about deprived citizens and about exiles. But the citizen whom we are seeking to define is a citizen in the strictest sense, against whom no such exception can be taken, and his special characteristic is that he shares in the administration of justice, and in offices. . . . But we must not forget that things of which the underlying principles differ in kind, one of them being first, another second, another third, have, when regarded in this relation, nothing, or hardly anything, worth mentioning in common. Now we see that governments differ in kind, and that some of them are prior and that others are posterior; those which are faulty or perverted are necessarily posterior to those which are perfect. (What we mean by perversion will be hereafter explained.) The citizen then of necessity differs under each form of government; and our definition is best adapted to the citizen of a democracy; but not necessarily to other states. For in some states the people are not acknowledged, nor have they any regular assembly, but only extraordinary ones; and suits are distributed by sections among the magistrates. At Lacedaemon, for instance, the Ephors determine suits about contracts, which they distribute among themselves, while the elders are judges of homicide, and other causes are decided by other magistrates. A similar principle prevails at Carthage; there certain magistrates decide all causes. We may, indeed, modify our definition of the citizen so as to include these states. In them it is the holder of a definite, not of an indefinite office, who legislates and judges, and to some or all such holders of definite offices is reserved the right of deliberating or judging about some things or about all things. The conception of the citizen now begins to clear up.

He who has the power to take part in the deliberative or judicial administration of any state is said by us to be a citizen of that state; and speaking generally, a state is a body of citizens sufficing for the purposes of life.

2 But in practice a citizen is defined to be one of whom both the parents are citizens; others insist on going further back; say to two or three or more ancestors. This is a short and practical definition; but there are some who raise the further question: How this third or fourth ancestor came to be a citizen? Gorgias

of Leontini, partly because he was in a difficulty, partly in irony, said—'Mortars are what is made by the mortar-makers, and the citizens of Larissa are those who are made by the magistrates; for it is their trade to make Larissaeans. Yet the question is really simple, for, if according to the definition just given they shared in the government, they were citizens. This is a better definition than the other. For the words, 'born of a father or mother who is a citizen', cannot possibly apply to the first inhabitants or founders of a state. . . .

3 Whether they ought to be so or not is a question which is bound up with the previous inquiry. For a parallel question is raised respecting the state, whether a certain act is or is not an act of the state; for example, in the transition from an oligarchy or a tyranny to a democracy. In such cases persons refuse to fulfil their contracts or any other obligations, on the ground that the tyrant, and not the state, contracted them; they argue that some constitutions are established by force, and not for the sake of the common good. But this would apply equally to democracies, for they too may be founded on violence, and then the acts of the democracy will be neither more nor less acts of the state in question than those of an oligarchy or of a tyranny. This question runs up into another:—on what principle shall we ever say that the state is the same, or different? It would be a very superficial view which considered only the place and the inhabitants (for the soil and the population may be separated and some of the inhabitants may live in one place and some in another). This, however, is not a very serious difficulty; we need only remark that the word 'state' is ambiguous.

It is further asked: When are men, living in the same place, to be regarded as a single city—what is the limit? Certainly not the wall of the city, for you might surround all Peloponnesus with a wall. Like this, we may say, is Babylon, and every city that has the compass of a nation rather than a city; Babylon, they say, had been taken for three days before some part of the inhabitants became aware of the fact. This difficulty may, however, with advantage be deferred to another occasion; the statesman has to consider the size of the state, and whether it should consist of more than one nation or not.

Again, shall we say that while the race of inhabitants, as well as their place of abode, remain the same, the city is also the same, although the citizens are always dying and being born, as we call rivers and fountains the same, although the water is always flowing away and coming again? Or shall we say that the generations of men, like the rivers, are the same, but that the state changes? For, since the state is a partnership, and is a partnership of citizens in a constitution, when the form of the government changes, and becomes different, then it may be supposed that the state is no longer the same, just as a tragic differs from a comic chorus, although the members of both may be identical. And in this manner we speak of every union or composition of elements as different when the form of their composition alters; for example, a scale containing the same sounds is said to be different, accordingly as the Dorian or the Phrygian mode is employed. And if this is true it is evident that the sameness of the state consists chiefly in the sameness of the constitution, and it may be called or not called by the same name, whether the inhabitants are the same or entirely different. It is quite another question, whether a state ought or ought not to fulfil engagements when the form of government changes.

4 There is a point nearly allied to the preceding: Whether the virtue of a good man and a good citizen is the same or not. But, before entering on this discussion, we must certainly first obtain some general notion of the virtue of the citizen. Like the sailor, the citizen is a member of a community. Now, sailors have different functions, for one of them is a rower, another a pilot, and a third a look-out man, a fourth is described by some similar term; and while the precise definition of each individual's virtue applies exclusively to him, there is, at the same time, a common definition applicable to them all. For they have all of them a common object, which is safety in navigation. Similarly, one citizen differs from another, but the salvation of the community is the common business of them all. This community is the constitution; the virtue of the citizen must therefore be relative to the constitution of which he is a member. If, then, there are many forms of government, it is evident that there is not one single

virtue of the good citizen which is perfect virtue. But we say that the good man is he who has one single virtue which is perfect virtue. Hence it is evident that the good citizen need not of necessity possess the virtue which makes a good man.

The same question may also be approached by another road, from a consideration of the best constitution. If the state cannot be entirely composed of good men, and yet each citizen is expected to do his own business well, and must therefore have virtue, still, inasmuch as all the citizens cannot be alike, the virtue of the citizen and of the good man cannot coincide. All must have the virtue of the good citizen—thus, and thus only, can the state be perfect; but they will not have the virtue of a good man, unless we assume that in the good state all the citizens must be good.

Again, the state, as composed of unlikes, may be compared to the living being: as the first elements into which a living being is resolved are soul and body, as soul is made up of rational principle and appetite, the family of husband and wife, property of master and slave, so of all these, as well as other dissimilar elements, the state is composed; and, therefore, the virtue of all the citizens cannot possibly be the same, any more than the excellence of the leader of a chorus is the same as that of the performer who stands by his side. I have said enough to show why the two kinds of virtue cannot be absolutely and always the same.

But will there then be no case in which the virtue of the good citizen and the virtue of the good man coincide? To this we answer that the good *ruler* is a good and wise man, and that he who would be a statesman must be a wise man. And some persons say that even the education of the ruler should be of a special kind, for are not the children of kings instructed in riding and military exercises? As Euripides says:

> 'No subtle arts for me, but what
> the state requires.'

As though there were a special education needed by a ruler. If then the virtue of a good ruler is the same as that of a good man, and we assume further that the subject is a citizen as well as the ruler, the virtue of the good citizen and the virtue of the good man cannot be absolutely the same, although in some cases they may; for the virtue of a ruler differs from that of a citizen. It was the sense of this difference which made Jason say that 'he felt hungry when he was not a tyrant', meaning that he could not endure to live in a private station. But, on the other hand, it may be argued that men are praised for knowing both how to rule and how to obey, and he is said to be a citizen of approved virtue who is able to do both. Now if we suppose the virtue of a good man to be that which rules, and the virtue of the citizen to include ruling and obeying, it cannot be said that they are equally worthy of praise. Since, then, it is sometimes thought that the ruler and the ruled must learn different things and not the same, but that the citizen must know and share in them both, the inference is obvious. There is, indeed, the rule of a master, which is concerned with menial offices—the master need not know how to perform these, but may employ others in the execution of them: the other would be degrading; and by the other I mean the power actually to do menial duties, which vary much in character and are executed by various classes of slaves, such, for example, as handicraftsmen, who, as their name signifies, live by the labour of their hands:—under these the mechanic is included. Hence in ancient times, and among some nations, the working classes had no share in the government—a privilege which they only acquired under the extreme democracy. Certainly the good man and the statesman and the good citizen ought not to learn the crafts of inferiors except for their own occasional use; if they habitually practise them, there will cease to be a distinction between master and slave.

This is not the rule of which we are speaking; but there is a rule of another kind, which is exercised over freemen and equals by birth—a constitutional rule, which the ruler must learn by obeying, as he would learn the duties of a general of cavalry by being under the orders of a general of cavalry, or the duties of a general of infantry by being under the orders of a general of infantry, and by having had the command of a regiment and of a company. It has been well said that 'he who has never learned to obey cannot be a good commander'. The two are not the same, but the good citizen ought to be capable of both; he should know how to govern like a freeman, and how to obey like a freeman—these are the virtues of a citizen. And, although the temperance and justice of a ruler are distinct from those of a subject, the virtue of a good man will include both; for the virtue of the good man who is free and also a subject, e.g. his justice, will not be one but will comprise distinct kinds, the one qualifying him to rule, the other to obey, and differing as the temperance and courage of men and women differ. For a man who be thought a coward if he had no more courage than a courageous woman, and a woman would be thought loquacious if she imposed no more restraint on her conversation than the good man; and indeed their part in the management of the household is different, for the duty of the one is to acquire, and of the other to preserve. Practical wisdom only is characteristic of the ruler: it would seem that all other virtues must equally belong to ruler and subject. The virtue of the subject is certainly not wisdom, but only true opinion; he may be compared to the maker of the flute, while his master is like the flute-player or user of the flute.

From these considerations may be gathered the answer to the question, whether the virtue of the good man is the same as that of the good citizen, or different, and how far the same, and how far different. . . .

Having determined these questions, we have next to consider whether there is only one form of government or many, and if many, what they are, and how many, and what are the differences between them.

A constitution is the arrangement of magistracies in a state, especially of the highest of all. The government is everywhere sovereign in the state, and the constitution is in fact the government. For example, in democracies the people are supreme, but in oligarchies, the few; and, therefore, we say that these two forms of government also are different; and so in other cases.

First, let us consider what is the purpose of a state, and how many forms of government there are by which human society is regulated. We have already said, in the first part of this treatise, when discussing household management and the rule of a master, that man is by nature a political animal. And therefore, men, even when they do not require one another's help, desire to live together; not but that they are also brought together by their common interests in proportion as they severally attain to any measure of well-being. This is certainly the chief end, both of individuals and of states. And also for the sake of mere life (in which there is possibly some noble element so long as the evils of existence do not greatly overbalance the good) mankind meet together and maintain the political community. And we all see that men cling to life even at the cost of enduring great misfortune, seeming to find in life a natural sweetness and happiness.

There is no difficulty in distinguishing the various kinds of authority; they have been often defined already in discussions outside the school. The rule of a master, although the slave by nature and the master by nature have in reality the same interests, is nevertheless exercised primarily with a view to the interest of the master, but accidentally considers the slave, since, if the slave perish, the rule of the master perishes with him. On the other hand, the government of a wife and children and of a household, which we have called household management, is exercised in the first instance for the good of the governed or for the common good of both parties, but essentially for the good of the governed, as we see to be the case in medicine, gymnastic, and the arts in general, which are only accidentally concerned with the good of the artists themselves. For there is no reason why the trainer may not sometimes practise gymnastics, and the helmsman is always one of the crew. The trainer or the helmsman considers the good of those committed to his care. But when he is one of the persons taken care of, he accidentally participates in the advantage, for the helmsman is also a sailor, and the trainer becomes one of those in training. And so in politics: when the state is framed upon the principle of equality and likeness, the citizens think that they ought to hold office by turns. Formerly, as is natural, every one would take his turn of service; and then again, somebody else would look after his interest, just as he, while in office, had looked after theirs. But nowadays, for the sake of the advantage which is to be gained from the public revenues and from office, men want to be always in office. One might imagine that the rulers, being sickly, were only kept in health while they continued in office; in that case we may be sure that they would be hunting after places. The conclusion is evident: that governments which have a regard to the common interest are constituted in accordance with strict principles of justice, and are therefore true forms; but those which regard only the interest of the rulers are all defective and perverted forms, for they are despotic, whereas a state is a community of freemen.

7 Having determined these points, we have next to consider how many forms of government there are, and what they are; and in the first place what are the true forms, for when they are determined the perversions of them will at once be apparent. The words constitution and government have the same meaning, and the government, which is the supreme authority in states, must be in the hands of one, or of a few, or of the many. The true forms of government, therefore, are those in which the one, or the few, or the many, govern with a view to the common interest; but governments which rule with a view to the private interest, whether of the one, or of the few, or of the many, are perversions. For the members of a state, if they are truly citizens, ought to participate in its advantages. Of forms of government in which one rules, we call that which regards the common interests, kingship or royalty; that in which more than one, but not many, rule, aristocracy; and it is so called, either because the rulers are the best men, or because they have at heart the best interests of the state and of the citizens. But when the citizens at large administer the state for the common interest, the government is called by the generic name—a constitution. And there is a reason for this use of language. One man or a few may excel in virtue; but as the number increases it becomes more difficult for them to attain perfection in every kind of virtue, though they may in military virtue, for this is found in the masses. Hence in a constitutional government the fighting-men have the supreme power, and those who possess arms are the citizens.

Of the above-mentioned forms, the perversions are as follows:—of royalty, tyranny; of aristocracy, oligarchy; of constitutional government, democracy. For tyranny is a kind of monarchy which has in view the interest of the monarch only; oligarchy has in view the interest of the wealthy; democracy, of the needy; none of them the common good of all. . . .

BOOK IV

1 In all arts and sciences which embrace the whole of any subject, and do not come into being in a fragmentary way, it is the province of a single art or science to consider all that appertains to a single subject. For example, the art of gymnastic considers not only the suitableness of different modes of training to different bodies, but what sort is absolutely the best; (for the absolutely best must suit that which is by nature best and best furnished with the means of life), and also what common form of training is adapted to the great majority of men. And if a man does not desire the best habit of body, or the greatest skill in gymnastics, which might be attained by him, still the trainer or the teacher of gymnastic should be able to impart any lower degree of either. The same principle equally holds in medicine and ship-building, and the making of clothes, and in the arts generally.

Hence it is obvious that government too is the subject of a single science, which has to consider what government is best and of what sort it must be, to be most in accordance with our aspirations, if there were no external impediment, and also what kind of government is adapted to particular states. For the best is often unattainable, and therefore the true legislator and statesman ought to be acquainted, not only with (1) that which is best in the abstract, but also with (2) that which is best relatively to circumstances. We should be able further to say how a state may be constituted under any given conditions (3); both how it is originally formed and, when formed, how it may be longest preserved; the supposed state being so far from having the best constitution that it is unprovided even with the conditions necessary for the best; neither is it the best under the circumstances, but of an inferior type.

He ought, moreover, to know (4) the form of government which is best suited to states in general; for political writers, although they have excellent ideas, are often unpractical. We should consider, not only what form of government is best, but also what is possible and what is easily attainable by all. There are some who would have none but the most perfect; for this many natural advantages are required. Others, again, speak of a more attainable form, and, although they reject the constitution under which they are living, they extol some one in particular, for example the Lacedaemonian. Any change of government which has to be introduced should be one which men, starting from their existing constitutions, will be both willing and able to adopt, since there is quite as much trouble in the reformation of an old constitution as in the establishment of a new one, just as to unlearn is as hard as to learn. And therefore, in addition to the qualifications of the statesman already mentioned, he should be able to find remedies for the defects of existing constitutions, as has been said before. This he cannot do unless he knows how many forms of government there are. It is often supposed that there is only one kind of democracy and one of oligarchy. But this is a mistake; and, in order to avoid such mistakes, we must ascertain what differences there are in the constitutions of states, and in how many ways they are combined. The same political insight will enable a man to know which laws are the best, and which are suited to different constitutions; for the laws are, and ought to be, relative to the constitution, and not the constitution to the laws. A constitution is the organization of offices in a state, and determines what is to be the governing body, and what is the end of each community. But laws are not to be confounded with the principles of the constitution; they are the rules according to which the magistrates should administer the state, and proceed against offenders. So that we must know the varieties, and the number of varieties, of each form of government, if only with a view to making laws. For the same laws cannot be equally suited to all oligarchies or to all democracies, since there is certainly more than one form both of democracy and of oligarchy.

2 In our original discussion about governments we divided them into three true forms: kingly rule, aristocracy, and constitutional government, and three corresponding perversions—tyranny, oligarchy, and democracy. Of kingly rule and of aristocracy we have already spoken, for the inquiry into the perfect state is the same thing with the discussion of the two forms thus named, since both imply a principle of virtue provided with external means. We have already determined in what aristocracy and kingly rule differ from one another, and when the latter should be established. In what follows we have to describe the so-called constitutional government, which bears the common name of all constitutions, and the other forms, tyranny, oligarchy, and democracy.

It is obvious which of the three perversions is the worst, and which is the next in badness. That which is the perversion of the first and most divine is necessarily the worst. And just as a royal rule, if not a mere name, must exist by virtue of some great personal superiority in the king, so tyranny, which is the worst of governments, is necessarily the farthest removed from a well-constituted form; oligarchy is little better, for it is a long way from aristocracy, and democracy is the most tolerable of all the three. . . .

11 We have now to inquire what is the best constitution for most states, and the best life for most men, neither assuming a standard of virtue which is above ordinary persons, nor an education which is exceptionally favoured by nature and circumstances, nor yet an ideal state which is an aspiration only, but having regard to the life in which the majority are able to share, and to the form of government which states in general can attain. As to those aristocracies, as they are called, of which we were just now speaking, they either lie beyond the possibilities of the greater number of states, or they approximate to the so-called constitutional government, and therefore need no separate discussion. And in fact the conclusion at which we arrive respecting all these forms rests upon the same grounds. For if what was said in the *Ethics* is true, that the happy life is the life according to virtue lived without impediment, and that virtue is a mean, then the life which is in a mean, and in a mean attainable by every one, must be the best. And the same principles of virtue and vice are characteristic of cities and of constitutions; for the constitution is in a figure the life of the city.

Now in all states there are three elements: one class is very rich, another very poor, and a third in a mean. It is admitted that moderation and the mean are best, and therefore it will clearly be best to possess the gifts of fortune in moderation; for in that condition of life men are most ready to follow rational principle. But he who greatly excels in beauty, strength, birth, or wealth, or on the other hand who is very poor, or very weak, or very much disgraced, finds it difficult to follow rational principle. Of these two the one sort grow into violent and great criminals, the others into rogues and petty rascals. And two sorts of offences correspond to them, the one committed from violence, the other from roguery. Again, the middle class is least likely to shrink from rule, or to be over-ambitious for it; both of which are injuries to the state. Again, those who have too much of the goods of fortune, strength, wealth, friends, and the like, are neither willing nor able to submit to authority. The evil begins at home; for when they are boys, by reason of the luxury in which they are brought up, they never learn, even at school, the habit of obedience. On the other hand, the very poor, who are in the opposite extreme, are too degraded. So that the one class cannot obey, and can only rule despotically; the other knows not how to command and must be ruled like slaves. Thus arise a city, not of freemen, but of masters and slaves, the one despising, the other envying; and nothing can be more fatal to friendship and good fellowship in states than this; for good fellowship springs from friendship; when men are at enmity with one another, they would rather not even share the same path. But a city ought to be composed as far as possible, of equals and similars; and these are generally the middle classes. Wherefore the city which is composed of middle-class citizens is necessarily best constituted in respect of the elements of which we say the fabric of the state naturally consists. And this is the class of citizens which is most secure in a state, for they do not, like the poor, covet their neighbours' goods; nor do others covet theirs, as the poor covets the goods of the rich; and as they neither plot against others, nor are themselves plotted against, they pass through life safely. Wisely then did Phocylides pray—'Many things are best in the mean; I desire to be of a middle condition in my city.'

Thus it is manifest that the best political community is formed by citizens of the middle class, and that those states are likely to be well-administered, in which the middle class is large, and stronger if possible than both the other classes, or at any rate than either singly; for the addition of the middle class turns the scale, and prevents either of the extremes from being dominant. Great then is the good fortune of a state in which the citizens have a moderate and sufficient property; for where some possess much, and the others nothing, there may arise an extreme democracy, or a pure oligarchy; or a tyranny may grown out of either extreme—either out of the most rampant democracy, or out of an oligarchy; but it is not so likely to arise out of the middle constitutions and those akin to them. The mean condition of states is clearly best, for no other is free from faction; and where the middle class is large, there are least likely to be factions and dissensions. For a similar reason large states are less liable to faction than small ones, because in them the middle class is large; whereas in small states it is easy to divide all the citizens into two classes who are either rich or poor, and to leave nothing in the middle. And democracies are safer and more permanent than oligarchies, because they have a middle class which is more numerous and has a greater share in the government; for when there is no middle class, and the poor greatly exceed in number, troubles arise, and the state soon comes to an end. A proof of the superiority of the middle class is that the best legislators have been of a middle condition; for example, Solon, as his own verses testify; and Lycurgus, for he was not a king; and Charondas, and almost all legislators.

These considerations will help us to understand why most governments are either democratical or oligarchical. The reason is that the middle class is seldom numerous in them, and whichever party, whether the rich or the common people, transgresses the mean and predominates, draws the constitution its own way, and thus arises either oligarchy or democracy. There is another reason—the poor and the rich quarrel with one another, and whichever side gets the better, instead of establishing a just or popular government, regards political supremacy as the prize of victory, and the one party sets up a democracy and the other an oligarchy. Further, both the parties which had the supremacy in Greece looked only to the interest of their own forms of government, and established in states, the one, democracies, and the other, oligarchies; they thought of their own advantage, of the public not at all. For these reasons the middle form of government has rarely, if ever, existed, and among a very few only. One man alone of all who ever ruled in Greece was induced to give this middle constitution to states. But it has now become a habit among the citizens of states, not even to care about equality; all men are seeking for dominion, or, if conquered, are willing to submit.

What then is the best form of government, and what makes it the best, is evident; and of other constitutions, since we say that there are many kinds of democracy and many of oligarchy, it is not difficult to see which has the first and which the second or any other place in the order of excellence, now that we have determined which is the best. For that which is nearest to the best must of necessity be better, and that which is furthest from it worse, if we are judging absolutely and not relatively to given conditions: I say 'relatively to given conditions', since a particular government may be preferable, but another form may be better for some people.

12 We have now to consider what and what kind of government is suitable to what and what kind of men. I may begin by assuming, as a general principle common to all governments, that the portion of the state which desires the permanence of the constitution ought to be stronger than that which desires the reverse. Now every city is composed of quality and quantity. But quality I mean freedom, wealth, education, good birth, and by quantity, superiority of numbers. Quality may exist in one of the classes which make up the state, and quantity in the other. For example, the meanly-born may be more in number than the well-born, or the poor than the rich, yet they may not so much exceed in quantity as they fall short in quality; and therefore there must be a comparison of quantity and quality. Where the number of the poor is more than proportioned to the wealth of the rich, there will naturally be a democracy, varying in form with the sort of people who compose it in each case. If, for example, the husbandmen exceed in number, the first form of democracy will then arise; if the artisans and labouring class, the last; and so with the intermediate forms. But where the rich and the notables exceed in quality more than they fall short in quantity, there oligarchy arises, similarly assuming various forms according to the kind of superiority possessed by the oligarchs.

The legislator should always include the middle class in his government; if he makes his laws oligarchical, to the middle class let him look; if he makes them democratical, he should equally by his laws try to attach this class to the state. There only can the government ever be stable where the middle class exceeds one or both of the others, and in that case there will be no fear that the rich will unite with the poor against the rulers. For neither of them will ever be willing to serve the other, and if they look for some form of government more suitable to both, they will find none better than this, for the rich and the poor will never consent to rule in turn, because they mistrust one another. The arbiter is always the one trusted, and he who is in the middle is an arbiter. The more perfect the admixture of the political elements, the more lasting will be the constitution. Many even of those who desire to form aristocratical governments make a mistake, not only in giving too much power to the rich, but in attempting to overreach the people. There comes a time when out of a false good there arises a true evil, since the encroachments of the rich are more destructive to the constitution than those of the people. . . .

BOOK VII

13 Returning to the constitution itself, let us seek to determine out of what and what sort of elements the state which is to be happy and well-governed should be composed. There are two things in which all well-being consists: one of them is the choice of a right end and aim of action, and the other the discovery of the actions which are means towards it; for the means and the end may agree or disagree.

Sometimes the right end is set before men, but in practice they fail to attain it; in other cases they are successful in all the means, but they propose to themselves a bad end; and sometimes they fail in both. Take, for example, the art of medicine; physicians do not always understand the nature of health, and also the means which they use may not effect the desired end. In all arts and sciences both the end and the means should be equally within our control.

The happiness and well-being which all men manifestly desire, some have the power of attaining, but to others, from some accident or defect of nature, the attainment of them is not granted; for a good life requires a supply of external goods, in a less degree when men are in a good state, in a greater degree when they are in a lower state. Others again, who possess the conditions of happiness, go utterly wrong from the first in the pursuit of it. But since our object is to discover the best form of government, that, namely, under which a city will be best governed, and since the city is best governed which has the greatest opportunity of obtaining happiness, it is evident that we must clearly ascertain the nature of happiness.

We maintain, and have said in the *Ethics,* if the arguments there adduced are of any value, that happiness is the realization and perfect exercise of virtue, and this not conditional, but absolute. And I used the term 'conditional' to express that which is indispensable, and 'absolute' to express that which is good in itself. Take the case of just actions; just punishments and chastisements do indeed spring from a good principle, but they are good only because we cannot do without them—it would be better that neither individuals nor states should need anything of the sort—but actions which aim at honour and advantage are absolutely the best. The conditional action is only the choice of a lesser evil; whereas these are the foundation and creation of good. A good man may make the best even of poverty and disease, and the other ills of life; but he can only attain happiness under the opposite conditions (for this also has been determined in accordance with ethical arguments, that the good man is he for whom, because he is virtuous, the things that are absolutely good are good; it is also plain that his use of these goods must be virtuous and in the absolute sense good). This makes men fancy that external goods are the cause of happiness, yet we might as well say that a brilliant performance on the lyre was to be attributed to the instrument and not to the skill of the performer.

It follows then from what has been said that some things the legislator must find ready to his hand in a state, others he must provide. And therefore we can only say: May our state be constituted in such a manner as to be blessed with the goods of which fortune disposes (for we acknowlege her power): whereas virtue and goodness in the state are not a matter of chance but the result of knowledge and purpose. A city can be virtuous only when the citizens who have a share in the government are virtuous, and in our state all the citizens share in the government; let us then inquire how a man becomes virtuous. For even if we could suppose the citizen body to be virtuous, without each of them being so, yet the latter would be better, for in the virtue of each the virtue of all is involved.

There are three things which make men good and virtuous; these are nature, habit, rational principle. In the first place, every one must be born a man and not some other animal; so, too, he must have a certain character, both of body and soul. But some qualities there is no use in having at birth, for they are altered by habit, and there are some gifts which by nature are made to be turned by habit to good or bad. Animals lead for the most part a life of nature, although in lesser particulars some are influenced by habit as well. Man has rational principle, in addition, and man only. Wherefore nature, habit, rational principle must be in harmony with one another; for they do not always agree; men do many things against habit and nature, if rational principle persuades them that they ought. We have already determined what natures are likely to be most easily moulded by the hands of the legislator. All else is the work of education; we learn some things by habit and some by instruction. . . .

Chapter IV –
The Quest For Values

Introduction

It would be difficult to name a great philosopher who, at one time or another in his career, did not find himself drawn to questions of ethics. For the questions that emerge from the moral experience of mankind are among the most perplexing in all of philosophy. All of us claim to have some understanding of the nature of right and wrong, yet we usually end up in confusion when asked to give an account of that understanding. Efforts to clarify moral issues are frequently tied to our total world outlook, and thus discussions of our knowledge of right and wrong lead quite often to questions concerning the nature of knowledge in general (epistemology), the nature of man and his place in nature (philosophical anthropology and metaphysics), and the relationship of individuals to the societies they inhabit (social philosophy).

If we confine ourselves specifically to ethical issues, we find that three sets of problems constitute the core of the Western tradition in ethics.

1. *What is the Good Life?* Although we placed selections from Plato and Aristotle in separate chapters of this anthology, it is to these men that the origin of ethics is traced. Before them, mankind merely assumed that the proper life for a person consisted in conformity to the ethos of his people and to the will of the gods. The choice of a course in life was transformed by Plato and Aristotle into one of the chief problems of life. In so doing they introduced the principle of human autonomy: man is not simply the slave of tradition or of the gods, but is responsible to himself and to others for the course he takes in life. Proper choice depends not upon fear of falling out of favor with men and

the gods, but upon knowledge of the true human good. And thus was initiated the quest for values. In Plato and Aristotle, this took the form of a search for the *summum bonum,* the *highest* human good, which Plato tentatively identified with the life of *justice,* or the total harmonious integration of the warring parts of the human soul, and which Aristotle identified with *eudaemonia,* or happiness achieved through a life of rational activity. Other philosophers have pursued the Good Life as a life lived in conformity to the nature of things in general (Epictetus and Stoicism), as a struggle to realize one's deepest potentials (self-realizationism), or simply as a pleasant or pleasurable life (Epicureanism) hedonism). In all cases, the question of man's highest good is pursued in the light of one simple but fundamental feature of the human situation: you have but one life to live, and if, when it comes time for you to die, you discover that you have not lived well, your failure is irremediable. It is clear that you could be living differently than you are at present; the question is, could you be living *better* than you now are, and if so, what is the nature of that better life, and how might you go about achieving it? A total, if simple vision of the world, of man's place in it, and of the Good Life for man, is found in the selection from Epictetus which opens this chapter.

2. *What is the nature of right and wrong?* It is easy to see that a person's vision of the Good Life might conflict with his views on the nature of right and wrong. The belief that happiness or pleasure is the proper end of life might lead a person to neglect his duties to others, or to engage in the exclusive pursuit of material or sensual pleasures. Again, the belief that the Good Life consists in conforming to the will of God and preparing for the next world might lead one to be unconcerned with the injustices of social systems in this world. However, a clarification of these issues depends upon an investigation of the nature of right and wrong themselves, for some philosophers have claimed that the Good Life and the morally upright life are in fact not in conflict.

Various theories of right and wrong action have been advanced over the centuries. All of them could be described according to the following pattern:

> "An action X of agent A is *right* if it meets condition(s) P (Q, R. . .);
> X is *wrong* if it fails to meet these conditions."

But what conditions (P, Q, R) have been suggested by philosophers? One obvious possibility is that P = "the will of God" (e.g., as expressed in the Decalogue). In that case, an action X of agent A is right if it does not break any of the Ten Commandments; and wrong if it does. Another everyday possibility is that P = "meets with the moral approval of A." In that case, "X is a right action" would mean that A (the person who performed the action) finds that it is right; this is the philosophy of "do your own thing." Other candidates for condition P are "X is approved of by the king (or pope, or sovereign);" this is the principle that "might makes right." Or "P is not illegal;" this is the principle of the moral authority of law. "P is approved by the person making the judgment;" this is the principle of subjectivism: as Hamlet said, nothing is good nor bad, but thinking makes it so.

All of the above moral theories have been attacked for considering the mere authority of some person, God, or institution the source of right and wrong. You will recall that in the *Euthyphro,* Socrates questions Euthyphro's contention that "holiness is what is loved by the gods," and concludes instead that the gods love what is holy (i.e., morally right). And powerful theories have been devised to support the view that moral goodness consists in more objective characteristics than the mere will of gods or man. Two such theories—perhaps the most powerful of all—are developed in this chapter.

For Immanuel Kant, the characteristic P that makes an action X good or bad must be sought in some characteristic of the action itself, and that characteristic he believes to consist in the motive for which the action is performed. A good action is one performed by a good will, that is, a will that desires to do what is right. But what then is the right thing to do? The good will desires to do its duty, i.e., to fulfill its obligations. But what are its obligations? To fulfill the moral law. And what is the moral law? Kant says that the moral law is inscribed upon our very hearts, and that I, for example, need but consult my reason to discover what I ought to do in any given situation. Should there be any doubt, I can ask myself whether the *subjective maxim* of my action (e.g., if I am contemplating telling a lie to get out of an embarrassing situation, the subjective maxim of my action would be "It is all right to tell lies") could be made a universal law, binding upon all mankind (clearly, this maxim could not, for if "It is all right to tell lies" were a universal law, no one would believe anyone, and lying would be impossible). If it cannot be made a universal law of conduct, then my action is clearly wrong, and if it can be, then I am in the sphere of moral action. For Kant, man dictates the moral law to himself; only the general form of obligation ("Do your duty!") appears to be imposed upon us from above.

John Stuart Mill believed that Kant's theory was mistaken to place the source of obligation in formal adherence to moral law itself. Rather, he believed, the moral law must justify itself in terms of the consequences that would flow from it if it were adhered to. The consequences of a moral law that make it worthy of adherence are the benefits that it produces for mankind. The goal of all human activity is happiness, and the rightness of any moral law or statute must consist in its contribution to mankind's happiness. Surely, Mill argues against Kant, it cannot be moral to adhere to a principle for its own sake alone, but rather for the happiness that such adherence brings. It would be absurd to refrain from telling a lie, when many lives could be saved thereby, just because it is wrong to tell lies! But moral rules cannot be broken with impunity, says Mill; always I must ask myself what will be achieved by adhering to, or breaking with time-tested moral rules: I must refer always to the general principle of utilitarianism: act so as to produce the greatest happiness for the greatest number of people. Thus, for Mill, the characteristic of an action X that qualifies it as a good action is the *utility* of the rule of which it is an instance: that the rule is more productive of happiness than of suffering for the majority of mankind.

3. *What is the nature of moral discourse?* The first two groups of questions discussed above are *normative* questions, that is, they attempt to discover and justify norms of human behavior, norms that we could use to praise or criticize our own conduct and that of others. This very effort, however, has raised some interesting questions. What sort of discourse is ethical discourse? When I claim, for example, that Abraham Lincoln was a good president, is my claim similar to the claim that Abraham Lincoln was assassinated in Ford's Theater? It will be said, of course, that the second claim is a factual claim, and the first claim is what we call a value judgment. But in what other respects are they different? Are both of them, for example, either true or false? Or is only the factual claim either true or false? I can easily imagine new discoveries being made that would falsify the second sentence—a contemporary document demonstrating that Lincoln was not at Ford's Theater the night he was shot, for example; but it is more difficult to say just how I might go about verifying or falsifying the claim "Abraham Lincoln was a good president."

Are value terms ("good," "just," "wise," "courageous"), then, different from terms used to describe states of affairs ("at Ford's Theater," "shot," "10 years old")? This is the claim made by G. E. Moore in the essay you will read in this chapter. He will argue that the value-term "good" refers not to sensible qualities of things, but rather to an *intuitable* quality of things by virtue of which we call them good. C. L. Stevenson is known for his development of the contrary claim that value-judgments are not descriptive of the qualities of things at all, whether sensible or intuitable. Rather, discourse about *values* has the function of expressing the attitudes of the speaker toward the thing spoken of. When I say that Abraham Lincoln was a good president, I am asserting that I like Lincoln, and I am suggesting that you ought to like him too. It is clear that if Stevenson is right on this point, then no normative ethical theory is possible, and philosophers will have to confine themselves to what is called metaethics, i.e., to the description of the ways in which people deliver themselves of ethical judgments.

In the twentieth century, thanks to the efforts of such philosophers as Moore and Stevenson, A. J. Ayer and R. M. Hare, K. Baier, Kai Nielsen, and many others, metaethics has succeeded in clarifying, to a great extent the nature of value judgments. But we should not forget that ethics remains one of the chief points at which philosophy speaks to us personally, and asks us what we are doing with our lives; indeed, it seeks to discover ways in which we can improve the *quality* of our lives, or, in the words of Socrates, to learn how to care for our souls. And it is in this spirit that the editors hope the following selections will be read.

Epictetus: The Values of Stoicism

I. Of things some are in our power, and others are not. In our power are opinion, movement toward a thing, desire, aversion (turning from a thing); and in a word, whatever are our own acts: not in our power are the body, property, reputation, offices (magisterial power), and in a word, whatever are not our own acts. And the things in our power are by nature free, not subject to restraint nor hindrance: but the things not in our power are weak, slavish, subject to restraint, in the power of others. Remember then that if you think the things which are by nature slavish to be free, and the things which are in the power of others to be your own, you will be hindered, you will lament, you will be disturbed, you will blame both gods and men: but if you think that only which is your own to be your own, and if you think that what is another's, as it really is, belongs to another, no man will ever compel you, no man will hinder you, you will never blame any man, you will accuse no man, you will do nothing involuntarily (against your will), no man will harm you, you will have no enemy, for you will not suffer any harm.

If then you desire such great things, remember that you must not lay hold of them with a small effort; but you must leave alone some things entirely, and postpone others for the present. But if you wish for these things also (such great things), and power and wealth, perhaps you will not gain even these very things (power and wealth) because you aim also at those former things (such great things): certainly you will fail in those things through which alone happiness and freedom are secured. Straightway then practice saying to every harsh appearance, You are an appearance, and in no manner what you appear to be. Then examine it by the rules which you possess, and by this first and chiefly, whether it relates to the things which are in our power or to the things which are not in our power: and if it relates to anything which is not in our power, be ready to say, that it does not concern you.

II. Remember that desire contains in it the hope of obtaining that which you desire; and the hope in aversion is that you will not fall into that which you attempt to avoid: and he who fails in his desire is unfortunate; and he who falls into that which he would avoid, is unhappy. If then you attempt to avoid only the things contrary to nature which are within your power, you will not be involved in any of the things which you would avoid. But if you attempt to avoid disease or death or poverty, you will be unhappy. Take away then aversion from all things which are not in our power, and transfer it to the things contrary to nature which are in our power. But destroy desire completely for the present. For if you desire anything which is not in our power, you must be unfortunate: but of the things in our power, and which it would be good to desire, nothing yet is before you. But employ only the power of moving toward an object and retiring from it; and these powers indeed only slightly and with exceptions and with remission.

Epictetus, *The Encheridion.* Translated by G. Long, 1890.

III. In everything which pleases the soul, or supplies a want, or is loved, remember to add this to the (description, notion); what is the nature of each thing, beginning from the smallest? If you love an earthen vessel, say it is an earthen vessel which you love; for when it has been broken, you will not be disturbed. If you are kissing your child or wife, say that it is a human being whom you are kissing, for when the wife or child dies, you will not be disturbed.

IV. When you are going to take in hand any act, remind yourself what kind of an act it is. If you are going to bathe, place before yourself what happens in the bath: some splashing the water, others pushing against one another, others abusing one another, and some stealing; and thus with more safety you will undertake the matter, if you say to yourself, I now intend to bathe, and to maintain my will in a manner conformable to nature. And so you will do in every act: for thus if any hindrance to bathing shall happen, let this thought be ready; it was not this only that I intended, but I intended also to maintain my will in a way conformable to nature; but I shall not maintain it so, if I am vexed at what happens.

V. Men are disturbed not by the things which happen, but by the opinions about the things: for example, death is nothing terrible, for if it were, it would have seemed so to Socrates; for the opinion about death, that it is terrible, is the terrible thing. When then we are impeded or disturbed or grieved, let us never blame others, but ourselves, that is, our opinions. It is the act of an ill-instructed man to blame others for his own bad condition; it is the act of one who has begun to be instructed, to lay the blame on himself; and of one whose instruction is completed, neither to blame another, nor himself.

VI. Be not elated at any advantage, which belongs to another. If a horse when he is elated should say, I am beautiful, one might endure it. But when you are elated, and say, I have a beautiful horse, you must know that you are elated at having a good horse. What then is your own? The use of appearances. Consequently when in the use of appearances you are conformable to nature, then be elated, for then you will be elated at something good which is your own.

VII. As on a voyage when the vessel has reached a port, if you go out to get water, it is an amusement by the way to pick up a shellfish or some bulb, but your thoughts ought to be directed to the ship, and you ought to be constantly watching if the captain should call, and then you must throw away all those things, that you may not be bound and pitched into the ship like sheep: so in life also, if there be given to you instead of a little bulb and a shell a wife and child, there will be nothing to prevent you from taking them. But if the captain should call, run to the ship, and leave all those things without regard to them. But if you are old, do not even go far from the ship, lest when you are called you make default.

VIII. Seek not that the things which happen should happen as you wish; but wish the things which happen to be as they are, and you will have a tranquil flow of life.

IX. Disease is an impediment to the body, but not to the will, unless the will itself chooses. Lameness is an impediment to the leg, but not to the will. And add this reflection on the occasion of everything that happens; for you will find it an impediment to something else, but not to yourself.

X. On the occasion of every accident that befalls you, remember to turn to yourself and inquire what power you have for turning it to use. If you see a fair man or a fair woman, you will find that the power to resist is temperance. If labor be presented to you, you will find that it is endurance. If it be abusive words, you will find it to be patience. And if you have been thus formed to the proper habit, the appearances will not carry you along with them.

XI. Never say about anything, I have lost it, but say I have restored it. Is your child dead? It has been restored. Is your wife dead? She has been restored. Has your estate been taken from you? Has not then this also been restored? But he who has taken it from me is a bad man. But what is it to you, by whose hands the giver demanded it back? So long as he may allow you, take care of it as a thing which belongs to another, as travelers do with their inn.

XII. If you intend to improve, throw away such thoughts as these: if I neglect my affairs, I shall not have the means of living: unless I chastise my slave, he will be bad. For it is better to die of hunger and so be released from grief and fear than to live in abundance with perturbation; and it is better for your slave to be bad than for you to be unhappy. Begin then from little things. Is the oil spilled? Is a little wine stolen? Say on the occasion, at such price is sold freedom from perturbation; at such price is sold tranquillity, but nothing is got for nothing. And when you call your slave, consider that it is possible that he does not hear; and if he does hear, that he will do nothing which you wish. But matters are not so well with him, but altogether well with you, that it should be in his power for you to be not disturbed.

XIII. If you would improve, submit to be considered without sense and foolish with respect to externals. Wish to be considered to know nothing: and if you shall seem to some to be a person of importance, distrust yourself. For you should know that it is not easy both to keep your will in a condition conformable to nature and to secure external things: but if a man is careful about the one, it is an absolute necessity that he will neglect the other.

XIV. If you would have your children and your wife and your friends to live forever, you are silly; for you would have the things which are not in your power to be in your power, and the things which belong to others to be yours. So if you would have your slave to be free from faults, you are a fool; for you would have badness not to be badness, but something else. But if you wish not to fail in your desires, you are able to do that. Practice then this which you are able to do. He is the master of every man who has the power over the things, which another person wishes or does not wish, the power to confer them on him or to take them away. Whoever then wishes to be free, let him neither wish for anything nor avoid anything which depends on others: if he does not observe this rule, he must be a slave.

XV. Remember that in life you ought to behave as at a banquet. Suppose that something is carried round and is opposite to you. Stretch out your hand and take a portion with decency. Suppose that it passes by you. Do not detain it. Suppose that it is not yet come to you. Do not send your desire forward to it, but wait till it is opposite to you. Do so with respect to children, so with respect to a wife, so with respect to magisterial offices, so with respect to wealth, and you will be some time a worthy partner of the banquets of the gods. But if you take none of the things which are set before you, and even despise them, then you will be not only a fellow-banqueter with the gods, but also a partner with them in power. For by acting thus Diogenes and Heracleitus and those like them were deservedly divine, and were so called.

XVI. When you see a person weeping in sorrow either when a child goes abroad or when he is dead, or when the man has lost his property, take care that the appearance does not hurry you away with it, as if he were suffering in external things. But straightway make a distinction in your own mind, and be in readiness to say, it is not that which has happened that afflicts this man, for it does not afflict another, but it is the opinion about this thing which afflicts the man. So far as words then do not be unwilling to show him sympathy, and even if it happens so, to lament with him. But take care that you do not lament internally also.

XVII. Remember that you are an actor in a play of such a kind as the teacher (author) may choose; if short, of a short one; if long, of a long one: if he wishes you to act the part of a poor man, see that you act the part naturally; if the part of a lame man, of a magistrate, of a private person, do the same. For this is your duty, to act well the part that is given to you; but to select the part, belongs to another. . . .

XX. Remember that it is not he who reviles you or strikes you, who insults you, but it is your opinion about these things as being insulting. When then a man irritates you, you must know that it is your own opinion which has irritated you. Therefore especially try not to be carried away by the appearance. For if you once gain time and delay, you will more easily master yourself.

XXI. Let death and exile and every other thing which appears dreadful be daily before your eyes; but most of all death: and you will never think of anything mean nor will you desire anything extravagantly.

XXII. If you desire philosophy, prepare yourself from the beginning to be ridiculed, to expect that many will sneer at you, and say, He has all at once returned to us as a philosopher; and whence does he get this supercilious look for us? Do not show a supercilious look; but hold on to the things which seem to you best as one appointed by God to this station. And remember that if you abide in the same principles, these men who first ridiculed will afterward admire you: but if you shall have been overpowered by them, you will bring on yourself double ridicule.

XXIII. If it should ever happen to you to be turned to externals in order to please some person, you must know that you have lost your purpose in life. Be satisfied then in everything with being a philosopher; and if you wish to seem also to any person to be a philosopher, appear so to yourself, and you will be able to do this.

XXIV. Let not these thoughts afflict you, I shall live unhonored and be nobody nowhere. For if want of honor is an evil, you cannot be in evil through the means of another any more than you can be involved in anything base. Is it then your business to obtain the rank of magistrate, or to be received at a banquet? By no means. How then can this be want of honor? And how will you be nobody nowhere, when you ought to be somebody in those things only which are in your power, in which indeed it is permitted to you to be a man of the greatest worth? But your friends will be without assistance! What do you mean by being without assistance? They will not receive money from you, nor will you make them Roman citizens. Who then told you that these are among the things which are in our power, and not in the power of others? And who can give to another what he has not himself? Acquire money then, your friends say, that we also may have something. If I can acquire money and also keep myself modest, and faithful and magnanimous, point out the way, and I will acquire it. But if you ask me to lose the things which are good and my own, in order that you may gain the things which are not good, see how unfair and silly you are. Besides, which would you rather have, money or a faithful and modest friend? For this end then rather help me to be such a man, and do not ask me to do this by which I shall lose that character. But my country, you say, as far as it depends on me, will be without my help. I ask again, what help do you mean? It will not have porticoes or baths through you. And what does this mean? For it is not furnished with shoes by means of a smith, nor with arms by means of a shoemaker. But it is enough if every man fully discharges the work that is his own: and if you provided it with another citizen faithful and modest, would you not be useful to it? Yes. Then you also cannot be useless to it. What place then, you say, shall I hold in the city? Whatever you can, if you maintain at the same time your fidelity and modesty. But if when you wish to be useful to the state, you shall lose these qualities, what profit could you be to it, if you were made shameless and faithless?

XXV. Has any man been preferred before you at a banquet, or in being saluted, or in being invited to a consultation? If these things are good, you ought to rejoice that he has obtained them: but if bad, be not grieved because you have not obtained them; and remember that you cannot, if you do not the same things in order to obtain what is not in our power, be considered worthy of the same things. For how can a man obtain an equal share with another when he does not visit a man's doors as that other man does, when he does not attend him when he goes abroad, as the other man does; when he does not praise him as another does? You will be unjust then and insatiable, if you do not part with the price, in return for which those things are sold, and if you wish to obtain them for nothing. Well, what is the price of lettuces? An obolus perhaps. If then a man gives up the obolus, and receives the lettuces, and if you do not give up the obolus and do not obtain the lettuces, do not suppose that you receive less than he who has got the lettuces; for as he has the lettuces, so you have the obolus which you did not give. In the same way then in the other matter also you have not been invited to a man's feast, for you did not give to the host the price at which the supper is sold; but he sells it for praise, he sells it for personal attention. Give then the price, if it is for your interest, for which it is sold. But if you wish both not to give the price and to obtain the things, you are insatiable and silly. Have you nothing then in place of the supper? You have indeed, you have the not flattering of him, whom you did not choose to flatter; you have the not enduring of the man when he enters the room. . . .

XXIX. In every act observe the things which come first, and those which follow it; and so proceed to the act. If you do not, at first you will approach it with alacrity, without having thought of the things which will follow; but afterward, when certain ugly things have shown themselves, you will be ashamed. A man wishes to conquer at the Olympic games. I also wish indeed, for it is a fine thing. But observe both the things which come first, and the things which follow; and then begin the act. You must do everything according to rule, eat according to strict orders, abstain from delicacies, exercise yourself as you are bid at appointed times, in heat, in cold, you must not drink cold water, nor wine as you choose; in a word, you must deliver yourself up to the exercise master as you do to the physician, and then proceed to the contest. And sometimes you will strain the hand, put the ankle out of joint, swallow much dust, sometimes be flogged, and after all this be defeated. When you have considered all this, if you still choose, go to the contest: if you do not, you will behave like children, who at one time play as wrestlers, another time as flute players, again as gladiators, then as trumpeters, then as tragic actors: so you also will be at one time an athlete, at another a gladiator, then a rhetorician, then a philosopher, but with your whole soul you will be nothing at all; but like an ape you imitate everything that you see, and one thing after another pleases you. For you have not undertaken anything with consideration, nor have you surveyed it well; but carelessly and with cold desire. Thus some who have seen a philosopher and having heard one speak, they wish to be philosophers themselves also. My man, first of all consider what kind of thing it is: and then examine your own nature, if you are able to sustain the character. Do you wish to be an athlete or a wrestler? Look at your arms, your thighs, examine your loins. For different men are formed by nature for different things. Do you think that if you do these things, you can eat in the same manner, drink in the same manner, and in the same manner loathe certain things? You must pass sleepless nights, endure toil, go away from your kinsmen, be despised by a slave, in every thing have the inferior part, in honor, in office, in the courts of justice, in every little matter. Consider these things, if you would exchange for them, freedom from passions, liberty, tranquillity. If not, take care that, like little children, you be not now a philosopher, then a servant of the publicani, then a rhetorician, then a procurator for Caesar. These things are not consistent. You must be one man, either good or bad. You must cultivate your own ruling faculty, or external things; you must either exercise your skill on internal things or on external things; that is you must either maintain the position of a philosopher or that of a common person.

XXX. Duties are universally measured by relations. Is a man a father? The precept is to take care of him, to yield to him in all things, to submit when he is reproachful, when he inflicts blows. But suppose that he is a bad father. Were you then by nature made akin to a good father? No; but to a father. Does a brother wrong you? Maintain then your own position toward him, and do not examine what he is doing, but what you must do that your will shall be conformable to nature. For another will not damage you, unless you choose: but you will be damaged then when you shall think that you are damaged. In this way then you will discover your duty from the relation of a neighbor, from that of a citizen, from that of a general, if you are accustomed to contemplate the relations.

XXXI. As to piety toward the Gods you must know that this is the chief thing, to have right opinions about them, to think that they exist, and that they administer the All well and justly; and you must fix yourself in this principle, to obey them, and yield to them in everything which happens, and voluntarily to follow it as being accomplished by the wisest intelligence. For if you do so, you will never either blame the Gods, nor will you accuse them of neglecting you. And it is not possible for this to be done in any other way than by withdrawing from the things which are not in our power, and by placing the good and the evil only in those things which are in our power. For if you think that any of the things which are not in our power is good or bad, it is absolutely necessary that, when you do not obtain what you wish, and when you fall into those things which you do not wish, you will find fault and hate those who are the cause of them; for every animal is formed by nature to this, to fly from and to turn from the things which appear harmful and the things which are the cause of the harm, but to follow and admire the things which are useful and the causes of the useful. It is impossible then for a person who thinks that he is harmed to be delighted with that which he thinks to be the cause of the harm, as it is also impossible to be pleased with the harm itself. For this reason also a father is reviled by his son, when he gives no part to his son of the things which are considered to be good. It is for this reason that the cultivator of the earth reviles the Gods, for this reason the sailor does, and the merchant, and for this reason those who lose their wives and their children. For where the useful (your interest) is, there also piety is. Consequently he who takes care to desire as he ought and to avoid as he ought, at the same time also cares after piety. But to make libations and to sacrifice and to offer first fruits according to the custom of our fathers, purely and not meanly nor carelessly nor scantily nor above our ability, is a thing which belongs to all to do.

XXXIII. Immediately prescribe some character and some form to yourself, which you shall observe both when you are alone and when you meet with men.

And let silence be the general rule, or let only what is necessary be said, and in few words. And rarely and when the occasion calls we shall say something; but about none of the common subjects, nor about gladiators, nor horse-races, nor about athletes, nor about eating or drinking, which are the usual subjects; and especially not about men, as blaming them or praising them, or comparing them. If then you are able, bring over by your conversation the conversation of your associates to that which is proper; but if you should happen to be confined to the company of strangers, be silent.

Let not your laughter be much, nor on many occasions, nor excessive.

Refuse altogether to take an oath, if it is possible: if it is not, refuse as far as you are able.

Avoid banquets which are given by strangers and by ignorant persons. But if ever there is occasion to join in them, let your attention be carefully fixed, that you slip not into the manners of the vulgar (the uninstructed). For you must know, that if your companion be impure, he also who keeps company with him must become impure, though he should happen to be pure.

Take the things which relate to the body as far as the bare use, as food, drink, clothing, house, and slaves: but exclude everything which is for show or luxury.

As to pleasure with women, abstain as far as you can before marriage: but if you do indulge in it, do it in the way which is conformable to custom. Do not however be disagreeable to those who indulge in these pleasures, or reprove them; and do not often boast that you do not indulge in them yourself.

If a man has reported to you, that a certain person speaks ill of you, do not make any defense to what has been told you: but reply, The man did not know the rest of my faults, for he would not have mentioned these only. . . .

XL. Women forthwith from the age of fourteen are called by the men mistresses. Therefore since they see that there is nothing else that they can obtain, but only the power of lying with men, they begin to decorate themselves, and to place all their hopes in this. It is worth our while then to take care that they may know that they are valued (by men) for nothing else than appearing decent and modest and discreet.

XLI. It is a mark of a mean capacity to spend much time on the things which concern the body, such as much exercise, much eating, much drinking, much easing of the body, much copulation. But these things should be done as subordinate things: and let all your care be directed to the mind.

XLII. When any person treats you ill or speaks ill of you, remember that he does this or says this because he thinks that it is his duty. It is not possible then for him to follow that which seems right to you, but that which seems right to himself. Accordingly if he is wrong in his opinion, he is the person who is hurt, for he is the person who has been deceived; for if a man shall suppose the true conjunction to be false, it is not the conjunction which is hindered, but the man who has been deceived about it. If you proceed then from these opinions, you will be mild in temper to him who reviles you: for say on each occasion, It seemed so to him. . . .

XLIV. These reasons do not cohere: I am richer than you, therefore I am better than you; I am more eloquent than you, therefore I am better than you. On the contrary these rather cohere, I am richer than you, therefore my possessions are greater than yours: I am more eloquent than you, therefore my speech is superior to yours. But you are neither possession nor speech.

XLV. Does a man bathe quickly? do not say that he bathes badly, but that he bathes quickly. Does a man drink much wine? do not say that he does this badly, but say that he drinks much. For before you shall have determined the opinion, how do you know whether he is acting wrong? Thus it will not happen to you to comprehend some appearances which are capable of being comprehended, but to assent to others.

XLVI. On no occasion call yourself a philosopher, and do not speak much among the uninstructed about theorems (philosophical rules, precepts): but do that which follows from them. For example at a banquet do not say how a man ought to eat, but eat as you ought to eat. For remember that in this way Socrates also altogether avoided ostentation: persons used to come to him and ask to be recommended by him to philosophers, and he used to take them to philosophers: so easily did he submit to being overlooked. Accordingly if any conversation should arise among uninstructed persons about any theorem, generally be silent; for there is great danger that you will immediately vomit up what you have not digested. And when a man shall say to you, that you know nothing, and you are not vexed, then be sure that you have begun the work of philosophy. For even sheep do not vomit up their grass and show to the shepherds how much they have eaten; but when they have internally digested the pasture, they produce externally wool and milk. Do you also show not your theorems to the uninstructed, but show the acts which come from their digestion. . . .

L. Whatever things are proposed to you for the conduct of life abide by them, as if they were laws, as if you would be guilty of impiety if you transgressed any of them. And whatever any man shall say about you, do not attend to it for this is no affair of yours. How long will you then still defer thinking yourself worthy of the best things, and in no matter transgressing the distinctive reason? Have you accepted the rules, which it was your duty to agree to, and have you agreed to them? what teacher then do you still expect that you defer to him the correction of yourself? You are no longer a youth, but already a full grown man. If then you are negligent and slothful, and are continually making procrastination after procrastination, and proposal after proposal, and fixing day after day, after which you will attend to yourself, you will not know that you are not making improvement, but you will continue ignorant (uninstructed) both while you live and till you die. Immediately then think it right to live as a full-grown man, and one who is making proficiency, and let everything which appears to you to be the best be to you a law which must not be transgressed. And if anything laborious, or pleasant or glorious or inglorious be presented to you, remember that now is the contest, now are the Olympic games, and they cannot be deferred; and that it depends on one defeat and one giving way that progress is either lost or maintained. Socrates in this way became perfect, in all things improving himself, attending to nothing except to reason. But you, though you are not yet a Socrates, ought to live as one who wishes to be a Socrates.

LI. The first and most necessary place in philosophy is the use of rules, for instance, that we must not lie: the second part is that of demonstrations, for instance, How is it proved that we ought not to lie: the third is that which is confirmatory of these two and explanatory, for example, How is this a demonstration? For what is demonstration, what is consequence, what is contradiction, what is truth, what is falsehood? The third part is necessary on account of the second, and the second on account of the first; but the most necessary and that on which we ought to rest is the first. But we do the contrary. For we spend our time on the third topic, and all our earnestness is about it: but we entirely neglect the first. Therefore we lie; but the demonstration that we ought not to lie we have ready to hand.

LII. In every thing we should hold these maxims ready to hand:

Lead me, O Zeus, and thou O Destiny,
The way that I am bid by you to go:
To follow I am ready. If I choose not,
I make myself a wretch, and still must
follow. But whoso nobly yields unto necessity,
We hold him wise, and skill'd in things
divine.

And the third also: O Crito, if so it pleases the Gods, so let it be; Anytus and Meletus are able indeed to kill me, but they cannot harm me.

Immanuel Kant: Duty and the Good Will

FIRST SECTION

TRANSITION FROM THE COMMON RATIONAL KNOWLEDGE OF MORALITY TO THE PHILOSOPHICAL.

Nothing can possibly be conceived in the world, or even out of it, which can be called good without qualification, except a Good Will. Intelligence, wit, judgment, and the other *talents* of the mind, however they may be named, or courage, resolution, perseverance, as qualities of temperament, are undoubtedly good and desirable in many respects; but these gifts of nature may also become extremely bad and mischievous if the will which is to make use of them, and which, therefore, constitutes what is called *character,* is not good. It is the same with the *gifts of fortune.* Power, riches, honour, even health, and the general well-being and contentment with one's condition which is called *happiness,* inspire pride, and often presumption, if there is not a good will to correct the influence of these on the mind, and with this also to rectify the whole principle of acting, and adapt it to its end. The sight of a being who is not adorned with a single feature of a pure and good will, enjoying unbroken prosperity, can never give pleasure to an impartial rational spectator. Thus a good will appears to constitute the indispensable condition even of being worthy of happiness.

There are even some qualities which are of service to this good will itself, and may facilitate its action, yet which have no intrinsic unconditional value, but always presuppose a good will, and this qualifies the esteem that we justly have for them, and does not permit us to regard them as absolutely good. Moderation in the affections and passions, self-control and calm deliberation are not only good in many respects, but even seem to constitute part of the intrinsic worth of the person; but they are far from deserving to be called good without qualification, although they have been so unconditionally praised by the ancients. For without the principles of a good will, they may become extremely bad, and the coolness of a villain not only makes him far more dangerous, but also directly makes him more abominable in our eyes than he would have been without it.

A good will is good not because of what it performs or effects, not by its aptness for the attainment of some proposed end, but simply by virtue of the volition, that is, it is good in itself, and considered by itself is to be esteemed much higher than all that can be brought about by it in favour of any inclination, nay, even of the sum total of all inclinations. Even if it should happen that, owing to special disfavour of fortune, or the niggardly provision of a step-motherly nature, this will should wholly lack power to accomplish its purpose, if with its greatest efforts it should yet achieve nothing, and there should remain only the good will (not, to be sure, a mere wish, but the summoning of all means in our power), then, like a jewel, it would still shine by its own light, as a thing which has its whole value in itself. Its usefulness or fruitlessness can neither add to nor take away anything from this value. It would be, as it were, only the setting to enable us to handle it the more conveniently in common commerce, or to attract to it the attention of those who are not yet connoisseurs, but not to recommend it to true connoisseurs, or to determine its value.

There is, however, something so strange in this idea of the absolute value of the mere will, in which no account is taken of its utility, that notwithstanding the thorough assent of even

From Immanuel Kant, *The Fundamental Principles of the Metaphysics of Morals* (selections), translated by T.K. Abbott, 1889.

common reason to the idea, yet a suspicion must arise that it may perhaps really be the product of mere high-flown fancy, and that we may have misunderstood the purpose of nature in assigning reason as the governor of our will. Therefore we will examine this idea from this point of view.

In the physical constitution of an organized being, that is, a being adapted suitably to the purposes of life, we assume it as a fundamental principle that no organ for any purpose will be found but what is also the fittest and best adapted for that purpose. Now in a being which has reason and a will, if the proper object of nature were its *conservation,* its *welfare,* in a word, its *happiness,* then nature would have hit upon a very bad arrangement in selecting the reason of the creature to carry out this purpose. For all the actions which the creature has to perform with a view to this purpose, and the whole rule of its conduct, would be far more surely prescribed to it by instinct, and that end would have been attained thereby much more certainly than it ever can be by reason. Should reason have been communicated to this favoured creature over and above, it must only have served it to contemplate the happy constitution of its nature, to admire it, to congratulate itself thereon, and to feel thankful for it to the beneficent cause, but not that it should subject its desires to that weak and delusive guidance, and meddle bunglingly with the purpose of nature. In a word, nature would have taken care that reason should not break forth into *practical exercise,* nor have the presumption, with its weak insight, to think out for itself the plan of happiness, and of the means of attaining it. Nature would not only have taken on herself the choice of the ends, but also of the means, and with wise foresight would have entrusted both to instinct.

And, in fact, we find that the more a cultivated reason applies itself with deliberate purpose to the enjoyment of life and happiness, so much the more does the man fail of true satisfaction. And from this circumstance there arises in many, if they are candid enough to confess it, a certain degree of *misology,* that is, hatred of reason, especially in the case of those who are most experienced in the use of it, because after calculating all the advantages they derive, I do not say from the invention of all the arts of common luxury, but even from the sciences (which seem to them to be after all only a luxury of the understanding), they find that they have, in fact, only brought more trouble on their shoulders, rather than gained in happiness; and they end by envying, rather than despising, the more common stamp of men who keep closer to the guidance of mere instinct, and do not allow their reason much influence on their conduct. And this we must admit, that the judgment of those who would very much lower the lofty eulogies of the advantages which reason gives us in regard to the happiness and satisfaction of life, or who would even reduce them below zero, is by no means morose or ungrateful to the goodness with which the world is governed, but that there lies at the root of these judgments the idea that our existence has a different and far nobler end, for which, and not for happiness, reason is properly intended, and which must, therefore, be regarded as the supreme condition to which the private ends of man must, for the most part, be postponed.

For as reason is not competent to guide the will with certainty in regard to its objects and the satisfaction of all our wants (which it to some extent even multiplies), this being an end to which an implanted instinct would have led with much greater certainty; and since, nevertheless, reason is imparted to us as a practical faculty, *i.e.* as one which is to have influence on the *will,* therefore, admitting that nature generally in the distribution of her capacities has adapted the means to the end, its true destination must be to produce a *will,* not merely good as a *means* to something else, but *good in itself,* for which reason was absolutely necessary. This will then, though not indeed the sole and complete good, must be the supreme good and the condition of every other, even of the desire of happiness. Under these circumstances, there is nothing inconsistent with the wisdom of nature in the fact that the cultivation of the reason, which is requisite for the first and unconditional purpose, does in many ways interfere, at least in this life, with the attainment of the second, which is always conditional, namely, happiness. Nay, it may even reduce it to nothing, without nature thereby failing of her purpose. For reason recognises the establishment of a good will as its highest practical destination, and in attaining this purpose is capable only of a satisfaction of its own proper kind, namely, that from the attainment of an end, which end again is determined by reason only, notwithstanding that this may involve many a disappointment to the ends of inclination.

We have then to develop the notion of a will which deserves to be highly esteemed for itself, and is good without a view to anything further, a notion which exists already in the sound natural understanding, requiring rather to be cleared up than to be taught, and which in estimating the value of our actions always takes the first place, and constitutes the condition of all the rest. In order to do this we will take the notion of duty, which includes that of a good will, although implying certain subjective restrictions and hindrances. These, however, far from concealing it, or rendering it unrecognisable, rather bring it out by contrast, and make it shine forth so much the brighter.

I omit here all actions which are already recognised as inconsistent with duty, although they may be useful for this or that purpose, for with these the question whether they are done *from duty* cannot arise at all, since they even conflict with it. I also set aside those actions which really conform to duty, but to which men have *no* direct *inclination,* performing them because they are impelled thereto by some other inclination. For in this case we can readily distinguish whether the action which agrees with duty is done *from duty,* or from a selfish view. It is much harder to make this distinction when the action accords with duty, and the subject has besides a *direct* inclination to it. For example, it is always a matter of duty that a dealer should not overcharge an inexperienced purchaser, and wherever there is much commerce the prudent tradesman does not overcharge, but keeps a fixed price for everyone, so that a child buys of him as well as any other. Men are thus *honestly* served; but this is not enough to make us believe that the tradesman has so acted from duty and from principles of honesty: his own advantage required it; it is out of the question in this case to suppose that he might besides have a direct inclination in favour of the buyers, so that, as it were, from love he should give no advantage to one over another. Accordingly the action was done neither from duty nor from direct inclination, but merely with a selfish view.

On the other hand, it is a duty to maintain one's life; and, in addition, every one has also a direct inclination to do so. But on this account the often anxious care which most men take for it has no intrinsic worth, and their maxim has no moral import. They preserve their life *as duty requires,* no doubt, but not *because duty requires.* On the other hand, if adversity and hopeless sorrow have completely taken away the relish for life; if the unfortunate one, strong in mind, indignant at his fate rather than desponding or dejected, wishes for death, and yet preserves his life without loving it—not from inclination or fear, but from duty—then his maxim has a moral worth.

To be beneficent when we can is a duty; and besides this, there are many minds so sympathetically constituted that, without any other motive of vanity or self-interest, they find a pleasure in spreading joy around them, and can take delight in the satisfaction of others so far as it is their own work. But I maintain that in such a case an action of this kind, however proper, however amiable it may be, has nevertheless no true moral worth, but is on a level with other inclinations, *e.g.* the inclination to honour, which, if it is happily directed to that which is in fact of public utility and accordant with duty, and consequently honourable, deserves praise and encouragement, but not esteem. For the maxim lacks the moral import, namely, that such actions be done *from duty,* not from inclination. Put the case that the mind of that philanthropist were clouded by sorrow of his own, extinguishing all sympathy with the lot of others, and that while he still has the power to benefit others in distress, he is not touched by their trouble because he is absorbed with his own; and now suppose that he tears himself out of this dead insensibility, and performs the action without any inclination to it, but simply from duty, then first has his action its genuine moral worth. Further still; if nature has put little sympathy in the heart of this or that man; if he, supposed to be an upright man, is by temperament cold and indifferent to the sufferings of others, perhaps because in respect of his own he is provided with the special gift of patience and fortitude, and supposes, or even requires, that others should have the same—and such a man would certainly not be the meanest product of nature—but if nature had not specially framed him for a philanthropist, would he not still find in himself a source from whence to give himself a far higher worth than that of a good-natured temperament could be? Unquestionably. It is just in this that the moral worth of the character is brought out which is incomparably the highest of all, namely, that he is beneficent, not from inclination, but from duty.

To secure one's own happiness is a duty, at least indirectly; for discontent with one's condition, under a pressure of many anxieties and amidst unsatisfied wants, might easily become a great *temptation to transgression of duty*. But here again, without looking to duty, all men have already the strongest and most intimate inclination to happiness, because it is just in this idea that all inclinations are combined in one total. But the precept of happiness is often of such a sort that it greatly interferes with some inclinations, and yet a man cannot form any definite and certain conception of the sum of satisfaction of all of them which is called happiness. It is not then to be wondered at that a single inclination, definite both as to what it promises and as to the time within which it can be gratified, is often able to overcome such a fluctuating idea, and that a gouty patient, for instance, can choose to enjoy what he likes, and to suffer what he may, since, according to his calculation, on this occasion at least, he has [only] not sacrificed the enjoyment of the present moment to a possibly mistaken expectation of a happiness which is supposed to be found in health. But even in this case, if the general desire for happiness did not influence his will, and supposing that in his particular case health was not a necessary element in this calculation, there yet remains in this, as in all other cases, this law, namely, that he should promote his happiness not from inclination but from duty, and by this would his conduct first acquire true moral worth.

It is in this manner, undoubtedly, that we are to understand those passages of Scripture also in which we are commanded to love our neighbour, even our enemy. For love, as an affection, cannot be commanded, but beneficence for duty's sake may; even though we are not impelled to it by any inclination—nay, are even repelled by a natural and unconquerable aversion. This is *practical* love, and not *pathological*—a love which is seated in the will, and not in the propensions of sense—in principles of action and not of tender sympathy; and it is this love alone which can be commanded.

The second[3] proposition is: That an action done from duty derives its moral worth, *not from the purpose* which is to be attained by it, but from the maxim by which it is determined, and therefore does not depend on the realization of the object of the action, but merely on the *principle of volition* by which the action has taken place, without regard to any object of desire. It is clear from what precedes that the purposes which we may have in view in our actions, or their effects regarded as ends and springs of the will, cannot give to actions any unconditional or moral worth. In what, then, can their worth lie, if it is not to consist in the will and in reference to its expected effect? It cannot lie anywhere but in the *principle of the will* without regard to the ends which can be attained by the action. For the will stands between its *à priori* principle, which is formal, and its *à posteriori* spring, which is material, as between two roads, and as it must be determined by something, it follows that it must be determined by the formal principle of volition when an action is done from duty, in which case every material principle has been withdrawn from it.

The third proposition, which is a consequence of the two preceding, I would express thus: *Duty is the necessity of acting from respect for the law.* I may have *inclination* for an object as the effect of my proposed action, but I cannot have *respect* for it, just for this reason, that it is an effect and not an energy of will. Similarly, I cannot have respect for inclination, whether my own or another's; I can at most, if my own, approve it; if another's, sometimes even love it; *i.e.* look on it as favourable to my own interest. It is only what is connected with my will as a principle, by no means as an effect—what does not subserve my inclination, but overpowers it, or at least in case of choice excludes it from its calculation—in other words, simply the law of itself, which can be an object of respect, and hence a command. Now an action done from duty must wholly exclude the influence of inclination, and with it every object of the will, so that nothing remains which can determine the will except objectively the *law,* and subjectively *pure respect* for this practical law, and consequently the maxim[4] that I should follow this law even to the thwarting of all my inclinations.

Thus the moral worth of an action does not lie in the effect expected from it, nor in any principle of action which requires to borrow its motive from this expected effect. For all these effects—agreeableness of one's condition, and even the promotion of the happiness of others—could have been also brought about by other causes, so that for this there would have been no need of the will of a rational being; whereas it is in this alone that the supreme and unconditional good can be found. The pre-eminent good which we call moral can therefore consist in nothing else than *the conception of law* in itself, *which certainly is only possible in a rational being,* in so far as this conception, and not the expected effect, determines the will. This is a good which is already present in the person who acts accordingly, and we have not to wait for it to appear first in the result.

But what sort of law can that be, the conception of which must determine the will, even without paying any regard to the effect expected from it, in order that this will may be called good absolutely and without qualification? As I have deprived the will of every impulse which could arise to it from obedience to any law, there remains nothing but the universal conformity of its actions to law in general, which alone is to serve the will as a principle, *i.e.* I am never to act otherwise than so *that I could also will that my maxim should become a universal law.* Here now, it is the simple conformity to law in general, without assuming any particular law applicable to certain actions, that serves the will as its principle, and must so serve it, if duty is not to be a vain delusion and a chimerical notion. The common reason of men in its practical judgments perfectly coincides with this, and always has in view the principle here suggested. Let the question be, for example: May I when in distress make a promise with the intention not to keep it? I readily distinguish here between the two significations which the question may have: Whether it is prudent, or whether it is right, to make a false promise. The former may undoubtedly often be the case. I see clearly indeed that it is not enough to extricate myself from a present difficulty by means of this subterfuge, but it must be well considered whether there may not hereafter spring from this lie much greater inconvenience than that from which I now free myself, and as, with all my supposed *cunning,* the consequences cannot be so easily foreseen but that credit once lost may be much more injurious to me than any mischief which I seek to avoid at present, it should be considered whether it would not be more *prudent* to act herein according to a universal maxim, and to make it a habit to promise nothing except with the intention of keeping it. But it is soon clear to me that such a maxim will still only be based on the fear of consequences. Now it is a wholly different thing to be truthful from duty, and to be so from apprehension of injurious consequences. In the first case, the very notion of the action already implies a law for me; in the second case, I must first look about elsewhere to see what results may be combined with it which would affect myself. For to deviate from the principle of duty is beyond all doubt wicked; but to be unfaithful to my maxim of prudence may often be very advantageous to me, although to abide by it is certainly safer. The shortest way, however, and an unerring one, to discover the answer to this question whether a lying promise is consistent with duty, is to ask myself, Should I be content that my maxim (to extricate myself from difficulty by a false promise) should hold good as a universal law, for myself as well as for others? and should I be able to say to myself, "Every one may make a deceitful promise when he finds himself in a difficulty from which he cannot otherwise extricate himself"? Then I presently become aware that while I can will the lie, I can by no means will that lying should be a universal law. For with such a law there would be no promises at all, since it would be in vain to allege my intention in regard to my future actions to those who would not believe this allegation, or if they over-hastily did so would pay me back in my own coin. Hence my maxim, as soon as it should be made a universal law, would necessarily destroy itself.

I do not, therefore, need any far-reaching penetration to discern what I have to do in order that my will may be morally good. Inexperienced in the course of the world, incapable of being prepared for all its contingencies, I only ask myself: Canst thou also will that thy maxim should be a universal law? If not, then it must be rejected, and that not because of a disadvantage accruing from it to myself or even to others, but because it cannot enter as a principle into a possible universal legislation, and reason extorts from me immediate respect for such legislation. I do not indeed as yet *discern* on what this respect is based (this the philosopher may inquire), but at least I understand this, that it is an estimation of the worth which far outweighs all worth of what is recommended by inclination, and that the necessity of acting from *pure* respect for the practical law is what constitutes duty, to which every other motive must give place, because it is the condition of a will being good *in itself,* and the worth of such a will is above everything.

Thus, then, without quitting the moral knowledge of common human reason, we have arrived at its principle. And although, no doubt, common men do not conceive it in such an abstract and universal form, yet they always have it really before their eyes, and use it as the standard of their decision. Here it would be easy to show how, with this compass in hand, men are well able to distinguish, in every case that occurs, what is good, what bad, conformably to duty or inconsistent with it, if, without in the least teaching them anything new, we only, like Socrates, direct their attention to the principles they themselves employ; and that therefore we do not need science and philosophy to know what we should do to be honest and good, yea, even wise and virtuous. Indeed we might well have conjectured beforehand that the knowledge of what every man is bound to do, and therefore also to know, would be within the reach of every man, even the commonest. Here we cannot forbear admiration when we see how great an advantage the practical judgment has over the theoretical in the common understanding of men. In the latter, if common reason ventures to depart from the laws of experience and from the perceptions of the senses it falls into mere inconceivabilities and self-contradictions, at least into a chaos of uncertainty, obscurity, and instability. But in the practical sphere it is just when the common understanding excludes all sensible springs from practical laws that its power of judgment begins to show itself to advantage. It then becomes even subtle, whether it be that it chicanes with its own conscience or with other claims respecting what is to be called right, or whether it desires for its own instruction to determine honestly the worth of actions; and, in the latter case, it may even have as good a hope of hitting the mark as any philosopher whatever can promise himself. Nay, it is almost more sure of doing so, because the philosopher cannot have any other principle, while he may easily perplex his judgment by a multitude of considerations foreign to the matter, and so turn aside from the right way. Would it not therefore be wiser in moral concerns to acquiesce in the judgment of common reason, or at most only to call in philosophy for the purpose of rendering the system of morals more complete and intelligible, and its rules more convenient for use (especially for disputation), but not so as to draw off the common understanding from its happy simplicity, or to bring it by means of philosophy into a new path of inquiry and instruction?

Innocence is indeed a glorious thing, only, on the other hand, it is very sad that it cannot well maintain itself, and is easily seduced. On this account even wisdom—which otherwise consists more in conduct than in knowledge—yet has need of science, not in order to learn from it, but to secure for its precepts admission and permanence. Against all the commands of duty which reason represents to man as so deserving of respect, he feels in himself a powerful counterpoise in his wants and inclinations, the entire satisfaction of which he sums up under the name of happiness. Now reason issues its commands unyieldingly, without promising anything to the inclinations, and, as it were, with disregard and contempt for these claims, which are so impetuous, and at the same time so plausible, and which will not allow themselves to be suppressed by any command. Hence there arises a natural *dialectic, i.e.* a disposition to argue against these strict laws of duty and to question their validity, or at least their purity and strictness; and, if possible, to make them more accordant with our wishes and inclinations, that is to say, to corrupt them at their very source, and entirely to destroy their worth—a thing which even common practical reason cannot ultimately call good.

Thus is the *common reason of man* compelled to go out of its sphere, and to take a step into the field of a *practical philosophy,* not to satisfy any speculative want (which never occurs to it as long as it is content to be mere sound reason), but even on practical grounds, in order to attain in it information and clear instruction respecting the source of its principle, and the correct determination of it in opposition to the maxims which are based on wants and inclinations, so that it may escape from the perplexity of opposite claims, and not run the risk of losing all genuine moral principles through the equivocation into which it easily falls. Thus, when practical reason cultivates itself, there insensibly arises in it a dialectic which forces it to seek aid in philosophy, just as happens to it in its theoretic use; and in this case, therefore, as well as in the other, it will find rest nowhere but in a thorough critical examination of our reason.

SECOND SECTION

TRANSITION FROM POPULAR MORAL PHILOSOPHY TO THE METAPHYSIC OF MORALS.

If we have hitherto drawn our notion of duty from the common use of our practical reason, it is by no means to be inferred that we have treated it as an empirical notion. On the contrary, if we attend to the experience of men's conduct, we meet frequent and, as we ourselves allow, just complaints that one cannot find a single certain example of the disposition to act from pure duty. Although many things are done in *conformity* with what *duty* prescribes, it is nevertheless always doubtful whether they are done strictly *from duty,* so as to have a moral worth. Hence there have, at all times, been philosophers who have altogether denied that this disposition actually exists at all in human actions, and have ascribed everything to a more or less refined self-love.[5] Not that they have on that account questioned the soundness of the conception of morality; on the contrary, they spoke with sincere regret of the frailty and corruption of human nature, which though noble enough to take as its rule an idea so worthy of respect, is yet too weak to follow it, and employs reason, which ought to give it the law only for the purpose of providing for the interest of the inclinations, whether singly or at the best in the greatest possible harmony with one another.

In fact, it is absolutely impossible to make out by experience with complete certainty a single case in which the maxim of an action, however right in itself, rested simply on moral grounds and on the conception of duty. Sometimes it happens that with the sharpest self-examination we can find nothing beside the moral principle of duty which could have been powerful enough to move us to this or that action and to so great a sacrifice; yet we cannot from this infer with certainty that it was not really some secret impulse of self-love, under the false appearance of duty, that was the actual determining cause of the will. We like then to flatter ourselves by falsely taking credit for a more noble motive; whereas in fact we can never, even by the strictest examination, get completely behind the secret springs of action; since when the question is of moral worth, it is not with the actions which we see that we are concerned, but with those inward principles of them which we do not see.

Moreover, we cannot better serve the wishes of those who ridicule all morality as a mere chimera of human imagination overstepping itself from vanity, than by conceding to them that notions of duty must be drawn only from experience (as from indolence, people are ready to think is also the case with all other notions); for this is to prepare for them a certain triumph. I am willing to admit out of love of humanity that even most of our actions are correct, but if we look closer at them we everywhere come upon the dear self which is always prominent, and it is this they have in view, and not the strict command of duty which would often require self-denial. Without being an enemy of virtue, a cool observer, one that does not mistake the wish for good, however lively, for its reality, may sometimes doubt whether true virtue is actually found anywhere in the world, and this especially as years increase and the judgment is partly made wiser by experience, and partly also more acute in observation. This being so, nothing can secure us from falling away altogether from our ideas of duty, or maintain in the soul a well-grounded respect for its law, but the clear conviction that although there should never have been actions which really sprang from such pure sources, yet whether this or that takes place is not at all the question; but that reason of itself, independent on all experience, ordains what ought to take place, that accordingly actions of which perhaps the world has hitherto never given an example, the feasibility even of which might be very much doubted by one who founds everything on experience, are nevertheless inflexibly commanded by reason; that, *ex. gr.* even though there might never yet have been a sincere friend, yet not a whit the less is pure sincerity in friendship required of every man, because, prior to all experience, this duty is involved as duty in the idea of a reason determining the will by *à priori* principles.

When we add further that, unless we deny that the notion of morality has any truth or reference to any possible object, we must admit that its law must be valid, not merely for men, but for all *rational creatures generally,* not merely under certain contingent conditions or with exceptions, but *with absolute necessity,* then it is clear that no experience could enable us to infer even the possibility of such apodictic laws. For with what right could we bring into unbounded respect as a universal precept for every rational nature that which perhaps holds only under the contingent conditions of humanity? Or how could laws of the determination of *our* will be regarded as laws of the determination of the will of rational beings generally, and for us only as such, if they were merely empirical, and did not take their origin wholly *à priori* from pure but practical reason?

Nor could anything be more fatal to morality than that we should wish to derive it from examples. For every example of it that is set before me must be first itself tested by principles of morality, whether it is worthy to serve as an original example, *i.e.* as a pattern, but by no means can it authoritatively furnish the conception of morality. Even the Holy One of the Gospels must first be compared with our ideal of moral perfection before we can recognise Him as such; and so He says of Himself, "Why call ye Me (whom you see) good; none is good (the model of good) but God only (whom ye do not see)?" But whence have we the conception of God as the supreme good? Simply from the *idea* of moral perfection, which reason frames *à priori,* and connects inseparably with the notion of a free-will. Imitation finds no place at all in morality, and examples serve only for encouragement, *i.e.* they put beyond doubt the feasibility of what the law commands, they make visible that which the practical rule expresses more generally, but they can never authorize us to set aside the true original which lies in reason, and to guide ourselves by examples. . . .

From what has been said, it is clear that all moral conceptions have their seat and origin completely *à priori* in the reason, and that, moreover, in the commonest reason just as truly as in that which is in the highest degree speculative; that they cannot be obtained by abstraction from any empirical, and therefore merely contingent knowledge; that it is just this purity of their origin that makes them worthy to serve as our supreme practical principle, and that just in proportion as we add anything empirical, we detract from their genuine influence, and from the absolute value of actions; that it is not only of the greatest necessity, in a purely speculative point of view, but is also of the greatest practical importance to derive these notions and laws from pure reason, to present them pure and unmixed, and even to determine the compass of this practical or pure rational knowledge, *i.e.* to determine the whole faculty of pure practical reason; and, in doing so, we must not make its principles dependent on the particular nature of human reason, though in speculative philosophy this may be permitted, or may even at times be necessary; but since moral laws ought to hold good for every rational creature, we must derive them from the general concept of a rational being. In this way, although for its *application* to man morality has need of anthropology, yet, in the first instance, we must treat it independently as pure philosophy, *i.e.* as metaphysic, complete in itself (a thing which in such distinct branches of science is easily done); knowing well that unless we are in possession of this, it would not only be vain to determine the moral element of duty in right actions for purposes of speculative criticism, but it would be impossible to base morals on their genuine principles, even for common practical purposes, especially of moral instruction, so as to produce pure moral dispositions, and to engraft them on men's minds to the promotion of the greatest possible good in the world.

But in order that in this study we may not merely advance by the natural steps from the common moral judgment (in this case very worthy of respect) to the philosophical, as has been already done, but also from a popular philosophy, which goes no further than it can reach by groping with the help of examples, to metaphysic (which does not allow itself to be checked by anything empirical, and as it must measure the whole extent of this kind of rational knowledge, goes as far as ideal conceptions, where even examples fail us), we must follow and clearly describe the practical faculty of reason, from the general rules of its determination to the point where the notion of duty springs from it.

Everything in nature works according to laws. Rational beings alone have the faculty of acting according *to the conception* of laws, that is according to principles, *i.e.* have a *will.* Since the deduction of actions from principles requires *reason,* the will is nothing but practical reason. If reason infallibly determines the will, then the actions of such a being which are recognised as objectively necessary are subjectively necessary also, *i.e.* the will is a faculty to choose *that only* which reason independent of inclination recognises as practically necessary, *i.e.* as good. But if reason of itself does not sufficiently determine the will, if the latter is subject also to subjective conditions (particular impulses) which do not always coincide with the objective conditions; in a word, if the will does not *in itself* completely accord with reason (which is actually the case with men), then the actions which objectively are recognised as necessary are subjectively contingent, and the determination of such a will according to objective laws is *obligation,* that is to say, the relation of the objective laws to a will that is not thoroughly good is conceived as the determination of the will of a rational being by principles of reason, but which the will from its nature does not of necessity follow.

The conception of an objective principle, in so far as it is obligatory for a will, is called a command (of reason), and the formula of the command is called an Imperative.

All imperatives are expressed by the word *ought* [or *shall*], and thereby indicate the relation of an objective law of reason to a will, which from its subjective constitution is not necessarily determined by it (an obligation). They say that something would be good to do or to forbear, but they say it to a will which does not always do a thing because it is conceived to be good to do it. That is practically *good,* however, which determines the will by means of the conceptions of reason, and consequently not from subjective causes, but objectively, that is on principles which are valid for every rational being as such. It is distinguished from the *pleasant,* as that which influences the will only by means of sensation from merely subjective causes, valid only for the sense of this or that one, and not as a principle of reason, which holds for every one.[6]

A perfectly good will would therefore be equally subject to objective laws (viz. laws of good), but could not be conceived as *obliged* thereby to act lawfully, because of itself from its subjective constitution it can only be determined by the conception of good. Therefore no imperatives hold for the Divine will, or in general for a *holy* will; *ought* is here out of place, because the volition is already of itself necessarily in unison with the law. Therefore imperatives are only formulae to express the relation of objective laws of all volition to the subjective imperfection of the will of this or that rational being, *e.g.* the human will.

Now all *imperatives* command either *hypothetically* or *categorically.* The former represent the practical necessity of a possible action as means to something else that is willed (or at least which one might possibly will).[7] The categorical imperative would be that which represented an action as necessary of itself without reference to another end, *i.e.* as objectively necessary.

Since every practical law represents a possible action as good, and on this account, for a subject who is practically determinable by reason, necessary, all imperatives are formulae determining an action which is necessary according to the principle of a will good in some respects. If now the action is good only as a means *to something else,* then the imperative is *hypothetical;* if it is conceived as good *in itself* and consequently as being necessarily the principle of a will which of itself conforms to reason, then it is *categorical.*

Thus the imperative declares what action possible by me would be good, and presents the practical rule in relation to a will which does not forthwith perform an action simply because it is good, whether because the subject does not always know that it is good, or because, even if it know this, yet its maxims might be opposed to the objective principles of practical reason.

Accordingly the hypothetical imperative only says that the action is good for some purpose, *possible* or *actual*. In the first case it is a Problematical, in the second an Assertorial practical principle. The categorical imperative which declares an action to be objectively necessary in itself without reference to any purpose, *i.e.* without any other end, is valid as an Apodictic (practical) principle.

Whatever is possible only by the power of some rational being may also be conceived as a possible purpose of some will; and therefore the principles of action as regards the means necessary to attain some possible purpose are in fact infinitely numerous. All sciences have a practical part, consisting of problems expressing that some end is possible for us, and of imperatives directing how it may be attained. These may, therefore, be called in general imperatives of Skill. Here there is no question whether the end is rational and good, but only what one must do in order to attain it. The precepts for the physician to make his patient thoroughly healthy, and for a poisoner to ensure certain death, are of equal value in this respect, that each serves to effect its purpose perfectly. Since in early youth it cannot be known what ends are likely to occur to us in the course of life, parents seek to have their children taught a *great many things,* and provide for their *skill* in the use of means for all sorts of arbitrary ends, of none of which can they determine whether it may not perhaps hereafter be an object to their pupil, but which it is at all events *possible* that he might aim at; and this anxiety is so great that they commonly neglect to form and correct their judgment on the value of the things which may be chosen as ends.

There is *one* end, however, which may be assumed to be actually such to all rational beings (so far as imperatives apply to them, viz. as dependent beings), and therefore, one purpose which they not merely *may* have, but which we may with certainty assume that they all actually *have* by a natural necessity, and this is *happiness.* The hypothetical imperative which expresses the practical necessity of an action as means to the advancement of happiness is Assertorial. We are not to present it as necessary for an uncertain and merely possible purpose, but for a purpose which we may presuppose with certainty and *à priori* in every man, because it belongs to his being. Now skill in the choice of means to his own greatest well-being may be called *prudence,* in the narrowest sense. And thus the imperative which refers to the choice of means to one's own happiness, *i.e.* the precept of prudence, is still always *hypothetical;* the action is not commanded absolutely, but only as means to another purpose.

Finally, there is an imperative which commands a certain conduct immediately, without having as its condition any other purpose to be attained by it. This imperative is Categorical. It concerns not the matter of the action, or its intended result, but its form and the principle of which it is itself a result; and what is essentially good in it consists in the mental disposition, let the consequence be what it may. This imperative may be called that of Morality.

There is a marked distinction also between the volitions on these three sorts of principles in the *dissimilarity* of the obligation of the will. In order to mark this difference more clearly, I think they would be most suitably named in their order if we said they are either *rules* of skill, or *counsels* of prudence, or *commands (laws)* of morality. For it is *law* only that involves the conception of an *unconditional* and objective necessity, which is consequently universally valid; and commands are laws which must be obeyed, that is, must be followed, even in opposition to inclination. *Counsels,* indeed, involve necessity, but one which can only hold under a contingent subjective condition, viz. they depend on whether this or that man reckons this or that as part of his happiness; the categorical imperative, on the contrary, is not limited by any condition, and as being absolutely, although practically, necessary, may be quite properly called a command. We might also call the first kind of imperatives *technical* (belonging to art), the second *pragmatic* (to welfare), the third *moral* (belonging to free conduct generally, that is, to morals).

Now arises the question, how are all these imperatives possible? This question does not seek to know how we can conceive the accomplishment of the action which the imperative ordains, but merely how we can conceive the obligation of the will which the imperative expresses. No special explanation is needed to show how an imperative of skill is possible. Whoever wills the end, wills also (so far as reason decides his conduct) the means in his power which are indispensably necessary thereto. This proposition is, as regards the volition, analytical; for, in willing an object as my effect, there is already thought the causality of myself as an acting cause, that is to say, the use of the means; and the imperative educes from the conception of volition of an end the conception of actions necessary to this end. Synthetical propositions must no doubt be employed in defining the means to a proposed end; but they do not concern the principle, the act of the will, but the object and its realization. *Ex. gr.*, that in order to bisect a line on an unerring principle I must draw from its extremities two intersecting arcs; this no doubt is taught by mathematics only in synthetical propositions; but if I know that it is only by this process that the intended operation can be performed, then to say that if I fully will the operation, I also will the action required for it, is an analytical proposition; for it is one and the same thing to conceive something as an effect which I can produce in a certain way, and to conceive myself as acting in this way.

If it were only equally easy to give a definite conception of happiness, the imperatives of prudence would correspond exactly with those of skill, and would likewise be analytical. For in this case as in that, it could be said, whoever wills the end, wills also (according to the dictate of reason necessarily) the indispensable means thereto which are in his power. But, unfortunately, the notion of happiness is so indefinite that although every man wishes to attain it, yet he never can say definitely and consistently what it is that he really wishes and wills. The reason of this is that all the elements which belong to the notion of happiness are altogether empirical, *i.e.* they must be borrowed from experience, and nevertheless the idea of happiness requires an absolute whole, a maximum of welfare in my present and all future circumstances. Now it is impossible that the most clear-sighted, and at the same time most powerful being (supposed finite) should frame to himself a definite conception of what he really wills in this. Does he will riches, how much anxiety, envy, and snares might he not thereby draw upon his shoulders? Does he will knowledge and discernment, perhaps it might prove to be only an eye so much the sharper to show him so much the more fearfully the evils that are now concealed from him, and that cannot be avoided, or to impose more wants on his desires, which already give him concern enough. Would he have long life, who guarantees to him that it would not be a long misery? would he at least have health? how often has uneasiness of the body restrained from excesses into which perfect health would have allowed one to fall? and so on. In short he is unable, on any principle, to determine with certainty what would make him truly happy; because to do so he would need to be omniscient. We cannot therefore act on any definite principles to secure happiness, but only on empirical counsels, *ex. gr.* of regimen, frugality, courtesy, reserve, &c.,which ,experience teaches, do, on the average, most promote well-being. Hence it follows that the imperatives of prudence do not, strictly speaking, command at all, that is, they cannot present actions objectively as practically *necessary;* that they are rather to be regarded as counsels (*consilia*) than precepts (*praecepta*) of reason, that the problem to determine certainly and universally what action would promote the happiness of a rational being is completely insoluble, and consequently no imperative respecting it is possible which should, in the strict sense, command to do what makes happy; because happiness is not an ideal of reason but of imagination, resting solely on empirical grounds, and it is vain to expect that these should define an action by which one could attain the totality of a series of consequences which is really endless. This imperative of prudence would however be an analytical proposition if we assume that the means to happiness could be certainly assigned; for it is distinguished from the imperative of skill only by this, that in the latter the end is merely possible, in the former it is given; as however both only ordain the means to that which we suppose to be willed as an end, it follows that the imperative which ordains the willing of the means to him who wills the end is in both cases analytical. Thus there is no difficulty in regard to the possibility of an imperative of this kind either.

On the other hand the question, how the imperative of *morality* is possible, is undoubtedly one, the only one, demanding a solution, as this is not at all hypothetical, and the objective necessity which it presents cannot rest on any hypothesis, as is the case with the hypothetical imperatives. Only here we must never leave out of consideration that we *cannot* make out *by any example*, in other words empirically, whether there is such an imperative at all; but it is rather to be feared that all those which seem to be categorical may yet be at bottom hypothetical. For instance, when the precept is: Thou shalt not promise deceitfully; and it is assumed that the necessity of this is not a mere counsel to avoid some other evil, so that it should mean: thou shalt not make a lying promise, lest if it become known thou shouldst destroy thy credit, but that an action of this kind must be regarded as evil in itself, so that the imperative of the prohibition is categorical; then we cannot show with certainty in any example that the will was determined merely by the law, without any other spring of action, although it may appear to be so. For it is always possible that fear of disgrace, perhaps also obscure dread of other dangers, may have a secret influence on the will. Who can prove by experience the non-existence of a cause when all that experience tells us is that we do not perceive it? But in such a case the so-called moral imperative, which as such appears to be categorical and unconditional, would in reality be only a pragmatic precept, drawing our attention to our own interests, and merely teaching us to take these into consideration.

We shall therefore have to investigate *à priori* the possibility of a categorical imperative, as we have not in this case the advantage of its reality being given in experience, so that [the elucidation of] its possibility should be requisite only for its explanation, not for its establishment. In the meantime it may be discerned beforehand that the categorical imperative alone has the purport of a practical law: all the rest may indeed be called *principles* of the will but not laws, since whatever is only necessary for the attainment of some arbitrary purpose may be considered as in itself contingent, and we can at any time be free from the precept if we give up the purpose: on the contrary, the unconditional command leaves the will no liberty to choose the opposite; consequently it alone carries with it that necessity which we require in a law.

Secondly, in the case of this categorical imperative or law of morality, the difficulty (of discerning its possibility) is a very profound one. It is an *à priori* synthetical practical proposition;[8] and as there is so much difficulty in discerning the possibility of speculative propositions of this kind, it may readily be supposed that the difficulty will be no less with the practical.

In this problem we will first inquire whether the mere conception of a categorical imperative may not perhaps supply us also with the formula of it, containing the proposition which alone can be a categorical imperative; for even if we know the tenor of such an absolute command, yet how it is possible will require further special and laborious study, which we postpone to the last section.

When I conceive a hypothetical imperative in general I do not know beforehand what it will contain until I am given the condition. But when I conceive a categorical imperative I know at once what it contains. For as the imperative contains besides the law only the necessity that the maxims[9] shall conform to this law, while the law contains no conditions restricting it, there remains nothing but the general statement that the maxim of the action should conform to a universal law, and it is this conformity alone that the imperative properly represents as necessary.

There is therefore but one categorical imperative, namely this: *Act only on that maxim whereby thou canst at the same time will that it should become a universal law.*

Now if all imperatives of duty can be deduced from this one imperative as from their principle, then, although it should remain undecided whether what is called duty is not merely a vain notion, yet at least we shall be able to show what we understand by it and what this notion means.

Since the universality of the law according to which effects are produced constitutes what is properly called *nature* in the most general sense (as to form), that is the existence of things so far as it is determined by general laws, the imperative of duty may be expressed thus: *Act as if the maxim of thy action were to become by thy will a Universal Law of Nature.*

We will now enumerate a few duties, adopting the usual division of them into duties to ourselves and to others, and into perfect and imperfect duties.

1. A man reduced to despair by a series of misfortunes feels wearied of life, but is still so far in possession of his reason that he can ask himself whether it would not be contrary to his duty to himself to take his own life. Now he inquires whether the maxim of his action could become a universal law of nature. His maxim is: From self-love I adopt it as a principle to shorten my life when its longer duration is likely to bring more evil than satisfaction. It is asked then simply whether this principle founded on self-love can become a universal law of nature. Now we see at once that a system of nature of which it should be a law to destroy life by means of the very feeling whose special nature it is to impel to the improvement of life would contradict itself, and therefore could not exist as a system of nature; hence that maxim cannot possibly exist as a universal law of nature, and consequently would be wholly inconsistent with the supreme principle of all duty.

2. Another finds himself forced by necessity to borrow money. He knows that he will not be able to repay it, but sees also that nothing will be lent to him, unless he promises stoutly to repay it in a definite time. He desires to make this promise, but he has still so much conscience as to ask himself: Is it not unlawful and inconsistent with duty to get out of a difficulty in this way? Suppose however that he resolves to do so, then the maxim of his action would be expressed thus: When I think myself in want of money, I will borrow money and promise to repay it, although I know that I never can do so. Now this principle of self-love or of one's own advantage may perhaps be consistent with my whole future welfare; but the question now is, Is it right? I change then the suggestion of self-love into a universal law, and state the question thus: How would it be if my maxim were a universal law? Then I see at once that it could never hold as a universal law of nature, but would necessarily contradict itself. For supposing it to be a universal law that everyone when he thinks himself in a difficulty should be able to promise whatever he pleases, with the purpose of not keeping his promise, the promise itself would become impossible, as well as the end that one might have in view in it, since no one would consider that anything was promised to him, but would ridicule all such statements as vain pretences.

3. A third finds in himself a talent which with the help of some culture might make him a useful man in many respects. But he finds himself in comfortable circumstances, and prefers to indulge in pleasure rather than to take pains in enlarging and improving his happy natural capacities. He asks, however, whether his maxim of neglect of his natural gifts, besides agreeing with his inclination to indulgence, agrees also with what is called duty. He sees then that a system of nature could indeed subsist with such a universal law although men (like the South Sea islanders) should let their talents rust, and resolve to devote their lives merely to idleness, amusement, and propagation of their species—in a word, to enjoyment; but he cannot possibly *will* that this should be a universal law of nature, or be implanted in us as such by a natural instinct. For, as a rational being, he necessarily wills that his faculties be developed, since they serve him, and have been given him, for all sorts of possible purposes.

4. A fourth, who is in prosperity, while he sees that others have to contend with great wretchedness and that he could help them, thinks: What concern is it of mine? Let everyone be as happy as heaven pleases, or as he can make himself; I will take nothing from him nor even envy him, only I do not wish to contribute anything to his welfare or to his assistance in distress! Now no doubt if such a mode of thinking were a universal law, the human race might very well subsist, and doubtless even better than in a state in which everyone talks of sympathy and good-will, or even takes care occasionally to put it into practice, but on the other side, also cheats when he can, betrays the rights of men, or otherwise violates them. But although it is possible that a universal law of nature might exist in accordance with that maxim, it is impossible to *will* that such a principle should have the universal validity of a law of nature. For a will which resolved this would contradict itself, inasmuch as many cases might occur in which one would have need of the love and sympathy of others, and in which, by such a law of nature, sprung from his own will, he would deprive himself of all hope of the aid he desires.

These are a few of the many actual duties, or at least what we regard as such, which obviously fall into two classes on one principle that we have laid down. We must be *able to will* that a maxim of our action should be a universal law. This is the canon of the moral appreciation of the action generally. Some actions are of such a character that their maxim cannot without contradiction be even *conceived* as a universal law of nature, far from it being possible that we should *will* that it *should* be so. In others this intrinsic impossibility is not found, but still it is impossible to *will* that their maxim should be raised to the universality of a law of nature, since such a will would contradict itself. It is easily seen that the former violate strict or rigorous (inflexible) duty; the latter only laxer (meritorious) duty. Thus it has been completely shown by these examples how all duties depend as regards the nature of the obligation (not the object of the action) on the same principle.

If now we attend to ourselves on occasion of any transgression of duty, we shall find that we in fact do not will that our maxim should be a universal law, for that is impossible for us; on the contrary we will that the opposite should remain a universal law, only we assume the liberty of making an *exception* in our own favour or (just for this time only) in favour of our inclination. Consequently if we considered all cases from one and the same point of view, namely, that of reason, we should find a contradiction in our own will, namely, that a certain principle should be objectively necessary as a universal law, and yet subjectively should not be universal, but admit of exceptions. As however we at one moment regard our action from the point of view of a will wholly conformed to reason, and then again look at the same action from the point of view of a will affected by inclination, there is not really any contradiction, but an antagonism of inclination to the precept of reason, whereby the universality of the principle is changed into a mere generality, so that the practical principle of reason shall meet the maxim half way. Now, although this cannot be justified in our own impartial judgment, yet it proves that we do really recognise the validity of the categorical imperative and (with all respect for it) only allow ourselves a few exceptions, which we think unimportant and forced from us.

We have thus established at least this much, that if duty is a conception which is to have any import and real legislative authority for our actions, it can only be expressed in categorical, and not at all in hypothetical imperatives. We have also, which is of great importance, exhibited clearly and definitely for every practical application the content of the categorical imperative, which must contain the principle of all duty if there is such a thing at all. We have not yet, however, advanced so far as to prove *à priori* that there actually is such an imperative, that there is a practical law which commands absolutely of itself, and without any other impulse, and that the following of this law is duty.

With the view of attaining to this it is of extreme importance to remember that we must not allow ourselves to think of deducing the reality of this principle from the *particular attributes of human nature.* For duty is to be a practical, unconditional necessity of action; it must therefore hold for all rational beings (to whom an imperative can apply at all) and *for this reason only* be also a law for all human wills. On the contrary, whatever is deduced from the particular natural characteristics of humanity, from certain feelings and propensions, nay even, if possible, from any particular tendency proper to human reason, and which need not necessarily hold for the will of every rational being; this may indeed supply us with a maxim, but not with a law; with a subjective principle on which we may have a propension and inclination to act, but not with an objective principle on which we should be *enjoined* to act, even though all our propensions, inclinations, and natural dispositions were opposed to it. In fact the sublimity and intrinsic dignity of the command in duty are so much the more evident, the less the subjective impulses favour it and the more they oppose it, without being able in the slighest degree to weaken the obligation of the law or to diminish its validity.

Here then we see philosophy brought to a critical position, since it has to be firmly fixed, notwithstanding that it has nothing to support it either in heaven or earth. Here it must show its purity as absolute dictator of its own laws, not the herald of those which are whispered to it by an implanted sense of who knows what tutelary nature. Although these may be better than nothing, yet they can never afford principles dictated by reason, which must have their source wholly *à priori* and thence their commanding authority, expecting everything from the supremacy of the law and the due respect for it, nothing from inclination, or else condemning the man to self-contempt and inward abhorrence.

Thus every empirical element is not only quite incapable of being an aid to the principle of morality, but is even highly prejudicial to the purity of morals, for the proper and inestimable worth of an absolutely good will consists just in this, that the principle of action is free from all influence of contingent grounds, which alone experience can furnish. We cannot too much or too often repeat our warning against this lax and even mean habit of thought which seeks for its principle amongst empirical motives and laws; for human reason in its weariness is glad to rest on this pillow, and in a dream of sweet illusions (in which, instead of Juno, it embraces a cloud) it substitutes for morality a bastard patched up from limbs of various derivation, which looks like anything one chooses to see in it; only not like virtue to one who has once beheld her in her true form.[10]

The question then is this: Is it a necessary law *for all rational beings* that they should always judge of their actions by maxims of which they can themselves will that they should serve as universal laws? If it is so, then it must be connected (altogether *à priori*) with the very conception of the will of a rational being generally. But in order to discover this connexion we must, however reluctantly, take a step into metaphysic, although into a domain of it which is distinct from speculative philosophy, namely, the metaphysic of morals. In a practical philosophy, where it is not the reasons of what *happens* that we have to ascertain, but the laws of what *ought to happen,* even although it never does, *i.e.* objective practical laws, there it is not necessary to inquire into the reasons why anything pleases or displeases, how the pleasure of mere sensation differs from taste, and whether the latter is distinct from a general satisfaction of reason; on what the feeling of pleasure or pain rests, and how from it desires and inclinations arise, and from these again maxims by the co-operation of reason: for all this belongs to an empirical psychology, which would constitute the second part of physics, if we regard physics as the *philosophy of nature,* so far as it is based on *empirical laws.* But here we are concerned with objective practical laws, and consequently with the relation of the will to itself so far as it is determined by reason alone, in which case whatever has reference to anything empirical is necessarily excluded; since if *reason of itself alone* determines the conduct (and it is the possibility of this that we are now investigating), it must necessarily do so *á priori.*

The will is conceived as a faculty of determining oneself to action *in accordance with the conception of certain laws.* And such a faculty can be found only in rational beings. Now that which serves the will as the objective ground of its self-determination is the *end,* and if this is assigned by reason alone, it must hold for all rational beings. On the other hand, that which merely contains the ground of possibility of the action of which the effect is the end, this is called the *means.* The subjective ground of the desire is the *spring,* the objective ground of the volition is the *motive*; hence the distinction between subjective ends which rest on springs, and objective ends which depend on motives valid for every rational being. Practical principles are *formal* when they abstract from all subjective ends, they are *material* when they assume these, and therefore particular springs of action. The ends which a rational being proposes to himself at pleasure as *effects* of his actions (material ends) are all only relative, for it is only their relation to the particular desires of the subject that gives them their worth, which therefore cannot furnish principles universal and necessary for all rational beings and for every volition, that is to say practical laws. Hence all these relative ends can give rise only to hypothetical imperatives.

Supposing, however, that there were something *whose existence* has *in itself* an absolute worth, something which, being *an end in itself,* could be a source of definite laws, then in this and this alone would lie the source of a possible categorical imperative, *i.e.* a practical law.

Now I say: man and generally any rational being *exists* as an end in himself, *not merely as a means* to be arbitrarily used by this or that will, but in all his actions, whether they concern himself or other rational beings, must be always regarded at the same time as an end. All objects of the inclinations have only a conditional worth, for if the inclinations and the wants founded on them did not exist, then their object would be without value. But the inclinations themselves being sources of want, are so far from having an absolute worth for which they should be desired, that on the contrary it must be the universal wish of every rational being to be wholly free from them. Thus the worth of any object which is *to be acquired* by our action is always conditional. Beings whose existence depends not on our will but on nature's, have nevertheless, if they are irrational beings, only a relative value as means, and are therefore called *things;* rational beings, on the contrary, are called *persons,* because their very nature points them out as ends in themselves, that is as something which must not be used merely as means, and so far therefore restricts freedom of action (and is an object of respect). These, therefore, are not merely subjective ends whose existence has a worth *for us* as an effect of our action, but *objective ends,* that is things whose existence is an end in itself: an end moreover for which no other can be substituted, which they should subserve *merely* as means, for otherwise nothing whatever would possess *absolute worth;* but if all worth were conditioned and therefore contingent, then there would be no supreme practical principle of reason whatever.

If then there is a supreme practical principle or, in respect of the human will, a categorical imperative, it must be one which, being drawn from the conception of that which is necessarily an end for every one because it is *an end in itself,* constitutes an *objective* principle of will, and can therefore serve as a universal practical law. The foundation of this principle is: *rational nature exists as an end in itself.* Man necessarily conceives his own existence as being so: so far then this is a *subjective* principle of human actions. But every other rational being regards its existence similarly, just on the same rational principle that holds for me:[11] so that it is at the same time an objective principle, from which as a supreme practical law all laws of the will must be capable of being deduced. Accordingly the practical imperative will be as follows: *So act as to treat humanity, whether in thine own person or in that of any other, in every case as an end withal, never as means only.* We will now inquire whether this can be practically carried out.

To abide by the previous examples:

Firstly, under the head of necessary duty to oneself: He who contemplates suicide should ask himself whether his action can be consistent with the idea of humanity *as an end in itself.* If he destroys himself in order to escape from painful circumstances, he uses a person merely as *a mean* to maintain a tolerable condition up to the end of life. But a man is not a thing, that is to say, something which can be used merely as means, but must in all his actions be always considered as an end in himself. I cannot, therefore, dispose in any way of a man in my own person so as to mutilate him, to damage or kill him. (It belongs to ethics proper to define this principle more precisely so as to avoid all misunderstanding, *e.g.* as to the amputation of the limbs in order to preserve myself; as to exposing my life to danger with a view to preserve it, &c. This question is therefore omitted here.)

Secondly, as regards necessary duties, or those of strict obligation, towards others; he who is thinking of making a lying promise to others will see at once that he would be using another man *merely as a mean,* without the latter containing at the same time the end in himself. For he whom I propose by such a promise to use for my own purposes cannot possibly assent to my mode of acting towards him, and therefore cannot himself contain the end of this action. This violation of the principle of humanity in other men is more obvious if we take in examples of attacks on the freedom and property of others. For then it is clear that he who transgresses the rights of men, intends to use the person of others merely as means, without considering that as rational beings they ought always to be esteemed also as ends, that is, as beings who must be capable of containing in themselves the end of the very same action.

Thirdly, as regards contingent (meritorious) duties to oneself; it is not enough that the action does not violate humanity in our own person as an end in itself, it must also *harmonise with* it. Now there are in humanity capacities of greater perfection, which belong to the end that nature has in view in regard to humanity in ourselves as the subject: to neglect these might perhaps be consistent with the *maintenance* of humanity as an end in itself, but not with the *advancement* of this end.

Fourthly, as regards meritorious duties

towards others: the natural end which all men have is their own happiness. Now humanity might indeed subsist, although no one should contribute anything to the happiness of others, provided he did not intentionally withdraw anything from it; but after all this would only harmonise negatively not positively with *humanity as an end in itself,* if every one does not also endeavour, as far as in him lies, to forward the ends of others. For the ends of any subject which is an end in himself, ought as far as possible to be *my* ends also, if that conception is to have its *full* effect with me.

This principle, that humanity and generally every rational nature is *an end in itself* (which is the supreme limiting condition of every man's freedom of action), is not borrowed from experience, *firstly,* because it is universal, applying as it does to all rational beings whatever, and experience is not capable of determining anything about them; *secondly,* because it does not present humanity as an end to men (subjectively), that is as an object which men do of themselves actually adopt as an end; but as an objective end, which must as a law constitute the supreme limiting condition of all our subjective ends, let them be what we will; it must therefore spring from pure reason. In fact the objective principle of all practical legislation lies (according to the first principle) in *the rule* and its form of universality which makes it capable of being a law (say, *e.g.,* a law of nature); but the *subjective* principle is in the *end;* now by the second principle the subject of all ends is each rational being, inasmuch as it is an end in itself. Hence follows the third practical principle of the will, which is the ultimate condition of its harmony with the universal practical reason, viz.: the idea of *the will of every rational being as a universally legislative will.*

On this principle all maxims are rejected which are inconsistent with the will being itself universal legislator. Thus the will is not subject simply to the law, but so subject that it must be regarded *as itself giving the law,* and on this ground only, subject to the law (of which it can regard itself as the author).

In the previous imperatives, namely, that based on the conception of the conformity of actions to general laws, as in a *physical system of nature,* and that based on the universal *prerogative* of rational beings as *ends* in themselves—these imperatives just because they were conceived as categorical, excluded from any share in their authority all admixture of any interest as a spring of action; they were however only *assumed* to be categorical, because such an assumption was necessary to explain the conception of duty. But we could not prove independently that there are practical propositions which command categorically, nor can it be proved in this section; one thing however could be done, namely, to indicate in the imperative itself by some determinate expression, that in the case of volition from duty all interest is renounced, which is the specific criterion of categorical as distinguished from hypothetical imperatives. This is done in the present (third) formula of the principle, namely, in the idea of the will of every rational being as a *universally legislating will.*

For although a will *which is subject to laws* may be attached to this law by means of an interest, yet a will which is itself a supreme lawgiver so far as it is such cannot possibly depend on any interest, since a will so dependent would itself still need another law restricting the interest of its self-love by the condition that it should be valid as universal law.

Thus the *principle* that every human will is *a will which in all its maxims gives universal laws,* provided it be otherwise justified, would be very *well adapted* to be the categorical imperative, in this respect, namely, that just because of the idea of universal legislation it is *not based on any interest,* and therefore it alone among all possible imperatives can be *unconditional.* Or still better, converting the proposition, if there is a categorical imperative (*i.e.,* a law for the will of every rational being), it can only command that everything be done from maxims of one's will regarded as a will which could at the same time will that it should itself give universal laws, for in that case only the practical principle and the imperative which it obeys are unconditional, since they cannot be based on any interest.

Looking back now on all previous attempts to discover the principle of morality, we need not wonder why they all failed. It was seen that man was bound to laws by duty, but it was not observed that the laws to which he is subject are *only those of his own giving,* though at the same time they are *universal,* and that he is only bound to act in conformity with his own will; a will, however, which is designed by nature to give universal laws. For when one has conceived man only as subject to a law (no matter what), then this law required some interest, either by way of attraction or constraint, since it did not originate as a law from *his own* will, but this will was according to a law obliged by *something else* to act in a certain manner. Now by this necessary consequence all the labour spent in finding a supreme principle of *duty* was irrevocably lost. For men never elicited duty, but only a necessity of acting from a certain interest. Whether this interest was private or otherwise, in any case the imperative must be conditional, and could not by any means be capable of being a moral command. I will therefore call this the principle of *Autonomy* of the will, in contrast with every other which I accordingly reckon as *Heteronomy.*

The conception of every rational being as one which must consider itself as giving in all the maxims of its will universal laws, so as to judge itself and its actions from this point of view—this conception leads to another which depends on it and is very fruitful, namely, that of *a kingdom of ends.*

By a *kingdom* I understand the union of different rational beings in a system by common laws. Now since it is by laws that ends are determined as regards their universal validity, hence, if we abstract from the personal differences of rational beings, and likewise from all the content of their private ends, we shall be able to conceive all ends combined in a systematic whole (including both rational beings as ends in themselves, and also the special ends which each may propose to himself), that is to say, we can conceive a kingdom of ends, which on the preceding principles is possible.

For all rational beings come under the *law* that each of them must treat itself and all others *never merely as means,* but in every case *at the same time as ends in themselves.* Hence results a systematic union of rational beings by common objective laws, *i.e.,* a kingdom which may be called a kingdom of ends, since what these laws have in view is just the relation of these beings to one another as ends and means. It is certainly only an ideal.

A rational being belongs as a *member* to the kingdom of ends when, although giving universal laws in it, he is also himself subject to these laws. He belongs to it *as sovereign* when, while giving laws, he is not subject to the will of any other.

A rational being must always regard himself as giving laws either as member or as sovereign in a kingdom of ends which is rendered possible by the freedom of will. He cannot, however, maintain the latter position merely by the maxims of his will, but only in case he is a completely independent being without wants and with unrestricted power adequate to his will.

Morality consists then in the reference of all action to the legislation which alone can render a kingdom of ends possible. This legislation must be capable of existing in every rational being, and of emanating from his will, so that the principle of this will is, never to act on any maxim which could not without contradiction be also a universal law, and accordingly always so to act *that the will could at the same time regard itself as giving in its maxims universal laws.* If now the maxims of rational beings are not by their own nature coincident with this objective principle, then the necessity of acting on it is called practical necessitation, i.e., *duty.* Duty does not apply to the sovereign in the kingdom of ends, but it does to every member of it and to all in the same degree.

The practical necessity of acting on this principle, *i.e.,* duty, does not rest at all on feelings, impulses, or inclinations, but solely on the relation of rational beings to one another, a relation in which the will of a rational being must always be regarded as *legislative,* since otherwise it could not be conceived as *an end in itself.* Reason then refers every maxim of the will, regarding it as legislating universally, to every other will and also to every action towards oneself; and this not on account of any other practical motive or any future advantage, but from the idea of the *dignity* of a rational being, obeying no law but that which he himself also gives.

In the kingdom of ends everything has either Value or Dignity. Whatever has a value can be replaced by something else which is *equivalent;* whatever, on the other hand, is above all value, and therefore admits of no equivalent, has a dignity.

Whatever has reference to the general inclinations and wants of mankind has a *market value;* whatever, without presupposing a want, corresponds to a certain taste, that is to a satisfaction in the mere purposeless play of our faculties, has a *fancy value;* but that which constitutes the condition under which alone anything can be an end in itself, this has not merely a relative worth, *i.e.,* value, but an intrinsic worth, that is *dignity.*

Now morality is the condition under which alone a rational being can be an end in himself, since by this alone is it possible that he should be a legislating member in the kingdom of ends. Thus morality, and humanity as capable of it, is that which alone has dignity. Skill and diligence in labour have a market value; wit, lively imagination, and humour, have fancy value; on the other hand, fidelity to promises, benevolence from principle (not from instinct), have an intrinsic worth. Neither nature nor art contains anything which in default of these it could put in their place, for their worth consists not in the effects which spring from them, not in the use and advantage which they secure, but in the disposition of mind, that is, the maxims of the will which are ready to manifest themselves in such actions, even though they should not have the desired effect. These actions also need no recommendation from any subjective taste or sentiment, that they may be looked on with immediate favour and satisfaction: they need no immediate propension or feeling for them; they exhibit the will that performs them as an object of an immediate respect, and nothing but reason is required to *impose* them on the will; not to *flatter* it into them, which, in the case of duties, would be a contradiction. This estimation therefore shows that the worth of such a disposition is dignity, and places it infinitely above all value, with which it cannot for a moment be brought into comparison or competition without as it were violating its sanctity.

What then is it which justifies virtue or the morally good disposition, in making such lofty claims? It is nothing less than the privilege it secures to the rational being of participating in the giving of universal laws, by which it qualifies him to be a member of a possible kingdom of ends, a privilege to which he was already destined by his own nature as being an end in himself, and on that account legislating in the kingdom of ends; free as regards all laws of physical nature, and obeying those only which he himself gives, and by which his maxims can belong to a system of universal law, to which at the same time he submits himself. For nothing has any worth except what the law assigns it. Now the legislation itself which assigns the worth of everything, must for that very reason possess dignity, that is an unconditional incomparable worth, and the word *respect* alone supplies a becoming expression for the esteem which a rational being must have for it. *Autonomy* then is the basis of the dignity of human and of every rational nature.

The three modes of presenting the principle of morality that have been adduced are at bottom only so many formulae of the very same law, and each of itself involves the other two. There is, however, a difference in them, but it is rather subjectively than objectively practical, intended namely to bring an idea of the reason nearer to intuition (by means of a certain analogy), and thereby nearer to feeling. All maxims, in fact, have—

1. A *form,* consisting in universality; and in this view the formula of the moral imperative is expressed thus, that the maxims must be so chosen as if they were to serve as universal laws of nature.

2. A *matter,* namely, an end, and here the formula says that the rational being, as it is an end by its own nature and therefore an end in itself, must in every maxim serve as the condition limiting all merely relative and arbitrary ends.

3. A *complete characterisation* of all maxims by means of that formula, namely, that all maxims ought by their own legislation to harmonise with a possible kingdom of ends as with a kingdom of nature.[12] There is a progress here in the order of the categories of *unity* of the form of the will (its universality), *plurality* of the matter (the objects, *i.e.,* the ends), and *totality* of the system of these. In forming our moral *judgment* of actions it is better to proceed always on the strict method, and start from the general formula of the categorical imperative: *Act according to a maxim which can at the same time make itself a universal law.* If, however, we wish to gain an *entrance* for the moral law, it is very useful to bring one and the same action under the three specified conceptions, and thereby as far as possible to bring it nearer to intuition.

We can now end where we started at the

beginning, namely, with the conception of a will unconditionally good. *That will* is *absolutely good* which cannot be evil, in other words, whose maxim, if made a universal law, could never contradict itself. This principle then is its supreme law: Act always on such a maxim as thou canst at the same time will to be a universal law; this is the sole condition under which a will can never contradict itself; and such an imperative is categorical. Since the validity of the will as a universal law for possible actions is analogous to the universal connexion of the existence of things by general laws, which is the formal notion of nature in general, the categorical imperative can also be expressed thus: *Act on maxims which can at the same time have for their object themselves as universal laws of nature.* Such then is the formula of an absolutely good will.

John Stuart Mill: Utilitarianism

CHAPTER I

GENERAL REMARKS

There are few circumstances among those which make up the present condition of human knowledge, more unlike what might have been expected, or more significant of the backward state in which speculation on the most important subjects still lingers, than the little progress which has been made in the decision of the controversy respecting the criterion of right and wrong. From the dawn of philosophy, the question concerning the *summum bonum,*[1] or, what is the same thing, concerning the foundation of morality, has been accounted the main problem in speculative thought, has occupied the most gifted intellects, and divided them into sects and schools, carrying on a vigorous warfare against one another. And after more than two thousand years the same discussions continue, philosophers are still ranged under the same contending banners, and neither thinkers nor mankind at large seem nearer to being unanimous on the subject, than when the youth Socrates listened to the old Protagoras, and asserted (if Plato's dialogue be grounded on real conversation) the theory of utilitarianism against the popular morality of the so-called sophist.

It is true that similar confusion and uncertainty, and in some cases similar discordance, exist respecting the first principles of all the sciences, not excepting that which is deemed the most certain of them, mathematics; without much impairing, generally indeed without impairing at all, the trustworthiness of the conclusions of those sciences. An apparent anomaly, the explanation of which is that the detailed doctrines of a science are not usually deduced from, nor depend for their evidence upon, what are called its first principles. Were it not so, there would be no science more precarious, or whose conclusions were more insufficiently made out, than algebra; which derives none of its certainty from what are commonly taught to learners as its elements, since these, as laid down by some of its most eminent teachers, are as full of fictions as English law, and of mysteries as theology. The truths which are ultimately accepted as the first principles of a science, are really the last results of metaphysical analysis, practiced on the elementary notions with which the science is conversant; and their relation to the science is not that of foundations to an edifice, but of roots to a tree, which may perform their office equally well though they be never dug down to and exposed to light. But though in science the particular truths precede the general theory, the contrary might be expected to be the case with a practical art, such as morals or legislation. All action is for the sake of some end, and rules of action, it seems natural to suppose, must take their whole character and color from the end to which they are subservient. When we engage in a pursuit, a clear and precise conception of what we are pursuing would seem to be the first thing we need, instead of the last we are to look forward to. A test of right and wrong must be the means, one would think, of ascertaining what is right or wrong,

From John Stuart Mill, *Utilitarianism* (selections).

and not a consequence of having already ascertained it.

The difficulty is not avoided by having recourse to the popular theory of a natural faculty, a sense or instinct, informing us of right and wrong. For—besides that the existence of such a moral instinct is itself one of the matters in dispute—those believers in it who have any pretensions to philosophy, have been obliged to abandon the idea that it discerns what is right or wrong in the particular case at hand, as our other senses discern the sight or sound actually present. Our moral faculty, according to all those of its interpreters who are entitled to the name of thinkers, supplies us only with the general principles of moral judgments; it is a branch of our reason, not of our sensitive faculty; and must be looked to for the abstract doctrines of morality, not for perception of it in the concrete. The intuitive, no less than what may be termed the inductive, school of ethics, insists on the necessity of general laws. They both agree that the morality of an individual action is not a question of direct perception, but of the application of a law to an individual case. They recognize also, to a great extent, the same moral laws; but differ as to their evidence, and the source from which they derive their authority. According to the one opinion, the principles of morals are evident *a priori,* requiring nothing to command assent, except that the meaning of the terms be understood. According to the other doctrine, right and wrong, as well as truth and falsehood, are questions of observation and experience. But both hold equally that morality must be deduced from principles; and the intuitive school affirms as strongly as the inductive that there is a science of morals. Yet they seldom attempt to make out a list of the *a priori* principles which are to serve as the premises of the science; still more rarely do they make any effort to reduce those various principles to one first principle, or common ground of obligation. They either assume the ordinary precepts of morals as of *a priori* authority, or they lay down as the common groundwork of those maxims some generality much less obviously authoritative than the maxims themselves, and which has never succeeded in gaining popular acceptance. Yet to support their pretensions there ought either to be some one fundamental principle or law, at the root of all morality, or if there be several, there should be a determinate order of precedence among them; and the one principal, or the rule for deciding between the various principles when they conflict, ought to be self-evident.

To inquire how far the bad effects of this deficiency have been mitigated in practice, or to what extent the moral beliefs of mankind have been vitiated or made uncertain by the absence of any distinct recognition of an ultimate standard, would imply a complete survey and criticism of past and present ethical doctrine. It would, however, be easy to show that whatever steadiness or consistency these moral beliefs have attained, has been mainly due to the tacit influence of a standard not recognized. Although the nonexistence of an acknowledged first principle has made ethics not so much a guide as a consecration of men's actual sentiments, still, as men's sentiments, both of favor and of aversion, are greatly influenced by what they suppose to be the effect of things upon their happiness, the principle of utility, or as Bentham latterly called it, the greatest happiness principle, has had a large share in forming the moral doctrines even of those who most scornfully reject its authority. Nor is there any school of thought which refuses to admit that the influence of actions on happiness is a most material and even predominant consideration in many of the details of morals, however unwilling to acknowledge it as the fundamental principle of morality, and the source of moral obligation. I might go much further, and say that to all those *a priori* moralists who deem it necessary to argue at all, utilitarian arguments are indispensable. It is not my present purpose to criticize these thinkers; but I cannot help referring, for illustration, to a systematic treatise by one of the most illustrious of them, the *Metaphysics of Ethics,* by Kant. This remarkable man, whose system of thought will long remain one of the landmarks in the history of philosophical speculation, does, in the treatise in question, lay down a universal first principle as the origin and ground of moral obligation; it is this:—"So act, that the rule on which thou actest would admit of being adopted as a law by all rational beings." But when he begins to deduce from this precept any of the actual duties of morality, he fails, almost grotesquely, to show that there would be any contradiction, any logical (not to say physical) impossibility, in the adoption by all rational beings of the most outrageously immoral rules of conduct. All he shows is that the *consequences* of their universal adoption would be such as no one would choose to incur.

On the present occasion, I shall, without further discussion of the other theories, attempt to contribute something towards the understanding and appreciation of the *utilitarian* or *happiness* theory, and towards such proof as it is susceptible of. It is evident that this cannot be proof in the ordinary and popular meaning of the term. Questions of ultimate ends are not amenable to direct proof. Whatever can be proved to be good, must be so by being shown to be a means to something admitted to be good without proof. The medical art is proved to be good by its conducing to health; but how is it possible to prove that health is good? The art of music is good, for the reason, among others, that it produces pleasure; but what proof is it possible to give that pleasure is good? If, then, it is asserted that there is a comprehensive formula, including all things which are in themselves good, and that whatever else is good, is not so as an end, but as a mean, the formula may be accepted or rejected, but is not a subject of what is commonly understood by proof. We are not, however, to infer that its acceptance or rejection must depend on blind impulse, or arbitrary choice. There is a larger meaning of the word proof, in which this question is as amenable to it as any other of the disputed questions of philosophy. The subject is within the cognizance of the rational faculty; and neither does that faculty deal with it solely in the way of intuition. Considerations may be presented capable of determining the intellect either to give or withhold its assent to the doctrine; and this is equivalent to proof.

We shall examine presently of what nature are these considerations; in what manner they apply to the case, and what rational grounds, therefore, can be given for accepting or rejecting the utilitarian formula. But it is a preliminary condition of rational acceptance or rejection, that the formula should be correctly understood. I believe that the very imperfect notion ordinarily formed of its meaning is the chief obstacle which impedes its reception; and that could it be cleared, even from only the grosser misconceptions, the question would be greatly simplified, and a large proportion of its difficulties removed. Before, therefore, I attempt to enter into the philosophical grounds which can be given for assenting to the utilitarian standard, I shall offer some illustrations of the doctrine itself; with the view of showing more clearly what it is, distinguishing it from what it is not, and disposing of such of the practical objections to it as either originate in, or are closely connected with, mistaken interpretations of its meaning. Having thus prepared the ground, I shall afterwards endeavor to throw such light as I can upon the question, considered as one of philosophical theory.

CHAPTER II

WHAT UTILITARIANISM IS

A passing remark is all that needs to be given to the ignorant blunder of supposing that those who stand up for utility as the test of right and wrong, use the term in that restricted and merely colloquial sense in which utility is opposed to pleasure. An apology is due to the philosophical opponents of utilitarianism, for even the momentary appearance of confounding them with anyone capable of so absurd a misconception; which is the more extraordinary, inasmuch as the contrary accusation, of referring everything to pleasure, and that too in its grossest form, is another of the common charges against utilitarianism: and, as has been pointedly remarked by an able writer, the same sort of persons, and often the very same persons, denounce the theory "as impracticably dry when the word utility precedes the word pleasure, and as too practicably voluptuous when the word pleasure precedes the word utility." Those who know anything about the matter are aware that every writer, from Epicurus to Bentham, who maintained the theory of utility, meant by it, not something to be contradistinguished from pleasure, but pleasure itself, together with exemption from pain; and instead of opposing the useful to the agreeable or the ornamental, have always declared that the useful means these, among other things. Yet the common herd, including the herd of writers, not only in newspapers, and periodicals, but in books of weight and pretension, are perpetually falling into this shallow mistake. Having caught up the word 'utilitarian,' while knowing nothing whatever about it but its sound, they habitually express by it the rejection, or the neglect, of pleasure in some of its forms: of beauty, of ornament, or of amusement. Nor is the term thus ignorantly misapplied solely in disparagement, but occasionally in compliment; as though it implied superiority to frivolity and the mere pleasures of the moment. And this perverted use is the only one in which the word is popularly known, and the one from which the new generation are acquiring their sole notion of its meaning. Those who introduced the word, but who had for many years discontinued it as a distinctive appellation, may well feel themselves called upon to resume it, if by doing so they can hope to contribute anything towards rescuing it from this utter degradation.

The creed which accepts as the foundation of morals *utility*, or the *greatest happiness principle*, holds that actions are right in proportion as they tend to promote happiness, wrong as they tend to produce the reverse of happiness. By 'happiness' is intended pleasure, and the absence of pain; by 'unhappiness,' pain, and the privation of pleasure. To give a clear view of the moral standard set up by the theory, much more requires to be said; in particular, what things it includes in the ideas of pain and pleasure; and to what extent this is left an open question. But these supplementary explanations do not affect the theory of life on which this theory of morality is grounded—namely, that pleasure, and freedom from pain, are the only things desirable as ends; and that all desirable things (which are as numerous in the utilitarian as in any other scheme) are desirable either for the pleasure inherent in themselves, or as means to the promotion of pleasure and the prevention of pain.

Now such a theory of life excites in many minds, and among them in some of the most estimable in feeling and purpose, inveterate dislike. To suppose that life has (as they express it) no higher end than pleasure—no better and nobler object of desire and pursuit—they designate as utterly mean and groveling; as a doctrine worthy only of swine, to whom the followers of Epicurus were, at a very early period, contemptuously likened; and modern holders of the doctrine are occasionally made the subject of equally polite comparisons by its German, French, and English assailants.

When thus attacked, the Epicureans have always answered that it is not they but their accusers who represent human nature in a degrading light; since the accusation supposes human beings to be capable of no pleasures except those of which swine are capable. If this supposition were true, the charge could not be gainsaid, but would then be no longer an imputation; for if the sources of pleasure were precisely the same to human beings and to swine, the rule of life which is good enough for the one would be good enough for the other. The comparison of the Epicurean life to that of beasts is felt as degrading, precisely because a beast's pleasures do not satisfy a human being's conceptions of happiness. Human beings have faculties more elevated than the animal appetites, and when once made conscious of them, do not regard anything as happiness which does not include their gratification. I do not, indeed, consider the Epicureans to have been by any means faultless in drawing out their scheme of consequences from the utilitarian principle. To do this in any sufficient manner, many Stoic, as well as Christian elements require to be included. But there is no known Epicurean theory of life which does not assign to the pleasures of the intellect, of the feelings and imagination, and of the moral sentiments, a much higher value as pleasures than to those of mere sensation. It must be admitted, however, that utilitarian writers in general have placed the superiority of mental over bodily pleasures chiefly in the greater permanency, safety, uncostliness, etc., of the former—that is, in their circumstantial advantages rather than in their intrinsic nature. And on all these points utilitarians have fully proved their case; but they might have taken the other, and, as it may be called, higher ground, with entire consistency. It is quite compatible with the principle of utility to recognize the fact, that some *kinds* of pleasure are more desirable and more valuable than others. It would be absurd that while, in estimating all other things, quality is considered as well as quantity, the estimation of pleasures should be supposed to depend on quantity alone.

If I am asked what I mean by difference of

quality in pleasures, or what makes one pleasure more valuable than another merely as a pleasure, except its being greater in amount, there is but one possible answer. Of two pleasures, if there be one to which all or almost all who have experience of both give a decided preference, irrespective of any feeling of moral obligation to prefer it, that is the more desirable pleasure. If one of the two is, by those who are competently acquainted with both, placed so far above the other that they prefer it, even though knowing it to be attended with a greater amount of discontent, and would not resign it for any quantity of the other pleasure which their nature is capable of, we are justified in ascribing to the preferred enjoyment a superiority in quality, so far outweighing quantity as to render it, in comparison, of small account.

Now it is an unquestionable fact that those who are equally acquainted with, and equally capable of appreciating and enjoying, both, do give a most marked preference to the manner of existence which employs their higher faculties. Few human creatures would consent to be changed into any of the lower animals, for a promise of the fullest allowance of a beast's pleasures; no intelligent human being would consent to be a fool, no instructed person would be an ignoramus, no person of feeling and conscience would be selfish and base, even though they should be persuaded that the fool, the dunce, or the rascal is better satisfied with his lot than they are with theirs. They would not resign what they possess more than he for the most complete satisfaction of all the desires which they have in common with him. If they ever fancy they would, it is only in cases of unhappiness so extreme, that to escape from it they would exchange their lot for almost any other, however undesirable in their own eyes. A being of higher faculties requires more to make him happy, is capable probably of more acute suffering, and certainly accessible to it at more points, than one of an inferior type; but in spite of these liabilities, he can never really wish to sink into what he feels to be a lower grade of existence. We may give what explanation we please of this unwillingness: we may attribute it to pride, a name which is given indiscriminately to some of the most and to some of the least estimable feelings of which mankind are capable; we may refer it to the love of liberty and personal independence, an appeal to which was with the Stoics one of the most effective means for the inculcation of it; to the love of power, or to the love of excitement, both of which do really enter into and contribute to it: but its most appropriate appellation is a sense of dignity, which all human beings possess in one form or other, and in some, though by no means in exact, proportion to their higher faculties, and which is so essential a part of the happiness of those in whom it is strong, that nothing which conflicts with it could be, otherwise than momentarily, an object of desire to them. Whoever supposes that this preference takes place at a sacrifice of happiness—that the superior being, in anything like equal circumstances, is not happier than the inferior—confounds the two very different ideas, of *happiness* and *contentment.* It is indisputable that the being whose capacities of enjoyment are low, has the greatest chance of having them fully satisfied; and a highly endowed being will always feel that any happiness which he can look for, as the world is constituted, is imperfect. But he can learn to bear its imperfections, if they are at all bearable; and they will not make him envy the being who is indeed unconscious of the imperfections, but only because he feels not at all the good which those imperfections qualify. It is better to be a human being dissatisfied than a pig satisfied; better to be Socrates dissatisfied than a fool satisfied. And if the fool, or the pig, are of a different opinion, it is because they only know their own side of the question. The other party to the comparison knows both sides.

It may be objected that many who are capable of the higher pleasures, occasionally, under the influence of temptation, postpone them to the lower. But this is quite compatible with a full appreciation of the intrinsic superiority of the higher. Men often, from infirmity of character, make their election for the nearer good, though they know it to be the less valuable; and this no less when the choice is between two bodily pleasures, than when it is between bodily and mental. They pursue sensual indulgences to the injury of health, though perfectly aware that health is the greater good. It may be further objected that many who begin with youthful enthusiasm for everything noble, as they advance in years sink into indolence and selfishness. But I do not believe that those who undergo this very common change, voluntarily choose the lower description of pleasures in preference to the higher. I believe that before they devote themselves exclusively to the one, they have already become incapable of the other. Capacity for the nobler feelings is in most natures a very tender plant, easily killed, not only by hostile influences, but by mere want of sustenance; and in the majority of young persons it speedily dies away if the occupations to which their position in life has devoted them, and the society into which it has thrown them, are not favorable to keeping that higher capacity in exercise. Men lose their high aspirations as they lose their intellectual tastes, because they have not time or opportunity for indulging them; and they addict themselves to inferior pleasures not because they deliberately prefer them, but because they are either the only ones to which they have access or the only ones which they are any longer capable of enjoying. It may be questioned whether anyone who has remained equally susceptible to both classes of pleasures, ever knowingly and calmly preferred the lower; though many, in all ages, have broken down in an ineffectual attempt to combine both.

From this verdict of the only competent judges I apprehend there can be no appeal. On a question which is the best worth having of two pleasures, or which of two modes of existence is the most grateful to the feelings, apart from its moral attributes and from its consequences, the judgment of those who are qualified by knowledge of both, or, if they differ, that of the majority among them, must be admitted as final. And there need be the less hesitation to accept this judgment respecting the quality of pleasures, since there is no other tribunal to be referred to even on the question of quantity. What means are there of determining which is the acutest of two pains, or the intensest of two pleasurable sensations, except the general suffrage of those who are familiar with both? Neither pains nor pleasures are homogeneous, and pain is always heterogeneous with pleasure. What is there to decide whether a particular pleasure is worth purchasing at the cost of a particular pain, except the feelings and judgment of the experienced? When, therefore, those feelings and judgment declare the pleasures derived from the higher faculties to be preferable *in kind,* apart from the question of intensity, to those of which the animal nature, disjoined from the higher faculties, is suspectible, they are entitled on this subject to the same regard.

I have dwelt on this point, as being a necessary part of a perfectly just conception of utility, or happiness, considered as the directive rule of human conduct. But it is by no means an indispensable condition to the acceptance of the utilitarian standard; for that standard is not the agent's own greatest happiness, but the greatest amount of happiness altogether; and if it may possibly be doubted whether a noble character is always the happier for its nobleness, there can be no doubt that it makes other people happier, and that the world in general is immensely a gainer by it. Utilitarianism, therefore, could only attain its end by the general cultivation of nobleness of character, even if each individual were only benefited by the nobleness of others, and his own, so far as happiness is concerned, were a sheer deduction from the benefit. But the bare enunciation of such an absurdity as this last renders refutation superfluous.

According to the 'greatest happiness principle,' as above explained, the ultimate end, with reference to and for the sake of which all other things are desirable (whether we are considering our own good or that of other people), is an existence exempt as far as possible from pain, and as rich as possible in enjoyments, both in point of quantity and quality; the test of quality, and the rule for measuring it against quantity, being the preference felt by those who in their opportunities of experience, to which must be added their habits of self-consciousness and self-observation, are best furnished with the means of comparison. This, being, according to the utilitarian opinion, the end of human action, is necessarily also the standard of morality; which may accordingly be defined, the rules and precepts for human conduct, by the observance of which an existence such as has been described might be, to the greatest extent possible, secured to all mankind; and not to them only, but, so far as the nature of things admits, to the whole sentient creation.

Against this doctrine, however, arises another

class of objectors, who say that happiness, in any form, cannot be the rational purpose of human life and action; because, in the first place, it is unattainable: and they contemptuously ask, what right hast thou to be happy?—a question which Mr. Carlyle[2] clenches by the addition, What right, a short time ago, hadst thou even *to be?* Next, they say that men can do *without* happiness; that all noble human beings have felt this, and could not have become noble but by learning the lesson of *Entsagen,* or renunciation; which lesson, thoroughly learnt and submitted to, they affirm to be the beginning and necessary condition of all virtue.

The first of these objections would go to the root of the matter were it well founded; for if no happiness is to be had at all by human beings, the attainment of it cannot be the end of morality, or of any rational conduct. Though, even in that case, something might still be said for the utilitarian theory; since utility includes not solely the pursuit of happiness, but the prevention or mitigation of unhappiness; and if the former aim be chimerical, there will be all the greater scope and more imperative need for the latter, so long at least as mankind think fit to live, and do not take refuge in the simultaneous act of suicide recommended under certain conditions by Novalis.[3] When, however, it is thus positively asserted to be impossible that human life should be happy, the assertion, if not something like a verbal quibble, is at least an exaggeration. If by happiness be meant a continuity of highly pleasurable excitement, it is evident enough that this is impossible. A state of exalted pleasure lasts only moments, or in some cases, and with some intermissions, hours or days, and is the occasional brilliant flash of enjoyment, not its permanent and steady flame. Of this the philosophers who have taught that happiness is the end of life were as fully aware as those who taunt them. The happiness which they meant was not a life of rapture; but moments of such, in an existence made up of few and transitory pains, many and various pleasures, with a decided predominance of the active over the passive, and having as the foundation of the whole, not to expect more from life than it is capable of bestowing. A life thus composed, to those who have been fortunate enough to obtain it, has always appeared worthy of the name of happiness. And such an existence is even now the lot of many, during some considerable portion of their lives. The present wretched education, and wretched social arrangements, are the only real hindrance to its being attainable by almost all.

The objectors perhaps may doubt whether human beings, if taught to consider happiness as the end of life, would be satisfied with such a moderate share of it. But great numbers of mankind have been satisfied with much less. The main constituents of a satisfied life appear to be two, either of which by itself is often found sufficient for the purpose: tranquillity and excitement. With much tranquillity, many find that they can be content with very little pleasure; with much excitement, many can reconcile themselves to a considerable quantity of pain. There is assuredly no inherent impossibility in enabling even the mass of mankind to unite both; since the two are so far from being incompatible that they are in natural alliance, the prolongation of either being a preparation for, and exciting a wish for, the other. It is only those in whom indolence amounts to a vice, that do not desire excitement after an interval of repose; it is only those in whom the need of excitement is a disease, that feel the tranquillity which follows excitement dull and insipid, instead of pleasurable in direct proportion to the excitement which preceded it. When people who are tolerably fortunate in their outward lot do not find in life sufficient enjoyment to make it valuable to them, the cause generally is, caring for nobody but themselves. To those who have neither public nor private affections, the excitements of life are much curtailed, and in any case dwindle in value as the time approaches when all selfish interests must be terminated by death; while those who leave after them objects of personal affection, and especially those who have also cultivated a fellow-feeling with the collective interests of mankind, retain as lively an interest in life on the eve of death as in the vigor of youth and health. Next to selfishness, the principal cause which makes life unsatisfactory is want of mental cultivation. A cultivated mind (I do not mean that of a philosopher, but any mind to which the fountains of knowledge have been opened, and which has been taught, in any tolerable degree, to exercise its faculties) finds sources of inexhaustible interest in all that surrounds it; in the objects of nature, the achievements of art, the imaginations of poetry, the incidents of history, the ways of mankind, past and present, and their prospects in the future. It is possible, indeed, to become indifferent to all this, and that too without having exhausted a thousandth part of it; but only when one has had from the beginning no moral or human interest in these things, and has sought in them only the gratification of curiosity.

Now there is absolutely no reason in the nature of things why an amount of mental culture sufficient to give an intelligent interest in these objects of contemplation, should not be the inheritance of everyone born in a civilized country. As little is there an inherent necessity that any human being should be a selfish egotist, devoid of every feeling or care but those which center in his own miserable individuality. Something far superior to this is sufficiently common even now, to give ample earnest of what the human species may be made. Genuine private affections, and a sincere interest in the public good, are possible, though in unequal degrees, to every rightly brought up human being. In a world in which there is so much to interest, so much to enjoy, and so much also to correct and improve, everyone who has this moderate amount of moral and intellectual requisites is capable of an existence which may be called enviable; and unless such a person, through bad laws, or subjection to the will of others, is denied the liberty to use the sources of happiness within his reach, he will not fail to find this enviable existence, if he escape the positive evils of life, the greater sources of physical and mental suffering—such as indigence, disease, and the unkindness, worthlessness, or premature loss of objects of affection. The main stress of the problem lies, therefore, in the contest with these calamities, from which it is a rare good fortune entirely to escape; which, as things now are, cannot be obviated, and often cannot be in any material degree mitigated. Yet no one whose opinion deserves a moment's consideration can doubt that most of the great positive evils of the world are in themselves removable, and will, if human affairs continue to improve, be in the end reduced within narrow limits. Poverty, in any sense implying suffering, may be completely extinguished by the wisdom of society, combined with the good sense and providence of individuals. Even that most intractable of enemies, disease, may be indefinitely reduced in dimensions by good physical and moral education, and proper control of noxious influences; while the progress of science holds out a promise for the future of still more direct conquests over this detestable foe. And every advance in that direction relieves us from some, not only of the chances which cut short our own lives, but, what concerns us still more, which deprive us of those in whom our happiness is wrapt up. As for vicissitudes of fortune, and other disappointments connected with worldly circumstances, these are principally the effect either of gross imprudence, of ill-regulated desires, or of bad or imperfect social institutions. All the grand sources, in short, of human suffering are in a great degree, many of them almost entirely, conquerable by human care and effort; and though their removal is grievously slow—though a long succession of generations will perish in the breach before the conquest is completed, and this world becomes all that, if will and knowledge were not wanting, it might easily be made—yet every mind sufficiently intelligent and generous to bear a part, however small and unconspicuous, in the endeavor, will draw a noble enjoyment from the contest itself, which he would not for any bribe in the form of selfish indulgence consent to be without.

And this leads to the true estimation of what is said by the objectors concerning the possibility, and the obligation, of learning to do without happiness. Unquestionably it is possible to do without happiness; it is done involuntarily by nineteen-twentieths of mankind, even in those parts of our present world which are least deep in barbarism; and it often has to be done voluntarily by the hero or the martyr, for the sake of something which he prizes more than his individual happiness. But this something, what is it, unless the happiness of others, or some of the requisites of happiness? It is noble to be capable of resigning entirely one's own portion of happiness, or chances of it: but, after all, this self-sacrifice must be for some end; it is not its own end; and if we are told that its end is not happiness, but virtue, which is better than happiness, I ask, would the sacrifice be made if the hero or martyr did not believe that it would earn for others immunity from similar sacrifices? Would it be made if he thought that his renunciation of happiness for himself would produce no fruit for any of his fellow creatures, but to make their lot like his, and place them also in the condition of persons who have renounced happiness? All honor to those who can abnegate for themselves the personal enjoyment of life, when by such renunciation they contribute worthily to increase the amount of happiness in the world; but he who does it, or professes to do it, for any other purpose, is no more deserving of admiration than the ascetic mounted on his pillar. He may be an inspiriting proof of what men *can* do, but assuredly not an example of what they *should.*

Though it is only in a very imperfect state of the world's arrangements that anyone can best serve the happiness of others by the absolute sacrifice of his own, yet so long as the world is in that imperfect state, I fully acknowledge that the readiness to make such a sacrifice is the highest virtue which can be found in man. I will add that in this condition of the world, paradoxical as the assertion may be, the conscious ability to do without happiness gives the best prospect of realizing such happiness as is attainable. For nothing except that consciousness can raise a person above the chances of life, by making him feel that, let fate and fortune do their worst, they have not power to subdue him; which, once felt, frees him from excess of anxiety concerning the evils of life, and enables him, like many a Stoic in the worst times of the Roman Empire, to cultivate in tranquillity the sources of satisfaction accessible to him, without concerning himself about the uncertainty of their duration, any more than about their inevitable end.

Meanwhile, let utilitarians never cease to claim the morality of self-devotion as a possession which belongs by as good a right to them, as either to the Stoic or to the Transcendentalist. The utilitarian morality does recognize in human beings the power of sacrificing their own greatest good for the good of others. It only refuses to admit that the sacrifice is itself a good. A sacrifice which does not increase, or tend to increase, the sum total of happiness, it considers as wasted. The only self-renunciation which it applauds, is devotion to the happiness, or to some of the means of happiness, of others; either of mankind collectively, or of individuals within the limits imposed by the collective interests of mankind.

I must again repeat, what the assailants of utilitarianism seldom have the justice to acknowledge, that the happiness which forms the utilitarian standard of what is right in conduct, is not the agent's own happiness, but that of all concerned. As between his own happiness and that of others, utilitarianism requires him to be as strictly impartial as a disinterested and benevolent spectator. In the golden rule of Jesus of Nazareth, we read the complete spirit of the ethics of utility. To do as you would be done by, and to love your neighbor as yourself, constitute the ideal perfection of utilitarian morality. As the means of making the nearest approach to this ideal, utility would enjoin, first, that laws and social arrangements should place the happiness, or (as speaking practically it may be called) the interest, of every individual, as nearly as possible in harmony with the interest of the whole; and secondly, that education and opinion, which have so vast a power over human character, should so use that power as to establish in the mind of every individual an indissoluble association between his own happiness and the good of the whole—especially between his own happiness and the practice of such modes of conduct, negative and positive, as regard for the universal happiness prescribes; so that not only he may be unable to conceive the possibility of happiness to himself, consistently with conduct opposed to the general good, but also that a direct impulse to promote the general good may be in every individual one of the habitual motives of action, and the sentiments connected therewith may fill a large and prominent place in every human being's sentient existence. If the impugners of the utilitarian morality represented it to their own minds in this its true character, I know not what recommendation possessed by any other morality they could possibly affirm to be wanting to it; what more beautiful or more exalted developments of human nature any other ethical system can be supposed to foster, or what springs of action, not accessible to the utilitarian, such systems rely on for giving effect to their mandates.

The objectors to utilitarianism cannot always be charged with representing it in a discreditable light. On the contrary, those among them who entertain anything like a just idea of its disinterested character sometimes find fault with its standard as being too high for humanity. They say it is exacting too much to require that people shall always act from the inducement of promoting the general interests of society. But this is to mistake the very meaning of a standard of morals, and confound the rule of action with the motive of it. It is the business of ethics to tell us what are our duties, or by what test we may know them; but no system of ethics requires that the sole motive of all we do shall be a feeling of duty; on the contrary, ninety-nine hundredths of all our actions are done from other motives, and rightly so done, if the rule of duty does not condemn them. It is the more unjust to utilitarianism that this particular misapprehension should be made a ground of objection to it, inasmuch as utilitarian moralists have gone beyond almost all others in affirming that the motive has nothing to do with the morality of the action, though much the worth of the agent. He who saves a fellow creature from drowning does what is morally right, whether his motive be duty, or the hope of being paid for his trouble; he who betrays the friend that trusts him, is guilty of a crime, even if his object be to serve another friend to whom he is under greater obligations. But to speak only of actions done from the motive of duty, and in direct obedience to principle: it is a misapprehension of the utilitarian mode of thought, to conceive it as implying that people should fix their minds upon so wide a generality as the world, or society at large. The great majority of good actions are intended not for the benefit of the world, but for that of individuals, of which the good of the world is made up; and the thoughts of the most virtuous man need not on these occasions travel beyond the particular persons concerned, except so far as is necessary to assure himself that in benefiting them he is not violating the rights, that is, the legitimate and authorized expectations, of anyone else. The multiplication of happiness is, according to the utilitarian ethics, the object of virtue: the occasions on which any person (except one in a thousand) has it in his power to do this on an extended scale, in other words to be a public benefactor, are but exceptional, and on these occasions alone is he called on to consider public utility; in every other case, private utility, the interest or happiness of some few persons, is all he has to attend to. Those alone the influence of whose actions extends to society in general, need concern themselves habitually about so large an object. In the case of abstinences indeed—of things which people forbear to do from moral considerations, though the consequences in the particular case might be beneficial—it would be unworthy of an intelligent agent not to be consciously aware that the action is of a class which, if practiced generally, would be generally injurious, and that this is the ground of the obligation to abstain from it. The amount of regard for the public interest implied in this recognition is no greater than is demanded by every system of morals, for they all enjoin to abstain from whatever is manifestly pernicious to society.

The same considerations dispose of another reproach against the doctrine of utility, founded on a still grosser misconception of the purpose of a standard of morality, and of the very meaning of the words right and wrong. It is often affirmed that utilitarianism renders men cold and unsympathizing; that it chills their moral feelings towards individuals; that it makes them regard only the dry and hard consideration of the consequences of actions, not taking into their moral estimate the qualities from which those actions emanate. If the assertion means that they do not allow their judgment respecting the rightness or wrongness of an action to be influenced by their opinion of the qualities of the person who does it, this is a complaint not against utilitarianism, but against having any standard of morality at all; for certainly no known ethical standard decides an action to be good or bad because it is done by a good or a bad man, still less because done by an amiable, a brave, or a benevolent man, or the contrary. These considerations are relevant, not to the estimation of actions, but of persons; and there is nothing in the utilitarian theory inconsistent with the fact that there are other things which interest us in persons besides the rightness and wrongness of their actions. The Stoics, indeed, with the paradoxical misuse of language which was part of their system, and by which they strove to raise themselves above all concern about anything but virtue, were fond of saying that he who has that has everything; that he, and only he, is rich, is beautiful, is a king. But no claim of this description is made for the virtuous man by the utilitarian doctrine. Utilitarians are quite aware that there are other desirable possessions and qualities besides virtue, and are perfectly willing to allow to all of them their full worth. They are also aware that a right action does not necessarily indicate a virtuous character, and that actions which are blamable, often proceed from qualities entitled to praise. When this is apparent in any particular case, it modifies their estimation, not certainly of the act, but of the agent. I grant that they are, notwithstanding, of opinion that in the long run the best proof of a good character is good actions; and resolutely refuse to consider any mental disposition as good, of which the predominant tendency is to produce bad conduct. This makes them unpopular with many people; but it is an unpopularity which they must share with everyone who regards the distinction between right and wrong in a serious light; and the reproach is not one which a conscientious utilitarian need be anxious to repel.

If no more be meant by the objection than that many utilitarians look on the morality of actions, as measured by the utilitarian standard, with too exclusive a regard, and do not lay sufficient stress upon the other beauties of character which go towards making a human being lovable or admirable, this may be admitted. Utilitarians who have cultivated their moral feelings, but not their sympathies nor their artistic perceptions, do fall into this mistake; and so do all other moralists under the same conditions. What can be said in excuse for other moralists is equally available for them, namely, that if there is to be any error, it is better that it should be on that side. As a matter of fact, we may affirm that among utilitarians as among adherents of other systems, there is every imaginable degree of rigidity and of laxity in the application of their standard: some are even puritanically rigorous, while others are as indulgent as can possibly be desired by sinner or by sentimentalist. But on the whole, a doctrine which brings prominently forward the interest that mankind have in the repression and prevention of conduct which violates the moral law, is likely to be inferior to no other in turning the sanctions of opinion against such violations. It is true, the question, "What does violate the moral law?" is one on which those who recognize different standards of morality are likely now and then to differ. But difference of opinion on moral questions was not first introduced into the world by utilitarianism, while that doctrine does supply, if not always an easy, at all events a tangible and intelligible mode of deciding such differences.

It may not be superfluous to notice a few more of the common misapprehensions of utilitarian ethics, even those which are so obvious and gross that it might appear impossible for any person of candor and intelligence to fall into them; since persons, even of considerable mental endowments, often give themselves so little trouble to understand the bearings of any opinion against which they entertain a prejudice, and men are in general so little conscious of this voluntary ignorance as a defect, that the vulgarest misunderstandings of ethical doctrines are continually met with in the deliberate writings of persons of the greatest pretensions both to high principle and to philosophy. We not uncommonly hear the doctrine of utility inveighed against as a *godless* doctrine. If it be necessary to say anything at all against so mere an assumption, we may say that the question depends upon what idea we have formed of the moral character of the Deity. If it be a true belief that God desires, above all things, the happiness of his creatures, and that this was his purpose in their creation, utility is not only not a godless doctrine, but more profoundly religious than any other. If it be meant that utilitarianism does not recognize the revealed will of God as the supreme law of morals, I answer that a utilitarian who believes in the perfect goodness and wisdom of God, necessarily believes that whatever God has thought fit to reveal on the subject of morals, must fulfil the requirements of utility in a supreme degree. But others besides utilitarians have been of opinion that the Christian revelation was intended, and is fitted, to inform the hearts and minds of mankind with a spirit which should enable them to find for themselves what is right, and incline them to do it when found, rather than to tell them, except in a very general way, what it is; and that we need a doctrine of ethics, carefully followed out, to *interpret* to us the will of God. Whether this opinion is correct or not, it is superfluous here to discuss; since whatever aid religion, either natural or revealed, can afford to ethical investigation, is as open to the utilitarian moralist as to any other. He can use it as the testimony of God to the usefulness or hurtfulness of any given course of action, by as good a right as others can use it for the indication of a transcendental law, having no connection with usefulness or with happiness.

Again, utility is often summarily stigmatized as an immoral doctrine by giving it the name of *expediency,* and taking advantage of the popular use of that term to contrast it with *principle.* But the *expedient,* in the sense in which it is opposed to the *right,* generally means that which is expedient for the particular interest of the agent himself; as when a minister sacrifices the interests of his country to keep himself in place. When it means anything better than this, it means that which is expedient for some immediate object, some temporary purpose, but which violates a rule whose observance is expedient in a much higher degree. The expedient, in this sense, instead of being the same thing with the useful, is a branch of the hurtful. Thus, it would often be expedient, for the purpose of getting over some momentary embarrassment, or attaining some object immediately useful to ourselves or others, to tell a lie. But inasmuch as the cultivation in ourselves of a sensitive feeling on the subject of veracity, is one of the most useful, and the enfeeblement of that feeling one of the most hurtful, things to which our conduct can be instrumental; and inasmuch as any, even unintentional, deviation from truth, does that much towards weakening the trustworthiness of human assertion, which is not only the principal support of all present social well-being, but the insufficiency of which does more than any one thing that can be named to keep back civilization, virtue, everything on which human happiness on the largest scale depends; we feel that the violation, for a present advantage, of a rule of such transcendent expediency, is not expedient, and that he who, for the sake of a convenience to himself or to some other individual, does what depends on him to deprive mankind of the good, and inflict upon them the evil, involved in the greater or less reliance which they can place in each other's word, acts the part of one of their worst enemies. Yet that even this rule, sacred as it is, admits of possible exceptions, is acknowledged by all moralists; the chief of which is when the withholding of some fact (as of information from a malefactor, or of bad news from a person dangerously ill) would save an individual (especially an individual other than oneself) from great and unmerited evil, and when the withholding can only be effected by denial. But in order that the exception may not extend itself beyond the need, and may have the least possible effect in weakening reliance on veracity, it ought to be recognized, and, if possible, its limits defined; and if the principle of utility is good for anything, it must be good for weighing those conflicting utilities against one another, and marking out the region within which one or the other preponderates.

Again, defenders of utility often find themselves called upon to reply to such objections as this—that there is not time, previous to action, for calculating and weighing the effects of any line of conduct on the general happiness. This is exactly as if anyone were to say that it is impossible to guide our conduct by Christianity, because there is not time, on every occasion on which anything has to be done, to read through the Old and New Testaments. The answer to the objection is that there has been ample time, namely, the whole past duration of the human species. During all that time, mankind have been learning by experience the tendencies of actions; on which experience all the prudence, as well as all the morality of life, are dependent. People talk as if the commencement of this course of experience had hitherto been put off, and as if, at the moment when some man feels tempted to meddle with the property or life of another, he had to begin considering for the first time whether murder and theft are injurious to human happiness. Even then I do not think that he would find the question very puzzling; but, at all events, the matter is now done to his hand. It is truly a whimsical supposition that, if mankind were agreed in considering utility to be the test of morality, they would remain without any agreement as to what *is* useful, and would take no measures for having their notions on the subject taught to the young, and enforced by law and opinion. There is no difficulty in proving any ethical standard whatever to work ill, if we suppose universal idiocy to be conjoined with it; but on any hypothesis short of that, mankind must by this time have acquired positive beliefs as to the effects of some actions on their happiness; and the beliefs which have thus come down are the rules of morality for the multitude, and for the philosopher until he has succeeded in finding better. That philosophers might easily do this, even now, on many subjects; that the received code of ethics is by no means of divine right; and that mankind have still much to learn as to the effects of actions on the general happiness, I admit, or rather, earnestly maintain. The corollaries from the principle of utility, like the precepts of every practical art, admit of indefinite improvement, and, in a progressive state of the human mind, their improvement is perpetually going on. But to consider the rules of morality as improvable, is one thing; to pass over the intermediate generalizations entirely, and endeavor to test each individual action directly by the first principle, is another. It is a strange notion that the acknowledgment of a first principle is inconsistent with the admission of secondary ones. To inform a traveler respecting the place of his ultimate destination, is not to forbid the use of landmarks and direction-posts on the way. The proposition that happiness is the end and aim of morality, does not mean that no road ought to be laid down to that goal, or that persons going thither should not be advised to take one direction rather than another. Men really ought to leave off taking a kind of nonsense on this subject, which they would neither talk nor listen to on other matters of practical concernment. Nobody argues that the art of navigation is not founded on astronomy, because sailors cannot wait to calculate the Nautical Almanac. Being rational creatures, they go to sea with it ready calculated; and all rational creatures go out upon the sea of life with their minds made up on the common questions of right and wrong, as well as on many of the far more difficult questions of wise and foolish. And this, as long as foresight is a human quality, it is to be presumed they will continue to do. Whatever we adopt as the fundamental principle of morality, we require subordinate principles to apply it by; the impossibility of doing without them, being common to all systems, can afford no argument against anyone in particular; but gravely to argue as if no such secondary principles could be had, and as if mankind had remained till now, and always must remain, without drawing any general conclusions from the experience of human life, is as high a pitch, I think, as absurdity has ever reached in philosophical controversy.

The remainder of the stock arguments against utilitarianism mostly consist in laying to its charge the common infirmities of human nature, and the general difficulties which embarrass conscientious persons in shaping their course through life. We are told that a utilitarian will be apt to make his own particular case an exception to moral rules, and when under temptation will see a utility in the breach of a rule greater than he will see in its observance. But is utility the only creed which is able to furnish us with excuses for evil-doing, and means of cheating our own conscience? They are afforded in abundance by all doctrines which recognize as a fact in morals the existence of conflicting considerations; which all doctrines do, that have been believed by sane persons. It is not the fault of any creed, but of the complicated nature of human affairs, that rules of conduct cannot be so framed as to require no exceptions, and that hardly any kind of action can safely be laid down as either always obligatory or always condemnable. There is no ethical creed which does not temper the rigidity of its laws by giving a certain latitude, under the moral responsibility of the agent, for accommodation to peculiarities of circumstances; and under every creed, at the opening thus made, self-deception and dishonest casuistry get in. There exists no moral system under which there do not arise unequivocal cases of conflicting obligation. These are the real difficulties, the knotty points both in the theory of ethics, and in the conscientious guidance of personal conduct. They are overcome practically, with greater or with less success, according to the intellect and virtue of the individual; but it can hardly be pretended that anyone will be the less qualified for dealing with them, from possessing an ultimate standard to which conflicting rights and duties can be referred. If utility is the ultimate source of moral obligations, utility may be invoked to decide between them when their demands are incompatible. Though the application of the standard may be difficult, it is better than none at all; while in other systems, the moral laws all claiming independent authority, there is no common umpire entitled to interfere between them: their claims to precedence one over another rest on little better than sophistry, and unless determined, as they generally are, by the unacknowledged influence of considerations of utility, afford a free scope for the action of personal desires and partialities. We must remember that only in these cases of conflict between secondary principles is it requisite that first principles should be appealed to. There is no case of moral obligation in which some secondary principle is not involved; and if only one, there can seldom be any real doubt which one it is, in the mind of any person by whom the principle itself is recognized.

CHAPTER III

OF THE ULTIMATE SANCTION OF THE PRINCIPLE OF UTILITY

The question is often asked, and properly so, in regard to any supposed moral standard—What is its sanction? what are the motives to obey it? or more specifically, what is the source of its obligation? whence does it derive its binding force? It is a necessary part of moral philosophy to provide the answer to this question; which, though frequently assuming the shape of an objection to the utilitarian morality, as if it had some special applicability to that above others, really arises in regard to all standards. It arises, in fact, whenever a person is called on to *adopt* a standard, or refer morality to any basis on which he has not been accustomed to rest in. For the customary morality, that which education and opinion have consecrated, is the only one which presents itself to the mind with the feeling of being *in itself* obligatory; and when a person is asked to believe that this morality *derives* its obligation from some general principle round which custom has not thrown the same halo, the assertion is to him a paradox; the supposed corollaries seem to have a more binding force than the original theorem; the superstructure seems to stand better without, than with, what is represented as its foundation. He says to himself, I feel that I am bound not to rob or murder, betray or deceive; but why am I bound to promote the general happiness? If my own happiness lies in something else, why may I not give that the preference?

If the view adopted by the utilitarian philosophy of the nature of the moral sense be correct, this difficulty will always present itself, until the influences which form moral character have taken the same hold of the principle which they have taken of some of the consequences—until, by the improvement of education, the feeling of unity with our fellow-creatures shall be (what it cannot be denied that Christ intended it to be) as deeply rooted in our character, and to our own consciousness as completely a part of our nature, as the horror of crime is in an ordinarily well brought up young person. In the meantime, however, the difficulty has no peculiar application to the doctrine of utility, but is inherent in every attempt to analyze morality and reduce it to principles; which, unless the principle is already in men's minds invested with as much sacredness as any of its applications, always seem to divest them of a part of their sanctity.

The principle of utility either has, or there is no reason why it might not have, all the sanctions which belong to any other system of morals. Those sanctions are either external or internal. Of the external sanctions it is not necessary to speak at any length. They are, the hope of favor and the fear of displeasure, from our fellow-creatures or from the Ruler of the Universe, along with whatever we may have of sympathy or affection for them, or of love and awe of Him, inclining us to do his will independently of selfish consequences. There is evidently no reason why all these motives for observance should not attach themselves to the utilitarian morality, as completely and as powerfully as to any other. Indeed, those of them which refer to our fellow-creatures are sure to do so, in proportion to the amount of general intelligence; for whether there be any other ground of moral obligation than the general happiness or not, men do desire happiness; and however imperfect may be their own practice, they desire and commend all conduct in others towards themselves, by which they think their happiness is promoted. With regard to the religious motive, if men believe, as most profess to do, in the goodness of God, those who think that conduciveness to the general happiness is the essence, or even only the criterion of good, must necessarily believe that it is also that which God approves. The whole force therefore of external reward and punishment, whether physical or moral, and whether proceeding from God or from our fellow men, together with all that the capacities of human nature admit of disinterested devotion to either, become available to enforce the utilitarian morality, in proportion as that morality is recognized; and the more powerfully, the more the appliances of education and general cultivation are bent to the purpose.

So far as to external sanctions. The internal sanction of duty, whatever our standard of duty may be, is one and the same—a feeling in our own mind: a pain, more or less intense, attendant on violation of duty, which in properly cultivated moral natures rises, in the more serious cases, into shrinking from it as an impossibility. This feeling, when disinterested, and connecting itself with the pure idea of duty, and not with some particular form of it, or with any of the merely accessory circumstances, is the essence of conscience; though in that complex phenomenon as it actually exists, the simple fact is in general all encrusted over with collateral associations, derived from sympathy, from love, and still more from fear; from all the forms of religious feeling; from the recollections of childhood and of all our past life; from self-esteem, desire of the esteem of others, and occasionally even self-abasement. This extreme complication is, I apprehend, the origin of the sort of mystical character which, by a tendency of the human mind of which there are many other examples, is apt to be attributed to the idea of moral obligation, and which leads people to believe that the idea cannot possibly attach itself to any other objects than those which, by a supposed mysterious law, are found in our present experience to excite it. Its binding force, however, consists in the existence of a mass of feeling which must be broken through in order to do what violates our standard of right, and which, if we do nevertheless violate that standard, will probably have to be encountered afterwards in the form of remorse. Whatever theory we have of the nature or origin of conscience, this is what essentially constitutes it.

The ultimate sanction, therefore, of all morality (external motives apart) being a subjective feeling in our own minds, I see nothing embarrassing to those whose standard is utility, in the question, what is the sanction of that particular standard? We may answer, the same as of all other moral standards—the conscientious feelings of mankind. Undoubtedly this sanction has no binding efficacy on those who do not possess the feelings it appeals to; but neither will these persons be more obedient to any other moral principle than to the utilitarian one. On them morality of any kind has no hold but through the external sanctions. Meanwhile the feelings exist, a fact in human nature, the reality of which, and the great power with which they are capable of acting on those in whom they have been duly cultivated, are proved by experience. No reason has ever been shown why they may not be cultivated to as great intensity in connection with the utilitarian, as with any other rule of morals.

NOTES

1. The highest good.

2. Thomas Carlyle (1795–1881). English conservative, antimaterialist philosopher and essayist. Helped to introduce German romanticism to England. Frequent opponent of Mill.

3. Novalis (1772–1801). German poet who gave highest expression to the romantic longing for perfections of beauty unattainable in this life.

George Edward Moore: Can We Define the Good?

1. It is very easy to point out some among our every-day judgments, with the truth of which Ethics is undoubtedly concerned. Whenever we say, 'So and so is a good man,' or 'That fellow is a villain'; whenever we ask, 'What ought I to do?' or 'Is it wrong for me to do like this?'; whenever we hazard such remarks as 'Temperance is a virtue and drunkenness a vice'—it is undoubtedly the business of Ethics to discuss such questions and such statements; to argue what is the true answer when we ask what it is right to do, and to give reasons for thinking that our statements about the character of persons or the morality of actions are true or false. In the vast majority of cases, where we make statements involving any of the terms 'virtue,' 'vice,' 'duty,' 'right,' 'ought,' 'good,' 'bad,' we are making ethical judgments; and if we wish to discuss their truth, we shall be discussing a point of Ethics.

So much as this is not disputed; but it falls very far short of defining the province of Ethics. That province may indeed be defined as the whole truth about that which is at the same time common to all such judgments and peculiar to them. But we have still to ask the question: What is it that is thus common and peculiar? And this is a question to which very different answers have been given by ethical philosophers of acknowleged reputation, and none of them, perhaps, completely satisfactory.

2. If we take such examples as those given above, we shall not be far wrong in saying that they are all of them concerned with the question of 'conduct'—with the question, what, in the conduct of us, human beings, is good, and what is bad, what is right, and what is wrong. For when we say that a man is good, we commonly mean that he acts rightly; when we say that drunkenness is a vice, we commonly mean that to get drunk is a wrong or wicked action. And this discussion of human conduct is, in fact, that with which the name 'Ethics' is most intimately associated. It is so associated by derivation; and conduct is undoubtedly by far the commonest and most generally interesting object of ethical judgments.

Accordingly, we find that many ethical philosophers are disposed to accept as an adequate definition of 'Ethics' the statement that it deals with the question what is good or bad in human conduct. They hold that its enquiries are properly confined to 'conduct' or to 'practice'; they hold that the name 'practical philosophy' covers all the matter with which it has to do. Now, without discussing the proper meaning of the word (for verbal questions are properly left to the writers of dictionaries and other persons interested in literature; philosophy, as we shall see, has no concern with them), I may say that I intend to use 'Ethics' to cover more than this—a usage, for which there is, I think, quite sufficient authority. I am using it to cover an enquiry for which, at all events, there is no other word: the general enquiry into what is good.

Ethics is undoubtedly concerned with the question what good conduct is; but, being concerned with this, it obviously does not start at the beginning, unless it is prepared to tell us what is good as well as what is conduct. For 'good conduct' is a complex notion: all conduct

From George Edward Moore, *Principia Ethica* (selections).

is not good; for some is certainly bad and some may be indifferent. And on the other hand, other things, beside conduct, may be good; and if they are so, then, 'good' denotes some property, that is common to them and conduct; and if we examine good conduct alone of all good things, then we shall be in danger of mistaking for this property, some property which is not shared by those other things: and thus we shall have made a mistake about Ethics even in this limited sense; for we shall not know what good conduct really is. This is a mistake which many writers have actually made, from limiting their enquiry to conduct. And hence I shall try to avoid it by considering first what is good in general; hoping, that if we can arrive at any certainty about this, it will be much easier to settle the question of good conduct: for we all know pretty well what 'conduct' is. This, then, is our first question: What is good? and What is bad? and to the discussion of this question (or these questions) I give the name of Ethics, since that science must, at all events, include it.

3. But this is a question which may have many meanings. If, for example, each of us were to say 'I am doing good now' or 'I had a good dinner yesterday,' these statements would each of them be some sort of answer to our question, although perhaps a false one. So, too, when A asks B what school he ought to send his son to, B's answer will certainly be an ethical judgment. And similarly all distribution of praise or blame to any personage or thing that has existed, now exists, or will exist, does give some answer to the question 'What is good?' In all such cases some particular thing is judged to be good or bad: the question 'What?' is answered by 'This.' But this is not the sense in which a scientific Ethics asks the question. Not one, of all the many million answers of this kind, which must be true, can form a part of an ethical system; although that science must contain reasons and principles sufficient for deciding on the truth of all of them. There are far too many persons, things and events in the world, past, present, or to come, for a discussion of their individual merits to be embraced in any science. Ethics, therefore, does not deal at all with facts of this nature, facts that are unique, individual, absolutely particular; facts with which such studies as history, geography, astronomy, are compelled, in part at least, to deal. And, for this reason, it is not the business of the ethical philosopher to give personal advice or exhortation.

4. But there is another meaning which may be given to the question 'What is good?' 'Books are good' would be an answer to it, though an answer obviously false; for some books are very bad indeed. And ethical judgments of this kind do indeed belong to Ethics; though I shall not deal with many of them. Such is the judgment 'Pleasure is good'—a judgment, of which Ethics should discuss the truth, although it is not nearly as important as that other judgment, with which we shall be much occupied presently—'Pleasure *alone* is good.' It is judgments of this sort, which are made in such books on Ethics as contain a list of 'virtues'—in Aristotle's 'Ethics' for example. But it is judgments of precisely the same kind, which form the substance of what is commonly supposed to be a study different from Ethics, and one much less respectable—the study of Casuistry. We may be told that Casuistry differs from Ethics, in that it is much more detailed and particular, Ethics much more general. But it is most important to notice that Casuistry does not deal with anything that is absolutely particular—particular in the only sense in which a perfectly precise line can be drawn between it and what is general. It is not particular in the sense just noticed, the sense in which this book is a particular book, and A's friend's advice particular advice. Casuistry may indeed be *more* particular and Ethics *more* general; but that means that they differ only in degree and not in kind. And this is universally true of 'particular' and 'general,' when used in this common, but inaccurate, sense. So far as Ethics allows itself to give lists of virtues or even to name constituents of the Ideal, it is indistinguishable from Casuistry. Both alike deal with what is general, in the sense in which physics and chemistry deal with what is general. Just as chemistry aims at discovering what are the properties of oxygen, *wherever it occurs,* and not only of this or that particular specimen of oxygen; so Casuistry aims at discovering what actions are good, *whenever they occur.* In this respect Ethics and Casuistry alike are to be classed with such sciences as physics, chemistry and physiology, in their absolute distinction from those of which history and geography are instances. And it is to

be noted that, owing to their detailed nature, casuistical investigations are actually nearer to physics and to chemistry than are the investigations usually assigned to Ethics. For just as physics cannot rest content with the discovery that light is propagated by waves of ether, but must go on to discover the particular nature of the ether-waves corresponding to each several colour; so Casuistry, not content with the general law that charity is a virtue, must attempt to discover the relative merits of every different form of charity. Casuistry forms, therefore, part of the ideal of ethical science: Ethics cannot be complete without it. The defects of Casuistry are not defects of principle; no objection can be taken to its aim and object. It has failed only because it is far too difficult a subject to be treated adequately in our present state of knowledge. The casuist has been unable to distinguish, in the cases which he treats, those elements upon which their value depends. Hence he often thinks two cases to be alike in respect of value, when in reality they are alike only in some other respect. It is to mistakes of this kind that the pernicious influence of such investigations has been due. For Casuistry is the goal of ethical investigation. It cannot be safely attempted at the beginning of our studies, but only at the end.

5. But our question 'What is good?' may have still another meaning. We may, in the third place, mean to ask, not what thing or things are good, but how 'good' is to be defined. This is an enquiry which belongs only to Ethics, not to Casuistry; and this is the enquiry which will occupy us first.

It is an enquiry to which most special attention should be directed; since this question, how 'good' is to be defined, is the most fundamental question in all Ethics. That which is meant by 'good' is, in fact, except its converse 'bad,' the *only* simple object of thought which is peculiar to Ethics. Its definition is, therefore, the most essential point in the definition of Ethics; and moreover a mistake with regard to it entails a far larger number of erroneous ethical judgments than any other. Unless this first question be fully understood, and its true answer clearly recognised, the rest of Ethics is as good as useless from the point of view of systematic knowledge. True ethical judgments, of the two kinds last dealt with, may indeed be made by those who do not know the answer to this question as well as by those who do; and it goes without saying that the two classes of people may lead equally good lives. But it is extremely unlikely that the *most general* ethical judgments will be equally valid, in the absence of a true answer to this question: I shall presently try to show that the gravest errors have been largely due to beliefs in a false answer. And, in any case, it is impossible that, till the answer to this question be known, any one should know *what is the evidence* for any ethical judgment whatsoever. But the main object of Ethics, as a systematic science, is to give correct *reasons* for thinking that this or that is good; and, unless this question be answered, such reasons cannot be given. Even, therefore, apart from the fact that a false answer leads to false conclusions, the present enquiry is a most necessary and important part of the science of Ethics.

6. What, then, is good? How is good to be defined? Now, it may be thought that this is a verbal question. A definition does indeed often mean the expressing of one word's meaning in other words. But this is not the sort of definition I am asking for. Such a definition can never be of ultimate importance in any study except lexicography. If I wanted that kind of definition I should have to consider in the first place how people generally used the word 'good'; but my business is not with its proper usage, as established by custom. I should, indeed, be foolish, if I tried to use it for something which it did not usually denote: if, for instance, I were to announce that, whenever I used the word 'good,' I must be understood to be thinking of that object which is usually denoted by the word 'table.' I shall, therefore, use the word in the sense in which I think it is ordinarily used; but at the same time I am not anxious to discuss whether I am right in thinking that it is so used. My business is solely with that object or idea, which I hold, rightly or wrongly, that the word is generally used to stand for. What I want to discover is the nature of that object or idea, and about this I am extremely anxious to arrive at an agreement.

But, if we understand the question in this sense, my answer to it may seem a very disappointing one. If I am asked 'What is good?' my answer is that good is good, and that is the end of the matter. Or if I am asked 'How is good to be defined?' my answer is that it cannot be defined, and that is all I have to say about it. But disappointing as these answers may appear, they are of the very last importance. To readers who are familiar with philosophic terminology, I can express their importance by saying that they amount to this: That propositions about the good are all of them synthetic and never analytic; and that is plainly no trivial matter. And the same thing may be expressed more popularly, by saying that, if I am right, then nobody can foist upon us such an axiom as that 'Pleasure is the only good' or that 'The good is the desired' on the pretence that this is 'the very meaning of the word.'

7. Let us, then, consider this position. My point is that 'good' is a simple notion, just as 'yellow' is a simple notion; that, just as you cannot, by any manner of means, explain to any one who does not already know it, what yellow is, so you cannot explain what good is. Definitions of the kind that I was asking for, definitions which describe the real nature of the object or notion denoted by a word, and which do not merely tell us what the word is used to mean, are only possible when the object or notion in a question is something complex. You can give a definition of a horse, because a horse has many different properties and qualities, all of which you can enumerate. But when you have enumerated them all, when you have reduced a horse to his simplest terms, then you can no longer define those terms. They are simply something which you think of or perceive, and to any one who cannot think of or perceive them, you can never, by any definition, make their nature known. It may perhaps be objected to this that we are able to describe to others, objects which they have never seen or thought of. We can, for instance, make a man understand what a chimaera is, although he has never heard of one or seen one. You can tell him that it is an animal with a lioness's head and body, with a goat's head growing from the middle of its back, and with a snake in place of a tail. But here the object which you are describing is a complex object; it is entirely composed of parts, with which we are all perfectly familiar—a snake, a goat, a lioness; and we know, too, the manner in which those parts are to be put together, because we know what is meant by the middle of a lioness's back, and where her tail is wont to grow. And so it is with all objects, not previously known, which we are able to define: they are all complex; all composed of parts, which may themselves, in the first instance, be capable of similar definition, but which must in the end be reducible to simplest parts, which can no longer be defined. But yellow and good, we say, are not complex: they are notions of that simple kind, out of which definitions are composed and with which the power of further defining ceases.

8. When we say, as Webster says, 'The definition of horse is "A hoofed quadruped of the genus Equus,"' we may, in fact, mean three different things. (1) We may mean merely: 'When I say "horse," you are to understand that I am talking about a hoofed quadruped of the genus Equus.' This might be called the arbitrary verbal definition: and I do not mean that good is indefinable in that sense. (2) We may mean, as Webster ought to mean: 'When most English people say "horse," they mean a hoofed quadruped of the genus Equus.' This may be called the verbal definition proper, and I do not say that good is indefinable in this sense either; for it is certainly possible to discover how people use a word: otherwise, we could never have known that 'good' may be translated by 'gut' in German and by 'bon' in French. But (3) we may, when we define horse, mean something much more important. We may mean that a certain object, which we all of us know, is composed in a certain manner: that it has four legs, a head, a heart, a liver, etc., etc., all of them arranged in definite relations to one another. It is in this sense that I deny good to be definable. I say that it is not composed of any parts, which we can substitute for it in our minds when we are thinking of it. We might think just as clearly and correctly about a horse, if we thought of all its parts and their arrangement instead of thinking of the whole: we could, I say, think how a horse differed from a donkey just as well, just as truly, in this way, as now we do, only not so easily; but there is nothing whatsoever which we could so substitute for good; and that is what I mean, when I say that good is indefinable.

9. But I am afraid I have still not removed the chief difficulty which may prevent acceptance of the proposition that good is indefinable. I do not mean to say that *the* good,

that which is good, is thus indefinable; if I did think so, I should not be writing on Ethics, for my main object is to help towards discovering that definition. It is just because I think there will be less risk of error in our search for a definition of 'the good,' that I am now insisting that *good* is indefinable. I must try to explain the difference between these two. I suppose it may be granted that 'good' is an adjective. Well 'the good, 'that which is good,' must therefore be the substantive to which the adjective 'good' will apply: it must be the whole of that to which the adjective will apply, and the adjective must *always* truly apply to it. But if it is that to which the adjective will apply, it must be something different from that adjective itself; and the whole of that something different, whatever it is, will be our definition of *the* good. Now it may be that this something will have other adjectives, besides 'good,' that will apply to it. It may be full of pleasure, for example; it may be intelligent: and if these two adjectives are really part of its definition, then it will certainly be true, that pleasure and intelligence are good. And many people appear to think that, if we say 'Pleasure and intelligence are good,' or if we say 'Only pleasure and intelligence are good,' we are defining 'good.' Well, I cannot deny that propositions of this nature may sometimes be called definitions; I do not know well enough how the word is generally used to decide upon this point. I only wish it to be understood that that is not what I mean when I say there is no possible definition of good, and that I shall not mean this if I use the word again. I do most fully believe that some true proposition of the form 'Intelligence is good and intelligence alone is good' can be found; if none could be found, our definition of *the* good would be impossible. As it is, I believe *the* good to be definable; and yet I still say that good itself is indefinable.

10. 'Good,' then, if we mean by it that quality which we assert to belong to a thing, when we say that the thing is good, is incapable of any definition, in the most important sense of that word. The most important sense of 'definition' is that in which a definition states what are the parts which invariably compose a certain whole; and in this sense 'good' has no definition because it is simple and has no parts. It is one of those innumerable objects of thought which are themselves incapable of definition, because they are the ultimate terms by reference to which whatever *is* capable of definition must be defined. That there must be an indefinite number of such terms is obvious, on reflection; since we cannot define anything except by an analysis, which, when carried as far as it will go, refers us to something, which is simply different from anything else, and which by that ultimate difference explains the peculiarity of the whole which we are defining: for every whole contains some parts which are common to other wholes also. There is, therefore, no intrinsic difficulty in the contention that 'good' denotes a simple and indefinable quality. There are many other instances of such qualities.

Consider yellow, for example. We may try to define it, by describing its physical equivalent; we may state what kind of light-vibrations must stimulate the normal eye, in order that we may perceive it. But a moment's reflection is sufficient to shew that those light-vibrations are not themselves what we mean by yellow. *They* are not what we perceive. Indeed we should never have been able to discover their existence, unless we had first been struck by the patent difference of quality between the different colours. The most we can be entitled to say of those vibrations is that they are what corresponds in space to the yellow which we actually perceive.

Yet a mistake of this simple kind has commonly been made about 'good.' It may be true that all things which are good are *also* something else, just as it is true that all things which are yellow produce a certain kind of vibration in the light. And it is a fact, that Ethics aims at discovering what are those other properties belonging to all things which are good. But far too many philosophers have thought that when they named those other properties they were actually defining good; that these properties, in fact, were simply not 'other,' but absolutely and entirely the same with goodness. This view I propose to call the 'naturalistic fallacy' and of it I shall now endeavour to dispose.

11. Let us consider what it is such philosophers say. And first it is to be noticed that they do not agree among themselves. They not only say that they are right as to what good is, but they endeavour to prove that other people who say that it is something else, are wrong.

One, for instance, will affirm that good is pleasure, another, perhaps, that good is that which is desired; and each of these will argue eagerly to prove that the other is wrong. But how is that possible? One of them says that good is nothing but the object of desire, and at the same time tries to prove that it is not pleasure. But from his first assertion, that good just means the object of desire, one of two things must follow as regards his proof:

(1) He may be trying to prove that the object of desire is not pleasure. But, if this be all, where is his Ethics? The position he is maintaining is merely a psychological one. Desire is something which occurs in our minds, and pleasure is something else which so occurs; and our would-be ethical philosopher is merely holding that the latter is not the object of the former. But what has that to do with the question in dispute? His opponent held the ethical proposition that pleasure was the good, and although he should prove a million times over the psychological proposition that pleasure is not the object of desire, he is no nearer proving his opponent to be wrong. The position is like this. One man says a triangle is a circle: another replies 'A triangle is a straight line, and I will prove to you that I am right: *for*' (this is the only argument) 'a straight line is not a circle.' 'That is quite true,' the other may reply; 'but nevertheless a triangle is a circle, and you have said nothing whatever to prove the contrary. What is proved is that one of us is wrong, for we agree that a triangle cannot be both a straight line and a circle: but which is wrong, there can be no earthly means of proving, since you define triangle as straight line and I define it as circle.'—Well, that is one alternative which any naturalistic Ethics has to face; if good is *defined* as something else, it is then impossible either to prove that any other definition is wrong or even to deny such definition.

(2) The other alternative will scarcely be more welcome. It is that the discussion is after all a verbal one. When A says 'Good means pleasant' and B says 'Good means desired,' they may merely wish to assert that most people have used the word for what is pleasant and for what is desired respectively. And this is quite an interesting subject for discussion: only it is not a whit more an ethical discussion than the last was. Nor do I think that any exponent of naturalistic Ethics would be willing to allow that this was all he meant. They are all so anxious to persuade us that what they call the good is what we really ought to do. 'Do, pray, act so, because the word "good" is generally used to denote actions of this nature': such, on this view, would be the substance of their teaching. And in so far as they tell us how we ought to act, their teaching is truly ethical, as they mean it to be. But how perfectly absurd is the reason they would give for it! 'You are to do this, because most people use a certain word to denote conduct such as this.' 'You are to say the thing which is not, because most people call it lying.' That is an argument just as good!—My dear sirs, what we want to know from you as ethical teachers, is not how people use a word; it is not even, what kind of actions they approve, which the use of this word 'good' may certainly imply: what we want to know is simply what *is* good. We may indeed agree that what most people do think good, is actually so; we shall at all events be glad to know their opinions: but when we say their opinions about what *is* good, we do mean what we say; we do not care whether they call that thing which they mean 'horse' or 'table' or 'chair,' 'gut' or 'bon'; we want to know what it is that they so call. When they say 'Pleasure is good,' we cannot believe that they merely mean 'Pleasure is pleasure' and nothing more than that.

12. Suppose a man says 'I am pleased'; and suppose that is not a lie or a mistake but the truth. Well, if it is true, what does that mean? It means that his mind, a certain definite mind, distinguished by certain definite marks from all others, has at this moment a certain definite feeling called pleasure. 'Pleased' *means* nothing but having pleasure, and though we may be more pleased or less pleased, and even, we may admit for the present, have one or another kind of pleasure; yet in so far as it is pleasure we have, whether there be more or less of it, and whether it be of one kind or another, what we have is one definite thing, absolutely indefinable, some one thing that is the same in all the various degrees and in all the various kinds of it that there may be. We may be able to say how it is related to other things: that, for example, it is in the mind, that it causes desire, that we are conscious of it, etc., etc. We can, I say, describe its relations to other things, but define it we can *not*. And if anybody tried to define pleasure for us as being any other

natural object; if anybody were to say, for instance, that pleasure *means* the sensation of red, and were to proceed to deduce from that that pleasure is a colour, we should be entitled to laugh at him and to distrust his future statements about pleasure. Well, that would be the same fallacy which I have called the naturalistic fallacy. That 'pleased' does not mean 'having the sensation of red,' or anything else whatever, does not prevent us from understanding what it does mean. It is enough for us to know that 'pleased' does mean 'having the sensation of pleasure,' and though pleasure is absolutely indefinable, though pleasure is pleasure and nothing else whatever, yet we feel no difficulty in saying that we are pleased. The reason is, of course, that when I say 'I am pleased,' I do *not* mean that 'I' am the same thing as 'having pleasure.' And similarly no difficulty need be found in my saying that 'pleasure is good' and yet not meaning that 'pleasure' is the same thing as 'good,' that pleasure *means* good, and that good *means* pleasure. If I were to imagine that when I said 'I am pleased,' I meant that I was exactly the same thing as 'pleased,' I should not indeed call that a naturalistic fallacy, although it would be the same fallacy as I have called naturalistic with reference to Ethics. The reason of this is obvious enough. When a man confuses two natural objects with one another, defining the one by the other, if for instance, he confuses himself, who is one natural object, with 'pleased' or with 'pleasure' which are others, then there is no reason to call the fallacy naturalistic. But if he confuses 'good,' which is not in the same sense a natural object, with any natural object whatever, then there is a reason for calling that a naturalistic fallacy; its being made with regard to 'good' marks it as something quite specific, and this specific mistake deserves a name because it is so common. As for the reasons why good is not to be considered a natural object, they may be reserved for discussion in another place. But, for the present, it is sufficient to notice this: Even if it were a natural object, that would not alter the nature of the fallacy nor diminish its importance one whit. All that I have said about it would remain quite equally true: only the name which I have called it would not be so appropriate as I think it is. And I do not care about the name: what I do care about is the fallacy. It does not matter what we call it, provided we recognise it when we meet with it. It is to be met with in almost every book on Ethics; and yet it is not recognised: and that is why it is necessary to multiply illustrations of it, and convenient to give it a name. It is a very simple fallacy indeed. When we say that an orange is yellow, we do not think our statement binds us to hold that 'orange' means nothing else than 'yellow,' or that nothing can be yellow but an orange. Supposing the orange is also sweet! Does that bind us to say that 'sweet' is exactly the same thing as 'yellow,' that 'sweet' must be defined as 'yellow'? And supposing it be recognised that 'yellow' just means 'yellow' and nothing else whatever, does that make it any more difficult to hold that oranges are yellow? Most certainly it does not: on the contrary, it would be absolutely meaningless to say that oranges were yellow, unless yellow did in the end mean just 'yellow' and nothing else whatever—unless it was absolutely indefinable. We should not get any very clear notion about things, which are yellow—we should not get very far with our science, if we were bound to hold that everything which was yellow, *meant* exactly the same thing as yellow. We should find we had to hold that an orange was exactly the same thing as a stool, a piece of paper, a lemon, anything you like. We could prove any number of absurdities; but should we be the nearer to the truth? Why, then, should it be different with 'good'? Why, if good is good and indefinable, should I be held to deny that pleasure is good? Is there any difficulty in holding both to be true at once? On the contrary, there is no meaning in saying that pleasure is good, unless good is something different from pleasure. It is absolutely useless, so far as Ethics is concerned, to prove, as Mr. Spencer tries to do, that increase of pleasure coincides with increase of life, unless good *means* something different from either life or pleasure. He might just as well try to prove that an orange is yellow by shewing that it always is wrapped up in paper.

13. In fact, if it is not the case that 'good' denotes something simple and indefinable, only two alternatives are possible: either it is a complex, a given whole, about the correct analysis of which there may be disagreement; or else it means nothing at all, and there is no such subject as Ethics. In general, however, ethical philosophers have attempted to define

good, without recognising what such an attempt must mean. They actually use arguments which involve one or both of the absurdities considered in § 11. We are, therefore, justified in concluding that the attempt to define good is chiefly due to want of clearness as to the possible nature of definition. There are, in fact, only two serious alternatives to be considered, in order to establish the conclusion that 'good' does denote a simple and indefinable notion. It might possibly denote a complex, as 'horse' does; or it might have no meaning at all. Neither of these possibilities has, however, been clearly conceived and seriously maintained, as such, by those who presume to define good; and both may be dismissed by a simple appeal to facts.

(1) The hypothesis that disagreement about the meaning of good is disagreement with regard to the correct analysis of a given whole, may be most plainly seen to be incorrect by consideration of the fact that, whatever definition be offered, it may be always asked, with significance, of the complex so defined, whether it is itself good. To take, for instance, one of the more plausible, because one of the more complicated, of such proposed definitions, it may easily be thought, at first sight, that to be good may mean to be that which we desire to desire. Thus if we apply this definition to a particular instance and say 'When we think that A is good, we are thinking that A is one of the things which we desire to desire,' our proposition may seem quite plausible. But, if we carry the investigation further, and ask ourselves 'Is it good to desire to desire A?' it is apparent, on a little reflection, that this question is itself as intelligible, as the original question 'Is A good?'—that we are, in fact, now asking for exactly the same information about the desire to desire A, for which we formerly asked with regard to A itself. But it is also apparent that the meaning of this second question cannot be correctly analysed into 'Is the desire to desire A one of the things which we desire to desire?': we have not before our minds anything so complicated as the question 'Do we desire to desire to desire to desire A?' Moreover any one can easily convince himself by inspection that the predicate of this proposition—'good'—is positively different from the notion of 'desiring to desire' which enters into its subject: 'That we should desire to desire A is good' is *not* merely equivalent to 'That A should be good is good.' It may indeed be true that what we desire to desire is always also good; perhaps, even the converse may be true: but it is very doubtful whether this is the case, and the mere fact that we understand very well what is meant by doubting it, shews clearly that we have two different notions before our minds.

(2) And the same consideration is sufficient to dismiss the hypothesis that 'good' has no meaning whatsoever. It is very natural to make the mistake of supposing that what is universally true is of such a nature that its negation would be self-contradictory: the importance which has been assigned to analytic propositions in the history of philosophy shews how easy such a mistake is. And thus it is very easy to conclude that what seems to be a universal ethical principle is in fact an identical proposition; that, if, for example, whatever is called 'good' seems to be pleasant, the proposition 'Pleasure is the good' does not assert a connection between two different notions, but involves only one, that of pleasure, which is easily recognised as a distinct entity. But whoever will attentively consider with himself what is actually before his mind when he asks the question 'Is pleasure (or whatever it may be) after all good?' can easily satisfy himself that he is not merely wondering whether pleasure is pleasant. And if he will try this experiment with each suggested definition in succession, he may become expert enough to recognise that in every case he has before his mind a unique object, with regard to the connection of which with any other object, a distinct question may be asked. Every one does in fact understand the question 'Is this good?' When he thinks of it, his state of mind is different from what it would be, were he asked 'Is this pleasant, or desired, or approved?' It has a distinct meaning for him, even though he may not recognise in what respect it is distinct. Whenever he thinks of 'intrinsic value,' or 'intrinsic worth,' or says that a thing 'ought to exist,' he has before his mind the unique object—the unique property of things—which I mean by 'good.' Everybody is constantly aware of this notion, although he may never become aware at all that it is different from other notions of which he is also aware. But, for correct ethical reasoning, it is extremely important that he

should become aware of this fact; and, as soon as the nature of the problem is clearly understood, there should be little difficulty in advancing so far in analysis.

14. 'Good,' then, is indefinable; and yet, so far as I know, there is only one ethical writer, Prof. Henry Sidgwick,[1] who has clearly recognised and stated this fact. We shall see, indeed, how far many of the most reputed ethical systems fall short of drawing the conclusions which follow from such a recognition. At present I will only quote one instance, which will serve to illustrate the meaning and importance of this principle that 'good' is indefinable, or, as Prof. Sidgwick says, an 'unanalysable notion.' It is an instance to which Prof. Sidgwick himself refers in a note on the passage, in which he argues that 'ought' is unanalysable.

'Bentham,' says Sidgwick, 'explains that his fundamental principle "states the greatest happiness of all those whose interest is in question as being the right and proper end of human action"'; and yet 'his language in other passages of the same chapter would seem to imply' that he *means* by the word "right" "conducive to the general happiness." Prof. Sidgwick sees that, if you take these two statements together, you get the absurd result that 'greatest happiness is the end of human action, which is conducive to the general happiness'; and so absurd does it seem to him to call this result, as Bentham calls it, 'the fundamental principle of a moral system,' that he suggests that Bentham cannot have meant it. Yet Prof. Sidgwick himself states elsewhere that Psychological Hedonism is 'not seldom confounded with Egoistic Hedonism'; and that confusion, as we shall see, rests chiefly on that same fallacy, the naturalistic fallacy, which is implied in Bentham's statements. Prof. Sidgwick admits therefore that this fallacy is sometimes committed, absurd as it is; and I am inclined to think that Bentham may really have been one of those who committed it. Mill, as we shall see, certainly did commit it. In any case, whether Bentham committed it or not, his doctrine, as above quoted, will serve as a very good illustration of this fallacy, and of the importance of the contrary proposition that good is indefinable.

Let us consider this doctrine. Bentham seems to imply, so Prof. Sidgwick says, that the word 'right' *means* 'conducive to general happiness.' Now this, by itself, need not necessarily involve the naturalistic fallacy. For the word 'right' is very commonly appropriated to actions which lead to the attainment of what is good; which are regarded as *means* to the ideal and not as ends-in-themselves. This use of 'right,' as denoting what is good as a means, whether or not it be also good as an end, is indeed the use to which I shall confine the word. Had Bentham been using 'right' in this sense, it might be perfectly consistent for him to *define* right as 'conducive to the general happiness,' *provided only* (and notice this proviso) he had already proved, or laid down as an axiom, that general happiness was *the* good, or (what is equivalent to this) that general happiness alone was good. For in that case he would have already defined *the* good as general happiness (a position perfectly consistent, as we have seen, with the contention that 'good' is indefinable), and, since right was to be defined as 'conducive to *the* good,' it would actually *mean* 'conducive to general happiness.' But this method of escape from the charge of having committed the naturalistic fallacy has been closed by Bentham himself. For his fundamental principle is, we see, that the greatest happiness of all concerned is the *right* and proper *end* of human action. He applies the word 'right,' therefore, to the end, as such, not only to the means which are conducive to it; and, that being so, right can no longer be defined as 'conducive to the general happiness,' without involving the fallacy in question. For now it is obvious that the definition of right as conducive to general happiness can be used by him in support of the fundamental principle that general happiness is the right end; instead of being itself derived from that principle. If right, by definition, means conducive to general happiness, then it is obvious that general happiness is the right end. It is not necessary now first to prove or assert that general happiness is the right end, before right is defined as conducive to general happiness—a perfectly valid procedure; but on the contrary the definition of right as conducive to general happiness proves general happiness to be the right end—a perfectly invalid procedure, since in this case the statement that 'general happiness is the right end of human action' is not an ethical principle at all, but either, as we have seen, a proposition about the meaning of words, or else a proposition about the *nature* of general happiness, not about its rightness or goodness.

Now, I do not wish the importance I assign to this fallacy to be misunderstood. The discovery of it does not at all refute Bentham's contention that greatest happiness is the proper end of human action, if that be understood as an ethical proposition, as he undoubtedly intended it. That principle may be true all the same; we shall consider whether it is so in succeeding chapters. Bentham might have maintained it, as Prof. Sidgwick does, even if the fallacy had been pointed out to him. What I am maintaining is that the *reasons* which he actually gives for his ethical proposition are fallacious ones so far as they consist in a definition of right. What I suggest is that he did not perceive them to be fallacious; that, if he had done so, he would have been led to seek for other reasons in support of his Utilitarianism; and that, had he sought for other reasons, he *might* have found none which he thought to be sufficient. In that case he would have changed his whole system—a most important consequence. It is undoubtedly also possible that he would have thought other reasons to be sufficient, and in that case his ethical system, in its main results, would still have stood. But, even in this latter case, his use of the fallacy would be a serious objection to him as an ethical philosopher. For it is the business of Ethics, I must insist, not only to obtain true results, but also to find valid reasons for them. The direct object of Ethics is knowledge and not practice; and any one who uses the naturalistic fallacy has certainly not fulfilled this first object, however correct his practical principles may be.

My objections to Naturalism are then, in the first place, that it offers no reason at all, far less any valid reason, for any ethical principle whatever; and in this it already fails to satisfy the requirements of Ethics, as a scientific study. But in the second place I contend that, though it gives a reason for no ethical principle, it is a *cause* of the acceptance of false principles—it deludes the mind into accepting ethical principles, which are false; and in this it is contrary to every aim of Ethics. It is easy to see that if we start with a definition of right conduct as conduct conducive to general happiness; then, knowing that right conduct is universally conduct conducive to the good, we very easily arrive at the result that the good is general happiness. If, on the other hand, we once recognise that we must start our Ethics without a definition, we shall be much more apt to look about us, before we adopt any ethical principle whatever; and the more we look about us, the less likely are we to adopt a false one. It may be replied to this: Yes, but we shall look about us just as much, before we settle on our definition, and are therefore just as likely to be right. But I will try to shew that this is not the case. If we start with the conviction that a definition of good can be found, we start with the conviction that good *can mean* nothing else than some one property of things; and our only business will then be to discover what that property is. But if we recognise that, so far as the meaning of good goes, anything whatever may be good, we start with a much more open mind. Moreover, apart from the fact that, when we think we have a definition, we cannot logically defend our ethical principles in any way whatever, we shall also be much less apt to defend them well, even if illogically. For we shall start with the conviction that good must mean so and so, and shall therefore be inclined either to misunderstand our opponent's arguments or to cut them short with the reply, 'This is not an open question: the very meaning of the word decides it; no one can think otherwise except through confusion.'

15. Our first conclusion as to the subject-matter of Ethics is, then, that there is a simple, indefinable, unanalysable object of thought by reference to which it must be defined. By what name we call this unique object is a matter of indifference, so long as we clearly recognise what it is and that it does differ from other objects. The words which are commonly taken as the signs of ethical judgments all do refer to it; and they are expressions of ethical judgments solely because they do so refer. But they may refer to it in two different ways, which it is very important to distinguish, if we are to have a complete definition of the range of ethical judgments. Before I proceeded to argue that there was such an indefinable notion involved in ethical notions, I stated (§ 4) that it was necessary for Ethics to enumerate all true universal judgments, asserting that such and such a thing was good, whenever it occurred. But, although all such judgments do refer to that

unique notion which I have called 'good,' they do not all refer to it in the same way. They may either assert that this unique property does always attach to the thing in question, or else they may assert only that the thing in question is a *cause or necessary condition* for the existence of other things to which this unique property does attach. The nature of these two species of universal ethical judgments is extremely different; and a great part of the difficulties, which are met with in ordinary ethical speculation, are due to the failure to distinguish them clearly. Their difference has, indeed, received expression in ordinary language by the contrast between the terms 'good as means' and 'good in itself,' 'value as a means' and 'intrinsic value.' But these terms are apt to be applied correctly only in the more obvious instances; and this seems to be due to the fact that the distinction between the conceptions which they denote has not been made a separate object of investigation ...

NOTE

1. Professor Henry Sidgwick (1838-1900), English philosopher, professor at Cambridge from 1869 until his death. His great work is *Methods of Ethics* (1874).

Charles L. Stevenson: Ethical Emotivism

I

Ethical questions first arise in the form "Is so and so good?" or "Is this alternative better than that?" These questions are difficult partly because we don't know what we are seeking. We are asking, "Is there a needle in that haystack?" without even knowing just what a needle is. So the first thing to do is to examine the questions themselves. We must try to make them clearer, either by defining the terms in which they are expressed, or by any other method that is available.

The present paper is concerned wholly with this preliminary step of making ethical questions clear. In order to help answer the question "Is X good?" we must *substitute* for it a question which is free from ambiguity and confusion.

It is obvious that in substituting a clearer question we must not introduce some utterly different kind of question. It won't do (to take an extreme instance of a prevalent fallacy) to substitute for "Is X good?" the question "Is X pink with yellow trimmings?" and then point out how easy the question really is. This would beg the original question, not help answer it. On the other hand, we must not expect the substituted question to be strictly "identical" with the original one. The original question may embody hypostatization, anthropomorphism, vagueness, and all the other ills to which our ordinary discourse is subject. If our substituted question is to be clearer, it must remove these ills. The questions will be identical only in the sense that a child is identical with the man he later becomes. Hence we must not demand that the substitution strike us, on immediate introspection, as making no change in meaning.

Just how, then, must the substituted question be related to the original? Let us assume (inaccurately) that it must result from replacing "good" by some set of terms which define it. The question then resolves itself to this: How must the defined meaning of "good" be related to its original meaning?

I answer that it must be *relevant.* A defined meaning will be called "relevant" to the original meaning under these circumstances: Those who have understood the definition must be able to say all that they then want to say by using the term in the defined way. They must never have occasion to use the term in the old, unclear sense. (If a person did have to go on using the word in the old sense, then to this extent his meaning would not be clarified, and the philosophical task would not be completed.) It frequently happens that a word is used so confusedly and ambiguously that we must give it *several* defined meanings, rather than one. In this case only the whole set of defined meanings will be called "relevant," and any one of them will be called "partially relevant." This is not a rigorous treatment of *relevance,* by any means; but it will serve for the present purposes.

Let us now turn to our particular task—that

Reprinted from *Mind* (1937) by permission of Basil Blackwell, Publisher, Oxford.

of giving a relevant definition of "good." Let us first examine some of the ways in which others have attempted to do this.

The word "good" has often been defined in terms of *approval*, or similar psychological attitudes. We may take as typical examples: "good" means *desired by me* (Hobbes); and "good" means *approved by most people* (Hume, in effect).* It will be convenient to refer to definitions of this sort as "interest theories," following Mr. R. B. Perry, although neither "interest" nor "theory" is used in the most usual way.

Are definitions of this sort relevant?

It is idle to deny their *partial* relevance. The most superficial inquiry will reveal that "good" is exceedingly ambiguous. To maintain that "good" is *never* used in Hobbes's sense, and never in Hume's, is only to manifest an insensitivity to the complexities of language. We must recognize, perhaps, not only these senses, but a variety of similar ones, differing both with regard to the kind of interest in question, and with regard to the people who are said to have the interest.

But this is a minor matter. The essential question is not whether interest theories are *partially* relevant, but whether they are *wholly* relevant. This is the only point for intelligent dispute. Briefly: Granted that some senses of "good" may relevantly be defined in terms of interest, is there some *other* sense which is *not* relevantly so defined? We must give this question careful attention. For it is quite possible that when philosophers (and many others) have found the question "Is X good?" so difficult, they have been grasping for this *other* sense of "good," and not any sense relevantly defined in terms of interest. If we insist on defining "good" in terms of interest, and answer the question when thus interpreted, we may be begging *their* question entirely. Of course this *other* sense of "good" may not exist, or it may be a complete confusion; but that is what we must discover.

Now many have maintained that interest theories are *far* from being completely relevant. They have argued that such theories neglect the very sense of "good" which is most vital. And certainly, their arguments are not without plausibility.

Only . . . what *is* this "vital" sense of "good"? The answers have been so vague, and so beset with difficulties, that one can scarcely determine.

There are certain requirements, however, with which this "vital" sense has been expected to comply—requirements which appeal strongly to our common sense. It will be helpful to summarize these, showing how they exclude the interest theories.

In the first place, we must be able seriously to *disagree* about whether something is "good." This condition rules out Hobbes's definition. For consider the following argument: "This is good." "That isn't so; it's not good." As translated by Hobbes, this becomes: "I desire this." "That isn't so, for *I* don't." The speakers are not contradicting one another, and think they are, only because of an elementary confusion in the use of pronouns. The definition, "good" means *desired by my community*, is also excluded, for how could people from different communities disagree?

In the second place, "goodness" must have, so to speak, a magnetism. A person who recognizes X to be "good" must *ipso facto* acquire a stronger tendency to act in its favor than he otherwise would have had. This rules out the Humian type of definition. For according to Hume, to recognize that something is "good" is simply to recognize that the majority approve of it. Clearly, a man may see that the majority approve of X without having, himself, a stronger tendency to favor it. This requirement excludes any attempt to define "good" in terms of the interest of people *other* than the speaker.

In the third place, the "goodness" of anything must not be verifiable solely by use of the scientific method. "Ethics must not be psychology." This restriction rules out all of the traditional interest theories, without exception. It is so sweeping a restriction that we must examine

* [The author has requested that the following note be added here: For a more adequate treatment of Hume's views see my *Ethics and Language* (Yale University Press, 1944), Chap. XII, Sect. 5. In the present paper the references to Hume are to be taken as references to the general *family* of definitions of which Hume's is typical; but Hume's own definition is somewhat different from any that is here specifically stated. Perhaps the same should be said of Hobbes.]

its plausibility. What are the methodological implications of interest theories which are here rejected?

According to Hobbes's definition, a person can prove his ethical judgments, with finality, by showing that he is not making an introspective error about his desires. According to Hume's definition, one may prove ethical judgments (roughly speaking) by taking a vote. *This* use of the empirical method, at any rate, seems highly remote from what we usually accept as proof, and reflects on the complete relevance of the definitions which imply it.

But aren't there more complicated interest theories which are immune from such methodological implications? No, for the same factors appear; they are only put off for a while. Consider, for example, the definition: "X is good" means *most people would approve of* X *if they knew its nature and consequences.* How, according to this definition, could we prove that a certain X was good? We should first have to find out, empirically, just what X was like, and what its consequences would be. To this extent the empirical method, as required by the definition, seems beyond intelligent objection. But what remains? We should next have to discover whether most people would approve of the sort of thing we had discovered X to be. This couldn't be determined by popular vote—but only because it would be too difficult to explain to the voters, beforehand, what the nature and consequences of X really were. Apart from this, voting would be a pertinent method. We are again reduced to counting noses, as a *perfectly final* appeal.

Now we need to scorn voting entirely. A man who rejected interest theories as irrelevant might readily make the following statement: "If I believed that X would be approved by the majority, when they knew all about it, I should be strongly *led* to say that X was good." But he would continue: "*Need* I say that X was good, under the circumstances? Wouldn't my acceptance of the alleged 'final proof' result simply from my being democratic? What about the more aristocratic people? They would simply say that the approval of most people, even when they knew all about the object of their approval, simply had nothing to do with the goodness of anything, and they would probably add a few remarks about the low state of people's interests." It would indeed seem, from these considerations, that the definition we have been considering has presupposed democratic ideals from the start; it has dressed up democratic propaganda in the guise of a definition.

The omnipotence of the empirical method, as implied by interest theories and others, may be shown unacceptable in a somewhat different way. Mr. G. E. Moore's familiar objection about the open question is chiefly pertinent in this regard. No matter what set of scientifically knowable properties a thing may have (says Moore, in effect), you will find, on careful introspection, that it is an open question to ask whether anything having these properties is *good.* It is difficult to believe that this recurrent question is a totally confused one, or that it seems open only because of the ambiguity of "good." Rather, we must be using some sense of "good" which is not definable, relevantly, in terms of anything scientifically knowable. That is, the scientific method is not sufficient for ethics.

These, then, are the requirements with which the "vital" sense of "good" is expected to comply: (1) goodness must be a topic for intelligent disagreement; (2) it must be "magnetic"; and (3) it must not be discoverable solely through the scientific method.

II

Let us now turn to my own analysis of ethical judgments. First let me present my position dogmatically, showing to what extent I vary from tradition.

I believe that the three requirements, given above, are perfectly sensible; that there is some *one* sense of "good" which satisfies all three requirements; and that no traditional interest theory satisfies them all. But this does not imply that "good" must be explained in terms of a Platonic Idea, or of a Categorical Imperative, or of an unique, unanalyzable property. On the contrary, the three requirements can be met by a *kind* of interest theory. *But we must give up a presupposition which all the traditional interest theories have made.*

Traditional interest theories hold that ethical statements are *descriptive* of the existing state of interests—that they simply *give information* about interests. (More accurately, ethical judgments are said to describe what the state of interests is, was, or will be, or to indicate what the state of interests *would* be under specified circumstances.) It is this emphasis on description, on information, which leads to their incomplete relevance. Doubtless there is always *some* element of description in ethical judgments, but this is by no means all. Their major use is not to indicate facts, but to *create an influence.* Instead of merely describing people's interests, they *change* or *intensify* them. They *recommend* an interest in an object, rather than state that the interest already exists.

For instance: When you tell a man that he oughtn't to steal, your object isn't merely to let him know that people disapprove of stealing. You are attempting, rather, to get *him* to disapprove of it. Your ethical judgment has a quasi-imperative force which, operating through suggestion, and intensified by your tone of voice, readily permits you to begin to *influence,* to *modify,* his interests. If in the end you do not succeed in getting *him* to disapprove of stealing, you will feel that you've failed to convince him that stealing is wrong. You will continue to feel this, even though he fully acknowledges that you disapprove of it, and that almost everyone else does. When you point out to him the consequences of his actions—consequences which you suspect he already disapproves of—these *reasons* which support your ethical judgment are simply a means of facilitating your influence. If you think you can change his interests by making vivid to him how others will disapprove of him, you will do so; otherwise not. So the consideration about other people's interest is just an additional means you may employ, in order to move him, and is not a part of the ethical judgment itself. Your ethical judgment doesn't merely describe interests to him, it directs his very interests. The difference between the traditional interest theories and my view is like the difference between describing a desert and irrigating it.

Another example: A munition maker declares that war is a good thing. If he merely meant that he approved of it, he would not have to insist so strongly, nor grow so excited in his argument. People would be quite easily convinced that he approved of it. If he merely meant that most people approved of war, or that most people would approve of it if they knew the consequences, he would have to yield his point if it were proved that this wasn't so. But he wouldn't do this, nor does consistency require it. He is not *describing* the state of people's approval; he is trying to *change* it by his influence. If he found that few people approved of war, he might insist all the more strongly that it was good, for there would be more changing to be done.

This example illustrates how "good" may be used for what most of us would call bad purposes. Such cases are as pertinent as any others. I am not indicating the *good* way of using "good." I am not influencing people, but am describing the way this influence sometimes goes on. If the reader wishes to say that the munition maker's influence is bad—that is, if the reader wishes to awaken people's disapproval of the man, and to make him disapprove of his own actions—I should at another time be willing to join in this undertaking. But this is not the present concern. I am not using ethical terms, but am indicating how they *are* used. The munition maker, in his use of "good," illustrates the persuasive character of the word just as well as does the unselfish man who, eager to encourage in each of us a desire for the happiness of all, contends that the supreme good is peace.

Thus ethical terms are *instruments* used in the complicated interplay and readjustment of human interests. This can be seen plainly from more general observations. People from widely separated communities have different moral attitudes. Why? To a great extent because they have been subject to different social influences. Now clearly this influence doesn't operate through sticks and stones alone; words play a great part. People praise one another, to encourage certain inclinations, and blame one another, to discourage others. Those of forceful personalities issue commands which weaker people, for complicated instinctive reasons, find it difficult to disobey, quite apart from fears of consequences. Further influence is brought to bear by writers and orators. Thus social influence is exerted, to an enormous extent, by means that have nothing to do with physical force or material reward. The ethical terms facilitate such influence. Being suited for use in *suggestion,* they are a means by which men's attitudes may be led this way or that. The reason, then, that we find a greater similarity in the moral attitudes of one community than in those of different communities is largely this: ethical judgments propagate themselves. One man says "This is good"; this may influence the approval of another person, who then makes the same ethical judgment, which in turn influences another person, and so on. In the end, by a process of mutual influence, people take up more or less the same attitudes. Between people of widely separated communities, of course, the influence is less strong; hence different communities have different attitudes.

These remarks will serve to give a general idea of my point of view. We must now go into more detail. There are several questions which must be answered: How does an ethical sentence acquire its power of influencing people—why is it suited to suggestion? Again, what has this influence to do with the *meaning* of ethical terms? And finally, do these considerations really lead us to a sense of "good" which meets the requirements mentioned in the preceding section?

Let us deal first with the question about *meaning*. This is far from an easy question, so we must enter into a preliminary inquiry about meaning in general. Although a seeming digression, this will prove indispensable.

III

Broadly speaking, there are two different *purposes* which lead us to use language. On the one hand we use words (as in science) to record, clarify, and communicate *beliefs*. On the other hand we use words to give vent to our feelings (interjections), or to create moods (poetry), or to incite people to actions or attitudes (oratory).

The first use of words I shall call "descriptive"; the second, "dynamic." Note that the distinction depends solely upon the *purpose* of the *speaker*.

When a person says "Hydrogen is the lightest known gas," his purpose *may* be simply to lead the hearer to believe this, or to believe that the speaker believes it. In that case the words are used descriptively. When a person cuts himself and says "Damn," his purpose is not ordinarily to record, clarify, or communicate any belief. The word is used dynamically. The two ways of using words, however, are by no means mutually exclusive. This is obvious from the fact that our purposes are often complex. Thus when one says "I want you to close the door," part of his purpose, ordinarily, is to lead the hearer to believe that he has this want. To that extent the words are used descriptively. But the major part of one's purpose is to lead the hearer to *satisfy* the want. To that extent the words are used dynamically.

It very frequently happens that the same sentence may have a dynamic use on one occasion, and may not have a dynamic use on another; and that it may have different dynamic uses on different occasions. For instance: A man says to a visiting neighbor, "I am loaded down with work." His purpose may be to let the neighbor know how life is going with him. This would *not* be a dynamic use of words. He may make the remark, however, in order to drop a hint. This *would* be dynamic usage (as well as descriptive). Again, he may make the remark to arouse the neighbor's sympathy. This would be a *different* dynamic usage from that of hinting.

Or again, when we say to a man, "Of course you won't make those mistakes any more," we *may* simply be making a prediction. But we are more likely to be using "suggestion," in order to encourage him and hence *keep* him from making mistakes. The first use would be descriptive; the second, mainly dynamic.

From these examples it will be clear that we can't determine whether words are used dynamically or not, merely by reading the dictionary—even assuming that everyone is faithful to dictionary meanings. Indeed, to know whether a person is using a word dynamically, we must note his tone of voice, his gestures, the general circumstances under which he is speaking, and so on.

We must now proceed to an important question: What has the dynamic use of words to do with their *meaning*? One thing is clear—we must not define "meaning" in a way that would make meaning vary with dynamic usage. If we did, we should have no use for the term. All that we could say about such "meaning" would be that it is very complicated, and subject to constant change. So we must certainly distinguish between the dynamic use of words and their meaning.

It doesn't follow, however, that we must define "meaning" in some non-psychological fashion. We must simply restrict the psychological field. Instead of identifying meaning with *all* the psychological causes and effects that attend a word's utterance, we must identify it with those that it has a *tendency* (causal property, dispositional property) to be connected with. The tendency must be of a particular kind, moreover. It must exist for all who speak the language; it must be persistent; and must be realizable more or less independently of determinate circumstances attending the word's utterance. There will be further restrictions dealing with the interrelation of words in different contexts. Moreover, we must include, under the psychological responses which the words tend to produce, not only immediately introspectable experiences, but *dispositions* to react in a given way with appropriate stimuli. I hope to go into these matters in a subsequent paper. Suffice it now to say that I think "meaning" may be thus defined in a way to include "propositional" meaning as an important kind. Now a word may *tend* to have causal relations which in fact it sometimes doesn't; and it may sometimes have causal relations which it *doesn't tend* to have. And since the tendency of words which constitutes their meaning must be of a particular kind, and may include, as responses, dispositions to reactions, of which any of *several* immediate experiences may be a sign, then there is nothing surprising in the fact that words have a permanent meaning, in spite of the fact that the immediately introspectable experiences which attend their usage are so highly varied.

When "meaning" is defined in this way, meaning will not include dynamic use. For although words are sometimes accompanied by dynamic purposes, they do not *tend* to be accompanied by them in the way above mentioned. E.g., there is no tendency realizable independently of the determinate circumstances under which the words are uttered.

There will be a kind of meaning, however, in the sense above defined, which has an intimate relation to dynamic usage. I refer to "emotive" meaning. The emotive meaning of a word is a tendency of a word, arising through the history of its usage, to produce (result from) *affective* responses in people. It is the immediate aura of feeling which hovers about a word. Such tendencies to produce affective responses cling to words very tenaciously. It would be difficult, for instance, to express merriment by using the interjection "alas." Because of the persistence of such affective tendencies (among other reasons) it becomes feasible to classify them as "meanings."

Just *what* is the relation between emotive meaning and the dynamic use of words? Let us take an example. Suppose that a man is talking with a group of people which includes Miss Jones, aged 59. He refers to her, without thinking, as an "old maid." Now even if his purposes are perfectly innocent—even if he is using the words purely descriptively—Miss Jones won't think so. She will think he is encouraging the others to have contempt for her, and will draw in her skirts, defensively. The man might have done better if instead of saying "old maid" he had said "elderly spinster." The latter words could have been put to the same descriptive use, and would not so readily have caused suspicions about the dynamic use.

"Old maid" and "elderly spinster" differ, to be sure, only in emotive meaning. From the example it will be clear that certain words, because of their emotive meaning, are suited to a certain kind of dynamic use—so well suited, in fact, that the hearer is likely to be misled when we use them in any other way. The more pronounced a word's emotive meaning is, the less likely people are to use it purely descriptively. Some words are suited to encourage people, some to discourage them, some to quiet them, and so on.

Even in these cases, of course, the dynamic purposes are not to be identified with any sort of meaning; for the emotive meaning accompanies a word much more persistently than do the dynamic purposes. But there is an important contingent relation between emotive meaning and dynamic purpose: the former assists the latter. Hence if we define emotively laden terms in a way that neglects their emotive meaning, we are likely to be confusing. *We lead people to think that the terms defined are used dynamically less often than they are.*

IV

Let us now apply these remarks in defining "good." This word may be used morally or non-morally. I shall deal with the non-moral usage almost entirely, but only because it is simpler. The main points of the analysis will apply equally well to either usage.

As a preliminary definition, let us take an inaccurate approximation. It may be more misleading than helpful, but will do to begin with. Roughly, then, the sentence "X is good" means *We like X.* ("We" includes the hearer or hearers.)

At first glance this definition sounds absurd. If used, we should expect to find the following sort of conversation: A. "This is good." B. "But I *don't* like it. What led you to believe that I did?" The unnaturalness of B's reply, judged by ordinary word-usage, would seem to cast doubt on the relevance of my definition.

B's unnaturalness, however, lies simply in this: he is assuming that "We like it" (as would occur implicitly in the use of "good") is being used descriptively. This won't do. When "We like it" is to take the place of "This is good," the former sentence must be used not purely descriptively, but dynamically. More specifically, it must be used to promote a very subtle (and for the non-moral sense in question, a very easily resisted) kind of *suggestion.* To the extent that "we" refers to the hearer, it must have the dynamic use, essential to suggestion, of leading the hearer to *make* true what is said, rather than merely to believe it. And to the extent that "we" refers to the speaker, the sentence must have not only the descriptive use of indicating belief about the speaker's interest, but the quasi-interjectory, dynamic function of giving direct expression to the interest. (This immediate expression of feelings assists in the process of suggestion. It is difficult to disapprove in the face of another's enthusiasm.)

For an example of a case where "We like this" is used in the dynamic way that "This is good" is used, consider the case of a mother who says to her several children, "One thing is certain, *we all like to be neat.*" If she really believed this, she wouldn't bother to say so. But she is not using the words descriptively. She is *encouraging* the children to like neatness. By telling them that they like neatness, she will lead them to *make* her statement true, so to speak. If, instead of saying "We all like to be neat" in this way, she had said "It's a good thing to be neat," the effect would have been approximately the same.

But these remarks are still misleading. Even when "We like it" is used for suggestion, it isn't quite like "This is good." The latter is more subtle. With such a sentence as "This is a good book," for example, it would be practically impossible to use instead "We like this book." When the latter is used, it must be accompanied by so exaggerated an intonation, to prevent its becoming confused with a descriptive statement, that the force of suggestion becomes stronger, and ludicrously more overt, than when "good" is used.

The definition is inadequate, further, in that the definiens has been restricted to dynamic usage. Having said that dynamic usage was different from meaning, I should not have to mention it in giving the *meaning* of "good."

It is in connection with this last point that we must return to emotive meaning. The word "good" has a pleasing emotive meaning which fits it especially for the dynamic use of suggesting favorable interest. But the sentence "We like it" has no such emotive meaning. Hence my definition has neglected emotive meaning entirely. Now to neglect emotive meaning is likely to lead to endless confusions, as we shall presently see; so I have sought to make up for the inadequacy of the definition by letting the restriction about dynamic usage take the place of emotive meaning. What I should do, of course, is to find a definiens whose emotive meaning, like that of "good," simply does *lead* to dynamic usage.

Why didn't I do this? I answer that it isn't possible, if the definition is to afford us increased clarity. No two words, in the first place, have quite the same emotive meaning. The most we can hope for is a rough approximation. But if we seek for such an approximation for "good," we shall find nothing more than synonyms, such as "desirable" or "valuable"; and these are profitless because they do not clear up the connection between "good" and favorable interest. If we reject such synonyms, in favor of non-ethical terms, we shall be highly misleading. For instance: "This is good" has something like the meaning of "I *do* like this; do so as well." But this is certainly not accurate. For the imperative makes an appeal to the conscious efforts of the hearer. Of course he can't like something just by trying. He must be led to like it through suggestion. Hence an ethical sentence differs from an imperative in that it enables one to make changes in a much more subtle, less fully conscious way. Note that the ethical sentence centers the hearer's attention not on his interests, but on the object of interest, and thereby facilitates suggestion. Because of its subtlety, moreover, an ethical sentence readily permits counter-suggestion, and leads to the give and take situation which is so characteristic of arguments about values.

Strictly speaking, then, it is impossible to define "good" in terms of favorable interest if emotive meaning is not to be distorted. Yet it is possible to say that "This is good" is *about* the favorable interest of the speaker and the hearer or hearers, and that it has a pleasing emotive meaning which fits the words for use in suggestion. This is a rough description of meaning, not a definition. But it serves the same clarifying function that a definition ordinarily does; and that, after all, is enough.

A word must be added about the moral use of "good." This differs from the above in that it is about a different kind of interest. Instead of being about what the hearer and speaker *like,* it is about a stronger sort of approval. When a person *likes* something, he is pleased when it prospers, and disappointed when it doesn't. When a person *morally approves* of something, he experiences a rich feeling of security when it prospers, and is indignant, or "shocked" when it doesn't. These are rough and inaccurate examples of the many factors which one would have to mention in distinguishing the two kinds of interest. In the moral usage, as well as in the non-moral, "good" has an emotive meaning which adapts it to suggestion.

And now, are these considerations of any importance? Why do I stress emotive meanings in this fashion? Does the omission of them really lead people into errors? I think, indeed, that the errors resulting from such omissions are enormous. In order to see this, however, we must return to the restrictions, mentioned in section I, with which the "vital" sense of "good" has been expected to comply.

V

The first restriction, it will be remembered, had to do with disagreement. Now there is clearly some sense in which people disagree on ethical points; but we must not rashly assume that all disagreement is modelled after the sort that occurs in the natural sciences. We must distinguish between "disagreement in belief" (typical of the sciences) and "disagreement in interest." Disagreement in belief occurs when A believes *p* and B disbelieves it. Disagreement in interest occurs when A has a favorable interest in X, when B has an unfavorable one in it, and when neither is content to let the other's interest remain unchanged.

Let me give an example of disagreement in interest. A. "Let's go to a cinema to-night." B. "I don't want to do that. Let's go to the symphony." A continues to insist on the cinema, B on the symphony. This is disagreement in a perfectly conventional sense. They can't agree on where they want to go, and each is trying to redirect the other's interest. (Note that imperatives are used in the example.)

It is disagreement in *interest* which takes place in ethics. When C says, "This is good," and D says "No, it's bad," we have a case of suggestion and counter-suggestion. Each man is trying to redirect the other's interest. There obviously need be no domineering, since each may be willing to give ear to the other's influence; but each is trying to move the other nonetheless. It is in this sense that they disagree. Those who argue that certain interest theories make no provision for disagreement have been misled, I believe, simply because the traditional theories, in leaving out emotive meaning, give the impression that ethical judgments are used descriptively only; and of course when judgments are used purely descriptively, the only disagreement that can arise is disagreement *in belief.* Such disagreement may be disagreement in belief *about* interests; but this is not the same as disagreement *in* interest. My definition doesn't provide for disagreement in belief about interests, any more than does Hobbes's; but that is no matter, for there is no reason to believe, at least on common-sense grounds, that this kind of disagreement exists. There is only disagreement *in* interest. (We shall see in a moment that disagreement in interest does not remove ethics from sober argument—that this kind of disagreement may often be resolved through empirical means.)

The second restriction, about "magnetism," or the connection between goodness and actions, requires only a word. This rules out *only* those interest theories which do *not* include the interest of the speaker, in defining "good." My account does include the speaker's interest; hence is immune.

The third restriction, about the empirical method, may be met in a way that springs naturally from the above account of disagreement. Let us put the question in this way: When two people disagree over an ethical matter, can they completely resolve the disagreement through empirical considerations, assuming that each applies the empirical method exhaustively, consistently, and without error?

I answer that sometimes they can, and sometimes they cannot; and that at any rate, even when they can, the relation between empirical knowledge and ethical judgments is quite different from the one which traditional interest theories seem to imply.

This can best be seen from an analogy. Let's return to the example where A and B couldn't agree on a cinema or a symphony. The example differed from an ethical argument in that imperatives were used, rather than ethical judgments; but was analogous to the extent that each person was endeavoring to modify the other's interest. Now how would these people argue the case, assuming that they were too intelligent just to shout at one another?

Clearly, they would give "reasons" to support their imperatives. A might say, "But you know, Garbo is at the Bijou." His hope is that B, who admires Garbo, will acquire a desire to go to the cinema when he knows what play will be there. B may counter, "But Toscanini is guest conductor tonight, in an all-Beethoven program." And so on. Each supports his imperative ("*Let's* do so and so") by reasons which may be empirically established.

To generalize from this: disagreement in interest may be rooted in disagreement in belief. That is to say, people who disagree in interest would often cease to do so if they knew the precise nature and consequences of the object of their interest. To this extent disagreement in interest may be resolved by securing agreement in belief, which in turn may be secured empirically.

This generalization holds for ethics. If A and B, instead of using imperatives, had said, respectively, "It would be *better* to go to the cinema," and "It would be better to go to the symphony," the reasons which they would advance would be roughly the same. They would each give a more thorough account of the object of interest, with the purpose of completing the redirection of interest which was begun by the suggestive force of the ethical sentence. On the whole, of course, the suggestive force of the ethical statement merely exerts enough pressure to start such trains of reasons, since the reasons are much more essential in resolving disagreement in interest than the persuasive effect of the ethical judgment itself.

Thus the empirical method is relevant to ethics simply because our knowledge of the world is a determining factor to our interests. But note that empirical facts are not inductive grounds from which the ethical judgment problematically follows. (This is what traditional interest theories imply.) If someone said "Close the door," and added the reason "We'll catch cold," the latter would scarcely be called an inductive ground of the former. Now imperatives are related to the reasons which support them in the same way that ethical judgments are related to reasons.

Is the empirical method *sufficient* for attaining ethical agreement? Clearly not. For empirical knowledge resolves disagreement in interest only to the extent that such disagreement is rooted in disagreement in belief. Not all disagreement in interest is of this sort. For instance: A is of a sympathetic nature, and B isn't. They are arguing about whether a public dole would be good. Suppose that they discovered all the consequences of the dole. Isn't it possible, even so, that A will say that it's good, and B that it's bad? The disagreement in interest may arise not from limited factual knowledge, but simply from A's sympathy and B's coldness. Or again, suppose, in the above argument, that A was poor and unemployed, and that B was rich. Here again the disagreement might not be due to different factual knowledge. It would be due to the different social positions of the men, together with their predominant self-interest.

When ethical disagreement is not rooted in disagreement in belief, is there *any* method by which it may be settled? If one means by "method" a *rational* method, then there is no method. But in any case there is a "way." Let's consider the above example, again, where disagreement was due to A's sympathy and B's coldness. Must they end by saying, "Well, it's just a matter of our having different temperaments"? Not necessarily. A, for instance, may try to *change* the temperament of his opponent. He may pour out his enthusiasms in such a moving way—present the sufferings of the poor with such appeal—that he will lead his opponent to see life through different eyes. He may build up, by the contagion of his feelings, an influence which will modify B's temperament, and create in him a sympathy for the poor which didn't previously exist. This is often the only way to obtain ethical agreement, if there is any way at all. It is persuasive, not empirical or rational; but that is no reason for neglecting it. There is no reason to scorn it, either, for it is only by such means that our personalities are able to grow, through our contact with others.

The point I wish to stress, however, is simply that the empirical method is instrumental to ethical agreement only to the extent that disgreement in interest is rooted in disagreement in belief. There is little reason to believe that all disagreement is of this sort. Hence the empirical method is not sufficient for ethics. In any case, ethics is not psychology, since psychology doesn't endeavor to *direct* our interests; it discovers facts about the ways in which interests are or can be directed, but that's quite another matter.

To summarize this section: my analysis of ethical judgments meets the three requirements for the "vital" sense of "good" that were mentioned in section I. The traditional interest theories fail to meet these requirements simply because they neglect emotive meaning. This neglect leads them to neglect dynamic usage, and the sort of disagreement that results from such usage, together with the method of resolving the disagreement. I may add that my analysis answers Moore's objection about the open question. Whatever scientifically knowable properties a thing may have, it *is* always open to question whether a thing having these (enumerated) qualities is good. For to ask whether it is good is to ask for *influence*. And whatever I may know about an object, I can still ask, quite pertinently, to be influenced with regard to my interest in it.

VI

And now, have I really pointed out the "vital" sense of "good"?

I suppose that many will still say "No," claiming that I have simply failed to set down *enough* requirements which this sense must meet, and that my analysis, like all others given in terms of interest, is a way of begging the issue. They will say: "When we ask 'Is X good?' we don't want mere influence, mere advice. We decidedly don't want to be influenced through persuasion, nor are we fully content when the influence is supported by a wide scientific knowledge of X. The answer to our question will, of course, modify our interests. But this is only because an unique sort of *truth* will be revealed to us—a truth which must be apprehended *a priori.* We want our interests to be guided by this truth, and by nothing else. To substitute for such a truth mere emotive meaning and suggestion is to conceal from us the very object of our search."

I can only answer that I do not understand. What is this truth to be *about*? For I recollect no Platonic Idea, nor do I know what to *try* to recollect. I find no indefinable property, nor do I know what to look for. And the "self-evident" deliverances of reason, which so many philosophers have claimed, seem, on examination, to be deliverances of their respective reasons only (if of anyone's) and not of mine.

I strongly suspect, indeed, that any sense of "good" which is expected both to unite itself in synthetic *a priori* fashion with other concepts, and to influence interests as well, is really a great confusion. I extract from this meaning the power of influence alone, which I find the only intelligible part. If the rest is confusion, however, then it certainly deserves more than the shrug of one's shoulders. What I should like to do is to *account* for the confusion—to examine the psychological needs which have given rise to it, and to show how these needs may be satisfied in another way. This is *the* problem, if confusion is to be stopped at its source. But it is an enormous problem, and my reflections on it, which are at present worked out only roughly, must be reserved until some later time.

I may add that if "X is good" is essentially a vehicle for suggestion, it is scarcely a statement which philosophers, any more than many other men, are called upon to make. To the extent that ethics predicates the ethical terms of anything, rather than explains their meaning, it ceases to be a reflective study. Ethical statements are social instruments. They are used in a co-operative enterprise in which we are mutually adjusting ourselves to the interests of others. Philosophers have a part in this, as do all men, but not the major part.

Chapter V – Man in Society

Introduction

The first attempt in the Western world to state the problem that will occupy us in this chapter is found in Plato's dialogue *The Crito* (see Chapter II). Crito has come to the cell in which Socrates is awaiting execution with the news that he and his friends are prepared to bribe Socrates' guards, and make possible his escape from Athens. But Socrates calls upon Crito to be mindful of the laws according to which he has been legally if unjustly convicted, and what they would say if he should attempt to escape their commands:

> What complaint have you to make against us (the laws), which justifies you in attempting to destroy us and the state? In the first place, did we not bring you into existence? . . . Were not the laws, which have the charge of education, right in commanding your father to train you in music and gymnastic? . . . He who has experience of the manner in which we order justice and administer the state, and still remains, has entered into an implied contract that he will do as we command him.

The key question, to which Socrates gives the answer proposed here, is: What is the responsibility of the individual to the state, and what is the responsibility of the state to the individual? Socrates' answer is clear: the responsibility of the state to the individual is to provide the social order and governmental administration that makes civilization possible, and the responsibility of the individual to the state is obedience.

This doctrine was sufficiently compelling to Socrates that he died in its name, and his courage in cleaving to the laws, despite the fact that they were unjustly applied in his case still has the power to inspire us. But closer scrutiny reveals difficulties in the doctrine giving rise to centuries of philosophical disputation. First of all, it appears that there is a difference between a law that is unjustly applied, and a law that is itself immoral. Laws may be used by evil judges and lawyers to commit what is called judicial murder, as in the case of Socrates, or, to take just one example from times closer to our own, as in the famous case of Sacco and Vanzetti. Socrates would argue that in such cases, the judges and lawyers are to be attacked, but the law itself remains unassailable. But may there not be laws that are themselves immoral? Think of the apartheid laws in the Republic of South Africa, or of the lawful commands of officers to shoot prisoners of war! *Wouldn't a person who submits to such laws be performing an immoral act even though he believes that obedience to the laws of his society is required of him?* Socrates provides two means of escape from this objection: a person who "does not like us (the laws) and the city may emigrate . . . and retain his property," or a man may attempt to "change the views of his city and country" as to what ought to be lawful and what not. But emigration may be impossible, and the influence of one man, even a great public figure like Socrates, is usually insufficient to change laws imposed by dictators or by an unfeeling majority. Although many thinkers have been dissatisfied with Socrates' stance, the question he first raised has not been forgotten. At least three groups of problems in political philosophy have the *question of the proper relationship of the individual to the state* as their locus.

1. *What are the proper goals of the state?* If we are to criticize the laws of our community in a responsible manner, we must do so on the basis of a coherent theory regarding the aims of government. Of course, it is the responsibility of a government to rule justly. But it is not clear that justice is the *sole* or *highest* goal of government; many people have argued that social order or progress are ideas to which perfect justice must occasionally be sacrificed. In the last century, for example, American pioneers, as well as the great majority of European Americans, tacitly approved the unjust treatment of native Americans on the grounds that progress is desirable. Thoreau, however, in the face of what he conceived to be his society's intolerable injustice towards slaves and their neighbors in Mexico, wrote that "this people (the Americans) must cease to hold slaves, and to make war on Mexico, though it cost them their existence as a people:" a view of justice that still appeals to revolutionaries, and fills partisans of the Establishment with consternation.

In Chapter III, we saw Aristotle propose a solution to the question of the proper ends of government that has become classic: the true interests of the government and the individual do not necessarily clash, he asserts. In fact, individual interests and the interests of the state as a whole are to a great extent in harmony. The goal of the individual is the realization of his potential for meaningful activity in a life of reason; the goal of civil society is to provide the individual with the challenges that will give scope to his talents. An evil government, therefore, is one that frustrates us in our pursuit of our natural end: happiness achieved through a life of reason. The best society is not that which achieves abstract justice, but assists us in the achievement of a valuable life. A society which fails to realize this end is subject to legitimate criticism.

2. *What is the source of legal obligation?* Still, Aristotle's theory does not dispose of the objection that the individual and the society may in fact clash at times, and legal means of protest may be insufficient to persuade the sovereign power to change the laws. The options available to the dissenting individual seem to be (1) either leaving the country or knuckling under, as Socrates holds; (2) civil disobedience, although this course, if widespread, might undermine civilization, which seems to depend upon the rule of law; or (3) violence, which might at times result in the destruction of some of the very people whose rights were being defended. Those who have taken a conservative position on this issue have striven to support the Socratic doctrine, while those who have taken a liberal standpoint have sought to weaken Socrates' position.

Although this argument has taken many forms, a key concept in the dispute, which is found in the above passage from *The Crito,* and will be encountered in the selections from Hobbes, Locke, and Rousseau in this chapter, concerns a putative *social contract* between the individual and the state. Socrates insists that the source of his obligation to submit to his execution is the implicit contract between himself and the laws: a contract in which *obedience* is the price of *civilization.* Hobbes, Locke, and Rousseau all agree that the relation of an individual to his society is analogous to a contract. They disagree as to the exact terms of that contract, however, and whether it contains an escape clause for cases in which the individual citizens become convinced that the government is not holding up its end of the contract. Again, liberal and conservative politics can be defined in terms of this philosophical conflict. Socrates' view is conservative: where there is a conflict between the individual and the society, the individual must give in. It is possible to reject the Socratic view and insist that the individual or a minority of citizens is justified in attempting a revolution, should the government not achieve the goals of society which are deemed proper by the protesters: justice, progress, or the pursuit of individual happiness. Locke's stand is especially ingenious, and should be subject to careful study by Americans, whose form of government it influenced greatly. Locke postulates two implicit contracts, one between the individual and society as a whole, and one between the individuals who make up society and their government. Sovereignty resides in the people, who ought to be free to dissolve the institutions of government, if the government fails in its purposes.

John Stuart Mill and Karl Marx, both represented by selections from their works in this chapter, insist even more strongly that the obligations of individuals to obey the law are contingent upon the success of their government. Mill warns us against a "tyranny of the majority" which threatens progress by the passage of laws that resist individual initiative. Marx is the chosen spokesman of all outcastes and scorned ones whom society ignores in their distress, though it be caused by no fault of their own. Their only recourse is the violent disruption of legal structures that are used to oppress them.

3. *What is the best form of government?* Even if we are aware of the proper *ends* of government, we are still not assured as to the best *means* for achieving those ends. Plato, who claimed that the proper end of government is the establishment of justice in the individual and in the structures of society, held that leadership should be placed in the hands of a ruling elite composed of philosophers who alone know the nature of justice and the means of leading mankind toward the ideal. But Plato was well aware that there were other possible forms of government. In *The Republic,* he presents a famous typography of possible governments, each of which he evaluates in terms of the good or evil they tend to produce. After his Utopia ruled by philosopher-kings, there is *timocracy,* or what we might call the rule of the generals, whose chief social goal is the maintenance of the honor and military power of the state; *oligarchy,* or capitalist republic, whose goal is material wealth; *democracy,* or rule of none, whose goal is the freedom of individuals to enjoy themselves; and *tyranny,* or the rule of one man, whose goal is the aggrandizement of the dictator. In the passages from Hobbes and Locke, you will also encounter the concept of *monarchy,* which was known, of course, in the ancient world, but constituted the dominant system of government in Europe during the seventeenth and eighteenth centuries. And in Rousseau and Marx you will find prefigured what has become one of the chief forms of government in the twentieth century: totalitarianism, which dissolves all the distinctions between the society and the state so as to institute a system of total control over the affairs of its citizens, presumably to insure that, as Marx demanded, to each will in fact be given according to his needs, and from each will be taken according to his abilities to produce. And the state thus becomes totally responsible not *to,* but *for* the individual "from the cradle to the grave" in return for the individual's total obedience to the law.

The search for better forms of government continues today, in the kibbutzim of Israel, the communes of China, the tentative gropings toward democratic rule in the emerging states of Africa and Asia, and the efforts of our own country to balance the often contradictory aims of the public and private sector. Our selections give the reader both the historical background and the philosophical vocabulary that are necessary for understanding the continuing struggle of individuals to assert their needs against legal and governmental systems, and of governments to provide for individuals while assuring their own survival.

Thomas Hobbes: Society and the State of Nature

OF THE DIFFERENCE OF MANNERS

By *manners,* I mean not here, decency of behavior; as how one should salute another, or how a man should wash his mouth, or pick his teeth before company, and such other points of the *small morals;* but those qualities of mankind, that concern their living together in peace, and unity. To which end we are to consider, that the felicity of this life, consisteth not in the repose of a mind satisfied. For there is no such *finis ultimus,* utmost aim, nor *summum bonum*, greatest good, as is spoken of in the books of the old moral philosophers. Nor can a man any more live, whose desires are at an end, than he, whose senses and imaginations are at a stand. Felicity is a continual progress of the desire, from one object to another; the attaining of the former, being still but the way to the latter. The cause whereof is, that the object of man's desire, is not to enjoy once only, and for one instant of time; but to assure for ever, the way of his future desire. And therefore the voluntary actions, and inclinations of all men, tend, not only to the procuring, but also to the assuring of a contented life; and differ only in the way: which ariseth partly from the diversity of passions in diverse men; and partly from the difference of the knowledge, or opinion each one has of the causes, which produce the effect desired.

So that in the first place, I put for a general inclination of all mankind, a perpetual and restless desire of power after power, that ceaseth only in death. And the cause of this, is not always that a man hopes for a more intensive delight, than he has already attained to; or that he cannot be content with a moderate power: but because he cannot assure the power and means to live well, which he hath present, without the acquisition of more. And from hence it is, that kings, whose power is greatest, turn their endeavors to the assuring it at home by laws, or abroad by wars; and when that is done, there succeedeth a new desire; in some, of fame from new conquest; in others, of ease and sensual pleasure; in others, of admiration, or being flattered for excellence in some art, or other ability of the mind. . . .

From Thomas Hobbes, *Leviathan* (selections).

OF THE NATURAL CONDITION OF MANKIND AS CONCERNING THEIR FELICITY, AND MISERY

Nature hath made men so equal, in the faculties of the body and mind; as that, though there be found one man sometimes manifestly stronger in body or of quicker mind than another, yet when all is reckoned together, the difference between man and man is not so considerable, as that one man can thereupon claim to himself any benefit, to which another may not pretend as well as he. For as to the strength of body, the weakest has strength enough to kill the strongest, either by secret machination, or by confederacy with others that are in the same danger with himself.

And as to the faculties of the mind—setting aside the arts grounded upon words, and especially that skill of proceeding upon general and infallible rules, called science; which very few have, and but in few things; as being not a native faculty, born with us; nor attained, as prudence, while we look after somewhat else—I find yet a greater equality amongst men, than that of strength. For prudence is but experience which equal time equally bestows on all men, in those things they equally apply themselves unto. That which may perhaps make such equality incredible, is but a vain conceit of one's own wisdom, which almost all men think they have in a greater degree than the vulgar; that is, than all men but themselves, and a few others, whom by fame, or for concurring with themselves, they approve. For such is the nature of men, that howsoever they may acknowledge many others to be more witty, or more eloquent, or more learned, yet they will hardly believe there be many so wise as themselves; for they see their own wit at hand, and other men's at a distance. But this proveth rather that men are in that point equal, than unequal. For there is not ordinarily a greater sign of the equal distribution of anything, than that every man is contented with his share.

From this equality of ability, ariseth equality of hope in the attaining of our ends. And therefore if any two men desire the same thing, which nevertheless, they cannot both enjoy, they become enemies; and in the way to their end, which is principally their own conservation, and sometimes their delectation only, endeavour to destroy, or subdue one another. And from hence it comes to pass that where an invader hath no more to fear than another man's single power; if one plant, sow, build, or possess a convenient seat, others may probably be expected to come prepared with forces united, to dispossess and deprive him, not only of the fruit of his labor, but also of his life or liberty. And the invader again is in the like danger of another.

And from this diffidence of one another, there is no way for any man to secure himself so reasonable as anticipation; that is, by force or wiles to master the persons of all men he can, so long, till he see no other power great enough to endanger him: and this is no more than his own conservation requireth, and is generally allowed. Also because there be some, that taking pleasure in contemplating their own power in the acts of conquest, which they pursue farther than their security requires; if others, that otherwise would be glad to be at ease within modest bounds, should not by invasion increase their power, they would not be able long time, by standing only on their defense, to subsist. And by consequence, such augmentation of dominion over men being necessary to a man's conservation, it ought to be allowed him.

Again, men have no pleasure, but on the contrary a great deal of grief, in keeping company, where there is no power able to overawe them all. For every man looketh that his companion should value him at the same rate he sets upon himself; and upon all signs of contempt, or undervaluing, naturally endeavors as far as he dares (which amongst them that have no common power to keep them in quiet, is far enough to make them destroy each other), to extort a greater value from his contemners by damage, and from others by the example.

So that in the nature of man, we find three principal causes of quarrel. First, competition; second, diffidence; thirdly, glory.

The first maketh men invade for gain; the second, for safety; and the third, for reputation. The first use violence to make themselves masters of other men's persons, wives, children, and cattle; the second, to defend them; the third, for trifles, as a word, a smile, a different opinion; and any other sign of undervalue, either direct in their persons, or by reflection in their kindred, their friends, their nation, their profession, or their name.

Hereby it is manifest that during the time men live without a common power to keep them all in awe, they are in that condition which is called war; and such a way as is of every man against every man. For *war* consisteth not in battle only, or the act of fighting, but in a tract of time wherein the will to contend by battle is sufficiently known, and therefore the notion of *time* is to be considered in the nature of war, as it is in the nature of weather. For as the nature of foul weather lieth not in a shower or two of rain, but in an inclination thereto of many days together; so the nature of war consisteth not in actual fighting, but in the known disposition thereto, during all the time there is no assurance to the contrary. All other time is *peace.*

Whatsoever therefore is consequent to a time of war, where every man is enemy to every man; the same is consequent to the time, wherein men live without other security than what their own strength and their own invention shall furnish them withal. In such condition there is no place for industry, because the fruit thereof is uncertain: and consequently no culture of the earth; no navigation, nor use of the commodities that may be imported by sea; no commodious building; no instruments of moving, and removing, such things as require much force; no knowledge of the face of the earth; no account of time; no arts; no letters; no society; and which is worst of all, continual fear, and danger of violent death; and the life of man, solitary, poor, nasty, brutish, and short.

It may seem strange to some man that has not well weighted these things, that nature should thus dissociate, and render men apt to invade and destroy one another; and he may, therefore, not trusting to this inference, made from the passions, desire perhaps to have the same confirmed by experience. Let him therefore consider with himself, when taking a journey, he arms himself and seeks to go well accompanied; when going to sleep, he locks his doors; when even in his house he locks his chests; and this when he knows there be laws, and public officers, armed, to revenge all injuries shall be done him: what opinion he has of his fellow-subjects, when he rides armed; of his fellow-citizens, when he locks his doors; and of his children, and servants, when he locks his chests. Does he not there as much accuse mankind by his actions, as I do by my words? But neither of us accuse man's nature in it. The desires, and other passions of man, are in themselves no sin. No more are the actions that proceed from those passions, till they know a law that forbids them: which till laws be made they cannot know; nor can any law be made, till they have agreed upon the person that shall make it.

It may peradventure be thought, there was never such a time nor condition of war as this; and I believe it was never generally so, over all the world: but there are many places where they live so now. For the savage people in many places of America, except the government of small families, the concord whereof dependeth on natural lust, have no government at all; and live at this time in that brutish manner, as I said before. Howsoever, it may be perceived what manner of life there would be, where there were no common power to fear; by the manner of life which men that have formerly lived under a peaceful government, use to degenerate into in a civil war.

But though there had never been any time wherein particular men were in a condition of war one against another; yet in all times, kings, and persons of sovereign authority, because of their independency, are in continual jealousies, and in the state and posture of gladiators; having their weapons pointing, and their eyes fixed on one another; that is, their forts, garrisons, and guns upon the frontiers of their kingdoms; and continual spies upon their neighbors; which is a posture of war. But because they uphold thereby the industry of their subjects, there does not follow from it that misery which accompanies the liberty of particular men.

To this war of every man against every man, this also is consequent: *that nothing can be unjust*. The notions of right and wrong, justice and injustice, have there no place. Where there is no common power, there is no law; where no law, no injustice. Force and fraud are in war the two cardinal virtues. Justice and injustice are none of the faculties neither of the body nor mind. If they were, they might be in a man that were alone in the world, as well as his senses and passions. They are qualities that relate to men in society, not in solitude. It is consequent also to the same condition, that there be no propriety, no dominion, no *mine* and *thine* distinct; but only that to be every man's, that he can get; and for so long as he can keep it. And thus much for the ill condition which man by mere nature is actually placed in; though with a possibility to come out of it, consisting partly in the passions, partly in his reason.

The passions that incline men to peace are fear of death, desire of such things as are necessary to commodious living, and a hope by their industry to obtain them. And reason suggesteth convenient articles of peace, upon which men may be drawn to agreement. These articles are they which otherwise are called the Laws of Nature whereof I shall speak more particularly in the two following chapters.

OF THE FIRST AND SECOND NATURAL LAWS, AND OF CONTRACTS

The right of nature, which writers commonly call *jus naturale,* is the liberty each man hath to use his own power, as he will himself, for the preservation of his own nature; that is to say, of his own life; and consequently, of doing anything, which in his own judgment and reason, he shall conceive to be the aptest means thereunto.

By *liberty,* is understood, according to the

proper signification of the word, the absence of external impediments: which impediments, may oft take away part of a man's power to do what he would; but cannot hinder him from using the power left him, according as his judgment and reason shall dictate to him.

A *law of nature, lex naturalis,* is a precept or general rule, found out by reason, by which a man is forbidden to do that which is destructive of his life, or taketh away the means of preserving the same; and to omit that by which he thinketh it may be best preserved. For though they that speak of this subject, use to confound *jus* and *lex*, *right* and *law*; yet they ought to be distinguished: because *right* consisteth in liberty to do or to forbear, whereas *law* determineth and bindeth to one of them; so that law, and right differ as much as obligation and liberty; which in one and the same matter are inconsistent.

And because the condition of man, as hath been declared in the precedent chapter, is a condition of war of everyone against everyone; in which case everyone is governed by his own reason, and there is nothing he can make use of that may not be a help unto him in preserving his life against his enemies: it followeth, that in such a condition every man has a right to everything; even to one another's body. And therefore, as long as this natural right of every man to everything endureth, there can be no security to any man, how strong or wise soever he be, of living out the time which nature ordinarily alloweth men to live. And consequently it is a precept, or general rule of reason, *that every man ought to endeavor peace, as far as he has hope of obtaining it; and when he cannot obtain it, that he may seek and use all helps and advantages of war.* The first branch of which rule containeth the first and fundamental law of nature; which is, *to seek peace and follow it.* The second, the sum of the right of nature; which is, *by all means we can, to defend ourselves.*

From this fundamental law of nature, by which men are commanded to endeavor peace, is derived this second law: *that a man be willing, when others are so too, as far forth as for peace and defense of himself he shall think it necessary, to lay down this right to all things; and be contented with so much liberty against other men, as he would allow other men against himself.* For as long as every man holdeth this right, of doing anything he liketh, so long are all men in the condition of war. But if other men will not lay down their right, as well as he, then there is no reson for anyone to divest himself of his: for that were to expose himself to prey, which no man is bound to, rather than to dispose himself to peace. This is that law of the Gospel: *whatsoever you require that others should do to you, that do ye to them.* And that law of all men, *quod tibi fieri non vis, alteri ne feceris* (do not do unto others what you do not wish them to do unto you).

To *lay down* a man's *right* to anything, is to *divest* himself of the *liberty,* of hindering another of the benefit of his own right to the same. For he that renounceth or passeth away his right, giveth not to any other man a right which he had not before; because there is nothing to which every man had not right by nature: but only standeth out of his way, that he may enjoy his own original right, without hindrance from him, not without hindrance from another. So that the effect which redoundeth to one man, by another man's defect of right, is but so much diminution of impediments to the use of his own right original.

Right is laid aside, either by simple renouncing it, or by transferring it to another. By *simply renouncing,* when he cares not to whom the benefit thereof redoundeth. By *transferring,* when he intendeth the benefit thereof to some certain person or persons. And when a man hath in either manner abandoned or granted away his right; then is he said to be *obliged,* or bound, not to hinder those to whom such right is granted or abandoned, from the benefit of it; and that he *ought,* and it is his *duty,* not to make void that voluntary act of his own; and that such hindrance is *injustice,* and *injury,* as being *sine jure*; the right being before renounced, or transferred. So that injury, or injustice, in the controversies of the world, is somewhat like to that, which in the disputations of scholars is called *absurdity.* For as it is there called an absurdity to contradict what one maintained in the beginning; so in the world, it is called injustice, and injury, voluntarily to undo that which from the beginning he had voluntarily done. The way by which a man either simply renounceth, or transferreth his right, is a declaration, or signification, by some voluntary and sufficient sign or signs, that he doth so renounce or transfer, or hath so renounced or transferred the same, to him that accepteth it. And these signs are either words only, or actions only, as it happeneth most often, both words and actions. And the same are the *bonds,* by which men are bound and obliged—bonds that have their strength, not from their own nature, for nothing is more easily broken than a man's word, but from fear of some evil consequence upon the rupture.

Whensoever a man transferreth his right, or renounceth it; it is either in consideration of some right reciprocally transferred to himself; or for some other good he hopeth for thereby. For it is a voluntary act; and of the voluntary act of every man, the object is some *good to himself.* And therefore there be some rights which no man can be understood by any words, or other signs, to have abandoned or transferred. As first a man cannot lay down the right of resisting them that assault him by force, to take away his life; because he cannot be understood to aim thereby, at any good to himself. The same may be said of wounds, and chains, and imprisonment: both because there is no benefit consequent to such patience, as there is to the patience of suffering another to be wounded or imprisoned; as also because a man cannot tell, when he seeth men proceed against him by violence, whether they intend his death or not. And lastly the motive, an end for which this renouncing and transferring of right is introduced, is nothing else but the security of a man's person, in his life, and in the means of so preserving life as not of to be weary of it. And therefore if a man by words, or others signs, seem to despoil himself of the end for which those signs were intended, he is not to be understood as if he meant it, or that it was his will, but that he was ignorant of how such words and actions were to be interpreted.

The mutual transferring of right, is what men call *contract.*

There is difference between transferring of right to the thing, and transferring, or tradition—that is delivery—of the thing itself. For the thing may be delivered together with the translation of the right, as in buying and selling with ready money, or exchange of goods, or lands; and it may be delivered sometime after.

Again, one of the contractors may deliver the thing contracted for on his part, and leave the other to perform his part at some determinate time after, and in the meantime be trusted; and then the contract on his part is called *pact,* or *covenant:* or both parts may contract now to perform hereafter; in which cases, he that is to perform in time to come, being trusted, his performance is called *keeping of promise,* or faith; and the failing of performance, if it be voluntary, *violation of faith.*

When the transferring of right is not mutual; but one of the parties transferreth, in hope to gain thereby friendship, or service from another, or from his friends; or in hope to gain the reputation of charity, or magnanimity; or to deliver his mind from the pain of compassion; or in hope of reward in heaven; this is not contract, but *gift, free-gift, grace:* which words signify one and the same thing.

Signs of contract, are either *express,* or *by inference.* Express, are words spoken with understanding of what they signify: and such words are either of the time *present,* or *past;* as, *I give, I grant, I have given, I have granted, I will that this be yours:* or of the future; as, *I will give, will grant:* which words of the future are called *promise.*

Signs by inference are sometimes the consequence of words; sometimes the consequence of silence; sometimes the consequence of actions; sometimes the consequence of forbearing an action; and generally a sign by inference, of any contract, is whatsoever sufficiently argues the will of the contractor.

Words alone, if they be of the time to come, and contain a bare promise, are an insufficient sign of a free-gift, and therefore not obligatory. For if they be of the time to come, as *tomorrow I will give,* they are a sign I have not given yet, and consequently that my right is not transferred, but remaineth till I transfer it by some other act. But if the words be of the time present, or past, as, *I have given, or, do give to be delivered tomorrow,* then is my tomorrow's right given away today; and that by the virtue of the words, though there were no other argument of my will. And there is a great difference in the signification of these words, *volo hoc tuum esse cras,* and *cras dabo;* that is, between *I will that this be thine tomorrow,* and, *I will it thee tomorrow:* for the word *I will,* in the former manner of speech, signifies an act of the will present; but in the latter, it signifies a promise of an act of the will to come: and therefore the former words, being of the present, transfer a future right; the latter, that be of the future, transfer nothing. But if there be other signs of the will to transfer a right, besides words; then, though the gift be free, yet may the right be understood to pass by words of the future: as if a man propound a prize to him that comes first to the end of a race, the gift is free; and though the words be of the future, yet the right passeth: for if he would not have his words so be understood, he should not have let them run.

In contracts, the right passeth, not only where the words are of the time present, or past, but also where they are of the future: because all contract is mutual translation, or change or right; and therefore he that promiseth only, because he hath already received the benefit for which he promiseth, is to be understood as if he intended the right should pass: for unless he had been content to have his words so understood, the other would not have performed his part first. And for that cause, in buying, and selling, and other acts of contract, a promise is equivalent to a convenant; and therefore obligatory.

He that performeth first in the case of a contract, is said to *merit* that which he is to receive by the performance of the other; and he hath it as *due*. Also when a prize is propounded to many, which is to be given to him only that winneth; or money is thrown amongst many, to be enjoyed by them that catch it; though this be a free gift; yet so to win, or so to catch, is to *merit*, and to have it as *due*. For the right is transferred in the propounding of the prize, and in throwing down the money; though it be not determined to whom, but by the event of the contention. But there is between these two sorts of merit, this difference, that in contract, I merit by virtue of my own power, and the contractor's need; but in this case of free gift, I am enabled to merit only by the benignity of the giver: in contract, I merit at the contractor's hand that he should depart with his right; in this case of gift, I merit not that the giver should part with his right; but that when he has parted with it, it should be mine, rather than another's. And this I think to be the meaning of that distinction of the Schools, between *meritum congrui*, and *meritum condigni*. For God Almighty, having promised Paradise to those men, hoodwinked with carnal desires, that can walk through this world according to the precepts, and limits prescribed by him; they say, he that shall so walk, shall merit Paradise *ex congruo*. But because no man can demand a right to it, by his own righteousness, or any other power in himself, but by the free grace of God only; they say, no man can merit Paradise *ex condigno*. This I say, I think is the meaning of that distinction; but because disputers do not agree upon the signification of their own terms of art, longer than it serves their turn; I will not affirm anything of their meaning: only this I say; when a gift is given indefinitely, as a prize to be contended for, he that winneth meriteth, and may claim the prize as due.

If a convenant be made, wherein neither of the parties perform presently, but trust one another; in the condition of mere nature, which is a condition of war of every man against every man, upon any reasonable suspicion, it is void: but if there be a common power set over them both, with right and force sufficient to compel performance, it is not void. For he that performeth first, has no assurance the other will perform after; because the bonds of words are too weak to bridle men's ambition, avarice, anger, and other passions, without the fear of some coercive power; which in the condition of mere nature, where all men are equal, and judges of the justness of their own fears, cannot possibly be supposed. And therefore he which performeth first, does but betray himself to his enemy; contrary to the right, he can never abandon, of defending his life, and means of living.

But in a civil estate, where there is a power set up to constrain those that would otherwise violate their faith, that fear is no more reasonable; and for that cause, he which by the covenant is to perform first, is obliged so to do.

OF THE RIGHTS OF SOVEREIGNS BY INSTITUTION

A commonwealth is said to be *instituted*, when a multitude of men do agree and covenant, everyone with everyone, that to whatsoever man, or assembly of men, shall be given by the major part the right to present the person of them all, that is to say, to be their *representative;* everyone, as well he that voted for it as he that voted against it, shall authorize all the actions and judgments of that man, or assembly of men, in the same manner as if they were his own, to the end to live peaceably amongst themselves and be protected against other men.

From this institution of a commonwealth are derived all the *rights* and *faculties* of him, or them, on whom sovereign power is conferred by the consent of the people assembled.

First, because they covenant, it is to be understood they are not obliged by former covenant to anything repugnant hereunto. And consequently they that have already instituted a commonwealth, being thereby bound by covenant to own the actions and judgments of one, cannot lawfully make a new covenant amongst themselves, to be obedient to any other, in anything whatsoever, without his permission. And therefore, they that are subject to a monarch, cannot without his leave cast off monarchy, and return to the confusion of a disunited multitude; not transfer their person from him that beareth it, to another man, or other assembly of men: for they are bound, every man to every man, to own, and be reputed author of all, that he that already is their sovereign shall do and judge fit to be done; so that any one man dissenting, all the rest should break their covenant made to that man, which is injustice: and they have also every man given the sovereignty to him that beareth their person; and therefore if they depose him, they take from him that which is his own, and so again it is injustice. Besides, if he that attempteth to depose his sovereign, be killed or punished by him for such attempt, he is author of his own punishment, as being by the institution, author of all his sovereign shall do; and because it is injustice for a man to do anything for which he may be punished by his own authority, he is also upon that title, unjust. And whereas some men have pretended for their disobedience to their sovereign, a new covenant, made not with men but with God, this also is unjust: for there is no covenant with God, but by mediation of somebody that representeth God's person; which none doth but God's lieutenant, who hath the sovereignty under God. But this pretense of covenant with God, is so evident a lie, even in the pretenders' own consciences, that it is not only an act of an unjust, but also of a vile and unmanly disposition.

Secondly, because the right of bearing a person of them all, is given to him they make sovereign, by covenant only of one to another, and not of him to any of them; there can happen no breach of covenant on the part of the sovereign; and consequently none of his subjects, by any pretense of forfeiture, can be freed from his subjection. That he which is made sovereign maketh no covenant with his subjects beforehand, is manifest; because either he must make it with the whole multitude, as one party to the covenant, or he must make a several covenant with every man. With the whole, as one party, it is impossible, because as yet they are not one person: and if he make so many several covenants as there be men, those covenants after he hath the sovereignty are void; because what act soever can be pretended by any one of them for breach thereof, is the act both of himself and of all the rest, because done in the person, and by the right of every one of them in particular. Besides, if any one, or more of them, pretend a breach of the covenant made by the sovereign at his institutions; and others; as one other of his subjects, or himself alone, pretend there was no such breach: there is in this case, no judge to decide the controversy; it returns therefore to the sword again; and every man recovereth the right of protecting himself by his own strength, contrary to the design they had in the institution. It is therefore in vain to grant sovereignty by way of precedent covenant. The opinion that any monarch receiveth his power by covenant, that is to say, on condition, proceedeth from want of understanding this easy truth, that convenants being but words and breath, have no force to oblige, contain, constrain, or protect any man, but what it has from the public sword; that is, from the untied hands of that man, or assembly of men that hath the sovereignty of them all, in him united. But when an assembly of men is made sovereign, then no man imagineth any such covenant to have passed in the institution; for no man is so dull as to say, for example, the people of Rome made a covenant with the Romans, to hold the sovereignty on such or such conditions; which not performed, the Romans might lawfully depose the Roman people. That men see not the reason to be alike in a monarchy and in a popular government, proceedeth from the ambition of some that are kinder to the government of an assembly, whereof they may hope to participate, than of monarchy, which they despair to enjoy,

Thirdly, because the major part hath by consenting voices declared a sovereign, he that dissented must now consent with the rest; that is, be contented to avow all the actions he shall do, or else justly be destroyed by the rest. For if he voluntarily entered into the congregation of them that were assembled, he sufficiently declared thereby his will, and therefore tacitly covenanted to stand to what the major part should ordain; and therefore if he refuse to stand thereto, or make protestation against any of their decrees, he does contrary to his covenant, and therefore unjustly. And whether he be of the congregation or not, and whether his consent be asked or not, he must either submit to their decrees, or be left in the condition of war he was in before; wherein he might without injustice be destroyed by any man whatsoever.

Fourthly, because every subject is by this institution author of all the actions and judgments of the sovereign instituted; it follows that whatsoever he doth, it can be no injury to any of his subjects, nor ought he to be by any of them accused to injustice. For he that doth anything by authority from another, doth therein no injury to him by whose authority he acteth: but by this institution of a commonwealth, every particular man is author of all the sovereign doth: and consequently he that complaineth of injury from his sovereign, complaineth of that whereof he himself is author; and therefore ought not to accuse any man but himself; nor himself of injury, because to do injury to one's self, is impossible. It is true that they that have sovereign power may commit iniquity, but not injustice, or injury, in the proper signification.

Fifthly, and consequently to that which was said last, no man that hath sovereign power can justly be put to death, or otherwise in any manner by his subjects punished. For seeing every subject is author of the actions of his sovereign, he punisheth another for the actions committed by himself.

And because the end of this institution, is the peace and defense of them all, and whosoever has right to the end has right to the means; it belongeth of right, to whatsoever man or assembly that hath the sovereignty, to be judge both of the means of peace and defense, and also of the hindrances and disturbances of the same; and to do whatsoever he shall think necessary to be done, both beforehand, for the preserving of peace and security, by prevention of discord at home and hostility from abroad. and, when peace and security are lost, for the recovery of the same. And therefore,

Sixthly, it is annexed to the sovereignty, to be judge of what opinions and doctrines are averse, and what conducing to peace; and consequently, on what occasions, how far, and what men are to be trusted withal, in speaking to multitudes of people; and who shall examine the doctrines of all books before they be published. For the actions of men proceed from their opinions; and in the well-governing of opinions consisteth the well-governing of men's actions, in order to their peace and concord. And though in matter of doctrine nothing ought to be regarded but the truth, yet this is not repugnant to regulating the same by peace. For doctrine repugnant to peace can no more be true, than peace and concord can be against the law of nature. It is true that in a commonwealth, where, by the negligence or unskillfulness of governors and teachers, false doctrines are by time generally received; the contrary truths may be generally offensive. Yet the most sudden and rough bursting in of a new truth that can be, does never break the peace, but only sometimes awake the war. For those men that are so remissly governed, that they dare take up arms to defend or introduce an opinion, are still in war; and their condition not peace, but only a cessation of arms for fear of one another; and they live, as it were, in the precincts of battle continually. It belongeth therefore to him that hath the sovereign power, to be judge, or constitute all judges of opinions and doctrines, as a thing necessary to peace; thereby to prevent discord and civil war.

Seventhly, is annexed to the sovereignty, the whole power of prescribing the rules, whereby every man may know what goods he may enjoy, and what actions he may do, without being molested by any of his fellow-subjects; and this is it men call *propriety*. For before constitution of sovereign power, as hath already been shown, all men had right to all things; which necessarily causeth war: and therefore this propriety, being necesary to peace, and depending on sovereign power, is the act of that power, in order to the public peace. These rules of propriety, or *meum* and *tuum*, and of good, evil, lawful, and unlawful in the actions of subjects, are the civil laws; that is to say the laws of each commonwealth in particular: though the name of civil law be now restrained to the ancient civil laws of the city of Rome; which being the head of a great part of the world, her laws at that time were in these parts the civil law.

Eighthly, is annexed to the sovereignty, the right of judicature; that is to say, of hearing and deciding all controversies which may arise concerning law, either civil or natural, or concerning fact. For without the decision of controversies, there is no protection of one subject against the injuries of another: the laws concerning *meum* and *tuum* are in vain; and to every man remaineth, from the natural and necessary appetite of his own conservation, the right of protecting himself by his private strength, which is the condition of war, and contrary to the end for which every commonwealth is instituted.

Ninthly, is annexed to the sovereignty, the right of making way and peace with other nations and commonwealths; that is to say, of judging when it is for the public good, and how great forces are to be assembled, armed, and paid for that end; and to levy money upon the subjects, to defray the expenses thereof. For the power by which the people are to be defended, consisteth in their armies; and the strength of an army, in the union of their strength under one command: which command the sovereign instituted, therefore hath; because the command of the militia, without other institution, maketh him that hath it sovereign. And therefore whosoever is made general of any army, he that hath the sovereign power is always generalissimo.

Tenthly, is annexed to the sovereignty, the choosing of all counsellors, ministers, magistrates, and offices, both in peace and war. For seeing the sovereign is charged with the end, which is the common peace and defense, he is understood to have power to use such means as he shall think most fit for his discharge.

Eleventhly, to the sovereign is committed the power of rewarding with riches, or honor, and of punishing with corporal or pecuniary punishment, or with ignominy, every subject according to the law he hath formerly made; or if there be no law made, according as he shall judge most to conduce to the encouraging of men to serve the commonwealth, or deterring of them from doing disservice to the same.

Lastly, considering what value men are naturally apt to set upon themselves, what respect they look for from others, and how little they value other men; from whence continually arise amongst them, emulation, quarrels, factions, and at last war, to the destroying of one another and diminution of their strength against a common enemy; it is necessary that there be laws of honor, and a public rate of the worth of such men as have deserved or are able to deserve well of the commonwealth; and that there be force in the hands of some or other, to put those laws in execution. But it hath already been shown, that not only the whole militia, or foces of the commonwealth, but also the judicature of all controveries, is annexed to the sovereignty. To the sovereign therefore it belongeth also to give titles of honor; and to appoint what order of place and dignity each man shall hold; and what signs of respect, in public or private meetings, they shall give to one another.

These are the rights which make the essence of sovereignty, and which are the marks whereby a man may discern in what man, or assembly of men, the sovereign power, is placed and resideth. For these are incommunicable and inseparable. The power to coin money, to dispose of the estate and persons of infant heirs, to have pre-emption in markets, and all other statute prerogatives, may be transferred by the sovereign; and yet the power to protect his subjects be retained. But if he transfer the militia, he retains the judicature in vain, for want of execution the laws; or if he gives away the power of raising money, the militia is in or if he give away the government of doctrines, men will be frighted into rebellion with the fear of spirits. And so if we consider any one of the said rights, we shall presently see that the holding of all the rest will produce no effect in the conservation of peace and justice, the end for which all commonwealths are instituted. And this division is it whereof it is said, *a kingdom divided in itself cannot stand:* for unless this division precede, division into opposite armies can never happen. If there had not first been an opinion received of the greatest part of England, that these powers were divided between the King and the Lords and the House of Commons, the people had never been divided and fallen into this civil war; first between those that disagreed in politics, and after between the dissenters about the liberty of religion: which have so instructed men in this point of sovereign right; and there be few now in England that do not see that these rights are inseparable, and will be so generally acknowledged at the next return of peace; and so continue till their miseries are forgotten; and no longer, except the vulgar be better taught than they have hitherto been.

And because they are essential and inseparable rights, it follows necessarily that in whatsoever words any of them seem to be granted away, yet if the sovereign power itself be not in direct terms renounced, and the name of sovereign no more given by the grantees to him that grants them, the grant is void: for when he has granted all he can, if we grant back the sovereignty, all is restored, as inseparably annexed thereunto.

This great authority being indivisible, and inseparably annexed to the sovereignty, there is little ground for the opinion of them that say of sovereign kings, though they be *singulis majores,* of greater power than every one of their subjects, yet they be *universis minores,* of less power than them all together. For if by 'all together' they mean not the collective body as one person, then 'all together' and 'every one' signify the same, and the speech is absurd. But if by 'all together' they understand them as one person, which person the sovereign bears, then the power of all together is the same with the sovereign's power, and so again the speech is absurd; which absurdity they see well enough when the sovereignty is in an assembly of the people, but in a monarch they see it not; and yet the power of sovereignty is the same in whomsoever it be placed.

And as the power, so also the honor of the sovereign, ought to be greater than that of any or all the subjects. For in the sovereignty is the fountain of honor. The dignities of lord, earl, duke, and prince are his creatures. As in the presence of the master, the servants are equal and without any honor at all; so are the subjects, in the presence of the sovereign. And though they shine some more, some less, when they are out of his sight; yet in his presence, they shine no more than the stars in the presence of the sun.

But a man may here object that the condition of subjects is very miserable, as being obnoxious to the lusts, and other irregular passions, of him or them that have so unlimited a power in their hands. And commonly they that live under a monarch, think it the fault of monarchy; and they that live under the government of democracy, or other sovereign assembly, attribute all the inconvenience to that form of commonwealth; whereas the power in all forms, if they be perfect enough to protect them, is the same: not considering that the state of man can never be without some incommodity or other; and that the greatest that in any form of government can possibly happen to the people in general, is scarce sensible, in respect to the miseries and horrible calamities that accompany a civil war, or that dissolute condition of masterless men, without subjection to laws and a coercive power to tie their hands from rapine and revenge; nor considering that the greatest pressure of sovereign governors, proceedeth not from any delight or profit they can expect in the damage or weakening of their subjects, in whose vigor consisteth their own strength and glory; but in the restiveness of themselves, that unwillingly contributing to their own defense, make it necessary for their governors to draw from them what they can in time of peace, that they may have means on any emergent occasion or sudden need, to resist or take advantage on their enemies. For all men are by nature provided of notable multiplying glasses, that is their passions and self-love, through which every little payment appeareth a great grievance; but are destitute of those prospective glasses, namely moral and civil science, to see afar off the miseries that hang over them, and cannot without such payment be avoided.

John Locke:
The Origins of Government

OF THE BEGINNING OF POLITICAL SOCIETIES

95. Men being, as has been said, by nature free, equal, and independent, no one can be put out of this estate, and subjected to the political power of another, without his own consent, which is done by agreeing with other men to join and unite into a community for their comfortable, safe, and peaceable living one amongst another, in a secure enjoyment of their properties, and a greater security against any that are not of it. This any number of men may do, because it injures not the freedom of the rest; they are left as they were in the liberty of the state of nature. When any number of men have so consented to make one community or government, they are thereby presently incorporated, and make one body politic, wherein the majority have a right to act and conclude the rest.

96. For when any number of men have, by the consent of every individual, make a community, they have thereby made that community one body, with a power to act as one body, which is only by the will and determination of the majority. For that which acts any community being only the consent of the individuals of it, and it being one body must move one way, it is necessary the body should move that way whither the greater force carries it, which is the consent of the majority; or else it is impossible it should act or continue one body, one community which the consent of every individual that united into it agreed that it should; and so everyone is bound by that consent to be concluded by the majority. And therefore we see that in assemblies empowered to act by positive laws, where no number is set by that positive law which empowers them, the act of the majority passes for the act of the whole, and of course determines, as having by the law of nature and reason the power of the whole.

97. And thus every man, by consenting with others to make one body politic under one government, puts himself under an obligation to every one of that society, to submit to the determination of the majority, and to be concluded by it; or else this original compact, whereby he with others incorporates into one society, would signify nothing, and be no compact, if he be left free and under no other ties than he was in before in the state of nature. For what appearance would there be of any compact? What new engagement if he were no farther tied by any decrees of the society, than he himself thought fit, and did actually consent to? This would be still as great a liberty as he himself had before his compact, or anyone else in the state of nature hath, who may submit himself and consent to any acts of it if he thinks fit.

98. For if the consent of the majority shall not in reason be received as the act of the whole and conclude every individual, nothing but the consent of every individual can make anything to be the act of the whole, which considering the infirmities of health and avocations of business, which in a number, though much less than that of a commonwealth, will necessarily keep many away from the public assembly, and the variety of opinions, and contrariety of interest, which unavoidably happen in all collections of men, 'tis next to impossible ever to be had. And therefore if the coming into society

From John Locke, *Two Treatises on Civil Government* (selections).

be upon such terms it will be only like Cato's coming into the theater, *tantum ut exiret.* Such a constitution as this would make the mighty leviathan of a shorter duration that the feeblest creatures, and not let it outlast the day it was born in; which cannot be supposed till we can think that rational creatures should desire and constitute societies only to be dissolved. For where the majority cannot conclude the rest, there they cannot act as one body, and consequently will be immediately dissolved again.

99. Whosoever therefore out of a state of nature unite into a community must be understood to give up all the power necessary to the ends for which they unite into society, to the majority of the community, unless they expressly agreed in any number greater than the majority. And this is done by barely agreeing to unite into one political society, which is all the compact that is, or needs be, between the individuals that enter into or make up a commonwealth. And thus that which begins and actually constitutes any political society is nothing but the consent of any number of freemen capable of a majority to unite and incorporate into such a society. And this is that, and that only, which did or could give beginning to any lawful government in the world.

OF THE ENDS OF POLITICAL SOCIETY AND GOVERNMENT

123. If man in the state of nature be so free, as has been said, if he be absolute lord of his own person and possessions, equal to the greatest, and subject to nobody, why will he part with his freedom, this empire, and subject himself to the dominion and control of any other power? To which, it is obvious to answer, that though in the state of nature he hath such a right, yet the enjoyment of it is very uncertain, and constantly exposed to the invasions of others. For all being kings as much as he, every man his equal, and the greater part no strict observers of equity and justice, the enjoyment of the property he has in this state is very unsafe, very unsecure. This makes him willing to quit this condition, which, however free, is full of fears and continual dangers; and it is not without reason that he seeks out and is willing to join in society with others, who are already united, or have in mind to unite, for the mutual preservation of their lives, liberties, and estates, which I call by the general name, property.

124. The great and chief end, therefore, of men's uniting into commonwealths, and putting themselves under government, is the preservation of their property; to which in the state of nature there are many things wanting.

First, There wants an established, settled, known law, received and allowed by common consent to be the standard of right and wrong, and the common measure to decide all controversies between them. For though the law of nature be plain and intelligible to all rational creatures; yet men, being biased by their interest, as well as ignorant for want of study of it, are not apt to allow of it as a law binding to them in the application of it to their particular cases.

125. Secondly, In the state of nature there wants a known and indifferent judge, with authority to determine all differences according to the established law. For everyone in that state, being both judge and executioner of the law of nature, men being partial to themselves, passion and revenge is very apt to carry them too far, and with too much heat in their own cases, as well as negligence and unconcernedness, to make them too remiss in other men's.

126. Thirdly, In the state of nature there often wants power to back and support the sentence when right, and to give it due execution. They who by any injustice offend, will seldom fail, where they are able to force to make good their injustice; such resistance many times makes the punishment dangerous, and frequently destructive to those who attempt it.

127. Thus mankind, notwithstanding all the privileges of the state of nature, being but in an ill condition, while they remain in it, are quickly driven into society. Hence it comes to pass that we seldom find any number of men live any time together in this state. The inconveniences that they are therein exposed to by the irregular and uncertain exercise of the power every man has of punishing the transgressions of others, make them take sanctuary under the established laws of government, and therein seek the preservation of their property. It is this makes them so willingly give up everyone his single power of punishing, to be exercised by such alone, as shall be appointed to it amongst them; and by such rules as the community, or those authorized by them to that

purpose, shall agree on. And in this we have the original right and rise of both the legislative and executive power, as well as of the governments and societies themselves.

128. For in the state of nature, to omit the liberty he has of innocent delights, a man has two powers.

The first is to do whatsoever he thinks fit for the preservation of himself, and others within the permission of the law of nature, by which law, common to them all, he and all the rest of mankind are of one community, make up one society, distinct from all other creatures. And were it not for the corruption and viciousness of degenerate men there would be no need of any other, no necessity that men should separate from this great and natural community, and associate into lesser combinations.

The other power a man has in the state of nature is the power to punish the crimes committed against that law. Both these he gives up when he joins in a private, if I may so call it, or particular political society, and incorporates into any commonwealth separate from the rest of mankind.

129. The first power, viz., of doing whatsoever he thought fit for the preservation of himself and the rest of mankind, he gives up to be regulated by laws made by the society, so far forth as the preservation of himself and the rest of that society shall require; which laws of the society in many things confine the liberty he had by the law of nature.

130. Secondly, The power of punishing he wholly gives up, and engages his natural force (which he might before employ in the execution of the law of nature, by his own single authority as he thought fit), to assist the executive power of the society, as the law thereof shall require. For being now in a new state, wherein he is to enjoy many conveniences, from the labor, assistance, and society of others in the same community, as well as protection from its whole strength; he has to part also with as much of his natural liberty, in providing for himself, as the good, property and safety of the society shall require; which is not only necessary but just, since the other members of the society do the like.

131. But though men when they enter into society give up the equality, liberty and executive power they had in the state of nature into the hands of the society, to be so far disposed of by the legislative as the good of the society shall require; yet it being only with an intention in everyone the better to preserve himself, his liberty and property (for no rational creature can be supposed to change his condition with an intention to the worse), the power of the society, or legislative constituted by them, can never be supposed to extend farther than the common good, but is obliged to secure everyone's property by providing against those three defects above-mentioned that made the state of nature so unsafe and uneasy. And so whoever has the legislative or supreme power of any commonwealth is bound to govern by established standing laws; promulgated and known to the people, and not by extemporary decrees; by indifferent and upright judges, who are to decide controversies by those laws; and to employ the force of the community at home only in the execution of such laws, or abroad, to prevent or redress foreign injuries, and secure the community from inroads and invasion. And all this to be directed to no other end but the peace, safety, and public good of the people.

OF THE FORMS OF A COMMONWEALTH

132. The majority having, as has been shown, upon men's first uniting into society, the whole power of the community, naturally in them, may employ all that power in making laws for the community from time to time, and executing those laws by officers of their own appointing: and then the form of the government is a perfect democracy; or else may put the power of making laws into the hands of a few select men, and their heirs or successors, and then it is an oligarchy; or else into the hands of one man and then it is a monarchy; if to him and his heirs, it is an hereditary monarchy; if to him only for life, but upon his death the power only of nominating a successor to return to them, an elective monarchy. And so accordingly of these, the community may make compounded and mixed forms of government, as they think good. And if the legislative power be at first given by the majority to one or more persons only for their lives, or any limited time, and then the supreme power to revert to them again; when it is so reverted, the community may dispose of it again anew into what hands they please, and so constitute a new form of government. For the form of government

depending upon the placing of the supreme power, which is the legislative, it being impossible to conceive that an inferior power should prescribe to a superior, or any but the supreme make laws, according as the power of making laws is placed, such is the form of the commonwealth.

133. By commonwealth, I must be understood all along to mean, not a democracy, or any form of government, but any independent community which the Latins signified by the word *civitas*, to which the word which best answers in our language is commonwealth, and most properly expresses such a society of men, which community does not, for there may be subordinate communities in a government; and city much less. And therefore to avoid ambiguity I crave leave to use the word commonwealth in that sense, in which I find it used by King James himself, which I think to be its genuine signification; which if anybody dislike, I consent with him to change it for a better.

OF THE SUBORDINATION OF THE POWERS OF THE COMMONWEALTH

149. Though in a constituted commonwealth, standing upon its own basis, and acting according to its own nature, that is, acting for the preservation of the community, there can be but one supreme power, which is the legislative, to which all the rest are and must be subordinate, yet the legislative being only of fiduciary power to act for certain ends, there remains still in the people a supreme power to remove or alter the legislative when they find the legislative act contrary to the trust reposed in them; for all power given with trust for the attaining an end, being limited by that end, wherever that end is manifestly neglected or opposed, the trust must necessarily be forfeited, and the power devolve into the hands of those that gave it who may place it anew where they shall think best for their safety and security. And thus the community perpetually retains a supreme power of saving themselves from the attempts and designs of anybody, even of their legislators wherever they shall be so foolish or so wicked as to lay and carry on designs against the liberties and properties of the subject; for no man or society of men, having a power to deliver up their preservation, or consequently the means of it to the absolute will and arbitrary dominion of another, whenever anyone shall go about to bring them into such a slavish, condition they will always have a right to preserve what they have not a power to part with; and to rid themselves of those who invade this fundamental, sacred and unalterable law of self-preservation for which they entered into society; and thus the community may be said in this resepct to be always the supreme power, but not as considered under any form of government, because this power of the people can never take place till the government be dissolved.

OF THE DISSOLUTION OF GOVERNMENT

211. He that will with any clearness speak of the dissolution of government ought, in the first place, to distinguish between the dissolution of the society and the dissolution of the government. That which makes the community, and brings men out of the loose state of nature into one politic society, is the agreement which everyone has with the rest to incorporate and act one body, and so be one distinct commonwealth. The usual and almost only way whereby this union is dissolved, is the inroad of foreign force making a conquest upon them. For in that case (not being able to maintain and support themselves as one entire and independent body) the union belonging to that body which consisted therein must necessarily cease, and so everyone return to the state he was in before, with a liberty to shift for himself and provide for his own safety as he thinks fit in some other society. Wherever the society is dissolved, it is certain the government of that society cannot remain. Thus conqueror's swords often cut up governments by the roots, and mangle societies to pieces, separating the subdued or scattered multitude from the protection of and dependence on that society which ought to have preserved them from violence. The world is too well instructed in, and too forward to allow of this way of dissolving of, governments to need any more to be said of it; and there wants not much argument to prove that where the society is dissolved, the government cannot remain—that being as impossible as for the frame of a house to subsist when the materials of it are scattered and displaced by a whirlwind, or jumbled into a confused heap by

an earthquake.

212. Besides this overturning from without, governments are dissolved from within.

First, When the legislative is altered. Civil society being a state of peace amongst those who are of it, from whom the state of war is excluded by the umpirage which they have provided in their legislative for the ending all differences that may arise amongst any of them, it is in their legislative that the members of a commonwealth are united and combined together in one coherent living body. This is the soul that gives form life, and unity to the commonwealth. From hence the several members have their mutual influence, sympathy, and connection. And, therefore, when the legislative is broken or dissolved, dissolution and death follow. For the essence and union of the society consisting in having one will, the legislative, when once established by the majority, has the declaring and, as it were, keeping of, that will. The constitution of the legislative is the first and fundamental act of the society, whereby provision is made for the continuation of their union, under the direction of persons and bonds of laws made by persons authorized thereunto by the consent and appointment of the people, without which no one man or number of men amongst them can have authority of making laws that shall be binding to the rest. When any one or more shall take upon them to make laws, whom the people have not appointed so to do, they make laws without authority, which the people are not therefore bound to obey; by which means they come again to be out of subjection, and may constitute to themselves a new legislative, as they think best, being in full liberty to resist the force of those who without authority would impose anything upon them. Everyone is at the disposure of his own will when those who had by the delegation of the society the declaring of the public will, are excluded from it, and others usurp the place who have no such authority or delegation.

213. This being usually brought about by such in the commonwealth who misuse the power they have, it is hard to consider it aright, and know at whose door to lay it, without knowing the form of government in which it happens. Let us suppose, then, the legislative placed in the concurrance of three distinct persons.

(1) A single hereditary person having the constant supreme executive power, and with it the power of convoking and dissolving the other two within certain periods of time.

(2) An assembly of hereditary nobility.

(3) An assembly of representatives chosen *pro tempore* by the people.

Such a form of government supposed, it is evident,

214. First, that when such a single person or prince sets up his own arbitrary will in place of the laws which are the will of the society, declared by the legislative, then the legislative is changed. For that being in effect the legislative whose rules and laws are put in execution and required to be obeyed when other laws set up, and other rules pretended and enforced, than what the legislative constituted by the society have enacted, it is plain that the legislative is changed. Whoever introduces new laws, not being thereunto authorized by the fundamental appointment of the society, or subverts the old, disowns and overturns the power by which they were made, and so sets up a new legislative.

215. Secondly, When the prince hinders the legislative from assembling in its due time, or from acting freely, pursuant to those ends for which it was constituted, the legislative is altered. For it is not a certain number of men, no, nor their meeting, unless they have also freedom of debating and lesiure of perfecting what is for the good of the society, wherein the legislative consists. When these are taken away or altered so as to deprive the society of the due exercise of their power, the legislative is truly altered. For it is not names that constitute governments, but the use and exercise of those powers that were intended to accompany them; so that he who takes away the freedom, or hinders the acting of the legislative in its due seasons, in effect takes away the legislative, and puts an end to the government.

216. Thirdly, When, by the arbitrary power of the prince, the electors or ways of elections are altered, without the consent and contrary to the common interest of the people, there also the legislative is altered. For if others than those whom the society hath authorized thereunto, do choose, or in another way than what the society hath prescribed, those chosen are not the legislative appointed by the people.

217. Fourthly, The delivery also of the people into the subjection of foreign power, either by

the prince, or by the legislative, is certainly a change of the legislative, and so a dissolution of the government. For the end why people entered into society being to be preserved one entire, free, independent society, to be governed by its own laws, this is lost whenever they are given up into the power of another.

218. Why, in such a constitution as this, the dissolution of the government in these cases is to be imputed to the prince is evidence, because he, having the force, treasure, and offices of the State to employ, and often persuading himself or being flattered by others, that, as supreme magistrate, he is incapable of control; he alone is in a condition to make great advances towards such changes under pretense of lawful authority, and has it in his hands to terrify or suppress oppressors as factious, seditious, and enemies to the government; whereas no other part of the legislative, or people, is capable by themselves to attempt any alteration of the legislative without open and visible rebellion, apt enough to be taken notice of, which when it prevails , produces effects very little different from foreign conquest. Besides, the prince, in such a form of government, having the power of dissolving the other parts of the legislative, and thereby rendering them private persons, they can never, in opposition to him, or without his concurrence, alter the legislative by a law, his consent being necessary to give any of their decrees that sanction. But yet so far as the other parts of the legislative any way contribute to any attempt upon the government, and do either promote, or not, what lies in them, hinder such designs, they are guilty, and partake in this, which is certainly the greatest crime men can be guilty of one towards another.

219. There is one way more whereby such a government may be dissolved, and that is, when he who has the supreme executive power neglects and abandons that charge, so that the laws already made can no longer be put in execution. This is demonstratively to reduce all to anarchy, and so effectually to dissolve the government. For laws not being made for themselves, but to be by their execution the bonds of the society, to keep every part of the body politic, in its due place and function, when that totally ceases, the government visibly ceases, and the people become a confused multitude without order or connection. Where there is no longer the administration of justice, for the securing of men's rights, nor any remaining power within the community to direct the force, or provide for the necessities of the public, there certainly is no government left. Where the laws cannot be executed, it is all one as if there were no laws; and a government without laws is, I suppose, a mystery in politics, inconceivable to human capacity, and inconsistent with human society.

220. In these and the like cases, when the government is dissolved, the people are at liberty to provide for themselves by erecting a new legislative, different from the other, by the change of persons, or form, or both, as they shall find it for their safety and good. For the society can never, by the fault of another, lose the native and original right it has to preserve itself, which can only be done by a settled legislative, and a fair and impartial execution of the laws made by it. But the state of mankind is not so miserable that they are not capable of using this remedy, till it be too late to look for any. To tell people they may provide for themselves by erecting a new legislative, when by oppression, artifice, or being delivered over to a foreign power, their old one is gone, is only to tell them they may expect relief when it is too late, and the evil is past cure. This is in effect no more than to bid them first be slaves, and then to take care of their liberty; and when their chains are on tell them they may act like free men. This, if barely, so, is rather mockery than relief; and men can never be secure from tyranny if there be no means to escape it till they are perfectly under it. And therefore it is that they have not only a right to get out of it, but to prevent it.

221. There is therefore secondly another way whereby governments are dissolved, and that is when the legislative or the prince, either of them, acts contrary to their trust.

First, The legislative acts against the trust reposed in them when they endeavor to invade the property of the subject, and to make themselves or any part of the community masters or abritrary disposers of the lives, liberties, or fortunes of the people.

222. The reason why men enter into society is the preservation of their property; and the end why they choose and authorize a legislative is that there may be laws made, and rules set, as guards and fences to the properties of all the

members of the society to limit the power and moderate the dominion of every part and member of the society. For since it can never be supposed to be the will of the society that the legislative should have a power to destroy that which everyone designs secure by entering into society, and for which the people submitted themselves to legislators of their own making, whenever the legislators endeavor to take away and destroy the property of the people, or to reduce them to slavery under arbitrary power, they put themselves into a state of war with the people, who are thereupon absolved from any further obedience, and are left to the common refuge which God hath provided for all men against force and violence. Whensoever, therefore, the legislative shall transgress this fundamental rule of society, and either by ambition, fear, folly, or corruption, endeavor to grasp themselves or put into the hands of any other an absolute power over the lives, liberties, and estates of the people, by this breach of trust they forfeit the power the people had put into their hands, for quite contrary ends, and it devolves to the people, who have a right to resume their original liberty, and by the establishment of the new legislative (such as they shall think fit) provide for their own safety and security, which is the end for which they are in society. What I have said here concerning the legislative in general, holds true also concerning the supreme executor, who having a double trust put in him, both to have a part in the legislative and the supreme execution of the law, acts against both when he goes about to set up his own arbitrary will as the law of the society. He acts also contrary to his trust when he either employs the force, treasure, and offices of the society, to corrupt the representatives, and gain them to his purposes; or openly pre-engages the electors, and prescribes to their choice such whom he has by solicitations, threats, promises, or otherwise won to his designs, and employs them to bring in such, who have promised beforehand what to vote and what to enact. Thus to regulate candidates and electors, and new-model the ways of election, what is it but to cut up the government by the roots, and poison the very fountain of public security? For the people having reserved to themselves the choice of their representatives as the fence to their properties, could do it for no other end but that they might always be freely chosen, and, so chosen, freely act and advise as the necessity of the commonwealth and the public good should upon examination and mature debate be judged to require. This those who give their votes before they hear the debate, and have weighed the reason on all sides, are not capable of doing. To prepare such an assembly as this, and endeavor to set up the declared abettors of his own will for the true representatives of the people and the lawmakers of the society, is certainly as great a breach of trust and as perfect a declaration of a design to subvert the government as is possible to be met with. To which if one shall add rewards and punishments visibly employed to the same end and all the arts of perverted law made use of to take off and destroy all that stand in the way of such a design, and will not comply and consent to betray the liberties of their country, it will be past doubt what is doing. What power they ought to have in the society who thus employ it contrary to the trust that went along with it in its first institution is easy to determine; and one cannot but see that he who has once attempted any such thing as this cannot any longer be trusted.

Jean-Jacques Rousseau: The Social Contract

SUBJECT OF THE FIRST BOOK

Man is born free, and everywhere he is in chains. Many a one believes himself the master of others, and yet he is a greater slave than they. How has this change come about? I do not know. What can render it legitimate? I believe that I can settle this question.

If I considered only force and the results that proceed from it, I should say that so long as a people is compelled to obey and does obey, it does well; but that, so soon as it can shake off the yoke and does shake it off, it does better; for, if men recover their freedom by virtue of the same right by which it was taken away, either they are justified in resuming it, or there was no justification for depriving them of it. But the social order is a sacred right which serves as a foundation for all others. This right, however, does not come from nature. It is therefore based on conventions. The question is to know what these conventions are. Before coming to that, I must establish what I have just laid down.

THE SOCIAL PACT

I assume that men have reached a point at which the obstacles that endanger their preservation in the state of nature overcome by their resistance the forces which each individual can exert with a view to maintaining himself in that state. Then this primitive condition cannot longer subsist, and the human race would perish unless it changed its mode of existence.

Now as men cannot create any new forces, but only combine and direct those that exist, they have no other means of self-preservation than to form by aggregation a sum of forces which may overcome the resistance, to put them in action by a single motive power, and to make them work in concert.

This sum of forces can be produced only by the combination of many; but the strength and freedom of each man being the chief instruments of his preservation, how can he pledge them without injuring himself, and without neglecting the cares which he owes to himself? This difficulty, applied to my subject, may be expressed in these terms:—

"To find a form of association which may defend and protect with the whole force of the community, the person and property of every associate, and by means of which, coalescing with all, may nevertheless obey only himself, and remain as free as before." Such is the fundamental problem of which the social contract furnishes the solution.

The clauses of this contract are so determined by the nature of the act that the slightest modification would render them vain and ineffectual; so that, although they have never perhaps been formally enunciated, they are everywhere the same, everywhere tacitly admitted and recognized, until, the social pact being violated, each man regains his original rights and recovers his natural liberty while losing the conventional liberty for which he renounced it.

These clauses, rightly understood, are reducible to one only, viz, the total alienation to the whole community of each associate with all his rights; for, in the first place, since each gives himself up entirely, the conditions are equal for all; and, the conditions being equal for all, no one has any interest in making them burdensome to others.

Further, the alienation being made without reserve, the union is as perfect as it can be, and an individual associate can no longer claim anything; for, if any rights were left to individuals, since there would be no common superior who could judge between them and the public, each, being on some point his own judge, would soon claim to be so on all; the state of nature would still subsist, and the association would necessarily become tyrannical or useless.

In short, each giving himself to all, gives himself to nobody; and as there is no one associate over whom we do not acquire the same rights which we concede to him over ourselves, we gain the equivalent of all that we lose, and more power to preserve what we have.

If, then, we set aside what is not of the essence of the social contract, we shall find that it is reducible to the following terms: "Each of us puts in common his person and his whole power under the supreme direction of the general will; and in return we receive every member as an indivisible part of the whole."

Forthwith, instead of the individual personalities of all the contracting parties, this act of association produces a moral and collective body, which is composed of as many members as the assembly has voices, and which receives from this same act its unity, its common self (*moi*), its life, and its will. This public person, which is thus formed by the union of all the individual members, formerly took the name of *city*, and now takes that of *republic* or *body politic*, which is called by its members *State* when it is passive, *sovereign* when it is active, *power* when it is compared to similar bodies. With regard to the associates, they take collectively the name of *people*, and are called individually *citizens*, as participating in the sovereign power, and *subjects*, as subjected to the laws of the State. But these terms are often confused and are mistaken one for another; it is sufficient to know how to distinguish them when they are used with complete precision.

THE SOVEREIGN

We see from this formula that the act of association contains a reciprocal engagement between the public and individuals, and that every individual, contracting so to speak with himself, is engaged in a double relation, viz, as a member of the sovereign toward individuals, and as a member of the State toward the sovereign. But we cannot apply here the maxim of civil law that no one is bound by engagements made with himself; for there is a great difference between being bound to oneself and to a whole of which one forms part.

We must further observe that the public resolution which can bind all subjects to the sovereign in consequence of the two different relations under which each of them is regarded cannot, for a contrary reason, bind the sovereign to itself; and that accordingly it is contrary to the nature of the body politic for the sovereign to impose on itself a law which it cannot transgress. As it can only be considered under one and the same relation, it is in the position of an individual contracting with himself; whence we see that there is not, nor can be, any kind of fundamental law binding upon the body of the people, not even the social contract. This does not imply that such a body cannot perfectly well enter into engagements with others in what does not derogate from this contract; for, with regard to foreigners, it becomes a simple being, an individual.

But the body politic or sovereign, deriving its existence only from the sanctity of the contract, can never bind itself, even to others, in anything that derogates from the original act, such as alienation of some portion of itself, or submission to another sovereign. To violate the act by which it exists would be to annihilate itself; and what is nothing produces nothing.

So soon as the multitude is thus united in one body, it is impossible to injure one of the members without attacking the body, still less to injure the body without the members feeling the effects. Thus duty and interest alike oblige the two contracting parties to give mutual assistance; and the men themselves should seek to combine in this twofold relationship all the advantages which are attendant on it.

Now, the sovereign, being formed only of the individuals that compose it, neither has nor can have any interest contrary to theirs; consequently the sovereign power needs no guarantee toward its subjects, because it is impossible that the body should wish to injure all its members; and we shall see hereafter that it can injure no one as an individual. The sovereign, for the simple reason that it is so, is always everything that it ought to be.

But this is not the case as regards the relation

of subjects to the sovereign, which, notwithstanding the common interest, would have no security for the performance of their engagements, unless it found means to ensure their fidelity.

Indeed, every individual may, as a man, have a particular will contrary to, or divergent from, the general will which he has as a citizen; his private interest may prompt him quite differently from the common interest; his absolute and naturally independent existence may make him regard what he owes to the common cause as a gratuitous contribution, the loss of which will be less harmful to others than the payment of it will be burdensome to him; and, regarding the moral person that constitutes the State as an imaginary being because it is not a man, he would be willing to enjoy the rights of a citizen without being willing to fulfill the duties of a subject. The progress of such injustice would bring about the ruin of the body politic.

In order, then, that the social pact may not be a vain formulary, it tacitly includes this engagement, which can alone give force to the others, that whoever refuses to obey the general will shall be constrained to do so by the whole body; which means nothing else than that he shall be forced to be free; for such is the condition which, uniting every citizen to his native land, guarantees him from all personal dependence, a condition that insures the control and working of the political machine, and alone renders legitimate civil engagements, which, without it, would be absurd and tyrannical, and subject to the most enormous abuses.

THE CIVIL STATE

The passage from the state of nature to the civil state produces in man a very remarkable change, by substituting in his conduct justice for instinct, and by giving his actions the moral quality that they previously lacked. It is only when the voice of duty succeeds physical impulse, and law succeeds appetite, that man, who till then had regarded only himself, sees that he is obliged to act on other principles, and to consult his reason before listening to his inclinations. Although, in this state, he is deprived of many advantages that he derives from nature, he acquires equally great ones in return; his faculties are exercised and developed; his ideas are expanded; his feelings are ennobled; his whole soul is exalted to such a degree that, if the abuses of this new condition did not often degrade him below that from which he has emerged, he ought to bless without ceasing the happy moment that released him from it for ever, and transformed him from a stupid and ignorant animal into an intelligent being and a man.

Let us reduce this whole balance to terms easy to compare. What man loses by the social contract is his natural liberty and an unlimited right to anything which tempts him and which he is able to attain: what he gains is civil liberty and property in all that he possesses. In order that we may not be mistaken about these compensations, we must clearly distinguish natural liberty, which is limited only by the powers of the individual, from civil liberty, which is limited by the general will; and possession, which is nothing but the result of force or the right of first occupancy, from property, which can be based only on a positive title.

Besides the preceding, we might add to the acquisitions of the civil state moral freedom, which alone renders man truly master of himself; for the impulse of mere appetite is slavery, while obedience to a self-prescribed law is liberty. But I have already said too much on this head, and the philosophical meaning of the term *liberty* does not belong to my present subject.

THAT SOVEREIGNTY IS INALIENABLE

The first and most important consequence of the principles above established is that the general will alone can direct the forces of the State according to the object of its institution, which is the common good; for if the opposition of private interests has rendered necessary the establishment of societies, the agreement of these same interests has rendered it possible. That which is common to these different interests forms the social bond; and unless there were some point in which all interests agree, no society could exist. Now, it is solely with regard to this common interest that the society should be governed.

I say, then, that sovereignty, being nothing but the exercise of the general will, can never be alienated, and that the sovereign power, which is only a collective being, can be represented by itself alone; power indeed can be transmitted, but not will.

In fact, if it is not impossible that a particular will should agree on some point with the general will, it is at least impossible that this agreement should be lasting and constant; for the particular will naturally tends to preferences, and the general will to equality. It is still more impossible to have a security for this agreement; even though it should always exist, it would not be a result of art, but of chance. The sovereign may indeed say: "I will now what a certain man wills, or at least what he says that he wills"; but he cannot say: "What that man wills to-morrow, I shall also will," since it is absurd that the will should bind itself as regards the future, and since it is not incumbent on any will to consent to anything contrary to the welfare of the being that wills. If then, the nation simply promises to obey, it dissolves itself by that act and loses its character as a people; the moment there is a master, there is no longer a sovereign, and forthwith the body politic is destroyed.

This does not imply that the orders of the chiefs cannot pass for decisions of the general will, so long as the sovereign, free to oppose them, refrains from doing so. In such a case the consent of the people should be inferred from the universal silence. This will be explained at greater length.

THAT SOVEREIGNTY IS INDIVISIBLE

For the same reason that sovereignty is inalienable it is indivisible; for the will is either general, or it is not; it is either that of the body of the people, or that of only a portion. In the first case, this declared will is an act of sovereignty and constitutes law; in the second case, it is only a particular will, or an act of magistracy —it is at most a decree.

But our publicists, being unable to divide sovereignty in its principle, divide it in its object. They divide it into force and will, into legislative power and executive power; into rights of taxation, of justice, and of war; into internal administration and power of treating with foreigners—sometimes confounding all these departments, and sometimes separating them. They make the sovereign a fantastic being, formed of connected parts; it is as if they composed a man of several bodies, one with eyes, another with arms, another with feet, and nothing else. The Japanese conjurers, it is said, cut up a child before the eyes of the spectators; then, throwing all its limbs into the air, they make the child come down again alive and whole. Such almost are the juggler's tricks of our publicists; after dismembering the social body by a deception worthy of the fair, they recombine its parts, nobody knows how.

This error arises from their not having formed exact notions about the sovereign authority, and from their taking as parts of this authority what are only emanations from it. Thus, for example, the acts of declaring war and making peace have been regarded as acts of sovereignty, which is not the case, since neither of them is a law, but only an application of the law, a particular act which determines the case of the law, as will be clearly seen when the idea attached to the word *law* is fixed.

By following out the other divisions in the same way it would be found that, whenever the sovereignty appears divided, we are mistaken in our supposition; and that the rights which are taken as parts of that sovereignty are all subordinate to it, and always suppose supreme wills of which these rights are merely executive.

It would be impossible to describe the great obscurity in which this want of precision has involved the conclusions of writers on the subject of political right when they have endeavored to decide upon the respective rights of kings and peoples on the principles that they had established. Every one can see in chapters III and IV of the first book of Grotius, how that learned man and his translator Barbeyrac became entangled and embarrassed in their sophisms, for fear of saying too much or not saying enough according to their views, and so offending the interests that they had to conciliate. Grotius, having taken refuge in France through discontent with his own country, and wishing to pay court to Louis XIII, to whom his book is dedicated, spares no pains to despoil the people of all their rights, and, in the most artful manner, bestow them on kings. This also would clearly have been the inclination of Barbeyrac, who dedicated his translation to the king of England, George I. But unfortunately the expulsion of James II, which he calls an abdication, forced him to be reserved and to equivocate and evade in order not to make William appear a usurper. If these two writers had adopted true principles, all difficulties would have been removed, and they would have been always consistent; but they would have spoken the truth with regret, and would have paid court only to the people. Truth, however, does not lead to fortune, and the people confer neither embassies, nor professorships, nor pensions.

WHETHER THE GENERAL WILL CAN ERR

It follows from what precedes that the general will is always right and always tends to the public advantage; but it does not follow that the resolutions of the people have always the same rectitude. Men always desire their own good, but do not always discern it; the people are never corrupted, though often deceived, and it is only then that they seem to will what is evil.

There is often a great deal of difference between the will of all and the general will; the latter regards only the common interest, while the former has regard to private interests, and is merely a sum of particular wills; but take away from these same wills the pluses and minuses which cancel one another, and the general will remains as the sum of the differences.

If the people come to a resolution when adequately informed and without any communication among the citizens, the general will would always result from the great number of slight differences, and the resolution would always be good. But when factions, partial associations, are formed to the detriment of the whole society the will of each of these associations becomes general with reference to its members, and particular with reference to the State; it may then be said that there are no longer as many voters as there are men, but only as many voters as there are associations. The differences become less numerous and yield a less general result. Lastly, when one of these associations becomes so great that it predominates over all the rest, you no longer have as the result a sum of small differences, but a single difference; there is then no longer a general will, and the opinion which prevails is only a particular opinion.

It is important, then, in order to have a clear declaration of the general will, that there should be no partial association in the State, and that every citizen should express only his own opinion. Such was the unique and sublime institution of the great Lycurgus. But if there are partial associations, it is necessary to multiply their number and prevent inequality, as Solon, Numa, and Servius did. These are the only proper precautions for insuring that the general will may always be enlightened, and that the people may not be deceived.

THAT THE GENERAL WILL IS INDESTRUCTIBLE

So long as a number of men in combination are considered as a single body, they have but one will, which relates to the common preservation and to the general well-being. In such a case all the forces of the State are vigorous and simple, and its principles are clear and luminous; it has no confused and conflicting interests; the common good is everywhere plainly manifest and only good sense is required to perceive it. Peace, union, and equality are foes to political subtleties. Upright and simple-minded men are hard to deceive because of their simplicity; allurements and refined pretexts do not impose upon them; they are not even cunning enough to be dupes. When, in the happiest nation in the world, we see troops of peasants regulating the affairs of the State under an oak and always acting wisely, can we refrain from despising the refinements of other nations, who make themselves illustrious and wretched with so much art and mystery?

A State thus governed needs very few laws; and in so far as it becomes necessary to promulgate new ones, this necessity is universally recognized. The first man to propose them only gives expression to what all have previously felt, and neither factions nor eloquence will be needed to pass into law what every one has already resolved to do, so soon as he is sure that the rest will act as he does.

What deceives reasoners is that, seeing only States that are ill-constituted from the beginning, they are impressed with the impossibility of maintaining such a policy in those States; they laugh to think of all the follies to which a cunning knave, an insinuating speaker, can persuade the people of Paris or London. They know not that Cromwell would have been put in irons by the people of Berne, and the Duke of Beaufort imprisoned by the Genevese.

But when the social bond begins to be relaxed and the State weakened, when private interests begin to make themselves felt and small associations to exercise an influence on the State, the common interest is injuriously affected and finds adversaries, unanimity no longer reigns in the voting; the general will is no longer the will of all; opposition and disputes arise, and the best counsel does not pass uncontested.

Lastly, when the State, on the verge of ruin, no longer subsists except in a vain and illusory form, when the social bond is broken in all hearts, when the basest interest shelters itself impudently under the sacred name of the public welfare, the general will becomes dumb; all, under the guidance of secret motives, no more express their opinions as citizens than if the State had never existed; and, under the name of laws, they deceitfully pass unjust decrees which have only private interest as their end.

Does it follow from this that the general will is destroyed or corrupted? No; it is always constant, unalterable, and pure; but it is subordinated to others which get the better of it. Each, detaching his own interest from the common interest, sees clearly that he cannot completely separate it; but his share in the injury done to the State appears to him as nothing in comparison with the exclusive advantage which he aims at appropriating to himself. This particular advantage being excepted, he desires the general welfare for his own interests quite as strongly as any other. Even in selling his vote for money, he does not extinguish in himself the general will, but eludes it. The fault that he commits is to change the state of the question, and to answer something different from what he was asked; so that, instead of saying by a vote: "It is beneficial to the State," he says: "It is beneficial to a certain man or a certain party that such or such a motion should pass." Thus the law of public order in assemblies is not so much to maintain in them the general will as to insure that it shall always be consulted and always respond.

I might in this place make many reflections on the simple right of voting in every act of sovereignty—a right which nothing can take away from the citizens—and on that of speaking, proposing, dividing, and discussing, which the government is always very careful to leave to its members only; but this important matter would require a separate treatise, and I cannot say everything in this one.

Karl Marx: Manifesto of the Communist Party

A spectre is haunting Europe—the spectre of Communism. All the Powers of old Europe have entered into a holy alliance to exorcise this spectre: Pope and Czar, Metternich and Guizot, French Radicals and German police-spies.

Where is the party in opposition that has not been decried as Communistic by its opponents in power? Where the Opposition that has not hurled back the branding reproach of Communism, against the more advanced opposition parties, as well as against its reactionary adversaries?

Two things result from this fact.

I. Communism is already acknowledged by all European Powers to be itself a Power.

II. It is high time that Communists should openly, in the face of the whole world, publish their views, their aims, their tendencies, and meet this nursery tale of the Spectre of Communism with a Manifesto of the party itself.

To this end, Communists of various nationalities have assembled in London, and sketched the following Manifesto, to be published in the English, French, German, Italian, Flemish and Danish languages.

The history of all hitherto existing society is the history of class struggles.

Freeman and slave, patrician and plebeian, lord and serf, guildmaster and journeyman, in a word, oppressor and oppressed, stood in constant opposition to one another, carried on an uninterrupted, now hidden, now open fight, a fight that each time ended, either in a revolutionary reconstitution of society at large, or in the common ruin of the contending classes.

In the earlier epochs of history, we find almost everywhere a complicated arrangement of society into various orders, a manifold gradation of social rank. In ancient Rome we have patricians, knights, plebeians, slaves; in the Middle Ages, feudal lords, vassals, guild-masters, journeymen, apprentices, serfs; in almost all of these classes, again, subordinate gradations.

The modern bourgeois society that has sprouted from the ruins of feudal society has not done away with class antagonisms. It has but established new classes, new conditions of oppression, new forms of struggle in place of the old ones.

Our epoch, the epoch of the bourgeoisie, possesses, however, this distinctive feature: It has simplified the class antagonisms. Society as a whole is more and more splitting up into two great hostile camps, into two great classes directly facing each other—bourgeoisie and proletariat.

From the serfs of the Middle Ages sprang the chartered burghers of the earliest towns. From these burgesses the first elements of the bourgeoisie were developed.

The discovery of America, the rounding of the Cape, opened up fresh ground for the rising bourgeoisie. The East-Indian and Chinese markets, the colonization of America, trade with the colonies, the increase in the means of exchange and in commodities generally, gave to commerce, to navigation, to industry, an impulse never before known, and thereby, to the revolutionary element in the tottering feudal society, a rapid development.

The feudal system of industry, in which industrial production was monopolized by closed guilds, now no longer sufficed for the growing wants of the new markets. The manufacturing system took its place. The guild-masters were pushed aside by the manufacturing middle class; division of labor between the different corporate guilds vanished in the face of division of labor in each single workshop.

Meantime the markets kept ever growing, the demand ever rising. Even manufacturing no longer sufficed. Thereupon, steam and machinery revolutionized industrial production. The place of manufacture was taken by the giant, modern industry, the place of the industrial middle class, by industrial millionaires—the leaders of whole industrial armies, the modern bourgeois.

Modern industry has established the world market, for which the discovery of America paved the way. This market has given an immense development to commerce, to navigation, to communication by land. This development has, in its turn, reacted on the extension of industry; and in proportion as industry, commerce, navigation, railways extended, in the same proportion the bourgeoisie developed, increased its capital, and pushed into the background every class handed down from the Middle Ages.

We see, therefore, how the modern bourgeoisie is itself the product of a long course of development, of a series of revolutions in the modes of production and of exchange.

Each step in the development of the bourgeoisie was accompanied by the corresponding political advance of that class. An oppressed class under the sway of the feudal nobility, it became an armed and self-governing association in the medieval commune; here independent urban republic (as in Italy and Germany), there taxable "third estate" of the monarchy (as in France); afterwards, in the period of manufacture proper, serving either the semi-feudal or the absolute monarchy as a counterpoise against the nobility, and, in fact, cornerstone of the great monarchies in general—the bourgeoisie has at last, since the establishment of modern industry and of the world market, conquered for itself, in the modern representative state, exclusive political sway. The executive of the modern state is but a committee for managing the common affairs of the whole bourgeoisie.

The bourgeoisie has played a most revolutionary role in history.

The bourgeoisie, wherever it has got the upper hand, has put an end to all feudal, patriarchal, idyllic relations. It has pitilessly torn asunder the motley feudal ties that bound man to his "natural superiors," and has left no other bond between man and man than naked self-interest, than callous "cash payment." It has drowned the most heavenly ecstasies of religious fervor, of chivalrous enthusiasm, of philistine sentimentalism, in the icy water of egotistical calculation. It has resolved personal worth into exchange value, and in place of the numberless indefeasible chartered freedoms, has set up that single, unconscionable freedom—Free Trade. In one word, for exploitation, veiled by religious and political illusions, it has substituted naked, shameless, direct, brutal exploitation. . . .

The bourgeoisie cannot exist without constantly revolutionizing the instruments of production, and thereby the relations of production, and with them the whole relations of society. Conservation of the old modes of production in unaltered form, was, on the contrary, the first condition of existence for all earlier industrial classes. Constant revolutionizing of production, uninterrupted disturbance of all social conditions, everlasting uncertainty and agitation distinguish the bourgeois epoch from all earlier ones. All fixed, fast-frozen relations, with their train of ancient and venerable prejudices and opinions, are swept away, all new-formed ones become antiquated before they can ossify. All that is solid melts into air, all that is holy is profaned, and man is at last compelled to face with sober senses his real conditions of life and his relations with his kind. . . .

The bourgeoisie, by the rapid improvements of all instruments of production, by the immensely facilitated means of communication, draws all nations, even the most barbarian, into civilization. The cheap prices of its commodities are the heavy artillery with which it batters down all Chinese walls, with which it forces the barbarians' intensely obstinate hatred of foreigners to capitulate. It compels all nations, on pain of extinction, to adopt the bourgeois mode of production, it compels them to introduce what it calls civilization into their midst, *i.e.,* to become bourgeois themselves. In a word, it creates a world after its own image. . . .

The bourgeoisie, during its rule of scarce one hundred years, has created more massive and more colossal productive forces than have all preceding generations together. Subjection of nature's forces to man, machinery, application of chemistry to industry and agriculture, steam-navigation, railways, electric telegraphs, clearing of whole continents for cultivation, canalization of rivers, whole populations conjured out of the ground—what earlier century had even a presentiment that such productive forces slumbered in the lap of social labor?

We see then that the means of production and of exchange, which served as the foundation for the growth of the bourgeoisie, were generated in feudal society. At a certain stage in the development of these means of production and of exchange, the conditions under which feudal society produced and exchanged, the feudal organization of agriculture and manufacturing industry, in a word, the feudal relations of property became no longer compatible with the already developed productive forces; they became so many fetters. They had to be burst asunder; they were burst asunder.

Into their place stepped free competition, accompanied by a social and political constitution adapted to it, and by the economic and political sway of the bourgeois class.

A similar movement is going on before our own eyes. Modern bourgeois society with its relations of production, of exchange and of property, a society that has conjured up such gigantic means of production and of exchange, is like the sorcerer who is no longer able to control the powers of the nether world whom he has called up by his spells. For many a decade past the history of industry and commerce is but the history of the revolt of modern productive forces against modern conditions of production, against the property relations that are the conditions for the existence of the bourgeoisie and of its rule. It is enough to mention the commercial crises that by their periodical return put the existence of the entire bourgeois society on trial, each time more threateningly. In these crises a great part not only of the existing products, but also of the previously created productive forces, are periodically destroyed. In these crises there breaks out an epidemic that, in all earlier epochs, would have seemed an absurdity—the epidemic of over-production. Society suddenly finds itself put back into a state of momentary barbarism; it appears as if a famine, a universal war of devastation had cut off the supply of every means of subsistence; industry and commerce seem to be destroyed. And why? Because there is too much civilization, too much means of subsistence, too much industry, too much commerce. The productive forces at the disposal of society no longer tend to further the development of the conditions of bourgeois property; on the contrary, they have become too powerful for these conditions, by which they are fettered, and no sooner do they overcome these fetters than they bring disorder into the whole of bourgeois society, endanger the existence of bourgeois property. The conditions of bourgeois society are too narrow to comprise the wealth created by them. And how does the bourgeoisie get over these crises? On the one hand by enforced destruction of a mass of productive forces; on the other, by the conquest of new markets, and by the more thorough exploitation of the old ones. That is to say, by paving the way for more extensive and more destructive crises, and by diminishing the means whereby crises are prevented.

The weapons with which the bourgeoisie felled feudalism to the ground are now turned against the bourgeoisie itself.

But not only has the bourgeoisie forged the weapons that bring death to itself; it has also called into existence the men who are to wield those weapons—the modern working class—the proletarians.

In proportion as the bourgeoisie, *i.e.,* capital, is developed, in the same proportion is the proletariat, the modern working class, developed—a class of laborers, who live only so long as they find work, and who find work only so long as their labor increases capital. These laborers, who must sell themselves piecemeal, are a commodity, like every other article of commerce, and are consequently exposed to all the vicissitudes of competition, to all the fluctuations of the market.

Owing to the extensive use of machinery and to division of labor, the work of the proletarians has lost all individual character, and, consequently, all charm for the workman. He becomes an appendage of the machine, and it is only the most simple, most monotonous, and most easily acquired knack, that is required of him. Hence, the cost of production of a workman is restricted, almost entirely, to the means of subsistence that he requires for his maintenance, and for the propagation of his race.

But the price of a commodity, and therefore also of labor, is equal to its costs of production. In proportion, therefore, as the repulsiveness of the work increases, the wage decreases. Nay more, in proportion as the use of machinery and division of labor increases, in the same proportion the burden of toil also increases, whether by prolongation of the working hours, by increase of the work exacted in a given time, or by increased speed of the machinery, etc.

Modern industry has converted the little workshop of the patriarchal master into the great factory of the industrial capitalist. Masses of laborers, crowded into the factory, are organized like soldiers. As privates of the industrial army they are placed under the command of a perfect hierarchy of officers and sergeants. Not only are they slaves of the bourgeois class, and of the bourgeois state; they are daily and hourly enslaved by the machine, by the supervisor, and, above all, by the individual bourgeois manufacturer himself. The more openly this despotism proclaims gain to be its end and aim, the more petty, the more hateful and the more embittering it is....

The proletariat goes through various stages of development. With its birth begins its struggle with the bourgeoisie. At first the contest is carried on by individual laborers, then by the work people of a factory, then by the operatives of one trade, in one locality, against the individual bourgeois who directly exploits them. They direct their attacks not against the bourgeois conditions of production, but against the instruments of production themselves; they destroy imported wares that compete with their labor, they smash machinery to pieces, they set factories ablaze, they seek to restore by force the vanished status of the workman of the Middle Ages.

At this stage the laborers still form an incoherent mass scattered over the whole country, and broken up by their mutual competition. If anywhere they unite to form more compact bodies, this is not yet the consequence of their own active union, but of the union of the bourgeoisie, which class, in order to attain its own political ends, is compelled to set the whole proletariat in motion, and is moreover still able to do so for a time. At this stage, therefore, the proletarians do not fight their enemies, but the enemies of their enemies, the remnants of absolute monarchy, the landowners, the nonindustrial bourgeois, the petty bourgeoisie. Thus the whole historical movement is concentrated in the hands of the bourgeoisie; every victory so obtained is a victory for the bourgeoisie.

But with the development of industry the proletariat not only increases in number; it becomes concentrated in greater masses, its strength grows, and it feels that strength more. The various interests and conditions of life within the ranks of the proletariat are more and more equalized, in proportion as machinery obliterates all distinctions of labor and nearly everywhere reduces wages to the same low level. The growing competition among the bourgeois, and the resulting commercial crises, make the wages of the workers ever more fluctuating. The unceasing improvement of machinery, ever more rapidly developing, makes their livelihood more and more precarious; the collisions between individual workmen and individual bourgeois take more and more the character of collisions between two classes. Thereupon the workers begin to form combinations (trade unions) against the bourgeoisie; they club together in order to keep up the rate of wages; they found permanent associations in order to make provision beforehand for these occasional revolts. Here and there the contest breaks out into riots.

Now and then the workers are victorious, but only for a time. The real fruit of their battle lies, not in the immediate results, but in the ever expanding union of the workers. This union is furthered by the improved means of communication which are created by modern industry, and which place the workers of different localities in contact with one another. It was just this contact that was needed to centralize the numerous local struggles, all of the same character, into one national struggle between classes. But every class struggle is a political struggle. And that union, to attain which the burghers of the Middle Ages, with their miserable highways, required centuries, the modern proletarians, thanks to railways, achieve in a few years.

This organization of the proletarians into a class, and consequently into a political party, is continually being upset again by the competition between the workers themselves, But it ever rises up again, stronger, firmer, mightier. It compels legislative recognition of particular interests of the workers, by taking advantage of the divisions among the bourgeoisie itself.

Thus the ten-hour bill in England was carried. . . .

Finally, in times when the class struggle nears the decisive hour, the process of dissolution going on within the ruling class, in fact within the whole range of old society, assumes such a violent, glaring character, that a small section of the ruling class cuts itself adrift, and joins the revolutionary class, the class that holds the future in its hands. Just as, therefore, at an earlier period, a section of the nobility went over to the bourgeoisie, so now a portion of the bourgeoisie goes over to the proletariat, and in particular, a portion of the bourgeois ideologists, who have raised themselves to the level of comprehending theoretically the historical movement as a whole.

Of all the classes that stand face to face with the bourgeoisie today, the proletariat alone is a really revolutionary class. The other classes decay and finally disappear in the face of modern industry; the proletariat is its special and essential product. . . .

The social conditions of the old society no longer exist for the proletariat. The proletarian is without property; his relation to his wife and children has no longer anything in common with bourgeois family relations; modern industrial labor, modern subjection to capital, the same in England as in France, in America as in Germany, has stripped him of every trace of national character. Law, morality, religion, are to him so many bourgeois prejudices, behind which lurk in ambush just as many bourgeois interests.

All the preceding classes that got the upper hand, sought to fortify their already acquired status by subjecting society at large to their conditions of appropriation. The proletarians cannot become masters of the productive forces of society, except by abolishing their own previous mode of appropriation, and thereby also every other previous mode of appropriation. They have nothing of their own to secure and to fortify; their mission is to destroy all previous securities for, and insurances of, individual property.

All previous historical movements were movements of minorities, or in the interest of minorities. The proletarian movement is the self-conscious, independent movement of the immense majority, in the interest of the immense majority. The proletariat, the lowest stratum of our present society, cannot stir, cannot raise itself up, without the whole superincumbent strata of official society being sprung into the air. . . .

Hitherto, every form of society has been based, as we have already seen, on the antagonism of oppressing and oppressed classes. But in order to oppress a class, certain conditions must be assured to it under which it can, at least, continue its slavish existence. The serf, in the period of serfdom, raised himself to membership in the commune, just as the petty bourgeois, under the yoke of feudal absolutism, managed to develop into a bourgeois. The modern laborer, on the contrary, instead of rising with the progress of industry, sinks deeper and deeper below the conditions of existence of his own class. He becomes a pauper, and pauperism develops more rapidly than population and wealth. And here it becomes evident, that the bourgeoisie is unfit any longer to be the ruling class in society, and to impose its conditions of existence upon society as an overriding law. It is unfit to rule because it is incompetent to assure an existence to its slave within his slavery, because it cannot help letting him sink into such a state, that it has to feed him, instead of being fed by him. Society can no longer live under this bourgeoisie, in other words, its existence is no longer compatible with society.

The essential condition for the existence and sway of the bourgeois class, is the formation and augmentation of capital; the condition for capital is wage-labor. Wage-labor rests exclusively on competition between the laborers. The advance of industry, whose involuntary promoter is the bourgeoisie, replaces the isolation of the laborers, due to competition, by their revolutionary combination, due to association. The development of modern industry, therefore, cuts from under its feet the very foundation on which the bourgeoisie produces and appropriates products. What the bourgeoisie therefore produces, above all, are its own grave-diggers. Its fall and the victory of the proletariat are equally inevitable. . . .

All property relations in the past have continually been subject to historical change consequent upon the change in historical conditions.

The French Revolution, for example, abolished feudal property in favor of bourgeois property.

The distinguishing feature of communism is not the abolition of property generally, but the abolition of bourgeois property. But modern bourgeois private property is the final and most complete expression of the system of producing and appropriating products that is based on class antagonisms, on the exploitation of the many by the few.

In this sense, the theory of the Communists may be summed up in the single sentence: Abolition of private property.

We Communists have been reproached with the desire of abolishing the right of personally acquiring property as the fruit of a man's own labor, which property is alleged to be the groundwork of all personal freedom, activity and independence.

Hard-won, self-acquired, self-earned property! Do you mean the property of the petty artisan and of the small peasant, a form of property that preceded the bourgeois form? There is no need to abolish that; the development of industry has to a great extent already destroyed it, and is still destroying it daily.

Or do you mean modern bourgeois private property?

But does wage-labor create any property for the laborer? Not a bit. It creates capital, *i.e.*, that kind of property which exploits wage-labor and which cannot increase except upon condition of begetting a new supply of wage-labor for fresh exploitation. Property, in its present form, is based on the antagonism of capital and wage-labor. Let us examine both sides of this antagonism.

To be a capitalist, is to have not only a purely personal but a social *status* in production. Capital is a collective product, and only by the united action of many members, nay, in the last resort, only by the united action of all members of society, can it be set in motion.

Capital is therefore not a personal, it is a social, power.

When, therefore, capital is converted into common property, into the property of all members of society, personal property is not thereby transformed into social property. It is only the social character of the property that is changed. It loses its class character.

Let us now take wage-labor.

The average price of wage-labor is the minimum wage, *i.e.*, that quantum of the means of subsistence which is absolutely requisite to keep the laborer in bare existence as a laborer. What, therefore, the wage-laborer appropriates by means of his labor, merely suffices to prolong and reproduce a bare existence. We by no means intend to abolish this personal appropriation of the products of labor, an appropriation that is made for the maintenance and reproduction of human life, and that leaves no surplus wherewith to command the labor of others. All that we want to do away with is the miserable character of this appropriation, under which the laborer lives merely to increase capital and is allowed to live only insofar as the interest of the ruling class requires it.

In bourgeois society, living labor is but a means to increase accumulated labor. In Communist society, accumulated labor is but a means to widen, to enrich, to promote the existence of the laborer.

In bourgeois society, therefore, the past dominates the present; in Communist society, the present dominates the past. In bourgeois society capital is independent and has individuality, while the living person is dependent and has no individuality.

And the abolition of this state of things is called by the bourgeois, abolition of individuality, bourgeois independence, and bourgeois freedom is undoubtedly aimed at.

By freedom is meant, under the present bourgeois conditions of production, free trade, free selling and buying.

But if selling and buying disappears, free selling and buying disappears also. This talk about free selling and buying, and all the other "brave words" of our bourgeoisie about freedom in general, have a meaning, if any, only in contrast with restricted selling and buying, with the fettered traders of the Middle Ages, but have no meaning when opposed to the Communist abolition of buying and selling, of the bourgeois conditions of production, and of the bourgeoisie itself.

You are horrified at our intending to do away with private property. But in your existing society, private property is already done away with for nine-tenths of the population; its existence for the few is solely due to its nonexistence in the hands of those nine-tenths. You reproach us, therefore, with intending to do away with a form of property, the necessary condition for whose existence is the nonexistence of any property for the immense majority of society.

In a word, you reproach us with intending to do away with your property. Precisely so; that is just what we intend.

From the moment when labor can no longer be converted into capital, money, or rent, into a social power capable of being monopolized, *i.e.*, from the moment when individual property can no longer be transformed into bourgeois property, into capital, from that moment, you say, individuality vanishes.

You must, therefore, confess that by "individual" you mean no other person than the bourgeois, than the middle-class owner of property. This person must, indeed, be swept out of the way, and made impossible.

Communism deprives no man of the power to appropriate the products of society; all that it does is to deprive him of the power to subjugate the labor of others by means of such appropriation. . . .

All objections urged against the Communist mode of producing and appropriating material products, have, in the same way, been urged against the Communist modes of producing and appropriating intellectual products. Just as, to the bourgeois, the disappearance of class property is the disappearance of production itself, so the disappearance of class culture is to him identical with the disappearance of all culture.

That culture, the loss of which he laments, is, for the enormous majority, a mere training to act as a machine.

But don't wrangle with us so long as you apply, to our intended abolition of bourgeois property, the standard of your bourgeois notions of freedom, culture, law, etc. Your very ideas are but the outgrowth of the conditions of your bourgeois production and bourgeois property, just as your jurisprudence is but the will of your class made into a law for all, a will whose essential character and direction are determined by the economic conditions of existence of your class.

The selfish misconception that induces you to transform into eternal laws of nature and of reason, the social forms springing from your present mode of production and form of property—historical relations that rise and disappear in the progress of production—this misconception you share with every ruling class that has preceded you. What you see clearly in the case of ancient property, what you admit in the case of feudal property, you are of course forbidden to admit in the case of your own bourgeois form of property. . . .

The charges against communism made from a religious, a philosophical, and, generally, from an ideological standpoint, are not deserving of serious examination.

Does it require deep intuition to comprehend that man's ideas, views, and conceptions, in one word, man's consciousness, changes with every change in the conditions of his material existence, in his social relations and in his social life?

What else does the history of ideas prove, than that intellectual production changes its character in proportion as material production is changed? The ruling ideas of each age have ever been the ideas of its ruling class.

When people speak of ideas that revolutionize society, they do but express the fact that within the old society the elements of a new one have been created, and that the dissolution of the old ideas keeps even pace with the dissolution of the old conditions of existence.

When the ancient world was in its last throes, the ancient religions were overcome by Christianity. When Christian ideas succumbed in the eighteenth century to rationalist ideas, feudal society fought its death-battle with the then revolutionary bourgeoisie. The ideas of religious liberty and freedom of conscience, merely gave expression to the sway of free competition within the domain of knowledge.

"Undoubtedly," it will be said, "religion, moral, philosophical and juridical ideas have been modified in the course of historical development. But religion, morality, philosophy, political science, and law, constantly survived this change."

"There are, besides, eternal truths, such as Freedom, Justice, etc., that are common to all states of society. But communism abolishes eternal truths, it abolished all religion, and all morality, instead of constituting them on a new basis; it therefore acts in contradiction to all past historical experience."

What does this accusation reduce itself to? The history of all past society has consisted in the development of class antagonisms, antagonisms that assumed different forms at different epochs.

But whatever form they may have taken, one

fact is common to all past ages, *viz.*, the exploitation of one part of society by the other. No wonder, then, that the social consciousness of past ages, despite all the multiplicity and variety it displays, moves within certain common forms, or general ideas, which cannot completely vanish except with the total disappearance of class antagonisms.

The Communist revolution is the most radical rupture with traditional property relations; no wonder that its development involves the most radical rupture with traditional ideas.

But let us have done with the bourgeois objections to communism.

We have seen above, that the first step in the revolution by the working class, is to raise the proletariat to the position of ruling class, to establish democracy.

The proletariat will use its political supremacy to west, by degrees, all capital from the bourgeoisie, to centralize all instruments of production in the hands of the state, *i.e.*, of the proletariat organized as the ruling class; and to increase the total of productive forces as rapidly as possible.

Of course, in the beginning, this cannot be effected except by means of despotic inroads on the rights of property, and on the conditions of bourgeois production; by means of measures, therefore, which appear economically insufficient and untenable, but which, in the course of the movement, outstrip themselves, necessitate further inroads upon the old social order, and are unavoidable as a means of entirely revolutionizing the mode of production. . . .

When, in the course of development, class distinctions have disappeared, and all production has been concentrated in the hands of a vast association of the whole nation, the public power will lose its political character. Political power, properly so called, is merely the organized power of one class for oppressing another. If the proletariat during its contest with the bourgeoisie is compelled, by the force of circumstances, to organize itself as a class, and, as such sweeps away by force the old conditions of production, then it will, along with these conditions, have swept away the conditions for the existence of class antagonisms, and of classes generally, and will thereby have abolished its own supremacy as a class.

In place of the old bourgeois society, with its classes and class antagonisms, we shall have an association, in which the free development of each is the condition for the free development of all.

John Stuart Mill: On Liberty

CHAPTER II

We have now recognized the necessity to the mental well-being of mankind (on which all their other well-being depends) of freedom of opinion, and freedom of the expression of opinion, on four distinct grounds, which we will now briefly recapitulate:

First, if any opinion is compelled to silence, that opinion may, for aught we can certainly know, be true. To deny this is to assume our own infallibility.

Secondly, though the silenced opinion be an error, it may, and very commonly does, contain a portion of truth; and since the general or prevailing opinion on any subject is rarely or never the whole truth, it is only by the collision of adverse opinions that the remainder of the truth has any chance of being supplied.

Thirdly, even if the received opinion be not only true, but the whole truth; unless it is suffered to be, and actually is, vigorously and earnestly contested, it will, by most of those who receive it, be held in the manner of a prejudice, with little comprehension or feeling of its rational grounds. And not only this, but, fourthly, the meaning of the doctrine of its vital effect on the character and conduct: the dogma becoming a mere formal profession, inefficacious for good, but cumbering the ground and preventing the growth of any real and heartfelt conviction from reason or personal experience. . . .

CHAPTER III

Such being the reasons which make it imperative that human beings should be free to form opinions and to express their opinions without reserve; and such the baneful consequences to the intellectual, and through that to the moral nature of man, unless this liberty is either conceded or asserted in spite of prohibition; let us next examine whether the same reasons do not require that men should be free to act upon their opinions—to carry these out in their lives without hindrance, either physical or moral, from their fellow men, so long as it is at their own risk and peril. This last proviso is of course indispensable. No one pretends that actions should be as free as opinions. On the contrary, even opinions lose their immunity when the circumstances in which they are expressed are such as to constitute their expression a positive instigation to some mischievous act. An opinion that corn dealers are starvers of the poor, or that private property is robbery, ought to be unmolested when simply circulated through the press, but may justly incur punishment when delivered orally to an excited mob assembled before the house of a corn dealer, or when handed about among the same mob in the form of a placard. Acts, of whatever kind, which without justifiable cause do harm to others may be, and in the more important cases absolutely require to be, controlled by the unfavorable sentiments, and, when needful, by the active interference of mankind. The liberty of the individual must be thus far limited; he must not make himself a nuisance to other people. But if he refrains from molesting others in what concerns them, and merely acts according to his own inclination and judgment in things which concern himself, the same reasons which show that opinion should be free prove also that he should be allowed, without molestation, to carry his opinions into practice at his own cost. That mankind are not infallible; that their truths, for the most part, are only half-truths; that unity of opinion, unless resulting from the fullest and freest comparison of opposite opinions, is not desirable, and diversity not an evil, but a good, until mankind are much more capable than at present of recognizing all sides of the truth, are principles applicable to men's modes of action not less than to their opinions. As it is useful that while mankind are imperfect there should be different opinions, so it is that there should be given to varieties of character, short of injury to others; and that the worth of different modes of life should be proved practically, when anyone thinks fit to try them. It is desirable, in short, that in things which do not primarily concern others individuality should assert itself. Where not the person's own character but the traditions or customs of other people are the rule of conduct, there is wanting one of the principal ingredients of human happiness, and quite the chief ingredient of individual and social progress.

In maintaining this principle, the greatest difficulty to be encountered does not lie in the appreciation of means toward an acknowledged end, but in the indifference of persons in general to the end itself. If it were felt that the free development of individuality is one of the leading essentials of well-being; that it is not only a co-ordinate element with all that is designated by the terms civilization, instruction, education, culture, but is itself a necessary part and condition of all those things, there would be no danger that liberty should be undervalued, and the adjustment of the boundaries between it and social control would present no extraordinary difficulty. But the evil is that individual spontaneity is hardly recognized by the common modes of thinking as having any intrinsic worth, or deserving any regard on its own account. The majority, being satisfied with the ways of mankind as they now are (for it is they who make them what they are), cannot comprehend why those ways should not be good enough for everybody; and what is more, spontaneity forms no part of the ideal of the majority of moral, and social reformers, but is rather looked on with jealousy as a troublesome and perhaps rebellious obstruction to the general acceptance of what these reformers, in their own judgment, think would be best for mankind. Few persons, out of Germany, even comprehend the meaning of the doctrine which Wilhelm von Humboldt, so eminent both as a *savant* and as a politician, made the text of a treatise—that "the end of man, or that which is prescribed by the eternal or immutable dictates of reason, and not suggested by vague and transient desires, is the highest and most harmonious development of his powers to a complete and consistent whole"; that, therefore, the object "toward which every human being must ceaselessly direct his efforts, and on which especially those who design to influence their fellow men must ever keep their eyes, is the individuality of power and development"; that for this there are two requisites, "freedom, and variety of situations"; and that from the union of these arise "individual vigor and manifold diversity," which combine themselves in "originality." . . .

Having said that the individuality is the same thing with development, and that it is only the cultivation of individuality which produces, or can produce, well-developed human beings, I might here close the argument: for what more or better can be said of any condition of human affairs than that it brings human beings themselves nearer to the best thing they can be? Or what worse can be said of any obstruction to good than that it prevents this? Doubtless, however, these considerations will not suffice to convince those who most need convincing; and it is necessary further to show that these developed human beings are of some use to the undeveloped—to point out to those who do not desire liberty, and would not avail themselves of it, that they may be in som intelligible manner rewarded for allowing other people to make use of it without hindrance.

In the first place, then, I would suggest that they might possibly learn something from them. It will not be denied by anybody that originality is a valuable element in human affairs. There is always need of persons not only to discover new truths and point out when what were once truths are true no longer, but also to commence new practices and set the example of more enlightened conduct and better taste and sense in human life. This cannot well be gain said by anybody who does not believe that the world has already attained perfection in all its ways and practices. It is true that this benefit is not capable of being rendered by everybody alike; there are but few persons, in comparison with the whole of mankind, whose experiments, if adopted by others, would be likely to be any improvement on established practice. But these few are the salt of the earth; without them, human life would become a stagnant pool. Not only is it they who introduce good things which did not before exist; it is they who keep the life in those which already exist. If there were nothing new to be done, would human intellect cease to be necessary? Would it be a reason why those who do the old things should forget why they are done, and do them like cattle, not like human beings? There is only too great a tendency in the best beliefs and practices to degenerate into the mechanical; and unless there were a succession of persons whose ever-recurring originality prevents the grounds of those beliefs and practices from becoming merely traditional, such dead matter would not resist the smallest shock from anything really alive, and there would be no reason why civilization should not die out, as in the Byzantine Empire. Persons of genius, it is true, are, and are always likely to be, a small minority; but in order to have them, it is necessary to preserve the soil in which they grow. Genius can only breathe freely in an *atmosphere* of freedom. Persons of genius are, *ex vi termini*, more individual than any other people—less capable, consequently, of fitting themselves, without hurtful compression, into any of the small number of molds which society provides in order to save its members the trouble of forming their own character. If from timidity they consent to be forced into one of these molds, and to let all that part of themselves which cannot expand under the pressure remain unexpanded, society will be little the better of their genius. If they are of strong character and break their fetters, they become a mark for the society which has not succeeded in reducing them to commonplace, to point out with solemn warning as "wild," "erratic," and the like—much as if one should complain of the Niagara river for not flowing smoothly between its banks like a Dutch canal.

I insist thus emphatically on the importance of genius and the necessity of allowing it to unfold itself freely both in thought and in practice, being well aware that no one will deny the position in theory, but knowing also that almost everyone, in reality, is totally indifferent to it. People think genius a fine thing if it enables a man to write an exciting poem or paint a picture. But in its true sense, that of originality in thought and action, though no one says that it is not a thing to be admired, nearly all, at heart, think that they can do very well without it. Unhappily this is too natural to be wondered at. Originality is the one thing which unoriginal minds cannot feel the use of. They cannot see what it is to do for them; how should they? If they could see what it would do for them, it would not be originality. The first service which originality has to render them is that of opening their eyes: which being once fully done, they would have a chance of being themselves original. Meanwhile, recollecting that nothing was ever done which someone was not the first to do, and that all good things which exist are the fruits of originality, let them be modest enough to believe that there is something still left for it to accomplish, and assure themselves that they are more in need of originality, the less they are conscious of the want.

Irving Kristol: About Equality

There would appear to be little doubt that the matter of equality has become, in these past two decades, a major political and ideological issue. The late Hugh Gaitskell proclaimed flatly that "socialism is about equality," and though this bold redefinition of the purpose of socialism must have caused Karl Marx to spin in his grave—he thought egalitarianism a vulgar, philistine notion and had only contemptuous things to say about it—nevertheless most socialist politicians now echo Mr. Gaitskell in a quite routine way. And not only socialist politicians: in the United States today, one might fairly conclude from the political debates now going on that capitalism, too, is "about equality," and will stand or fall with its success in satisfying the egalitarian impulse. To cap it all, a distinguished Harvard professor, John Rawls, recently published a serious, massive, and widely acclaimed work in political philosophy whose argument is that a social order is just and legitimate *only* to the degree that it is directed to the redress of inequality. To the best of my knowledge, no serious political philosopher ever offered such a proposition before. It is a proposition, after all, that peremptorily casts a pall of illegitimacy over the entire political history of the human race—that implicitly indicts Jerusalem and Athens and Rome and Elizabethan England, all of whom thought inequality was necessary to achieve a particular ideal of human excellence, both individual and collective. Yet most of the controversy about Professor Rawls's extraordinary thesis has revolved around the question of whether he has demonstrated it with sufficient analytical meticulousness. The thesis itself is not considered controversial.

One would think, then, that with so much discussion "about equality," there would be little vagueness as to what equality itself is about—what one means by "equality." Yet this is not at all the case. I think I can best illustrate this point by recounting a couple of my editorial experiences at the journal, *The Public Interest,* with which I am associated.

It is clear that some Americans are profoundly and sincerely agitated by the existing distribution of income in this country, and these same Americans—they are mostly professors of course—are constantly insisting that a more equal distribution of income is a matter of considerable urgency. Having myself no strong prior opinion as to the "proper" shape of an income-distribution curve in such a country as the United States, I have written to several of these professors asking them to compose an article that would describe a proper redistribution of American income. In other words, in the knowledge that they are discontented with our present income distribution, and taking them at their word that when they demand "more equality" they are not talking about an absolute leveling of all incomes, I invited them to give our readers a picture of what a "fair" distribution of income would be like.

I have never been able to get that article, and I have come to the conclusion that I never shall get it. In two cases I was promised such an

---

Reprinted by kind permission of the author.

analysis, but it was never written. In the other cases, no one was able to find the time to devote to it. Despite all the talk "about equality," no one seems willing to commit himself to a precise definition from which statesmen and social critics can take their bearings.

As with economists, so with sociologists. Here, instead of income distribution, the controversial issue is social stratification, i.e., the "proper" degree of intergenerational social mobility. The majority of American sociologists seem persuaded that American democracy has an insufficient degree of such mobility, and it seemed reasonable to me that some of them—or at least one of them!—could specify what degree would be appropriate. None of them, I am sure, envisages a society that is utterly mobile, in which *all* the sons and daughters of the middle and upper classes end up in the very lowest social stratum, where they can live in anticipation of *their* sons and daughters rising again toward the top, and then of their grandsons and granddaughters moving downward once again! On the other hand, there is much evident dissatisfaction with what social mobility we do have. So why not find out what pattern of social mobility would be "fair" and "just" and "democratic"?

I regret to report that one will not find this out by consulting any issue of *The Public Interest*. I further regret to report that nowhere in our voluminous sociological literature will one find any such depiction of the ideally mobile society. Our liberal sociologists, like our liberal economists, are eloquent indeed in articulating their social discontents, but they are also bewilderingly modest in articulating their social goals.

Now, what is one to infer from this experience? One could, of course, simply dismiss the whole thing as but another instance of the intellectual irresponsibility of our intellectuals. That such irresponsibility exists seems clear enough, but *why* it exists is not clear at all. I do not believe that our intellectuals and scholars are genetically destined to be willfully or mischievously irresponsible. They are, I should say, no more perverse than the rest of mankind, and if they act perversely there must be a reason, even if they themselves cannot offer us a reason.

I, for one, am persuaded that though these people talk most earnestly about equality, it is not really equality that interests them. Indeed, it does not seem to me that equality *per se* is much of an issue for anyone. Rather, it is a surrogate for all sorts of other issues, some of them of the highest importance; these involve nothing less than our conception of what constitutes a just and legitimate society, a temporal order of things that somehow "makes sense" and seems "right."

A just and legitimate society, according to Aristotle, is one in which inequalities—of property, or station, or power—are generally perceived by the citizenry as necessary for the common good. I do not see that this definition has ever been improved on, though generations of political philosophers have found it unsatisfactory and have offered alternative definitions. In most cases, the source of this dissatisfaction has been what I would call the "liberal" character of the definition: it makes room for many different and even incompatible kinds of just and legitimate societies. In some of these societies, large inequalities are accepted as a necessary evil, whereas in others they are celebrated as the source of positive excellence. The question that this definition leaves open is the relation between a particular just and legitimate society and the "best" society. Aristotle, as we know, had his own view of the "best" society: he called it a "mixed regime," in which the monarchical, aristocratic, and democratic principles were all coherently intermingled. But he recognized that his own view of the "best" regime was of a primarily speculative nature—that is to say, a view always worth holding in mind but usually not relevant to the contingent circumstances (the "historical" circumstances, we should say) within which actual statesmen have to operate.

Later generations found it more difficult to preserve this kind of philosophic detachment from politics. The influence of Christianity, with its messianic promises, made the distinction between "the best" and "the legitimate" ever harder to preserve against those who insisted that *only* the best regime was legitimate. (This, incidentally, is an assumption that Professor Rawls makes as a matter of course.) The Church tried—as an existing and imperfect institution it had to try—to maintain this distinction, but it could only do so by appearing somewhat less Christian than it had promised to be. When the messianic impulse was secularized in early modernity, and science and reason and technology took over the promise of redemptive power—of transforming this dismal world into the wonderful place it "ought" to be—that same difficulty persisted. Like the Church, all the political regimes of modernity have had to preserve their legitimacy either by claiming an ideal character which in obvious truth they did not possess, or by making what were taken to be "damaging admissions" as to their inability to transform the real into the ideal.

The only corrective to this shadow of illegitimacy that has hovered threateningly over the politics of Western civilization for nearly two millennia now was the "common sense" of the majority of the population, which had an intimate and enduring relation to mundane realities that was relatively immune to speculative enthusiasm. This relative immunity was immensely strengthened by the widespread belief in an afterlife, a realm in which, indeed, whatever existed would be utterly perfect. I think it possible to suggest that the decline of the belief in personal immortality has been the most important *political* fact of the last hundred years; nothing else has so profoundly affected the way in which the masses of people experience their worldly condition. But even today, the masses of people tend to be more "reasonable," as I would put it, in their political judgments and political expectations than are our intellectuals. The trouble is that our society is breeding more and more "intellectuals" and fewer common men and women.

I use quotation marks around the term "intellectuals" because this category has, in recent decades, acquired a significantly new complexion. The enormous expansion in higher education, and the enormous increase in the college-educated, means that we now have a large class of people in our Western societies who, though lacking intellectual distinction (and frequently lacking even intellectual competence), nevertheless believe themselves to be intellectuals. A recent poll of American college teachers discovered that no fewer than 50 percent defined themselves as "intellectuals." That gives us a quarter of a million American intellectuals on our college faculties alone; if one adds all those in government and in the professions who would also lay claim to the title, the figure would easily cross the million mark! And if one also adds the relevant numbers of college students, one might pick up another million or so. We are, then, in a country like America today, talking about a mass of several millions of "intellectuals" who are looking at their society in a highly critical way and are quick to adopt an adversary posture toward it.

It is this class of people who are most eloquent in their denunciations of inequality, and who are making such a controversial issue of it. Why? Inequality of income is no greater today than it was twenty years ago, and is certainly less than it was fifty years ago. Inequality of status and opportunity have visibly declined since World War II, as a result of the expansion of free or nearly-free higher education. (The percentage of our leading business executives who come from modest socioeconomic backgrounds is much greater today than in 1910.) Though there has been a mushrooming of polemics against the inequalities of the American condition, most of this socioeconomic literature is shot through with disingenuousness, sophistry, and unscrupulous statistical maneuvering. As Professor Seymour Martin Lipset has demonstrated, by almost any socioeconomic indicator one would select, American society today is—as best we can determine—*more* equal than it was one hundred years ago. Yet, one hundred years ago most Americans were boasting of the historically unprecedented equality that was to be found in their nation, whereas today many seem convinced that inequality is at least a problem and at worst an intolerable scandal.

The explanation, I fear, is almost embarrassingly vulgar in its substance. A crucial clue was provided several years ago by Professor Lewis Feuer, who made a survey of those American members of this "new class" of the college-educated—engineers, scientists, teachers, social scientists, psychologists, etc.—who had visited the Soviet Union in the 1920s and 1930s, and had written admiringly of what they saw. In practically all cases, what they saw was power and status in the possession of their own kinds of people. The educators were enthusiastic about the "freedom" of educators in the USSR to run things as they saw fit. Ditto the engineers, the psychologists, and the rest. Their perceptions were illusory, of course, but this is less significant than the wishful thinking that so evidently law behind the illusions. The same illusions, and the same wishful thinking, are now to be noticed among our academic tourists to Mao's China.

The simple truth is that the professional classes of our modern bureaucratized societies are engaged in a class struggle with the business community for status and power. Inevitably, this class struggle is conducted under the banner of "equality"—a banner also raised by the bourgeoisie in *its* revolutions. Professors are genuinely indignant at the expense accounts when business executives have and which they do not. They are, in contrast, utterly convinced that *their* privileges are "rights" that are indispensable to the proper workings of a good society. Most academics and professional people are even unaware that they are among the "upper" classes of our society. When one points this out to them, they refuse to believe it.*

The animus toward the business class on the part of members of our "new class" is expressed in large ideological terms. But what it comes down to is that our *nuovi uomini* are persuaded they can do a better job of running our society and feel entitled to have the opportunity. This is what *they* mean by "equality."

Having said this, however, one still has to explain the authentic moral passion that motivates our egalitarians of the "new class." They are not motivated by any pure power-lust; very few people are. They clearly dislike—to put it mildly—our liberal, bourgeois, commercial society, think it unfit to survive, and seek power to reconstruct it in some unspecified but radical way. To explain this, one has to turn to the intellectuals—the real ones—who are the philosophical sources of their ideological discontent.

Any political community is based on a shared conception of the common good, and once this conception becomes ambiguous and unstable, then the justice of any social order is called into question. In a democratic civilization, this questioning will always take the form of an accusation of undue privilege. Its true meaning, however, is to be found behind the literal statements of the indictment.

It is interesting to note that, from the very beginnings of modern bourgeois civilization, the class of people we call intellectuals—poets, novelists, painters, men of letters—has never accepted the bourgeois notion of the common good. This notion defines the common good as consisting mainly of personal security under the law, personal liberty under the law, and a steadily increasing material prosperity for those who apply themselves to that end. It is, by the standards of previous civilizations, a "vulgar" conception of the common good: there is no high nobility of purpose, no selfless devotion to transcendental ends, no awe-inspiring heroism. It is, therefore, a conception of the common good that dispossesses the intellectual of his traditional prerogative, which was to celebrate high nobility of purpose, selfless devotion to transcendental ends, and awe-inspiring heroism. In its place, it offered the intellectuals the freedom to write or compose as they pleased and then to sell their wares in the marketplace as best they could. This "freedom" was interpreted by—one can even say experienced by—intellectuals as a base servitude to philistine powers. They did not accept it two hundred years ago; they do not accept it today.

The original contempt of intellectuals for bourgeois civilization was quite explicitly "elitist," as we should now say. It was the spiritual egalitarianism of bourgeois civilization that offended them, not any material inequalities. They anticipated that ordinary men and women would be unhappy in bourgeois civilization precisely because it was a civilization of and for the "common man"—and it was their conviction that common men could only find true happiness when their lives were subordinated to and governed by uncommon ideals, as conceived and articulated by intellectuals. It was, and is, a highly presumptuous and self-serving argument to offer—though I am not so certain that it was or is altogether false. In any case, it was most evidently not an egalitarian

*One of the reasons they are so incredulous is that they do not count as "income"—as they should—such benefits as tenure, long vacations, relatively short working hours, and all of their other prerogatives. When a prerogative is construed as a "right," it ceases to be seen as a privilege.

argument. It only became so in our own century, when aristocratic traditions had grown so attenuated that the only permissible anti-bourgeois arguments had to be framed in "democratic" terms. The rise of socialist and communist ideologies made this transition a relatively easy one. A hundred years ago, when an intellectual became "alienated" and "radicalized," he was as likely to move "Right" as "Left." In our own day, his instinctive movement will almost certainly be to the "Left."

With the mass production of "intellectuals" in the course of the 20th century, traditional intellectual attitudes have come to permeate our college-educated upper-middle classes, and most especially the children of these classes. What has happened to the latter may be put with a simplicity that is still serviceably accurate: they have obtained enough of the comforts of bourgeois civilization, and have a secure enough grip upon them, to permit themselves the luxury of reflecting uneasily upon the inadequacies of their civilization. They then discover that a life that is without a sense of purpose creates an acute experience of anxiety, which in turn transforms the universe into a hostile, repressive place. The spiritual history of mankind is full of such existential moments which are the seedbeds of gnostic and millenarian movements—movements that aim at both spiritual and material reformations. Radical egalitarianism is, in our day, exactly such a movement.

The demand for greater equality has less to do with any specific inequities of bourgeois society than with the fact that bourgeois society is seen as itself inequitable because it is based on a deficient conception of the common good. The recent history of Sweden is living proof of this proposition. The more egalitarian Sweden becomes—and it is already about as egalitarian as it is ever likely to be—the more *enragés* are its intellectuals, the more guilt-ridden and uncertain are its upper-middle classes, the more "alienated" are its college-educated youth. Though Swedish politicians and journalists cannot bring themselves to believe it, it should be obvious by now that there are *no* reforms that are going to placate the egalitarian impulse in Swedish society. Each reform only invigorates this impulse the more, because the impulse is not, in the end, about equality at all but about the quality of life in bourgeois society.

In Sweden, as elsewhere, it is only the common people who remain loyal to the bourgeois ethos. As well they might: it is an ethos devised for their satisfaction. Individual liberty and security—in the older, bourgeois senses of these terms—and increasing material prosperity are still goals that are dear to the hearts of the working classes of the West. They see nothing wrong with a better, bourgeois life: a life without uncommon pretensions, a life to be comfortably lived by common men. This explains two striking oddities of current politics: (1) The working classes have, of all classes, been the most resistant to the spirit of radicalism that has swept the upper levels of bourgeois society; and (2) once a government starts making concessions to this spirit—by announcing its dedication to egalitarian reforms—the working class is rendered insecure and fearful, and so becomes more militant in *its* demands. These demands may be put in terms of greater equality of income and privilege—but, of course, they also and always mean greater inequality vis-à-vis other sections of the working class and those who are outside the labor force.

Anyone who is familiar with the American working class knows—as Senator McGovern discovered—that they are far less consumed with egalitarian bitterness or envy than are college professors or affluent journalists. True, they do believe that in a society where so large a proportion of the national budget is devoted to the common defense, there ought to be some kind of "equality of sacrifice," and they are properly outraged when tax laws seem to offer wealthy people a means of tax avoidance not available to others. But they are even more outraged at the way the welfare state spends the large amounts of tax moneys it does collect. These moneys go in part to the nonworking population and in part to the middle-class professionals who attend to the needs of nonworking population (teachers, social workers, lawyers, doctors, dieticians, civil servants of all description). The "tax rebellion" of recent years has been provoked mainly by the rapid growth of this welfare state, not by particular inequities in the tax laws—inequities, which, though real enough, would not, if abolished, have any significant impact on the workingman's tax burden. After all, the 20 billion dollars—a highly exaggerated figure, in my opinion—that Senator McGovern might "capture" by tax reforms would just about pay for his day-care center proposals, which the working class has not displayed much interest in.

Still, though ordinary people are not significantly impressed by the assertions and indignations of egalitarian rhetoric, they cannot help but be impressed by the fact that the ideological response to this accusatory rhetoric is so feeble. Somehow, bourgeois society seems incapable of explaining and justifying its inequalities and how they contribute to or are consistent with the common good. This, I would suggest, derives from the growing bureaucratization of the economic order, a process which makes bourgeois society even more efficient economically, but also ever more defenseless before its ideological critics.

For any citizen to make a claim to an unequal share of income, power, or status, his contribution has to be—and has to be seen to be—a human and personal thing. In no country are the huge salaries earned by film stars or popular singers or professional athletes a source of envy or discontent. More than that: in most countries—and especially in the United States—the individual entrepreneur who builds up his own business and becomes a millionaire is rarely attacked on egalitarian grounds. In contrast, the top executives of our large corporations, most of whom are far less wealthy than Frank Sinatra or Bob Hope or Mick Jagger or Wilt Chamberlain, cannot drink a martini on the expense account without becoming the target of a "populist" politician. These faceless and nameless personages (who is the president of General Electric?) have no clear title to their privileges—and I should say the reason is precisely that they are nameless and faceless. One really has no way of knowing what they are doing "up there," and whether what they are doing is in the public interest or not.

It was not always so. In the 19th century, at the apogee of the bourgeois epoch, the perception of unequal contributions was quite vivid indeed. The success of a businessman was taken to be testimony to his personal talents and character—especially character, than which there is nothing more personal. This explains the popularity of biographies of successful entrepreneurs, full of anecdotes about the man and with surprisingly little information about his economic activities. In the 20th century, "entrepreneurial history," as written in our universities, becomes the history of the firm rather than the biography of a man. To a considerable extent, of course, this reflects the fact that most businessmen today are not "founding fathers" of a firm but temporary executives in a firm: the bureaucratization of modern society empties the category of the bourgeois of its human content. To the best of my knowledge, the only notable biography of a living businessman to have appeared in recent years was that of Alfred P. Sloan, who made his contribution to General Motors a good half century ago.

Nor is it only businessmen who are so affected. As the sociological cast of mind has gradually substituted itself for the older bourgeois moral-individualist cast of mind, military men and statesmen have suffered a fate similar to that of businessmen. Their biographies emphasize the degree to which they shared all our common human failings; their contributions to the common good, when admitted at all, are ascribed to larger historical forces in whose hands they were little more than puppets. They are all taken to be representative men, not exceptional men.

But when the unequal contributions of individuals are perceived as nothing but the differential functions of social or economic or political roles, then only those inequalities absolutely needed to perform these functions can be publicly justified. The burden of proof is heavy indeed, as each and every inequality must be scrutinized for its functional purport. True, that particular martini, drunk in that place, in that time, in that company, might contribute to the efficiency and growth of the firm and the economy. But would the contribution really have been less if the executive in question had been drinking water?

So this, it appears to me, is what the controversy "about equality" is really about. We have an intelligentsia which so despises the ethos of bourgeois society, and which is so guilt-ridden at being implicated in the life of this society, that it is inclined to find even collective suicide preferable to the status quo. (How else can one explain the evident attraction which totalitarian regimes possess for so many of our writers and artists?) We have a "New Class" of self-designated "intellectuals" who share much of this basic attitude—but who, rather than committing suicide, pursue power in the name of equality. (The children of this "New Class," however, seemed divided in their yearnings for suicide via drugs, and in their lust for power via "revolution.") And then we have the ordinary people, working-class and lower-middle-class, basically loyal to the bourgeois order but confused and apprehensive at the lack of clear meaning in this order—a lack derived from the increasing bureaucratization (and accompanying impersonalization) of political and economic life. All of these discontents tend to express themselves in terms of "equality"—which is in itself a quintessentially bourgeois ideal and slogan.

It is neither a pretty nor a hopeful picture. None of the factors contributing to this critical situation is going to go away; they are endemic to our 20th-century liberal-bourgeois society. Still, one of the least appreciated virtues of this society is its natural recuperative powers—its capacity to change, as we say, but also its capacity to preserve itself, to adapt and survive. The strength of these powers always astonishes us, as we anticipate (even proclaim) an imminent apocalypse that somehow never comes. And, paradoxically enough, this vitality almost surely has something to do with the fact that the bourgeois conception of equality, so vehemently denounced by the egalitarian, is "natural" in a way that other political ideas—egalitarian or anti-egalitarian—are not. Not necessarily in all respects superior, but more "natural." Let me explain.

The founding fathers of modern bourgeois society (John Locke, say, or Thomas Jefferson) all assumed that biological inequalities among men—inequalities in intelligence, talent, abilities of all kinds—were not extreme, and therefore did not justify a society of hereditary privilege (of "two races," as it were). This assumption we now know to be true, demonstrably true, as a matter of fact. Human talents and abilities, as measured, do tend to distribute themselves along a bell-shaped curve, with most people clustered around the middle, and with much smaller percentages at the lower and higher ends. That men are "created equal" is not a myth or a mere ideology—unless, of course, one interprets that phrase literally, which would be patently absurd and was never the bourgeois intention. Moreover, it is a demonstrable fact that in all modern, bourgeois societies, the distribution of income is also roughly along a bell-shaped curve, indicating that in such an "open" society the inequalities that do emerge are not inconsistent with the bourgeois notion of equality.

It is because of this "natural tyranny of the bell-shaped curve," in the conditions of a commercial society, that contemporary experiments in egalitarian community-building—the Israeli kibbutz, for instance—only work when they recruit a homogeneous slice of the citizenry, avoiding a cross-section of the entire population. It also explains why the aristocratic idea—of a distribution in which the right-hand section of the bell curve is drastically shrunken—is so incongruent with the modern world, so that modern versions of superior government by a tiny elite (which is what the communist regimes are) are always fighting against the economic and social tendencies inherent in their own societies. Purely egalitarian communities are certainly feasible—but only if they are selective in their recruitment and are relatively indifferent to economic growth and change, which encourages differentiation. Aristocratic societies are feasible, too—most of human history consists of them—but only under conditions of relative economic lethargy, so that the distribution of power and wealth is insulated from change. But once you are committed to the vision of a predominantly commercial society, in which flux and change are "normal"—in which men and resources are expected to move to take advantage of new economic opportunities—then you find yourself tending toward the limited inequalities of a bourgeous kind.

This explains one of the most extraordinary (and little-noticed) features of 20th-century societies: how relatively invulnerable the distribution of income is to the efforts of politicians and ideologues to manipulate it. In all the Western nations—the United States, Sweden, the United Kingdom, France, Germany—despite the varieties of social and economic policies of their governments, the distribution of income is strikingly similar. Not identical; politics is not entirely impotent, and the particular shape of the "bell" can be modified—but only with immense effort, and only slightly, so that to the naked eye of the visitor the effect is barely visible.* Moreover, available statistics suggest that the distribution of income in the communist regimes of Russia and Eastern Europe, despite both their egalitarian economic ideologies and aristocratic political structure, moves closer every year to the Western model, as these regimes seek the kind of economic growth that their "common men" unquestionably desire. And once the economic structure and social structure start assuming the shape of this bell-shaped curve, the political structure—the distribution of political power—follows along the same way, however slowly and reluctantly. The "Maoist" heresy within communism can best be understood as a heroic—but surely futile—rebellion against the gradual submission of communism to the constraints of the bell-shaped curve.

So bourgeois society—using this term in its larger sense, to include such "mixed economies" as prevail in Israel or Sweden or even Yugoslavia—is not nearly so fragile as its enemies think or its friends fear. Only a complete reversal of popular opinion toward the merits of material prosperity and economic growth would destroy it, and despite the fact that some of our citizens seem ready for such a reversal, that is unlikely to occur.

The concern and distress of our working- and lower-middle classes over the bureaucratization of modern life can, I think, be coped with. One can envisage reforms that would encourage their greater "participation" in the corporate structures that dominate our society; or one can envisage reforms that would whittle down the size and power of these structures returning part way to a more traditional market economy; or one can envisage a peculiar—and, in pure principle, incoherent—combination of both. My own view is that this last alternative, an odd amalgam of the prevailing "Left" and "Right" viewpoints, is the most realistic and the most probable. And I see no reason why it should not work. It will not be the "best" of all possible societies. But the ordinary man like Aristotle, is no utopian, and he will settle for a "merely satisfactory" set of social arrangements and is prepared to grant them a title of legitimacy.

The real trouble is not sociological or economic at all. It is that the "middling" nature of a bourgeois society falls short of corresponding adequately to the full range of man's spiritual nature, which makes more than middling demands upon the universe, and demands more than middling answers. This weakness of bourgeois society has been highlighted by its intellectual critics from the very beginning. And it is this weakness that generates continual dissatisfaction, especially among those for whom material problems are no longer so urgent. They may speak about "equality"; they may even be obsessed with statistics and pseudo-statistics about equality; but it is a religious vacuum—a lack of meaning in their own lives, and the absence of a sense of larger purpose in their society—that terrifies them and provokes them to "alienation" and unappeasable indignation. It is not too much to say that it is the death of God, not the emergence of any new social or economic trends, that haunts bourgeois society. And *this* problem is far beyond the competence of politics to cope with.

*It must be kept in mind, of course that retaining the shape of the curve is not inconsistent with *everyone* getting richer or poorer. The bell itself then moves toward a new axis.

Paul Kurtz: The Democratic Ethic

THE MEANING OF DEMOCRACY

Democracy is still the most radical social philosophy in the world today—radical because there are so many opposed to it and so few who genuinely understand or believe in it, and because, if adopted, it would mean a fundamental change in human institutions. Nevertheless it is espoused by people on all sides of the political spectrum. Liberals praise democracy; so do conservatives and reactionaries; even Marxist communists defend what they call "people's democratic republics." Democracy, like other noble ideals, is thought to confer virtue by association. Yet not all those who pay lip service to it are democrats. Democracy has been betrayed by totalitarians and humanitarians of all kinds—by those who believe in government for the people, if not necessarily of or by them—and has been undermined by apostles of the far right and the far left.

One source of this confusion is that many of those who appeal for democracy are uncertain of its nature, or else choose to misapply it. What is "democracy"? How is it to be applied? Are there any limits that a society calling itself democratic should not exceed? What is essential to democracy?

THE ETHICAL DIMENSIONS OF DEMOCRACY

The term "democracy" may be used in different senses. We talk of political, economic, racial, social democracy. The essential factor, in my judgment, is that democracy expresses an ethical dimension: It advocates first and foremost a normative ideal—one that recommends how we shall treat people, and how we should live and work together as individuals in community. Although the democratic ideal has many different interpretations and applications, it cannot be implemented without recognition of its basic moral foundations.

What are the moral principles that it expresses? As we have seen, the democratic philosophy involves at the very least a commitment to the principles of liberty and equality. But as we also have seen, if the principle of liberty is overemphasized, it may lead to an extreme laissez-faire individualism or anarchism that may deny the rights of others; it may ignore the need for equality of treatment; and it may lead to an unjust society in which large sections of the population are disenfranchised socially and economically and excluded from the good things of life. Indeed, the principle of freedom if allowed to reign alone may eventually lead to an exclusive class society in which some individuals or groups would possess power, while large numbers of people are bypassed or excluded from effective involvement. On the other hand, an egalitarian society which is excessively protective of equal rights might so restrict individual freedom that the right of choice and initiative would be thwarted. Societies that emphasize egalitarianism and ignore libertarianism generally tend to become totalitarian,

---

From Chapter VIII of *The Fullness of Life* by Paul Kurtz, Horizon Press, 1974. Reprinted by the kind permission of the author

willing to trample on freedoms of thought, action, and dissent.

In its concern for the worth and dignity of the individual democracy recognizes his right to do what he wishes and restricts undue interference in the sphere of individual choice and action. It provides the opportunity and conditions for personal realization and growth.

The democratic ethic recognizes that insofar as we respect an individual's right to personal freedom, we contribute not only to his growth but to our own; insofar as we can appreciate others we can learn to share their stores of experience, wisdom, truth. In being tolerant of diversity, the democratic approach enlarges our horizons for discovery and insight; it permits creative growth in the community, for it eliminates undue limitations on uniqueness. Insofar as I am willing to listen to another, to consider him as a being entitled to equal consideration and fair treatment, I contribute to both my development and his.

The democratic ethic is also based on the idea of freely given consent; its institutions strive as nearly as possible to base their policies on the consent of the greatest number of people. This consent is not mere acquiescence; it must be freely given in active approval of the main directions being taken and confidence in the key officials who are to carry them out.

Consent alone is never enough. We should always seek to enlist real participation in the affairs of the state, the sharing of power and responsibility on all levels. Since each one has an equal stake in society and in life, each should have a commensurate role. The true democrat has some measure of faith in the "ordinary man," in his ingrained wisdom and practical judgment, particularly in that which concerns his self-interest. The democratic ethic denies that any group or class has special knowledge or moral virtue that enables it to judge better what is good for others than they can judge for themselves. No claim to power based upon privilege, wealth, prestige, birth or background entitles any group to exercise rule.

There are, of course, many interpretations of cooperative participation. Some believe that democracy requires consensus, even unanimity. Yet, although in democratic decisions one tries to arouse wide, if possible unanimous, support for a policy or program, it is rarely if ever attained. In small groups where decisions are made face-to-face in daily encounter, it may be possible to reach consensus; the method is persuasion and negotiation. In a large social context, with diversity of opinion, the next best thing is majority rule. Majorities are often lumbering and in error, but they are fairer to a greater number of interests than the minority, even though the minority may be correct.

What is crucial for democracy is the method by which decisions are reached. The most desirable method is that of peaceful deliberation, discussion, persuasion, the widest possible dialogue between opposing conceptions. In recognizing that no individual or group may possess all the truth, democracy leaves open the possibilities for the class of competing views, and thrives on heresy and nonconformity.

BASIC COMMITMENTS

Of course, democracy can only survive if its citizens abide by certain rules. Provided that you are willing to listen to me or to those who represent me, and possibly be persuaded to change, I will try to convince you, says the democrat, but if I cannot I will go along in general with what the majority wants. What is essential is the willingness to negotiate differences and to reach common ground. If the democratic method of shared decision-making is to be effective, it presupposes that certain concomitant policies and procedures be present. What is of first importance is that there be a common framework of values and ideals; for a democracy to operate there must be some consensual agreement that the ethic of democracy is just and humane. Those who live in the community may dissent from current policies and pursue a plurality of life styles or hold different belief systems; yet they should have some intelligent commitment to the framework, that is, to the method by which social change is made possible, policies are enacted, and leaders are selected. If large sections of the population do not believe in democracy and are willing to abandon it for a more efficient, more orderly, or what seems to promise a more just system, the democratic ethic will break down; and if an underdeveloped nation, there is no heritage of democratic values, it is hardly likely to accept democracy, which presupposes some allegiance to common values. The serious problem that some Western countries now face is that large sections of the populace, whether of the New Left or Old Right, are no longer really loyal to the moral premises of democracy.

AN OPEN SOCIETY: FREE EDUCATION AND INFORMATION

Public knowledge and access to truth are pre-conditions of a democratic society. If public decisions are to be made wisely, it is important that state secrets be at a minimum and truly concern national security.

Democracy requires some system of universal education. This does not mean that all men are entitled to pursue programs in all fields, or be admitted to all institutions of higher education without qualification; as we have seen, rewards should depend upon merit. What it does mean is that basic opportunities are to be available for all. As John Dewey recommended, an appreciation for democratic values should be developed in the young, the capacity for shared experience and toleration, and most vitally, the cultivation of the arts of intelligence. For only an informed citizenry, capable of distinguishing the true from the false, is the most reliable safeguard for a democracy.

If the citizens are to reach their decisions wisely, moreover, it is also essential that there be free access to *all* sources of inquiry. Thus, freedom of opinion, research, investigation, and publication are essential: The key public value is cooperative inquiry. This is not possible where there is no marketplace in which ideas can be examined. We have seen how in totalitarian societies the ministries of information control the sources of information—radio, TV, cinema, magazines, newspapers, book publishing, education; and so we must fundamentally oppose those societies in which elementary freedoms are denied, and not be misled by those who label as "democratic" the communist societies closed to free inquiry. In capitalist and quasi-democratic societies in the West, on the other hand, it is vital that large commercial interests not be allowed to control the mass media. A genuine threat to freedom of information in the United States has emerged because the control of television is concentrated in only a few national networks and only two or three wire services predominate—an unfortunate narrowing of points of view. The development of large conglomerates in the book, newspaper, and magazine publishing fields must also be viewed with alarm.

The problem of free communication and access to information is of course related to economics. If democracy is to be effective it is necessary that the media be free of undue control by advertising merchants. It is said that the mass media, based upon the profit motive, need to sell their services to advertisers if they are to be supported. But from the standpoint of the public interest, the first duty of the media should be to inform and only secondarily to profit. There can be no quibbling on this point and no compromise. We would surely complain if our public school system were run primarily for profit rather than for service. It is one thing to have the profit motive rule in manufacturing automobiles or selling shoes; it is quite another to allow it to dominate in the sensitive area of ideas, the mainstays of a viable democratic society.

Democracy cannot operate where there is fear or intimidation of opinion, nor where pressures compel people against their better judgment. In dictatorships the threat of imprisonment and torture effectively prevents expression of ideas, but other forms of sanctions operate more subtly in a democracy to undermine an individual's courage—fear of losing security or status, of ecclesiastical pressure threatening excommunication or penance, or social discrimination or racial prejudice.

An increasing peril is the misuse of the mass media. Here too we have seen how dictatorships use them to indoctrinate, to keep people misinformed and docile. The mass media are used in subtle or unscrupulous ways by advertisers, who by conditioning techniques persuade consumers to buy shoddy products. When such techniques are used to sell the presidency or other political offices, the whole fabric of a democratic polity is undermined. I am not objecting to advertising *per se* as the informed description of products and services, not surely to the use of the mass media by contenders for political office. What I do condemn is the increasingly abusive manipulation of the air waves by political hucksters. The members of modern society are consumers but they are also citizens and the mass media should not be allowed to cater to one role while they neglect the other. I am not arguing for state control of advertisers and the mass media—we have seen how political power can be as offensive as economic power—but for democratic mechanisms of regulation and of support. Consumer unions and groups, for example, should also be allowed to advertise and analyze products sold through the mass media. It is essential that the consumer have some power over what is fed to him and that corporate organizations be democratized and regulated so that the public interest will never be overlooked.

INDIVIDUAL AND MINORITY RIGHTS

If democracy is rule by the people, can the people ever suspend the rights of individuals or of minorities even if they are offensive? If democracy is rule by the majority, can a majority ever abrogate the rights of those with whom it disagrees? Can it suppress recalcitrant minorities? There is considerable confusion here, even among some of the best-intentioned of democrats: After all, if we agree to abide by the majority decision, how can we intervene when it goes against what we like? Must we not suffer in silence, hoping to persuade the majority to reverse itself?

The majority is not sacred; nor does majority rule remain inviolable under every circumstance. Democracy rests upon still more fundamental principles—liberty, equality, toleration, civil disobedience—which are higher on the scale of values. Majority rule does not have an intrinsic value in itself. It is only a mechanism to ensure conditions of social harmony and peace and is used because it entails fewer risks and dangers to social welfare than other methods of decision-making. Majority rule is justified only because it safeguards individual rights; it must not be used to suppress them; and opposing minorities and individuals have obligations to the majority—not to impose their beliefs by non-democratic means. The protection of minority rights is a pre-condition of any democratic society, in which majorities are free to determine public policy but not to undermine the ethical presuppositions of democracy.

Am I not bringing in a doctrine of natural rights that are prior to political policy? No, I reject any such fiction. Nor do I accept the notion of a social contract. All individual and minority rights are social; they are claims made upon the community, which lay down certain restrictions upon political power. To say that certain liberties and rights should be recognized is to make a normative claim. It is to prescribe or direct future action. How should we regard or treat individuals in society? They are entitled to equal consideration and freedom even if the majority disagrees with them.

How are these principles to be justified? They are not derived from a divine or natural law, nor do they have any special metaphysical status. They are rules offered to govern how we shall behave. They can be justified only by reference to their results. Societies that nourish the rights of individuals and minorities will, in the long run, be happier, more humane, and just. Societies willing to suspend individual rights whenever immediate purposes seem to require it will be liable to disharmony. The respect for those rights is justified because they are more likely to ensure the common good and the conditions whereby individuals may discover the fullness of life.

THE RULE OF LAW

A democratic society is also based upon respect for due process and the rule of law. There are those who indict "legalism" and "parliamentarianism," and who attack the slow-moving character of democratic societies committed to legal processes, in which policies rest upon precedent. There is a temptation for some to prefer rule by fiat in order to get things done rapidly, independently of legal tradition or bureaucratic red tape. Yet if there is one conclusion to be drawn from the history of political and social philosophy, it is the collective wisdom of the law. Plato in *The Republic* wanted philosopher-kings to rule, and to apply their wisdom and knowledge for the social good. Utopianists and totalitarians ever since have decried laws that have stood in their way and have defended "reason" and "revelation." Yet Plato himself recognized in *The Laws* that in the absence of a philosopher-king, laws are the best guarantors of freedom. Alas, such philosopher-kings have not yet been discovered; nor does the easy temptation today to resort to behavioral scientists as our messiahs promise anything better. Laws still seem a more reliable way of running a society. Laws, however, provide us only with general guides for behavior; how they work out depends upon the context. In a just society laws are applied without discrimination. In the absence of law there would be no possibility of security; fear and indecision would be our constant companions. Of course provisions must be allowed for equity in interpreting and adjusting them to new situations. Further, a just society should try to minimize the regulation of our lives, to leave to individual citizens the widest possible latitude; where regulation is necessary, it should be based upon legal development.

A recurrent problem arises when in the name of civil disobedience and equal rights, some partisans flout the law and argue that it is corrupt. They dramatize crime in the ghettoes, minimize its consequences, and explain it by attributing it to unjust conditions. There is of course a good deal of truth to this claim, particularly for disadvantaged minorities who have often been brutalized by excessive police power and denied their rights. We also need to decriminalize much of the law; as the discussion in Chapter VI shows, many so-called criminal offenses ought not to be so considered.

Of course, law does not guarantee freedom. History has taught us how it can be oppressive and arbitrary, especially in fascist or closed societies. The ideal is for laws to come into being and to become modified by the parliamentary process, and to be applied impartially and humanely. If law is essential to a democracy, it is equally essential that it must not become sacrosanct, that it be responsive to the will of the people, and tested by its consequences in action.

THE JUSTIFICATION OF THE DEMOCRATIC IDEAL

The above is a mere outline suggestive of some features of a democratic society. Does such a society exist? Obviously not. Democracy is an ideal and any definition of it must be ideal. Naturally there is a descriptive element in the definition. "Democracy" does not refer to some theoretical entity independent of the real world. Many societies have had democratic features, but none has ever been a pure democracy. Hence the concept is comparative, a standard by which we may criticize, classify, and compare existing states, and a guide and incentive to greater democracy in the future. So the definition of democracy is normative and prescriptive for the development of society, and for the ethical principles by which we may evaluate policies and systems and reform them.

We have recently heard indictments of so-called democratic societies. Young idealists accuse them of being hypocritical and of betraying their ideals in practice—the result of defects in the democratic ideal. It is said that democracy doesn't work; we need something else. But as I have pointed out, no society—not America nor Britain nor the Scandinavian countries nor ancient Athens—has ever fully implemented the democratic ideal. Then how justify continued commitment to democracy? How would we go about proving its efficacy and power?

One should, to begin with, have a mature and realistic attitude about social systems and ideals. Although there has been immense progress in human affairs, only a pure visionary would expect to see all problems solved or utopia achieved. The justification of democracy is always relative, not rooted in metaphysics or science; it cannot have a deductive or necessary proof. The demand for that kind of justification is, like the demand for the justification of life, an expression of religious need. Democracy can only be vindicated practically and empirically. And what of the alternatives—dictatorship, oligarchy, aristocracy? At least democracy has a wider concern for a greater number of people; even the lowliest have a stake in it, and so it has a more extensive appeal. But also, in comparative terms, it provides fewer dangers and fewer negative consequences than other systems. There is always the danger that self-interest may be confused with the common good. Power has corrupted and blinded rulers throughout history to their own imperfections; it is dangerous to entrust power to an individual or group without proper checks and balances. This has been the collective wisdom of human experience. Antidemocratic societies, which award power on the basis of class, wealth, or military force, tend to degenerate into self-interested rule.

Since in a democracy those who are responsible can be called to account there is less likelihood of excessive duplicity or cruelty. Of course injustices and mistakes occur in a democracy, but at least where a society is open injustices can be examined by the critical eye of the public.

Consequently, in democratic societies muckraking is an important tradition for exposing graft and corruption, whereas people in totalitarian societies usually live in illusion, far less aware of social problems. It has been said by Marxist critics that America, and other Western democracies, are in decay, whereas the Soviet Union and some Eastern European countries are coalescing and advancing. So it may seem on the surface, but is that not due in part to the fact that the West has some freedom of the press, which tends to dramatize its problems—from alcoholism and crime to political corruption and wiretapping, from poverty to racism, among others? It is universally recognized that totalitarian societies, though they have similar problems, withhold them from public view by controlling the press. We need to be mindful of putting things in perspective. At least, free societies can know about problems which closed societies cannot.

Surely democracy has the potential for the widest realization of happiness for the largest number. It provides the richest soil for both individual development and social cooperation. With a role in society and a stake in the future, man becomes a devoted member of the cause that provides such noble opportunities; his alienation is reduced, his creative commitment and loyalty enhanced. In an age of crisis in religious commitment, democracy is more amenable to meaningful identification with worthwhile goals. It is more likely to be creative and innovative, more receptive to invention and discovery than a closed, hierarchical, or fixed society. Thus, if viewed in terms of desirable consequences, more people will tend to find a more satisfying life on the whole in a democratic system than in a non-democratic one. There are those who have had no experience of freedom, who either go wild when they first taste it or flee in fear and seek to escape it. Democracy presupposes that the experience of freedom in the young will develop an understanding of its responsible application so that it will become ingrained in the mores of the society.

POLITICAL DEMOCRACY

This discussion has been a general one, concerning the ideal normative features of democracy viewed in its ethical and social dimensions. But it is the *way* that these principles work out in practice that is important. Some institutions of a society are democratic, some not. With respect to institutions, most democrats believe that an essential pre-condition for the realization of any genuinely ethical system is political democracy. But many Marxists who claim to be "democratic" deny the importance of this and debunk the definition of liberal political democracy as mere "bourgeois deception."

What is a democratic *political* system? The term "political system" refers primarily to the operations of state and government, the control of decision-making and power. In large nation states, the only feasible method of rule is by means of representation. Although democracy encourages decentralization, enlisting the largest degree of involvement at all levels, some policies cannot be adequately arrived at by a local unit and have to be enunciated for the whole society. The only practical way to implement the democratic philosophy is for the people to delegate power by electing representatives to carry out the main programs. In a large society we cannot elect all the government officials (the United States, for example, has some 12 million government workers), but only key leaders. Nor can the people by means of elections determine all the policies of the state (there are of course many thousands of governmental rules and regulations, many of them highly technical), but only general guidelines. The presumption is that the major policies are fully discussed before they are adopted. Accordingly, the operation of majority rule, though not a "pure" form of democracy, is the most feasible method of expressing the will of the people. Free elections are the necessary ingredient in a democratic polity, local, state, and federal, as well as in the control of political parties.

Concomitant with this is the legal right of the individual not only to disagree but to make known his opposition to leaders and programs.

Where there is no right to oppose the government, to submit its policies to critical scrutiny, and to offer alternatives, there is no democracy. One-party states, where leaders are selected by acclamation, where there are no alternative programs available, and no mechanisms for making known the views of those in opposition, are not democratic, even though totalitarians attempt to co-opt the term "democracy."

Democracy allows the representatives of the people the right to exercise some independence and autonomous judgment. But since most citizens do not have the time, energy, or interest to be concerned with every decision, a bureaucracy or elite will often emerge. A democracy therefore functions best when there is some intelligent distrust of leaders—if not of motives, certainly of policies and consequences. Excessive criticism, however, and unwillingness to allow them some latitude in judgment and some authority in acting, will undermine their ability to govern, both on the international and domestic levels. On the other hand, the glorification of leaders is antithetical to a democratic milieu. Many who remain in office for ten or twenty years become removed from the people; unresponsiveness sets in; history has taught us how important it is that leadership be refurbished.

In the last analysis a political democracy can be effective only if its citizens are interested in the affairs of government and participate in it by way of constant discussion, letter writing, free association and publication. In the absence of such interest, democracy will become inoperative; an informed electorate is the best guarantee of its survival.

SOCIAL DEMOCRACY

But to talk about the instrumentalities of *political* democracy would be merely rhetorical, if *social* democracy did not exist along with it. What is social democracy? I wish to focus first on two aspects: (a) the elimination of discrimination, racial, ethnic and sexual; and (b) the destruction of a closed class society.

Democracy requires an *open* society. Political democracy by itself is not a sufficient guarantee that the society will be one. Invidious distinctions drawn between individuals and groups prevent the full realization of the ethics of democracy. The most notorious, as we have seen, are the forms of exclusiveness based upon racial, religious, ethnic, or sexual grounds. That such discrimination is undemocratic no longer needs to be stressed. It is universally understood. One may argue that the state should respect free choice, and not force people of different backgrounds and interests to live together if they do not wish to. But in order that the principle of equal opportunity may prevail, false barriers in housing, employment, education, medical treatment, and recreational facilities must be broken down. As I have stressed, the chief method of change should be voluntary and persuasive. I would in principle prefer, for example, voluntary to compulsory busing to achieve racial balance. Where constitutional liberties are denied, however, the courts must intervene to guarantee individual rights and equal opportunity.

Many political democracies, as in Latin America or Europe, may be purely formal. In a closed society, there are strong class lines and a hierarchy, based upon wealth, birth, or tradition, making it virtually impossible for one from a lower station in society to break through. An open society would allow full mobility. It would, as far as possible, break down class lines, and thus make interaction, intermarriage, and fraternization possible. In England and France, old class societies, such mobility has been difficult. In the United States and the Soviet Union less so.

We are often told that the United States is a class society; hence, its bourgeois democracy is deceptive. What is the meaning of "class"? The 19th-century Marxist definition does not seem strictly applicable to the current scene. In an advanced agricultural technology less than six percent of the population are now needed on the farms. Hence, the peasantry which once made up a significant part of society has virtually disappeared. The percentage of industrial workers engaged in production is also becoming a smaller part of the labor force; skilled labor is replacing unskilled; the expert technician is assuming a more important role; the number of people in service occupations, in the professions, and in governmental service is growing significantly and is now greater than those in production.

The increasing tendency of corporations to

get larger—large-scale industries and trusts prevail in socialist as well as capitalist societies—is harmful to decentralization and democracy. In the United States, where there is a separation between ownership and management, the capitalists alone do not run industry. Consequently, the over-simplified model of the proletarian class on one side of the barricades and the capitalist class on the other is a romantic fiction that Marxists attempt to keep alive, but that has little applicability to contemporary conditions. Recently some Marxists have lumped students and blacks into the proletarian class in an effort to increase its size, but this destroys the classical model, for the basis of the distinction here is age and race rather than economic interest.

Is class based upon property? Two-thirds of American families own their own homes, and large numbers own stocks or bonds. Is class based upon earnings from interest, rent, dividends? Virtually everyone draws earnings from interest in savings accounts; many people earn money from rent. Millions of workers and retired people own insurance annuities or have retirement plans, drawing dividends and capital gains. One can not deny the maldistribution of wealth and other inequities in capitalist society, but these do not follow strict class lines. Presumably progressive taxation and other feasible kinds of adjustment could rectify these inequities.

The notion of class makes most sense not simply as an economic term, but in its reference to the existence of a power structure, and to distinctions in power and responsibility based upon role and function. There is a power elite that makes decisions and directs the affairs of institutions. But socialist societies have discovered that they too need bureaucrats to direct the large-scale state trusts, industries, and communes, much like the managers in so-called capitalist societies. Given this reality there is a need to democratize the power structure and to see that large institutions come under effective democratic political control. But there is also a need to change the character and selection of elites within these institutions. Anti-democratic tendencies in elites can only be modified where the principles of liberty and equality operate. To have elites is not in itself wicked. It is hard to see how a complex modern society can exist without them. What is important is that membership in an elite group be based upon proven merit and talent, that it be made responsive to public needs, and that it not be overladen with privileges and rights that are unavailable to others.

ORGANIZATIONAL DEMOCRACY

It is unfortunate that, in the history of political theory, many democrats have concentrated upon political or social democracy in the government and state as if these were the only areas where democracy might be applied. A large and significant struggle has been waged in which the people have attempted to extract concessions from authoritarian governments, and in which the principles of liberty and equality have been recognized by the state. But the democratic ideal will not be fulfilled without being extended to other institutions.

Thus, the new democratic frontier is to be found in a variety of organizations, associations, and institutions within society. It is often not the state or the government that is the oppressive instrument which exposes the individual to alienating forces, but rather the church, the economy, the school, the family. Such organizations as General Motors, I.T.T., the Mormon Church, McGraw-Hill, the AFL-CIO, the University of California, are complex, imperial structures. They have become in some instances larger than many national governments or states. We have been aware of this serious development for some time. Berle and Means pointed out back in the 'thirties the danger of the growth of the corporation, the concentration of economic power in a limited number of hands, the divorce between ownership and control. But we have since become aware that it is not simply the growth of economic corporations that is the characteristic of our society (or of other complex industrial societies), but the growth of organizations in general—even though other organizations have been influenced by the corporate model: labor unions, farmers' groups, cooperatives, political parties, government bureaus, colleges and universities, hospitals, prisons, churches, television networks, newspaper chains, publishing houses, associations, clubs of all sorts. The organizational growth trend is not necessarily toward monopoly, but oligopoly—i.e., a limited number of large organizations dominating a field.

The result of this concentration is that we are faced with a new dilemma which did not exist for liberal democrats in the nineteenth century or even in the early part of the twentieth: the displacement of personality by "organizality" and the surrender of the individual to the organization. What is clear is that our theories of ethical duty and responsibility have failed to diagnose the condition of contemporary man or to provide adequate proposals for its solution. Indeed, one of the reasons why the individual today frequently feels powerless to affect decision-making processes in his society is that decisions emanate from organizations, not individuals. The entrepreneur of Adam Smith's day, the writer or free thinker of John Stuart Mill's day, are rapidly being replaced by the corporate organization, the publishing firm, or the multiversity. If we analyze the term "responsibility," we find that if viewed in terms of the individual it has lost much of its meaning, for to say that someone ought to do something implies that he has the power to act and to effect change. The point is that individuals by themselves have been shorn of power. Hence responsibility is organizational insofar as power and capacity are organizational.

Mankind has for centuries had huge organizations: the Roman Empire, the Catholic Church, among others. But with the vast increase of population and the economic development of society, the tendency toward organization—vast and impersonal—has increased. Organization is one of the basic keys to human progress. It is founded on the discovery that specialization and the division of labor are the keys to productivity and efficiency. The organized factory system and mass production made possible rapid industrialization. Organizations have also made possible large systems of distribution and communication, mass education, teams for scientific research, efficient armies, and the fulfillment of many other social purposes. The organizational revolution is an essential part of the technological revolution.

PARTICIPATORY DEMOCRACY

From the standpoint of democracy, it is important that organizations be reformed and the democratic ethos extended to them. What we need is to develop an "organizational bill of rights," an emancipation proclamation by means of which we can build a plurality of democratic organizations. What should be done is always relative, but some general observations can nonetheless be made.

We have examined the position of the anarchist who demands that large organizations be abolished: "Man is born free but is everywhere in organizations." Hence to liberate human beings we must destroy organizations. It is clear that this proposal is sheer utopianism; modern life is so complex that without some organizational structures there would be a breakdown of civilized life. There are too many services and functions to be performed which only the ordering of energies can accomplish. It is conceivable that with a vast increase of automation the necessity for organizations may be lessened; but their withering away at this stage of development is not feasible.

There is also the recommendation of Marxists that organizations, particularly economic corporations, be nationalized and placed under state control. This proposal has had an allure for liberals who look to the government as a countervailing power, in a position to restrict the power of monopoly formations, but there is no guarantee that still another superbureacracy will correct the defects of an organizational society, or that it will not bring in its wake the still more terrible effects of a totalitarian society. The Soviet Union is an organizational society, but it has hardly solved the problem of the suppressed individual. A society in which there is a plurality of organizations guarantees a higher measure of freedom for the individual than one in which the state dominates organizations. The panacea of central government planning of organizational life must be seriously questioned. But this does not preclude, and indeed one may argue for, government regulation of organizations and indeed governmental ownership of a limited number (a mixed economy). The Securities and Exchange Commission, Federal Communication Commission, National Labor Relations Board, or Congressional investigations of industry, illustrate the therapeutic role that government can play by regulating rather than by outright control; and partial nationalization, as of the railroads and banks in Europe, or the TVA in the United States, shows the important stimulus that this can have on the economy.

There are other avenues of reform beyond complete nationalization. The legal system and the courts can be enlisted to guarantee due process within institutions, and there is the power of public opinion and of moral suasion. All organizations—business, labor, education, the churches, and private associations—must be constantly examined publicly, for many large organizations have become quasi-legal and in some sense public properties. There is a method of control, however ineffective it sometimes is, that can be exerted by the clientele of the corporate organizations: Consumers can protest by refusing to buy products, and by complaining to sponsors of the mass media; voters can make known their objections to their Congressmen, students can protest bad teaching and bad administration, and parishioners can refuse to attend churches. It is the responsibility of the organization to fulfill its service functions, and where it distorts the process the users have a right to insist that it cease and desist, and to demand quality of performance. There is a growing awareness of this power in our consumer unions and student cooperatives, in the professional associations and groups which set proper standards for organizations (American Association of University Professors, American Bar Association, American Civil Liberties Union, etc.); and we can create new organizations to combat nondemocratic organizations.

It is also important that public members concerned with the public interest be appointed to Boards of Directors. Here the consumer interest needs to be respected and the needs of the community for ecological and environmental concern. In this, it seems to me, lies the importance of Naderism as a movement. Perhaps we need to extend stockholder ownership of the corporations extensively and make the workers the real owners of their own industries. The point is, we need to be open to creative, alternative methods of developing democracy in all large organizations, particularly in economic institutions.

I do not believe, however, that these modes of reform by themselves are sufficient. They do not fully appreciate the centrality of the humanistic ethical principle which finds individuality a positive good and which seeks to rescue the individual from the forces that negate him. In the light of this principle, what we need to do is to reform and transform organizations by the men in the organizations themselves.

There are various types of government within organization: monarchic rule by family inheritance, autocratic tyranny, oligarchical rule by an elite (the dominant mode in our corporate and financial trusts), or rule by democracy. It is the democratic process within the organization that we should defend. It is there that our true hope rests.

Some insist that an organization requires an administrative structure if it is to be efficient, that democracy will not work. It is of course clear that in their need for leaders organizations cannot avoid hierarchical structures; an elite is bound to develop to some extent. The same thing is inevitably true in the political field. The matters here at issue are rather the procedures employed in selecting leaders, in changing elites, and in making hierarchies sensitive to criticism. The democrat may argue that representative government is essential even in organizations (which are too complex for town-hall-meeting governments), that the leaders should in some sense represent all members of an organization, that organization personnel have some stake in their selection, and that rule should not be imposed from above.

Unfortunately directors of large corporations often represent self-perpetuating oligarchies, they are rarely elected by the stockholders, or by the workers and foremen in the plants. It is regrettable as well that many officials or labor unions establish closed dynasties which are very difficult to break, and that ecclesiastical hierarchies still dominate many of the churches. Many of our educational institutions have introduced some measure of democratic participation by faculties and students, but it is clear that the real power of most institutions of higher learning still lies with absentee Boards of Trustees (in many cases self-appointed), and that the officials they elect to carry out their policies are more often responsive to them than to the people within their organizations.

What I am stressing is the need to respect participation at all levels in the decision-making process. We need decentralization of our organizational structures so that decisions may also be made on the lower rungs. Above all, what we need is the principle of *freedom of dissent* and the *right of opposition* within the organization itself. At times this may even mean the right of *corporate disobedience.* If there are no legal mechanisms for a change in policies or for the redress of grievances, one has a right to disobey—within the limits of prudence and balance—in accordance with, not in violation of, civil laws. Corporate organizations all too rarely tolerate or respect disagreements, all too rarely admit honest differences of opinion (outside of the elite). They prefer to impose sanctions and penalties upon those who resist the organizational system and who dissent from policies—cutting off increments and promotions, reducing salaries, or ultimately ordering expulsions. The counter methods available to workers—the picket line, the slowdown, the strike, resignation, accepting another position—have shown how sharp a cutting edge there is in mobility. The point is, a person has a right to continue to be part of an organized group to which he has devoted his time and energy even if he dissents from or disobeys its policy directives.

Contemporary American society is often said to be quasi-competitive; the real competition exists more among organizations than individuals. To compete, we are told, an organization must be efficient; hence the argument for administrative coercion. But the fear of coercion should not be the sole determinant of an employee's motivation. There are other subtle factors, among them confidence in the administration and belief that what one is doing is worthwhile.

We need to develop pluralistic democracies in organizations which would encourage responsible individuals to speak out against malpractices and to defend what they hold to be worthwhile without fear of reprisals. Of course private industries, even if they are controlled by those who work within them, may continue to be self-interested and to that extent perhaps against the public good.

COMPETENCE AND THE LIMITS OF PARTICIPATION

As I have said earlier in regard to the principles of liberty and equality, general principles are guides for policy and action, to be tested by their consequences and in pragmatic terms. Participatory democracy, though a general principle that I defend, must be applied in context if it is to be meaningful. Individual participation must of course be related to the functions of the particular organization. Participatory democracy in an army, for example, has its uses up to a point, but it also obviously has its limitations. If a nation wants to win a war, a certain degree of discipline must be enforced and military orders and regulations obeyed, else chaos will result, and an army will become a mob.

The German General Staff created in the Wehrmacht an army of unquestioning obedience to orders; but it might be argued, in defense of participatory democracy, that if an army's loyalty were based upon intelligent commitment and participation rather than fear, it would contribute to morale and efficiency; that an obedient mass is no substitute for individual initiative, intelligence, and skill; that the stupidities and mistakes of an "infallible" officer class may be unmasked by the practical wisdom of noncommissioned officers and enlisted men; and that a citizens' militia in a democracy is to be preferred to sole dependence upon a professional army cadre. The democratization of the ranks may thus contribute to the performance of the chief function of the military organization. Yet we all recognize that some limitation on democracy is necessary as long as nation-states and armies exist. One cannot debate whether to go into battle when an opposing army menaces.

There are comparable advantages in the democratization of prisons and other penal institutions but within obvious limits. A prison where inmates can participate to some degree in decisions affecting their welfare, where individuality is not destroyed by constraint, and where prisoners are able to develop potentialities, is bound to be able to rehabilitate them better than one run by compulsion and command. Yet if incarceration is deemed necessary, participatory democracy has its limitations when order must be imposed. It is obvious that each institution must be democratized in a specifically characteristic way.

One might argue, for example, that hospital patients should be consulted concerning treatment and care, food and fees and have the final say as to whether they want to be treated; but doctors and nurses are usually better able on the basis of knowledge and skill than patients to evaluate the wisdom of a course of treatment.

The most frequent confusion in the relationship of participatory democracy to competence may be seen in the universities, which are for the most part hierarchial organizations made up of three estates: administration, faculty, and students. From one side comes the demand that faculty participate in important policy decisions and wrest power from administrations. The imposition by Boards of Regents and Trustees of administrative officials—often success-achievers—upon faculty, and the view that professors are "employees," primarily passive and security-oriented, are archaic. As a result faculty members often become ambivalent toward their universities. But what after all is a top-flight university, if it is not its faculty? Who should run the university, if not the faculty? The overemphasis upon bureaucracy is to be deplored; the same degree of centralization does not exist in comparable European institutions. Administrators, where necessary, should be elected by the faculty, serve as their representatives, with power only as delegated by faculty. The argument of competence or special qualifications does not apply here; one may argue that administrators are no more competent than the faculty, probably less so.

From still another quarter comes the demand that students should participate in all decisions and share power equally with the faculty and the administration. The student often finds the multiversity remote from his interests, hierarchical, conservative, and bureaucratic. From his point of view the faculty often represents an elite whose first commitment is to narrow specialization. The student is considered an unimportant element within the knowledge factory. No wonder that students often have felt alienated, like plastic-wrapped consumer products, standardized, replaceable, largely irrelevant. The archaic university stands in relation to its students as a parent does, and it can control their conduct to virtually the same extent that parents can. In many universities the student is an outsider whose chief virtue is submission to authority. Students must knuckle under to rules and regulations; those who are "difficult" may be disciplined by suspension or expulsion.

The arguments in favor of granting some measure of personal involvement to students are numerous. An excellent university should not be organized along corporate authoritarian lines, but to activate the creative potential in both students and faculty. The two estates should share in the common enterprise of learning and research and thus become a community of scholars in the full sense. What better way for students to learn if not by personal identification with the process of education? What better way to be stimulated toward goals than by participating in creating them? Students are entitled to be treated as adults and individuals; and they should join with professors in the noble effort of developing the university.

Yet, after all is said, the university is a peculiar kind of organization; it is by its nature hierarchical, though this (in theory at least) is based not upon birth, class, or wealth, but upon scholarly attainment. In most universities of quality there are careful processes of selection and standards of tenure; in order to be appointed a faculty member, to be promoted and receive the emoluments required, one must demonstrate qualifications in education, and experience. Tenure, an essential component in all great universities, protects the academic freedom of the professor, *Lehrfreiheit,* without fear of censorship or reprisal, and it assures promotion with the highest standards of excellence. There is always the danger that an entrenched oligarchy of senior professors will attempt to keep out new ideas and fresh blood. Junior faculty need safeguards against prejudical treatment, and they need a method for redress of grievances.

Freedom and tenure are the essential principles upon which a university committed to the free pursuit of knowledge is based. If the students' right to learn cannot be questioned, however, it does not qualify them for the rights and privileges which faculty members of demonstrated competence possess: to teach and to further research.

Students should be given the opportunity to participate, but not to control academic policies. They are not qualified to teach higher mathematics or advanced philosophy, nor can they be responsible for the curriculum. They cannot make up or grade examinations, or set standards for the granting of degrees. They are not competent to judge the quality of a professor's research, though they may judge his teaching to some extent. Learning is the primary responsibility of the student, teaching and research the primary responsibilities of the faculty, and the functions should not be confused. Besides competence in a field of specialization, there are certain professional standards which faculty members possess, as doctors and lawyers do. It is absurd to expect medical or law students to qualify as doctors or lawyers before they have graduated or pass the bar exams but they should be given every opportunity to learn by doing, and to contribute to the educational process. It would be similarly absurd to expect students to qualify as professional educators. The policy of allowing each vote—of student and faculty member—to count for one is made even more untenable by the fact that students are apt to be transient whereas educators have a lifetime involvement in education.

There are other dangers. Devotees of an ethical principle may be so carried away by its virtues that they fail to make distinctions. Participation does not mean politicizing the university. It does not mean that the purposes of the university can be dominated by political pressure groups. It does not mean that vocal minorities, or *a fortiori* suppressive majorities, can intimidate the community of scholarship. It does not mean that force can be used to coerce faculties. It does mean that a university is a place for reason and moderation, for responsible criticism and the free market of ideas, committed to the involvement of students, faculty, and administrators in the educational process.

The crucial question often asked is: if students and faculty share in the common task of education, which decisions are to be made by students and which by faculty? It is clear that students should be primarily concerned with those standards which concern their behavior and moral choices. *In loco parentis* is no longer justifiable. The private lives and social activities of students are their own business, including what they do off and on campuses, within the bounds of civil law.

They should have the freedom to invite speakers to campus, to organize groups, to publish newspapers and magazines. They should have the full protection of those freedoms which are the right of all other citizens in a democracy, all consistent with the idea of an open campus. Students should be permitted to grade their professors as a contribution to the improvement of university teaching; they should assist in selecting scholars in residence or visiting professors, within the limits of the budget; and permitted to suggest new courses and programs. They should be consulted about university facilities, the library, bookstore, cafeteria, transportation, fees, and tuition—they should be involved in all matters which concern their welfare directly.

Certain decisions should be left to the faculty, among them standards for admission and graduation, grading of student performance, curricular content and subject matter of courses, the goals of the university, the character of faculty or university-sponsored research, faculty appointments, promotions, and tenure, the free expression of ideas. These prerogatives appropriately follow from their professional competence.

There are decisions which concern both students and faculty. They should always maintain continuous dialogue on a number of issues: facilities which the faculty also use, such as the library, bookstore, and cafeteria, the university calendar, the initiation of new programs, new services, long-range goals, and so on. There are many creative methods by which cooperative ventures may be enacted: a university-wide senate in which the faculty is predominant, should contain student representation; student participation in committees—perhaps not in all but in those which concern student affairs and policy directly; open discussion of issues by faculty and students in the classroom, in forums and debates, in publications, and so on. The life blood of a university is one in which there is a free give and take on all sides.

Participatory democracy in those institutions where competence and knowledge are basic does not entail egalitarianism or unbridled liberty. To paraphrase Aristotle, it involves a form of proportional equality, relative to the competence of the participants, which must not be indiscriminately applied. Organizations may claim specialized competence as a basis for excluding personnel from decision-making. Such exclusion would be fraudulent in many cases; it may, as we have seen, be meaningful in the university, but only insofar as it achieves the furtherance of learning.

Participatory democracy should allow competence to emerge; it provides the best opportunities for commitment and talent. It does not deny leadership, or the emergence of elites of demonstrated merit, but seeks to make them representative. The premise of the democratic value system is that "he who wears the shoe best knows where it pinches." The most reliable way to direct an organization is to give the people in it a chance to contribute to its functioning.

Society has presented us with the new and complex phenomenon of large-scale organizalities ready to suffocate the individual. We need to reawaken the sense of democratic community within organizations. There are dimensions of responsibility that can only be expressed by the individual in terms of his hopes and ideals, which cannot be relinquished to any organization. Our humanist concern is based upon a concern for this individual freedom.

To repeat, the institutions of society are tested by whether or not they help individuals to express their talents and contribute to the common good. If so, they will help to resolve the problem of alienation in the postmodern world.

Chapter VI — The Mind and the World

Introduction

Two highly interrelated branches of philosophy are considered in this chapter. They are *epistemology,* or the theory of knowledge, and *metaphysics,* or the search for ultimate reality. Like most branches of Western philosophy, they originated among the ancient Greeks. You have already encountered some fundamental epistemological and metaphysical doctrines in the writings of Plato and Aristotle. We will point these out in a moment and then proceed to describe the more modern doctrines that you will encounter in this chapter.

Epistemology comes from the Greek words *episteme,* or knowledge (for Plato, the highest form of knowledge), and *logos,* or reason. Epistemology is therefore to be understood as the attempt to give an account of knowledge. A certain philosophical spice is added to what would seem at first sight to be a rather dull undertaking by the fact that the question seems to be self-defeating: how, it might be asked, is it possible to know what knowledge is without first *knowing* something? And how can we be sure we really know something without knowing what knowledge is? What a frightful paradox! And it is one that has plagued philosophy and science up to this day. Put in more simple terms, we might state this *first fundamental question* of epistemology as follows: knowledge occurs when thought corresponds to reality, but does the claim to knowledge made by the previous sentence correspond to reality? How could we know this to be the case? Only by knowing what knowledge is! *Any* theory of knowledge will fall prey to this logical difficulty, even the theory of knowledge called skepticism, which holds that genuine knowledge is impossible.

For how could we know that there is no knowledge, unless we know what knowledge is?

The answers given to this perplexing question have usually depended upon the prior assumption of some examples of knowledge or of knowing as genuine. For Plato, as for Descartes who followed him, the model of knowledge is geometry, while for Locke it was the mechanistic physics of Johannes Kepler and Isaac Newton, and for most modern philosophers including Kant the model of knowledge has been the totality of what is called "scientific" knowledge, that is, a body of beliefs subject to criticism, change, and evolution by means of universally accepted techniques of research and verification. Once one is satisfied that a given model of knowledge is genuine, the problem of epistemology is to provide an *account* of that knowledge, that is, to show how it is possible, and how it is obtained, and then to *defend* the view that all genuine claims to knowledge must measure up to that model.

Metaphysics can now be seen as the correlative, in a certain sense, of epistemology. For insofar as knowledge is always of some subject or other (or, more broadly, knowledge is always about some aspect of "the world"), our understanding of what knowledge is will condition our understanding of the nature of what is known. Conversely, our beliefs concerning the ultimate nature of the world will condition our understanding of the nature of genuine knowledge. The word "metaphysics" comes from a Greek expression meaning "after the physics," which an ancient editor used for an untitled work of Aristotle that appeared after his *Physics.* In that later work, Aristotle treats of the question of existence itself, or what he calls "Being simply as being." This is the most abstract study of all, where we are concerned not with any specific things that exist or "have being" in one way or another, but simply with being itself. To understand how Aristotle could ask himself such an abstract question, we must go back to the pre-Socratics and to Plato.

The early Greek thinkers were concerned with the problem of change. Specifically, they wanted to know what *undergoes* change. If I take a piece of wood and throw it into a fire, I get a piece of charcoal. Wood and charcoal: two different things, are they not? But *what is it that once was wood and now is charcoal?* If you say that there is nothing underlying the change, then the fact of change becomes incomprehensible (Try this on yourself: there is a big difference between the person you are now and the person you were at the age of four. What has undergone these changes? You, yourself, you say? But now give us an account of this "you, yourself" that was once four and is now forty. . .). Yet it is difficult to make a plausible case for some one substance that underlies all others. The first philosopher, Thales, suggested that the primary substance or *arche* was water, but this interpretation was rejected as inadequate by his immediate successors. Another of the great thinkers of antiquity, who lived approximately at the same time as Plato, was Democritus, whose theory prefigures the preferred present-day solution to this question: the ultimate constituents of all physical objects are *atoms,* he held, and the changing configurations of atoms among themselves produce the visible changes in things.

But more to the point of Aristotle's thought are the metaphysical doctrines of his great teacher Plato, who held that existence was always of four kinds. The broadest division in existence is that between the realm of ideas, or Forms, and the changing objects of the world of sense, or what Plato calls the realm of becoming. Implicit in this metaphysical dualism is the belief that the realm of Forms is qualitatively *higher* than that of becoming and change, for ideas are the permanent unchanging structures of reality. This doctrine has immediate implications for epistemology, for, according to Plato, genuine knowledge, i.e., knowledge that is permanent because certain, must always be knowledge of Forms. But how do we know the Forms? Surely not through our senses, which give us only "knowledge" of the realm of becoming. Rather, we know the Forms in acts of *intuition,* or with what Plato calls the "eye of the mind," as we know, for example, that a "triangle" is essentially a "three-sided plane figure," or that the shortest distance between two points on a plane is described by a straight line. Knowledge of individual objects (e.g., "this object I have in my hand is a pen") is not knowledge at all, but merely "opinion." The question that Aristotle's metaphysics attempts to answer is clear, given this background: are there in fact two realms of being, a realm of Forms and a realm of becoming? If so, can we use the realm of Forms to explain the fact of change in the visible world (this is the question of the relationship of the two realms of being to each other, one of the thorniest questions in Plato's entire philosophy)? And if not, then how is change possible? Moreover, if there is no realm of Forms, the knowledge of which could serve as the model of all knowledge, then we must return to the starting point of all epistemology, and ask anew: what is knowledge, and how is it possible? In fact, Aristotle does reject Plato's metaphysics and epistemology, and proposes a new model of knowledge and of the world, which we studied briefly in Chapter III.

But it is not our task here to investigate proposed solutions to metaphysical and epistemological problems in detail. Let us, instead, move into the modern world, and describe how these fundamental problems were encountered and analyzed by the thinkers you will meet in this chapter. Descartes is the first modern metaphysician. Dissatisfied with the philosophical picture of the world he had received during his years at school, and uncertain as to what models of knowledge he should accept as genuine, he reverted to a total skepticism. We recall that the skeptic's claim is also subject to criticism, for how can we be sure that there is no knowledge if we do not at least know what knowledge is? But Descartes's skepticism was not simply a renunciation of philosophy, or an excuse to stop thinking about epistemological and metaphysical problems, as it so often has been in the past. Rather Descartes became a systematic or methodological skeptic: he attempted to doubt everything in order to see what, if anything, is absolutely indubitable, and upon that foundation to erect a system of principles that assure us when we make some claim (e.g., that $2+2=4$), that the claim is true or false. In this way, he hoped to undercut the objections of skeptics, and place the search for new knowledge on a sound footing. Out of his efforts has arisen a set of metaphysical and epistemological theories that, despite ferocious criticism in our own century, continues to influence philosophy even today.

If Descartes, like Plato before him, attempted to use geometry as his model science, and to place knowledge of the world upon the firm footing of intuition, the British empiricists Locke, Berkeley, and Hume rejected this rationalist approach, and insisted that the primary model of knowledge be just that which Plato had relegated to the level of opinion: e.g., "This object I have in my hand is a pen." For while Descartes had noted that it is always possible to doubt the testimony of our senses (I might be dreaming or subject to a hallucinatory image of a pen), the empiricists noted that at the very least I cannot doubt that I *see* a pen, regardless of whether the pen in fact exists apart from my seeing it. This furious metaphysical debate as to the *starting point of all knowledge*—in the mind (geometry), or in the senses—raged for some two hundred years before reaching an impasse. That impasse can be described in terms of the following simplification.

The Cartesian claims that all genuine knowledge must be as intuitive and certain as is the knowledge we have of geometry. Such intuitive knowledge is called *a priori,* and is contrasted with knowledge *a posteriori,* or knowledge through the senses, which the empiricists believe to be the source of genuine knowledge. Now both kinds of knowledge appear to have their drawbacks. *A priori* knowledge is certain, but the number of things that can be known in this way seems to be quite limited, despite Descartes's optimism that the *a priori* principles underlying all knowledge claims can be discovered. On the other hand, *a posteriori* knowledge, though in many cases at least apparently certain, and surely quite abundant, cannot assure us as to the existence of the objects we perceive, or the principles that underlie them: hence you will see George Berkeley, the radical empiricist, deny the existence of material objects, insofar as their material basis cannot be observed. After all, if experience is the ultimate source of knowledge, how can we ever learn what *underlies* experience? In this way, a metaphysics of the world beyond my perceptions of it would appear to be impossible. "This pen exists"—that means, I see it and feel it; its existence consists in the perceptions I have of it. Again, thanks to an epistemological thesis, Berkeley draws a metaphysical conclusion: whatever exists are either minds or ideas in minds.

At this point, David Hume introduced an important linguistic distinction. All statements must concern either *relations of ideas* or *matters of fact,* he said. The first kind of statement is today called *analytic,* and is exemplified by such sentences as "All husbands have wives," or "A triangle is a three-sided plane figure." Such statements are easily known to be true by reflecting upon the meanings of the terms that comprise them. "All husbands have wives is true because by "husband" we *mean* "having a wife." Statements asserting matters of fact are today called *synthetic* statements, such as: "This is a pen I have in my hand," or "Bears live in caves." Now it is easy to see that analytic statements can be known to be true or false by Descartes's preferred method of intuition. We know their truth or falsity *a priori,* without reference to sense-experience. And synthetic statements, if knowable at all, are knowable *a posteriori,* or through the senses, the preferred avenue to knowledge of the empiricists. But now observe that analytical statements, though knowable *a priori,* do not appear to give us any new factual information about the world. And this is just what all modern thinkers, whether Cartesians or empiricists, were desirous of obtaining: scientific knowledge, knowledge not just about ideas, but about the way things are in the world. And synthetic statements, though knowable *a posteriori,* appear to lack the universality and certainty of *a priori* knowledge. Hence Hume, who first discovered and drew the consequences of this distinction, appears to return to skepticism: the world in its ultimate structures is not knowable with certainty; certain knowledge is available, but is (alas) not about the world, but only about our own ideas.

Hume did, however, make a suggestion for a new start in philosophy that was later taken up by our most recent author in this chapter, Immanuel Kant. Perhaps, Hume thought, we could imagine our knowledge of the world to be dependent upon the structure of our minds. For example, I believe that if I were to jump out of the window, I would fall to the ground. How do I know this? Not *a posteriori,* because I haven't experienced my jump as yet. And not *a priori,* for it is not intuitively certain that all unsupported objects fall; that is a synthetic, not an analytic statement. Nevertheless, past experience conditions my present responses, and constrains me to believe that I will fall if I jump. Hume thus reminds us that in such matters we have no certainty, yet nature itself prohibits us from falling into total skepticism.

This seminal idea suggests that the mind is active in the construction of what we call knowledge; or, conversely, that knowledge is not a question of the mind's forming an adequate idea of reality, but of it determining, at least in part, what shall count as real. And Kant took this notion and created what he called the Copernican revolution in philosophy. That is, he attempted to discover the way in which our knowledge of the external world is rendered possible by the very structure of our senses and our understanding. In so doing, he produced a synthesis of Cartesian rationalism and empiricism, and his philosophy is now looked upon as a great watershed in the history of Western philosophy.

Very briefly, Kant considered the possibility of discovering an *a priori* basis for synthetic statements. As we have seen, general statements of fact, such as "If you jump out of a window you will fall to the ground," cannot be known *a priori,* just because they refer to specific facts that can be given only through the senses. But what about statements that *condition* our experience of facts? For example, the synthetic *a priori* statement, "Every event has a cause" conditions our experience with respect to our investigation of facts; or the synthetic *a priori* statements of geometry conditions our experience with respect to space and time. Such synthetic *a priori* knowledge is highly general, and guarantees no specific factual claim, but it is *certain,* at least for the realm of experience, says Kant. I may be sure that I will always find a cause of any given event if I look long enough for it; I may be certain that any object I encounter will have spatial dimensions, and that no physical plane will ever be so structured that a triangle inscribed upon it will have interiori angles that total more or less than 180°. The structure of my mind itself guarantees that, he believes. And in the selection from his works that you will read here, Kant proposes a "transcendental deduction" of the synthetic *a priori* categories that condition our experience of the world. In this way, we may learn how certain knowledge of the structural elements of the world we experience is possible, however much the key to ultimate reality may elude us.

Alas, contemporary science has proven Kant at least partially wrong in that belief, and we will encounter a certain philosophical reaction against the fundamental Kantian insights in the final chapter of this book. But now to the struggle for clarity! Begin by rereading the selections from Plato's *Republic* and from Aristotle's *Metaphysics* in Chapter II. You will probably find the selections in this chapter to be the most difficult of all to master. But the world and our vague knowledge of it is complex and confusing; why should the works of those who are audacious enough to try and understand it be any less so?

René Descartes: Mind and Matter

OF THE THINGS ON WHICH WE MAY DOUBT

Several years have now elapsed since I first became aware that I had accepted, even from my youth, many false opinions for true, and that consequently what I afterward based on such principles was highly doubtful; and from that time I was convinced of the necessity of undertaking once in my life to rid myself of all the opinions I had adopted, and of commencing anew the work of building from the foundation, if I desired to establish a firm and abiding superstructure in the sciences. But as this enterprise appeared to me to be one of great magnitude, I waited until I had attained an age so mature as to leave me no hope that at any stage of life more advanced I should be better able to execute my design. On this account, I have delayed so long that I should henceforth consider I was doing wrong were I still to consume in deliberation any of the time that now remains for action. To-day, then, since I have opportunely freed my mind from all cares [and am happily disturbed by no passions], and since I am in the secure possession of leisure in a peaceable retirement, I will at length apply myself earnestly and freely to the general overthrow of all my former opinions. But, to this end, it will not be necessary for me to show that the whole of these are false—a point, perhaps, which I shall never reach; but as even now my reason convinces me that I ought not the less carefully to withhold belief from what is not entirely certain and indubitable, than from what is manifestly false, it will be sufficient to justify the rejection of the whole if I shall find in each some ground for doubt. Nor for this purpose will it be necessary even to deal with each belief individually, which would be truly an endless labor; but, as the removal from below of the foundation necessarily involves the downfall of the whole edifice, I will at once approach the criticism of the principles on which all my former beliefs rested.

All that I have, up to this moment, accepted as possessed of the highest truth and certainty, I received either from or through the senses. I observed, however, that these sometimes misled us; and it is the part of prudence not to place absolute confidence in that by which we have even once been deceived.

But it may be said, perhaps, that, although the senses, occasionally mislead us respecting minute objects, and such as are so far removed from us as to be beyond the reach of close observation, there are yet many other of their informations (presentations), of the truth of which it is manifestly impossible to doubt; as for example, that I am in this place, seated by the fire, clothed in a winter dressing gown, that I hold in my hands this piece of paper, with other intimations of the same nature. But how could I deny that I possess these hands and this body, and withal escape being classed with persons in a state of insanity, whose brains are so disordered and clouded by dark bilious vapors as to cause them pertinaciously to assert that they are monarchs when they are in the greatest poverty; or clothed [in gold] and purple when destitute of any covering; or that their head is made of clay, their body of glass, or that they are gourds? I should certainly be not less insane than they, were I to regulate my procedure according to examples so extravagant.

Though this be true, I must nevertheless here consider that I am a man, and that, consequently, I am in the habit of sleeping, and representing to myself in dreams those same

From Rene Descartes, *Meditations* (1 and 2).

things, or even sometimes others less probable, which the insane think are presented to them in their waking moments. How often have I dreamt that I was in these familiar circumstances, that I was dressed, and occupied this place by the fire, when I was lying undressed in bed? At the present moment, however, I certainly look upon this paper with eyes wide awake; the head which I now move is not asleep; I extend this hand consciously and with express purpose, and I perceive it; the occurrences in sleep are not so distinct as all this. But I cannot forget that, at other times I have been deceived in sleep by similar illusions; and, attentively considering those cases, I perceive too clearly that there exist no certain marks by which the state of waking can ever be distinguished from sleep, that I feel greatly astonished; and in amazement I almost persuade myself that I am now dreaming.

Let us suppose, then, that we are dreaming, and that all these particulars—namely, the opening of the eyes, the motion of the head, the forth-putting of the hands—are merely illusions; and even that we really possess neither an entire body nor hands such as we see. Nevertheless it must be admitted at least that the objects which appear to us in sleep are, as it were, painted representations which could not have been formed unless in the likeness of realities; and, therefore, that those general objects, at all events, namely, eyes, a head, hands, and an entire body, are not simply imaginary, but really existent. For, in truth, painters themselves, even when they study to represent sirens and satyrs by forms the most fantastic and extraordinary, cannot bestow upon them natures absolutely new, but can only make a certain medley of the members of different animals; or if they chance to imagine something so novel that nothing at all similar has ever been seen before, and such as is, therefore, purely fictitious and absolutely false, it is at least certain that the colors of which this is composed are real.

And on the same principle, although these general objects, viz, eyes, a head, hands, and the like, be imaginary, we are nevertheless absolutely necessitated to admit the reality at least of some other objects still more simple and universal than these, of which, just as of certain real colors, all those images of things, whether true and real, or false and fantastic, that are found in our consciousness (*cogitatio*), are formed.

To this class of objects seem to belong corporeal nature in general and its extension; the figure of extended things, their quantity or magnitude, and their number, as also the place in, and the time during, which they exist, and other things of the same sort. We will not, therefore, perhaps reason illegitimately if we conclude from this that Physics, Astronomy, Medicine, and all the other sciences that have for their end the consideration of composite objects, are indeed of a doubtful character; but that Arithmetic, Geometry, and the other sciences of the same class, which regard merely the simplest and most general objects, and scarcely inquire whether or not these are really existent, contain somewhat that is certain and indubitable: for whether I am awake or dreaming, it remains true that two and three make five, and that a square has but four sides; nor does it seem possible that truths so apparent can ever fall under a suspicion of falsity [or incertitude].

Nevertheless, the belief that there is a God who is all powerful, and who created me, such as I am, has, for a long time, obtained steady possession of my mind. How, then, do I know that he has not arranged that there should be neither earth, nor sky, nor any extended thing, nor figure, nor magnitude, nor place, providing at the same time, however, for [the rise in me of the perceptions of all these objects, and] the persuasion that these do not exist otherwise than as I perceive them? And further, as I sometimes think that others are in error respecting matters of which they believe themselves to possess a perfect knowledge, how do I know that I am not also deceived each time I add together two and three, or number the sides of a square, or form some judgment still more simple, if more simple indeed can be imagined? But perhaps God has not been willing that I should be thus deceived, for he is said to be supremely good. If, however, it were repugnant to the goodness of God to have created me subject to constant deception, it would seem likewise to be contrary to his goodness to allow me to be occasionally deceived; and yet it is clear that this is permitted. Some, indeed, might perhaps be found who would be disposed rather to deny the existence of a Being so powerful than to believe that there is nothing certain. But let us for the present refrain from opposing this opinion, and grant that all which is here said of a God is fabulous: nevertheless, in whatever way it be supposed that I reach the state in which I exist, whether by fate, or chance, or by an endless series of antecedents and consequents, or by any other means, it is clear (since to be deceived and to err is a certain defect) that the probability of my being so imperfect as to be the constant victim of deception, will be increased exactly in proportion as the power possessed by the cause, to which they assign my origin, is lessened. To these reasonings I have assuredly nothing to reply, but am constrained at last to avow that there is nothing of all that I formerly believed to be true of which it is impossible to doubt, and that not through thoughtlessness or levity, but from cogent and maturely considered reasons; so that henceforward, if I desire to discover anything certain, I ought not the less carefully to refrain from assenting to those same opinions than to what might be shown to be manifestly false.

But it is not sufficient to have made these observations; care must be taken likewise to keep them in remembrance. For those old and customary opinions perpetually recur—long and familiar usage giving them the right of occupying my mind, even almost against my will, and subduing my belief; nor will I lose the habit of deferring to them and confiding in them so long as I shall consider them to be what in truth they are, viz, opinions to some extent doubtful, as I have already shown, but still highly probable, and such as it is much more reasonable to believe than deny. It is for this reason I am persuaded that I shall not be doing wrong, if, taking an opposite judgment of deliberate design, I become my own deceiver, by supposing, for a time, that all those opinions are entirely false and imaginary, until at length, having thus balanced my old by my new prejudices, my judgment shall no longer be turned aside by perverted usage from the path that may conduct to the perception of truth. For I am assured that, meanwhile, there will arise neither peril nor error from this course, and that I cannot for the present yield too much to distrust, since the end I now seek is not action but knowledge.

I will suppose, then, not that God, who is sovereignly good and the fountain of truth, but that some malignant demon, who is at once exceedingly potent and deceitful, has employed all his artifice to deceive me; I will suppose that the sky, the air, the earth, colors, figures, sounds, and all external things, are nothing better than the illusions of dreams, by means of which this being has laid snares for my credulity; I will consider myself as without hands, eyes, flesh, blood, or any of the senses, and as falsely believing that I am possessed of these; I will continue resolutely fixed in this belief, and if indeed by this means it be not in my power to arrive at the knowledge of truth, I shall at least do what is in my power, viz [suspend my judgment], and guard with settled purpose against giving my assent to what is false, and being imposed upon by this deceiver, whatever be his power and artifice.

But this undertaking is arduous, and a certain indolence insensibly leads me back to my ordinary course of life; and just as the captive, who, perchance, was enjoying in his dreams an imaginary liberty, when he begins to suspect that it is but a vision, dreads awakening, and conspires with the agreeable illusions that the deception may be prolonged; so I, of my own accord, fall back into the train of my former beliefs, and fear to arouse myself from my slumber, lest the time of laborious wakefulness that would succeed this quiet rest, in place of bringing any light of day, should prove inadequate to dispel the darkness that will arise from the difficulties that have now been raised.

OF THE NATURE OF THE HUMAN MIND; AND THAT IT IS MORE EASILY KNOWN THAN THE BODY

The Meditation of yesterday has filled my mind with so many doubts, that it is no longer in my power to forget them. Nor do I see, meanwhile, any principle on which they can be resolved; and, just as if I had fallen all of a sudden into very deep water, I am so greatly disconcerted as to be unable either to plant my feet firmly on the bottom or sustain myself by swimming on the surface. I will, nevertheless, make an effort, and try anew the same path on which I had entered yesterday, that is, proceed by casting aside all that admits of the slightest doubt, not less than if I had discovered it to be absolutely false; and I will continue always in this track until I shall find somethng that is certain, or at least, if I can do nothing more, until I shall know with certainty that there is nothing certain. Archimedes, that he might transport the entire globe from the place it occupied to another, demanded only a point that was firm and immovable; so, also, I shall be entitled to entertain the highest expectations, if I am fortunate enough to discover only one thing that is certain and indubitable.

I suppose, accordingly, that all the things which I see are false (fictitious); I believe that none of those objects which my fallacious memory represents ever existed; I suppose that I possess no senses; I believe that body, figure, extension, motion, and place are merely fictions of my mind. What is there, then, that can be esteemed true? Perhaps this only, that there is absolutely nothing certain.

But how do I know that there is not something different altogether from the objects I have now enumerated, of which it is impossible to entertain the slightest doubt? Is there not a God, or some being, by whatever name I may designate him, who causes these thoughts to arise in my mind? But why suppose such a being, for it may be I myself am capable of producing them? Am I, then, at least not something? But I before denied that I possessed senses or a body; I hesitate, however, for what follows from that? Am I so dependent on the body and the senses that without these I cannot exist? But I had the persuasion that there was absolutely nothing in the world, that there was no sky and no earth, neither minds nor bodies; was I not, therefore, at the same time, persuaded that I did not exist? Far from it; I assuredly existed, since I was persuaded. But there is I know not what being, who is possessed at once of the highest power and the deepest cunning, who is constantly employing all his ingenuity in deceiving me. Doubtless, then, I exist, since I am deceived; and, let him deceive me as he may, he can never bring it about that I am nothing, so long as I remain conscious that I am something. So that it must, in fine, be maintained, all things being maturely and carefully considered, that this proposition (*pronunciatum*) I am, I exist, is necessarily true each time it is expressed by me, or conceived in my mind.

But I do not yet know with sufficient clearness what I am, though assured that I am; and hence, in the next place, I must take care, lest perchance I inconsiderately substitute some other object in room of what is properly myself, and thus wander from truth, even in that knowledge (cognition) which I hold to be of all others the most certain and evident. For this reason, I will now consider anew what I formerly believed myself to be, before I entered on the present train of thought; and of my previous opinion I will retrench all that can in the least be invalidated by the grounds of doubt I have adduced, in order that there may at length remain nothing but what is certain and indubitable. What then did I formerly think I was? Undoubtedly I judged that I was a man. But what is a man? Shall I say a rational animal? Assuredly not; for it would be necessary forthwith to inquire into what is meant by animal, and what by rational, and thus, from a single question, I should insensibly glide into others, and these more difficult than the first; nor do I now possess enough of leisure to warrant me in wasting my time amid subtleties of this sort. I prefer here to attend to the thoughts that sprung up of themselves in my mind, and were inspired by my own nature alone, when I applied myself to the consideration of what I was. In the first place, then, I thought that I possessed a countenance, hands, arms, and all the fabric of members that appears in a corpse, and which I called by the name of body. It further occurred to me that I was nourished, that I walked, perceived, and thought, and all those actions I referred to the soul; but what the soul itself was I either did not stay to consider, or, if I did, I imagined that it was something extremely rare and subtile, like wind, or flame, or ether, spread through my grosser parts. As regarded the body, I did not even doubt of its nature, but thought I distinctly knew it, and if I had wished to describe it according to the notions I then entertained, I should have explained myself in this manner: By body I understand all that can be terminated by a certain figure; that can be comprised in a certain place, and so fill a certain space as therefrom to exclude every other body; that can be perceived either by touch, sight, hearing, taste, or smell; that can be moved in different ways, not indeed of itself, but by something foreign to it by which it is touched and from which it receives the impression; for the power of self-motion, as likewise that of perceiving and thinking, I held as by no means pertaining to the nature of body; on the contrary, I was somewhat astonished to find such faculties existing in some bodies.

But as to myself, what can I now say that I am, since I suppose there exists an extremely powerful, and, if I may so speak, malignant being, whose whole endeavors are directed toward deceiving me? Can I affirm that I possess any one of all those attributes of which I have lately spoken as belonging to the nature of body? After attentively considering them in my own mind, I find none of them that can properly be said to belong to myself. To recount them were idle and tedious. Let us pass, then, to the attributes of the soul. The first mentioned were the powers of nutrition and walking; but, if it be true that I have no body, it is true likewise that I am capable neither of walking nor of being nourished. Perception is another attribute of the soul; but perception too is impossible without the body; besides, I have frequently, during sleep, believed that I perceived objects which I afterward observed I did not in reality perceive. Thinking is another attribute of the soul; and here I discover what properly belongs to myself. This alone is inseparable from me. I am—I exist: this is certain; but how often? As often as I think; for perhaps it would even happen, if I should wholly cease to think, that I should at the same time altogether cease to be. I now admit nothing that is not necessarily true. I am therefore, precisely speaking, only a thinking thing, that is, a mind (*mens sive animus*), understanding, or reason, terms whose signification was before unknown to me. I am, however, a real thing, and really existent; but what thing? The answer was, a thinking thing. The question now arises, am I something besides? I will stimulate my imagination with a view to discover whether I am not still something more than a thinking being. Now it is plain I am not the assemblage of members called the human body; I am not a thin and penetrating air diffused through all these members, or wind, or flame, or vapor, or breath, or any of all the things I can imagine; for I supposed that all these were not, and, without changing the supposition, I find that I still feel assured of my existence.

But it is true, perhaps, that those very things which I suppose to be non-existent, because they are unknown to me, are not in truth different from myself whom I know. This is a point I cannot determine, and do not now enter into any dispute regarding it. I can only judge of things that are known to me: I am conscious that I exist, and I who know that I exist inquire into what I am. It is, however, perfectly certain that the knowledge of my existence, thus precisely taken, is not dependent on things, the existence of which is as yet unknown to me: and consequently it is not dependent on any of the things I can feign in imagination. Moreover, the phrase itself, I frame an image (*effingo*), reminds me of my error; for I should in truth frame one if I were to imagine myself to be anything, since to imagine is nothing more than to contemplate the figure or image of a corporeal thing; but I already know that I exist, and that it is possible at the same time that all those images, and in general all that relates to the nature of body, are merely dreams or chimeras. From this I discover that it is not more reasonable to say, I will excite my imagination that I may know more distinctly what I am, than to express myself as follows: I am now awake, and perceive something real; but because my perception is not sufficiently clear, I will of express purpose go to sleep that my dreams may represent to me the object of my perception with more truth and clearness. And, therefore, I know that nothing of all that I can embrace in imagination belongs to the knowledge which I have of myself, and that there is need to recall with the utmost care the mind from this mode of thinking, that it may be able to know its own nature with perfect distinctness.

But what, then, am I? A thinking thing, it has been said. But what is a thinking thing? It is a thing that doubts, understands, conceives, affirms, denies, wills, refuses; that imagines also, and perceives. Assuredly it is not little, if all these properties belong to my nature. But why should they not belong to it? Am I not that very being who now doubts of almost everything; who, for all that, understands and conceives certain things; who affirms one alone as true, and denies the others; who desires to know more of them, and does not wish to be deceived; who imagines many things, sometimes even despite his will; and is likewise percipient of many, as if through the medium of the senses. Is there nothing of all this as true as that I am, even although I should be always dreaming, and although he who gave me being employed all his ingenuity to deceive me? Is there also any one of these attributes that can be properly distinguished from my thought, or that can be said to be separate from myself? For it is of itself so evident that it is I who doubt, I who understand, and I who desire, that it is here unnecessary to add anything by way of rendering it more clear. And I am as certainly the same being who imagines; for although it may be (as I before supposed) that nothing I imagine is true, still the power of imagination does not cease really to exist in me and to form part of my thought. In fine, I am the same being who perceives, that is, who apprehends certain objects as by the organs of sense, since, in truth, I see light, hear a noise, and feel heat. But it will be said that these presentations are false, and that I am dreaming. Let is be so. At all events it is certain that I seem to see light, hear a noise, and feel heat; this cannot be false, and this is what in me is properly called perceiving (*sentire*), which is nothing else than thinking. From this I begin to know what I am with somewhat greater clearness and distinctness than heretofore.

But, nevertheless, it still seems to me, and I cannot help believing, that corporeal things, whose images are formed by thought which fall under the senses, and are examined by the same, are known with much greater distinctness than that I know not what part of myself which is not imaginable; although, in truth, it may seem strange to say that I know and comprehend with greater distinctness things whose existence appears to me doubtful, that are unknown, and do not belong to me, than others of whose reality I am persuaded, that are known to me, and appertain to my proper nature; in a word, than myself. But I see clearly what is the state of the case. My mind is apt to wander, and will not yet submit to be restrained within the limits of truth. Let us therefore leave the mind to itself once more, and, according to it every kind of liberty permit it to consider the objects that appear to it from without, in order that, having afterward withdrawn it from these gently and opportunely and fixed it on the consideration of its being and the properties it finds in itself, it may then be the more easily controlled.

Let us now accordingly consider the objects that are commonly thought to be the most easily, and likewise *the most distinctly known,* viz, the bodies we touch and see; not, indeed, bodies in general, for these general notions are usually somewhat more confused, but one body in particular. Take, for example, this piece of wax; it is quite fresh, having been but recently taken from the beehive; it has not yet lost the sweetness of the honey it contained; it still retains somewhat of the odor of the flowers from which it was gathered; its color, figure, size, are apparent (to the sight); it is hard, cold, easily handled; and sounds when struck upon with the finger. In fine, all that contributes to make a body as distinctly known as possible, is found in the one before us. But, while I am speaking, let it be placed near the fire—what remained of the taste exhales, the smell evaporates, the color changes, its figure is destroyed, its size increases, it becomes liquid, it grows hot, it can hardly be handled, and, although struck upon, it emits no sound. Does the same wax still remain after this change? It must be admitted that it does remain; no one doubts it, or judges otherwise. What then was it I knew with so much distinctness in the piece of wax? Assuredly, it could be nothing of all that I observed by means of the senses, since all the things that fell under taste, smell, sight, touch, and hearing are changed, and yet the same wax remains. It was perhaps what I now think, viz, that this wax was neither the sweetness of honey, the pleasant odor of flowers, the whiteness, the figure, nor the sound, but only a body that a little before appeared to me conspicuous under these forms, and which is now perceived under others. But, to speak precisely, what is it that I imagine when I think of it in this way? Let it be attentively considered, and, retrenching all that does not belong to the wax, let us see what remains. There certainly remains nothing, except something extended, flexible, and movable. But what is meant by flexible and movable? Is it not that I imagine that the piece of wax, being round, is capable of becoming square, or of passing from a square into a triangular figure? Assuredly such is not the case, because I conceive that it admits of an infinity of similar changes; and I am, moreover, unable to compass this infinity by imagination, and consequently this conception which I have of the wax is not the product of the faculty of imagination. But what now is this extension? Is it not also unknown? for it becomes greater when the wax is melted, greater when it is boiled, and greater still when the heat increases; and I should not conceive clearly and according to truth, the wax as it is, if I did not suppose that the piece we are considering admitted even of a wider variety of extension than I ever imagined. I must, therefore, admit that I cannot even comprehend by imagination what the piece of wax is, and that it is the mind alone which perceives it. I speak of one piece in particular; for as to wax in general, this is still more evident. But what is the piece of wax that can be perceived only by the understanding or mind? It is certainly the same which I see, touch, imagine. But (and this it is of moment to observe) the perception of it is neither an act of sight, of touch, nor of imagination, and never was either of these, though it might formerly seem so, but is simply an intuition (*inspectio*) of the mind, which may be imperfect and confused, as it formerly was, or very clear and distinct, as it is at present, according as the attention is more or less directed to the elements which it contains, and of which it is composed.

But, meanwhile, I feel greatly astonished when I observe the weakness of my mind, and its proneness to error. For although, without at all giving expression to what I think, I consider all this in my own mind, words yet occasionally impede my progress, and I am almost led into error by the terms of ordinary language. We say, for example, that we see the same wax when it is before us, and not that we judge it to be the same from its retaining the same color and figure: whence I should forthwith be disposed to conclude that the wax is known by the act of sight, and not by the intuition of the mind alone, were it not for the analogous instance of human beings passing on in the street below, as observed from a window. In this case I do not fail to say that I see the men themselves, just as I say that I see the wax; and yet what do I see from the window beyond hats and cloaks that might cover artificial machines, whose motions might be determined by springs? But I judge that there are human beings from these appearances, and thus I comprehend, by the faculty of judgment alone which is in the mind, what I believed I saw with my eyes.

The man who makes it his aim to rise to knowledge superior to the common, ought to be ashamed to seek occasions of doubting from the vulgar forms of speech: instead, therefore, of doing this, I shall proceed with the matter in hand, and inquire whether I had a clearer and more perfect perception of the piece of wax when I first saw it, and when I thought I knew it by means of the external sense itself, or, at all events, by the common sense (*sensus communis*), as it is called, that is, by the imaginative faculty; or whether I rather apprehend it more clearly at present, after having examined with greater care, both what it is, and in what way it can be known. It would certainly be ridiculous to entertain any doubt on this point. For what, in that first perception, was there distinct? What did I perceive which any animal might not have perceived? But when I distinguish the wax from its exterior forms, and when, as if I had stripped it of its vestments, I consider it quite naked, it is certain, although some error may still be found in my judgment, that I cannot, nevertheless, thus apprehend it without possessing a human mind.

But, finally, what shall I say of the mind itself, that is, of myself? for as yet I do not admit that I am anything but mind. What, then! I who seem to possess so distinct an apprehension of the piece of wax, do I not know myself, both with greater truth and certitude, and also much more distinctly and clearly? For if I judge that the wax exists because I see it, it assuredly follows, much more evidently, that I myself am or exist, for the same reason: for it is possible that what I see may not in truth be wax, and that I do not even possess eyes with which to see anything; but it cannot be that when I see, or, which comes to the same thing, when I think I see, I myself who think am nothing. So likewise, if I judge that the wax exists because I touch it, it will also follow that I am; and if I determine that my imagination, or any other cause, whatever it be, persuades me of the existence of the wax, I will still draw the same conclusion. And what is here remarked of the piece of wax, is applicable to all the other things that are external to me. And further, if the (notion or) perception of wax appeared to me more precise and distinct, after that not only sight and touch, but many other causes besides, rendered it manifest to my apprehension, with how much greater distinctness must I now know myself, since all the reasons that contribute to the knowledge of the nature of wax, or of any body whatever, manifest still better the nature of my mind? And there are besides so many other things in the mind itself that contribute to the illustration of its nature, that those dependent on the body, to which I have here referred, scarcely merit to be taken into account.

But, in conclusion, I find I have insensibly reverted to the point I desired; for, since it is now manifest to me that bodies themselves are not properly perceived by the senses nor by the faculty of imagination, but by the intellect alone; and since they are not perceived because they are seen and touched, but only because they are understood (or rightly comprehended by thought), I readily discover that there is nothing more easily or clearly apprehended than my own mind. But because it is difficult to rid one's self so promptly of an opinion to which one has been long accustomed, it will be desirable to tarry for some time at this stage, that, by long continued meditation, I may more deeply impress upon my memory this new knowledge.

John Locke: The Structure of the Mind

INTRODUCTION

1. *An inquiry into the understanding, pleasant and useful.*—Since it is the *understanding* that sets man above the rest of sensible beings, and gives him all the advantage and dominion which he has over them, it is certainly a subject, even for its nobleness, worth our labor to inquire into. The understanding, like the eye, whilst it makes us see and perceive all other things, takes no notice of itself; and it requires art and pains to set it at a distance, and make it its own object. But whatever be the difficulties that lie in the way of this inquiry, whatever it be that keeps us so much in the dark to ourselves, sure I am that all the light we can let in upon our own minds, all the acquaintance we can make with our own understandings, will not only be very pleasant, but bring us great advantage in directing our thoughts in the search of other things.

2. *Design.*—This, therefore, being my purpose, to inquire into the original, certainty, and extent of *human knowledge*, together with the grounds and degrees of *belief, opinion,* and *assent,* I shall not at present meddle with the physical consideration of the mind, or trouble myself to examine wherein its essence consists or by what motions of our spirits, or alteration of our bodies, we come to have any sensation by our organs, or any *ideas* in our understandings; and whether those ideas do, in their formation, any or all of them, depend on matter or not. These are speculations, which, however curious and entertaining, I shall decline, as lying out of my way in the design I am now upon. It shall suffice to my present purpose, to consider the discerning faculties of a man, as they are employed about the objects which they have to do with. And I shall imagine I have not wholly misemployed myself in the thoughts I shall have on this occasion, if, in this historical, plain method, I can give any account of the ways whereby our understandings come to attain those notions of things we have, and can set down any measures of the certainty of our knowledge, or the grounds of those persuasions which are to be found amongst men, so various, different, and wholly contradictory; and yet asserted somewhere or other with such assurance and confidence, that he that shall take a view of the opinions of mankind, observe their opposition, and at the same time consider the fondness and devotion wherewith they are embraced, the resolution and eagerness wherewith they are maintained, may perhaps have reason to suspect that either there is no such thing as truth at all or that mankind hath no sufficient means to attain a certain knowledge of it.

3. *Method.*—It is therefore worth while to search out the bounds between opinions and knowledge, and examine by what measures, in things whereof we have no certain knowledge, we ought to regulate our assent, and moderate our persuasions. In other whereunto, I shall pursue this following method:—

First, I shall inquire into the original of those *ideas,* notions, or whatever else you please to call them, which a man observes, and is conscious to himself he has in his mind; and the ways whereby the understanding comes to be furnished with them.

Secondly, I shall endeavor to show what *knowledge* the understanding hath by those ideas, and the certainty, evidence, and extent to it.

From John Locke, *Essay Concerning Human Understanding* (selections).

Thirdly, I shall make some inquiry into the nature and grounds of *faith* or *opinion*; whereby I mean, that assent which we give to any proposition as true, of whose truth yet we have no certain knowledge and here we shall have occasion to examine the reasons and degrees of assent.

4. *Useful to know the extent of our comprehension.*—If by this inquiry into the nature of the understanding, I can discover the powers thereof, how far they reach, to what things they are in any degree proportionate, and where they fail us, I suppose it may be of use to prevail with the busy mind of man to be more cautious in meddling with things exceeding its comprehension, to stop when it is at the utmost extent of its tether, and to sit down in a quiet ignorance of those things which, upon examination, are found to be beyond the reach of our capacities. We should not then, perhaps, be so forward, out of an affectation of an universal knowledge, to raise questions, and perplex ourselves and others with disputes, about things to which our understandings are not suited, and of which we cannot frame in our minds any clear or distinct perceptions, or whereof (as it has, perhaps, too often happened) we have not any notions at all. If we can find out how far the understanding can extend its view, how far it has faculties to attain certainty, and in what cases it can only judge and guess, we may learn to content ourselves with what is attainable by us in this state.

5. *Our capacity suited to our state and concerns.*—For though the comprehension of our understandings comes exceeding short of the vast extent of things, yet we shall have cause enough to magnify the bountiful Author of our being for that proportion and degree of knowledge He has bestowed on us, so far above all the rest of the inhabitants of this our mansion. Men have reason to be well satisfied with what God hath thought fit for them, since He has given them, as St. Peter says, whatsoever is necessary for the conveniences of life, and information of virtue; and has put within the reach of their discovery, the comfortable provision for this life and the way that leads to a better. How short soever their knowledge may come of an universal or perfect comprehension of whatsoever is, it yet secures their great concernments that they have light enough to lead them to the knowledge of their Maker, and the sight of their own duties. Men may find matter sufficient to busy their heads and employ their hands with variety, delight, and satisfaction, if they will not boldly quarrel with their own constitution, and throw away the blessings their hands are filled with, because they are not big enough to grasp everything. We shall not have much reason to complain of the narrowness of our minds, if we will but employ them about what may be of use to us; for of that they are very capable; and it will be an unpardonable as well as childish peevishness, if we undervalue the advantages of our knowledge, and neglect to improve it to the ends for which it was given us, because there are some things that are set out of the reach of it. It will be no excuse to an idle and untoward servant, who would not attend his business by candlelight, to plead that he had not broad sunshine. The candle that it set up in us shines bright enough for all our purposes. The discoveries we can make with this ought to satisfy us; and we shall then use our understandings right, when we entertain all objects in that way and proportion that they are suited to our faculties, and upon those grounds they are capable of being proposed to us; and not peremptorily or intemperately require demonstration, and demand certainty, where probability only is to be had, and which is sufficient to govern all our concernments. If we will disbelieve everything because we cannot certainly know all things, we shall do much-what as wisely as he who would not use his legs, but sit still and perish because he had no wings to fly.

6. *Knowledge of our capacity a cure of scepticism and idleness.*—When we know our own strength, we shall the better know what to undertake with hopes of success; and when we have well surveyed the *powers* of our own minds, and made some estimate what we may expect from them, we shall not be inclined either to sit still, and not set our thoughts on work at all, in despair of knowing anything; nor, on the other side, question everything and disclaim all knowledge, because some things are not to be understood. It is of great use to the sailor to know the length of his line, though he cannot with it fathom all the depths of the ocean; it is well he knows that it is long enough to reach the bottom at such places as are necessary to direct his voyage, and caution him against running upon shoals that may ruin him. Our business here is not to know all things, but

those which concern our conduct. If we can find out those measures whereby a rational creature, put in that state which man is in this world, may and ought to govern his opinions and actions depending thereon, we need not be troubled that some other things escape our knowledge. . . .

8. *What 'idea' stands for.*—I must here, in the entrance, beg pardon of my reader for the frequent use of the word 'idea' which he will find in the following treatise. It being that term which, I think, serves best to stand for whatsoever is the *object* of the understanding when a man thinks, I have used it to express whatever is meant by phantasm, notion, species, or whatever it is which the mind can be employed about in thinking; and I could not avoid frequently using it.

I presume it will be easily granted me, that there are such *ideas* in men's minds. Everyone is conscious of them in himself; and men's words and actions will satisfy him that they are in others.

Our first inquiry, then, shall be, how they come into the mind. . . .

NO INNATE SPECULATIVE PRINCIPLES

1. It is an established opinion amongst some men, that there are in the understanding certain *innate principles*; some primary notions, Kolivoci evvoloci, characters, as it were stamped upon the mind of man; which the soul receives in its very first being, and brings into the world with it. It would be sufficient to convince unprejudiced readers of the falseness of this supposition, if I should only show (as I hope I shall in the following parts of this Discourse) how men, barely by the use of their natural faculties, may attain to all the knowledge they have, without the help of any innate impressions; and may arrive at certainty, without any such original notions or principles. For I imagine any one will easily grant that it would be impertinent to suppose the ideas of colours innate in a creature to whom God hath given sight, and a power to receive them by the eyes from external objects: and no less unreasonable would it be to attribute several truths to the impressions of nature, and innate characters, when we may observe in ourselves faculties fit to attain as easy and certain knowledge of them as if they were originally imprinted on the mind.

But because a man is not permitted without censure to follow his own thoughts in the search of truth, when they lead him ever so little out of the common road, I shall set down the reasons that made me doubt of the truth of that opinion, as an excuse for my mistake, if I be in one; which I leave to be considered by those who, with me, dispose themselves to embrace truth wherever they find it.

2. There is nothing more commonly taken for granted than that there are certain *principles,* both *speculative* and *practical,* (for they speak of both), universally agreed upon by all mankind: which therefore, they argue, must needs be the constant impressions which the souls of men receive in their first beings, and which they bring into the world with them, as necessarily and really as they do any of their inherent faculties.

3. This argument, drawn from universal consent, has this misfortune in it, that if it were true in matter of fact, that there were certain truths wherein all mankind agreed, it would not prove them innate, if there can be any other way shown how men may come to that universal agreement, in the things they do consent in, which I presume may be done.

4. But, which is worse, this argument of universal consent, which is made use of to prove innate principles, seems to me a demonstration that there are none such: because there are none to which all mankind give an universal assent. I shall begin with the speculative, and instance in those magnified principles of demonstration, 'Whatsoever is, is,' and 'It is impossible for the same thing to be and not to be'; which, of all others, I think have the most allowed title to innate. These have so settled a reputation of maxims universally received, that it will no doubt be thought strange if any one should seem to question it. But yet I take liberty to say, that these propositions are so far from having an universal assent, that there are a great part of mankind to whom they are not so much as known.

5. For, first, it is evident, that all children and idiots have not the least apprehension or thought of them. And the want of that is enough to destroy that universal assent which must needs be the necessary concomitant of all innate truths: it seeming to me near a contradiction to say, that there are truths imprinted

on the soul, which it perceives or understands not: imprinting, if it signify anything, being nothing else but the making certain truths to be perceived. For to imprint anything on the mind without the mind's perceiving it, seems to me hardly intelligible. If therefore children and idiots have souls, have minds, with those impressions upon them, *they* must unavoidably perceive them, and necessarily know and assent to these truths; which since they do not, it is evident that there are no such impressions. For if they are not notions naturally imprinted, how can they be innate? and if they are notions imprinted, how can they be unknown? To say a notion is imprinted on the mind, and yet at the same time to say, that the mind is ignorant of it, and never yet took notice of it, is to make this impression nothing. No proposition can be said to be in the mind which it never yet knew, which it was never yet conscious of. For if any one may, then, by the same reason, all propositions that are true, and the mind is capable ever of assenting to, may be said to be in the mind, and to be imprinted: since, if any one can be said to be in the mind, which it never yet knew, it must be only because it is capable of knowing it; and so the mind is of all truths it ever shall know. Nay, thus truths may be imprinted on the mind which it never did, nor ever shall now; for a man may live long, and die at last in ignorance of many truths which his mind was capable of knowing, and that with certainty. So that if the capacity of knowing be the natural impression contended for, all the truths a man ever comes to know will, by this account, be every one of them innate; and this great point will amount to no more, but only to a very improper way of speaking; which, whilst it pretends to assert the contrary, says nothing different from those who deny innate principles. For nobody, I think, ever denied that the mind was capable of knowing several truths. The capacity, they say, is innate; the knowledge acquired. But then to what end such contest for certain innate maxims? If truths can be imprinted on the understanding without being perceived, I can see no difference there can be between any truths the mind is *capable* of knowing in respect of their original: they must all be innate or all adventitious: in vain shall a man go about to distinguish them. He therefore that talks of innate notions in the understanding, cannot (if he intend thereby any distinct sort of truths) mean such truths to be in the understanding as it never perceived, and is yet wholly ignorant of. For if these words 'to be in the understanding' have any propriety, they signify to be understood. So that to be in the understanding, and not to be understood; to be in the mind and never to be perceived, is all one as to say anything is and is not in the mind or understanding. If therefore these two propositions, 'Whatsoever is, is,' and 'It is impossible for the same thing to be and not to be,' are by nature imprinted, children cannot be ignorant of them: infants, and all that have souls, must necessarily have them in their understandings, know the truth of them, and assent to it.

6. To avoid this, it is usually answered, that all men know and assent to them, *when they come to the use of reason*; and this is enough to prove them innate, I answer:

7. Doubtful expressions, that have scarce any significance, go for clear reasons to those who, being prepossessed, take not the pains to examine even what they themselves say. For, to apply this answer with any tolerable sense to our present purpose, it must signify one of these two things: either that as soon as men come to the use of reason these supposed native inscriptions come to be known and observed by them; or else, that the use and exercise of men's reason, assists them in the discovery of these principles, and certainly makes them known to them.

8. If they mean, that by the use of reason men may discover these principles, and that this is sufficient to prove them innate; their way of arguing will stand thus, viz. that whatever truths reason can certainly discover to us, and make us firmly assent to, those are all naturally imprinted on the mind; since that universal assent, which is made the mark of them, amounts to no more but this,—that by the use of reason we are capable to come to a certain knowledge of and assent to them; and, by this means, there will be no difference between the maxims of the mathematicians, and theorems they deduce from them: all must be equally allowed innate; they being all discoveries made by the use of reason, and truths that a rational creature may certainly come to know, if he apply his thoughts rightly that way.

9. But how can these men think the use of reason necessary to discover principles that are supposed innate, when reason (if we may

believe them) is nothing else but the faculty of deducing unknown truths from principles or propositions that are already known? That certainly can never be thought innate which we have need of reason to discover; unless as I have said, we will have all the certain truths that reason ever teaches us, to be innate. We may as well think the use of reason necessary to make our eyes discover visible objects, as that there should be need of reason, or the exercise thereof, to make the understanding see what is originally engraven on it, and cannot be in the understanding before it be perceived by it. So that to make reason discover those truths thus imprinted, is to say, that the use of reason discovers to a man what he knew before: and (if men have those innate impressed truths originally, and before the use of reason, and yet are always ignorant of them till they come to the use of reason, it is in effect to say, that men know and know them not at the same time). . . .

15. The senses at first let in *particular ideas*, and furnish the yet empty cabinet, and the mind by degrees growing familiar with some of them, they are lodged in the memory, and names got to them. Afterwards, the mind proceeding further, abstracts them, and by degrees learns the use of general names. In this manner the mind comes to be furnished with ideas, and language, the *materials* about which to exercise its discursive faculty. And the use of reason becomes daily more visible, as these materials that give it employment increase. But though the having of general ideas and the use of general words and reason usually grow together, yet I see not how this any way proves them innate. The knowledge of some truths, I confess, is very early in the mind; but in a way that shows them not to be innate. For, if we will observe, we shall find it still to be about ideas, not innate, but acquired; it being about those first which are imprinted by external things, with which infants have earliest to do, which make the most frequent impressions on their senses. In ideas thus got, the mind discovers that some agree and others differ, probably as soon as it has any use of memory; as soon as it is able to retain and perceive distinct ideas. But whether it be then or no, this is certain, it does so long before it has the use of words; or comes to that which we commonly call 'the use of reason.' For a child knows as certainly before it can speak the difference between the ideas of sweet and bitter (i.e. that sweet is not bitter), as it knows afterwards (when it comes to speak; that wormwood and sugarplums are not the same thing. . . .

BOOK II: OF IDEAS

CHAPTER I

OF IDEAS IN GENERAL, AND THEIR ORIGINAL

1. *Idea is the object of thinking.*—Every man being conscious to himself that he thinks, and that which his mind is applied about whilst thinking being the ideas that are there, it is past doubt that men have in their mind several ideas, such as are those expressed by the words whiteness, hardness, sweetness, thinking, motion, man, elephant, army, drunkenness, and others: it is in the first place then to be inquired, How he comes by them? I know it is a received doctrine, that men have native ideas and original characters stamped upon their minds in their very first being. This opinion I have at large examined already; and, I suppose, what I have said in the foregoing book will be much more easily admitted, when I have shown whence the understanding may get all the ideas it has, and by what ways and degrees they may come into the mind; for which I shall appeal to everyone's own observation and experience.

2. *All ideas come from sensation or reflection.*—Let us then suppose the mind to be, as we say, white paper, void of all characters, without any ideas; how comes it to be furnished? Whence comes it by that vast store, which the busy and boundless fancy of man has painted on it with an almost endless variety? Whence has it all the materials of reason and knowledge? To this I answer, in one word, from experience. In that all our knowledge is founded, and from that it ultimately derives itself. Our observation, employed either about external sensible objects, or about the internal operations of our minds, perceived and reflected on by ourselves, is that which supplies our understandings with all the materials of thinking. These two are the fountains of knowledge, from whence all the ideas we have, or can naturally have, do spring.

3. *The object of sensation one source of ideas.*— First, our senses, conversant about

particular sensible objects, do convey into the mind several distinct perceptions of things, according to those various ways wherein those objects do affect them; and thus we come by those ideas we have of yellow, white, heat, cold, soft, hard, bitter, sweet, and all those which we call sensible qualities; which when I say the senses convey into the mind, I mean, they from external objects convey into the mind what produces these those perceptions. This great source of most of the ideas we have, depending wholly upon our senses, and derived by them to the understanding, I call *sensation.*

4. *The operations of our minds the other source of them.*—Secondly, the other fountain, from which experience furnisheth the understanding with ideas, is the perception of the operations of our own mind within us, as it is employed about the ideas it has got; which operations when the soul comes to reflect on and consider, do furnish the understanding with another set of ieas which could not be had from things without; and such are perception, thinking, doubting, believing, reasoning, knowing, willing, and all the different actings of our own minds; which we, being conscious of, and observing in ourselves, do from these receive into our understandings as distinct ideas, we do from bodies affecting our senses. This source of ideas every man has wholly in himself; and though it be not sense as having nothing to do with external objects, yet it is very like it, and might properly enough be called *internal sense.* But as I call the other sensation, so I call this *reflection,* the ideas it affords being such only as the mind gets by reflecting on its own operations within itself. By reflection, then, in the following part of this discourse, I could be understood to mean that notice which the mind takes of its own operations, and the manner of them, by reason whereof there come to be ideas of these operations in the understanding. These two, I say, viz., external material things as the object of sensation, and the operations of our own minds within as the objects of sensation, and, to me, the only originals from whence all our ideas take their beginnings. The term *operations* here, I use in a large sense, as comprehending not barely the actions of the mind about its ideas, but some sort of passions arising sometimes from them, such as is the satisfaction or uneasiness arising from any thought.

5. *All our ideas are of the one or the other of these.*—The understanding seems to me not to have the least glimmering of any ideas which it doth not receive from one of these two. *External objects* furnish the mind with the ideas of sensible qualities, which are all those different perceptions they produce in us; and *the mind* furnishes the understanding with ideas of its own operations.

These, when we have taken a full survey of them, and their several modes, [combinations, and relations,] we shall find to contain all our whole stock of ideas; and that we have nothing in our minds which did not come in one of these two ways. Let anyone examine his own thoughts, and thoroughly search into his understanding, and then let him tell me, whether all the original ideas he has there, are any other than of the objects of his senses, or of the operations of his mind considered as objects of his reflection; and how great a mass of knowledge soever he imagines to be lodged there, he will, upon taking a strict view, see that he has not any idea in his mind but what one of these two have imprinted, though perhaps with infinite variety compounded and enlarged by the understanding, as we shall see hereafter. . . .

CHAPTER II

OF SIMPLE IDEAS

1. *Uncompounded appearances.*—The better to understand the nature, manner, and extent of our knowledge, one thing is carefully to be observed concerning the ideas we have; and that is, that some of them are *simple,* and some *complex.*

Though the qualities that affect our senses are, in the things themselves, so united and blended that there is no separation, no distance between them; yet it is plain the ideas they produce in the mind enter by the senses simple and unmixed. For though the sight and touch often take in from the same object, at the same time, different ideas—as a man sees at once motion and color, the hand feels softness and warmth in the same piece of wax—yet the simple (ideas thus united in the same subjects are as perfectly distinct as those that come in by different senses; the coldness and hardness which a man feels in a piece of ice being as distinct ideas in the mind as the smell and whiteness of a lily, or as the taste of sugar and smell of a rose: and there is nothing can be plainer to a man than the clear and distinct perception he has of those simple ideas; which, being each in itself uncompounded, contains in it nothing but *one uniform appearance or conception in the mind,* and is not distinguishable into different ideas.

2. *The mind can neither make nor destroy them.*—These simple ideas, the materials of all our knowledge, are suggested and furnished to the mind only by those two ways above mentioned, viz., sensation and reflection. When the understanding is once stored with these simple ideas, it has the power to repeat, compare, and unite them, even to an almost infinite variety, and so can make at pleasure new complex ideas. But it is not in the power of the most exalted wit or enlarged understanding, by any quickness or variety of thought, to *invent* or *frame* one new simple idea in the mind, not taken in by the ways before mentioned; nor can any force of the understanding *destroy* those that are there: the dominion of man in this little world of his own understanding, being muchwhat the same as it is in the great world of visible things; wherein his power, however managed by art and skill, reaches no farther than to compound and divide the materials that are made to his hand but can do nothing towards the making the least particle of new matter, or destroying one atom of what is already in being. The same inability will everyone find in himself, who shall go about to fashion in his understanding any simple idea not received in by his senses from external objects, or by reflection from the operations of his own mind about them. I would have anyone try to fancy any taste which had never affected his palate, or frame the idea of a scent he had never smelt; and when he can do this, I will also conclude that a blind man hath *ideas* of colors, and a deaf man true, distinct notions of sounds.

3. *Only the qualities that affect the senses are imaginable.*—This is the reason why, though we cannot believe it impossible to God to make a creature with other organs, and more ways to convey into the understanding the notice of corporeal things than those five as they are usually counted, which He has given to man; yet I think it is not possible for anyone to imagine any other qualities in bodies, howsoever constituted, whereby they can be taken notice of, besides sounds, tastes, smells, visible and tangible qualities. . . .

CHAPTER IV

IDEA OF SOLIDITY

1. *We receive this idea from touch.*—The idea of *solidity* we receive by our touch; and it arises from the resistance which we find in body to the entrance of any other body into the place it possesses, till it has left it. There is no idea which we receive more constantly from sensation than solidity. Whether we move or rest, in what posture soever we are, we always feel something under us that supports us, and hinders our farther sinking downwards; and the bodies which we daily handle make us perceive that whilst they remain between them, they do, by an insurmountable force, hinder the approach of the parts of our hands that press them. *That which thus hinders the approach of two bodies, when they are moving one towards another, I call solidity.* I will not dispute whether this acceptation of the word solid be nearer to its original signification than that which mathematicians use it in; it suffices that, I think, the common notion of solidity, will allow, if not justify, this use of it; but if any one think it better to call it *impenetrability*, he has my consent. Only I have thought the term solidity the more proper to express this idea, not only because of its vulgar use in that sense, but also because it carried something more of positive in it than impenetrability, which is negative, and is, perhaps, more a consequence of solidity than solidity itself. This of all others, seems the idea most intimately connected with and essential to body, so as nowhere else to be found or imagined but only in matter and though our senses take notice of it but in masses of matter, of a bulk sufficient to cause a sensation in us; yet the mind, having once got this idea from such grosser sensible bodies, traces it farther and considers it, as well as figure, in the minutest particle of matter that can exist, and finds it inseparably inherent in body, wherever or however modified.

2. *Solidity fills space.*—This is the idea which belongs to body, whereby we conceive it to fill space. The idea of which filling of space is, that where we imagine any space taken up by a solid substance, we conceive it so to possess it

that it excludes all other solid substances, and will for ever hinder any two other bodies, that move towards one another in a straight line, from coming to touch one another, unless it removes from between them in a line not parallel to that which they move in. This idea of it, the bodies which we ordinarily handle sufficiently furnish us with.

3. *Distinct from space.*—This resistance, whereby it keeps other bodies out of the space which it possesses, is so great that no force, how great soever, can surmount it. All the bodies in the world, pressing a drop of water on all sides, will never be able to overcome the resistance which it will make, as soft as it is, to their approaching one another, till it be removed out of their way: whereby our idea of solidity is distinguished both from pure space, which is capable neither of resistance nor motion, and from the ordinary idea of hardness. For a man may conceive two bodies at a distance so as they may approach one another without touching or displacing any solid thing till their superficies come to meet; whereby, I think, we have the clear idea of space without solidity. For (not to go so far as annihilation of any particular body), I ask, whether a man cannot have the idea of the motion of one single body alone, without any other succeeding immediately into its place? I think it is evident he can: the idea of motion in one body no more including the idea of motion in another, than the idea of a square figure in one body includes the idea of a square figure in another. I do not ask, whether bodies do so *exist,* that the motion of one body cannot really be without the motion of another. To determine this either way is to beg the question for or against a *vacuum.* But my question is, whether one cannot have the idea of one body moved, whilst others are at rest? And I think this no one will deny. If so, then the place it deserted gives us the idea of pure space without solidity, whereinto another body may enter without either resistance or protrusion of anything. When the sucker in a pump is drawn, the space it filled in the tube is certainly the same, whether any other body follows the motion of the sucker or not; nor does it imply a contradiction that upon the motion of one body, another that is only contiguous to it should not follow it. The necessity of such a motion is built only on the supposition that the world is full, but not on the distinct ideas of space and solidity; which are as different as resistance and not-resistance, protrusion and not-protrusion. And that men have ideas of space without body, their very disputes about a vacuum plainly demonstrate, as is showed in another place.

5. *On solidity depend impulse, resistance, and protrusion.*—By this idea of solidity is the extension of body distinguished from the extension of space: the extension of body being nothing but the cohesion or continuity of solid, separable, movable parts; and the extension of space, the continuity of unsolid, inseparable, and immovable parts. Upon the solidity of bodies also depend their mutual impulse, resistance, and protrusion. Of pure space, then, and solidity, there are several (amongst which I confess myself one) who persuade themselves they have clear and distinct ideas; and that they can think on space without anything in it that resists or is protruded by body. This is the idea of pure space, which they think they have as clear as any idea they can have of the extension of body: the idea of the distance between the opposite parts of a concave superficies being equally as clear without as with the idea of any solid parts between; and on the other side they persuade themselves that they have, distinct from that of pure space, the idea of something that fills space, that can be protruded by the impulse of other bodies, or resist their motion. If there be others that have not these two ideas distinct, but confound them, and make but one of them, I know not how men who have the same idea under different names, or different ideas under the same name, can in that case talk with one another, any more than a man who, not being blind or deaf, has distinct ideas of the color of scarlet and the sound of a trumpet, would discourse concerning scarlet color with the blind man I mention in another place, who fancied that the idea of scarlet was like the sound of a trumpet....

CHAPTER VIII

8. Whatsoever the mind perceives in itself, or is the immediate object of perception, thought, or understanding, that I call *idea;* and the power to produce any idea in our mind, I call *quality* of the subject wherein that power is. Thus a snowball having the power to produce in us the ideas of white, cold, and round, the

powers to produce those ideas in us as they are in the snowball, I call qualities; and as they are sensations or perceptions in our understandings, I call them ideas; which ideas, if I speak of them sometimes as the things themselves, I would be understood to mean those qualities in the objects which produce them in us.

9. *Primary qualities.*—[Qualities thus considered in bodies are: *First* such as are utterly inseparable from the body, in what estate soever it be;] and such as, in all the alterations and changes it suffers, all the force can be used upon it, it constantly keeps; and such as sense constantly finds in every particle of matter which has bulk enough to be perceived, and the mind finds inseparable from every particle of matter, though less than to make itself singly be perceived by our senses: v.g., take a grain of wheat, divide it into two parts, each part has still solidity, extension, figure, and mobility, divide it again, and it retains still the same qualities: and so divide it on till the parts become insensible, they must retain still each of them all those qualities. For, division (which is all that a mill or pestle or any other body does upon another, in reducing it to insensible parts) can never take away either solidity, extension, figure, or mobility from any body, but only makes two or more distinct separate masses of matter of that which was but one before; all which distinct masses, reckoned as so many distinct bodies, after division, make a certain number. [These I call *original* or *primary qualities* of body, which I think we may observe to produce simple ideas in us, viz., solidity, extension, figure, motion or rest, and number.

10. *Secondary qualities.—Secondly,* such qualities, which in truth are nothing in the objects themselves, but powers to produce various sensations in us by their primary qualities, i.e., by the bulk, figure, texture, and motion of their insensible parts, as colors, sounds, tastes, etc., these I call *secondary* qualities. To these might be added a third sort, which are allowed to be barely powers, though they are as much real qualities in the subject as those which I, to comply with the common way of speaking, call qualities, but, for distinction, *secondary* qualities. For, the power in fire to produce a new color or consistency in wax or clay, by its primary qualities, is as much a quality in fire as the power it has to produce in me a new idea or sensation of warmth or burning, which I felt not before, by the same primary qualities, viz., the bulk, texture, and motion of its insensible parts.]

11. [*How primary qualities produce ideas in us.*—The next thing to be considered is, how bodies produce ideas in us; and that is manifestly by impulse, the only way which we can conceive bodies to operate in.]

12. If, then, external objects be not united to our minds when they produce ideas herein, and yet we perceive these original qualities in such of them as singly fall under our senses, it is evident that some motion must be thence continued by our nerves, or animal spirits, by some parts of our bodies, to the brain or the seat of sensation, there to produce in our minds the particular ideas we have to them. And since the extension, figure, number, and motion of bodies of an observable bigness, may be perceived at a distance by the sight, it is evident some singly imperceptible bodies must come from them to the eyes, and thereby convey to the brain some motion which produces these ideas which we have of them in us.

13. *How secondary.*—After the same manner that the ideas of these original qualities are produced in us, we may conceive that the ideas of secondary qualities are also produced, viz., by the operation of insensible particles on our senses. For it being manifest that there are bodies, and good store of bodies, each whereof are so small that we cannot by any of our senses discover either their bulk, figure, or motion (as is evident in the particles of the air and water, and others extremely smaller than those, perhaps as much smaller than the particles of air or water as the particles of air or water are smaller than peas or hailstones): let us suppose at present that the different motions and figures, bulk and number, of such particles, affecting the several organs of our senses, produce in us these different sensations which we have from the colors and smells of bodies, v.g., that a violet, by the impulse of such insensible particles of matter of peculiar figures and bulks, and in different degrees and modifications of their motions, causes the ideas of the blue color and sweet scent of that flower to be produced in our minds; it being no more impossible to conceive that God should annex such ideas to such motions, with which they

have no similitude, than that He should annex the idea of pain to the motion of a piece of steel dividing our flesh, with which the idea hath no resemblance.

14. What I have said concerning colors and smells may be understood also of tastes and sounds, and other the like sensible qualities; which, whatever reality we by mistake attribute to them, are in truth nothing in the objects themselves, but powers to produce various sensations in us, and depend on those primary qualities, viz., bulk figure, texture, and motion of parts [as I have said].

15. *Ideas of primary qualities are resemblances; of secondary, not.*—From whence I think it is easy to draw this observation, that the ideas of primary qualities of bodies are resemblances of them, and their patterns do really exist in the bodies themselves; but the ideas produced in us by these secondary qualities have no resemblance of them at all. There is nothing like our ideas existing in the bodies themselves. They are, in the bodies we denominate from them, only a power to produce those sensations in us; and what is sweet, blue, or warm in idea, is but the certain bulk, figure, and motion of the insensible parts of the bodies themselves, which we call so.

16. Flame is denominated hot and light; snow, white, and cold; and manna, white and sweet, from the ideas they produce in us, which qualities are commonly thought to be the same in those bodies that those ideas are in us, the one the perfect resemblance of the other, as they are in a mirror; and it would by most men be judged very extravagant, if one should say otherwise. And yet he that will consider that the same fire that at one distance produces in us the sensation of warmth, does at a nearer approach produce in us the far different sensation of pain, ought to bethink himself what reason he has to say, that this idea of warmth which was produced in him by the fire, is actually in the fire, and his idea of pain which the same fire produced in him the same way is not in the fire. Why are whiteness and coldness in snow and pain not, when it produces the one and the other idea in us, and can do neither but by the bulk, figure, number, and motion of its solid parts?

17. The particular bulk, number, figure, and motion of the parts of fire or snow are really in them, whether anyone's senses perceive them or no; and therefore they may be called *real* qualities, because they really exist in those bodies. But light, heat, whiteness, or coldness, are no more really in them than sickness or pain is in manna. Take away the sensation of them; let not the eyes see light or colors, nor the ears hear sounds; let the palate not taste, nor the nose smell; and all colors, tastes, odors, and sounds, as they are such particular ideas, vanish and cease, and are reduced to their causes, i.e., bulk, figure, and motion of parts. . . .

19. Let us consider the red and white colors in porphyry; hinder light but from striking on it, and its colors vanish; it no longer produces any such ideas in us. Upon the return of light, it produces these appearances on us again. Can anyone think any real alterations are made in the porphyry by the presence or absence of light, and that those ideas of whiteness and redness are really in porphyry in the light, when it is plain it has no color in the dark? It has indeed such a configuration of particles, both night and day, as are apt, by the rays of light rebounding from some parts of that hard stone, to produce in us the idea of redness, and from others the idea of whiteness. But whiteness or redness are not in it at any time, but such a texture that hath the power to produce such a sensation in us. . . .

22. I have, in what just goes before, been engaged in physical inquiries a little farther than perhaps I intended. But it being necessary to make the nature of sensation a little understood, and to make the difference between the qualities in bodies, and the ideas produced by them in the mind, to be distinctly conceived, without which it were impossible to discourse intelligibly of them, I hope I shall be pardoned this little excursion into natural philosophy, it being necessary in our present inquiry to distinguish the primary and real qualities of bodies, which are always in them (viz., solidity, extension, figure, number, and motion on rest, and are sometimes perceived by us, viz., when the bodies they are in are big enough singly to be discerned), from those secondary and imputed qualities, which are but the powers of several combinations of those primary ones, when they operate without being distinctly discerned; whereby we also may come to know what ideas

are, and what are not, resemblances of something really existing in the bodies we denominate from them. . . .

CHAPTER XII

OF COMPLEX IDEAS

1. *Made by the mind out of simple ones.*—We have hitherto considered those ideas, in the reception whereof the mind is only passive, which are those simple ones received from sensation and reflection before mentioned, whereof the mind cannot make one to itself, nor have any ideas which does not wholly consist of them. [But as the mind is wholly passive in the reception of all its simple ideas, so it exerts several acts of its own, whereby out of its simple ideas, as the materials and foundations of the rest, the others are framed. The acts of the mind wherein its exerts its power over its simple ideas are chiefly these three: (1) Combining several simple ideas into one compound one; and thus all *complex ideas* are made. (2) The second is bringing two ideas, whether simple or complex, together, and setting them by one another, so as to take a view of them at once, without uniting them into one; by which way it gets all its *ideas of relations.* (3) The third is separating them from all other ideas that accompany them in their real existence; this is called abstraction: and thus all its *general ideas* are made. This shows man's power and its way of operation to be much the same in the material and intellectual world. For, the materials in both being such as he had no power over, either to make or destroy, all that man can do is either to unite them together, or to set them by one another, or wholly separate them. I shall here begin with the first of these in the consideration of complex ideas, and come to the other two in their due places.] As simple ideas are observed to exist in several combinations united together so the mind has a power to consider several of them united together as one idea; and that not only as they are united in external objects, but as itself has joined them. Ideas thus made up of several simple ones put together I call *complex*; such as are beauty, gratitude, a man, an army, the universe; which, though complicated of various simple ideas or complex ideas made up of simple ones, yet are, when the mind pleases, considered each by itself as one entire thing, and signified by one name.

2. *Made voluntarily.*—In this faculty of repeating and joining together its ideas, the mind has great power in varying and multiplying the objects of its thoughts infinitely beyond what sensation or reflection furnished it with; but all this still confined to those simple ideas which it received from those two sources, and which are the ultimate materials of all its compositions. For, simple ideas are all from things themselves; and of these the mind can have no more nor other than what are suggested to it. It can have no other ideas of sensible qualities than what come from without by the senses, nor any ideas of other kind of operations of a thinking substance than what it finds in itself. But when it has once got these simple ideas, it is not confined barely to observation, and what offers itself from without; it can, by its own power, put together those ideas it has, and make new complex ones which it never received so united.

3. *Complex ideas are either of modes, substances, or relations.*—Complex ideas, however compounded and decompounded, though their number be infinite, and the variety endless wherewith they fill and entertain the thoughts of men, yet I think they may be all reduced under these three heads: (1) Modes. (2) Substances. (3) Relations.

4. *Ideas of modes.*—First, *modes* I call such complex ideas which, however compounded, contain not in them the supposition of subsisting by themselves, but are considered as dependences on, or affections of, substances; such are the ideas signified by the words, triangle, gratitude, murder, etc. And if in this I use the word mode in somewhat a different sense from its ordinary signification, I beg pardon; it being unavoidable in discourses differing from the ordinary received notions, either to make new words or to use old words in somewhat a new signification: the latter whereof, in our present case, is perhaps the more tolerable of the two. . . .

6. *Ideas of substances, single or collective.*—Secondly, the ideas of *substances* are such combinations of simple ideas as are taken to represent distinct *particular* things subsisting by themselves, in which the supposed or confused idea of substance, such as it is, is always the first and chief. Thus, if to substance be joined the simple idea of a certain dull, whitish color,

with certain degrees of weight, hardness, ductility, and fusibility, we have the idea of lead; and a combination of the ideas of a certain sort of figure, with the powers of motion, thought, and reasoning, joined to substance, make the ordinary idea of a man. Now of substances also there are two sorts of ideas, one of single substances, as they exist separately, as of a man or a sheep; the other of several of those put together, as an army of men or flock of sheep; which collective ideas of several substances thus put together, are as much each of them one single idea as that of a man or an unit.

7. *Relation.*—Thirdly, the last sort of complex ideas is that we call *relation*, which consists in the consideration and comparing one idea with another. Of these several kinds we shall treat in their order.

8. *The abstrusest ideas are from the two sources.*—If we trace the progress of our minds, and with attention observe how it repeats, adds together, unites its simple ideas received from sensation or reflection, it will lead us further than at first perhaps we should have imagined. And I believe we shall find, if we warily observe the originals of our notions, that even the most abstruse ideas, how remote soever they may seem from sense, or from any operation of our own minds, are yet only such as the standing frames to itself, by repeating and joining together ideas that it had either from objects of sense, or from its own operations about them: so that those even large and abstract ideas are derived from sensation or reflection, being no other than what the mind, by the ordinary use of its own faculties, employed about ideas received from objects of sense, or from the operations it observes in itself about them, may and does attain unto. This I shall endeavor to show in the ideas we have of space, time, and infinity, and some few other that seem the most remote from those originals. . . .

CHAPTER XXIII

OF OUR COMPLEX IDEAS OF SUBSTANCES

1. *Ideas of particular substances, how made.*—The mind being, as I have declared, furnished with a great number of the simple ideas conveyed in by the senses, as they are found in exterior things, or by reflection on its own operations, takes notice, also, that a certain number of these simple ideas go constantly together; which being presumed to belong to one thing, and words being suited to common apprehensions, and made use of for quick despatch, are called, so united in one subject, by one name; which, by inadvertency, we are apt afterward to talk of and consider as one simple idea, which indeed is a complication of many ideas together: because, as I have said, not imagining how these simple ideas can subsist by themselves, we accustom ourselves to suppose some *substratum* wherein they do subsist, and from which they do result; which therefore we call *substance*.

2. *Our obscure idea of substance in general.*—So that if anyone will examine himself concerning his notion of pure substance in general, he will find he has no other idea of it at all, but only a supposition of he knows not what support of such qualities which are capable of producing simple ideas in us; which qualities are commonly called accidents. If anyone should be asked, what is the subject wherein color or weight inheres, he would have nothing to say, but, the solid extended parts. And if he were demanded, what is that solidity and extension inhere in, he would not be in a much better case than the Indian before mentioned, who, saying that the world was supported by a great elephant, was asked, what the elephant rested on; to which his answer was, a great tortoise; but being again pressed to know what gave support to the broad-backed tortoise, replied—something, he knew not what. And thus here, as in all other cases where we use words without having clear and distinct ideas, we talk like children: who, being questioned what such a thing is which they know not, readily give this satisfactory answer, that it is *something*; which in truth signifies no more, when so used either by children or men, but that they know not what; and that the thing they pretend to know and talk of, is what they have no distinct idea of at all, and so are perfectly ignorant of it, and in the dark. The idea, then, we have, to which we give the *general* name substance, being nothing but the supposed, but unknown, support of those qualities we find existing, which we imagine cannot subsist *sine re substante*, "without something to support them," we call that support *substantia;* which, according to the true import of the word, is, in plain

English, standing under, or upholding.

3. *Of the sorts of subtances.*—An obscure and relative idea of substance in general being thus made, we come to have the ideas of particular sorts of substances, by collecting such combinations of simple ideas as are by experience and observation of men's senses taken notice of to exist together, and are therefore supposed to flow from the particular internal constitution or unknown essence of that substance. Thus we come to have the ideas of a man, horse, gold, water, etc., of which substances, whether anyone has any other clear idea, farther than of certain simple ideas coexistent together, I appeal to everyone's own experience. It is the ordinary qualities observable in iron or a diamond, put together, that make the true complex idea of those substances, which a smith or a jeweler commonly knows better than a philosopher; who, whatever substantial forms he may talk of, has no other idea of those substances than what is framed by a collection of those simple ideas which are to be found in them. Only we must take notice that our complex ideas of substances, besides all these simple ideas they are made up of, have always the confused idea of something to which they belong, and in which they subsist: and therefore when we speak of any sort of substance, we say it is a thing having such or such qualities; as, body is a thing, that is extended, figured, and capable of motion; spirit, a thing capable of thinking; and so hardness, friability, and power to draw iron, we say, are qualities to be found in a loadstone. These and the like fashions of speaking, intimate that the substance is supposed always something, besides the extension, figure, solidity, motion, thinking, or other observable ideas, though we know not what it is.

4. *No clear or distinct idea of substance in general.*—Hence, when we talk or think of any particular sort of corporeal substances, as horse, stone, etc., though the idea we have of either of them be but the complication or collection of those several simple ideas of sensible qualities which we used to find united in the thing called horse or stone; yet because we cannot conceive how they should subsist alone, nor one in another, we suppose them existing in, and supported by, some common subject; which support we denote by the name substance, though it be certain we have no clear or distinct idea of that thing we suppose a support.

5. *As clear an idea of spirit as body.*—The same happens concerning the operations of the mind; viz., thinking, reasoning, fearing, etc., which we, concluding not to subsist of themselves, nor apprehending how they can belong to body, or be produced by it, we are apt to think these the actions of some other substance, which we call *spirit*; whereby yet it is evident, that having no other idea or notion of matter but something wherein those many sensible qualities which affect our senses do subsist; by supposing a substance wherein thinking knowing, doubting, and a power of moving, etc., do subsist, we have as clear a notion of the substance of spirit as we have of body: the one being supposed to be (without knowing what it is) the *substratum* to those simple ideas we have from without; and the other supposed (with a like ignorance of what it is) to be the *substratum* to those operations which we experiment in ourselves within. It is plain, then, that the idea of *corporeal substance* in matter is as remote from our conceptions and apprehensions as that of *spiritual substance,* or spirit; and therefore, from our not having any notion of the substance of spirit, we can no more conclude its non-existence than we can, for the same reason, deny the existence of body: it being as rational to affirm there is no body, because we have no clear and distinct idea of the substance of matter, as to say there is no spirit, because we have no clear and distinct idea of the substance of a spirit.

6. *Our ideas of particular sorts of substances.*—Whatever therefore be the secret and abstract nature of substance in general, all the ideas we have of particular, distinct sorts of substances, are nothing but several combinations of simple ideas coexisting in such, though unknown, cause of their union, as makes the whole subsist of itself. It is by such combinations of simple ideas, and nothing else, that we represent particular sorts of substances to ourselves, such are the ideas we have of their several species in our minds; and such only do we, by their specific names, signify to others, v.g., man, horse, sun, water, iron; upon hearing which words everyone who understands the language, frames in his mind a combination of

those several simple ideas which he has usually observed or fancied to exist together under that denomination; all which he supposed to rest in, and be, as it were, adherent to, that unknown common subject, which inheres not in anything else. Though in the meantime it be manifest, and everyone upon inquiry into his own thoughts will find, that he has no other ideas of any substance, v.g., let it be gold, horse, iron, man, vitriol, bread, but what he has barely of those sensible qualities which he supposes to inhere with a supposition of such a *substratum* as gives, as it were, a support to those qualities, or simple ideas, which he has observed to exist united together. Thus, the idea of the sun,—what is it but an aggregate of those several simple ideas—bright, hot, roundish, having a constant regular motion, at a certain distance from us, and perhaps some other: as he who thinks and discourses of the sun has been more or less accurate in observing those sensible qualities, ideas, or properties which are in that thing which he calls the sun. . . .

11. *The now secondary qualities of bodies would disappear, if we could discover the primary ones of their minute parts.*—Had we senses acute enough to discern the minute particles of bodies, and the real constitution on which their sensible qualities depend, I doubt not but they would produce quite different ideas in us, and that which is now the yellow color of gold would then disappear, and instead of it we should see an admirable texture of parts of a certain size and figure. This microscopes plainly discover to us; for, what to our naked eyes produces a certain color is, by thus augmenting the acuteness of our senses, discovered to be quite a different thing; and the thus altering, as it were, the proportion of the bulk of the minute parts of a colored object to our usual sight, produces different ideas from what it did before. Thus sand, or pounded glass, which is opaque and white to the naked eye, is pellucid in a microscope; and a hair seen this way loses its former color, and is in a great measure pellucid, with a mixture of some bright sparkling colors, such as appear from the refraction of diamonds and other pellucid bodies. Blood to the naked eye appears all red; but by a good microscope, wherein its lesser parts appear, shows only some few globules of red, swimming in a pellucid liquor; and how these red globules would appear, if glasses could be found that yet could magnify them one thousand or ten thousand times more, is uncertain. . . .

15. *Idea of spiritual substances as clear as of bodily substances.*—Besides the complex ideas we have of material sensible substances, of which I have last spoken, by the simple ideas we have taken from those operations of our own minds, which we experiment daily in ourselves, as thinking, understanding, willing, knowing, and power of beginning motion, etc., co-existing in some substance, we are able to frame the *complex idea of an immaterial spirit.* And thus, by putting together the ideas of thinking, perceiving, liberty, and power of moving themselves and other things, we have as clear a perception and notion of immaterial substances as we have of material. For putting together the ideas of thinking willing, or the power of moving or quieting corporeal motion, joined to substance, of which we have no distinct idea, we have the idea of an immaterial spirit; and by putting together the ideas of coherent, solid parts, and a power of being moved, joined with substance, of which, likewise we have no positive idea, we have the idea of matter. The one is as clear and distinct an idea as the other: the idea of thinking and moving a body being as clear and distinct ideas as the ideas of extension, solidity, and begin moved. For our idea of substance is equally obscure, or none at all, in both; it is but a supposed I-know-not-what, to support those ideas we call accidents. [It is for want of reflection that we are apt to think that our senses show us nothing but material things. Every act of sensation, when duly considered, gives us an equal view of both parts of nature, the corporeal and spiritual. For whilst I know, by seeing or hearing, etc., that there is some corporeal being without me, the object of that sensation, I do more certainly know that there is some spiritual being within me that sees and hears. This I must be convinced cannot be the action of bare insensible matter, nor ever could be without an immaterial thinking being.]

16. *No idea of abstract substance.*—By the complex idea of extended, figured, colored, and all other sensible qualities, which is all that we know of it, we are as far from the idea of the substance of body as if we knew nothing at all; nor after all the acquaintance and familiarity

which we imagine we have with matter, and the many qualities men assure themselves they perceive and know in bodies, will it, perhaps, upon examination be found that they have any more or clearer primary ideas belonging to body than they have belonging to immaterial spirit.

17. *The cohesion of solid parts and impulse, the primary ideas of body.*—The primary ideas we have peculiar to body, as contradistinguished to spirit, are the *cohesion of solid and consequently separable parts,* and a *power of communicating motion by impulse.* These, I think, are the original ideas proper and peculiar to body; for figure is but the consequence of finite extension.

18. *Thinking and motivity, the primary ideas of spirit.*—The ideas we have belonging and peculiar to spirit are *thinking,* and *will*, or a *power of putting body into motion by thought*, and, which is consequent to it, *liberty.* For as body cannot but communicate its motion by impulse to another body, which it meets with at rest; so the mind can put bodies into motion, or forbear to do so, as it pleases. The ideas of existence, duration, and mobility are common to them both. . . .

29. To conclude: Sensation convinces us that there are solid, extended substances; and reflection, that there are thinking ones; experience assures us of the existence of such beings; and that the one hath a power to move body by impulse, the other by thought; this we cannot doubt of. Experience, I say, every moment furnishes us with the clear ideas both of the one and the other. But beyond these ideas, as received from their proper sources, our faculties will not reach. If we would inquire farther into their nature, causes, and manner, we perceive not the nature of extension clearer than we do of thinking. If we would explain them any farther, one is as easy as the other; and there is no more difficulty to conceive how a substance we know not should by impulse set body into motion. So that we are no more able to discover wherein the ideas belonging to body consist, than those belonging to spirit. From whence it seems probable to me that the simple ideas we receive from sensation and reflection are the boundaries of our thoughts; beyond which, the mind, whatever efforts it would make, is not able to advance one jot; nor can it make any discoveries, when it would pry into the nature and hidden causes of those ideas. . . .

33. *Idea of God.*—For if we examine the idea we have of the incomprehensible Supreme Being, we shall find that we come by it the same way; and that the complex ideas we have both of God and separate spirits are made of the simple ideas we receive from reflection: v.g., having, from what we experiment in ourselves, got the ideas of existence and duration, of knowledge and power, of pleasure and happiness, and of several other qualities and powers which it is better to have than to be without; when we would frame an idea the most suitable we can to the Supreme Being, we enlarge every one of these with our idea of infinity; and so, putting them together, make our complex idea of God For that the mind has such a power of enlarging some of its ideas, received from sensation and reflection, has been already showed.

34. If I find that I know some few things, and some of them, or all, perhaps, imperfectly; I can frame an idea of knowing twice as many, which I can double again as often as I can add to number; and thus enlarge my idea of knowledge, by extending its comprehension to all things existing or possible. The same also I can do of knowing them more perfectly, i.e., all their qualities, powers, causes, consequences, and relations, etc., till all be perfectly known that is in them, or can any way relate to them; and thus frame the idea of infinite or boundless knowledge. The same may also be done of power, till we come to that we call infinite; and also of the duration of existence without beginning or end; and so frame the idea of an eternal being. The degrees or extent, wherein we ascribe existence, power, wisdom, and all other perfections (which we can have any ideas of), to that Sovereign Being which we call God, being all boundless and infinite, we frame the best idea of Him our minds are capable of: all which is done, I say, by enlarging those simple ideas we have taken from the operations of our own minds by reflection, or by our senses from exterior things, to that vastness to which infinity can extend them.

35. For it is infinity which, joined to our ideas of existence, power, knowledge, etc., makes that complex idea whereby we represent to ourselves, the best we can, the Supreme Being. For though in His own essence, which certainly we do not know (not knowing the real essence of a

pebble, or a fly, or of our own selves), God be simple and uncompounded; yet, I think, I may say we have no other idea of Him but a complex one of existence, knowledge, power, happiness, etc., infinite and eternal: which are all distinct ideas, and some of them being relative are again compounded of others; all which, being, as has been shown, originally got from sensation and reflection, go to make up the idea or notion we have of God. . . .

37. *Recapitulation.*—And thus we have seen what kind of ideas we have of substances of all kinds, wherein they consist, and how we came by them. From whence, I think, it is very evident:—

First, that all our ideas of the several sorts of substances are nothing but collections of simple ideas, with a supposition of something to which they belong, and in which they subsist; though of this supposed something we have no clear distinct idea at all.

Secondly, that all the simple ideas that, thus united in one common substratum, make up our complex ideas of several sorts of substances, are no other but such as we have received from sensation or reflection. So that even in those which we think we are most intimately acquainted with, and that come nearest the comprehension of our most enlarged conceptions, we cannot reach beyond those simple ideas. And even in those which seem most remote from all we have to do with, and do infinitely surpass anything we can perceive in ourselves by reflection, or discover by sensation in other things, we can attain to nothing but those simple ideas which we originally received from sensation or reflection; as is evident in the complex ideas we have of angels, and particularly of God Himself.

Thirdly, that most of the simple ideas that make up our complex ideas of substances, when truly considered, are only powers, however we are apt to take them for positive qualities: v.g., the greatest part of the ideas that make our complex idea of gold are yellowness, great weight, ductility, fusibility, and solubility in *aqua regia,* etc., all united together in an unknown substratum; all which ideas are nothing else but so many relations to other substances, and are not really in the gold considered barely in itself, though they depend on those real and primary qualities of its internal constitution, whereby it has a fitness differently to operate and be operated on by several other substances.

David Hume: The Nature of Human Understanding

SECTION II

OF THE ORIGIN OF IDEAS

Everyone will readily allow that there is a considerable difference between the perceptions of the mind, when a man feels the pain of excessive heat, or the pleasure of moderate warmth, and when he afterwards recalls to his memory this sensation, or anticipates it by his imagintion. These faculties may mimic or copy the perceptions of the senses; but they never can entirely reach the force and vivacity of the original sentiment. The utmost we say of them, even when they operate with greatest vigor, is, that they represent their object in so lively a manner, that we could *almost* say we feel or see it: But, except the mind be disordered by disease or madness, they never can arrive at such a pitch of vivacity, as to render these perceptions altogether undistinguishable. All the colors of poetry, however splendid, can never paint natural objects in such a manner as to make the description be taken for a real landscape. The most lively thought is still inferior to the dullest sensation.

We may observe a like distinction to run through all the other perceptions of the mind. A man in a fit of anger, is actuated in a very different manner from one who only thinks of that emotion. If you tell me, that any person is in love, I easily understand your meaning, and form a just conception of his situation; but never can mistake that conception for the real disorders and agitations of the passion. When we reflect on our past sentiments and affections, our thought is a faithful mirror, and copies its objects truly; but the colors which it employs are faint and dull, in comparison of those in which our original perceptions were clothed. It requires no nice discernment or metaphysical head to mark the distinction between them.

Here therefore we may divide all the perceptions of the mind into two classes or species, which are distinguished by their different degrees of force and vivacity. The less forcible and lively are commonly denominated *thoughts* or *ideas.* The other species want a name in our language, and in most others; I suppose, because it was not requisite for any, but philosophical purposes, to rank them under a general term or appellation. Let us, therefore, use a little freedom, and call them *impressions;* employing that word in a sense somewhat different from the usual. By the term *impression,* then, I mean all our more lively perceptions, when we hear, or see, or feel, or love, or hate, or desire, or will. And impressions are distinguished from ideas, which are the less lively perceptions, of which we are conscious, when we reflect on any of those sensations or movements above mentioned.

Nothing, at first view, may seem more unbounded than the thought of man, which not only escapes all human power and authority, but is not even restrained within the limits of nature and reality. To form monsters, and join incongruous shapes and appearances, costs the imagination no more trouble than to conceive the most natural and familiar objects. And while the body is confined to one planet, along which it creeps with pain and difficulty; the thought can in an instant transport us into the most distant regions of the universe; or even beyond the universe, into the unbounded chaos,

From David Hume, *An Enquiry Concerning Human Understanding.*

where nature is supposed to lie in total confusion. What never was seen, or heard of, may yet be conceived; nor is anything beyond the power of thought, except what implies an absolute contradiction.

But though our thought seems to possess this unbounded liberty, we shall find, upon a nearer examination, that it is really confined within very narrow limits, and that all this creative power of the mind amounts to no more than the faculty of compounding, transposing, augmenting, or diminishing the materials afforded us by the senses and experience. When we think of a golden mountain, we only join two consistent ideas, *gold*, and *mountain*, with which we were formerly acquainted. A virtuous horse we can conceive; because, from our own feeling, we can conceive virtue; and this we may unite to the figure and shape of a horse, which is an animal familiar to us. In short, all the materials of thinking are derived either from our outward or inward sentiment: the mixture and composition of these belongs alone to the mind and will. Or, to express myself in philosophical language, all our ideas or more feeble perceptions are copies of our impressions or more lively ones.

To prove this, the two following arguments will, I hope, be sufficient. First, when we analyze our thoughts or ideas, however compounded or sublime, we always find that they resolve themselves into such simple ideas as were copied from a precedent feeling or sentiment. Even those ideas, which, at first view, seem the most wide of this origin, are found, upon a nearer scrutiny, to be derived from it. The idea of God, as meaning an infinitely intelligent, wise, and good Being, arises from reflecting on the operations of our own mind, and augmenting, without limit, those qualities of goodness and wisdom. We may prosecute this inquiry to what length we please; where we shall always find, that every idea which we examine is copied from a similar impression. Those who would assert that this position is not universally true nor without exception, have only one, and that an easy method of refuting it; by producing that idea, which, in their opinion, is not derived from this source. It will then be incumbent on us, if we would maintain our doctrine, to produce the impression, or lively perception, which corresponds to it.

Secondly. If it happen, from a defect of the organ, that a man is not susceptible of any species of sensation, we always find that he is as little susceptible of the correspondent ideas. A blind man can form no notion of colors; a deaf man of sounds. Restore either of them that sense in which he is deficient; by opening this new inlet for his sensations, you also open an inlet for the ideas; and he finds no difficulty in conceiving these objects. The case is the same, if the object, proper for exciting any sensation, has never been applied to the organ. A Laplander or Negro has no notion of the relish of wine. And though there are few or no instances of a like deficiency in the mind, where a person has never felt or is wholly incapable of a sentiment or passion that belongs to his species; yet we find the same observation to take place in a less degree. A man of mild manners can form no idea of inveterate revenge or cruelty; nor can a selfish heart easily conceive the heights of friendship and generosity. It is readily allowed, that other beings may possess many senses of which we can have no conception; because the ideas of them have never been introduced to us in the only manner by which an idea can have access to the mind, to wit, by the actual feeling and sensation.

There is, however, one contradictory phenomenon, which may prove that it is not absolutely impossible for ideas to arise, independent of their correspondent impressions. I believe it will readily be allowed, that the several distinct ideas of color, which enter by the eye, or those of sound, which are conveyed by the ear, are really different from each other; though, at the same time, resembling. Now if this be true of different colors, it must be no less so of the different shades of the same color; and each shade produces a distinct idea, independent of the rest. For if this should be denied, it is possible, by the continual gradation of shades, to run a color insensibly into what is most remote from it; and if you will not allow any of the means to be different, you cannot, without absurdity, deny the extremes to be the same. Suppose, therefore, a person to have enjoyed his sight for thirty years, and to have become perfectly acquainted with colors of all kinds except one particular shade of blue, for instance, which it never has been his fortune to meet with. Let all the different shades of that color, except that single one, be placed before him, descending gradually from the deepest to the lightest; it is plain that he will perceive a blank, where that shade is wanting, and will be sensible that there is a greater distance in that place between the contiguous colors than in any other. Now I ask, whether it be possible for him, from his own imagination, to supply this deficiency, and raise up to himself the idea of that particular shade, though it had never been conveyed to him by his senses? I believe there are few but will be of opinion that he can: and this may serve as a proof that the simple ideas are not always, in every instance, derived from the correspondent impressions; though this instance is so singular, that it is scarcely worth our observing, and does not merit that for it alone we should alter our general maxim.

Here, therefore, is a proposition, which not only seems, in itself, simple and intelligible; but, if a proper use were made of it, might render every dispute equally intelligible, and banish all that jargon, which has so long taken possession of metaphysical reasonings, and drawn disgrace upon them. All ideas, especially abstract ones, are naturally faint and obscure: the mind has but a slender hold of them: they are apt to be confounded with other resembling ideas; and when we have often employed any term, though without a distinct meaning, we are apt to imagine it has a determinate idea annexed to it. On the contrary, all impressions, that is, all sensations, either outward or inward, are strong and vivid: the limits between them are more exactly determined: nor is it easy to fall into any error or mistake with regard to them. When we entertain, therefore, any suspicion that a philosophical term is employed without any meaning or idea (as is but too frequent), we need but inquire, *from what impression is that supposed idea derived*? And if it be impossible to assign any, this will serve to confirm our suspicion. By bringing ideas into so clear a light we may reasonably hope to remove all dispute, which may arise, concerning their nature and reality.

SECTION III

OF THE ASSOCIATION OF IDEAS

It is evident that there is a principle of connection between the different thoughts or ideas of the mind, and that, in their appearance to the memory or imagination, they introduce each other with a certain degree of method and regularity. In our more serious thinking or discourse this is so observable that any particular thought, which breaks in upon the regular tract or claim of ideas, is immediately remarked and rejected. And even in our wildest and most wandering reveries, nay in our very dreams, we shall find, if we reflect, that the imagination ran not altogether at adventures, but that there was still a connection upheld among the different ideas, which succeeded each other. Were loosest and freest conversation to be transcribed, there would immediately be observed something which connected it in all its transitions. Or where this is wanting, the person who broke the thread of discourse might still inform you, that there had secretly revolved in his mind a sucession of thought, which had gradually led him from the subject of conversation. Among different languages, even where we cannot suspect the least connection or communication, it is found, that the words, expressive of ideas, the most compounded, do yet nearly correspond to each other: a certain proof that the simple ideas, comprehended in the compound ones, were bound together by some universal principle, which had an equal influence on all mankind.

Though it be too obvious to escape observation, that different ideas are connected together; I do not find that any philosopher has attempted to enumerate or class all the principles of association; a subject, however, that seems worthy of curiosity. To me, there appear to be only three principles of connection among ideas, namely, *resemblance, contiguity* in time or place, and *cause* or *effect.*

That these principles serve to connect ideas will not, I believe, be much doubted. A picture naturally leads our thoughts to the original: the mention of one apartment in a building naturally introduces an inquiry or discourse concerning the others; and if we think of a wound, we can scarcely forbear reflecting on the pain which follows it. But that this enumeration is complete, and that there are no other principles of association except these, may be difficult to prove to the satisfaction of the reader, or even to a man's own satisfaction. All we can do, in such cases, is to run over several instances, and examine carefully the principle which binds the different thoughts to each other, never stopping till we render the principle as general as possible. The more instances we examine, and the more care we employ, the more assurance shall we acquire, that the enumeration, which we form from the whole, is complete and entire.

SECTION IV

SCEPTICAL DOUBTS CONCERNING THE OPERATIONS OF THE UNDERSTANDING

Part I

All the objects of human reason or inquiry may naturally be divided into two kinds, to wit, *relations of ideas,* and *matters of fact.* Of the first kind are the sciences of geometry, algebra, and arithmetic; and in short, every affirmation which is either intuitively or demonstratively certain. *That the square of the hypothenuse is equal to the squares of the two sides,* is a proposition which expressed a relation between these figures. *That three times five is equal to the half of thirty,* expresses a relation between these numbers. Propositions of this kind are discoverable by the mere operation of thought, without dependence on what is anywhere existent in the universe. Though there never was a circle or triangle in nature, the truths demonstrated by Euclid would for ever retain their certainty and evidence.

Matters of fact, which are the second objects of human reason, are not ascertained in the same manner; nor is our evidence of their truth, however great, of a like nature with the foregoing. The contrary of every matter of fact is still possible; because it can never imply a contradiction, and is conceived by the mind with the same facility and distinctness, as if ever so comformable to reality. *That the sun will not rise tomorrow* is no less intelligible a proposition, and implies no more contradiction than the affirmation, *that it will rise.* We should in vain, therefore, attempt to demonstrate its falsehood. Were it demonstratively false, it would imply a contradiction, and could never be distinctly conceived by the mind.

It may, therefore, be a subject worthy of curiosity, to inquire what is the nature of that evidence which assures us of any real existence and matter of fact, beyond the present testimony of our senses, or the records of our memory. This part of philosophy, it is observable, has been little cultivated, either by the ancients or moderns; and therefore our doubts and errors, in the prosecution of so important an inquiry, may be the more excusable; while we march through such difficult paths without any guide or direction. They may even prove useful, by exciting curiosity, and destroying that implicit faith and security, which is the bane of all reasoning and free inquiry. The discovery of defects in the common philosophy, if any such there be, will not, I presume, be a discouragement, but rather an incitment, as is usual, to attempt something more full and satisfactory than has yet been proposed to the public.

All reasonings concerning matter of fact seem to be founded on the relation of *cause* and *effect.* By means of that relation alone we can go beyond the evidence of our memory and senses. If you were to ask a man, why he believes any matter of fact, which is absent; for instance, that his friend is in the country, or in France; he would give you a reason; and this reason would be some other fact; as a letter received from him, or the knowledge of his former resolutions and promises. A man finding a watch or any other machine in a desert island, would conclude that there had once been men in that island. All our reasonings concerning fact are of the same nature. And here it is constantly supposed that there is a connection between the present fact and that which is inferred from it. Were there nothing to bind them together, the inference would be entirely precarious. The hearing of an articulate voice and rational discourse in the dark assures us of the presence of some person: Why? because these are the effects of the human make and fabric, and closely connected with it. If we anatomize all the other reasonings of this nature, we shall find that they are founded on the relation of cause and effect, and that this relation is either near or remote, direct or collateral. Heat and light are collateral effects of fire, and the one effect may justly be inferred from the other.

If we would satisfy ourselves, therefore, concerning the nature of that evidence, which assures us of matters of fact, we must inquire how we arrive at the knowledge of cause and effect.

I shall venture to affirm, as a general proposition, which admits of no exception, that the knowledge of this relation is not, in any instance, attained by reasonings *a priori*; but arises entirely from experience, when we find that any particular objects are constantly conjoined with each other. Let an object be presented to a man of ever so strong natural reason and abilities; if that object be entirely new to him, he will not be able, by the most accurate examination of its sensible qualities, to discover any of its causes or effects. Adam, though his rational faculties be supposed, at the very first, entirely pefect, could not have inferred from the fluidity and transparency of water that it would suffocate him, or from the light and warmth of fire that it would consume him. No object ever discovers, by the qualities which appear to the senses, either the causes which produced it, or the effects which will arise from it; nor can our reason, unassisted by experience, ever draw any inference concerning real existence and matter of fact.

This proposition, *that causes and effects are discoverable, not by reason but by experience,* will readily be admitted with regard to such objects, as we remember to have once been altogether unknown to us; since we must be conscious of the utter inability, which we then lay under, of foretelling what would arise from them. Present two smooth pieces of marble to a man who has no tincture of natural philosophy; he will never discover that they will adhere together in such a manner as to require great force to separate them in a direct line, while they make so small a resistance to a lateral pressure. Such events, as bear little analogy to the common course of nature, are also readily confessed to be known only by experience; nor does any man imagine that the explosion of gunpowder, or the attraction of a loadstone, could ever be discovered by arguments *a priori*. In like manner, when an effect is supposed to depend upon an intricate machinery or secret structure of parts, we make no difficulty in attributing all our knowledge of it to experience. Who will assert that he can give the ultimate reason, why milk or bread is proper nourishment for a man, not for a lion or a tiger?

But the same truth may not appear, at first sight, to have the same evidence with regard to events, which have become familiar to us from our first appearance in the world, which bear a close analogy to the whole course of nature, and which are supposed to depend on the simple qualities of objects, without any secret structure of parts. We are apt to imagine that we could discover these effects by the mere operation of our reason, without experience. We fancy, that were we brought on a sudden into this world, we could at first have inferred that one billiard ball would communicate motion to another upon impulse; and that we needed not to have waited for the event, in order to pronounce with certainty concerning it. Such is the influence of custom, that, where it is strongest, it not only covers our natural ignorance, but even conceals itself, and seems not to take place, merely because it is found in the highest degree.

But to convince us that all the laws of nature, and all the operations of bodies without exception, are known only by experience, the following reflections may, perhaps, suffice. Were any object presented to us, and were we required to pronounce concerning the effect, which will result from it, without consulting past observation; after what manner, I beseech you, must the mind proceed in this operation? It must invent or imagine some event, which it ascribes to the object as its effect; and it is plain that this invention must be entirely arbitrary. The mind can never possibly find the effect in the supposed cause, by the most accurate scrutiny and examination. For the effect is totally different from the cause, and consequently can never be discovered in it. Motion in the second billiard ball is a quite distinct event from motion in the first: nor is there anything in the one to suggest the smallest hint of the other. A stone or piece of metal raised into the air, and left without any support, immediately falls: but to consider the matter *a priori*, is there anything we discover in this situation which can beget the idea of a downward, rather than an upward, or any other motion, in the stone or metal?

And as the first imagination or invention of a particular effect, in all natural operations, is arbitrary, where we consult not experience; so must we also esteem the supposed tie or connection between the cause and effect, which binds them together, and renders it impossible that any other effect could result from the operation of that cause. When I see, for instance, a billiard ball moving in a straight line towards another; even suppose motion in the second ball should by accident be suggested to me, as the result of their contact or impulse;

may I not conceive, that a hundred different events might as well follow from that cause? May not both these balls remain at absolute rest? May not the first ball return in a straight line, or leap off from the second in any line or direction? All these suppositions are consistent and conceivable. Why then should we give the preference to one, which is no more consistent or conceivable than the rest? All our reasonings *a priori* will never be able to show us any foundation for this preference.

In a word, then, every effect is a distinct event from its cause. It could not, therefore, be discovered in the cause, and the first invention or conception of it, *a priori*, must be entirely arbitrary. And even after it is suggested, the conjunction of it with the cause must appear equally arbitrary; since there are always many other effects, which, to reason, must seem fully as consistent and natural. In vain, therefore, should we pretend to determine any single event, or infer any cause or effect, without the assistance of observation and experience.

Hence we may discover the reason why no philosopher, who is rational and modest, has ever pretended to assign the ultimate cause of any natural operation, or to show distinctly the action of that power, which produces any single effect in the universe. It is confessed, that the utmost effort of human reason is to reduce the principles, productive of natural phenomena, to a greater simplicity, and to resolve the many particular effects into a few general causes, by means of reasonings from analogy, experience, and observation. But as to the causes of these general causes, we should in vain attempt their discovery; nor shall we ever be able to satisfy ourselves, by any particular explication of them. These ultimate springs and principles are totally shut up from human curiosity and inquiry. Elasticity, gravity, cohesion of parts, communication of motion by impulse; these are probably the ultimate causes and principles which we ever discover in nature; and we may esteem ourselves sufficiently happy, if, by accurate inquiry and reasoning, we can trace up the particular phenomena to, or near to, these general principles. The most perfect philosophy of the natural kind only staves off our ignorance a little longer: as perhaps the most perfect philosophy of the moral or metaphysical kind serves only to discover larger portions of it. Thus the observation of human blindness and weakness is the result of all philosophy, and meets us at every turn, in spite of our endeavors to elude or avoid it.

Nor is geometry, when taken into the assistance of natural philosophy, ever able to remedy this defect, or lead us into the knowledge of ultimate causes, by all that accuracy of reasoning for which it is so justly celebrated. Every part of mixed mathematics proceeds upon the supposition that certain laws are established by nature in her operations; and abstract reasonings are employed, either to assist experience in the discovery of these laws, or to determine their influence in particular instances, where it depends upon any precise degree of distance and quantity. Thus, it is a law of motion, discovered by experience, that the moment or force of any body in motion is in the compound ratio or proportion of its solid contents and its velocity; and consequently, that a small force may remove the greatest obstacle or raise the greatest weight, if, by any contrivance or machinery, we can increase the velocity of that force, so as to make it an overmatch for its antagonist. Geometry assists us in the application of this law, by giving us the just dimensions of all the parts and figures which can enter into any species of machine; but still the discovery of the law itself is owing merely to experience, and all the abstract reasonings in the world could never lead us one step towards the knowledge of it. When we reason *a priori*, and consider merely any object or cause, as it appears to the mind, independent of all observation, it never could suggest to us the notion of any distinct object, such as its effects; much less, show us the inseparable and inviolable connection between them. A man must be very sagacious who could discover by reasoning that crystal is the effect of heat, and ice of cold, without being previously acquainted with the operation of these qualities.

Part II

But we have not yet attained any tolerable satisfaction with regard to the question first proposed. Each solution still gives rise to a new question as difficult as the foregoing, and leads us on to farther inquiries. When it is asked, *What is the nature of all our reasonings concerning matter of fact?* the proper answer seems to be, that they are founded on the relation of cause and effect. When again it is asked, *What is the foundation of all our reasonings and conclusions concerning that relation?* it may be replied in one word, *experience.* But if we still carry on our sifting humor, and ask, *What is the foundation of all conclusions from experience?* this implies a new question, which may be of more difficult solution and explication. Philosophers, that give themselves airs of superior wisdom and sufficiency, have a hard task when they encounter persons of inquisitive dispositions, who push them from every corner to which they retreat, and who are sure at last to bring them to some dangerous dilemma. The best expedient to prevent this confusion, is to be modest in our pretensions; and even to discover the difficulty ourselves before it is objected to us. By this means, we may make a kind of merit of our very ignorance.

I shall content myself, in this section, with an easy task, and shall pretend only to give a negative answer to the question here proposed. I say then, that, even after we have experience of the operations of cause and effect, our conclusions from that experience are *not* founded on reasoning, or any process of the understanding. This answer we must endeavor both to explain and to defend.

It must certainly be allowed, that nature has kept us at a great distance from all her secrets, and has afforded us only the knowledge of a few superficial qualities of objects; while she conceals from us those powers and principles on which the influence of those objects entirely depends. Our senses inform us of the color, weight, and consistence of bread; but neither sense nor reason can ever inform us of those qualities which fit it for the nourishment and support of a human body. Sight or feeling conveys an idea of the actual motion of bodies; but as to that wonderful force or power, which would carry on a moving body for ever in a continued change of place, and which bodies never lose but by communicating it to others; of this we cannot form the most distant conception. But notwithstanding this ignorance of natural powers and principles, we always presume, when we see like sensible qualities, that they have like secret powers, and expect that effects, similar to those which we have experienced, will follow from them. If a body of like color and consistence with that bread, which we have formerly eat, be presented to us, we make no scruple of repeating the experiment, and foresee, with certainty, like nourishment and support. Now this is a process of the mind or thought, of which I would willingly know the foundation. It is allowed on all hands that there is no known connection between the sensible qualities and the secret powers; and consequently, that the mind is not led to form such a conclusion concerning their constant and regular conjunction, by anything which it knows of their nature. As to past *experience,* it can be allowed to give *direct* and *certain* information of those precise objects only, and that precise period of time, which fell under its cognizance: but why this experience should be extended to future times, and to other objects, which, for aught we know, may be only in appearance similar; this is the main question on which I would insist. The bread, which I formerly eat, nourished me; that is, a body of such sensible qualities was, at that time, endued with such secret powers: but does it follow, and that like sensible qualities must always be attended with like secret powers? The consequence seems no wise necessary. At least, it must be acknowledged that there is here a consequence drawn by the mind; that there is a certain step taken; a process of thought, and an inference, which wants to be explained. These two propositions are far from being the same, *I have found that such an object has always been attended with such an effect,* and *I foresee, that other objects, which are, in appearance, similar, will be attended with similar effects.* I shall allow, if you please, that the one proposition may justly be inferred from the other; I know, in fact, that is always inferred. But if you insist that the inference is made by a chain of reasoning, I desire you to produce that reasoning. The connection between these propositions is not intuitive. There is required a medium, which may enable the mind to draw such an inference, if indeed it be drawn by reasoning and argument. What that medium is, I must confess, passes my comprehension; and it is incumbent on those to produce it, who assert that it really exists, and is the origin of all our conclusions concerning matter of fact.

This negative argument must certainly, in process of time, become altogether convincing, if many penetrating and able philosophers shall turn their inquiries this way and no one be ever able to discover any connecting proposition or intermediate step, which supports the understanding in this conclusion. But as the question is yet new, every reader may not trust so far to his own penetration, as to conclude, because an argument escapes his inquiry, that therefore it does not really exist. For this reason it may be requisite to venture upon a more difficult task; and enumerating all the branches of human knowledge, endeavor to show that none of them can afford such an argument.

All reasonings may be divided into two kinds, namely demonstrative reasoning, or that concerning relations of ideas, and moral reasoning, or that concerning matter of fact and existence. That there are no demonstrative arguments in the case seems evident; since it implies no contradiction that the course of nature may change, and that an object, seemingly like those which we have experienced, may be attended with different or contrary effects. May I not clearly and distinctly conceive that a body, falling from the clouds, and which, in all other respects, resembles snow, has yet the taste of salt or feeling of fire? Is there any more intelligible proposition than to affirm, that all the trees will flourish in December and January, and decay in May and June? Now whatever is intelligible, and can be distinctly conceived, implies no contradiction, and can never be proved false by any demonstrative argument or abstract reasoning *a priori*.

If we be, therefore, engaged by arguments to put trust in past experience, and make it the standard of our future judgment, these arguments must be probable only, so such as regard matter of fact and real existence, according to the division above mentioned. But that there is no argument of this kind, must appear, if our explication of that species of reasoning be admitted as solid and satisfactory. We have said that all arguments concerning existence are founded on the relation of cause and effect; that our knowledge of that relation is derived entirely from experience; and that all our experimental conclusions proceed upon the supposition by probable arguments, or arguments regarding existence, must be evidently going in a circle, and taking that for granted, which is the very point in question.

In reality, all arguments from experience are founded on the similiarity which we discover among natural objects, and by which we are induced to expect effects similar to those which we have found to follow from such objects. And though none but a fool or madman will ever pretend to dispute the authority of experience, or to reject that great guide of human life, it may surely be allowed a philosopher to have so much curiosity at least as to examine the principle of human nature, which gives this mighty authority to experience, and makes us draw advantage from that similarity which nature has placed among different objects. From causes which appear *similar* we expect similar effects. This is the sum of all our experimental conclusions. Now it seems evident that, if this conclusion were formed by reason, it would be as perfect at first, and upon one instance, as after ever so long a course of experience. But the case is far otherwise. Nothing so like as eggs; yet no one, on account of this appearing similarity, expects the same taste and relish in all of them. It is only after a long course of uniform experiments in any kind, that we attain a firm reliance and security with regard to a particular event. Now where is that process of reasoning which, from one instance, draws a conclusion, so different from that which it infers from a hundred instances that are nowise different from that single one? This question I propose as much for the sake of information, as with an intention of raising difficulties. I cannot find, I cannot imagine any such reasoning. But I keep my mind still open to instruction, if anyone will vouchsafe to bestow it on me.

Should it be said that, from a number of uniform experiments, we *infer* a connection between the sensible qualities and the secret powers; this, I must confess, seems the same difficulty, couched in different terms. The question still recurs, on what process of argument this *inference* is founded? Where is the medium, the interposing ideas, which join propositions so very wide of each other? It is confessed that the color, consistence, and other sensible qualities of bread appear not, of themselves, to have any connection with the secret powers of nourishment and support. For otherwise we could infer these secret powers from the first appearance of these sensible qualities, without the aid of experience; contrary to the sentiment of all philosophers, and contrary to plain matter of fact. Here, then, is our natural state of ignorance with regard to the powers and influence of all objects. How is this remedied by experience? It only shows us a number of uniform effects, resulting from certain objects, and teaches us that those particular objects, at that particular time, were endowed with such powers and forces. When a new object, endowed with similar sensible qualities, is produced, we expect similar powers and forces, and look for a like effect. From a body of like color and consistence with bread we expect like nourishment and support. But this surely is a step or progress of the mind, which wants to be explained. When a man says, *I have found, in all past instances, such sensible qualities conjoined with such secret powers*: And when he says, *Similar sensible qualities will always be conjoined with similar secret powers*, he is not guilty of a tautology, nor are these propositions in any respect the same. You say that the one proposition is an inference from the other. But you must confess that the inference is not intuitive; neither is it demonstrative: Of what nature is it, then? To say it is experimental, is begging the question. For all inferences from experience suppose, as their foundation, that the future will resemble the past, and that similar powers will be conjoined with similar sensible qualities. If there be any suspicion that the course of nature may change, and that the past may be no rule for the future, all experience becomes useless, and can give rise to no inference or conclusion. It is impossible, therefore, that any arguments from experience can prove this resemblance of the past to the future; since all these arguments are founded on the supposition of that resemblance. Let the course of things be allowed hitherto ever so regular; that without some new argument or inference, proves not that, for the future, it will continue so. In vain do you pretend to have learned the nature of bodies from your past experience. Their secret nature, and consequently all their effects and influence, may change, without any change in their sensible qualities. This happens sometimes, and with regard to some objects: Why may it not happen always, and with regard to all objects? What logic, what process of argument secures you against this supposition? My practice, you say, refutes my doubts. But you mistake the purport of my question. As an agent, I am quite satisfied in the point; but as a philosopher, who has some share of curiosity, I will not say scepticism, I want to learn the foundation of this inference. No reading, no inquiry has yet been able to remove my difficulty, or give me satisfaction in a matter of such importance. Can I do better than propose the difficulty to the public, even though, perhaps, I have small hopes of obtaining a solution? We shall, at least, by this means, be sensible of our ignorance, if we do not augment our knowledge.

I must confess that a man is guilty of unpardonable arrogance who concludes, because an argument has escaped his own investigation, that therefore it does not really exist. I must also confess that, though all the learned, for several ages, should have employed themselves in fruitless search upon any subject, it may still, perhaps, be rash to conclude positively that the subject must, therefore, pass all human comprehension. Even though we examine all the sources of our knowledge, and conclude them unfit for such a subject, there may still remain a suspicion, that the enumeration is not complete, or the examination not accurate. But with regard to the present subject, there are some considerations which seem to remove all this accusation of arrogance or suspicion of mistake.

It is certain that the most ignorant and stupid peasants—nay infants, nay even brute beasts—improve by experience, and learn the qualities of natural objects, by observing the effects which result from them. When a child has felt the sensation of pain from touching the flame of a candle, he will be careful not to put his hand near any candle; but will expect a similar effect from a cause which is similar in its sensible qualities and appearance. If you assert, therefore, that the understanding of the child is led into this conclusion by any process of argument or ratiocination, I may justly require you to produce that argument; nor have you any pretense to refuse so equitable a demand. You cannot say that the argument is abstruse, and may possibly escape your inquiry; since you confess that it is obvious to the capacity of a mere infant. If you hesitate, therefore, a moment, or if, after reflection, you produce any intricate or profound argument, you, in a manner, give up the question, and confess that it is not reasoning which engages us to suppose the past resembling the future, and to expect similar effects from causes which are, to appearance, similar. This is the proposition which I intended to enforce in the present section. If I be right, I pretend not to have made any mighty discovery. And if I be wrong, I must acknowledge myself to be indeed a very backward scholar; since I cannot now discover an argument which, it seems, was perfectly familiar to me long before I was out of my cradle.

SECTION V

SCEPTICAL SOLUTION OF THESE DOUBTS

Part I

The passion for philosophy, like that for religion, seems liable to this inconvenience, that, thought it aims at the correction of our manners, and extirpation of our vices, it may only serve, by imprudent management, to foster a predominant inclination, and push the mind, with more determined resolution, towards that side which already *draws* too much, by the bias and propensity of the natural temper. It is certain that, while we aspire to the magnanimous firmness of the philosophic sage, and endeavor to confine our pleasures altogether within our own minds, we may, at last, render our philosophy like that of Epictetus, and other *stoics*, only a more refined system of selfishness, and reason ourselves out of all virtue as well as social enjoyment. While we study with attention the vanity of human life, and turn all our thoughts towards the empty and transitory nature of riches and honors, we are, perhaps, all the while flattering our natural indolence, which, hating the bustle of the world, and drudgery of business, seeks a pretense of reason to give itself a full and uncontrolled indulgence. There is, however, one species of philosophy which seems little liable to this inconvenience, and that because it strikes in with no disorderly passion of the human mind, nor can mingle itself with any natural affection or propensity; and that is the *academic* or *sceptical* philosophy. The academics always talk of doubt and suspense of judgment, of danger in hasty determinations, of confining to very narrow bounds the inquiries of the understanding, and of renouncing all speculations which lie not within the limits of common life and practice. Nothing, therefore, can be more contrary than such a philosophy to the supine indolence of the mind, its rash arrogance, its lofty pretensions, and its superstitious credulity. Every passion is mortified by it, except the love of truth; and that passion never is, nor can be, carried to too high a degree. It is surprising, therefore, that this philosophy, which, in almost every instance, must be harmless and innocent, should be the subject of so much groundless reproach and obloquy. But, perhaps, the very circumstance which renders it so innocent is what chiefly exposes it to the public hatred and resentment. By flattering no irregular passion, it gains few partisans: By opposing so many vices and follies, it raises to itself abundance of enemies, who stigmatize it as libertine, profane, and irreligious.

Nor need we fear that this philosophy, while it endeavors to limit our inquiries to common life, should ever undermine the reasonings of common life, and carry its doubts so far as to destroy all action, as well as speculation. Nature will always maintain her rights, and prevail in the end over any abstract reasoning whatsoever. Though we should conclude, for instance, as in the foregoing section, that, in all reasonings from experience, there is a step taken by the mind which is not supported by any argument or process of the understanding; there is no danger that these reasonings, on which almost all knowledge depends, will ever be affected by such a discovery. If the mind be not engaged by argument to make this step, it must be induced by some other principle of equal weight and authority; and that principle will preserve its influence as long as human nature remains the same. What that principle is may well be worth the pains of inquiry.

Suppose a person, though endowed with the strongest faculties of reason and reflection, to be brought on a sudden into this world; he would, indeed, immediately observe a continual succession of objects, and one event following another; but he would not be able to discover anything farther. He would not, at first, by any reasoning, be able to reach the idea of cause and effect; since the particular powers, by which all natural operations are performed, never appear to the senses; nor is it reasonable to conclude, merely because one event, in one instance, precedes another, that therefore the one is the cause, the other the effect. Their conjunction may be arbitrary and casual. There may be no reason to infer the existence of one from the appearance of the other. And in a word, such a person, without more experience, could never employ his conjecture or reasoning concerning any matter of fact, or be assured of anything beyond what was immediately present to his memory and senses.

Suppose, again, that he has acquired more experience, and has lived so long in the world as to have observed familiar objects or events to be constantly conjoined together; what is the consequence of this experience? He immediately infers the existence of one object from the appearance of the other. Yet he has not, by all his experience, acquired any idea or knowledge of the secret power by which the one object produces the other; nor is it, by any process of reasoning, he is engaged to draw this inference. But still he finds himself determined to draw it: And though he should be convinced that his understanding has no part in the operation, he would nevertheless continue in the same course of thinking. There is some other principle which determines him to form such a conclusion.

This principle is *custom* or *habit*. For wherever the repetition of any particular act or operation produces a propensity to renew the same act or operation, without being impelled by any reasoning or process of the understanding, we always say, that this propensity is the effect of *custom*. By employing the word, we pretend not to have given the ultimate reason of such a propensity. We only point out a principle of human nature, which is universally acknowledged, and which is well known by its effects. Perhaps we can push our inquiries no farther, or pretend to give the cause of this cause; but must rest contented with it as the ultimate principle, which we can assign, of all our conclusions from experience. It is sufficient satisfaction, that we can go so far, without repining at the narrowness of our faculties because they will carry us no farther. And it is certain we here advance a very intelligible proposition at least, if not a true one, when we assert that, after the constant conjunction of two objects—heat and flame, for instance, weight and solidity—we are determined by custom alone to expect the one from the appearance of the other. This hypothesis seems even the only one which explains the difficulty, why we draw, from a thousand instances, an inference which we are not able to draw from one instance, that is, in no respect, different from them. Reason is incapable of any such variation. The conclusions which it draws from considering one circle are the same which it would form upon surveying all the circles in the universe. But no man, having seen only one body move after being impelled by another, could infer that every other body will move after a like impulse. All inferences from experience, therefore, are effects of custom, not of reasoning.

Custom, then, is the great guide of human life. It is that principle alone which renders our experience useful to us, and makes us expect, for the future, a similar train of events with those which have appeared in the past. Without the influence of custom, we should be entirely ignorant of every matter of fact beyond what is immediately present to the memory and senses. We should never know how to adjust means to ends, or to employ our natural powers in the production of any effect. There would be an end at once of all action, as well as of the chief part of speculation.

But here it may be proper to remark, that though our conclusions from experience carry us beyond our memory and senses, and assure us of matters of fact which happened in the most distant places and most remote ages, yet some fact must always be present to the senses or memory, from which we may first proceed in drawing these conclusions. A man, who should find in a desert country the remains of pompous buildings, would conclude that the country had, in ancient times, been cultivated by civilized inhabitants; but did nothing of this nature occur to him, he could never form such an inference. We learn the events of former ages from history; but then we must peruse the volumes in which this instruction is contained, and thence carry up our inferences from one testimony to another, till we arrive at the eyewitnesses and spectators of these distant events. In a word, if we proceed not upon some fact, present to the memory or senses, our reasonings would be merely hypothetical; and however the particular links might be connected with each other, the whole chain of inferences would have nothing to support it, nor could we ever, by its means, arrive at the knowledge of any real existence. If I ask why you believe any particular matter of fact, which you relate, you must tell me some reason; and this reason will be some other fact, connected with it. But as you cannot proceed after this manner, *in infinitum*, you must at last terminate in some fact, which is present to your memory or senses; or must allow that your belief is entirely without foundation. . . .

Here, then, is a kind of pre-established harmony between the course of nature and the succession of our ideas; and though the powers and forces, by which the former is governed, be wholly unknown to us; yet our thoughts and conceptions have still, we find, gone on in the same train with the other works of nature. Custom is that principle, by which this correspondence has been effected; so necessary to the subsistence of our species, and the regulation of our conduct, in every circumstance and occurrence of human life. Had not the presence of an object, instantly excited the idea of those objects, commonly conjoined with it, all our knowledge must have been limited to the narrow sphere of our memory and senses; and we should never have been able to adjust means to ends, or employ our natural powers, either to the producing of good, or avoiding of evil. Those, who delight in the discovery and contemplation of *final causes*, have here ample subject to employ their wonder and admiration.

George Berkeley: Does Matter Really Exist?

1. It is evident to any one who takes a survey of the objects of human knowledge, that they are either *ideas* actually imprinted on the senses; or else such as are perceived by attending to the passions and operations of the mind; or lastly, *ideas* formed by help of memory and imagination—either compounding, dividing, or barely representing those originally perceived in the aforesaid ways.—By sight I have the ideas of light and colours, with their several degrees and variations. By touch I perceive hard and soft, heat and cold, motion and resistance, and of all these more and less either as to quantity or degree. Smelling furnishes me with odours; the palate with tastes; and hearing conveys sounds to the mind in all their variety of tone and composition.—And as several of these are observed to accompany each other, they come to be marked by one name, and so to be reputed as one THING. Thus, for example, a certain colour, taste, smell, figure and consistence having been observed to go together, are accounted one distinct thing, signified by the name *apple;* other collections of ideas constitute a stone, a tree, a book, and the like sensible things—which as they are pleasing or disagreeable excite the passions of love, hatred, joy, grief, and so forth.

2. But, besides all that endless variety of ideas or objects of knowledge, there is likewise something which knows or perceives them; and exercises divers operations, as willing, imagining, remembering, about them. This perceiving, active being is what I call MIND, SPIRIT, SOUL, or MYSELF. By which words I do not denote any one of my ideas, but a thing entirely distinct from them, wherein they exist, or, which is the same thing, whereby they are perceived—for the existence of an idea consists in being perceived.

3. That neither our thoughts, nor passions, nor ideas formed by the imagination, exist without the mind, is what everybody will allow.—And to me it is no less evident that the various SENSATIONS, or *ideas imprinted on the sense,* however blended or combined together (that is, whatever *objects* they compose), cannot exist otherwise than in a mind perceiving them—I think an intuitive knowledge may be obtained of this by any one that shall attend to *what is meant by the term 'exist' when applied to sensible things.* The table I write on I say exists, that is, I see and feel it; and if I were out of my study I should say it existed—meaning thereby that if I was in my study I might perceive it, or that some other spirit actually does perceive it. There was an odour, that is, it was smelt; there was a sound, that is, it was heard; a colour or figure, and it was perceived by sight or touch. This is all that I can understand by these and the like expressions.—For as to what is said of the absolute existence of unthinking things without any relation to their being perceived, that is to me perfectly unintelligible. Their *esse* is *percipi,* nor is it possible they should have any existence out of the minds or thinking things which perceive them.

4. It is indeed an opinion strangely prevailing

The selection has been taken from Part I of Berkeley's *The Principles of Human Knowledge.*

amongst men, that houses, mountains, rivers, and in a word all sensible objects, have an existence, natural or real, distinct from their being perceived by the understanding. But, with how great an assurance and acquiescence soever this principle may be entertained in the world, yet whoever shall find in his heart to call it in question may, if I mistake not, perceive it to involve a manifest contradiction. For, what are the forementioned objects but the things we perceive by sense? and what do we perceive besides our own ideas or sensations? and is it not plainly repugnant that any one of *these,* or any combination of them, should exist unperceived?

5. If we thoroughly examine this tenet it will, perhaps, be found at bottom to depend on the doctrine of *abstract ideas.* For can there be a nicer strain of abstraction than to distinguish the *existence* of sensible objects from their *being perceived,* so as to conceive them existing unperceived? Light and colours, heat and cold, extension and figures—in a word the things we see and feel—what are they but so many sensations, notions, ideas, or impressions on the sense? and is it possible to separate, even in thought, any of these from perception? For my part, I might as easily divide a thing from itself. I may, indeed, divide in my thoughts, or conceive apart from each other, those things which, perhaps, I never perceived by sense so divided. Thus, I imagine the trunk of a human body without the limbs, or conceive the smell of a rose without thinking on the rose itself. So far, I will not deny, I can abstract—if that may properly be called *abstraction* which extends only to the conceiving separately such objects as it is possible may really exist or be actually perceived asunder. But my conceiving or imagining power does not extend beyond the possibility of real existence or perception. Hence, as it is impossible for me to see or feel anything without an actual sensation of that thing, so is it impossible for me to conceive in my thoughts any sensible thing or object distinct from the sensation or perception of it.

6. Some truths there are so near and obvious to the mind that a man need only open his eyes to see them. Such I take this important one to be, viz. that all the choir of heaven and furniture of the earth, in a word all those bodies which compose the mighty frame of the world, have not any subsistence without a mind—that their *being* is *to be perceived or known;* that consequently so long as they are not actually perceived by me, or do not exist in my mind or that of any other created spirit, they must either have no existence at all, or else subsist in the mind of some Eternal Spirit—it being perfectly unintelligible, and involving all the absurdity of abstraction, to attribute to any single part of them an existence independent of a spirit. To be convinced of which, the reader need only reflect, and try to separate in his own thoughts the *being* of a sensible thing from its *being perceived.*

7. From what has been said it is evident there is not any other Substance than SPIRIT, or *that which perceives.* But, for the fuller demonstration of this point, let it be considered the sensible qualities are colour, figure, motion, smell, taste, &c., *i.e.* the ideas perceived by sense. Now, for an idea to exist in an unperceiving thing is a manifest contradiction; for to have an idea is all one as to perceive; that therefore wherein colour, figure, &c. exist must perceive them; hence it is clear there can be no unthinking substance or *substratum* of those ideas.

8. But say you, though the ideas themselves do not exist without the mind, yet there may be things like them, whereof they are copies or resemblances, which things exist without the mind in an unthinking substance. I answer, an idea can be like nothing but an idea; a colour or figure can be like nothing but another colour or figure. If we look but ever so little into our own thoughts, we shall find it impossible for us to conceive a likeness except only between our ideas. Again, I ask whether those supposed originals or external things, of which our ideas are the pictures or representations, be themselves perceivable or no? If they are, then they are ideas and we have gained our point; but if you say they are not, I appeal to any one whether it be sense to assert a colour is like something which is invisible; hard or soft, like something which is intangible; and so of the rest.

9. Some there are who make a distinction between *primary* and *secondary* qualities. By the former they mean extension, figure, motion, rest, solidity, impenetrability, and

number; by the latter they denote all other sensible qualities, as colours, sounds, tastes, and so forth. The ideas we have of these last they acknowledge not to be the resemblances of anything existing without the mind, or unperceived, but they will have our ideas of the primary qualities to be patterns or images of things which exist without the mind, in an unthinking substance which they call *inert, senseless substance, in which extension, figure and motion do actually subsist.* But it is evident, from what we have already shown, that extension, figure, and motion are only ideas existing in the mind, and that an idea can be like nothing but another idea, and that consequently neither they nor their archetypes can exist in an unperceiving substance. Hence, it is plain that the very notion of what is called *Matter* or *corporeal substance* involves a contradiction in it.

10. They who assert that figure, motion, and the rest of the primary or original qualities do exist without the mind, in unthinking substances, do at the same time acknowledge that colours, sounds, heat, cold, and suchlike secondary qualities, do not—which they tell us are sensations existing in the mind alone, that depend on and are occasioned by the different size, texture, and motion of the minute particles of matter. This they take for an undoubted truth, which they can demonstrate beyond all exception. Now, if it be certain that those original qualities are inseparably united with the other sensible qualities, and not, even in thought, capable of being abstracted from them, it plainly follows that they exist only in the mind. But I desire any one to reflect and try whether he can, by any abstraction of thought, conceive the extension and motion of a body without all other sensible qualities. For my own part, I see evidently that it is not in my power to frame an idea of a body extended and moving, but I must withal give it some colour or other sensible quality which is acknowledged to exist only in the mind. In short, extension, figure, and motion, abstracted from all other qualities, are inconceivable. Where therefore the other sensible qualities are, there must these be also, to wit, in the mind and nowhere else.

11. Again, *great* and *small, swift* and *slow,* are allowed to exist nowhere without the mind, being entirely relative, and changing as the frame or position of the organs of sense varies. The extension therefore which exists without the mind is neither great nor small, the motion neither swift nor slow, that is, they are nothing at all. But, say you, they are extension in general, and motion in general: thus we see how much the tenet of extended moveable substances existing without the mind depends on that strange doctrine of *abstract* ideas. And here I cannot but remark how nearly the vague and indeterminate description of Matter or corporeal substance, which the modern philosophers are run into by their own principles, resembles that antiquated and so much ridiculed notion of *materia prima,* to be met with in Aristotle and his followers. Without extension solidity can be conceived; since therefore it has been shown that extension exists not in an unthinking substance, the same must also be true of solidity.

12. That number is entirely the creature of the mind, even though the other qualities be allowed to exist without, will be evident to whoever considers that the same thing bears a different denomination of number as the mind views it with different respects. Thus, the same extension is one, or three, or thirty-six, according as the mind considers it with reference to a yard, a foot, or an inch. Number is so visibly relative, and dependent on men's understanding, that it is strange to think how any one should give it an absolute existence without the mind. We say one book, one page, one line, &c.; all these are equally units, though some contain several of the others. And in each instance, it is plain, the unit relates to some particular combination of ideas arbitrarily put together by the mind.

13. Unity I know some will have to be a simple or uncompounded idea, accompanying all other ideas into the mind. That I have any such idea answering the word *unity* I do not find; and if I had, I think I could not miss finding it: on the contrary, it should be the most familiar to my understanding, since it is said to accompany all other ideas, and to be perceived by all the ways of sensation and reflexion. To say no more, it is an *abstract* idea.

14. I shall further add, that, after the same manner as modern philosophers prove certain sensible qualities to have no existence in Matter,

or without the mind, the same thing may be likewise proved of all other sensible qualities whatsoever. Thus, for instance, it is said that heat and cold are affections only of the mind, and not at all patterns of real beings existing in the corporeal substances which excite them, for that the same body which appears cold to one hand seems warm to another. Now, why may we not as well argue that figure and extension are not patterns or resemblances of qualities existing in Matter, because to the same eye at different stations, or eyes of a different texture at the same station, they appear various, and cannot therefore be the images of anything settled and determinate without the mind? Again, it is proved that sweetness is not really in the sapid thing, because the thing remaining unaltered the sweetness is changed into bitter, as in case of a fever or otherwise vitiated palate. Is it not as reasonable to say that motion is not without the mind, since if the succession of ideas in the mind become swifter the motion, it is acknowledged, shall appear slower without any alteration in any external object.

15. In short, let any one consider those arguments which are thought manifestly to prove that colours and tastes exist *only* in the mind, and he shall find they may with equal force be brought to prove the same thing of extension, figure, and motion.—Thought it must be confessed this method of arguing does not so much prove that there is no extension or colour in an outward object, as that *we* do not know by *sense* which is the *true* extension or colour of the object. But the arguments foregoing plainly show it to be impossible that any colour or extension at all, or other sensible quality whatsoever, should exist in an unthinking subject without the mind, or in truth, that there should be any such thing as an outward object.

16. But let us examine a little the received opinion.—It is said extension is a mode or accident of Matter, and that Matter is the *substratum* that supports it. Now I desire that you would explain to me what is meant by Matter's *supporting* extension. Say you, I have no idea of Matter and therefore cannot explain it. I answer, though you have no positive, yet, if you have any meaning at all, you must at least have a relative idea of Matter; though you know not what it is, yet you must be supposed to know what relation it bears to accidents, and what is meant by its supporting them. It is evident 'support' cannot here be taken in its usual or literal sense—as when we say that pillars support a building; in what sense therefore must it be taken?

17. If we inquire into what the most accurate philosophers declare themselves to mean by *material substance,* we shall find them acknowledge they have no other meaning annexed to those sounds but the idea of *being in general,* together with the relative notion of its *supporting accidents.* The general idea of Being appeareth to me the most abstract and incomprehensible of all other; and as for its supporting accidents, this, as we have just now observed, cannot be understood in the common sense of those words; it must therefore be taken in some other sense, but what that is they do not explain. So that when I consider the two parts or branches which make the signification of the words *material substance,* I am convinced there is no distinct meaning annexed to them. But why should we trouble ourselves any farther, in discussing this material *substratum* or 'support' of figure, and motion, and other sensible qualities? Does it not suppose *they* have an existence without the mind? And is not this a direct repugnancy, and altogether inconceivable?

18. But, though it were possible that solid, figure, moveable *substances* may exist without the mind, corresponding to the ideas we have of bodies, yet how is it possible for us to know this? Either we must know it by Sense or by Reason.—As for our senses, by them we have the knowledge only of our sensations, ideas, or those things that are immediately perceived by sense, call them what you will: but they do not inform us that things exist without the mind, or unperceived, like to those which are perceived. This the Materialists themselves acknowledge.—It remains therefore that if we have any knowledge at all of external things, it must be by Reason inferring their existence from what is immediately perceived by sense. But what reason can induce us to believe the existence of bodies without the mind, from what we perceive, since the very patrons of Matter themselves do not pretend there is any *necessary* connexion between them and our ideas? I say it is granted on all hands—and what happens in dreams, frenzies, and the like,

puts it beyond dispute—that it is possible we might be affected with all the ideas we have now, though there were no bodies existing without resembling them. Hence, it is evident the supposition of external bodies is not necessary for producing our ideas; since it is granted they are produced sometimes, and might possibly be produced always in the same order we see them in at present, without their concurrence.

19. But, though we might possibly have all our sensations without them, yet perhaps it may be thought easier to conceive and explain the manner of their production, by supposing external bodies in their likeness rather than otherwise; and so it might be at least probable there are such things as bodies that excite their ideas in our minds. But neither can this be said; for, though we give the materialists their external bodies, they by their own confession are never the nearer knowing *how* our ideas are produced; since they own themselves unable to comprehend in what manner body can act upon spirit, or how it is possible it should imprint any idea in the mind. Hence it is evident the production of ideas or sensations in our minds can be no reason why we should suppose Matter or corporeal substances, since *that* is acknowledged to remain equally inexplicable with or without this supposition. If therefore it were possible for bodies to exist without the mind, yet to hold they do so must needs be a very precarious opinion; since it is to suppose, without any reason at all, that God has created innumerable beings that are entirely useless, and serve to no manner of purpose.

20. In short, if there were external bodies, it is impossible we should ever come to know it; and if there were not, we might have the very same reasons to think there were that we have now. Suppose—what no one can deny possible—an intelligence *without the help of external bodies,* to be affected with the same train of sensations or ideas that you are, imprinted in the same order and with like vividness in his mind. I ask whether that intelligence has not all the reason to believe the existence of corporeal substances, represented by his ideas, and exciting them in his mind, that you can possibly have for believing the same thing? Of this there can be no question—which one consideration were enough to make any reasonable person suspect the strength of whatever arguments he may think himself to have, for the existence of bodies without the mind.

21. Were it necessary to add any further proof against the Existence of Matter, after what has been said, I could instance several of those errors and difficulties (not to mention impieties) which have sprung from that tenet. It has occasioned numberless controversies and disputes in philosophy, and not a few of far greater moment in religion. But I shall not enter into the detail of them in this place, as well because I think arguments *a posteriori* are unnecessary for confirming what has been, if I mistake not, sufficiently demonstrated *a priori,* as because I shall hereafter find occasion to speak somewhat of them.

22. I am afraid I have given cause to think I am needlessly prolix in handling this subject. For, to what purpose is it to dilate on that which may be demonstrated with the utmost evidence in a line or two, to any one that is capable of the least reflection? It is but looking into your own thoughts, and so trying whether you can conceive it possible for a sound, or figure, or motion, or colour to exist without the mind or unperceived. This easy trial may perhaps make you see that what you contend for is a downright contradiction. Insomuch that I am content to put the whole upon this issue:—If you can but conceive it possible for one extended moveable substance, or, in general, for any one idea, or anything like an idea, to exist otherwise than in a mind perceiving it, I shall readily give up the cause. And, as for all that compages of external bodies you contend for, I shall grant you its existence, though you cannot either give me any reason why you believe it exists, or assign any use to it when it is supposed to exist. I say, the bare possibility of your opinions being true shall pass for an argument that it is so.

23. But, say you, surely there is nothing easier than for me to imagine trees, for instance, in a park, or books existing in a closet, and nobody by to perceive them. I answer, you may so, there is no difficulty in it; but what is all this, I beseech you, more than framing in *your* mind certain ideas which you call books and trees, and at the same time omitting to frame the idea of any one that may perceive them? But do not you yourself perceive or think

of them all the while? This therefore is nothing to the purpose: it only shows you have the power of imagining or can conceive it possible the objects of your thought may exist without the mind. To make out this, it is necessary that *you* conceive them existing unconceived or unthought of, which is a manifest repugnancy. When we do our utmost to conceive the existence of external bodies, we are all the while only contemplating our own ideas. But the mind, *taking no notice of itself,* is deluded to think it can and does conceive bodies existing unthought of or without the mind, though at the same time they are apprehended by or exist in itself. A little attention will discover to any one the truth and evidence of what is here said, and make it unnecessary to insist on any other proofs against the existence of *material substance.*

24. It is very obvious, upon the least inquiry into our own thoughts, to know whether it be possible for us to *understand* what is meant by the *absolute* existence of sensible objects *in themselves,* or *without the mind.* To me it is evident those words mark out either a direct contradiction, or else nothing at all. And to convince others of this, I know no readier or fairer way than to entreat they would calmly attend to their own thoughts; and if by this attention the emptiness or repugnancy of those expressions does appear, surely nothing more is requisite for their conviction. It is on this therefore that I insist, to wit, that the absolute existence of unthinking things are words without a meaning, or which include a contradiction. This is what I repeat and inculcate, and earnestly recommended to the attentive thoughts of the reader.

25. All our ideas, sensations, notions, or the things which we perceive, by whatsoever names they may be distinguished, are visibly inactive—there is nothing of Power or Agency included in them. So that one idea or object of thought cannot produce or make any alteration in another.—To be satisfied of the truth of this, there is nothing else requisite but a bare observation of our ideas. For, since they and every part of them exist only in the mind, it follows that there is nothing in them but what is perceived: but whoever shall attend to his ideas, whether of sense or reflection, will not perceive in them any power or activity; there is, therefore, no such thing contained in them. A little attention will discover to us that the very being of an idea implies passiveness and inertness in it, insomuch that it is impossible for an idea to do anything, or, strictly speaking, to be the cause of anything: neither can it be the resemblance or pattern of any active being, as it is evident from sect. 8. Whence it plainly follows that extension, figure, and motion cannot be the cause of our sensations. To say, therefore, that these are the effects of powers resulting from the configuration, number, motion, and size of corpuscles, must certainly be false.

26. We perceive a continual *succession* of ideas; some are anew excited, others are changed or totally disappear. There is therefore some Cause of these ideas, whereon they depend, and which produces and changes them. That this cause cannot be any quality, or idea, or combination of ideas is clear from the preceding section. It must therefore be a substance; but it has been shown that there is no corporeal or material substance: it remains therefore that the cause of ideas is an incorporeal active substance or Spirit.

27. A Spirit is one simple, undivided, active being—as it *perceives* ideas it is called the *Understanding,* and as it *produces* or otherwise *operates* about them it is called the *Will.* Hence there can be no *idea* formed of a soul or spirit; for, all ideas whatever, being passive and inert (see sect. 25,) cannot represent unto us, by way of image or likeness, that which acts. A little attention will make it plain to any one that to have an idea which shall be *like* that active principle of motion and change of ideas is absolutely impossible. Such is the nature of Spirit, or that which acts, that it cannot be of itself perceived, but only by the effects which it produces.—If any man shall doubt of the truth of what is here delivered, let him but reflect and try if he can frame the idea of any Power or Active Being; and whether he has ideas of two principal powers, marked by the names *Will* and *Understanding,* distinct from each other, as well as from a third idea of Substance or Being in general, with a relative notion of its supporting or being the subject of the aforesaid powers—which is signified by the name Soul or Spirit. This is what some hold; but, so far as I can see, the words *will, soul, spirit,* do not stand for different ideas, or, in truth, for

any idea at all, but for something which is very different from ideas, and which, being an Agent, cannot be like unto, or represented by, any idea whatsoever. . . .

29. But, whatever power I may have over my own thoughts, I find the ideas actually perceived by Sense have not a like dependence on my will. When in broad daylight I open my eyes, it is not in my power to choose whether I shall see or no, or to determine what particular objects shall present themselves to my view; and so likewise as to the hearing and other senses, the ideas imprinted on them are not creatures of my will. There is therefore some *other* Will or Spirit that produces them.

30. The ideas of Sense are more strong, lively, and distinct than those of the Imagination; they have likewise a steadiness, order, and coherence, and are not excited at random, as those which are the effects of human wills often are, but in a regular train or series—the admirable connexion whereof sufficiently testifies the wisdom and benevolence of its Author. Now the set rules or established methods wherein the Mind we depend on excites in us the ideas of sense, are called the *laws of nature;* and these we learn by experience, which teaches us that such and such ideas are attended with such and such other ideas, in the ordinary course of things.

31. This gives us a sort of foresight which enables us to regular our actions for the benefit of life. And without this we should be eternally at a loss; we could not know how to act anything that might procure us the least pleasure, or remove the least pain of sense. That food nourishes, sleep refreshes, and fire warms us; that to sow in the seedtime is the way to reap in the harvest; and in general that to obtain such or such ends, such or such means are conducive—all this we know, not by discovering any *necessary connexion* between our ideas, but only by the *observation* of the settled laws of nature, without which we should be all in uncertainty and confusion, and a grown man no more know how to manage himself in the affairs of life than an infant just born.

32. And yet this consistent uniform working, which so evidently plays the goodness and wisdom of that Governing Spirit whose Will constitutes the laws of nature, is so far from leading our thoughts to Him, that it rather sends them wandering after second causes. For, when we perceive certain ideas of Sense constantly followed by other ideas, and we know this is not of our own doing, we forthwith attribute power and agency to the ideas themselves, and make one the cause of another, that which nothing can be more absurd and unintelligible. Thus, for example, having observed that when we perceive by sight a certain round luminous figure we at the same time perceive by touch the idea or sensation called heat, we do from thence conclude the sun to be the *cause* of heat. And in like manner perceiving the motion and collision of bodies to be attended with sound, we are inclined to think the latter the *effect* of the former.

33. The ideas imprinted on the Senses by the Author of nature are called *real things:* and those excited in the Imagination being less regular, vivid, and constant, are more properly termed *ideas;* or *images of things,* when they copy and represent. But then our sensations, be they never so vivid and distinct, are nevertheless ideas, that is, they exist in the mind, or are perceived by it, as truly as the ideas of its own framing. The ideas of Sense are allowed to have more reality in them, that is, to be more strong, orderly, and coherent than the creatures of the mind; but this is no argument that they exist without the mind. They are also less dependent on the spirit, or thinking substance which perceives them, in that they are excited by the will of another and more powerful Spirit; yet still they are *ideas,* and certainly no idea, whether faint or strong, can exist otherwise than in a mind perceiving it. . . .

Immanuel Kant: Critical Idealism

INTRODUCTION

There are learned men, to whom the history of philosophy (both ancient and modern) is philosophy itself; for such the present Prolegomena are not written. They must wait till those who endeavor to draw from the fountain of reason itself have made out their case; it will then be the historians' turn to inform the world of what has been done. Moreover, nothing can be said, which in their opinion has not been said already, and indeed this may be applied as an infallible prediction to all futurity; for as the human reason has for many centuries pursued with ardour infinitely various objects in various ways, it is hardly to be expected that we should not be able to match every new thing with some old thing not unlike it.

My object is to persuade all who think Metaphysics worth studying, that it is absolutely necessary to adjourn for the present this (historical) labour, to consider all that has been done as undone, and to start first of all with the question, 'Whether such a thing as metaphysic be at all possible?'

If it be a science, how comes it that it cannot, like other sciences, obtain for itself an universal and permanent recognition? If not, how is it ever making constant pretensions, under this supposition, and keeping the human mind in suspense with hopes that never fade, and yet are never fulfilled? Whether then, as a result, we demonstrate our knowledge or our ignorance, we must come once for all to a definite conclusion about the nature of this pretended science, which cannot possibly remain on its present footing. It seems almost ridiculous, while every other science is continually advancing, that in this, which would be very Wisdom, at whose oracle all men inquire, we should perpetually revolve round the same point, without gaining a single step. And so its followers having melted away, we do not find men who feel able to shine in other sciences venturing their reputation here, where everybody, however ignorant in other matters, pretends to deliver a final verdict, as in this domain there is as yet no certain weight and measure to distinguish sound knowledge from shallow talk.

But after long elaboration of a science, when men begin to wonder how far it has advanced, it is not without precedent that the question should at last occur, whether and how such a science be even possible? For the human reason is so constructive, that it has already several times built up a tower, and then razed it to examine the nature of the foundation. It is never too late to mend; but if the change comes late, there is always more difficulty in setting it going.

The question whether a science be possible, presupposes a doubt as to its actuality. But such a doubt offends the men whose whole possessions consist of this supposed jewel; hence he who raises the doubt must expect opposition from all sides. Some, in the proud consciousness of their possessions, which are ancient, and therefore considered legitimate, will take their metaphysical compendia in their hands, and look down on him with contempt; others, who never see anything except it be identical with what they have seen before, will not understand him, and everything will remain for a time, as if nothing had happened to excite the concern, or the hope, for an impending change.

Nevertheless, I venture to predict that the

From Immanuel Kant, *Prolegomena to Any Future Metaphysic,* translated by J.P. Mahaffy.

independent reader of these Prolegomena will not only doubt his previous science, but ultimately be fully persuaded, that it cannot exist without satisfying the demands here stated, on which its possibility depends; and, as this has never been done, that there is, as yet, no such thing as Metaphysic. But as it can never cease to be in demand—

> 'Rusticus expectat, dum defluat amnis, at ille
> Labitur et labetur in omne volubilis aevum;'—

since the interests of mankind are interwoven with it so intimately, he must confess that a radical reform, or rather a new birth of the science after an original plan, must be unavoidably at hand, however men may struggle against it for a while.

Since the Essays of Locke and Leibnitz, or rather since the origin of metaphysic so far as we know its history, nothing has ever happened which might have been more decisive to the fortunes of the science than the attack made upon it by David Hume. He threw no light on this species of knowledge, but he certainly struck a spark from which light might have been obtained, had it caught a proper substance to nurture and develop the flame.

Hume started chiefly from a single but important concept in Metaphysic—that of Cause and Effect (including the deduced notions of action and power). He calls on reason, which pretends to have generated this notion from itself, to answer him with what right it thinks anything to be so constituted, that if granted, something else must necessarily be granted thereby; for this is the meaning of the concept of cause. He demonstrated irresistibly that it was perfectly impossible for reason to think such a combination by means of concepts and *a priori*—a combination that contains necessity. We cannot at all see why, in consequence of the existence of one thing, another must necessarily exist, or how the concept of one thing, another must necessarily exist, or how the concept of such a combination can arise *a priori*. Hence he inferred, that reason was altogether deluded by this concept, which it considered erroneously as one of its children, whereas in reality the concept was nothing but the bastard offspring of the imagination, impregnated by experience, and so bringing certain representations under the Law of Association. The subjective necessity, that is, the custom which so arises, is then substituted for an objective necessity from real knowledge. Hence he inferred that reason had no power to think such combinations, even generally, because its concepts would then be mere inventions, and all its pretended *a priori* cognitions nothing but common experiences marked with a false stamp. In plain language there is not, and cannot be, any such thing as metaphysic at all. This conclusion, however hasty and mistaken, was at least founded upon investigation, and the investigation deserved to have suggested to the brighter spirits of his day a combined attempt at a happy solution of the problem proposed by him, if such solution were possible. Thus a complete reform of the science must have resulted.

But the perpetual hard fate of metaphysic would not allow him to be understood. We cannot without a certain sense of pain consider how utterly his opponents, Reid, Oswald, Beattie, and even Priestley, missed the point of the problem. For while they were ever assuming as conceded what he doubted, and demonstrating with eagerness and often with arrogance what he never thought of disputing, they so overlooked his indication towards a better state of things, that everything remained undisturbed in its old condition.

The question was not whether the concept of cause was right, useful, and even indispensable with regard to our knowledge of nature, for this Hume had never doubted. But the question to which Hume expected an answer was this, whether that concept could be thought by reason *a priori*, and whether it consequently possesses an inner truth, independent of all experience, and therefore applied more widely than to the mere objects of experience. It was surely a question concerning the *origin*, not concerning the *indispensable use* of the concept. Had the former question been determined, the conditions of the use and valid application of the concept would have been given *ipso facto*.

But the opponents of the greater thinker should have probed very deeply into the nature of reason, so far as it concerns pure thinking, if they would satisfy the conditions of the problem—a task which did not suit them. They therefore discovered a more convenient means of putting on a bold face without any proper insight into the question, by appealing to the *common sense of mankind.* It is indeed a great gift of God, to possess right, or (as they now call it) plain common sense. But this common sense must be shown practically, by well-considered and reasonable thoughts and words, not by appealing to it as an oracle, when you can advance nothing rational in justification of yourself. To appeal to common sense, when insight and science fail, and no sooner—this is one of the subtile discoveries of modern times, by means of which the most vapid babbler can safely enter the lists with the most thorough-going thinker, and hold his own. But as long as a particle of insight remains, no one would think of having recourse to this subterfuge. For what is it, but an appeal to the opinion of the multitude, of whose applause the philosopher is ashamed, while the popular and superficial man glories and confides in it? I should think Hume might fairly have laid as much claim to sound sense as Beattie, and besides to a critical understanding (such as the latter did not possess), which keeps common sense within such limits as to prevent it from speculating, or, if it does speculate, keeps it from wishing to decide when it cannot satisfy itself concerning its own principles. By this means alone can common sense remain sound sense. Chisels and hammers may suffice to work a piece of wood, but for steel-engraving we require a special instrument. Thus common sense and speculative understanding are each serviceable in their own way, the former in judgments which apply immediately to experience, the latter when we judge universally from mere concepts, as in metaphysic, where that which calls itself (often *per antiphrasin*) sound common sense has no right to judge at all.

I honestly confess, the suggestion of David Hume was the very thing, which many years ago first interrupted my dogmatic slumber, and gave my investigations in the field of speculative philosophy quite a new direction. I am far from following him in all his conclusions, which only resulted from his regarding not the whole of his problem, but a part, which by itself can give us no information. If we start from a well-founded, but undeveloped, thought, which another has bequeathed to us, we may well hope by continued reflection to advance farther than the acute man, to whom we owe the first spark of light.

I therefore first tried whether Hume's objection could not be put into a general form, and soon found that the concept of the connexion of cause and effect was by no means the only one by which the understanding thinks the connexion of things *a priori*, but rather that metaphysic consists altogether of such connexions. I sought to make certain of their number, and when I had succeeded in this to my expectation, by starting from a single principle, I proceeded to the deduction of these concepts, which I was now certain were not deduced from experience, as Hume had apprehended, but sprang from the pure understanding. This deduction, which seemed impossible to my acute predecessor, which had never even occurred to any one else, though they were all using the concepts unsuspiciously without questioning the basis of their objective validity—this deduction was the most difficult task ever undertaken in aid of metaphysic. More especially, no existing metaphysic could assist me in the least, because this deduction must prove the very possibility of metaphysic. But as soon as I had succeeded in solving Hume's problem not merely in a particular case, but with respect to the whole faculty of pure reason. I could proceed safely, though slowly, to determine the whole sphere of pure reason completely and from general principles, in its bounds, as well as in its contents. This was what metaphysic required, in order to construct its system safely.

But I fear that the *carrying out* of Hume's problem in its widest extent (see my Critique of the Pure Reason) will fare as the *problem* itself fared, when first proposed. It will be misjudged because it is misunderstood, and misunderstood because men choose to skim through the book, and not to *think* through it—a disagreeable task, because the work is dry, obscure, opposed to all ordinary notions, and moreover voluminous. I confess, however, I did not expect to hear from philosophers complaints of want of popularity, entertainment, and facility, when the existence of a highly esteemed and to us indispensable cognition is at stake, which cannot be established otherwise than by the strictest rules of scholastic accuracy. Popularity may follow, but is inadmissible at the commencement. Yet as regards a certain obscurity, arising partly from the extent of the plan, in which the principal points of the investigation cannot be easily gathered into view, the complaint is partly just, and I intend to remove it by the present Prolegomena.

The work which represents the pure faculty of reason in its whole compass and bounds will always remain the groundwork to which the Prolegomena, as a preliminary exercise, refer; for we must have that Critique completed as a science, systematically, in its minutest details, before we can think of letting Metaphysics appear on the scene, or even have the most distant hope of attaining it.

We have been long accustomed to seeing antiquated knowledge produced as new by being taken out of its former context, and fitted into a suit of any fancy pattern under new titles. Most readers will set out by expecting nothing else from the Critique; but these Prolegomena may persuade him that it is a perfectly new science, of which no one has ever even thought, the very idea of which was unknown, and for which nothing hitherto accomplished can be of the smallest use, except it be the indication suggested by Hume's doubts. Yet even he did not suspect such a formal science, but ran his ship ashore, for safety's sake, on scepticism, there to let it lie and rot; whereas my object is rather to give it a pilot, who, by means of safe astronomical principles drawn from a knowledge of the globe, and provided with a complete chart and compass, may steer the ship safely, whither he listeth.

If we proceed to a perfectly isolated and peculiar new science, with the presupposition that we can judge it by means of a supposed science that has been already acquired, whereas the reality of this latter must be first of all thoroughly questioned—if we do this, it will make men think they merely recognize old knowledge. For the terms are similar, with this difference, that everything must appear distorted, absurd, and unintelligible, because men start from a mental attitude not the author's, but their own, which through long habit has become a second nature. But the voluminous character of the work, so far as it depends on the subject, and not the exposition, its consequent unavoidable dryness, and its scholastic accuracy—these are qualities which can only benefit the science, though they may damage the book.

Few writers are gifted with the subtlety, and at the same time with the grace of David Hume, or with the depth, as well as the elegance, of Moses Mendelssohn. Yet I flatter myself I might have made my own exposition popular, had my object been merely to sketch out a plan, and leave its completion to others, instead of having my heart in the welfare of the science that I had so long pursued; in truth, it required no little constancy, and even self-denial, to postpone the sweets of an immediate success to the prospect of a slower, but more lasting reputation.

Making plans is often the occupation of a luxurious and boastful mind, which thus obtains the reputation of a creative genius, by demanding what it cannot itself supply; by censuring, what it cannot improve; and by proposing, what it knows not where to find. And yet something more should belong to a sound plan of a general Critique of the Pure Reason than mere conjectures, if this plan is to be other than the usual declamation of pious aspirations. But pure reason is a sphere so separate and self-contained, that we cannot touch a part without affecting all the rest. We can therefore do nothing without first determining the position of each part, and its relation to the rest; for, as our judgment cannot be corrected by anything without, the validity and use of every part depends upon the relation in which it stands to all the rest within reason.

So in the structure of an organized body, the end of each member can only be deduced from the full conception of the whole. It may, then, be said of such a Critique, that it is never trustworthy except it be *perfectly complete,* down to the smallest elements of the reason. In the sphere of this faculty you can determine either *everything* or *nothing*.

But altogether a mere sketch, preceding the Critique of Pure Reason, would be unintelligible, unreliable and useless, it is all the more useful as a sequel. For so we are abie to grasp the whole, to examine in detail the chief points of importance in the science, and to improve in many respects our exposition, as compared with the first execution of the work.

Such is the plan sketched out in the following pages, which, after the completion of the work, may be carried out *analytically,* though the work itself must absolutely be executed in the *synthetical* method, in order that the science may present all its articulations, as the structure of a peculiar cognitive faculty, in their natural combination. But should any reader find this plan, which I publish as the Prolegomena to any future Metaphysics, itself difficult, let him consider that every one is not bound to study Metaphysics, that there are many minds which succeed very well, in genuine and even deep sciences more closely allied to intuition, while they cannot succeed in investigations proceeding only by means of abstract concepts. In such cases men should apply their talents to other subjects. But he that undertakes to judge, or still more to construct a system of Metaphysics, must satisfy the demands here made, either by adopting my solution, or by thoroughly refuting it, and substituting another. To evade it is impossible.

In conclusion, let it be remembered that this much-abused obscurity—a very common cloak for men's own laziness or stupidity—has its uses, since all who in other sciences observe a prudent silence, in this speak authoritatively, and decide boldly, because their ignorance is not here contrasted with the knowledge of others. . . .

This is the proper place to remove Hume's difficulty. He justly maintains, that we can by no means see by reason the possibility of Causality, that is, of the reference of the existence of one thing to the existence of another, which is necessitated by the former. I add, that we comprehend just as little the concept of Subsistence, that is, the necessity that at the foundation of the existence of things there lies a subject which cannot itself be a predicate of any other thing; nay, we cannot even form a notion of the possibility of such a thing (though we can point out examples of its use in experience). The very same incomprehensibility affects the Community of things, as we cannot comprehend how from the state of one thing an inference to the state of quite another thing beyond it, and *vice versa*, can be drawn, and how substances which have each their own separate existence should depend upon one another necessarily. But I am very far from holding these concepts to be derived merely from experience, and the necessity represented in them, to be imaginary and a mere illusion produced in us by long habit. On the contrary, I have amply shown, that the principles [derived] from them are firmly established *a priori*, or before all experience, and have their undoubted objective value, though only with regard to experience.

I have indeed no notion of such a connexion of things in themselves, that they can either exist as substances, or act as causes, or stand in community with others (as parts of a real whole), and I can just as little conceive such properties in phenomena as such, because those concepts contain nothing that lies in the phenomena, but what the understanding alone must think. But we have a concept of such connexion of representations in our understanding, and in judgments generally—a concept that representations appear in one sort of judgments as subject in relation to predicate, in another as reason in relation to consequence, and in a third as parts, which constitute together a total possible cognition. Besides we cognise *a priori* that without considering the representation of an object as determined in some of these respects, we can have no valid cognition of the object, and, if we should occupy ourselves about the object *per se*, there is no possible attribute, by which I could know that it is determined under any of these aspects, that is, under the concept either of substance, or of cause, or (in relation to other substances) of community, for I have no notion of the possibility of such a connexion of existence [*per se*]. But the question is not how things in themselves, but how the empirical cognition of things is determined, as regards the above aspects of judgments in general, that is, how things, as objects of experience, can and shall be subsumed under these concepts of the understanding. And then it is clear, that I completely comprehend not only the possibility, but also the necessity of subsuming all phenomena under these concepts, that is, of using them for principles of the possibility of experience.

Let us make an experiment with Hume's problematical concept (his *crux metaphysicorum*), the concept of cause. In the first place I am given *a priori*, by means of logic, the form of a conditional judgment in general, that is, one given cognition as antecedent and another as consequent. But it is possible, that in perception we may meet with a rule of relation, which runs thus: that a certain phenomenon is constantly followed by another (though not conversely), and this is a case for me to use the hypothetical judgment, and, for instance, to say, if the sun shines long enough upon a body, it grows warm. Here there is indeed as yet no necessity of connexion, or concept of cause. But I proceed and say, that if the [above] proposition, which is merely a subjective connexion of perceptions, is to be a judgment of experience, it must be considered as necessary and universally valid. Such a proposition would be, 'the sun is by its light the cause of heat.' The empirical rule is now considered as a law, and as valid not merely of phenomena, but valid of them for the purposes of a possible experience which requires thoroughly and therefore necessarily valid rules. I therefore easily comprehend the concept of cause, as a concept necessarily belonging to the mere form of experience, and its possibility as a synthetical union of perceptions in consciousness generally; but I do not at all comprehend the possibility of a thing generally as a cause, because the concept of cause denotes a condition not at all belonging to things, but to experience. It is nothing in fact but an objectively valid cognition of phenomena and of their succession, so far as the antecedent can be conjoined with the consequent according to the rule of hypothetical judgments.

Hence to the pure concepts of the understanding, if they quit objects of experience and would refer to things in themselves, (*noumena*) have no signification whatever. They serve, as it were, only to spell phenomena, that we may be able to read them as experience; the principles which arise from their reference to the sensible world, only serve our understanding for empirical use. Beyond this they are arbitrary combinations, without objective reality, and we can neither cognise their possibility *a priori*, nor verify their reference to objects or make it intelligible by any example; because examples can be borrowed from some possible experience, consequently the objects of these concepts can be found nowhere but in a possible experience.

This complete (though to its originator unexpected) solution of Hume's problem preserves therefore to the pure concepts of the understanding their *a priori* origin, and to the universal laws of nature their validity, as laws of the understanding, yet so that their use is limited to experience, because their possibility depends solely on the reference of the understanding to experience; but not by deriving them from experience, but by deriving it from them, a completely reversed mode of connexion which never occurred to Hume.

This is therefore the result of all our foregoing inquiries: all synthetical principles *a priori* are nothing more than principles of possible experience, and can never be referred to things in themselves, but to phenomena as objects of experience. And hence pure mathematic as well as pure physic can never be referred to anything more than mere phenomena, and can only represent either that which makes experience generally possible, or else that which, as it is derived from these principles, must always be capable of being represented in some possible experience. . . .

SECOND PART OF THE GENERAL TRANSCENDENTAL PROBLEM

How is the Pure Science of Nature possible?

Nature is the *existence* of things, so far as it is determined according to universal laws. Should nature signify the existence of things *in themselves,* we could never cognise nature either *a priori* or *a posteriori*. Not *a priori*, for how can we know what belongs to things in themselves, since this never can be done by the dissection of our concepts (analytical judgments)? For we do not want to know what is contained in our concept of a thing (for this [content] belongs to its logical being), but what is in the actuality of the thing superadded to our concept, and by what the thing itself is determined in its existence outside the concept. Our understanding, and the conditions on which alone it can connect the determinations of things in their existence, do not prescribe any rule to things themselves; these do not conform to our understanding, but it must conform itself to them; they must therefore be first given us in order to gather these determinations from them, wherefore they would not be cognised *a priori*.

A cognition of the nature of things in themselves *a posteriori* would be equally impossible. For, if experience is to teach us *laws*, to which the existence of things is subject, these laws, if they regard things in themselves, must belong to them *of necessity* even outside our experience. But experience teaches us what exists and how it exists, but never that it must necessarily exist so and not otherwise. Experience therefore can never teach us the nature of things in themselves....

How is Nature itself possible?

This question—the highest point that transcendental philosophy can ever reach, and to which, as its boundary and completion, it must proceed—properly contains two [subordinate] questions.

First: How is nature at all possible in the *material* sense, as to intuition, [I mean nature] considered as the complex of phenomena; how are space, time, and that which fills both—the object of sensation, in general possible? The answer is: By means of the constitution of our Sensibility, according to which it is specifically affected by objects, which are in themselves unknown to it, and totally distinct from those phenomena. This answer is given in the *Critique* itself in the transcendental Aesthetic, and in these *Prolegomena* by the solution of the first general problem.

Secondly: How is nature possible in the formal sense, nature as the complex of the rules, under which all phenomena must come, in order to be thought as connected in experience? The answer must be this: It is only possible by means of the constitution of our Understanding, according to which all the above representations of the sensibility are necessarily referred to a consciousness, and by which the peculiar way in which we think (that is, by rules), and hence experience also, are possible, but must be clearly distinguished from an insight into the objects in themselves. This answer is given in the *Critique* itself in the transcendental Logic, and in these *Prolegomena,* in the course of the solution of the second main problem.

But how this peculiar property of our sensibility itself is possible, or that of our understanding and of the apperception which is necessarily its basis and that of all thinking—this cannot be further resolved or answered, because we require these [faculties] for all our answers and for all our thinking about objects.

There are many laws of nature, which we can only know by means of experience; but conformity to law in the connexion of phenomena, that is, nature in general, we cannot discover by any experience, because experience itself requires laws, which are *a priori* at the basis of its possibility.

The possibility of experience in general is therefore at the same time the universal law of nature, and the principles of the former (experience) are the very laws of the latter (nature). For we do not know nature but as the complex of the phenomena, that is, of representations in us, and hence can only derive the laws of its connexion from the principles of their connexion in us, that is, from the conditions of their necessary union in consciousness, which union constitutes the possibility of experience.

Even the main proposition expounded throughout this section—that universal laws of nature can be distinctly cognised *a priori*—leads naturally to the proposition: that the highest legislation of nature must lie in ourselves (that is, in our understanding), and that we must not seek the universal laws of nature in nature by means of experience, but conversely must seek nature, as to its universal conformity to law, in the conditions of the possibility of experience, which lie in our sensibility and in our understanding. For how were it otherwise possible to know *a priori* these laws, as they are not rules of analytical cognition, but really synthetical extensions of it? Such a necessary agreement of the principles of possible experience with the laws of the possibility of nature, can only proceed from one of two reasons: either these laws are drawn from nature by means of experience, or conversely nature is derived from the laws of the possibility of experience in general, and is quite the same as the mere universal conformity to law of the latter. The former is self-contradictory, for the universal laws of nature can and must be cognised *a priori* (that is, independent of all experience), and be the foundation of all empirical use of the understanding; the latter alternative therefore alone remains.

But we must distinguish the empirical laws of nature, which always presuppose particular perceptions, from the pure or universal laws of nature, which, without being based on particular perceptions, contain merely the conditions of their necessary union in experience. In relation to the latter, nature and *possible* experience are quite the same, and as the conformity to law here depends upon the necessary connexion of phenomena in experience (without which we cannot cognise any object whatever in the sensible world), consequently upon the original laws of the understanding, it seems at first strange, but is not the less certain, to says as regards the latter: *The understanding does not draw its laws (a priori) from nature, but prescribes them to it.*

We shall illustrate this apparently daring proposition by an example which will show that laws, which we discover in objects of sensuous intuition (especially when these laws are cognised as necessary), are commonly held to be such as the understanding has placed in them, though they are similar in all points to the laws of nature, which we ascribe to experience.

If we consider the properties of the circle, by which this figure unites so many arbitrary determinations of space in itself, and therefore in a universal rule, we cannot avoid attributing a nature to this geometrical thing. Two right lines, for example, which intersect one another and the circle, however they may be drawn, are always divided so that the rectangle under the segments of the one is equal to that under the segments of the other. The question now is: Does this law lie in the circle or in the understanding? Does this figure, independently of the understanding, contain in itself the ground of the law, or does the understanding, having constructed according to its concepts (according to the equality of the radii) the figure itself, introduce into it this law of the chords cutting one another in geometrical proportion? When we follow the proofs of this law, we soon perceive, that it can only be derived from the condition on which the understanding founds the construction of this figure, and which is that of the equality of the radii. But, if we enlarge this concept, to pursue further the unity of various properties of geometrical figures under common laws, and consider the circle as a conic section, which of course is subject to the same fundamental conditions of construction as other conic sections, we shall find, that all the chords, which intersect within the ellipse, parabola, and hyperbola, always intersect so that the rectangles under their segments are not indeed equal, but always bear a constant ratio to one another [the directions of the chords being fixed]. If we proceed still farther, to the fundamental laws of physical astronomy, we find a physical law of reciprocal attraction diffused over all material nature, the rule of which attraction is: 'that it decreases inversely as the square of the distance from each attracting point, that is, as the spherical surfaces, over which this power diffuses itself—increase,' which law seems to be necessarily inherent in the very nature of things, and hence is usually propounded as cognisable *a priori*. Simple as the sources of this law are, merely resting upon the relation of spherical surfaces of different radii, its consequences are so valuable with regard to the variety of their agreement and its regularity, that not only are all possible orbits of the celestial bodies conic sections, but such a relation of these orbits to each other results, that no other law of attraction, than that of the inverse square of the distance, can be imagined as fit for a cosmical system.

Here then is a Nature that rests upon laws which the understanding cognises *a priori*, and chiefly from the universal principles of the determination of space. And the question now is: Do the laws of nature lie in space, and does the understanding learn them by merely endeavouring to find out the fruitful meaning that lies in space; or do they inhere in the understanding and in the way in which it determines space according to the conditions of the synthetical unity in which its concepts are all centred? Space is something so uniform and as to all particular properties so indeterminate, that we should certainly not seek a store of laws of nature in it. Whereas that which determines space to the form of a circle or to the figures of a sphere, is the understanding, so far as it contains the ground of the unity of their constructions. The mere universal form of intuition, called space, must therefore be the substream of all intuitions determinable to particular objects, and in it of course the condition of the possibility and of the variety of these intuitions lies. But the unity of the objects is entirely determined by the understanding, and on conditions which lie in its own nature; and thus the understanding is the origin of the universal order of nature, in that it comprehends all appearances under its own law, and thereby first constructs, *a priori*, experience (as to its form), by means of which whatever is to be cognised only by experience, is subjected to its laws necessarily. For we are not now concerned with the nature of things in themselves, which is independent of the conditions both of our sensibility and our understanding, but with nature, as an object of possible experience, and in this case the understanding, whilst it makes experience possible, thereby insists that the sensuous world is either not an object of experience at all, or must be Nature.

Chapter VII — God and Religion

Introduction

What is studied by the philosophy of religion? In order to answer this question clearly, we will have to make several distinctions.

Religion is one of the most universal practices of mankind. Some anthropologists have gone so far as to claim that from the earliest times to the present, no genuine human community has been without some form of religion. But the religious experience of mankind has taken many forms. It may involve the worship of spirits believed to inhabit the clouds, the rivers, and the forests; such practices are called *animistic.* It may involve the worship of many gods (polytheism), or just one (monotheism). The gods may be viewed as the Lords of Nature and of man, as in ancient Greek religion, or they may be seen as personifications of higher, more spiritual forces, as in Hinduism. Again, a religion may view the dieties simply as forces that must be placated through sacrifice and ritual, or it may take on an ethical element, in the sense that God or the gods are thought to be themselves morally good and therefore desirous of moral behavior on the part of mankind.

Religion is a social as well as an individual phenomenon, and is subject to variations throughout human history along with society itself. In universities today, the study of the origins, the kinds, and the social dimensions or religious practices may be the province of anthropology, of history, of comparative religion, or of sociology. The philosophy of religion may presuppose such studies, but it is not concerned with them directly. Indeed, the philosophical tradition of the West has normally not concerned itself with the religious experience of mankind as a whole, but rather only with that of its own culture, that is, with Judaism, Christianity, and Islam, and with the one God worshipped by Jews, Christians, and Moslems. But it is *not* concerned with articulating the content of these religions, either descriptively, as in the case of history and comparative religion, or substantively, i.e., by developing a system of religious belief. The latter study is one of the tasks of *theology*. Theology is the attempt to give an account of God, His relation to the world we inhabit, and His designs for mankind. Theology has traditionally taken two forms. One is *revealed* theology, where the special revelations of God to man in the Holy Books are accepted as genuine, and where these books are then searched in the hope of finding further insight into the nature of the Divine. The other is called *natural* theology; this study begins with the world as the creation of God, and seeks to understand the ways of God by studying His handiwork. What, for example, does the apparent evil in this world have to tell us about the nature of God? Does it suggest that God is not all good? Or that He is not all powerful, that is, He is incapable of preventing some evils? Or perhaps what we call evil is not evil in the eyes of God? These are theological questions, not philosophical ones, but they share with philosophy a concern for consistency, an emphasis upon rational argumentation, and a desire to speculate about the unknown on the basis of what is known.

In the great religions of the Western world, a further distinction can be made between *positive* or *objective,* and *subjective* religion. Positive religion refers to what is sometimes called institutional religion: an organized church, with its ecclesiastical hierarchy, its rites and rituals, its scriptures and dogmas, its congregation. Subjective religion, on the other hand, refers to the individual worshipper and his experience of God. Here belong the phenomena associated with *faith*: the individual who "gives himself over to God," who prays, who feels the presence of God in the world, who seeks his salvation with fear and trembling before the might of God.

The philosophy of religion is not concerned, of course, with either strengthening or weakening the religious institutions of its community, or with reinforcing or subverting religious faith, although some philosophers may in fact attempt to do one or the other. However, the philosophy of religion normally begins with an exploration of the edifices of belief and experience upon which organized religion and personal faith are erected. Philosophy approaches religion from the outside, as it were, and reflects systematically upon the claims to truth projected by the religious institutions and the religious way of life. The typical questions that it asks of religion are as follows:

1. *What reasons do we have for believing in the existence of God?* The world, at least at first sight, appears to be without a God. God is not part of the visible furniture of the universe; neither the objects beneath our feet, nor those in the most remote depths of outer space, which we probe with our optical and radio telescopes, have revealed to us the presence of something divine. Of course it might be that God is supernaturally present in the world about us, that He is beyond the world as its ultimate creator, and within the world as our

judge. But what reasons do we have for believing this to be so? The approach to this question which has attracted the most attention from philosophers is the efforts of some thinkers to develop a rational *argument* for the existence of God. These efforts are usually classified under three rubrics: the *ontological* argument, the *cosmological* argument, and the *teleological* argument. The *ontological* argument asserts that the existence of God is implied by our very concept of God. You will encounter such an argument in the selection from Descartes in this chapter, and the core concept of the argument is usually traced to the eleventh-century philosopher and theologian Saint Anselm. The *cosmological* argument begins with the fact of physical events and occurrences in the world, and argues that these events could not have occurred without the agency of God. How could there be change at all, argues Saint Thomas Aquinas, unless God at some point initiated change? Indeed, how could there be a world of changing things at all unless a being *beyond* the world created it? And there is the *teleological* argument, which you will find in the selection from Saint Thomas, and elaborated upon in the essay by William Paley. This argument is a form of the cosmological argument, for it goes from a set of facts about the world to the conclusion that God must exist as the ultimate ground of these facts. In the teleological argument, the relevant facts are those which reveal an underlying order or structure in the events of nature. How is it possible that such an incredibly complex, yet orderly and goal-directed instrument as the human brain could come to be without the directing hand of a supernatural and infinitely intelligent and powerful deity? Just as the existence of the watch points to the existence of a watchmaker, so does the world point to the existence of its Creator. But the nineteenth-century philosopher John Stuart Mill, who gives us a more contemporary statement of the cosmological argument, attempts to show that modern standards of scientific and logical analysis fail to support the principles that underlie it. "The world does not, by its mere existence," Mill says, "bear witness to a God."

However, religion is not founded upon rational argument alone. Another pillar of faith is found in the Holy Books—the Old Testament, the New Testament, and the Koran—works which, in their sublimity and profundity, appear to the religious believer to be the Word of God itself. Although the Bible does not contain any proofs for the existence of God, it has always had the power to inspire men to faith. The philosopher, approaching religion from the outside, will ask whether any book could justify its own authority. Clearly, I may be able to tell whether the claims made by my daily newspaper are true by conducting my own investigation, but how could I judge whether the claim made by the Bible, that it represents the Word of God, is true? No investigation seems to be possible; we are left only with faith, or the lack of it. And in the essay entitled "The Will to Believe," William James inquires as to whether it could ever be reasonable to believe in God in the absence of formal proof, or at least without more evidence than the testimony of the Bible itself. His conclusions are quite controversial, but challenging, and may have the power to draw you closer to religion, as James himself was drawn to it.

If one is not led to religious belief by the power of Holy Scripture, however, there is still the possibility that your own experience of the religious dimensions of the world will convince you that God exists. For many persons have claimed that each of us possesses, at least potentially, a special mode of awareness, called "insight" or the "sense of the noumenal" or "mystical states of consciousness" that gives us access to God. If this is so, the philosophers may ask, what is the nature of those states, and how can one ever be sure that one has had such an experience? In our final chapter, Bertrand Russell takes up the claims of mystics—that they possess special powers of insight which give them direct knowledge of things divine—and submits them to philosophical scrutiny. His efforts are typical of the attitudes of naturalistic and pragmatic philosophers, and constitute a contribution to the philosophy of religion that has today become classic.

2. *What is the value of positive religion?* It has long been debated by philosophers whether religious institutions and religious education have had a salutary or a destructive influence upon mankind. It has been argued on the one hand, that religion is *destructive* of human good: it justifies warfare against neighboring peoples who practice a religion different from one's own; it may be used as an instrument to oppress the lower classes, promising happiness in the world to come in return for obedience in this world (note the anti-religious attitudes expressed by Karl Marx and Friedrich Engels in the *Communist Manifesto,* Chapter IV). What is more, religious dogma may be inimical to the free expression of new and potentially valuable ideas (e.g., the suppression of the Copernican theory of a heliocentric solar system by the Catholic Inquisition), and, because of its apparent belief that life in this world is merely a preparation for heaven, detract from the values inherent in this life, suggesting instead that the enjoyment of life for its own sake is sinful.

On the other hand, it has also been argued that established religion has made positive contributions to mankind. It has provided us with a sense of being part of a universal community, which, under the fatherhood of God, has worked to further the brother and sisterhood of all mankind. Churches have worked for the alleviation of poverty, contributed to the aid of the outcast and the scorned, and have, far more often than not, supported institutions of learning, and the development of secular knowledge. Perhaps most importantly, religions have brought a moral message to all mankind, namely that we must do good to others for the love of God. And it is this message that is investigated by Denis Diderot in the dialogue you will read in this chapter. If religion were abandoned by mankind, and the moral message of the churches should be heard no more, with its promise of heaven and its threat of hell, wouldn't people return to barbarism? Wouldn't we decide that everything is allowed, and begin to act like beasts? Nonsense, says Diderot, and his character Crudeli tries to demonstrate to the Maréchale that the churches in fact contribute to, rather than correct, the evil dispositions of men.

3. *What is the value of faith as a personal attitude toward life?* In the nineteenth century, the Danish philosopher and theologian Søren Kierkegaard

contended that since the arguments for the existence of God are unconvincing, and the authority of the Bible as the Word of God can be questioned on historical grounds, those who would be truly religious are required to take a "leap of faith"—to believe in God although His existence is objectively uncertain. And in Chapter VIII, we will encounter Kierkegaard's interpretation of *truth* as something to be achieved by subjectively appropriating an uncertain belief to myself, and organizing my life around that belief. Granting that Kierkegaard is correct in his assessment of religion as subjectively uncertain and as requiring a leap, it remains to be asked why anyone might wish to take such a leap. Why not choose instead to live the life of the atheist, content with the meanings and values discoverable in this life alone? One may simply seek the Good Life for man, and abandon the perennial search for the Infinite and the Divine. Friedrich Nietzsche argues for this point of view in the selections from his works to be found in Chapter VIII. Belief in God is dying out in the Western world in any case, says Nietzsche; but instead of succumbing to the view that life is meaningless because there is no God and no immortality, let us instead have the courage to create our own values and meanings.

This attitude toward religion was later reinforced by psychology. Sigmund Freud, for example, claimed that broad philosophical or religious theories of the nature of the world and the meaning of life are projections of unconscious attitudes that can be explained in terms of the dynamic psychic processes common to all mankind. Far better, Freud thought, to abandon religion and seek happiness in this world by applying our newly developed knowledge of the origins of human behavior to the improvement of that behavior. His view that religious belief is a manifestation of a mild neurosis has done much to destroy the credibility of religion in our own day, even though it does not disprove God's existence: after all, a belief could be founded in neurosis and yet be true. Many philosophers, including Martin Buber, argue against a psychological interpretation of religious experience, and insist upon searching the human spirit for the sources of our sense of the divine Presence in the world.

Finally, the school of philosophy known as existentialism, which is represented in Chapter VIII by the contemporary French thinker Jean-Paul Sartre, has numbered many religious believers, like Kierkegaard, among its ranks. Existentialists have normally stressed the same incomprehensibleness of God that the positivists complain about; for such as Kierkegaard, this remoteness of God from human understanding simply forces faith to become that much more "subjective." But Sartre, who is an atheist, believes that even if God did exist, it would make little difference to an appraisal of the human situation. In any case, he says, men are condemned to be free: we are forced to decide what will be the meaning of our lives. If I believe that God commands me to live in a certain way, it is still I myself who must appropriate the divine commands to myself; I alone must decide which of God's commands are authentic. Religious belief, Sartre appears to suggest, may serve the weak-minded as a crutch supporting their failed lives; but for those men who realize the extent of their own freedom, God will have little significance.

It will not come as a surprise to you that the twentieth century has generally come down hard upon religious belief. Perhaps this antipathy is due to the influence of science and the scientific method. After all, most people think that if you can't know something scientifically, then you can't know it at all—and no one today would suggest that God could or should become the subject of scientific investigation. But you ought not to conclude that genuine religious belief is no longer possible for an intelligent, educated person, or that your own religious belief or lack of it has nothing to gain from a discussion of past thinkers. Our selections in this chapter and the next will give you a broad philosophical perspective upon religion. If you are not afraid to think through their criticism of your stance towards religion, and to try to criticize them in turn, you will profit from them.

Saint Anselm of Canterbury: The Ontological Argument

And so, Lord, do thou, who dost give understanding to faith, give me, so far as thou knowest it to be profitable, to understand that thou art as we believe; and that thou art that which we believe. And, indeed, we believe that thou art a being than which nothing greater can be conceived. Or is there no such nature, since the fool hath said in his heart, there is no God? (Psalms xiv. 1). But, at any rate, this very fool, when he hears of this being of which I speak—a being than which nothing greater can be conceived—understands what he hears, and what he understands is in his understanding; although he does not understand it to exist.

For, it is one thing for an object to be in the understanding, and another to understand that the object exists. When a painter first conceives of what he will afterwards perform, he has it in his understanding, but he does not yet understand it to be, because he has not yet performed it. But after he has made the painting, he both has it in his understanding, and he understands that it exists, because he has made it.

Hence, even the fool is convinced that something exists in the understanding, at least, than which nothing greater can be conceived. For, when he hears of this, he understands it. And whatever is understood, exists in the understanding. And assuredly that, than which nothing greater can be conceived, cannot exist in the understanding alone. For, suppose it exists in the understanding alone: the it can be conceived to exist in reality; which is greater.

Therefore, if that, than which nothing greater can be conceived, exists in the understanding alone, the very being, than which nothing greater can be conceived, is one, than which a greater can be conceived. But obviously this is impossible. Hence, there is no doubt that there exists a being, than which nothing greater can be conceived, and it exists both in the understanding and in reality.

And it assuredly exists so truly, that it cannot be conceived not to exist. For, it is possible to conceive of a being which cannot be conceived not to exist; and this is greater than one which can be conceived not to exist. Hence, if that, than which nothing greater can be conceived, can be conceived not to exist, it is not that, than which nothing greater can be conceived. But this is an irreconcilable contradiction. There is, then, so truly a being than which nothing greater can be conceived to exist, that it cannot even be conceived not to exist; and this being thou art, O Lord, our God.

So truly, therefore, dost thou exist, O Lord, my God, that thou canst not be conceived not to exist; and rightly. For, if a mind could conceive of a being better than thee, the creature would rise above the Creator; and this is most absurd. And, indeed, whatever else there is, except thee alone, can be conceived not to exist. To thee alone, therefore, it belongs to exist more truly than all other beings, and hence in a higher degree than all others. For, whatever else exists does not exist so truly, and hence in a less degree it belongs to it to exist. Why, then, has the fool said in his heart, there is no God (Psalms, xiv. 1), since it is so evident, to a rational mind, that thou dost exist in the highest degree of all? Why, except that he is dull and a fool?

But how has the fool said in his heart what he could not conceive; or how is it that he could not conceive what he said in his heart? since it is the same to say in the heart, and to conceive.

But, if really, nay, since really, he both conceived, because he said in his heart; and did not say in his heart because he could not conceive. there is more than one way in which a thing is said in the heart or conceived. For, in one sense, an object is conceived, when the word signifying it is conceived; and in another, when the very entity, which the object is, is understood.

In the former sense, then, God can be conceived not to exist; but in the latter, not at all. For no one who understands what fire and water are can conceive fire to be water, in accordance with the nature of the facts themselves, although this is possible according to the words. So, then, no one who understands what God is can conceive that God does not exist; although he says these words in his heart, either without any, or with some foreign signification. For God is that than which a greater cannot be conceived. And he who thoroughly understands this, assuredly understands that this being so truly exists, that not even in concept can it be non-existent. Therefore, he who understands that God so exists, cannot conceive that he does not exist.

I thank thee, gracious Lord, I thank thee; because what I formerly believed by thy bounty, I now so understand by thine illumination, that if I were unwilling to believe that thou dost exist, I should not be able not to understand this to be true.

René Descartes: Of God: That He Exists

I will now close my eyes, I will stop my ears, I will turn away my senses from their objects, I will even efface from my consciousness all the images of corporeal things; or at least, because this can hardly be accomplished, I will consider them as empty and false; and thus, holding converse only with myself, and closely examining my nature, I will endeavor to obtain by degrees a more intimate and familiar knowledge of myself. I am a thinking (conscious) thing, that is, a being who doubts, affirms, denies, knows a few objects, and is ignorant of many,—(who loves, hates), wills, refuses, who imagines likewise, and perceives; for, as I before remarked, although the things which I perceive or imagine are perhaps nothing at all apart from me (and in themselves), I am nevertheless assured that those modes of consciousness which I call perceptions and imaginations, in as far only as they are modes of consciousness, exist in me. And in the little I have said I think I have summed up all that I really know, or at least all that up to this time I was aware I knew. Now, as I am endeavoring to extend my knowledge more widely, I will use circumspection, and consider with care whether I can still discover in myself anything further which I have not yet hitherto observed. I am certain that I am a thinking thing; but do I not therefore likewise know what is required to render me certain of a truth? In this first knowledge, doubtless, there is nothing that gives me assurance of its truth except the clear and distinct perception of what I affirm, which would not indeed be sufficient to give me the assurance that what I say is true, if it could ever happen that anything I thus clearly and distinctly perceived should prove false; and accordingly it seems to me that I may now take as a general rule, that all that is very clearly and distinctly apprehended (conceived) is true.

Nevertheless I before received and admitted many things as wholly certain and manifest, which yet I afterward found to be doubtful. What, then, were those? They were the earth, the sky, the stars, and all the other objects which I was in the habit of perceiving by the senses. But what was it that I clearly and distinctly perceived in them? Nothing more than that the ideas and the thoughts of those objects were presented to my mind. And even now I do not deny that these ideas are found in my mind. But there was yet another thing which I affirmed, and which, from having been accustomed to believe it, I thought I clearly perceived, although, in truth, I did not perceive it at all; I mean the existence of objects external to me, from which those ideas proceeded, and to which they had a perfect resemblance; and it was here I was mistaken, or if I judged correctly, this assuredly was not to be traced to any knowledge I possessed.

But when I considered any matter in arithmetic and geometry, that was very simple and easy, as, for example, that two and three added together make five, and things of this sort, did I not view them with at least sufficient clearness to warrant me in affirming their truth? Indeed, if I afterward judged that we ought to doubt of these things, it was for no other reason than because it occurred to me that a God might perhaps have given me such a nature as that I should be deceived, even respecting the

The selection has been taken from Descartes' *Meditations* (3).

matters that appeared to me the most evidently true. But as often as this preconceived opinion of the sovereign power of a God presents itself to my mind, I am constrained to admit that it is easy for him, if he wishes it, to cause me to err, even in matters where I think I possess the highest evidence; and, on the other hand, as often as I direct my attention to things which I think I apprehend with great clearness, I am so persuaded of their truth that I naturally break out into expressions such as these: Deceive me who may, no one will yet ever be able to bring it about that I am not, so long as I shall be conscious that I am, or at any future time cause it to be true that I have never been, it being now true that I am, or make two and three more or less than five, in supposing which, and other like absurdities, I discover a manifest contradiction.

And in truth, as I have no ground for believing that God is deceitful, and as, indeed, I have not even considered the reasons by which the existence of God of any kind is established, the ground of doubt that rests only on this supposition is very slight, and, so to speak, metaphysical. But, that I may be able wholly to remove it, I must inquire whether there is a God, as soon as an opportunity of doing so shall present itself; and if I find that there is a God, I must examine likewise whether he can be a deceiver; for, without the knowledge of these two truths, I do not see that I can ever be certain of anything. And that I may be enabled to examine this without interrupting the order of meditation I have proposed to myself which is, to pass by degrees from the notions that I shall find first in my mind to those I shall afterward discover in it, it is necessary at this stage to divide all my thoughts into certain classes, and to consider in which of these classes truth and error are, strictly speaking, to be found.

Of my thoughts some are, as it were, images of things, and to these alone properly belong the name ideas; as when I think [represent to my mind] a man, a chimera, the sky, an angel or God. Others, again, have certain other forms; as when I will, fear, affirm, or deny, I always, indeed, apprehend something as the object of my thought, but I also embrace in thought something more than the representation of the object; and of this class of thoughts some are called volitions or affections, and others judgments.

Now, with respect to ideas, if these are considered only in themselves, and are not referred to any object beyond them, they cannot, properly speaking, be false; for, whether I imagine a goat or chimera, it is not less true that I imagine the one than the other. Nor need we fear that falsity may exist in the will or affections; for, although I may desire objects that are wrong, and even that never existed, it is still true that I desire them. There thus only remain our judgments, in which we must take diligent heed that we be not deceived. But the chief and most ordinary error that arises in them consists in judging that the ideas which are in us are conformed to the things that are external to us; for assuredly, if we but considered the ideas themselves as certain modes of our thought (consciousness), without referring them to anything beyond, they could hardly afford any occasion of error.

But among these ideas, some appear to me to be innate, others adventitious, and others to be made by myself (factitious); for, as I have the power of conceiving what is called a thing, or a truth, or a thought, it seems to me that I hold this power from no other source than my own nature; but if I now hear a noise, if I see the sun, or if I feel heat, I have all along judged that these sensations proceeded from certain objects existing out of myself; and, in fine, it appears to me that sirens, hippogryphs, and the like, are inventions of my own mind. But I may even perhaps come to be of opinion that all my ideas are of the class which I call adventitious, or that they are all innate, or that they are all factitious; for I have not yet clearly discovered their true origin; and what I have here principally to do is to consider, with reference to those that appear to come from certain objects without me, what grounds there are for thinking them like these objects.

The first of these grounds is that it seems to me I am so taught by nature; and the second that I am conscious that those ideas are not dependent on my will, and therefore not in myself, for they are frequently presented to me against my will, as at present, whether I will or not, I feel heat; and I am thus persuaded that this sensation or idea (*sensum vel ideam*) of heat is produced in me by something different from myself, viz., by the heat of the fire by which I sit. And it is very reasonable to suppose that this object impresses me with its own likeness rather than any other thing.

But I must consider whether these reasons are sufficiently strong and convincing. When I speak of being taught by nature in this matter, I understand by the word nature only a certain spontaneous impetus that impels me to believe in a resemblance between ideas and their objects, and not a natural light that affords a knowledge of its truth. But these two things are widely different; for what the natural light shows to be true can be in no degree doubtful, as, for example, that I am because I doubt, and other truths of the like kind; inasmuch as I possess no other faculty whereby to distinguish truth from error, which can teach me the falsity of what the natural light declares to be true, and which is equally trustworthy; but with respect to seemingly natural impulses, I have observed, when the question related to the choice of right or wrong in action, that they frequently led me to take the worse part; nor do I see that I have any better ground for following them in what relates to truth and error. Then, with respect to the other reason, which is that because these ideas do not depend on my will, they must arise from objects existing without me, I do not find it more convincing than the former; for just as those natural impulses, of which I have lately spoken, are found in me, notwithstanding that they are not always in harmony with my will, so likewise it may be that I possess some power not sufficiently known to myself capable of producing ideas without the aid of external objects, and, indeed, it has always hitherto appeared to me that they are formed during sleep, by some power of this nature, without the aid of something external. And, in fine, although I should grant that they proceeded from those objects, it is not a necessary consequence that they must be like them. On the contrary, I have observed, in a number of instances, that there was a great difference between the object and its idea. Thus, for example, I find in my mind two wholly diverse ideas of the sun; the one, by which it appears to me extremely small draws its origin from the senses; and should be placed in the class of adventitious ideas; the other, by which it seems to be many times larger than the whole earth, is taken up on astronomical grounds, that is, elicited from certain notions born with me, or is framed by myself in some other manner. These two ideas cannot certainly both resemble the same sun; and reason teaches me that the one which seems to have immediately emanated from it is the most unlike. And these things sufficiently prove that hitherto it has not been from a certain and deliberate judgment, but only from a sort of blind impulse, that I believe in the existence of certain things different from myself, which, by the organs of sense, or by whatever other means it might be, conveys their ideas or images into my mind and impressed it with their likenesses.

But there is still another way of inquiring whether, of the objects whose ideas are in my mind, there are any that exist out of me. If ideas are taken in so far only as they are certain modes of consciousness, I do not remark any difference or inequality among them, and all seem, in the same manner, to proceed from myself; but, considering them as images, of which one represents one thing and another a different, it is evident that a great diversity obtains among them. For, without doubt, those that represent substances are something more, and contain in themselves, so to speak, more objective reality [that is, participate by representation in higher degrees of being or perfection], than those that represent only modes or accidents; and again, the idea by which I conceive a God sovereign, eternal, infinite, immutable, all-knowing, all-powerful, and the creator of all things that are out of himself, this, I say, has certainly in it more objective reality than those ideas by which finite substances are represented.

Now, it is manifest by the natural light that there must at least be as much reality in the efficient and total cause as in its effect; for whence can the effect draw its reality if not from its cause? And how could the cause communicate to it this reality unless it possessed it in itself? And hence it follows, not only that what is cannot be produced by what is not, but likewise that the more perfect, in other words, that which contains in itself more reality, cannot be the effect of the less perfect; and this is not only evidently true of those effects, whose reality is actual or formal, but likewise of ideas, whose reality is only considered as objective. Thus, for example, the stone that is not yet in existence, not only cannot now commence to be, unless it be produced by that which possesses in itself, formally or eminently, all that enters into its composition, [in other words, by that which contains in itself the same properties that are in the stone, or others superior to them]; and heat can only be produced in a subject that was before devoid of it, by a cause that is of an order, degree or kind, at least as perfect as heat; and so of the others. But further, even the idea of the heat, or of the stone, cannot exist in me unless it be put there by a cause that contains, at least, as much reality as I conceive existent in the heat or in the stone: for although that cause may not transmit into my idea anything of its actual or formal reality, we ought not on this account to imagine that it is less real; but we ought to consider, that, as every idea is a work of the mind, its nature is such as of itself to demand no other formal reality than that which it borrows from our consciousness, of which it is but a mode [that is, a manner or way of thinking]. But in order that an idea may contain this objective reality rather than that, it must doubtless derive it from some cause in which is found at least as much formal reality as the idea contains of objective; for, if we suppose that there is found in an idea anything which was not in its cause, it must of course derive this from nothing.

But, however, imperfect may be the mode of existence by which a thing is objectively [or by representation] in the understanding by its idea, we certainly cannot, for all that, allege that this mode of existence is nothing, nor, consequently, that the idea owes its origin to nothing. Nor must it be imagined that, since the reality which is considered in these ideas is only objective, the same reality need not be formally (actually) in the causes of these ideas, but only objectively: for, just as the mode of existing objectively belongs to ideas by their peculiar nature, so likewise the mode of existing formally appertains to the causes of these ideas (at least to the first and principal), by their peculiar nature. And although an idea may give rise to another idea, this regress cannot, nevertheless, be infinite; we must in the end reach a first idea, the cause of which is, as it were, the archetype in which all the reality [or perfection] that is found objectively in these ideas is contained formally. I am thus clearly taught by the natural light that ideas exist in me as pictures or images, which may, in truth, readily fall short of the perfection of the objects from which they are taken, but can never contain anything greater or more perfect.

And in proportion to the time and care with which I examine all those matters, the conviction of their truth brightens and becomes distinct. But, to sum up, what conclusion shall I draw from it all? It is this: if the objective reality [or perfection] of any one of my ideas be such as clearly to convince me, that this same reality exists in me neither formally nor eminently, and if, as follows from this, I myself cannot be the cause of it, it is a necessary consequence that I am not alone in the world, but that there is besides myself some other being who exists as the cause of that idea; while, on the contrary, if no such idea be found in my mind, I shall have no sufficient ground of assurance of the existence of any other being besides myself; for, after a most careful search, I have, up to this moment, been unable to discover any other ground.

But, among these my ideas, besides that which represents myself, respecting which there can be here no difficulty, there is one that represents a God; others that represent corporeal and inanimate things; others angels; other animals; and, finally, there are some that represent men like myself. But with respect to the ideas that represent other men, or animals, or angels, I can easily suppose that they were formed by the mingling and composition of the other ideas which I have of myself, of corporeal things, and of God, although they were, apart from myself, neither men, animals, nor angels. And with regard to the ideas of corporeal objects, I never discovered in them anything so great or excellent which I myself did not appear capable of originating; for, by considering these ideas closely and scrutinizing them individually, in the same way that I yesterday examined the idea of wax, I find that there is but little in them that is clearly and distinctly perceived. As belonging to the class of things that are clearly apprehended, I recognize the following, viz, magnitude or extension in length, breadth, and depth; figure, which results from the termination of extension; situation, which bodies of diverse figures preserve with reference to each other; and motion or the change of situation; to which may be added substance, duration, and number. But with regard to light, colors, sounds, odors, tastes, heat, cold, and the other tactile qualities, they are thought with so much obscurity and confusion, that I cannot determine even whether they are true or false;

in other words, whether or not the ideas I have of these qualities are in truth the ideas of real objects. For although I before remarked that it is only in judgments that formal falsity, or falsity properly so called, can be met with, there may nevertheless be found in ideas a certain material falsity, which arises when they represent what is nothing as if it were something.

Thus, for example, the ideas I have of cold and heat are so far from being clear and distinct, that I am unable from them to discover whether cold is only the privation of heat, or heat the privation of cold; or whether they are or are not real qualities; and since, ideas being as it were images there can be none that does not seem to us to represent some object, the idea which represents cold as something real and positive will not improperly be called false, if it be correct to say that cold is nothing but a privation of heat; and so in other cases. To ideas of this kind, indeed, it is not necessary that I should assign any author besides myself: for if they are false, that is, represent objects that are unreal, the natural light teaches me that they proceed from nothing; in other words, that they are in me only because something is wanting to the perfection of my nature; but if these ideas are true, yet because they exhibit to me so little reality that I cannot even distinguish the object represented from non-being, I do not see why I should not be the author of them.

With reference to those ideas of corporeal things that are clear and distinct, there are some which, as appears to me, might have been taken from the idea I have of myself, as those of substance, duration, number, and the like. For when I think that a stone is a substance, or a thing capable of existing of itself, and that I am likewise a substance, although I conceive that I am a thinking and non-extended thing, and that the stone, on the contrary, is extended and unconscious, there being thus the greatest diversity between the two concepts, yet these two ideas seem to have this in common that they both represent substances. In the same way, when I think of myself as now existing, and recollect besides that I existed some time ago, and when I am conscious of various thoughts whose number I know, I then acquire the ideas of duration and number, which I can afterward transfer to as many objects as I please. With respect to the other qualities that go to make up the ideas of corporeal objects, viz, extension, figure, situation, and motion, it is true that they are not formally in me, since I am merely a thinking being; but because they are only certain modes of substance, and because I myself am a substance, it seems possible that they may be contained in me eminently.

There only remains, therefore, the idea of God, in which I must consider whether there is anything that cannot be supposed to originate with myself. By the name God, I understand a substance infinite, eternal, immutable, independent, all-knowing, all-powerful, and by which I myself, and every other thing that exists, if any such there be, were created. But these properties are so great and excellent, that the more attentively I consider them the less I feel persuaded that the idea I have of them owes its origin to myself alone. And thus it is absolutely necessary to conclude, from all that I have before said, that God exists: for though the idea of substance be in my mind owing to this, that I myself am a substance, I should not, however, have the idea of an infinite substance, seeing I am a finite being, unless it were given me by some substance in reality infinite.

And I must not imagine that I do not apprehend the infinite by a true idea, but only by the negation of the finite, in the same way that I comprehend repose and darkness by the negation of motion and light: since, on the contrary, I clearly perceive that there is more reality in the infinite substance than in the finite, and therefore that in some way I possess the perception (notion) of the infinite before that of the finite, that is, the perception of God before that of myself, for how could I think that I doubt, desire, or that something is wanting to me, and that I am not wholly perfect, if I possessed no idea of a being more perfect than myself, by comparison of which I knew the deficiencies of my nature?

And it cannot be said that this idea of God is perhaps materially false, and consequently that it may have arisen from nothing [in other words, that it may exist in me from my imperfection], as I before said of the ideas of heat and cold, and the like: for, on the contrary, as this idea is very clear and distinct, and contains in itself more objective reality than any other, there can be no one of itself more true, or less open to the suspicion of falsity.

The idea, I say, of a being supremely perfect, and infinite, is in the highest degree true; for although, perhaps, we may imagine that such a being does not exist, we cannot, nevertheless, suppose that his idea represents nothing real, as I have already said of the idea of cold. It is likewise clear and distinct in the highest degree, since whatever the mind clearly and distinctly conceives as real or true, and as implying any perfection, is contained entire in this idea. And this is true, nevertheless, although I do not comprehend the infinite, and although there may be in God an infinity of things that I cannot comprehend, nor perhaps even compass by thought in any way; for it is of the nature of the infinite that it should not be comprehended by the finite; and it is enough that I rightly understand this, and judge that all which I clearly perceive, and in which I know there is some perfection, and perhaps also an infinity of properties of which I am ignorant, are formally or eminently in God, in order that the idea I have of him may become the most true, clear, and distinct of all the ideas in my mind.

But perhaps I am something more than I suppose myself to be, and it may be that all those perfections which I attribute to God, in some way exist potentially in me, although they do not yet show themselves, and are not reduced to act. Indeed, I am already conscious that my knowledge is being increased and perfected by degrees; and I see nothing to prevent it from thus gradually increasing to infinity, nor any reason why, after such increase and perfection, I should not be able thereby to acquire all the other perfections of the Divine nature; nor, in fine, why the power I possess of acquiring those perfections, if it really now exist in me, should not be sufficient to produce the ideas of them. Yet in looking more closely into the matter, I discover that this cannot be; for, in the first place, although it were true that my knowledge daily acquired new degrees of perfection, and although there were potentially in my nature much that was not as yet actually in it, still all these excellences make not the slightest approach to the idea I have of God in whom there is no perfection merely potentially [but all actually] existent; for it is even an unmistakable token of imperfection in my knowledge, that it is augmented by degrees. Further, although my knowledge increase more and more, nevertheless I am not, therefore, induced to think that it will ever be actually infinite, since it can never reach that point beyond which it shall be incapable of further increase. But I conceive God as actually infinite, so that nothing can be added to his perfection. And, in fine, I readily perceive that the objective being of an idea cannot be produced by a being that is merely potentially existent, which, properly speaking, is nothing, but only by a being existing formally or actually.

And, truly, I see nothing in all that I have now said which it is not easy for anyone, who shall carefully consider it, to discern by the natural light; but when I allow my attention in some degree to relax, the vision of my mind being obscured, and, as it were, blinded by the images of sensible objects, I do not readily remember the reason why the idea of a being more perfect than myself, must of necessity have proceeded from a being in reality more perfect. On this account I am here desirous to inquire further, whether I, who possess this idea of God, could exist supposing there were no God. And I ask, from whom could I, in that case, derive my existence? Perhaps from myself, or from my parents, or from some other causes less perfect than God; for anything more perfect, or even equal to God, cannot be thought or imagined. But if I were independent of every other existence, and were myself the author of my being, I should doubt of nothing, I should desire nothing, and, in fine, no perfection would be awanting to me; for I should have bestowed upon myself every perfection of which I possess the idea, and I should thus be God.

And it must not be imagined that what is now wanting to me is perhaps of more difficult acquisition than that of which I am already possessed; for, on the contrary, it is quite manifest that it was a matter of much higher difficulty that I, a thinking being, should arise from nothing, than it would be for me to acquire the knowledge of many things of which I am ignorant, and which are merely the accidents of a thinking substance; and certainly, if I possessed of myself the greater perfection of which I have now spoken [in other words, if I were the author of my own existence], I would not at least have denied to myself things that may be more easily obtained [as that infinite variety of knowledge of which I am at present destitute]. I could not, indeed, have denied to myself any property which I perceive is contained in the idea of God, because there is none of these that seems to me to be more difficult to make or acquire; and if there were any that should happen to be more difficult to acquire, they would certainly appear so to me because I should discover in them a limit to my power. And though I were to suppose that I always was as I now am, I should not, on this ground, escape the force of these reasonings, since it would not follow, even on this supposition, that no author of my existence needed to be sought after. For the whole time of my life may be divided into an infinity of parts, each of which is in no way dependent on any other; and, accordingly, because I was in existence a short time ago, it does not follow that I must now exist, unless in this moment some cause create me anew as it were, that is, conserve me. In truth, it is perfectly clear and evident to all who will attentively consider the nature of duration, that the conservation of a substance, in each moment of its duration, requires the same power and act that would be necessary to create it, supposing it were not yet in existence; so that it is manifestly a dictate of the natural light that conservation and creation differ merely in respect of our mode of thinking and not in reality. All that is here required, therefore, is that I interrogate myself to discover whether I possess any power by means of which I can bring it about that I, who now am, shall exist a moment afterward: for, since I am merely a thinking thing (or since, at least, the precise question, in the meantime, is only of that part of myself), if such a power resided in me, I should, without doubt, be conscious of it; but I am conscious of no such power, and thereby I manifestly know that I am dependent upon some being different from myself.

But perhaps the being upon whom I am dependent is not God, and I have been produced either by my parents, or by some causes less perfect than God. This cannot be: for, as I before said, it is perfectly evident that there must at least be as much reality in the cause as in its effect; and accordingly, since I am a thinking thing and possess in myself an idea of God, whatever in the end be the cause of my existence, it must of necessity be admitted that it is likewise a thinking being, and that it possesses in itself the idea and all the perfections I attribute to God. Then it may again be inquired whether this cause owes its origin and existence to itself, or to some other cause. For if it be self-existent, it follows, from what I have before laid down, that this cause is God; for since it possesses the perfection of self-existence, it must likewise, without doubt, have the power of actually possessing every perfection of which it has the idea—in other words, all the perfections I conceive to belong to God. But if it owe its existence to another cause than itself, we demand again, for a similar reason, whether this second cause exists of itself or through some other, until, from stage to stage, we at length arrive at an ultimate cause, which will be God. And it is quite manifest that in this matter there can be no infinite regress of causes, seeing that the question raised respects not so much the cause which once produced me, as that by which I am at this present moment conserved.

Nor can it be supposed that several causes concurred in my production, and that from one I received the idea of one of the perfections I attribute to God, and from another the idea of some other, and thus that all those perfections are indeed found somewhere in the universe, but do not all exist together in a single being who is God; for, on the contrary, the unity, the simplicity, or inseparability of all the properties of God, is one of the chief perfections I conceive him to possess; and the idea of this unity of all the perfections of God could certainly not be put into my mind by any cause from which I did not likewise receive the ideas of all the other perfections; for no power could enable me to embrace them in an inseparable unity, without at the same time giving me the knowledge of what they were and of their existence in a particular mode.

Finally, with regard to my parents [from whom it appears I sprung], although all that I believed respecting them be true, it does not, nevertheless, follow that I am conserved by them, or even that I was produced by them, in so far as I am a thinking being. All that, at the most, they contributed to my origin was the giving of certain dispositions (modifications) to the matter in which I have hitherto judged that I or my mind, which is what alone I now consider to be myself, is inclosed; and thus there can here be no difficulty with respect to them, and it is absolutely necessary to conclude from this alone that I am, and possess the idea of a being absolutely perfect, that is, of God, that his existence is most clearly demonstrated.

There remains only the inquiry as to the way in which I received this idea from God; for I have not drawn it from the senses, nor is it even presented to me unexpectedly, as is usual with the ideas of sensible objects, when these are presented or appear to be presented to the external organs of the senses; it is not even a pure production or fiction of my mind, for it is not in my power to take from or add to it; and consequently there but remains the alternative that it is innate, in the same way as is the idea of myself. And, in truth, it is not to be wondered at that God, at my creation, implanted this idea in me, that it might serve, as it were, for the mark of the workman impressed on his work; and it is not also necessary that the mark should be something different from the work itself; but considering only that God is my creator, it is highly probable that he in some way fashioned me after his own image and likeness, and that I perceive this likeness, in which is contained the idea of God, by the same faculty by which I apprehend myself, in others words, when I make myself the object of reflection, I only find that I am an incomplete, [imperfect] and dependent being, and one who unceasingly aspires after something better and greater than he is. At the same time, I am assured likewise that he upon whom I am dependent possesses in himself all the goods after which I aspire [and the ideas of which I find in my mind], and they not merely indefinitely and potentially, but infinitely and actually, and that he is thus God. And the whole force of the argument of which I have here availed myself to establish the existence of God, consists in this, that I perceive I could not possibly be of such a nature as I am, and yet have in my mind the idea of a God, if God did not in reality exist—this same God, I say, whose idea is in my mind—that is, a being who possesses all those lofty perfections, of which the mind may have some slight conception, without, however, being able fully to comprehend them, and who is wholly superior to all defect [and has nothing that marks imperfection]: whence it is sufficiently manifest that he cannot be a deceiver, since it is a dictate of the natural light that all fraud and deception spring from some defect.

But before I examine this with more attention, and pass on to the consideration of other truths that may be evolved out of it, I think it proper to remain here for some time in the contemplation of God himself—that I may ponder at leisure his marvelous attributes—and behold, admire, and adore the beauty of this light so unspeakably great, as far, at least, as the strength of my mind, which is to some degree dazzled by the sight, will permit. For just as we learn by faith that the supreme felicity of another life consists in the contemplation of the Divine majesty alone, so even now we learn from experience that a like meditation, though incomparably less perfect, is the source of the highest satisfaction of which we are susceptible in this life. . . .

Saint Thomas Aquinas: The Existence of God

The existence of God can be proved in five ways.

The first and more manifest way is the argument from motion. It is certain, and evident to our senses, that in the world some things are in motion. Now whatever is in motion is put in motion by another, for nothing can be in motion except it is in potentiality to that towards which it is in motion; whereas a thing moves inasmuch as it is in act. For motion is nothing else than the reduction of something from potentiality to actuality. But nothing can be reduced from potentiality to actuality, except by something in a state of actuality. Thus that which is actually hot, as fire, makes wood, which is potentially hot, to be actually hot, and thereby moves and changes it. Now is it not possible that the same thing should be at once in actuality and potentiality in the same respect, but only in different respects. For what is actually hot cannot simultaneously be potentially hot; but it is simultaneously potentially cold. It is therefore impossible that in the same respect and in the same way a thing should be both mover and moved, *i.e.,* that it should move itself. Therefore, whatever is in motion must be put in motion by another. If that by which it is put in motion be itself put in motion, then this also must needs be put in motion by another, and that by another again. But this cannot go on to infinity, because then there would be no first mover, and, consequently, no other mover; seeing that subsequent movers move only inasmuch as they are put in motion by the first mover; as the staff moves only because it is put in motion by the hand. Therefore it is necessary to arrive at a first mover, put in motion by no other; and this everyone understands to be God.

The second way is from the nature of the efficient cause. In the world of sense we find there is an order of efficient causes. There is no case known (neither is it, indeed, possible) in which a thing is found to be the efficient cause of itself; for so it would be prior to itself, which is impossible. Now in efficient causes it is not possible to go on to infinity, because in all efficient causes following in order, the first is the cause of the intermediate cause, and the intermediate is the cause of the ultimate cause, whether the intermediate cause be several, or one only. Now to take away the cause is to take away the effect. Therefore, if there be no first cause among efficient causes, there will be no ultimate, nor any intermediate cause. But if in efficient causes it is possible to go on to infinity, there will be no first efficient cause, neither will there be an ultimate effect, nor any intermediate efficient causes; all of which is plainly false. Therefore it is necessary to admit a first efficient cause, to which everyone gives the name of God.

The third way is taken from possibility and necessity, and runs thus. We find in nature things that are possible to be and not to be, since they are found to be generated, and to corrupt, and consequently, they are possible to be and not to be. But it is impossible for these always to exist, for that which is possible not to be at some time is not. Therefore, if everything is possible not to be, then at one time there could have been nothing in existence. Now if this were true, even now there would be nothing in existence, because that which does not exist only begins to exist by something already existing. Therefore, if at one time nothing was in existence, it would have been impossible for anything to have begun to exist; and thus even now nothing would be in existence—which is absurd. Therefore, not all beings are merely possible, but there must exist something the existence of which is necessary. But every necessary thing either has its necessity caused by another, or not. Now it is impossible to go on to infinity in necessary things which have their necessity caused by another, as has been already proved in regard to efficient causes. Therefore we cannot but postulate the existence of some being having of itself its own necessity, and not receiving it from another, but rather causing in others their necessity. This all men speak of as God.

The fourth way is taken from the gradation to be found in things. Among beings there are some more and some less good, true, noble, and the like. But "more" and "less" are predicated of different things, according as they resemble in their different ways something which is the maximum, as a thing is said to be hotter according as it more nearly resembles that which is hottest; so that there is something which is truest, something best, something noblest, and consequently, something which is uttermost being; for those things that are greatest in truth are greatest in being. Now the maximum in any genus is the cause of all in that genus; as fire, which is the maximum of heat, is the cause of all hot things. Therefore there must also be something which is to all beings the cause of their being, goodness, and every other perfection; and this we call God.

The fifth way is taken from the governance of the world. We see that things which lack intelligence, such as natural bodies, act for an end, and this is evident from their acting always, or nearly always, in the same way, so as to obtain the best result. Hence it is plain that not fortuitously, but designedly, do they achieve their end. Now whatever lacks intelligence cannot move towards an end, unless it be directed by some being endowed with knowledge and intelligence; as the arrow is shot to its mark by the archer. Therefore some intelligent being exists by whom all natural things are directed to their end; and this being we call God.

David Hume: Of Miracles

PART I

. . . A miracle is a violation of the laws of nature; and as a firm and unalterable experience has established these laws, the proof against a miracle, from the very nature of the fact, is as entire as any argument from experience can possibly be imagined. Why is it more than probable, that all men must die; that lead cannot, of itself, remain suspended in the air; that fire consumes wood, and is extinguished by water; unless it be, that these events are found agreeable to the laws of nature, and there is required, a violation of these laws, or in other words, a miracle to prevent them? Nothing is esteemed a miracle, if it ever happen in the common course of nature. It is no miracle that a man, seemingly in good health, should die on a sudden: because such a kind of death, though more unusual than any other, has yet been frequently observed to happen. But it is a miracle, that a dead man should come to life; because that has never been observed in any age or country. There must, therefore, be a uniform experience against every miraculous event, otherwise the event would not merit that appellation. And as a uniform experience amounts to a proof, there is here a direct and full *proof,* from the nature of the fact, against the existence of any miracle; nor can such a proof be destroyed, or the miracle rendered credible, but by an opposite proof, which is superior. Sometimes an event may not, *in itself,* seem to be contrary to the laws of nature, and yet, if it were real, it might, by reason of some circumstances, be denominated a miracle; because, *in fact*, it is contrary to these laws. Thus if a person, claiming a divine authority, should command a sick person to be well, a healthful man to fall down dead, the clouds to pour rain, the winds to blow, in short, should order many natural events, which immediately follow upon his command; these might justly be esteemed miracles, because they are really, in this case, contrary to the laws of nature. For if any suspicion remain, that the event and command concurred by accident, there is no miracle and no transgression of the laws of nature. If this suspicion be removed, there is evidently a miracle, and a transgression of these laws; because nothing can be more contrary to nature than that the voice or command of a man should have such an influence. A miracle may be accurately defined, *a transgression of a law of nature by a particular volition of the Deity, or by the interposition of some invisible agent.* A miracle may either be discoverable by men or not. This alters not its nature and essence. The raising of a house or ship into the air is a visible miracle. The raising of a feather, when the wind wants ever so little of a force requisite for that purpose, is as real a miracle, though not so sensible with regard to us.

The plain consequence is (and it is a general maxim worthy of our attention), 'That no testimony is sufficient to establish a miracle, unless the testimony be of such a kind, that its falsehood would be more miraculous, than the fact, which it endeavors to establish; and even in that case there is a mutual destruction of arguments, and the superior only gives us an assurance suitable to that degree of force, which remains, after deducting the inferior.' When anyone tells me, that he saw a dead man restored to life, I immediately consider with myself, whether it be more probable, that this

From David Hume, *An Enquiry Concerning Human Understanding.*

person should either deceive or be deceived, or that the fact, which he relates should really have happened. I weigh the one miracle against the other; and according to the superiority, which I discover, I pronounce my decision, and always reject the greater miracle. If the falsehood of his testimony would be more miraculous, than the event which he relates; then, and not till then, can he pretend to command my belief or opinion.

Part II

In the foregoing reasoning we have supposed, that the testimony, upon which a miracle is founded, may possibly amount to an entire proof, and that the falsehood of that testimony would be a real prodigy. But it is easy to show, that we have been a great deal too liberal in our concession, and that there never was a miraculous event established on so full an evidence.

For *first,* there is not to be found, in all history, any miracle attested by a sufficient number of men, of such unquestioned good sense, education, and learning, as to secure us against all delusion in themselves; of such undoubted integrity, as to place them beyond all suspicion of any design to deceive others; of such credit and reputation in the eyes of mankind, as to have a great deal to lose in case of their being detected in any falsehood; and at the same time, attesting facts performed in such a public manner and in so celebrated a part of the world, as to render the detection unavoidable: all which circumstances are requisite to give us a full assurance in the testimony of men.

Secondly. We may observe in human nature a principle which, if strictly examined, will be found to diminish extremely the assurance, which we might, from human testimony, have in any kind of prodigy. The maxim, by which we commonly conduct ourselves in our reasonings, is, that the objects, of which we have no experience, resemble those, of which we have; that what we have found to be most usual is always most probable; and that where there is an opposition of arguments, we ought to give the preference to such as are founded on the greatest number of past observations. But though, in proceeding by this rule, we readily reject any fact which is unusual and incredible in an ordinary degree; yet in advancing farther, the mind observes not always the same rule; but when anything is affirmed utterly absurd and miraculous, it rather the more readily admits of such a fact, upon account of that very circumstance, which ought to destroy all its authority. The passion of *surprise* and *wonder,* arising from miracles, being an agreeable emotion, gives a sensible tendency towards the belief of those events, from which it is derived. And this goes so far, that even those who cannot enjoy this pleasure immediately, nor can believe those miraculous events, of which they are informed, yet love to partake of the satisfaction at second hand or by rebound, and place a pride and delight in exciting the admiration of others. . . .

. . . The many instances of forged miracles, and prophecies, and supernatural events, which, in all ages, have either been detected by contrary evidence, or which detect themselves by their absurdity, prove sufficiently the strong propensity of mankind to the extraordinary and marvellous, and ought reasonably to beget a suspicion against all relations of this kind. This is our natural way of thinking, even with regard to the most common and most credible events. For instance: there is no kind of report which rises so easily, and spreads so quickly, especially in country places and provincial towns, as those concerning marriages; insomuch that two young persons of equal condition never see each other twice, but the whole neighborhood immediately join them together. The pleasure of telling a piece of news so interesting, of propagating it, and of being the first reporters of it, spreads the intelligence. And this is so well known, that no man of sense gives attention to these reports, till he find them confirmed by some greater evidence. Do not the same passions, and others still stronger, incline the generality of mankind to believe and report, with the greatest vehemence and assurance, all religious miracles?

Thirdly. It forms a strong presumption against all supernatural and miraculous relations, that they are observed chiefly to abound among ignorant and barbarous nations; or if a civilized people has ever given admissions to any of them, that people will be found to have received them from ignorant and barbarous ancestors, who transmitted them with that inviolable sanction and authority, which always attend received opinions. When we peruse the first histories of all nations, we are apt to imagine ourselves transported into some new world; where the whole frame of nature is disjointed, and every element performs its operations in a different manner, from what it does at present. Battles, revolutions, pestilence, famine and death, are never the effect of those natural causes, which we experience. Prodigies, omens, oracles, judgments, quite obscure the few natural events, that are intermingled with them. But as the former grow thinner every page, in proportion as we advance nearer the enlightened ages, we soon learn, that there is nothing mysterious or supernatural in the case, but that all proceeds from the usual propensity of mankind towards the marvellous, and that, though this inclination may at intervals receive a check from sense and learning, it can never be thoroughly extirpated from human nature. . . .

. . . I may add a *fourth* reason, which diminishes the authority of prodigies, that there is no testimony for any, even those which have not been expressly detected, that is not opposed by an infinite number of witnesses; so that not only the miracle destroys the credit of testimony, but the testimony destroys itself. To make this the better understood, let us consider, that, in matters of religion, whatever is different is contrary; and that it is impossible the religions of ancient Rome, of Turkey, of Siam, and of China should, all of them, be established on any solid foundation. Every miracle, therefore, pretended to have been wrought in any of these religions (and all of them abound in miracles), as its direct scope is to establish the particular system to which it is attributed; so has it the same force, though more indirectly, to overthrow every other system. In destroying a rival system, it likewise destroys the credit of those miracles, on which that system was established; so that all the prodigies of different religions are to be regarded as contrary facts, and the evidences of these prodigies, whether weak or strong, as opposite to each other. According to this method of reasoning, when we believe any miracle of Mahomet or his successors, we have for our warrant the testimony of a few barbarous Arabians. And on the other hand, we are to regard the authority and witnesses, Grecian, Chinese, and Roman Catholic, who have related any miracle in their particular religion; I say, we are to regard their testimony in the same light as if they had mentioned that Mohammedan miracle, and had in express terms contradicted it, with the same certainty as they have for the miracle they relate. This argument may appear oversubtle and refined; but is not in reality different from the reasoning of a judge, who supposes, that the credit of two witnesses, maintaining a crime against anyone, is destroyed by the testimony of two others, who affirm him to have been two hundred leagues distant, at the same instant when the crime is said to have been committed. . . .

Upon the whole, then, it appears, that no testimony for any kind of miracle has ever amounted to a probability, much less to a proof; and that, even supposing it amounted to a proof, it would be opposed by another proof; derived from the very nature of the fact, which it would endeavor to establish. It is experience only, which gives authority to human testimony; and it is the same experience, which assures us of the laws of nature. When, therefore, these two kinds of experience are contrary, we have nothing to do but substract the one from the other, and embrace an opinion, either on one side or the other, with that assurance which arises from the remainder. But according to the principle here explained, this substraction, with regard to all popular religions, amounts to an entire annihilation; and therefore we may establish it as a maxim, that no human testimony can have such force as to prove a miracle, and make it a just foundation for any such system of religion.

I beg the limitations here made may be remarked, when I say, that a miracle can never be proved, so as to be the foundation of a system of religion. For I own, that otherwise, there may possibly be miracles, or violations of the usual course of nature, of such a kind as to admit of proof from human testimony; though, perhaps, it will be impossible to find any such in all the records of history. Thus, suppose, all authors, in all languages, agree, that, from the first of January 1600, there was a total darkness over the whole earth for eight days: suppose that the tradition of this extraordinary event is still strong and lively among the people: that all travelers, who return from foreign countries, bring us accounts of the same tradition, without the least variation or contradiction: it is evident, that our present philosophers, instead of doubting the fact, ought to receive it as certain, and ought to search for the causes whence it might be derived. The decay, corruption, and dissolution of nature, is an event rendered probable by so many analogies, that any phenomenon, which seems to have a tendency towards that catastrophe, comes within the reach of human testimony, if that testimony be very extensive and uniform.

William Paley: The Argument from Design

In crossing a heath, suppose I pitched my foot against a *stone,* and were asked how the stone came to be there, I might possibly answer, that for anything I knew to the contrary it had lain there forever; nor would it, perhaps, be very easy to show the absurdity of this answer. But suppose I had found a *watch* upon the ground, and it should be inquired how the watch happened to be in that place, I should hardly think of the answer which I had before given, that for anything I knew the watch might have always been there. Yet why should not this answer serve for the watch as well as for the stone; why is it not as admissible in the second case as in the first? For this reason, and for no other, namely, that when we come to inspect the watch, we perceive—what we could not discover in the stone—that its several parts are framed and put together for a purpose, e.g. that they are so formed and adjusted as to produce motion, and that motion so regulated as to point out the hour of the day; that if the different parts had been differently shaped from what they are, or placed after any other manner or in any other order than that in which they are placed, either no motion at all would have been carried on in the machine, or none which would have answered the use that is now served by it. To reckon up a few of the plainest of these parts and of their offices, all tending to one result: We see a cylindrical box containing a coiled elastic spring, which, by its endeavor to relax itself, turns round the box. We next observe a flexible chain—artificially wrought for the sake of flexure—communicating the action of the spring from the box to the fusee. We then find a series of wheels, the teeth of which catch in and apply to each other, conducting the motion from the fusee to the balance and from the balance to the pointer, and at the same time, by the size and shape of those wheels, so regulating that motion as to terminate in causing an index, by an equal and measured progression, to pass over a given space in a given time. We take notice that the wheels are made of brass, in order to keep them from rust; the springs of steel, no other metal being so elastic; that over the face of the watch there is placed a glass, a material employed in no other part of the work, but in the room of which, if there had been any other than a transparent substance, the hour could not be seen without opening the case. This mechanism being observed—it requires indeed an examination of the instrument, and perhaps some previous knowledge of the subject, to perceive and understand it; but being once, as we have said, observed and understood, the inference we think is inevitable, that the watch must have had a maker—that there must have existed, at some time and at some place or other, an artificer or artificers who formed it for the purpose which we find it actually to answer, who comprehended its construction and designed its use.

I. Nor would it, I apprehend, weaken the conclusion, that we had never seen a watch made—that we had never known an artist capable of making one—that we were altogether incapable of executing such a piece of workmanship ourselves, or of understanding in what manner it was performed; all this being no more than what is true of some exquisite remains of ancient art, or some lost arts, and,

From William Paley, *Natural Theology.*

to the generality of mankind, of the more curious productions of modern manufacture. Does one man in a million know how oval frames are turned? Ignorance of this kind exalts our opinion of the unseen and unknown artist's skill, if he be unseen and unknown, but raises no doubt in our minds of the existence and agency of such an artist, at some former time and in some place or other. Nor can I perceive that it varies at all the inference, whether the question arise concerning a human agent or concerning an agent of a different species, or an agent possessing in some respects a different nature.

II. Neither, secondly, would it invalidate our conclusion, that the watch sometimes went wrong or that it seldom went exactly right. The purpose of the machinery, the design, and the designer might be evident, and in the case supposed, would be evident, in whatever way we accounted for the irregularity of the movement, or whether we could account for it or not. It is not necessary that a machine be perfect, in order to show with what design it was made: still less necessary, where the only question is whether it were made with any design at all.

III. Nor, thirdly, would it bring any uncertainty into the argument, if there were a few parts of the watch, concerning which we could not discover or had yet discovered in what manner they conduced to the general effect; or even some parts, concerning which we could not ascertain whether they conduced to that effect in any manner whatever. For, as to the first branch of the case, if by the loss, or disorder, or decay of the parts in question, the movement of the watch were found in fact to be stopped, or disturbed, or retarded, no doubt would remain in our minds as to the utility or intention of these parts, although we should be unable to investigate the manner according to which, or the connection by which, the ultimate effect depended upon their action or assistance; and the more complex the machine, the more likely is this obscurity to arise. Then, as to the second thing supposed, namely, that there were parts which might be spared without prejudice to the movement of the watch, and that we had proved this by experiment, these superfluous parts, even if we were completely assured that they were such, would not vacate the reasoning which we had instituted concerning other parts. The indication of contrivance remained, with respect to them, nearly as it was before.

IV. Nor, fourthly, would any man in his senses think the existence of the watch with its various machinery accounted for, by being told that it was one out of possible combinations of material forms; that whatever he had found in the place where he found the watch, must have contained some internal configuration or other; and this configuration might be the structure now exhibited, namely, of the works of a watch, as well as a different structure.

V. Nor, fifthly, would it yield his inquiry more satisfaction, to be answered that there existed in things a principle of order, which had disposed the parts of the watch into their present form and situation. He never knew a watch made by the principle of order; nor can he ever form to himself an idea of what is meant by a principle of order, distinct from the intelligence of the watchmaker.

VI. Sixthly, he would be surprised to hear that the mechanism of the watch was no proof of contrivance, only a motive to induce the mind to think so.

VII. And not less surprised to be informed, that the watch in his hand was nothing more than the result of the laws of *metallic* nature. It is a perversion of language to assign any law as the efficient, operative cause of any thing. A law presupposes an agent; for it is only the mode according to which an agent proceeds: it implies a power; for it is the order according to which that power acts. Without this agent, without this power, which are both distinct from itself, the *law* does nothing, is nothing. The expression, "the law of metallic nature," may sound strange and harsh to a philosophic ear; but it seems quite as justifiable as some others which are more familiar to him, such as "the law of vegetable nature," "the law of animal nature," or, indeed, as "the law of nature" in general, when assigned as the cause of phenomena, in exclusion of agency and power, or when it is substituted into the place of these.

VIII. Neither, lastly, would our observer be driven out of his conclusion or from his confidence in its truth, by being told that he knew nothing at all about the matter. He knows enough for his argument; he knows the utility of the end; he knows the subserviency and adaptation of the means to the end. These points being known, his ignorance of other points, his doubts concerning other points, affect not the certainty of his reasoning. The consciousness of knowing little need not beget a distrust of that which he does know.

. . . Every indication of contrivance, every manifestation of design which existed in the watch, exists in the works of nature, with the difference on the side of nature of being greater and more, and that in a degree which exceeds all computation. I mean, that the contrivances of nature surpass the contrivances of art, in the complexity, subtilty, and curiosity of the mechanism; and still more, if possible, do they go beyond them in number and variety; yet, in a multitude of cases, are not less evidently mechanical, not less evidently contrivances, not less evidently accommodated to their end or suited to their office, than are the most perfect productions of human ingenuity.

[From the above considerations, Paley concludes that the existence of God is a fact that becomes evident as one contemplates the Universe at large and its details in particular. The wonderful organization of nature, the universal design of all things, and the contrivances found in natural objects,—all point to the undeniable presence of a supreme organizer and architect whom we call God.—*Eds.*]

John Stuart Mill: Theism

Though I have defined the problem of Natural Theology, to be that of the existence of God or of a God, rather than of Gods, there is the amplest historical evidence that the belief in Gods is immeasurably more natural to the human mind than the belief in one author and ruler of nature; and that this more elevated belief is, compared with the former, an artificial product, requiring (except when impressed by early education) a considerable amount of intellectual culture before it can be reached. For a long time, the supposition appeared forced and unnatural that the diversity we see in the operations of nature can all be the work of a single will. To the untaught mind, and to all minds in pre-scientific times, the phenomena of nature seem to be the result of forces altogether heterogeneous, each taking its course quite independently of the others; and though to attribute them to conscious wills is eminently natural, the natural tendency is to suppose as many such independent wills as there are distinguishable forces of sufficient importance and interest to have been remarked and named. There is no tendency in polytheism as such to transform itself spontaneously into monotheism. It is true that in polytheistic systems generally the deity whose special attributes inspire the greatest degree of awe, is usually supposed to have a power of controlling the other deities; and even in the most degraded perhaps of all such systems, the Hindoo, adulation heaps upon the divinity who is the immediate object of adoration, epithets like those habitual to believers in a single God. But there is no real acknowledgment of one Governor. Every God normally rules his particular department though there may be a still stronger God whose power when he chooses to exert it can frustrate the purposes of the inferior divinity. There could be no real belief in one Creator and Governor until mankind had begun to see in the apparently confused phenomena which surrounded them, a system capable of being viewed as the possible working out of a single plan. This conception of the world was perhaps anticipated (though less frequently than is often supposed) by individuals of exceptional genius, but it could only become common after a rather long cultivation of scientific thought.

The special mode in which scientific study operates to instil Monotheism in place of the more natural Polytheism, is in no way mysterious. The specific effect of science is to show by accumulating evidence, that every event in nature is connected by laws with some fact or facts which preceded it, or in other words, depends for its existence on some antecedent; but yet not so strictly on one, as not to be liable to frustration or modification from others: for these distinct chains of causation are so entangled with one another; the action of each cause is so interfered with by other causes, though each acts according to its own fixed law; that every effect is truly the result rather of the aggregate of all causes in existence than of any one only; and nothing takes place in the world of our experience without spreading a perceptible influence of some sort through a greater or less portion of Nature, and making perhaps every portion of it slightly different from what it would have been if that event had not taken place. Now, when once the double conviction has found entry into the mind—that every event depends on antecedents; and at the same time that to bring it about many antecedents must concur, perhaps all the antecedents in Nature, insomuch that a slight difference in any one of them might have prevented the phenomenon, or materially altered its character—the conviction follows that no one event, certainly no one kind of events, can be absolutely preordained or governed by any Being but one who holds in his hand the reins of all Nature and not of some department only. At least if a plurality be supposed, it is necessary to assume so complete a concert of action and unity of will among them that the difference is for most purposes immaterial between such a theory and that of the absolute unity of the Godhead.

The reason, then, why Monotheism may be accepted as the representative of Theism in the abstract, is not so much because it is the Theism of all the more improved portions of the human race, as because it is the only Theism which can claim for itself any footing on scientific ground. Every other theory of the government of the universe by supernatural beings, is inconsistent either with the carrying on of that government through a continual series of natural antecedents according to fixed laws, or with the interdependence of each of these series upon all the rest, which are the two most general results of science.

Setting out therefore from the scientific view of nature as one connected system, or united whole, united not like a web composed of separate threads in passive juxtaposition with one another, but rather like the human or animal frame, an apparatus kept going by perpetual action and reaction among all its parts; it must be acknowledged that the question, to which Theism is an answer, is at least a very natural one, and issues from an obvious want of the human mind. Accustomed as we are to find, in proportion to our means of observation, a definite beginning to each individual fact; and since wherever there is a beginning we find that there was an antecedent fact (called by us a cause), a fact but for which, the phenomenon which thus commences would not have been; it was impossible that the human mind should not ask itself whether the whole, of which these particular phenomena are a part, had not also a beginning, and if so, whether that beginning was not an origin; whether there was not something antecedent to the whole series of causes and effects that we term Nature, and but for which Nature itself would not have been. From the first recorded speculation this question has never remained without an hypothetical answer. The only answer which has long continued to afford satisfaction is Theism.

Looking at the problem, as it is our business to do, merely as a scientific inquiry, it resolves itself into two questions. First: Is the theory, which refers the origin of all the phenomena of nature to the will of a Creator, consistent or not with the ascertained results of science? Secondly, assuming it to be consistent, will its proofs bear to be tested by the principles of evidence and canons of belief by which our long experience of scientific inquiry has proved the necessity of being guided?

First, then: there is one conception of Theism which is consistent, another which is radically inconsistent, with the most general truths that have been made known to us by scientific investigation.

The one which is inconsistent is the conception of a God governing the world by acts of variable will. The one which is consistent, is the conception of a God governing the world by invariable laws.

The primitive, and even in our own day the vulgar, conception of the divine rule, is that the one God, like the many Gods of antiquity, carries on the government of the world by special decrees. Although supposed to be omniscient as well as omnipotent, he is thought not to make up his mind until the moment of action; or at least not so conclusively, but that his intentions may be altered up to the very last moment by appropriate solicitation. Without entering into the difficulties of reconciling this view of the divine government with the prescience and the perfect wisdom ascribed to the Deity, we may content ourselves with the fact that it contradicts what experience has taught us of the manner in which things actually take place. The phenomena of Nature do take place according to general laws. They do originate from definite natural antecedents. Therefore if their ultimate design is derived from a will, that will must have established the general laws and willed the antecedents. If there be a Creator, his intention must have been that events should depend upon antecedents and be produced according to fixed laws. But this being conceded, there is nothing in scientific experience inconsistent with the belief that those laws and sequences are themselves due to a divine will. Neither are we obliged to suppose that the divine will exerted itself once for all, and after putting a power into the system which enabled it to go on of itself, has ever since let it alone. Science contains nothing repugnant to the supposition that every event which takes place results from a specific volition of the presiding Power, provided that this Power adheres in its particular volitions to general laws laid down by itself. The common opinion is that this hypothesis tends more to the glory of the Deity than the supposition that the universe was made so that it could go on of itself. There have been thinkers however—of no ordinary eminence (of whom Leibnitz was one)—who thought the last the only supposition worthy of the Deity, and protested against likening God to a clockmaker whose clock will not go unless he puts his hand to the machinery and keeps it going. With such considerations we have no concern in this place. We are looking at the subject not from the point of view of reverence but from that of science; and with science both these suppositions as to the mode of the divine action are equally consistent.

We must now, however, pass to the next question. There is nothing to disprove the creation and government of Nature by a sovereign will; but is there anything to prove it? Of what nature are its evidences; and weighed in the scientific balance, what is their value?

THE EVIDENCES OF THEISM

The evidences of a Creator are not only of several distinct kinds but of such diverse characters, that they are adapted to minds of very different descriptions, and it is hardly possible for any mind to be equally impressed by them all. The familiar classification of them into proofs *à priori* and *à posteriori,* marks that when looked at in a purely scientific view they belong to different schools of thought. Accordingly though the unthoughtful believer whose creed really rests on authority gives an equal welcome to all plausible arguments in support of the belief in which he has been brought up, philosophers who have had to make a choice between the *à priori* and the *à posteriori* methods in general science seldom fail, while insisting on one of these modes of support for religion, to speak with more or less of disparagement of the other. It is our duty in the present inquiry to maintain complete impartiality and to give a fair examination to both. At the same time I entertain a strong conviction that one of the two modes of argument is in its nature scientific, the other not only unscientific but condemned by science. The scientific argument is that which reasons from the facts and analogies of human experience as a geologist does when he infers the past states of our terrestrial globe, or an astronomical observer when he draws conclusions respecting the physical composition of the heavenly bodies. This is the *à posteriori* method, the principal application of which to Theism is the argument (as it is called) of design. The mode of reasoning which I call unscientific, though in the opinion of some thinkers it is also a legitimate mode of scientific procedure, is that which infers external objective facts from ideas or convictions of our minds. I say this independently of any opinion of my own respecting the origin of our ideas or convictions; for even if we were unable to point out any manner in which the idea of God, for example, can have grown up from the impressions of experience, still the idea can only prove the idea, and not the objective fact, unless indeed the fact is supposed (agreeably to the book of Genesis) to have been handed down by tradition from a time when there was direct personal intercourse with the Divine Being; in which case the argument is no longer *à priori.* The supposition that an idea, or a wish, or a need, even if native to the mind, proves the reality of a corresponding object, derives all its plausibility from the belief already in our minds that we were made by a benignant Being who would not have implanted in us a groundless belief, or a want which he did not afford us the means of satisfying; and is therefore a palpable *petitio principii* if adduced as an argument to support the very belief which it presupposes.

At the same time, it must be admitted that all *à priori* systems whether in philosophy or religion, do, in some sense profess to be founded on experience, since though they affirm the possibility of arriving at truths which transcend experience, they yet make the facts of experience their starting point (as what other starting point is possible?). They are entitled to consideration in so far as it can be shown that experience gives any countenance either to them or to their method of inquiry. Professedly *à priori* arguments are not unfrequently of a mixed nature, partaking in some degree of the *à posteriori* character, and may often be said to be *à posteriori* arguments in disguise; the *à priori* considerations acting chiefly in the way of making some particular *à posteriori* argument tell for more than its worth. This is emphatically true of the argument for Theism which I shall first examine, the necessity of a First Cause. For this has in truth a wide basis of experience in the universality of the relation of Cause and Effect among the phenomena of nature; while at the same time, theological philosophers have not been content to let it rest upon this basis, but have affirmed Causation as a truth of reason apprehended intuitively by its own light.

ARGUMENT FOR A FIRST CAUSE

The argument for a First Cause admits of being, and is, presented as a conclusion from the whole of human experience. Everything that we know (it is argued) had a cause, and owed its existence to that cause. How then can it be but that the world, which is but a name for the aggregate of all that we know, has a cause to which it is indebted for its existence?

The fact of experience however, when correctly expressed, turns out to be, not that everything which we know derives its existence from a cause, but only every event or change. There is in Nature a permanent element, and also a changeable: the changes are always the effects of previous changes; the permanent existences, so far as we know, are not effects at all. It is true we are accustomed to say not only of events, but of objects, that they are produced by causes, as water by the union of hydrogen and oxygen. But by this we only mean that when they begin to exist, their beginning is the effect of a cause. But their beginning to exist is not an object, it is an event. If it be objected that the cause of a thing's beginning to exist may be said with propriety to be the cause of the thing itself, I shall not quarrel with the expression. But that which in an object begins to exist, is that in it which belongs to the changeable element in nature; the outward form and the properties depending on mechanical or chemical combinations of its component parts. There is in every object another and a permanent element, viz., the specific elementary substance or substances of which it consists and their inherent properties. These are not known to us as beginning to exist: within the range of human knowledge they had no beginning, consequently no cause; though they themselves are causes or con-causes of everything that takes place. Experience therefore, affords no evidences, not even analogies, to justify our extending to the apparently immutable, a generalization grounded only on our observation of the changeable.

As a fact of experience, then, causation cannot legitimately be extended to the material universe itself, but only to its changeable phenomena; of these, indeed, causes may be affirmed without any exception. But what causes? The cause of every change is a prior change; and such it cannot but be; for if there were no new antecedent, there would not be a new consequent. If the state of facts which brings the phenomenon into existence had existed always or for an indefinite duration, the effect also would have existed always or been produced an indefinite time ago. It is thus a necessary part of the fact of causation, within the sphere of our experience, that the causes as well as the effects had a beginning in time, and were themselves caused. It would seem therefore that our experience, instead of furnishing an argument for a first cause, is repugnant to it; and that the very essence of causation as it exists within the limits of our knowledge, is incompatible with a First Cause.

But it is necessary to look more particularly into the matter, and analyse more closely the nature of the causes of which mankind have experience. For if it should turn out that though all causes have a beginning, there is in all of them a permanent element which had no beginning, this permanent element may with some justice be termed a first or universal cause, inasmuch as though not sufficient of itself to cause anything, it enters as a con-cause into all causation. Now it happens that the last result of physical inquiry, derived from the converging evidences of all branches of physical science, does, if it holds good, land us so far as the material world is concerned, in a result of this sort. Whenever a physical phenomenon is traced to its cause, that cause when analysed is found to be a certain quantum of Force, combined with certain collocations. And the last great generalization of science, the Conservation of Force, teaches us that the variety in the effects depends partly upon the *amount* of the force, and partly upon the diversity of the collocations. The force itself is essentially one and the same; and there exists of it in nature a fixed quantity, which (if the theory be true) is never increased or diminished. Here then we find, even in the changes of material nature, a permanent element; to all appearance the very one of which we were in quest. This it is apparently to which if to anything we must assign the character of First Cause, the cause of the material universe. For all effects may be traced up to it, while it cannot be traced up, by our experience, to anything beyond: its transformations alone can be so traced, and of them the cause always includes the force itself: the same quantity of force, in some previous form. It would seem then that in the only sense in which experience supports in any shape the doctrine of a First Cause, viz., as the primaeval and universal element in all causes, the First Cause can be no other than Force.

We are, however, by no means at the end of the question. On the contrary, the greatest stress of the argument is exactly at the point which we have now reached. For it is maintained that Mind is the only possible cause of Force; or rather perhaps, that Mind is a Force, and that all other force must be derived from it inasmuch as mind is the only thing which is capable of originating change. This is said to be the lesson of human experience. In the phenomena of inanimate nature the force which works is always a pre-existing force, not originated, but transferred. One physical object moves another by giving out to it the force by which it has first been itself moved. The wind communicates to the waves, or to a windmill, or a ship, part of the motion which has been given to itself by some other agent. In voluntary action alone we see a commencement, an origination of motion; since all other causes appear incapable of this origination experience is in favour of the conclusion that all the motion in existence owed its beginning to this one cause, voluntary agency, if not that of man, then of a more powerful Being.

This argument is a very old one. It is to be found in Plato; not as might have been expected, in the *Phaedon,* where the arguments are not such as would now be deemed of any weight, but in his latest production, the *Leges.* And it is still one of the most telling arguments with the more metaphysical class of defenders of Natural Theology.

Now, in the first place, if there be truth in the doctrine of the Conservation of Force, in other words the constancy of the total amount of Force in existence, this doctrine does not change from true to false when it reaches the field of voluntary agency. The will does not, any more than other causes, create Force: granting that it originates motion, it has no means of doing so but by converting into that particular manifestation a portion of Force which already existed in other forms. It is known that the source from which this portion of Force is derived, is chiefly, or entirely, the Force evolved in the processes of chemical composition and decomposition which constitute the body of nutrition: the force so liberated becomes a fund upon which every muscular and even every merely nervous action, as of the brain in thought, is a draft. It is in this sense only that, according to the best lights of science, volition is an originating cause. Volition, therefore, does not answer to the idea of a First Cause; since Force must in every instance be assumed as prior to it; and there is not the slightest colour, derived from experience, for supposing Force itself to have been created by a volition. As far as anything can be concluded from human experience Force has all the attributes of a thing eternal and uncreated.

This, however, does not close the discussion. For though whatever verdict experience can give in the case is against the possibility that Will ever originates Force, yet if we can be assured that neither does Force originate Will, Will must be held to be an agency, if not prior to Force yet coeternal with it: and if it be true that Will can originate, not indeed Force but the transformation of Force from some other of its manifestations into that of mechanical motion, and that there is within human experience no other agency capable of doing so, the argument for a Will as the originator, though not of the universe, yet of the kosmos, or order of the universe, remains unanswered.

But the case thus stated is not comformable to fact. Whatever volition can do in the way of creating motion out of other forms of force, and generally of evolving force from a latent into a visible state, can be done by many other causes. Chemical action, for instance; electricity; heat; the mere presence of a gravitating body; all these are causes of mechanical motion on a far larger scale than any volitions which experience presents to us: and in most of the effects thus produced the motion given by one body to another, is not, as in the ordinary cases of mechanical action, motion that has first been given to that other by some third body. The phenomenon is not a mere passing on of mechanical motion, but a creation of it out of a force previously latent or manifesting itself in some other form. Volition, therefore, regarded as an agent in the material universe, has no exclusive privilege of origination: all that it can originate is also originated by other transforming agents. If it be said that those other agents must have had the force they give out put into them from elsewhere, I answer, that this is no less true of the force which volition disposes of. We know that this force comes from an external source, the chemical action of the food and air. The force by which the phenomena of the material world are produced, circulates through all physical agencies in a never ending though sometimes intermitting stream. I am, of course, speaking of volition only in its action on the material world. We have nothing to do here with the freedom of the will itself as a mental phenomenon—with the *vexata questio* whether volition is self-determining or determined by causes. To the question now in hand it is only the effects of volition that are relevant, not its origin. The assertion is that physical nature must have been produced by a Will, because nothing but Will is known to us as having the power of originating the production of phenomena. We have seen that, on the contrary, all the power that Will possesses over phenomena is shared, as far as we have the means of judging, by other and much more powerful agents, and that in the only sense in which those agents do not originate, neither does Will originate. No prerogative, therefore, can, on the ground of experience, be assigned to volition above other natural agents, as a producing cause of phenomena. All that can be affirmed by the strongest assertor of the Freedom of the Will, is that volitions are themselves uncaused and are therefore alone fit to be the first or universal Cause. But, even assuming volitions to be uncaused, the properties of matter, so far as experience discloses, are uncaused also, and have the advantage over any particular volition, in being so far as experience can show, eternal. Theism, therefore, in so far as it rests on the necessity of a First Cause, has no support from experience.

To those who, in default of Experience, consider the necessity of a first cause as matter of intuition, I would say that it is needless, in this discussion, to contest their premises; since admitting that there is and must be a First Cause, it has now been shown that several other agencies than Will can lay equal claim to that character. One thing only may be said which requires notice here. Among the facts of the universe to be accounted for, it may be said, is Mind; and it is self-evident that nothing can have produced Mind but Mind.

The special indications that mind is deemed to give, pointing to intelligent contrivance, belong to a different portion of this inquiry. But if the mere existence of Mind is supposed to require, as a necessary antecedent, another Mind greater and more powerful, the difficulty is not removed by going one step back: the creating mind stands as much in need of another mind to be the source of its existence, as the created mind. Be it remembered that we have no direct knowledge (at least apart from Revelation) of a Mind which is even apparently eternal, as Force and Matter are: an eternal mind is, as far as the present argument is concerned, a simple hypothesis to account for the minds which we know to exist. Now it is essential to an hypothesis that if admitted it should at least remove the difficulty and account for the facts. But it does not account for Mind to refer one mind to a prior mind for its origin. The problem remains unsolved, the difficulty undiminished, nay, rather increased.

To this it may be objected that the causation of every human mind is matter of fact, since we know that it had a beginning in time. We even know, or have the strongest grounds for believing that the human species itself had a beginning in time. For there is a vast amount of evidence that the state of our planet was once such as to be incompatible with animal life, and that human life is of very much more modern origin than animal life. In any case, therefore, the fact must be faced that there must have been a cause which called the first human mind, nay the very first germ of organic life, into existence. No such difficulty exists in the supposition of an External Mind. If we did not know that Mind on our earth began to exist, we might suppose it to be uncaused; and we may still suppose this of the mind to which we ascribe its existence.

To take this ground is to return into the field of human experience, and to become subject to its canons, and we are then entitled to ask where is the proof that nothing can have caused a mind except another mind. From what, except from experience, can we know what can produce what—what causes are adequate to what effects? That nothing can *consciously* produce Mind but Mind, is self-evident, being involved in the meaning of the words; but that there cannot be unconscious production must not be assumed, for it is the very point to be proved. Apart from experience, and arguing on what is called reason, that is on supposed self-evidence, the notion seems to be, that no causes can give rise to products of a more precious or elevated kind than themselves. But this is at variance with the known analogies of Nature. How vastly nobler and more precious, for instance, are the higher vegetables and animals than the soil and manure out of which, and by the properties of which they are raised up! The tendency of all recent speculation is towards the opinion that the development of inferior orders of existence into superior, the substitution of greater elaboration and higher organization for lower, is the general rule of Nature. Whether it is so or not, there are at least in Nature a multitude of facts bearing that character, and this is sufficient for the argument.

Here, then, this part of the discussion may stop. The result it leads to is that the First Cause argument is in itself of no value for the establishment of Theism: because no cause is needed for the existence of that which has no beginning; and both Matter and Force (whatever metaphysical theory we may give of the one or the other) have had, so far as our experience can teach us, no beginning—which cannot be said of Mind. The phenomena or changes in the universe have indeed each of them a beginning and a cause, but their cause is always a prior change; nor do the analogies of experience give us any reason to expect, from the mere occurrence of changes, that if we could trace back the series far enough we should arrive at a Primaeval Volition. The world does not, by its mere existence, bear witness to a God: if it gives indications of one, these must be given by the special nature of the phenomena, by what they present that resembles adaptation to an end: of which hereafter. If, in default of evidence from experience, the evidence of intuition is relied upon, it may be answered that if Mind, as Mind, presents intuitive evidence of having been created, the Creative Mind must do the same, and we are no nearer to the First Cause than before. But if there be nothing in the nature of mind which in itself implies a Creator, the minds which have a beginning in time, as all minds have which are known to our experience, must indeed have been caused, but it is not necessary that their cause should have been a prior Intelligence.

William James:
The Will to Believe

In the recently published Life by Leslie Stephen of his brother, Fitz-James, there is an account of a school to which the latter went when he was a boy. The teacher, a certain Mr. Guest, used to converse with his pupils in this wise: "Gurney, what is the difference between justification and sanctification?—Stephen, prove the omnipotence of God!" etc. In the midst of our Harvard freethinking and indifference we are prone to imagine that here at your good old orthodox College conversation continues to be somewhat upon this order; and to show you that we at Harvard have not lost all interest in these vital subjects, I have brought with me tonight something like a sermon on justification by faith to read to you—I mean an essay in justification of faith, a defence of our right to adopt a believing attitude in religious matters, in spite of the fact that our merely logical intellect may not have been coerced. "The Will to Believe," accordingly, is the title of my paper.

I have long defended to my own students the lawfulness of voluntarily adopted faith; but as soon as they have got well imbued with the logical spirit, they have as a rule refused to admit my contention to be lawful philosophically, even though in point of fact they were personally all the time chock-full of some faith or other themselves. I am all the while, however, so profoundly convinced that my own position is correct, that your invitation has seemed to me a good occasion to make my statements more clear. Perhaps your minds will be more open than those with which I have hitherto had to deal. I will be as little technical as I can, though I must begin by setting up some technical distinctions that will help us in the end.

1

Let us give the name of *hypothesis* to anything that may be proposed to our belief; and just as the electricians speak of live and dead wires, let us speak of any hypothesis as either *live* or *dead*. A live hypothesis is one which appeals as a real possibility to him to whom it is proposed. If I ask you to believe in the Mahdi, the notion makes no electric connection with your name—it refuses to scintillate with any credibility at all. As an hypothesis it is completely dead. To an Arab, however (even if he be not one of the Mahdi's followers), the hypothesis is among the mind's possibilities: it is alive. This shows that deadness and liveness in an hypothesis are not intrinsic properties, but relations to the individual thinker. They are measured by his willingness to act. The maximum of liveness in an hypothesis means willingness to act irrevocably. Practically, that means belief; but there is some believing tendency wherever there is willingness to act at all.

Next, let us call the decision between two hypotheses an *option*. Options may be of several kinds. They may be—first, *living* or *dead*; secondly, *forced* or *avoidable;* thirdly, *momentous* or *trivial*; and for our purposes we may call an option a *genuine* option when it is of the forced, living, and momentous kind.

1. A living option is one in which both hypotheses are live ones. If I say to you: "Be a theosophist or be a Mohammedan," it is probably a dead option, because for you neither hypothesis is likely to be alive. But if I say: "Be an agnostic or be a Christian," it is otherwise: trained as you are, each hypothesis makes some appeal, however small, to your belief.

2. Next, if I say to you: "Choose between going out with your umbrella or without it," I do not offer you a genuine option, for it is not forced. You can easily avoid it by not going out at all. Similarly, if I say, "Either love me or hate me," "Either call my theory true or call it false," your option is avoidable. You may remain indifferent to me, neither loving nor hating, and you may decline to offer any judgment as to my theory. But if I say, "Either accept this truth or go without it," I put on you a forced option, for there is no standing place outside of the alternative. Every dilemma based on a complete logical disjunction, with no possibility of not choosing, is an option of this forced kind.

3. Finally, if I were Dr. Nansen and proposed to you to join my North Pole expedition, your option would be momentous; for this would probably be your only similar opportunity, and your choice now would either exclude you from the North Pole sort of immortality altogether or put at least the chance of it into your hands. He who refuses to embrace a unique opportunity loses the prize as surely as if he tried and failed. *Per contra,* the option is trivial when the opportunity is not unique, when the stake is insignificant, or when the decision is reversible if it later proves unwise. Such trivial options abound in the scientific life. A chemist finds an hypothesis live enough to spend a year in its verification: he believes in it to that extent. But if his experiments prove inconclusive either way, he is quit for his loss of time, no vital harm being done.

It will facilitate our discussion if we keep all these distinctions well in mind.

2

The next matter to consider is the actual psychology of human opinion. When we look at certain facts, it seems as if our passional and volitional nature lay at the root of all our convictions. When we look at others, it seems as if they could do nothing when the intellect had once said its say. Let us take the latter facts up first.

Does it not seem preposterous on the very fact of it to talk of our opinions being modifiable at will? Can our will either help or hinder our intellect in its perceptions of truth? Can we, by just willing it, believe that Abraham Lincoln's existence is a myth, and that the portraits of him in *McClure's Magazine* are all of some one else: Can we, by any effort of our will, or by any strength of wish that it were true, believe outselves well and about when we are roaring with rheumatism in bed, or feel certain that the sum of the two one-dollar bills in our pocket must be a hundred dollars? We can say any of these things, but we are absolutely impotent to beleive them; and of just such things is the whole fabric of the truths that we do believe in made up—matters of fact, immediate or remote, as Hume said, and relations between ideas, which are either there or not there for us if we see them so, and which if not there cannot be put there by any action of our own.

In Pascal's *Thoughts* there is a celebrated passage known in literature as Pascal's wager. In it he tries to force us into Christianity by reasoning as if our concern with truth resembled our concern with the stakes in a game of chance. Translated freely his words are these: You must either believe or not believe that God is—which will you do? Your human reason cannot say. A game is going on between you and the nature of things which at the day of judgment will bring out either heads or tails. Weigh what your gains and your losses would be if you should stake all you have on heads, or God's existence: if you win in such case, you gain eternal beatitude; if you lose, you lose nothing at all. If there were an infinity of chances, and only one of God in this wager, still you ought to stake your all on God; for though you surely risk a finite loss by this procedure, any finite loss is reasonable, even a certain one is reasonable, if there is but the possibility of infinite gain. Go, then, and take holy water, and have masses said; belief will come and stupefy your scruples—*Cela vous fera croire et vous abetira.* Why should you not? At bottom, what have you to lose?

You probably feel that when religious faith expresses itself thus, in the language of the gaming-table, it is put to its last trumps. Surely Pascal's own personal belief in masses and holy water had far other springs; and this celebrated page of his is but an argument for others, a last desperate snatch at a weapon against the hardness of the unbelieving heart. We feel that a faith in masses and holy water adopted wilfully after such a mechanical calculation would lack the inner soul of faith's reality; and if we were ourselves in the place of the Deity, we should probably take particular pleasure in cutting off believers of this pattern from their infinite reward. It is evident that unless there be some pre-existing tendency to believe in masses and holy water, the option offered to the will by Pascal is not a living option. Certainly no Turk ever took to masses and holy water on its account; and even to us Protestants these means of salvation seem such foregone impossibilities that Pascal's logic, invoked for them specifically, leaves us unmoved. As well might the Mahdi write to us, saying, "I aı the Expected One whom God has created in his effulgence. You shall be infinitely happy if you confess me; otherwise you shall be cut off from the light of the sun. Weigh, then, your infinite gain if I am genuine against your finite sacrifice if I am not!" His logic would be that of Pascal; but he would vainly use it on us, for the hypothesis he offers us is dead. No tendency to act on it exists in us to any degree.

The talk of believing by our volition seems, then, from one point of view, simply silly. From another point of view it is worse than silly, it is vile. When one turns to the magnificent edifice of the physical sciences, and sees how it was reared; what thousands of disinterested moral lives of men lie buried in its mere foundations; what patience and postponement, what choking down of preference, what submission to the icy laws of outer fact are wrought into its very stones and mortar; how absolutely impersonal it stands in its vast augustness—then how besotted and contemptible seems every little sentimentalist who comes blowing his voluntary smoke-wreaths, and pretending to decide things from out of his private dream! Can we wonder if those bred in the rugged and manly school of science should feel like spewing such subjectivism out of their mouths? The whole system of loyalities which grow up in the schools of science go dead against its toleration; so that it is only natural that those who have caught the scientific fever should pass over to the opposite extreme, and write sometimes as if the incorruptibly truthful intellect ought positively to prefer bitterness and unacceptableness to the heart in its cup.

It fortifies my soul to know
That though I perish, Truth is so—

sings Clough, while Huxley exclaims: "My own consolation lies in the reflection that, however bad our posterity may become, so far as they hold by the plain rule of not pretending to believe what they have no reason to believe, because it may be to their advantage so to pretend [the word 'pretend' is surely here redundant], they will not have reached the lowest depth of immorality." And that delicious *enfant terrible* Clifford writes: "Belief is desecrated when given to unproved and unquestioned statements for the solace and private pleasure of the believer. . . . Whoso would deserve well of his fellows in this matter will guard the purity of his belief with a very fanaticism of jealous care, lest at any time it should rest on an unworthy object, and catch a stain which can never be wiped away. . . . If [a] belief has been accepted on insufficient evidence [even though the beleif be true, as Clifford on the same page explains] the pleasure is a stolen one. . . . It is sinful because it is stolen in defiance of our duty to mankind. That duty is to guard ourselves from such beliefs as from a pestilence which may shortly master our own body and then spread to the rest of the town. . . . It is wrong always, everywhere, and for every one, to believe anything upon insufficient evidence."

3

All this strikes one as healthy, even when expressed, as by Clifford, with somewhat too much of robustious pathos in the voice. Free will and simple wishing do seem, in the matter of our credences, to be only fifth wheels to the coach. Yet if any one should thereupon assume that intellectual insight is what remains after wish and will and sentimental preference have taken wing, or that pure reason is what then settles our opinions, he would fly quite as directly in the teeth of the facts.

It is only our already dead hypotheses that our willing nature is unable to bring to life again. But what has made them dead for us is for the most part a previous action of our willing nature of an antagonistic kind. When I say "willing nature," I do not mean only such deliberate volitions as may have set up habits of belief that we cannot now escape from—I mean all such factors of belief as fear and hope, prejudice and passion, imitation and partisanship the circumpressure of our caste and set. As a matter of fact we find ourselves believing, we hardly know how or why. Mr. Balfour gives the name of "authority" to all those influences, born of the intellectual climate, that make hypotheses possible or impossible for us, alive or dead. Here in this room, we all of us believe in molecules and the conservation of energy, in democracy and necessary progress, in Protestant Christianity and the duty of fighting for "the doctrine of the immortal Monroe," all for no reasons worthy of the name. We see into these matters with no more inner clearness, and probably with much less, than any disbeliever in them might possess. His unconventionality would probably have some grounds to show for its conclusions; but for us, not insight, but the *prestige* of the opinions, is what makes the spark shoot from them and light up our sleeping magazines of faith. Our reason is quite satisfied, in nine hundred and ninety-nine cases out of every thousand of us, if it can find a few arguments that will do to recite in case our credulity is criticized by some one else. Our faith is faith in some one else's faith, and in the greatest matters this is most the case. Our belief in truth itself, for instance, that there is a truth, and that our minds and it are made for each other—what is it but a passionate affirmation of desire, in which our social system backs us up? We want to have a truth; we want to beleive that our experiments and studies and discussions must put us in a continually better and better position towards it; and on this line we agree to fight out our thinking lives. But if a Pyrrhonistic sceptic asks us *how we know* all this, can our logic find a reply? No! certainly it cannot. It is just one volition against another—we willing to go in for life upon a trust or assumption which he, for his part, does not care to make.

As a rule we disbelieve all facts and theories for which we have no use. Clifford's cosmic emotions find no use for Christian feelings. Huxley belabors the bishops because there is no use for sacerdotalism in his scheme of life. Newman, on the contrary, goes over to Romanism, and finds all sorts of reasons good for staying there, because a priestly system is for him an organic need and delight. Why do so few "scientists" even look at the evidence for telepathy, so called? Because they think, as a leading biologist, now dead, once said to me, that even if such a thing were true, scientists ought to band together to keep it suppressed and concealed. It would undo the uniformity of Nature and all sorts of other things without which scientists cannot carry on their pursuits. But if this very man had been shown something which as a scientist he might *do* with telepathy, he might not only have examined the evidence, but even have found it good enough. This very law which the logicians would impose upon us —if I may give the name of logicians to those who would rule out our willing nature here—is based on nothing but their own natural wish to exclude all elements for which they, in their professional quality of logicians, can find no use.

Evidently, then, our non-intellectual nature does influence our convictions. There are passional tendencies and volitions which run before and others which come after belief, and it is only the latter that are too late for the fair; and they are not too late when the previous passional work has been already in their own direction. Pascal's argument, instead of being powerless, then seems a regular clincher, and is the last stroke needed to make our faith in masses and holy water complete. The state of things is evidently far from simple; and pure insight and logic, whatever they might do ideally, are not the only things that really do produce our creeds.

4

Our next duty, having recognized this mixed-up state of affairs, is to ask whether it be simply reprehensible and pathological, or whether, on the contrary, we must treat it as a normal element in making up our minds. The thesis I defend is, briefly stated, this: *Our passional nature not only lawfully may, but must, decide an option between propositions, whenever it is a genuine option that cannot by its nature be decided on intellectual grounds; for to say, under such circumstances, "Do not decide, but leave the question open," is itself a passional decision—just like deciding yes or no—and is attended with the same risk of losing the truth.* The thesis thus abstractly expressed will, I trust, soon become quite clear. But I must first indulge in a bit more of preliminary work.

5

It will be observed that for the purposes oı this discussion we are on "dogmatic" ground—ground, I mean, which leaves systematic philosophical scepticism altogether out of account. The postulate that there is truth, and that it is the destiny of our minds to attain it, we are deliberately resolving to make, though the sceptic will not make it. We part company with him, therefore, absolutely, at this point. But the faith that truth exists, and that our minds can find it, may be held in two ways. We may talk of the *empiricist* way and of the *absolutist* way of believing in truth. The absolutists in this matter say that we not only can attain to knowing truth, but we can *know when* we have attained to knowing it; while the empiricists think that although we may attain it, we cannot infallibly know when. To *know* is one thing, and to know for certain *that* we know is another. One may hold to the first being possible without the second; hence the empiricists and the absolutists, although neither of them is a sceptic in the usual philosophic sense of the term, show very different degrees of dogmatism in their lives.

If we look at the history of opinions, we see that the empiricist tendency has largely prevailed in science, while in philosophy the absolutist tendency has had everything its own way. The characteristic sort of happiness, indeed, which philosophies yield has mainly consisted in the conviction felt by each successive school or system that by it bottom-certitude had been attained. "Other philosophies are collections of opinions, mostly false; *my* philosophy gives standing-ground forever"—who does not recognize in this the key-note of every system worthy of the name? A system, to be a system at all, must come as a *closed* system, reversible in this or that detail, perchance, but in its essential features never!

Scholastic orthodoxy, to which one must always go when one wishes to find perfectly clear statement, has beautifully elaborated this absolutist conviction in a doctrine which it calls that of "objective evidence." If, for example, I am unable to doubt that I now exist before you, that two is less than three, or that if all men are mortal then I am mortal too, it is because these things illumine my intellect irresistibly. The final ground of this objective evidence possessed by certain propositions is the *adaequatio intellectus nostri cum re.* The certitude it brings involves an *aptitudinem ad extorquendum certum assensum* on the part of the truth envisaged, and on the side of the subject a *quietem in cognitione*, when once the object is mentally received, that leaves no possibility of doubt behind; and in the whole transaction nothing operates but the *entitas ipsa* of the object and the *entitas ipsa* of the mind. We slouchy modern thinkers dislike to talk in Latin,—indeed, we dislike to take in set terms at all; but at bottom our own state of mind is very much like this whenever we uncritically abandon ourselves: You believe in objective evidence, and I do. Of some things we feel that we are certain: we know, and we know that we do know. There is something that gives a click inside of us, a bell that strikes twelve, when the hands of our mental clock have swept the dial and meet over the meridian hour. The greatest empiricists among us are only empiricists on reflection: when left to their instincts, they dogmatize like infallible popes. When the Cliffords tell us how sinful it is to be Christians on such "insufficient evidence," insufficiency is really the last thing they have in mind. For them the evidence is absolutely sufficient, only it makes the other way. They believe so completely in an anti-Christian order of the universe that there is no living option: Christianity is a dead hypothesis from the start.

6

But now, since we are all such absolutists by instinct, what in our quality of students of philosophy ought we to do about the fact? Shall we espouse and indorse it? Or shall we treat it as a weakness of our nature from which we must free ourselves, if we can?

I sincerely believe that the latter course is the only one we can follow as reflective men. Objective evidence and certitude are doubtless very fine ideals to play with, but where on this moonlit and dream-visited planet are they found? I am, therefore, myself a complete empiricist so far as my theory of human knowledge goes. I live, to be sure, by the practical faith that we must go on experiencing and thinking over our experience, for only thus can our opinions grow more true; but to hold any one of them—I absolutely do not care which—as if it never could be reinterpretable or corrigible, I believe to be a tremendously mistaken attitude, and I think that the whole history of philosophy will bear me out. There is but one indefectibly certain truth, and that is the truth that Pyrrhonistic scepticism itself leaves standing—the truth that the present phenomenon of consciousness exists. That, however, is the bare starting-point of knowledge, the mere admission of a stuff to be philosophized about. The various philosophies are but so many attempts at expressing what this stuff really is. And if we repair to our libraries what disagreement do we discover! Where is a certainly true answer found? Apart from abstract propositions of comparison (such as two and two are the same as four), propositions which tell us nothing by themselves about concrete reality, we find no proposition ever regarded by any one as evidently certain that has not either been called a falsehood, or at least had its truth sincerely questioned by some one else. The transcending of the axioms of geometry, not in play but in earnest, by certain of our contemporaries (as Zollner and Charles H. Hinton), and the rejection of the whole Aristotelian logic by the Hegelians, are striking instances in point.

No concrete test of what is really true has ever been agreed upon. Some make the criterion external to the moment of perception, putting it either in revelation, the *consensue gentium*, the instincts of the heart, or the systematized experience of the race. Others make the perceptive moment its own test—Descartes, for instance, with his clear and distinct ideas guaranteed by the veracity of God; Reid with his "commonsense"; and Kant with his forms of synthetic judgment *a priori*. The inconceivability of the opposite; the capacity to be vertified by sense; the possession of complete organic unity or self-relation, realized when a thing is its own other—are standards which, in turn, have been used. The much lauded objective evidence is never triumphantly there; it is a mere aspiration or *Grenzhegriff*, marking the infinitely remote ideal of our thinking life. To claim that certain truths now possess it, is simply to say that when you think them true and they *are* true, then their evidence is objective, otherwise it is not. But practically one's conviction that the evidence one goes by is of the real objective brand, is only one more subjective opinion added to the lot. For what a contradictory array of opinions have objective evidence and absolute certitude been claimed! The world is rational through and through—its existence is an utlimate brute fact; there is a personal God—a personal God is inconceivable; there is an extra-mental physical world immediately known—the mind can only know its own ideas; a moral imperative exists—obligation is only the resultant of desires; a permanent spiritual principle is in every one—there are only shifting states of mind; there is an endless chain of causes—there is an absolute first cause; an eternal necessity—a freedom; a purpose—no purpose; a primal One—a primal Many; a universal continuity—an essential discontinuity in things; an infinity—no infinity. There is this—there is that; there is indeed nothing which some one has not thought absolutely true, while his neighbor deemed it absolutely false; and not an absolutist among them seems ever to have considered that the trouble may all the time be essential, and that the intellect, even with truth directly in its grasp, may have no infallible signal for knowing whether it be truth or no. When one remembers that the most striking practical application to life of the doctrine of objective certitude has been the conscientious labors of the Holy Office of the Inquisition, one feels less tempted than ever to lend the doctrine a respectful ear.

But please observe, now, that when as empiricists we give up the doctrine of objective certitude, we do not thereby give up the quest or hope of truth itself. We still pin our faith on its existence, and still believe that we gain an even better position towards it by systematically continuing to roll up experiences and think. Our great difference from the scholastic lies in the way we face. The strength of his system lies in the principles, the origin, the *terminus a quo* of his thought; for us the strength is in the outcome, the upshot, the *terminus ad quem*. Not where it comes from but what it leads to is to decide. It matters not to an empiricist from what quarter an hypothesis may come to him: he may have acquired it by fair means or by foul; passion may have whispered or accident suggested it; but if the total drift of thinking continues to confirm it, that is what he means by its being true.

7

One more point, small but important, and our preliminaries are done. There are two ways of looking at our duty in the matter of opinion—ways entirely different, and yet ways about whose difference the theory of knowledge seems hitherto to have shown very little concern. *We must know the truth;* and *we must avoid error*—these are our first and great commandments as would-be knowers; but they are not two ways of stating an identical commandment, they are two separable laws. Although it may indeed happen that when we believe the truth *A*, we escape as an incidental consequence from believing that falsehood *B*, it hardly ever happens that by merely disbelieving *B* we necessarily believe *A*. We may in escaping *B* fall into believing other falsehoods, *C* or *D*, just as bad as *B*; or we may escape *B* by not believing anything at all, not even *A*.

Believe truth! Shun error!—these, we see, are two materially different laws; and by choosing between them we may end by coloring differently our whole intellectual life. We may regard the chase for truth as paramount, and the avoidance of error as secondary; or we may, on the other hand, treat the avoidance of error as more imperative, and let truth take its chance. Clifford, in the instructive passage which I have quoted, exhorts us to the latter course. Believe nothing, he tells us, keep your mind in suspense forever, rather than by closing it on insufficient evidence incur the awful risk of believing lies. You, on the other hand, may think that the risk of being in error is a very small matter when compared with the blessings of real knowledge, and be ready to be duped many times in your investigation rather than postpone indefinitely the chance of guessing true. I myself find it impossible to go with Clifford. We must remember that these feelings of our duty about either truth or error are in any case only expressions of our passional life. Biologically considered, our minds are as ready to grind out falsehood as veracity, and he who says, "Better go without belief forever than believe a lie!" merely shows his own preponderant private horror of becoming a dupe. He may be critical of many of his desires and fears, but this fear he slavishly obeys. He cannot imagine any one questioning its binding force. For my own part, I have also a horror of being duped; but I can believe that worse things than being duped may happen to a man in this world: so Clifford's exhortation has to my ears a thoroughly fantastic sound. It is like a general informing his soldiers that it is better to keep out of battle forever than to risk a single wound. Not so are victories either over enemies or over nature gained. Our errors are surely not such awfully solemn things. In a world where we are so certain to incur them in spite of all our caution, a certain lightness of heart seems healthier than this excessive nervousness on their behalf. At any rate, it seems the fittest thing for the empiricist philosopher.

8

And now, after all this introduction, let us go straight at our question. I have said, and now repeat it, that not only as a matter of fact do we find our passional nature influencing us in our opinions, but that there are some options between opinions in which this influence must be regarded both as an inevitable and as a lawful determinant of our choice.

I fear here that some of you my hearers will begin to scent danger, and lend an inhospitable ear. Two first steps of passion you have indeed had to admit as necessary—we must think so as to avoid dupery, and we must think so as to gain truth; but the surest path to those ideal consummations, you will probably consider, if from now onwards to take no further passional step.

Well, of course, I agree as far as the facts will allow. Whether the option between losing truth and gaining it is not momentous, we can throw the chance of *gaining truth* away, and at any rate save ourselves from any chance of *believing falsehood*, by not making up our minds at all till objective evidence has come. In scientific questions, this is almost always the case; and even in human affairs in general, the need of acting is seldom so urgent that a false belief to act on is better than no belief at all. Law courts, indeed, have to decide on the best evidence attainable to the moment, because a judge's duty is to make law as well as to ascertain it, and (as a learned judge once said to me) few cases are worth spending much time over: the great thing is to have them decided on *any* acceptable principles, and got out of the way. But in our dealings with objective nature we obviously are recorders, not makers, of the truth; and decisions for the mere sake of deciding promptly and getting on to the next business would be wholly out of place. Throughout the breadth of physical nature facts are what they are quite independently of us, and seldom is there any such hurry about them that the risks of being duped by believing a premature theory need be faced. The questions here are always trivial options, the hypotheses are hardly living (at any rate not living for us spectators) the choice between believing truth or falsehood is seldom forced. The attitude of sceptical balance is therefore the absolutely wise one if we would escape mistakes. What difference, indeed, does it make to most of us whether we have or have not a theory of the Rontgen rays, whether we believe or not in mind-stuff, or have a conviction about the causality of conscious states? It makes no difference. Such options are not forced on us. On every account it is better not to make them, but still keep weighing reasons *pro et contra* with an indifferent hand.

I speak, of course, here of the purely judging mind. For purposes of discovery such indifference is to be less highly recommended, and science would be far less advanced than she is if the passionate desires of individuals to get their own faiths confirmed had been kept out of the game. See for example the sagacity which Spencer and Weismann now display. On the other hand, if you want an absolute duffer in an investigation, you must, after all, take the man, who has no interest whatever in its results: he is the warranted incapable, the positive fool. The most useful investigator, because the most sensitive observer, is always he whose eager interest in one side of the question is balanced by an equally keen nervousness lest he become deceived. Science has organized this nervousness into a regular *technique*, her so-called method of verification; and she has fallen so deeply in love with the method that one may even say she has ceased to care for truth by itself at all. It is only truth as technically verified that interests her. The truth of truths might come in merely affirmative form, and she would decline to touch it. Such truths as that, she might repeat with Clifford, would be stolen in defiance of her duty to mankind. Human passions, however, are stronger than technical rules. "*Le coeur a ses raisons,*" as Pascal says, "*que la raison ne connait pas*"; and however indifferent to all but the bare rules of the game the umpire, the abstract intellect, may be, the concrete players who furnish him the materials to judge of are usually, each one of them, in love with some pet "live hypothesis" of his own. Let us agree, however, that wherever there is no forced option, the dispassionately judicial intellect with no pet hypothesis, saving us, as it does, from dupery at any rate, ought to be ideal.

The question next arises: Are there not somewhere forced options in our speculative questions, and can we (as men who may be interested at least as much in positively gaining truth as in merely escaping dupery) always wait with impunity till the coercive evidence shall have arrived? It seems *a priori* improbable that the truth should be so nicely adjusted to our needs and powers as that. In the great boarding-house of nature, the cakes and the butter and the syrup seldom come out so even and leave the plates so clean. Indeed, we should view them with scientific suspicion if they did.

9

Moral questions immediately present themselves as questions whose solution cannot wait for sensible proof. A moral question is a question not of what sensibly exists, but of what is good, or would be good if it did exist. Science can tell us what exists; but to compare the *worths*, both of what exists and of what does not exist, we must consult not science, but what Pascal calls our heart. Science herself consults her heart when she lays it down that the infinite ascertainment of fact and correction of false belief are the supreme goods for man. Challenge the statement, and science can only repeat it oracularly, or else prove it by showing that such ascertainment and correction bring man all sorts of other goods which man's heart in turn declares. The question of having moral beliefs at all or not having them is decided by our will. Are our moral preferences true or false, or are they only odd biological phenomena, making things good or bad for *us*, but in themselves indifferent? How can your pure intellect decide? If your heart does not *want* a world of moral reality, your head will assuredly never make you believe in one. Mephistophelian scepticism, indeed, will satisfy the head's play-instincts much better than any rigorous idealism can. Some men (even at the student age) are so naturally cool-hearted that the moralistic hypothesis never has for them any pungent life, and in their supercilious presence the hot young moralist always feels strangely ill at ease. The appearance of knowingness is on their side, of *naivete* and gullibility on his. Yet, in the inarticulate heart of him, he clings to it that he is not a dupe, and that there is a realm in which (as Emerson says) all their wit and intellectual superiority is no better than the cunning of a fox. Moral scepticism can no more be refuted or proved by logic than intellectual scepticism can. When we stick to it that there *is* truth (be it of either kind), we do so with our whole nature, and resolve to stand or fall by the results. The sceptic with his whole nature adopts the doubting attitude; but which of us is the wiser, Omniscience only knows.

Turn now from these wide questions of good to a certain class of questions of fact, questions concerning personal relations, states of mind between one man and another. *Do you like me or not?*—for example. Whether you do or not depends, in countless instances, on whether I meet you half-way, am willing to assume that you must like me, and show you trust and expectation. The previous faith on my part in your liking's existence is in such cases what makes your liking come. But if I stand aloof, and refuse to budge an inch until I have objective evidence, until you shall have done something apt, as the absolutists say, *ad extorquendum assensum meum*, ten to one your liking never comes. How many women's hearts are vanquished by the mere sanguine insistence of some man that they *must* love him! he will not consent to the hypothesis that they cannot. The desire for a certain kind of truth here brings about that special truth's existence; and so it is in innumerable cases of other sorts. Who gains promotions, boons, appointments, but the man in whose life they are seen to play the part of live hypotheses, who discounts them, sacrifices other things for their sake before they have come, and takes risks for them in advance? His faith acts on the power above him as a claim, and creates its own verification.

A social organism of any sort whatever, large or small, is what it is because each member proceeds to his own duty with a trust that the other members will simultaneously do theirs. Wherever a desired result is achieved by the cooperation of many independent persons, its existence as a fact is a pure consequence of the precursive faith in a commercial system, a ship, a college, an athletic team, all exist on this condition, without which not only is nothing achieved, but nothing is even attempted. A whole train of passengers (individually brave enough) will be looted by a few highwaymen, simply because the latter can count on one another, while each passenger fears that if he makes a movement of resistance, he will be shot before any one else backs him up. If we believed that the whole car-full would rise at once with us, we should each severally rise, and train-robbing would never even be attempted. There are, then, cases where a fact cannot come at all unless a preliminary faith exists in its coming. *And where faith in a fact can help create the fact,* that would be an insane logic which should say that faith running ahead of scientific evidence is the "lowest kind of immorality" into which a thinking being can fall. Yet such is the logic by which our scientific absolutists pretend to regulate our lives!

10

In truths dependent on our personal action, then, faith based on desire is certainly a lawful and possibly an indispensable thing.

But now, it will be said, these are all childish human cases, and have nothing to do with great cosmical matters, like the question of religious faith. Let us then pass on to that. Religions differ so much in their accidents that in discussing the religious question we must make it very generic and broad. What then do we now mean by the religious hypothesis? Science says things are; morality says some things are better than other things; and religion says essentially two things.

First, she says that the best things are the more eternal things, the overlapping things, the things in the universe that throw the last stone, so to speak, and say the final word. "Perfection is eternal"—this phrase of Charles Secrétan seems a good way of putting this first affirmation of religion, an affirmation which obviously cannot yet be verified scientifically at all.

The second affirmation of religion is that we are better off even now if we believe her first affirmation to be true.

Now, let us consider what the logical elements of this situation are *in case the religious hypothesis in both its branches be really true.* (Of course, we must admit that possibility at the outset. If we are to discuss the question at all, it must involve a living option. If for any of you religion be a hypothesis that cannot, by any living possibility, be true, then you need go no farther. I speak to the "saving remnant" alone.) So proceeding, we see, first, that religion offers itself as a *momentous* option. We are supposed to gain, even now, by our belief, and to lose by our non-belief a certain vital good. Secondly, religion is a *forced* option, so far as that good goes. We cannot escape the issue by remaining sceptical and waiting for more light, because, although we do avoid error in that way if *religion be untrue*, we lose the good, *if it be true,* just as certainly as if we positively chose to disbelieve. It is as if a man should hesitate indefinitely to ask a certain woman to marry him because he was not perfectly sure that she would prove an angel after he brought her home. Would he not cut himself off from that particular angel-possibility as decisively as if he went and married some one else? Scepticism, then, is not avoidance of option; it is option of a certain particular kind of risk. *Better risk loss of truth than chance of error*—that is your faith-vetoer's exact position. He is actively playing his stake as much as the believer is; he is backing the field against the religious hypothesis, just as the believer is backing the religious hypothesis against the field. To preach scepticism to us as a duty until "sufficient evidence" for religion be found, is tantamount therefore to telling us, when in presence of the religious hypothesis, that to yield to our fear of its being error is wiser and better than to yield to our hope that it may be true. It is not intellect against all passions, then; it is only intellect with one passion laying down its law. And by what, forsooth, is the supreme wisdom of this passion warranted? Dupery for dupery, what proof is there that dupery through hope is so much worse than dupery through fear? I, for one, can see no proof; and I simply refuse obedience to the scientists command to imitate his kind of option, in a case where my own sake is important enough to give me the right to choose my own form of risk. If religion be true and the evidence for it be still insufficient, I do not wish, by putting your extinguisher upon my nature (which feels to me as if it had after all some business in this matter), to forfeit my sole chance in life of getting upon the winning side—that chance depending, of course, on my willingness to run the risk of acting as if my passional need of taking the world religiously might be prophetic and right.

All this is on the supposition that it really may be prophetic and right, and that, even to us who are discussing the matter, religion is a live hypothesis which may be true. Now, to most of us religion comes in a still further way that makes a veto on our active faith even more illogical. The more perfect and more eternal aspect of the universe is represented in our religions as having personal form. The universe is no longer a mere *It* to us, but a *Thou*, if we are religious; and any relation that may be possible from person to person might be possible here. For instance, although in one sense we are passive portions of the universe, in another we show a curious autonomy, as if we were small active centres on our own account. We feel, too, as if the appeal of religion to us were made to our own active good-will, as if evidence might be forever withheld from us unless we met the hypothesis half-way. To take a trivial illustration: just as a man who in a company of gentlemen made no advances, asked a warrant for every concession, and believed no one's word without proof, would cut himself off by such churlishness from all the social rewards that a more trusting spirit would earn—so here, one who should shut himself up in snarling logicality and try to make the gods extort his recongition willy-nilly, or not get it at all, might cut himself off forever from his only opportunity of making the gods' acquaintance. This feeling, forced on us we know not whence, that by obstinately believing that there are gods (although not to do so would be so easy both for our logic and our life) we are doing the universe the deepest service we can, seems part of the living essence of the religious hypothesis. If the hypothesis *were* true in all its part, including this one, then pure intellectualism, with its veto on our making willing advances, would be an absurdity; and some participation of our sympathetic nature would be logically required, I, therefore, for one, cannot see my way to accepting the agnostic rules for truth-seeking, or willfully agree to keep my willing nature out of the game. I cannot do so for this plain reason, that *a rule of thinking which would absolutely prevent me from acknowledging certain kinds of truth if those kinds of truth were really there, would be an irrational rule.* That for me is the long and short of the formal logic of the situation, no matter what the kinds of truth might materially be.

I confess I do not see how this logic can be escaped. But sad experience makes me fear that some of you may still shrink from radically saying with me, in *abstractor*, that we have the right to believe at our own risk any hypothesis that is live enough to tempt our will. I suspect, however, that if this is so, it is because you have got away from the abstract logical point of view altogether, and are thinking (perhaps without realizing it) of some particular religious hypothesis which for you is dead. The freedom to "believe what we will" you apply to the case of some patent superstition; and the faith you think of is the faith defined by the schoolboy when he said, "Faith is when you believe something that you know ain't true." I can only repeat that this is misapprehension. *In concreto,* the freedom to believe can only cover living options which the intellect of the individual cannot by itself resolve; and living options never seem absurdities to him who has them to consider. When I look at the religious question as it really puts itself to concrete men, and when I think of all the possibilities which both practically and theoretically it involves, then this command that we shall put a stopper on our heart, instincts, and courage, and *wait*—acting of course meanwhile more or less as if religion were *not* true—till doomsday, or till such time as our intellect and senses working together may have raked in evidence enough—this command, I say, seems to me the queerest idol ever manufactured in the philosophic cave. Were we scholastic absolutists, there might be more excuse. If we had an infallible intellect with its objective certitudes, we might feel ourselves disloyal to such a perfect organ of knowledge in not trusting to it exclusively, in not waiting for its releasing word. But if we are empiricists, if we believe that no bell in us tolls to let us know for certain when truth is in our grasp, then it seems a piece of idle fantasticality to preach so solemnly our duty of waiting for the bell. Indeed we *may* wait if we will—I hope you do not think that I am denying that—but if we do so, we do so at our peril as much as if we believed. In either case we *act,* taking our life in our hands. No one of us ought to issue vetoes to the other, nor should we bandy words of abuse. We ought, on the contrary, delicately and profoundly to respect one another's mental freedom: then only shall we bring about the intellectual republic; then only shall we have that spirit of inner intolerance without which all our outer tolerance is soulless, and which is empiricism's glory; then only shall we live and let live, in speculative as well as in practical things.

I began by a reference to Fitz-James Stephen; let me end by a quotation from him. "What do you think of yourself? What do you think of the world? . . . These are questions with which all must deal as it seems good to them. They are riddles of the Sphinx, and in some way or other we must deal with them. . . . In all important transactions of life we have to take a leap in the dark. . . . If we decide to leave the riddles unanswered, that is a choice; if we waver in our answer, that, too, is a choice: but whatever choice we make, we make it at our peril. If a man chooses to turn his back altogether on God and the future, no one can prevent him; no one can show beyond reasonable doubt that he is mistaken. If a man thinks otherwise and acts as he thinks, I do not see that any one can prove that *he* is mistaken. Each must act as he thinks best; and if he is wrong, so much the worse for him. We stand on a mountain pass in the midst of whirling snow and blinding mist, through which we get glimpses now and then of paths which may be deceptive. If we stand still we shall be frozen to death. If we take the wrong road we shall be dashed to pieces. We do not certainly know whether there is any right one. What must we do? 'Be strong and of a good courage.' Act for the best, hope for the best, and take what comes. . . . If death ends all, we cannot meet death better."

Denis Diderot: A Dialogue on Religion

I had some business or other with Maréchal de ———. I went to his house one morning. He was out. I was shown in to Madame la Maréchale. She is a charming woman, beautiful and pious as an angel: and she has a tone of voice and naïveté of speech which entirely suit her face. She was dressing. A chair is drawn up. I sit down and we talk. As a result of some observations on my part which edified and surprised her (for she holds that the man who denies the Blessed Trinity is a ruffian who will end on the gallows), she said to me:

Are you not M. Crudeli?

CRUDELI. Yes.

MARECHALE. The man who believes in nothing?

CRUDELI. I am.

MARECHALE. But your morals are the same as a believer's.

CRUDELI. Why not, if that believer is an honest man?

MARECHALE. And you put that morality into practice?

CRUDELI. As well as I can.

MARECHALE. What! you do not steal, or kill, or pillage?

CRUDELI. Very rarely.

MARECHALE. Then what do you get out of not believing?

CRUDELI. Nothing; but does one believe in order to get something out of it?

MARECHALE. I do not know. But a little self-interest comes in useful both for this world and the next.

CRUDELI. I am a little sorry for our poor human race, to be no better than that.

MARECHALE. So you do not steal at all?

CRUDELI. I promise you, not.

MARECHALE. But if you are neither a thief nor an assassin, you must admit you are hardly consistent.

CRUDELI. Why so?

MARECHALE. Because I think if I had nothing to fear or to hope, after death, I should allow myself a good many little pleasures here below. I admit I lend to God at a stiff rate of interest.

CRUDELI. So you think, perhaps.

MARECHALE. It is not a matter of thinking. It is a fact.

CRUDELI. But might one ask, What are those things you would allow yourself, if you did not believe?

MARECHALE. One might not. They are only for my confessor's ears.

CRUDELI. For my part, I never expect any return on my money.

MARECHALE. All beggars are in that situation.

CRUDELI. You would rather I were a usurer?

MARECHALE. Why, yes. One can be as usurious with God as one pleases. He cannot be ruined. It is hardly delicate, I know. But what does that matter? As the essential thing is to get into Heaven either by cunning or by force, we must use every means, and neglect no source of profit. Alas! whatever we do, we shall get but scanty recognition compared with what we had looked for. And you, you look for nothing?

CRUDELI. Nothing.

MARECHALE. But that is very sad. Agree then—you are either a rogue or a madman.

CRUDELI. But I cannot.

MARECHALE. But what motive can an unbeliever have for being good, unless he be mad?

CRUDELI. I shall tell you.

MARECHALE. I shall be most grateful.

CRUDELI. Do you think a man can be born with such a happy disposition as to find real pleasure in doing good?

MARECHALE. I do.

CRUDELI. And that he may have received an excellent education, which will strengthen his natural leaning towards benevolence.

MARECHALE. Certainly.

CRUDELI. And that, in later life, experience may have convinced us that on the whole it is better for one's happiness in this world to be an honest man than a rogue.

MARECHALE. Why, yes. But how can he be an honest man, when evil principles united with the passions involve us in evil?

CRUDELI. By inconsistency. And is there anything commoner than inconsistency?

MARECHALE. Alas! Unfortunately not. We believe, yet every day we behave as though we did not.

CRUDELI. And without believing, one behaves very much as if one did.

MARECHALE. If you like. But what can be the harm in having one reason the more, religion, for doing good, and one reason the less, unbelief, for doing wrong?

CRUDELI. None, if religion were a motive for doing good and unbelief for doing wrong.

MARECHALE. But can there be any doubt about it? What is the essence of religion but to check our vile corrupted nature, and that of unbelief but to abandon it to its own wickedness by relieving it of fear?

CRUDELI. That is going to involve us in a long discussion.

MARECHALE. What of that? The Maréchal will not be back for a bit. And we are better employed in rational discussion than in slandering our neighbours.

CRUDELI. Then I must go back a little.

MARECHALE. As far as you like, provided you make yourself understood.

CRUDELI. If I do not, it will be entirely my fault.

MARECHALE. That is very polite of you. But you must know I have hardly read anything but my Prayer Book, and I do almost nothing but study the Gospels and breed children.

CRUDELI. Two duties you have admirably fulfilled.

MARECHALE. As regards the children, yes. Here are six round me and in a few days you will be able to see a seventh on my knee. But begin.

CRUDELI. Well. Is there any good in this world which has not got its drawbacks?

MARECHALE. None.

CRUDELI. And any evil which has not got its advantages?

MARECHALE. None.

CRUDELI. What then do you call a good or an evil?

MARECHALE. An evil is that which has more drawbacks than advantages, and a good that which has more advantages than drawbacks.

CRUDELI. I hope you will be good enough to remember your definition of good and evil?

MARECHALE. I will. But do you call that a definition?

CRUDELI. Yes.

MARECHALE. Then it is philosophy?

CRUDELI. And very good philosophy, too.

MARECHALE. So I have made philosophy!

CRUDELI. So you are convinced that religion has more advantages than drawbacks. Hence you call it a good?

MARECHALE. Yes.

CRUDELI. And for my part, I have no doubt your bailiff robs you a little less just before Easter than he does a few days afterwards, and that from time to time religion prevents a number of small evils and produces a number of small goods.

MARECHALE. Little by little, that tots up.

CRUDELI. But do you think that these poky little advantages make up adequately for the terrible ravages religion has caused in the past and will cause in the future? Remember it has created and now perpetuates the most violent national hatreds. No Mussulman but believes he is doing an action agreeable to God and the holy prophet in exterminating every Christian. And the Christians on their side are scarcely more tolerant. Think how it has created and still perpetuates in the same country divisions rarely suppressed without the shedding of blood. Our own history offers us examples all too recent and too tragic. Think how it has created and still perpetuates, in society between citizens, and in the family between relatives, the most violent and most lasting of hatreds. Christ said he had come to separate husband from wife, mother from children, brother from sister, friend from friend. And his prediction has been all too faithfully fulfilled.

MARECHALE. These are abuses, not the essentials, of the thing.

CRUDELI. It is, if abuses and essentials are inseparable.

MARECHALE. And how can you demonstrate that religion and its abuses are inseparable?

CRUDELI. Very easily. Suppose a misanthrope had set out to harm the human race, what could he have invented better than belief in an incomprehensible being about whom men should never agree and to whom they should attach more importance than to their own lives. Now is it possible to separate from the notion of a Divinity the most profound incomprehensibility and the greatest importance?

MARECHALE. No.

CRUDELI. Your conclusion, then?

MARECHALE. My conclusion is that it is an idea which might well be disastrous, if lunatics got hold of it.

CRUDELI. And you may add that lunatics always have been and always will be in the vast majority; and that the most dangerous lunatics are those made so by religion, and that the disturbers of society know how to make good use of them when occasion arises.

MARECHALE. But we must have something with which to frighten men off those actions, which escape the severity of the laws. Destroy religion, and what will you put in its place?

CRUDELI. And suppose I had nothing to put in its place, there would always be one terrible prejudice the less. Besides, in no century and with no nation have religious opinions been the basis of national morals. The gods adored by the ancient Greeks and Romans, the most virtuous of people, were the merest scum: a Jupiter who should have been burnt alive: a Venus fit for a reformatory: a Mercury who ought to be in a jail.

MARECHALE. So you think it does not matter at all whether we be Christians or pagans; that we should be none the worse for being pagans and are none the better for being Christians?

CRUDELI. Honestly, I am certain of it, unless we should be slightly merrier for being pagans.

MARECHALE. That cannot be.

CRUDELI. But are there any Christians? I have never seen one.

MARECHALE. And you say that to me?

CRUDELI. No, not to you, but to one of my neighbours, who is as honest and pious as you: who thinks herself a Christian in all sincerity just as you do.

MARECHALE. And you made her admit she was wrong?

CRUDELI. In a moment.

MARECHALE. And how?

CRUDELI. I opened a New Testament, which she had used a great deal, for it was very worn. I read her the Sermon on the Mount, and after each article I asked her—Do you do that? Or that? Or even that? I went one further. She is very beautiful, and although most good and pious, she is well aware of the fact. She has a very white skin, and although she does not attach any great importance to this slender merit, she does not mind it being praised. Her throat is as handsome as throat can be: and although she is very modest, she thinks it as well that this should be noticed.

MARECHALE. But if only herself and her husband know it?

CRUDELI. Certainly, I think her husband knows it better than anyone else. But for a woman who prides herself on being such a tremendous Christian this is not enough. I said to her: "Is it not written in the Gospel that he who lusts after his neighbour's wife has committed adultery in his heart?"

MARECHALE. And she answered Yes.

CRUDELI. And I said: And is not adultery committed in the heart as surely damned as adultery of the most thoroughgoing kind?

MARECHALE. And she answered Yes.

CRUDELI. And I said: And if the man is damned for the adultery he has committed in his heart, what will be the fate of the woman who invites all those who come near her to commit this crime? This last question embarrassed her.

MARECHALE. I understand; for she did not, very carefully, cover up this throat of hers, which is handsome as throat can be.

CRUDELI. That is so. She replied it was a convention, as if anything were more conventional than to call oneself a Christian and not be one. And also that one must not dress absurdly, as if there could be any comparison between a trifling little absurdity and one's eternal damnation, as well as the damnation of one's neighbour. And also that she was in the hands of her dressmaker, as if it were not better to change one's dressmaker than to throw over one's religion. And that it was the whim of her husband, as if a husband were sufficiently insensate to demand from his wife the forgetfulness of decency and duty, and as if a true Christian should push obedience to a preposterous husband to the point of sacrificing the will of God and despising the threats of her Redeemer.

MARECHALE. I knew all those childish answers before you mentioned them. And perhaps I should have employed them like your neighbour. And we should both have been insincere. But what line did she take after your protest?

CRUDELI. The day after our conversation (it was a festival of the Church), as I was going up to my room, my beautiful and pious neighbour was coming down, on the way to Mass.

MARECHALE. Dressed as usual.

CRUDELI. Dressed as usual. I smiled. She smiled. We passed each other without speaking. And she, an honest woman! a Christian! a pious woman! And after this sample, and one hundred thousand others exactly like it, what real influence can I allow religion to have on morals? Practically none, and so much the better.

MARECHALE. What! so much the better?

CRUDELI. Yes. If twenty thousand Parisians took it into their heads to base their conduct strictly on the Sermon on the Mount . . .

MARECHALE. Well, there would be a few handsome throats better covered.

CRUDELI. And so many lunatics that the commissioner of police would not know what to do with them: for our asylums would never hold them. There are two moralities in Inspired Books. One general and common to all nations and all religions, which is more or less observed: the other, peculiar to each nation and each religion in which people believe, which they preach in church and praise up at home, but which is not observed at all.

MARECHALE. And to what is this preposterous state of affairs due?

CRUDELI. To the impossibility of subjecting a nation to a rule which suits only a few melancholiacs, who have imposed it on their characters. It is with religious as with monastic institutions; they relax with time. They are lunacies which cannot hold out against the constant impulse of nature, which brings us back under her law. See to it that private good be so closely united to public good that a citizen can hardly harm society without harming himself. Promise virtue its reward, as you have promised wickedness its punishment. Let virtue lead to high offices of state, without distinction of faith, wherever virtue is to be found. Then you need only count on a small number of wicked men, who are involved in vice by a perversity of nature which nothing can correct. No. Temptation is too near: hell too far off. Look for nothing worth the attention of a wise lawgiver from a system of fantastic opinions, which imposes only on children: which encourages crime by its convenient system of penances: which sends the guilty man to ask pardon of God for harm done to man, and which degrades the order of natural and moral duties by subordinating it to an order of imaginary duties.

MARECHALE. I do not follow.

CRUDELI. Let me explain. But I think I hear the Maréchal's carriage coming back just in time to prevent my saying something silly.

MARECHALE. Say it. I shall not understand you. I am an adept at understanding only what gives me pleasure.

CRUDELI. I went up to her and said quite low in her ear: "Ask the vicar of your parish, which of the two crimes is, in his opinion, the more heinous—to piss into a sacred vessel or to blacken the reputation of an honest woman. He will shudder with horror at the first, and the civil law, which scarcely notices calumny while punishing sacrilege with fire, will complete the confusion of ideas and the corruption of the intelligence."

MARECHALE. I know more than one woman who would never eat meat on a Friday and who . . . I was going to make my silly contribution. Go on.

CRUDELI. But I simply must speak to the Maréchal.

MARECHALE. One moment more, and then we will go and see him together. I do not quite see how to answer you, but you have not made me change my opinion.

CRUDELI. I did not set out to change it. It is with religion as with marriage. Marriage, which has wrecked so many lives, has made for your happiness and for that of the Maréchal. You have both of you done well to marry. Religion, which has made, does make, and will make so many men wicked, has made you better still: you do well to keep it. It is sweet to you to imagine beside you, and above your head, a great and powerful being who sees you walk upon the earth, and this idea strengthens your steps. Continue to be happy in this august guarantor of your thoughts, in this spectator, in this sublime model for your actions.

MARECHALE. I see you have not got the proselytizing mania.

CRUDELI. Not in the least.

MARECHALE. I think the better of you for it.

CRUDELI. I allow everyone to think as he pleases, provided I am allowed to think as I please. And then those who exist in order to free themselves from these prejudices are scarcely in need of being catechized.

MARECHALE. Do you think man can get along without superstition?

CRUDELI. Not as long as he remains ignorant and timid.

MARECHALE. Well then, superstition for superstition, ours is as good as another.

CRUDELI. I do not think so.

MARECHALE. Now tell me sincerely. Does the idea of being nothing after death not distress you?

CRUDELI. I would rather exist, though I do not know why a Being who has been once capable of making me wretched for no reason should not enjoy doing so twice.

MARECHALE. But if, despite this drawback, the hope of a life to come appear to you consoling and sweet, why tear it from us?

CRUDELI. I do not entertain this hope because desire for it has not blinded me to its hollowness; but I take it away from no one else. If anyone can believe they will see without eyes, hear without ears, think without a head, love without a heart, feel without senses, exist without being anywhere, and be something without place or size, very well.

MARECHALE. But who made this world?

CRUDELI. I ask you.

MARECHALE. God.

CRUDELI. And what is God?

MARECHALE. A spirit.

CRUDELI. And if a spirit makes matter, why should not matter make a spirit!

MARECHALE. And why should it?

CRUDELI. Because I see it do so every day. Do you believe animals have souls?

MARECHALE. Certainly I do.

CRUDELI. Could you tell me, for example, what happens to the soul of the Peruvian serpent, hung on the chimney and exposed to the smoke for two years together while it is drying?

MARECHALE. How can it matter to me what happens to it?

CRUDELI. So you do not know that this serpent, after being dried and smoked, is resuscitated and reborn?

MARECHALE. I do not believe it for a moment.

CRUDELI. Yet a very clever man, Bouguer, asserts it.

MARECHALE. Your clever man is a liar.

CRUDELI. But suppose he were telling the truth?

MARECHALE. I should get off with believing that animals are machines.

CRUDELI. And man, who is only a machine a little more perfected than any other. . . . But the Maréchal.

MARECHALE. One more question and it is the last. Does your unbelief leave you calm?

CRUDELI. As calm as it is possible to be.

MARECHALE. But suppose you were mistaken?

CRUDELI. Suppose I were?

MARECHALE. Suppose everything you believe false were true and you were damned. Monsieur Crudeli, it is a terrible thing to be damned. To burn through eternity. It is a long time.

CRUDELI. La Fontaine thought we should be as comfortable as fishes in water.

MARECHALE. Yes, yes, but your La Fontaine became very serious at the end, and I expect the same of you.

CRUDELI. I can answer for nothing when my brain has softened. But if I end with one of those illnesses which leave the dying man in possession of his powers, I shall be no more distressed at the expected moment than I am now.

MARECHALE. Your fearlessness amazes me.

CRUDELI. I am much more amazed at the fearlessness of the dying man who believes in a severe judge, in one who weighs our most secret thoughts, and in whose balance the justest man would be lost through vanity if he did not tremble to find himself too light. If this dying man could choose between being wiped out and going before this tribunal, I should be much more amazed by his fearlessness if he hesitated to choose the first: unless, indeed, he were more insensate than the companion of Saint Bruno or more intoxicated with his own merits than Bohola.

MARECHALE. I have read the account of the associate of Saint Bruno, but I have never heard of your Bohola.

CRUDELI. He was a Jesuit of the College at Pinsk in Lithuania, who left at his death a casket full of money with a note written and signed in his own hand.

MARECHALE. And the note?

CRUDELI. . . . was as follows: "I want my dear colleague, to whom I hand over this casket, to open it when I have performed miracles. The money inside will go to the expenses in connection with my beatification. I have added some authentic memoirs in confirmation of my virtues which will be useful to those engaged on writing my life."

MARECHALE. But it is a roaring farce.

CRUDELI. To me, yes; but not to you: your God has got no sense of humour.

MARECHALE. That is so.

CRUDELI. It is very easy to sin grievously against your law.

MARECHALE. I agree. It is.

CRUDELI. The justice that will decide your fate is very stern.

MARECHALE. True.

CRUDELI. And if you believe in the oracles of your creed, the number of the saved is small.

MARECHALE. Oh, I am no Jansenist: I look only at the bright side of the medal. In my eyes the blood of Jesus Christ has flowed far. I should think it very odd if the Devil, who never sacrificed his son, nevertheless got the lion's share.

CRUDELI. Do you damn Socrates, Phocion, Aristides, Cato, Trajan, Marcus Aurelius?

MARECHALE. Gracious me, no! Only wild beasts can believe that. Saint Paul said everyone will be judged by his own law and Saint Paul is right.

CRUDELI. And by what law will the unbeliever be judged?

MARECHALE. Your case is rather different. You are one of those cursed inhabitants of Corozaïn and Betzaïda who shut their eyes to the light that shone on them, and put wax in their ears so as not to hear the voice of reason which spoke to them.

CRUDELI. But these Corozaïnians and Betzaïdans were unique if they were free to believe or not to believe.

MARECHALE. They saw prodigies enough to have raised the price of sackcloth and ashes in Tyre and Sidon.

CRUDELI. These inhabitants of Tyre and Sidon were intelligent, the Corozaïnian and Betzaïdan mere fools. But is it for him who made them fools to punish them for their folly? Just now I related to you an actual occurrence. Now I want to tell you a story: A young Mexican . . . But the Maréchal?

MARECHALE. I will send to find out if we can see him. Well then, your young Mexican?

CRUDELI. Tired of his work, walked one day upon the seashore. He saw a plank with one end in the water and the other on the beach. He takes his seat on the plank; and turning his gaze on the huge space stretched out before him, said: "It is certain my grandmother is talking nonsense when she romances about some inhabitants or other who, God knows when, came here heaven knows where from, but from some country beyond the seas. Why, there is no commonsense in it. Cannot I see the sea merging in the sky? And can I believe, against the evidence of my senses, an old story of unknown date, which everyone rearranges to suit himself, which is a mere farrago of preposterous incidents over which men eat their hearts out, and tear out the whites of their eyes." As he reasoned thus, the undulating waters rocked him on his plank and he fell asleep. As he sleeps, the wind gets up, the waves carry the barque away, and behold our young reasoner started on his voyage.

MARECHALE. Alas! that is just like us. We are each on his plank: the wind blows and the waves carry us away.

CRUDELI. He was already far from the mainland when he awoke. And who was mighty surprised to find himself on the open sea? Why, our young Mexican. And who was more surprised still? He again, when the sea seemed to merge in the sky on every side, now that he had lost sight of the beach where he had been walking only a moment before. Then he began to suspect that he might have been mistaken, and that if the wind continued in the same quarter he might be carried on shore, amongst those inhabitants of whom his mother had talked to him so often.

MARECHALE. But you say nothing about his agitation.

CRUDELI. He felt none. He said to himself: "What does that matter to me, as long as I get on shore? I have argued like a fool, certainly. But I was sincere with myself, and that is all that can be expected of me. If it be not a virtue to be intelligent, it is not a crime to be a fool." Meanwhile, the wind went on blowing, the man and the plank drifted along, and the unknown shore began to appear. He touches land, and there he is!

MARECHALE. We shall meet again there one day, M. Crudeli.

CRUDELI. I sincerely hope so. Wherever it may be, I shall always be flattered to pay you my addresses. Scarcely had he left his plank and set foot on the sand when he perceived a venerable old man standing by his side. The Mexican asked him where he was and whom he had the honour of addressing. "I am the sovereign of the country," answered the old man. At once the young man prostrated himself. "Get up," said the old man; "you have denied my existence?" "I have." "And the existence of my empire?" "I have." "I forgive you that because you acted in good faith. But the rest of your thoughts and actions have not been equally innocent." Then the old man, who held him by the ear, recalled to him all the errors of his life. And at each article the young Mexican bowed his head and beat his breast and prayed for pardon. . . . There now. Put yourself a moment in the place of the old man and tell me what you would have done. Would you have taken this insensate young man by the hair and joyfully dragged him along the beach for ever?

MARECHALE. To tell you the truth, no.

CRUDELI. And if one of your six pretty children, after escaping from the paternal roof, and committing every conceivable sort of folly, came home repentant?

MARECHALE. I should run to meet him. I should clasp him in my arms and bathe him with my tears. But his father the Maréchal would not take the thing so lightly.

CRUDELI. The Maréchal is not a tiger.

MARECHALE. Far from it.

CRUDELI. He would make rather a scene about it. But he would forgive in the end.

MARECHALE. Certainly.

CRUDELI. Especially if he came to reflect that, before becoming the father of the child, he had known all that was going to happen to it, and that punishing him for his faults would be of no use to himself, the guilty one, or his brothers.

MARECHALE. The Maréchal and the old man are two different people.

CRUDELI. You mean to say that the Maréchal is better than the old man?

MARECHALE. Heaven forbid! I mean to say that if my notion of justice is not the same as the Maréchal's perhaps the notion of the Maréchal will not be the same as the old man's.

CRUDELI. But you cannot have realized the consequences of that answer. Either the general definition applies equally to you, to the Maréchal, to me, to the young Mexican and the old man, or I can no longer say what is what, or how one pleases or displeases the old man.

We had reached this point when we were told that the Maréchal expected us. As I gave his wife my hand, she said: It is enough to make one's head go round, is it not?

CRUDELI. Why, if one's head is a good one?

MARECHALE. After all, the simplest course is to act on the assumption that the old man exists.

CRUDELI. Even when one does not believe it?

MARECHALE. And when one does believe it, not to rely too much on his good nature.

CRUDELI. That is the safest way, if not the politest.

MARECHALE. By the way, if you had to state your principles to the magistrates, would you make a clean breast of them?

CRUDELI. I should do my best to hinder the magistrates performing a brutal act.

MARECHALE. Oh, you coward! And if you were at the point of death, would you submit to the ceremonies of the Church?

CRUDELI. I should not fail to do so.

MARECHALE. Oh, you wretched hypocrite!

John Wisdom: Gods

1. *The existence of God is not an experimental issue in the way it was.* An atheist or agnostic might say to a theist "You still think there are spirits in the trees, nymphs in the streams, a God of the world." He might say this because he noticed the theist in time of drought pray for rain and make a sacrifice and in the morning look for rain. But disagreement about whether there are gods is now less of this experimental or betting sort than it used to be. This is due in part, if not wholly, to our better knowledge of why things happen as they do.

It is true that even in these days it is seldom that one who believes in God has no hopes or fears which an atheist has not. Few believers now expect prayer to still the waves, but some think it makes a difference to people and not merely in ways the atheist would admit. Of course with people, as opposed to waves and machines, one never knows what they won't do next, so that expecting prayer to make a difference to them is not so definite a thing as believing in its mechanical efficacy. Still, just as primitive people pray in a business-like way for rain so some people still pray for others with a real feeling of doing something to help. However, in spite of this persistence of an experimental element in some theistic belief, it remains true that Elijah's method on Mount Carmel of settling the matter of what god or gods exist would be far less appropriate to-day than it was then.

2. *Belief in gods is not merely a matter of expectation of a world to come.* Someone may say "The fact that a theist no more than an atheist expects prayer to bring down fire from heaven or cure the sick does not mean that there is no difference between them as to the facts, it does not mean that the theist has no expectations different from the atheist's. For very often those who believe in God believe in another world and believe that God is there and that we shall go to that world when we die."

This is true, but I do not want to consider here expectations as to what one will see and feel after death nor what sort of reasons these logically unique expectations could have. So I want to consider those theists who do not believe in a future life, or rather, I want to consider the differences between atheists and theists in so far as these differences are not a matter of belief in a future life.

3. *What are these differences? And is it that theists are superstitious or that atheists are blind?* A child may wish to sit a while with his father and he may, when he has done what his father dislikes, fear punishment and feel distress at causing vexation, and while his father is alive he may feel sure of help when danger threatens and feel that there is sympathy for him when disaster has come. When his father is dead he will no longer expect punishment or help. Maybe for a moment an old fear will come or a cry for help escape him, but he will at once remember that this is no good now. He may feel that his father is no more until perhaps someone says to him that his father is still

---

Reprinted by permission of the Aristotelian Society.

alive though he lives now in another world and one so far away that there is no hope of seeing him or hearing his voice again. The child may be told that nevertheless his father can see him and hear all he says. When he has been told this the child will still fear no punishment nor expect any sign of his father, but now, even more than he did when his father was alive, he will feel that his father sees him all the time and will dread distressing him and when he has done something wrong he will feel separated from his father until he has felt sorry for what he has done. Maybe when he himself comes to die he will be like a man who expects to find a friend in the strange country where he is going, but even when this is so, it is by no means all of what makes the difference between a child who believes that his father lives still in another world and one who does not.

Likewise one who believes in God may face death differently from one who does not, but there is another difference between them besides this. This other difference may still be described as belief in another world, only this belief is not a matter of expecting one thing rather than another here or hereafter, it is not a matter of a world to come but of a world that now is, though beyond our senses.

We are at once reminded of those other unseen worlds which some philosophers "believe in" and others "deny," while non-philosophers unconsciously "accept" them by using them as models with which to "get the hang of" the patterns in the flux of experience. We recall the timeless entities whose changeless connections we seek to represent in symbols, and the values which stand firm amidst our flickering satisfaction and remorse, and the physical things which, though not beyond the corruption of moth and rust, are yet more permanent than the shadows they throw upon the screen before our minds. We recall, too, our talk of souls and of what lies in their depths and is manifested to us partially and intermittently in our own feelings and the behaviour of others. The hypothesis of mind, of other human minds and of animal minds, is reasonable because it explains for each of us why certain things behave so cunningly all by themselves unlike even the most ingenious machines. Is the hypothesis of minds in flowers and trees reasonable for like reasons? Is the hypothesis of a world mind reasonable for like reasons—someone who adjusts the blossom to the bees, someone whose presence may at times be felt—in a garden in high summer, in the hills when clouds are gathering, but not, perhaps, in a cholera epidemic?

4. *The question "Is belief in gods reasonable?" has more than one source.* It is clear now that in order to grasp fully the logic of belief in divine minds we need to examine the logic of belief in animal and human minds. But we cannot do that here and so for the purposes of this discussion about divine minds let us acknowledge the reasonableness of our belief in human minds without troubling ourselves about its logic. The question of the reasonableness of belief in divine minds then becomes a matter of whether there are facts in nature which support claims about divine minds in the way facts in nature support our claims about human minds.

In this way we resolve the force behind the problem of the existence of gods into two components, one metaphysical and the same which prompts the question "Is there *ever any* behaviour which gives reason to believe in *any* sort of mind?" and one which finds expression in "Are there other mind-patterns in nature beside the human and animal patterns which we can all easily detect, and are these other mind-patterns super-human?"

Such over-determination of a question syndrome is common. Thus, the puzzling questions "Do dogs think?", "Do animals feel?" are partly metaphysical puzzles and partly scientific questions. They are not purely metaphysical; for the reports of scientists about the poor performances of cats in cages and old ladies' stories about the remarkable performances of their pets are not irrelevant. But nor are these questions purely scientific; for the stories never settle them and therefore they have other sources. One other source is the metaphysical source we have already noticed, namely, the difficulty about getting behind an animal's behaviour to its mind, whether it is a non-human animal or a human one.

But there's a third component in the force behind these questions, these disputes have a third source, and it is one which is important in the dispute which finds expression in the words "I believe in God," "I do not." This source comes out well if we consider the question "Do flowers feel?" Like the questions about dogs and animals this question about flowers comes partly from the difficulty we sometimes feel over inference from *any* behaviour to thought or feeling and partly from ignorance as to what behaviour is to be found. But these questions, as opposed to a like question about human beings, comes also from hesitation as to whether the behaviour in question is *enough* mind-like, that is, is it enough similar to or superior to human behaviour to be called "mind-proving"? Likewise, even when we are satisfied that human behaviour shows mind and even when we have learned whatever mind-suggesting things there are in nature which are not explained by human and animal minds, we may still ask "But are these things sufficiently striking to be called a mind-pattern? Can we fairly call them manifestations of a divine being?"

"The question," someone may say, "has then become merely a matter of the application of a name. And 'What's in a name?'"

5. *But the line between a question of fact and a question or decision as to the application of a name is not so simple as this way of putting things suggests.* The question "What's in a name?" is engaging because we are inclined to answer both "Nothing" and "Very much." And this "Very much" has more than one source. We might have tried to comfort Heloise by saying "It isn't that Abelard no longer loves you, for this man isn't Abelard"; we might have said to poor Mr. Tebrick in Mr. Garnet's *Lady into Fox* "But this is no longer Silvia." But if Mr. Tebrick replied "Ah, but it is!" this might come not at all from observing facts about the fox which we have not observed, but from noticing facts about the fox for which we had missed, although we had in a sense observed all that Mr. Tebrick had observed. It is possible to have before one's eyes all the items of a pattern and still to miss the pattern. Consider the following conversation:

" 'And I think Kay and I are pretty happy. We've always been happy.'

"Bill lifted up his glass and put it down without drinking.

" 'Would you mind saying that again?' he asked.

" 'I don't see what's so queer about it. Taken all in all, Kay and I have really been happy.'

" 'All right,' Bill said gently, 'Just tell me how you and Kay have been happy.'

"Bill had a way of being amused by things which I could not understand.

" 'It's a little hard to explain,' I said. 'It's like taking a lot of numbers that don't look alike and that don't mean anything until you add them all together.'

"I stopped, because I hadn't meant to talk to him about Kay and me.

" 'Go ahead,' Bill said. 'What about the numbers.' And he began to smile.

" 'I don't know why you think it's so funny," I said. 'All the things that two people do together, two people like Kay and me, add up to something. There are the kids and the house and the dog and all the people we have known and all the times we've been out to dinner. Of course, Kay and I do quarrel sometimes but when you add it all together, all of it isn't as bad as the parts of it seem. I mean, maybe that's all there is to anybody's life.'

"Bill poured himself another drink. He seemed about to say something and checked himself. He kept looking at me."

Or again, suppose two people are speaking of two characters in a story which both have read or of two friends which both have known, and one says "Really she hated him," and the other says "She didn't, she loved him." Then the first may have noticed what the other has not although he knows no incident in the lives of the people they are talking about which the other doesn't know too, and the second speaker may say "She didn't, she loved him" because he hasn't noticed what the first noticed, although he can remember every incident the first can remember. But then again he may say "She didn't, she loved him" not because he hasn't noticed the patterns in time which the first has noticed but because though he has noticed them he doesn't feel he still needs to emphasize them with "Really she hated him." The line between using a name because of how we feel and because of what we have noticed isn't sharp. "A difference as to the facts," "a discovery," "a revelation," these phrases cover many things. Discoveries have been made not only by Christopher Columbus and Pasteur, but also by Tolstoy and Dostoevsky and Freud. Things are revealed to us not only by the scientists with microscopes, but also by the poets, the prophets, and the painters. What is so isn't merely a matter of "the facts." For sometimes when there is agreement as to the facts there is still argument as to whether defendant did or did not "exercise reasonable care," was or was not "negligent."

And though we shall need to emphasize how much "There is a God" evinces an attitude to the familiar we shall find in the end that it also evinces some recognition of patterns in time easily missed and that, therefore, difference as to there being any gods is in part a difference as to what is so and therefore as to the facts, though not in the simple ways which first occurred to us.

6. Let us now approach these same points by a different road.

6.1. *How it is that an explanatory hypothesis, such as the existence of God, may start by being experimental and gradually become something quite different can be seen from the following story:*

Two people return to their long neglected garden and find among the weeds a few of the old plants surprisingly vigorous. One says to the other "It must be that a gardener has been coming and doing something about these plants." Upon inquiry they find that no neighbour has ever seen anyone at work in their garden. The first man says to the other "He must have worked while people slept." The other says "No, someone would have heard him and besides, anybody who cared about the plants would have kept down these weeds." The first man says "Look at the way these are arranged. There is purpose and a feeling for beauty here. I believe that someone comes, someone invisible to mortal eyes. I believe that the more carefully we look the more we shall find confirmation of this." They examine the garden ever so carefully and sometimes they come on new things suggesting that a gardener comes and sometimes they come on new things suggesting the contrary and even that a malicious person has been at work. Besides examining the garden carefully they also study what happens to gardens left without attention. Each learns all the other learns about this and about the garden. Consequently, when after all this, one says "I still believe a gardener comes" while the other says "I don't" their different words now reflect no difference as to what they have found in the garden, no difference as to what they would find in the garden if they looked further and no difference about how fast untended gardens fall into disorder. At this stage, in this context, the gardener hypothesis has ceased to be experimental, the difference between one who accepts and one who rejects it is now not a matter of the one expecting something the other does not expect. What is the difference between them? The one says "A gardener comes unseen and unheard. He is manifested only in his works with which we are all familiar," the other says "There is no gardener" and with this difference in what they say about the gardener goes a difference in how they feel towards the garden, in spite of the fact that neither expects anything of it which the other does not expect.

But is this the whole difference between them—that the one calls the garden by one name and feels one way towards it, while the other calls it by another name and feels in another way towards it? And if this is what the difference has become then is it any longer appropriate to ask "Which is right?" or "Which is reasonable?"

And yet surely such questions *are* appropriate when one person says to another "You still think the world's a garden and not a wilderness, and that the gardener has not forsaken it" or "You still think there are nymphs of the streams, a presence in the hills, a spirit of the world." Perhaps when a man sings "God's in His heaven" we need not take this as more than an expression of how he feels. But when Bishop Gore or Dr. Joad writes about belief in God and young men read them in order to settle their religious doubts the impression is not simply that of persons choosing exclamations with which to face nature and the "changes and chances of this mortal life." The disputants speak as if they are concerned with a matter of scientific fact, or of trans-sensual, trans-scientific and metaphysical fact, but still of fact and still a matter about which reasons for and against may be offered, although no scientific reasons in the sense of field surveys for fossils or experiments on delinquents are to the point.

6.2. *Now can an interjection have a logic?* Can the manifestation of an attitude in the utterance of a word, in the application of a name, have a logic? When all the facts are known how can there still be a question of fact? How can there still be a question? Surely as Hume says "... after every circumstance, every relation is known, the understanding has no further room to operate"?

6.3. When the madness of these questions leaves us for a moment *we can all easily recollect disputes which though they cannot be settled by experiment are yet disputes in which one party may be right and the other wrong* and in which both parties may offer reasons and the one better reasons than the other. *This may happen in pure and applied mathematics and logic.* Two accountants or two engineers provided with the same data may reach different results and this difference is resolved not by collecting further data but by going over the calculations again. Such differences indeed share with differences as to what will win a race, the honour of being among the most "settlable" disputes in the language.

6.4. *But it won't do to describe the theistic issue as one settlable by such calculation,* or as one about what can be deduced in this *vertical* fashion from the facts we know. No doubt dispute about God has sometimes, perhaps especially in mediaeval times, been carried on in this fashion. But nowadays it is not and we must look for some other analogy, some other case in which a dispute is settled but not by experiment.

6.5. *In courts of law* it sometimes happens that opposing counsel are agreed as to the facts and are not trying to settle a question of further fact, are not trying to settle whether the man who admittedly had quarrelled with the deceased did or did not murder him, but are concerned with whether Mr. A who admittedly handed his long-trusted clerk signed blank cheques did or did not exercise reasonable care, whether a ledger is or is not a document, whether a certain body was or was not a public authority.

In such cases we notice that the process of argument is not a *chain* of demonstrative reasoning. It is a presenting and representing of those features of the case which *severally cooperate* in favour of the conclusion, in favour of saying what the reasoner wishes said, in favour of calling the situation by the name by which he wishes to call it. The reasons are like the legs of a chair, not the links of a chain. Consequently although the discussion is *a priori* and the steps are not a matter of experience, the procedure resembles scientific argument in that the reasoning is not *vertically* extensive but *horizontally* extensive—it is a matter of the cumulative effect of several independent premises, not of the repeated transformation of one or two. And because the premises are severally inconclusive the process of deciding the issue becomes a matter of weighing the cumulative effect of one group of severally inconclusive items against the cumulative effect of another group of severally inconclusive items, and thus lends itself to description in terms of conflicting "probabilities." This encourages the feeling that the issue is one of fact—that it is a matter of guessing from the premises at a further fact, at what is to come. But this is a muddle. *The dispute does not cease to be* a priori *because it is a matter of the cumulative effect of severally inconclusive premises.* The logic of the dispute is not that of a chain of deductive reasoning as in a mathematic calculation. But nor is it a matter of collecting from several inconclusive items of information an expectation as to something further, as when a doctor from a patient's symptoms guesses at what is wrong, or a detective from many clues guesses the criminal. It has its own sort of logic and its own sort of end—the solution of the question at issue is a decision, a ruling by the judge. But it is not an arbitrary decision though the rational connections are neither quite like those in vertical deductions nor like those in inductions in which from many signs we guess at what is to come; and though the decision manifests itself in the application of a name it is no more merely the application of a name than is the pinning on of a medal merely the pinning on of a bit of metal. Whether a lion with stripes is a tiger or a lion is, if you like, merely a matter of the application of a name. Whether Mr. So-and-So of whose conduct we have so complete a record did or did not exercise reasonable care is not merely a matter of the application of a name or, if we choose to say it is, then we must remember that with this name a game is lost and won and a game with very heavy stakes. With the judges' choice of a name for the facts goes an attitude, and the declaration, the ruling, is an exclamation evincing that attitude. But *it is an exclamation which not only has a purpose but also has a logic,* a logic surprisingly like that of "futile," "deplorable," "graceful," "grand," "divine."

6.6. *Suppose two people are looking at a picture or natural scene.* One says "Excellent" or "Beautiful" or "Divine"; the other says "I don't see it." He means he doesn't see the beauty. And this reminds us of how we felt the theist accuse the atheist of blindness and the atheist accuse the theist of seeing what isn't there. And yet surely each sees what the other sees. It isn't that one can see part of the picture while the other can't see. So the difference is in a sense not one as to the facts. And so it cannot be removed by the one disputant discovering to the other what so far he hasn't seen. It isn't that the one sees the picture in a different light and so, as we might say, sees a different picture. Consequently the difference between them cannot be resolved by putting the picture in a different light. And yet surely this is just what can be done in such a case—not by moving the picture but by talk perhaps. To settle a dispute as to whether a piece of music is good or better than another we listen again, with a picture we look again. Someone perhaps points to emphasize certain features and we see it in a different light. Shall we call this "field work" and "the last of observation" or shall we call it "reviewing the premises" and "the beginning of deduction (horizontal)"?

If in spite of all this we choose to say that a difference as to whether a thing is beautiful is not a factual difference we must be careful to remember that there is a procedure for settling these differences and that this consists not only in reasoning, and redescription as in the legal case, but also in a more literal re-setting-before with re-looking or re-listening.

6.7. *And if we say as we did at the beginning that when a difference as to the existence of a God is not one as to future happenings then it is not experimental and therefore not as to the facts, we must not forthwith assume that there is no right and wrong about it,* no rationality or irrationality, no appropriateness or inappropriateness, no procedure which tends to settle it, *nor even that this procedure is in no sense a discovery of new facts.* After all even in science this is not so. Our two gardeners even when they had reached the stage when neither expected any experimental result which the other did not, might yet have continued the dispute, each presenting and re-presenting the features of the garden favouring his hypothesis, that is, fitting his model for describing the accepted fact; each emphasizing the pattern he wishes to emphasize. True, in science, there is seldom or never a pure instance of this sort of dispute, for nearly always with difference of hypothesis goes some difference of expectation as to the facts. But scientists argue about rival hypotheses with a vigour which is not exactly proportioned to difference in expectations of experimental results.

The difference as to whether a God exists involves our feelings more than most scientific disputes and in this respect is more like a difference as to whether there is beauty in a thing.

7. *The Connecting Technique.* Let us consider again the technique used in revealing or proving beauty, in removing a blindness, in inducing an attitude which is lacking, in reducing a reaction that is inappropriate. Besides running over in a special way the features of the picture, tracing the rhythms, making sure that this and that are not only seen but noticed, and their relation to each other—besides all this—there are other things we can do to justify our attitude and alter that of the man who cannot see. For features of the picture may be brought out by setting beside it other pictures; just as the merits of an argument may be brought out, proved, by setting beside it other arguments, in which striking but irrelevant features of the original are changed and relevant features emphasized; just as the merits and demerits of a line of action may be brought out by setting beside it other actions. To use Susan Stebbing's example: Nathan brought out for David certain features of what David had done in the matter of Uriah the Hittite by telling him a story about two sheepowners. This is the kind of thing we very often do when someone is "inconsistent" or "unreasonable." This is what we do in referring to other cases of law. The paths we need to trace from other cases to the case in question are often numerous and difficult to detect and the person with whom we are discussing the matter may well draw attention to connections which, while not incompatible with those we have tried to

emphasize, are of an opposite inclination. A may have noticed in B subtle and hidden likenesses to an angel and reveal these to C, while C has noticed in B subtle and hidden likenesses to a devil which he reveals to A.

Imagine that a man picks up some flowers that lie half withered on a table and gently puts them in water. Another man says to him "You believe flowers feel." He says this although he knows that the man who helps the flowers doesn't expect anything of them which he himself doesn't expect; for he himself expects the flowers to be "refreshed" and to be easily hurt, injured, I mean, by rough handling, while the man who puts them in water does not expect them to whisper "Thank you." The Sceptic says "You believe flowers feel" because something about the way the other man lifts the flowers and puts them in water suggests an attitude to the flowers which he feels inappropriate although perhaps he would not feel it inappropriate to butterflies. He feels that this attitude to flowers is somewhat crazy *just as it is sometimes felt that a lover's attitude is somewhat crazy even when this is not a matter of his having false hopes about how the person he is in love with will act.* It is often said in such cases that reasoning is useless. But the very person who says this feels that the lover's attitude is crazy, is inappropriate like some dreads and hatreds, such as some horrors of enclosed places. And often one who says "It is useless to reason" proceeds at once to reason with the lover, nor is this reasoning always quite without effect. We may draw the lover's attention to certain things done by her he is in love with and trace for him a path to these from things done by others at other times which have disgusted and infuriated him. And by this means we may weaken his admiration and confidence, make him feel it unjustified and arouse his suspicion and contempt and make him feel our suspicion and contempt reasonable. It is possible, of course, that he has already noticed the analogies, the connections, we point out and that he has accepted them—that is, he has not denied them nor passed them off. He has recognized them and they have altered his attitude, altered his love, but he still loves. We then feel that perhaps it is we who are blind and cannot see what he can see.

8. *Connecting and Disconnecting.* But before we confess ourselves thus inadequate there are other fires his admiration must pass through. For when a man has an attitude which it seems to us he should not have or lacks one which it seems to us he should have, then, not only do we suspect that he is not influenced by connections which we feel should influence him and draw his attention to these, but also we suspect he is influenced by connections which should not influence him and draw attention to these. It may, for a moment, seem strange that we should draw his attention to connections which we feel should not influence him, and which, since they do influence him, he has in a sense already noticed. But we do—such is our confidence in "the light of reason."

Sometimes the power of these connections comes mainly from a man's mismanagement of the language he is using. This is what happens in the Monte Carlo fallacy, where by mismanaging the laws of chance a man passes from noticing that a certain colour or number has not turned up for a long while to an improper confidence that now it soon will turn up. In such cases our showing up of the false connections is a process we call "explaining a fallacy in reasoning." To remove fallacies in reasoning we urge a man to call a spade a spade, ask him what he means by "the State" and having pointed out ambiguities and vaguenesses ask him to reconsider the steps in his argument.

9. *Unspoken Connections. Usually, however, wrongheadedness or wrongheartedness in a situation, blindness to what is there or seeing what is not, does not arise merely from mismanagement of language but is more due to connections which are not mishandled in language, for the reason that they are not put into language at all.* And often these misconnections too, weaken in the light of reason, if only we can guess where they lie and turn it on them. In so far as these connections are not presented in language the process of removing their power is not a process of correcting the mismanagement of language. But it is still akin to such a process; for though it is not a process of setting out fairly what has been set out unfairly, it is a process of setting out fairly what has not been set out at all. And we must remember that the line between connections ill-presented or half-presented in language and connections operative but not presented in language, or only hinted at, is not a sharp one.

Whether or not we call the process of showing up these connections "reasoning to remove bad unconscious reasoning" or not, it is certain that in order to settle in ourselves what weight we shall attach to someone's confidence or attitude we not only ask him for his reasons but also look for unconscious reasons both good and bad; that is, for reasons which he can't put into words, isn't explicitly aware of, is hardly aware of, isn't aware of at all—perhaps it's long experience which he *doesn't* recall which let him know a squall is coming, perhaps it's old experience which he *can't* recall which makes the cake in the tea mean so much and makes Odette so fascinating.

I am well aware of the distinction between the question "What reasons are there for the belief that S is P?" and the question "What are the sources of beliefs that S is P?" There are cases where investigation of the rationality of a claim which certain persons make is done with very little inquiry into why they say what they do, into the causes of their beliefs. This is so when we have very definite ideas about what is really logically relevant to their claim and what is not. Offered a mathematical theorem we ask for the proof; offered the generalization that parental discord causes crime we ask for the correlation co-efficients. But even in this last case, if we fancy that only the figures are reasons we underestimate the complexity of the logic of our conclusion; and yet it is difficult to describe the other features of the evidence which have weight and there is apt to be disagreement about the weight they should have. In criticizing other conclusions and especially conclusions which are largely the expression of an attitude, we have not only to ascertain what reasons there are for them but also to decide what things are reasons and how much. This latter process of sifting reasons from causes is part of the critical process for every belief, but in some spheres it has been done pretty fully already. In these spheres we don't need to examine the actual processes to belief and distil from them a logic. But in other spheres this remains to be done. Even in science or on the stock exchange or in ordinary life we sometimes hesitate to condemn a belief or a hunch merely because those who believe it cannot offer the sort of reasons we had hoped for. And now suppose Miss Gertrude Stein finds excellent the work of a new artist while we see nothing in it. We nervously recall, perhaps, how pictures by Picasso, which Miss Stein admired and others rejected, later came to be admired by many who gave attention to them, and we wonder whether the case is not a new instance of her perspicacity and our blindness. But if, upon giving all our attention to the work in question, we still do not respond to it, and we notice that the subject matter of the new pictures is perhaps birds in wild places and learn that Miss Stein is a birdwatcher, then we begin to trouble ourselves less about her admiration.

It must not be forgotten that our attempt to show up misconnections in Miss Stein may have an opposite result and reveal to us connections we had missed. Thinking to remove the spell exercised upon his patient by the old stories of the Greeks, the psycho-analyst may himself fall under that spell and find in them what his patient has found and, incidentally, what made the Greeks tell those tales.

10. *Now what happens, what should happen, when we inquire in this way into the reasonableness, the propriety of belief in Gods?* The answer is: A double and opposite-phased change. Wordsworth writes:

> . . . And I have felt
> A presence that disturbs me with the joy
> Of elevated thoughts; a sense sublime
> Of something far more deeply interfused,
> Whose dwelling is the light of setting suns,
> And the round ocean and the living air,
> And the blue sky, and in the mind of man:
> A motion and a spirit, that impels
> All thinking things, all objects of all thought,
> And rolls through all things . . .

We most of us know this feeling. But is it well placed like the feeling that here is first-rate work, which we sometimes rightly have even before we have fully grasped the picture we are looking at or the book we are reading? Or is it misplaced like the feeling in a house that has long been empty that someone secretly lives there still. Wordsworth's feeling *is* the feeling that the world is haunted, that something watches in the hills and manages the stars. The child feels that the stone tripped him when he stumbled, that the bough struck him when it flew back in his face. He has to learn that the wind isn't buffeting him, that there is not a devil in it, that he was wrong, that his attitude was inappropriate. And as he learns that the wind wasn't hindering him so he also learns it wasn't helping him. But we know how, though he learns, his attitude lingers. It is plain that Wordsworth's feeling is of this family.

Belief in gods, it is true, is often very different from belief that stones are spiteful, the sun kindly. For the gods appear in human form and from the waves and control these things and by so doing reward and punish us. But varied as are the stories of the gods they have a family likeness and we have only to recall them to feel sure of the other main sources which co-operate with animism to produce them.

What are the stories of the gods? What are our feelings when we believe in God? They are feelings of awe before power, dread of the thunderbolts of Zeus, confidence in the everlasting arms, unease beneath the all-seeing eye. They are feelings of guilt and inescapable vengeance, of smothered hate and of a security we can hardly do without. We have only to remind ourselves of these feelings and the stories of the gods and goddesses and heroes in which these feelings find expression, to be reminded of how we felt as children to our parents and the big people of our childhood. Writing of a first telephone call from his grandmother, Proust says: ". . . it was rather that this isolation of the voice was like a symbol, a presentation, a direct consequence of another isolation, that of my grandmother, separated for the first time in my life, from myself. The orders or prohibitions which she addressed to me at every moment in the ordinary course of my life, the tedium of obedience or the fire of rebellion which neutralized the affection that I felt for her were at this moment eliminated. . . . "Granny!" I cried to her . . . but I had beside me only that voice, a phantom, as unpalpable as that which would come to revisit me when my grandmother was dead. 'Speak to me!' but then it happened that, left more solitary still, I ceased to catch the sound of her voice. My grandmother could no longer hear me . . . I continued to call her, sounding the empty night, in which I felt that her appeals also must be straying. I was shaken by the same anguish which, in the distant past, I had felt once before, one day when, a little child, in a crowd, I had lost her."

Giorgio de Chirico, writing of Courbet, says: "The word yesterday envelops us with its yearning echo, just as, on waking, when the sense of time and the logic of things remain a while confused, the memory of a happy hour we spent the day before may sometimes linger reverberating within us. At times we think of Courbet and his work as we do of our own father's youth."

When a man's father fails him by death or weakness how much he needs another father, one in the heavens with whom is "no variableness nor shadow of turning."

We understood Mr. Kenneth Graham when he wrote of the Golden Age we feel we have lived in under the Olympians. Freud says: "The ordinary man cannot imagine this Providence in any other form but that of a greatly exalted father, for only such a one could understand the needs of the sons of men, or be softened by their prayers and be placated by the signs of their remorse. The whole thing is so patently infantile, so incongruous with reality. . . . So incongruous with reality"! It cannot be denied.

But here a new aspect of the matter may strike us. For the very facts which make us feel that now we can recognize systems of superhuman, sub-human, elusive, beings for what they are—the persistent projections of infantile phantasies—include facts which make these systems less fantastic. What are these facts? They are patterns in human reactions which are well described by saying that we are as if there were hidden within us powers, persons, not ourselves and stronger than ourselves. That this is so may perhaps be said to have been common knowledge yielded by ordinary observation of people, but we did not know the degree in which this is so until recent study of extraordinary cases in extraordinary conditions had revealed it. I refer, of course, to the study of multiple personalities and the wider studies of psycho-analysts. Even when the results of this work are reported to us that is not the same as tracing the patterns in the details of the cases on which the results are based; and even that is not the same as taking part in the studies oneself. One thing not sufficiently realized is that some of the things shut within us are not bad but good.

Now the gods, good and evil and mixed, have always been mysterious powers outside us rather than within. But they have also been within. It is not a modern theory but an old saying that in each of us a devil sleeps. Eve said: "The serpent beguiled me." Helen says to Menelaus:

> . . . And yet how strange it is!
> I ask not thee; I ask my own sad thought,
> What was there in my heart, that I forgot
> My home and land and all I loved, to fly
> With a strange man? Surely it was not I,
> But Cypris there!

Elijah found that God was not in the wind, nor in the thunder, but in a still small voice. The kingdom of Heaven is within us, Christ insisted, though usually about the size of a grain of mustard seed, and he prayed that we should become one with the Father in Heaven.

New knowledge made it necessary either to give up saying "The sun is sinking" or to give the words a new meaning. In many contexts we preferred to stick to the old words and give them a new meaning which was not entirely new but, on the contrary, *practically* the same as the old. The Greeks did not speak of the dangers of repressing instincts but they did speak of the dangers of thwarting Dionysos, of neglecting Cypris for Diana, of forgetting Poseidon for Athena. We have eaten of the fruit of a garden we can't forget though we were never there, a garden we still look for though we can never find it. Maybe we look for too simple a likeness to what we dreamed. Maybe we are not as free as we fancy from the old idea that Heaven is a happy hunting ground, or a city with streets of gold. Lately Mr. Aldous Huxley has recommended our seeking not somewhere beyond the sky or late in time but a timeless state not made of the stuff of this world, which he rejects, picking it into worthless pieces. But this sounds to me still too much a looking for another place, not indeed one filled with sweets but instead so empty that some of us would rather remain in the Lamb or the Elephant, where, as we know, they stop whimpering with another bitter and so far from sneering at all things, hang pictures of winners at Kempton and stars of the 'nineties. Something good we have for each other is freed there, and in some degree and for a while the miasma of time is rolled back without obliging us to deny the present.

The artists who do most for us don't tell us only of fairylands. Proust, Manet, Breughel, even Botticelli and Vermeer show us reality. And yet they give us for a moment exhilaration without anxiety, peace without boredom. And those who, like Freud, work in a different way against that which too often comes over us and forces us into deadness or despair, also deserve critical, patient and courageous attention. For they, too, work to release us from human bondage into human freedom.

Many have tried to find ways of salvation. The reports they bring back are always incomplete and apt to mislead even when they are not in words but in music or paint. But they are by no means useless; and not the worst of them are those which speak of oneness with God. But in so far as we become one with Him He becomes one with us. St. John says he is in us as we love one another.

This love, I suppose, is not benevolence but something that comes of the oneness with one another of which Christ spoke. Sometimes it momentarily gains strength. Hate and the Devil do too. And what is oneness without otherness?

Chapter VIII — Recent Philosophical Trends

Introduction

The twentieth century, for all its other merits and its many demerits, will probably be remembered as a century of great achievement in philosophy. Its accomplishments have taken place amidst great intellectual ferment and conflict, for this has not been a time in which one or two thinkers or schools have dominated all the rest—a frequent occurrence in past centuries. In philosophy, as in the fine arts and literature, the decades that have passed since the beginning of our century have seen a proliferation of schools and movements, each claiming a certain uniqueness for itself, and questioning the right to be of the others. For this reason, it is difficult to pin a label upon twentieth-century philosophy, one that would sum up its basic nature, as "empiricism" or "Enlightenment" might do for the eighteenth century, or "scholasticism" does so well for the thirteenth. Moreover, twentieth-century philosophy presents the added problem of being almost exclusively the affair of university professors, and, perhaps as a consequence of this academic inbreeding, it is written in a jargon that only other professors (and a few of their students) can understand. That philosophy has drifted away from the public marketplace is not a twentieth-century phenomenon, of course; since the time of Immanuel Kant, philosophy has tended to withdraw into the groves of academe, much as science forbids entry to all but those who have received advanced training in its mysteries.

To the outsider, then, what goes on within philosophy today may seem like a jumble of academic conflicts, none of which has direct relevance to anything of importance to mankind. As Freud somewhat contemptuously observed of philosophy, "philosophy has no direct influence on the great mass of mankind; it is of interest only to a small number even of the top layer of intellectuals and is scarcely intelligible to anyone else." But is this an *indictment* of philosophy, or is philosophy's remoteness from the prejudices and the narrow vision of the "common man" a source of its strength? Let us not exaggerate the force of Freud's remark. Few people may be aware of the technical niceties of the problems argued about by philosophers today, but this does not mean that the masses are unaffected by these problems. Let us consider again what it is that philosophers do.

Philosophers, as we have seen throughout this book, have always concerned themselves with the intellectual and spiritual problems posed by their historical situation. Plato, for example, was concerned with improving the fortunes of the declining city-state system of ancient Greece, and Descartes was desirous of giving a methodological basis to the new system of scientific knowledge that was emerging in his day. No one living at the times when they fashioned their views could have been untouched by the problems they addressed. However, philosophers tend to go about the investigation of issues with more energy and tenacity than most people have time for, and their thoroughness may lead them into technical difficulties that seem far afield from their starting-point only to those persons who have not taken the trouble to follow the argument. Nevertheless the problems of the age remain.

Many of the questions you will encounter in this chapter have very simple origins, though they may be raised to dizzying heights by our authors. (1) I am losing my faith in God. But if God does not exist, does that mean that life is without meaning? (Nietzsche) (2) Scientific questions are those that can be investigated empirically, and empirical investigation alone can give us knowledge. Science therefore represents one legitimate pursuit of knowledge; almost everyone today would agree to that. But are there other legitimate avenues to knowledge, such as religion, or poetry, or art, or even drugs? Or are all genuine questions scientific questions? (3) Some people claim to have a special faculty called insight that gives them knowledge of God or of the nature of ultimate reality. But are such claims genuine? How could we know that they are or are not? (Russell) (4) I am a human being, and apparently different from the other animals and from physical objects in some respects. But in just what respects? What is the peculiar nature of man, and what is our special destiny in the world? (Sartre) Hardly everyday questions, these; they are genuine and living questions, however, and the common man—even if he be Sigmund Freud—ignores such questions and what philosophers have to say about them at his own peril.

Nevertheless, the remoteness and technicality of some of the answers given to these questions and others like them is hardly a merit in itself. When I was at college, a friend of mine who was majoring in one of the sciences, and who had been raised as a Catholic, was encountering serious perplexities concerning his faith in God. He turned to one of the greatest Catholic philosophers and intellectuals of our time, Jacques Maritain, to seek guidance. What does a Catholic philosopher have to say to a man who is in danger of losing his faith? To his great disappointment, my friend found that he could not understand a word of Maritain's book entitled: *The Degrees of Knowledge.* "They might as well have not bothered to translate it from the French," he said, "it seems to have nothing to do with anything I can understand." And so he dismissed philosophy as irrelevant—to him, at any rate.

There is an interesting debate going on among philosophers themselves about this issue. As we write this, a struggle is taking place within the American Philosophical Association, an organization representing professional philosophers and philosophy professors in this country. The struggle is between the Analysts, who usually belong to the schools of logical positivism or linguistic analysis, and the Pluralists, who may represent such European schools of philosophy as existentialism and phenomenology. Some Pluralists may be individuals who draw their inspiration from the earlier history of philosophy, or they may be Marxists. The Analysts dominate the faculties of our best universities, and there is a preponderance of their work in the leading philosophical journals. Their claim to superiority rests in part upon technical virtuosity and high standards of logical rigor. The Pluralists criticize the Analysts for their narrowness of outlook: a refusal to look beyond the problems and techniques of their own school, and a failure to concern themselves with the broad issues that have traditionally been the province of philosophy. A Pluralist might remark, for example, that it is odd for Analysts in ethics to be so concerned with frighteningly technical questions in metaethics, while the fundamental premises of relativism and empiricism usually assumed by them seem to deny the possibility of a normative ethical system. Why be concerned with developing a philosophy of the language of ethics, if philosophy must renounce all pretensions to answer the broader ethical question, "How should I live?"

These are important issues, and, in this case at least, they have great practical consequences for those who engage in them. For the American Philosophical Association has tremendous political power in the world of academic philosophy. Those who dominate it have the power to endorse huge private and federal grants, to support or withdraw support to research projects at specific universities, to choose to give or withhold publicity to scholarly achievement, and thus to make or break careers. Hardly a game for innocent academicians, or for pure thinkers in an ivory-tower world! But such, it seems, are the social underpinnings of much of the intellectual world today. And none of this detracts from the achievements of philosophers in this century; in fact, it might again be a source of its strength. Let us briefly sketch some of the leading schools of twentieth-century philosophy, and describe the relation of our authors to each of these schools.

1. *Pragmatism.* William James assures us that the leading idea of pragmatism is as old as philosophy itself: it holds that questions, in order to be genuine, must relate to the living, practical concerns of people. Endless arguments about the nature of Absolute Reality, or whether the world is Spirit, Will, Idea,

or just a congeries of atoms, are without such a relationship, and should be forgotten. But modern pragmatism is more than just a name for a hard-nosed, practical attitude toward life and philosophy. It is a theory of truth and meaning as well, and these subjects furnish the topics of James's lecture which you are about to read. For, after all, if all genuine questions must relate to concrete human tasks, what then of Absolute Truth, the perennial Holy Grail of philosophy, which, by its very nature, is indifferent to human concerns? James argues that there is no Absolute Truth; truth by its very nature can only be a truth for some person, community, or for mankind as a whole. Quoting C. S. Peirce, James contends that beliefs are rules for action, and the truth or falsity of beliefs must be measured by their ability to solve our problems, answer our questions, and guide our actions as we search for satisfying solutions to genuine perplexities. The meaning of a belief, then, can be found in how it affects our action; and you will recall James's claim in our previous chapter that the meaningfulness of that statement "God exists" lies in the influence one's belief in God has on the conduct of that person's life.

2. *Linguistic Analysis.* Pragmatism was developed at the very outset of our century, and most of its leading ideas appear to be well assimilated today; at least it would be quite unusual to find a philosopher at meetings of the American Philosophical Association who was searching for Ultimate Reality or Absolute Truth. Linguistic or analytic philosophy operates well within the parameters of pragmatism. Its fundamental principles are traceable to the later philosophy of Ludwig Wittgenstein, whose works are too difficult and too fragmentary to include in a book of introductory readings in philosophy. But the essay by John Wisdom in the previous chapter is a good contemporary example of linguistic analysis. Wisdom is exploring the logic of words in his essay; he is concerned with what people think they are communicating when they use terms such as "God" or "belief in God;" he examines differences between factual disputes and semantical disputes, and seeks thereby to establish the practical difference between believing in God and not believing in God. Note, too, the pragmatic aspect of Wisdom's analysis. He speaks of two men disputing the statement "Flowers can feel." Is their dispute a practical one, i.e., is there some experiment that could be performed to decide who is right? Or is the dispute one of *attitudes* towards the facts? Note the parallel here with James's discussion of whether the man who goes around a tree also goes around a squirrel that is clinging to the tree and keeping the tree between himself and the hunter. The question here, as for linguistic philosophers, is: what do we *mean* by "to go around"? Won't a *practical decision* on how to interpret the meaning of a term decide the issue, and not an experiment? How facts and language interact to create the world we inhabit!

3. *Logical Positivism.* The difficulty with linguistic analysis and pragmatism, as some philosophers see it, is that they appear to concern themselves only with traditional philosophical questions in the light of "ordinary" language. But contemporary physics and mathematics have created extremely rigorous languages that are capable of much greater precision than ordinary

speech. Why not, therefore, apply these languages to an understanding of the logical relationships obtaining between things and events? And Bertrand Russell has been in the vanguard of the revolution in logical techniques that is one of the great accomplishments of twentieth-century philosophy. A primary statement of the principles of logical positivism can be traced to the works of members of the *Vienna Circle,* which met between the world wars. Men such as Moritz Schlick and Rudolf Carnap argued that the *meaningfulness* of statements consists in their *verifiability.* This means that if no evidence could be described that is relevant to the truth or falsity of a given statement, then the statement lacks meaning. Recall, for example, Bishop Berkeley's claim that "to exist is to be perceived." However logical the reasons may be that impelled him to that conclusion, what conceivable experimental evidence could corroborate the claim? A similar objection could of course be made about the materialist contention! We cannot imagine what it would be like to "experience" the underlying, ultimate nature of experience itself, so therefore what meaning could claims about its ultimate nature possibly have? And, the pragmatist might add, what difference does it make to the conduct of my life if Berkeley is right or his opponents are? Unfortunately, however, the verifiability criterion of meaningfulness was never capable of an exact formulation. It seemed frequently to prescribe a case of throwing out the baby with the bath-water, for it made not only religion and metaphysics into meaningless pursuits, but ethics, art criticism, and even itself meaningless as well. Indeed, how could one verify experimentally the statement "unverifiable statements are meaningless"?

Still, as is usual in the errors of great men, the core idea of positivism, like that of pragmatism, is a salutary one. It helped clear away accumulated intellectual garbage—much as Descartes's methodical doubt had done three hundred years earlier—and it reminded us once more of the frailty of all human claims to know something. In his essay, Russell applies the spirit of logical positivism to a demolition of mysticism. The mystic's claim to a special sort of insight that serves as a basis for his claims to know something about God and the world, are never in themselves adequate, but must be confirmed, if at all, by what we as a community of human beings searching for knowledge can *see* and *feel,* what we can corroborate *through our senses.* The spirit of mysticism may inspire some of our best scientific minds; but as a substitute for careful research it will never do.

Are Russell and Carnap merely bowing to the new god of science now that they have buried all the old gods? I believe not; they appear less as prophets of a new religion than as tentative supporters of a technique of inquiry that has provided us with more reliable and comprehensive knowledge than any previous method. Peirce said simply that he had "taken science as his bride"—no more than that. Science is not a goddess promising us ultimate answers to ultimate questions, but a reliable companion whose accomplishments merit our faithfulness, if not our slavish obedience.

4. *Existentialism.* As opposed to the three schools of philosophy just mentioned, all of which developed in the English-speaking countries (although

logical positivism, at least, was born in Vienna after World War I), existentialism was conceived and developed in continental Europe. Although it has gone through many stages since its birth in the nineteenth century, and little seems to hold its adherents together except a concern for similar questions, there is one thread of continuity internal and one tie with the Anglo-American schools: that is, the emphasis upon *subjectivity*. The pragmatists, linguistic analysts, and logical positivists all insist that truth is not something that can exist apart from the human way of existing. While the Anglo-American schools tend to interpret that way of existing as fundamentally conditioned by our biological evolution by means of natural selection, the existentialists tend to abstract from the question of the genesis of man, and try to describe the human situation from within, and from the point of view of the individual who is struggling to make sense out of his life. Thus Kierkegaard, a nineteenth-century thinker who has influenced existentialism in this century perhaps more than any other, developed a theory of truth that has certain parallels with James's theory, but is strangely different also. Truth consists in an "objective uncertainty" grasped by the individual in an act of subjective passion—a passion inspired by the fact that although *science may give me an understanding of the world, it cannot instruct me on how to live.* But I must live; I must choose meanings to live by—and life has provided me with no assurances, no guarantees, no fixed goal posts to strive for. Alone and uncertain of who and what he is, says Kierkegaard, man must search not only for understanding, but for meaning, value, and direction.

The twentieth century, with its incessant and seemingly senseless violence and destruction, has caused these questions to loom before our eyes like an evil destiny in the midst of abundance. How much we have learned about the world and about ourselves during this century! How much we know; how confident we are that there is much more that we can learn! How our knowledge has produced so many useful implements, which can be and have been used to improve our material well-being! And yet: who are we; where are we going; how long the road—and I, an individual, what ought I to do with my life? The gods have left their temples, the signposts have been removed; we are forced to begin anew at every instant, for nothing remains fixed, not nations, not families, not systems of government.

The terrible pathos of words like these are only comprehensible in a world gone mad with war and destruction. James's desire to make every question into a practical question is only possible in the cool and quiet of peaceful walks in the country, as he so much liked to do. When we are swimming in the dark over seventy fathoms of water, as Kierkegaard says we are, or where we are continuously forced to risk our lives for what we believe in, as was Jean-Paul Sartre's experience during the German occupation of France, then questions of practicality seem nugatory. What counts is not so much what is believed, but rather how well one holds to one's beliefs, how resolutely one takes them to the very grave. Let us say, then, that existentialism is a theory of the human situation, of how persons exist in the world and how they can exist. Perhaps Sartre's essay will reveal something of yourself to you.

In addition to these four, other important schools of philosophy have developed in the Western world during the twentieth century. One is Marxism, a school that seeks to make the social criticism of Marx both *relevant* to the capitalist societies as they have evolved during the hundred years since the death of Marx, and *politically effective* in opposing what it sees as unjust social structures. Philosophy in the hands of Marx and our contemporary Marxists refuses in principle to confine itself to academic disputes; to Marxists, the academic world itself becomes suspect, for it is an adjunct to an evil social system. But if we had room for everything that contemporary philosophy has to offer, we would have a much longer book! Our second selection is from the nineteenth-century "existentialist" Friedrich Nietzsche, who speaks with the passion of a man for whom the world has grown strange, and the foundations of life uncertain. "Alas!" he once wrote, "for those who have *lost their home.*" He is a good introduction to the twentieth century.

Søren Kierkegaard: Truth Is Subjectivity

In the principle that subjectivity, inwardness, is the truth, there is comprehended the Socratic wisdom, whose everlasting merit it was to have become aware of the essential significance of existence, of the fact that the knower is an existing individual. For this reason Socrates was in the truth by virtue of his ignorance, in the highest sense in which this was possible within paganism. To attain to an understanding of this, to comprehend that the misfortune of speculative philosophy is again and again to have forgotten that the knower is an existing individual, is in our objective age difficult enough. But to have made an advance upon Socrates without even having understood what he understood, is at any rate not "Socratic."

Let us now start from this point, and as was attempted in the *Fragments,* seek a determination of thought which will really carry us further. I have nothing here to do with the question of whether this proposed thought-determination is true or not, since I am merely experimenting; but it must at any rate be clearly manifest that the Socratic thought is understood within the new proposal, so that at least I do not come out behind Socrates.

When subjectivity, inwardness, is the truth, the truth becomes objectively a paradox; and the fact that the truth is objectively a paradox shows in its turn that subjectivity is the truth. For the objective situation is repellent; and the expression for the objective repulsion constitutes the tension and the measure of the corresponding inwardness. The paradoxical character of the truth is its objective uncertainty; this uncertainty is an expression for the passionate inwardness, and this passion is precisely the truth. So far the Socratic principle. The eternal and essential truth, the truth which has an essential relationship to an existing individual because it pertains essentially to existence (all other knowledge being from the Socratic point of view accidental, its scope and degree a matter of indifference), is a paradox. But the eternal essential truth is by no means in itself a paradox; but it becomes paradoxical by virtue of its relationship to an existing individual. The Socratic ignorance gives expression to the objective uncertainty attaching to the truth, while his inwardness in existing is the truth. To anticipate here what will be developed later, let me make the following remark. The Socratic ignorance is an analogue to the category of the absurd, only that there is still less of objective certainty in the absurd, and in the repellent effect that the absurd exercises. It is certain only that it is absurd, and precisely on that account it incites to an infinitely greater tension in the corresponding inwardness. The Socratic inwardness in existing is an analogue to faith; only that the inwardness of faith, corresponding as it does, not to the repulsion of the Socratic ignorance, but to the repulsion exerted by the absurd, is infinitely more profound.

Socratically the external essential truth is by no means in its own nature paradoxical, but

Selections from *Concluding Unscientific Postcript.*

Reprinted by permission of Princeton University Press.

only in its relationship to an existing individual. This finds expression in another Socratic proposition, namely, that all knowledge is recollection. This proposition is not for Socrates a cue to the speculative enterprise, and hence he does not follow it up; essentially it becomes a Platonic principle. Here the way swings off; Socrates concentrates essentially upon accentuating existence, while Plato forgets this and loses himself in speculation. Socrates' infinite merit is to have been an *existing* thinker, not a speculative philosopher who forgets what it means to exist. For Socrates therefore the principle that all knowledge is recollection has at the moment of his leave-taking and as the constantly rejected possibility of engaging in speculation, the following two-fold significance: (1) that the knower is essentially *integer*, and that with respect to the knowledge of the eternal truth he is confronted with no other difficulty than the circumstance that he exists; which difficulty, however, is so essential and decisive for him that it means that existing, the process of transformation to inwardness in and by existing, is the truth; (2) that existence in time does not have any decisive significance, because the possibility of taking oneself back into eternity through recollection is always there, though this possibility is constantly nullified by utilizing the time, not for speculation, but for the transformation to inwardness in existing.

The infinite merit of the Socratic position was precisely to accentuate the fact that the knower is an existing individual, and that the task of existing is his essential task. Making an advance upon Socrates by failing to understand this, is quite a mediocre achievement. This Socratic principle we must therefore bear in mind, and then inquire whether the formula may not be so altered as really to make an advance beyond the Socratic position.

Subjectivity, inwardness, has been posited as the truth; can any expression for the truth be found which has a still higher degree of inwardness? Aye, there is such an expression, provided the principle that subjectivity or inwardness is the truth begins by positing the opposite principle: that subjectivity is untruth. Let us not at this point succumb to such haste as to fail in making the necessary distinctions. Speculative philosophy also says that subjectivity is untruth, but says it in order to stimulate a movement in precisely the opposite direction, namely, in the direction of the principle that objectivity is the truth. Speculative philosophy determines subjectivity negatively as tending toward objectivity. This second determination of ours, however, places a hindrance in its own way while proposing to begin, which has the effect of making the inwardness far more intensive. Socratically speaking, subjectivity is untruth if it refuses to understand that subjectivity is truth, but, for example, desires to become objective. Here, on the other hand, subjectivity in beginning upon the task of becoming the truth through a subjectifying process, is in the difficulty that it is already untruth. Thus, the labor of the task is thrust backward, backward, that is, in inwardness. So far is it from being the case that the way tends in the direction of objectivity, that the beginning merely lies still deeper in subjectivity.

But the subject cannot be untruth eternally, or eternally be presupposed as having been untruth; it must have been brought to this condition in time, or here become untruth in time. The Socratic paradox consisted in the fact that the eternal was related to an existing individual, but now existence has stamped itself upon the existing individual a second time. There has taken place so essential an alteration in him that he cannot now possibly take himself back into the eternal by way of recollection. To do this is to speculate; to be able to do this, but to reject the possibility by apprehending the task of life as a realization of inwardness in existing, is the Socratic position. But now the difficulty is that what followed Socrates on his way as a rejected possibility, has become an impossibility. If engaging in speculation was a dubious merit even from the point of view of the Socratic, it is now neither more nor less than confusion.

The paradox emerges when the eternal truth and existence are placed in juxtaposition with one another; each time the stamp of existence is brought to bear, the paradox becomes more clearly evident. Viewed Socratically the knower was simply an existing individual, but now the existing individual bears the stamp of having been essentially altered by existence.

Let us now call the untruth of the individual *Sin*. Viewed eternally he cannot be sin, nor can he be eternally presupposed as having been in sin. By coming into existence therefore (for the beginning was that subjectivity is untruth), he becomes a sinner. He is not born as a sinner in the sense that he is presupposed as being a sinner before he is born, but he is born in sin and as a sinner. This we might call *Original Sin.* But if existence has in this manner acquired a power over him, he is prevented from taking himself back into the eternal by way of recollection. If it was paradoxical to posit the eternal truth in relationship to an existing individual, it is now absolutely paradoxical to posit it in relationship to such an individual as we have here defined. But the more difficult it is made for him to take himself out of existence by way of recollection, the more profound is the inwardness that his existence may have in existence; and when it is made impossible for him, when he is held so fast in existence that the back door of recollection is forever closed to him, then his inwardness will be the most profound possible. But let us never forget that the Socratic merit was to stress the fact that the knower is an existing individual; for the more difficult the matter becomes, the greater the temptation to hasten along the easy road of speculation, away from fearful dangers and crucial decisions, to the winning of renown and honors and property, and so forth. If even Socrates understood the dubiety of taking himself speculatively out of existence back into the eternal, although no other difficulty confronted the existing individual except that he existed, and that existing was his essential task, now it is impossible. Forward he must, backward he cannot go.

Subjectivity is the truth. By virtue of the relationship subsisting between the eternal truth and the existing individual, the paradox came into being. Let us now go further, let us suppose that the eternal essential truth is itself a paradox. How does the paradox come into being? By putting the eternal essential truth into juxtaposition with existence. Hence when we posit such a conjunction within the truth itself, the truth becomes a paradox. The eternal truth has come into being in time: this is the paradox. If in accordance with the determinations just posited, the subject is prevented by sin from taking himself back into the eternal, now he need not trouble himself about this; for now the eternal essential truth is not behind him but in front of him, through its being in existence or having existed, so that if the individual does not existentially and in existence lay hold of the truth, he will never lay hold of it.

Existence can never be more sharply accentuated than by means of these determinations. The evasion by which speculative philosophy attempts to recollect itself out of existence has been made impossible. With reference to this, there is nothing for speculation to do except to arrive at an understanding of this impossibility; every speculative attempt which insists on being speculative shows *eo ipso* that it has not understood it. The individual may thrust all this away from him, and take refuge in speculation; but it is impossible first to accept it, and then to revoke it by means of speculation; since it is definitely calculated to prevent speculation.

When the eternal truth is related to an existing individual it becomes a paradox. The paradox repels in the inwardness of the existing individual, through the objective uncertainty and the corresponding Socratic ignorance. But since the paradox is not in the first instance itself paradoxical (but only in its relationship to the existing individual), it does not repel with a sufficient intensive inwardness. For without risk there is no faith, and the greater the risk the greater the faith; the more objective security the less inwardness (for inwardness is precisely subjectivity), and the less objective security the more profound the possible inwardness. When the paradox is paradoxical in itself, it repels the individual by virtue of its absurdity, and the corresponding passion of inwardness is faith. But subjectivity, inwardness, is the truth; for otherwise we have forgotten what the merit of the Socratic position is. But there can be no stronger expression for inwardness than when the retreat out of existence into the eternal by way of recollection is impossible; and when, with truth confronting the individual as a paradox, gripped in the anguish and pain of sin, facing the tremendous risk of the objective insecurity, the individual believes. But without risk no faith, not even the Socratic form of faith, much less the form of which we here speak.

When Socrates believed that there was a

God, he held fast to the objective uncertainty with the whole passion of his inwardness, and it is precisely in this contradiction and in this risk, that faith is rooted. Now it is otherwise. Instead of the objective uncertainty, there is here a certainty, namely, that objectively it is absurd; and this absurdity, held fast in the passion of inwardness, is faith. The Socratic ignorance is as a witty jest in comparison with the earnestness of facing the absurd; and the Socratic existential inwardness is as Greek light-mindedness in comparison with the grave strenuosity of faith.

What now is the absurd? The absurd is—that the eternal truth has come into being in time, that God has come into being, has been born, has grown up, and so forth, precisely like any other individual human being, quite indistinguishable from other individuals. For every assumption of immediate recognizability is pre-Socratic paganism, and from the Jewish point of view, idolatry; and every determination of what really makes an advance beyond the Socratic must essentially bear the stamp of having a relationship to God's having come into being; for faith *sensu strictissimo,* refers to becoming. When Socrates believed that there was a God, he saw very well that where the way swings off there is also an objective way of approximation, for example by the contemplation of nature and human history, and so forth. His merit was precisely to shun this way, where the quantitative siren song enchants the mind and deceives the existing individual.

In relation to the absurd, the objective approximation-process is like the comedy, *Misunderstanding upon Misunderstanding,* which is generally played by *Privatdocents* and speculative philosophers. The absurd is precisely by its objective repulsion the measure of the intensity of faith in inwardness. Suppose a man who wishes to acquire faith; let the comedy begin. He wishes to have faith, but he wishes also to safeguard himself by means of an objective inquiry and its approximation-process. What happens? With the help of the approximation-process the absurd becomes something different; it becomes probable, it becomes increasingly probable, it becomes extremely and emphatically probable. Now he is ready to believe it, and he ventures to claim for himself that he does not believe as shoemakers and tailors and simple folk believe, but only after long deliberation. Now he is ready to believe it; and lo, now it has become precisely impossible to believe it. Anything that is almost probable, or probable, or extremely and emphatically probable, is something he can almost know, or as good as know, or extremely and emphatically almost *know*—but it is impossible to *believe.* For the absurd is the object of faith, and the only object that can be believed.

Or suppose a man who says that he has faith, but desires to make his faith clear to himself, so as to understand himself in his faith. Now the comedy again begins. The object of faith becomes almost probable, as good as probable, extremely and emphatically probable. He has completed his investigations, and he ventures to claim for himself that he does not believe as shoemakers and tailors and other simple folk believe, but that he has also understood himself in his believing. Strange understanding! On the contrary, he has in fact learned something else about faith than when he believed; and he has learned that he no longer believes, since he almost knows, or as good as knows, or extremely and emphatically almost knows.

In so far as the absurd comprehends within itself the factor of becoming, one way of approximation will be that which confuses the absurd fact of such a becoming (which is the object of faith) with a simple historical fact, and hence seeks historical certainty for that which is absurd, because it involves the contradiction that something which can become historical only in direct opposition to all human reason, has become historical. It is this contradiction which constitutes the absurd, and which can only be believed. If historical certainty with respect to it is assumed, the certainty attained is merely that the something which is thus assumed as certain is not the thing in question. A witness can testify that he has believed it, and hence that so far from being a historical certainty it is directly contrary to his own reason; but such a witness thrusts the individual away in precisely the same sense that the absurd itself does. And a witness who does not so repel is *eo ipso* a deceiver, or a man who talks about something quite different, and can help only to obtain certainty about something quite different. A hundred thousand individual witnesses, who are individual witnesses precisely on account of the peculiar character of their testimony (that they have believed the absurd), cannot *en masse* become anything else, so as to make the absurd less absurd—and why less absurd? Because a hundred thousand human beings have separately, each one for himself, believed that it was absurd? On the contrary, these hundred thousand witnesses again exercise a repellent influence in nearly the same way that the absurd itself exercises it.

But this I need not here expound in greater detail. In the *Fragments* (especially where the distinction between the disciple at first-hand and at second-hand is shown to be illusory), and in the first part of this book, I have already carefully enough expounded the thesis that all approximation is useless, since on the contrary it behooves us to get rid of introductory guarantees of security, proofs from consequences, and the whole mob of public pawnbrokers and guarantors, so as to permit the absurd to stand out in all its clarity—in order that the individual may believe if he wills it; I merely say that it must be strenuous in the highest degree so to believe.

If speculative philosophy wishes to take cognizance of this, and say as always, that there is no paradox when the matter is viewed eternally, divinely, theocentrically—then I admit that I am not in a position to determine whether the speculative philosopher is right, for I am only a poor existing human being, not competent to contemplate the eternal either eternally or divinely or theocentrically, but compelled to content myself with existing. So much is certain, however, that speculative philosophy carries everything back, back past the Socratic position, which at least comprehended that for an existing individual existence is essential; to say nothing of the failure of speculative philosophy to take time to grasp what it means to be so critically situated in existence as the existing individual in the experiment. . . .

Friedrich Nietzsche: The Superman and Eternal Return

Thus Spoke Zarathustra

PART I

ZARATHUSTRA'S PROLOGUE

(Zarathustra has spent ten years living in solitude upon a mountainside, developing his wisdom and deepening his joy in life. At the age of forty, he decides that he needs disciples. What happiness would the sun have, he asks himself, had it no one to shine upon? And thus he decides to return to the cities below and to speak to mankind.)

2.

Zarathustra descended the mountainside alone, and he encountered no one. But suddenly, as he came into the forest, an old man stood before him, who had left his holy cottage to seek roots to eat in the forest. And the old man spoke thus to Zarathustra:

"This wanderer is not unknown to me: many years ago he passed by this place. Zarathustra is his name; but he is greatly changed.

"Then you carried your ashes to the mountain; now you will carry your fire into the valleys? Are you not afraid to be punished as an incendiary?

"Yes, I know Zarathustra. His eye is clear, and there is no sign of disgust about his lips. Does he not walk about like a dancer?

"Transformed is Zarathustra, Zarathustra has become as a child, an Awakened One is Zarathustra; what do you have to seek among those who sleep?

"As in the sea you lived in your solitude, and the sea carried you. Alas, you now wish to return to the land? Alas, you wish to carry your own bones once again?"

Zarathustra answered, "I love mankind."

"Why," said the holy man, "did I go into the forest and the wilderness? Was it not because I loved mankind all too much?

"Now I love God: man I love no more. Man is far too incomplete: love of man would kill me."

Zarathustra answered: "What did I speak of love! I bring mankind a gift."

"Give them nothing," said the holy man. "Rather take something from them and help them to carry it: that will be best for them, if only it is good for you!

"And if you wish to give them something, let it be no more than an alms, and let them beg for it as well!"

"No," said Zarathustra, "I shall give no alms; for that I am not poor enough."

The holy man laughed at Zarathustra and said: "So see to it, then, that they accept your treasures! They are suspicious of hermits, and do not believe that we come with gifts.

"Our steps sound too lonely to them as we go through the streets. And when they hear a man walking by as they take to their beds in the night, they ask themselves: what is the thief about?

"Do not go to man; stay in your forest! Rather go to the animals! Be as I am: a bear

---

Nietzsche, *Thus Spoke Zarathustra*. Translated by Eugene Kelly, 1980.

among bears, a bird among birds."

"And what does the holy man do here in his forest?" asked Zarathustra.

The holy man answered: "I make songs and sing them, and when I make songs, I laugh, weep, and hum: in this way I praise God.

With singing, weeping, laughing and humming, I praise the God who is my God. But what is it you bring us as a gift?"

When Zarathustra heard these words, he said farewell to the holy man and said: "What might I have to give to you? But let me go quickly, lest I take something from you!"

And so they parted, the old saint and the man, laughing as two children laugh.

But when Zarathustra was alone, he spoke thus unto his heart: "Could it be possible! This old holy man in his forest has not heard that *God is dead?*"

3.

When Zarathustra entered the nearest town that lay upon the forest rim, he found there many people collected in the marketplace; for they had been told that a tightrope walker would perform. And Zarathustra spoke thus unto the people:

"*I teach you the Superman.* Man is something that must be overcome. What have you done to overcome him?

"All beings up to now have created something beyond themselves. And do you wish to be the ebb of this great upward flood, and rather return to the beasts than to overcome man?

"What is the ape to man? A painful joke or an object of scorn. And just so should man be to the superman: a painful joke or an object of scorn.

"You have traveled the road from the worm to man, and much in you is still worm. Once you were apes, and even now man is more an ape than any ape.

"He who is the wisest among you is still but a discordant hybrid of plant and phantom. But do I teach you to be like plants or phantoms?

"Behold, I teach you the Superman!

"The Superman is the meaning of the earth. May your will say: The Superman *shall be* the meaning of the earth!

"I beseech you, my brothers, to *remain true to the earth,* and believe them not who speak of otherworldly hopes! They are mixers of poisons, whether they know it or not.

"Despisers of life they are; they move toward extinction, poisoned by their own hands: the earth is tired of them; may they move on quickly!

"Once the greatest sin was the sin against God; but God died, and with him these sinners died as well. To sin against the earth is now the greatest blasphemy, and to show more reverence to the mere entrails of the incomprehensible than to the meaning of the earth!

"Once the soul looked contemptuously upon the body: and this contempt was then the highest of attitudes—the soul desired the body to be emaciated, ugly, starving. Thus the soul hoped to escape from it and from the earth.

"Oh, this soul was itself emaciated, ugly, and starving; and cruelty was the passion of this soul!

"But you too, my brothers, tell me: what does your body reveal about your soul? Is your soul not poverty and filth and miserable complacency?

"Truly, man is a polluted stream. One must be the sea itself to be able to absorb such pollution without becoming polluted oneself.

"Behold, I teach you the Superman. He is this sea in which your contempt may be submerged.

"What is the greatest thing that you can experience? It is the hour of great contempt. The hour in which even your happiness becomes disgusting to you, along with your reason and your virtue.

"The hour in which you say, 'what good is my happiness?! It is poverty and filth and a miserable complacency! But my happiness should justify existence itself!'

"The hour in which you say, 'what good is my reason? Does it desire knowledge like the lion its prey? It is poverty and filth and miserable complacency!'

"The hour in which you say, 'what good my virtue? It has not yet put me in a rage. How sick am I of my good and my evil! All that is poverty and filth and miserable complacency!'

"The hour in which you say, 'what good my justice? I have not yet become a fiery coal! But justice is fire and coal!'"

"The hour in which you say, 'what good my pity? Is not pity the cross upon which he who loved mankind was nailed? But my pity is not crucifixion.'

"Have you ever spoken thus? Have you ever cried out thus? Oh, that I might have heard you cry out thus!

"Not just your sins but your complacency cries out to heaven, the very cautious frugality with which you sin cries out to heaven!

"Where is the lightning that will burn you with its tongue? Where is the madness with which to inoculate you?

"Behold, I teach you the Superman: he is the lightning, he is the madness!—"

When Zarathustra had spoken thus, a man called out from among the people: "Now we have heard enough about the tightrope walker, now let us see him!" And the people laughed at Zarathustra. The tightrope walker, who thought they were talking about him, began his performance.

4.

But Zarathustra looked at the people and was amazed. Then he spoke thus:

"Man is a rope between the ape and the Superman, a rope stretched across an abyss.

"A dangerous glance to the other side, a dangerous way across, a dangerous looking back, a dangerous trembling and stopping.

"What is great in man is that he is a bridge and not a goal: what can be loved about man is that he is a *going-across* and a *going-down*.

"I love them who do not know how to live except by going down to destruction, for they are the ones who will go across to the other side.

"I love those who are full of contempt, for they are the ones who are full of esteem, and are like arrows longing to reach the other shore.

"I love them who do not seek beyond the clouds for a reason to go down to destruction as a sacrificial victim, but who sacrifice themselves to the earth, that the earth may one day see the Superman.

"I love him who lives that he may know, and who wants to know so that the Superman may live. And thus he desires his own destruction.

"I love him who works and invents, that he may build a house for the Superman, and who prepares earth, animals, and plants for him: for in this way he wills his own destruction.

"I love him who loves his virtue, for virtue is the will to destruction and the arrow of longing for the other shore.

"I love him who does not hold a drop of spirit for himself, but who wishes to be entirely the spirit of his virtue: he will go as spirit across the bridge.

"I love him who makes of his virtue his aptitude and his destiny [seinen Hang und sein Behaengnis] for he desires to live for the sake of his virtue, and to live no more.

"I love him who does not desire too many virtues. One virtue is more virtue than two, because it is more of a knot upon which destiny hangs.

"I love him whose soul uses itself up, who will not be thanked, and who gives nothing back: for he gives always, and will not save himself.

"I love him who is ashamed when the dice roll to his advantage, and who then asks: have I cheated?—for he wills his own destruction.

"I love him who speaks golden words before his actions, and produces more than he has promised: for he desires his own destruction.

"I love him who justifies the people of the future and who brings salvation to those in the past: for he desires his own destruction at the hands of his contemporaries.

"I love him who punishes his God because he loves Him: for he will find his destruction in the wrath of his God.

"I love him whose soul is deep even when it is amazed, and who is destroyed even through a trifle: he will gladly cross the bridge.

"I love him whose soul is overfull, that he forgets himself, and all things are in him: thus all things will be his destruction.

"I love all those who are like heavy droplets, which fall one after the other out of the dark clouds that hang over mankind: they bear witness that the lightning is coming, and they are destroyed as witness-bearers.

"Behold, I bear witness to this lightning, and am a heavy droplet out of the cloud: this lightning is called the *Superman*."

7.

When Zarathustra had spoken these words, he looked again upon the people and fell silent. "There they stand," he said unto his heart, "there they laugh: they do not understand me, I am not the mouth for these ears.

"Must I break their ears in pieces, that they may learn to hear with their eyes? Must I rattle like a tin drum, or like the preachers of sin? Or do they believe only the stammerer?

"They have something of which they are proud. What do they call this source of their pride? They call it culture; it distinguishes them from the goatherds.

"For that reason they do not like to hear the word 'contempt.' Therefore I will address myself to their pride.

"I will speak to them of what is most contemptible: I will speak of the *last man.*"

And Zarathustra spoke thus unto the people:

"It is time that man set a goal for himself. It is time that man plant the seed of his highest hope.

"The soil of man is not yet ready for this seed. But one day this soil shall become poor and unfertile, and no higher tree will be able to grow from it.

"Alas! The time will come in which man will no longer be able to hurl the arrow of longing for something beyond himself, when he will have forgotten to draw his own bowstring!

"I say unto you: you must have chaos in yourselves if you are to give birth to a dancing star. I say unto you: you still possess this chaos.

"Alas! The time is coming in which man will no longer be able to give birth to a star. Alas! The time of the most contemptible man is coming, the man who can no longer feel contempt for himself.

"Behold, I show you the most contemptible man.

"'What is love? What is creation? What is desire? What is a star?' the last man asks himself, and blinks.

"The earth will then have become small, and out of it will come hopping the last man, who makes everything small. His race is as indestructible as that of the flea; the last man lives the longest.

"'We have invented happiness,' say the last men, and they blink.

"They have left the regions where life was the hardest; after all, does one not need warmth? They still love their neighbors, and they rub up against them: does one not need warmth?

"To become sick, to be suspicious, is sinful to them; one walks cautiously. A fool is he, they say, who still trips over stones or men!

"Now and then let us inject a bit of poison into life: that will give us pleasant dreams. And finally we will take a lot of poison: that makes death more pleasant!

"They still work, for work is a pastime, after all. But they are careful that the pastime does not weaken them.

"They no longer become either rich or poor: both are too troublesome. Who wants to rule? Who wants to obey? Both are too troublesome.

"No shepherd and no flock! Everyone has the same desires, everyone is the same: anyone who disagrees goes of his own free will to the madhouse.

"'Once the whole world had gone mad,' say these refined people, and they blink.

"They have become wise, and know everything about the past: thus they have no present to laugh at. They still argue and fight, but are soon reconciled: otherwise they might disturb their digestion.

"They have a little vice for the day and a little vice for the night; but 'one takes care of one's health.'

"'We invented happiness,' say the last men, and they blink."

At this point the first speech of Zarathustra comes to a close, which is called also "The Preface": for at this moment the cries and the laughter of the crowd interrupted him. "Give us this last man, O Zarathustra," they cried, "make us like unto these last men! Then we will give you the superman!" And the people roared and clucked their tongues. But Zarathustra became sad and said unto his heart:

"They do not understand me: I am not the mouth for these ears.

"Too long have I lived in the mountains, too long I listened to the rivers and the trees: now I speak to them like the goatherd.

"My soul is calm and bright as the mountain at midmorning. But they think I am cold and a scoffer with fearsome jests.

"And now they look at me and laugh: and while they laugh, they hate me: there is ice in their laughter."

(Zarathustra decides that he will not speak to the masses of men, but will seek disciples to whom he will teach independence of mind and joy of life, that they become themselves independent and joyful, and may go off to seek their own way, as did Zarathustra himself. The greater part of *Thus Spoke Zarathustra* contains the speeches that Zarathustra is supposed to have made to his disciples. We reproduce one of them here.)

ON A THOUSAND AND ONE GOALS

Many lands and many peoples were visited by Zarathustra; thus he discovered the good and evil of many peoples. Zarathustra found no greater power on earth than the power of good and evil.

"No people could live that did not value; if a people wishes to continue to exist, it must value differently than its neighbor.

"Many things that one people calls good is a mockery and a disgrace to another: thus I have seen. Many things I found in one place to be called evil was clothed in purple in another.

"Never did one people understand its neighbor: always their souls were astonished at the madness and wickedness of their neighbors.

"A list of goods hangs over the heads of each people. Behold, this is the list of its overcomings; behold, it is the voice of its will to power.

"They call that praiseworthy which is difficult for them; what is necessary and difficult they call good; and what frees them from the highest need, that which is strangest and most difficult of all—that they call holy.

"What enables them to rule and be victorious, to excel and to reduce their neighbors to fear and envy: that they call the Highest, the First, the standard of all, the meaning of all things.

"Truly my brothers, when you learn the needs and the land and the heaven and the neighbors of a people, then you will understand the law of their overcomings, and why they climb to the object of their hopes upon this ladder.

"'You must always be the first, and tower over the others: no one shall love your jealous soul, unless he be your friend': this thought made the soul of the Greek tremble: upon it he trod the path of his greatness.

"'Speak the truth, and be excellent with bow and arrow': so thought the people from whom I have taken my name to be words dear and hard: and their name is at once dear and hard to me.

"'Honor your father and mother, and be willing to serve them to the very roots of your soul': this list of overcomings was set above themselves by another people, and with them they became powerful and eternal.

"'Be loyal, and for the sake of loyalty risk life and honor even in dangerous and evil undertakings': thus admonishing itself, another people overcame itself, and thus overcoming, became heavy and pregnant with great hopes.

"Truly, man has given himself all his good and evil. Truly, he did not take them, did not find them; they fell upon him as a voice from heaven.

"Man placed values in things that he might live—he created the meaning of all things, a human-meaning! Thus he calls himself 'man': that is, the valuer.

"Valuing is creating: hear this, you creative ones! Valuing is itself the treasure and the jewel of all valued things.

"Only through valuing does value come to be: and without valuing the very core of life would be hollow. Hear this, you creative ones!

"The transformation of values—that is, the transformation of the one who values. He who will be a creator will be a destroyer.

"Once peoples placed lists of goods above their heads. A love that wishes to command, and a love that wishes to obey, together created such lists of goods.

"The joy in the herd is older than the joy in the self: and as long as good conscience is called 'herd', bad conscience will say 'I'."

Truly, the clever one, the loveless one, the one that seeks its good in the good of others: this self is not the origin of the herd, but rather its destruction.

Always loving selves and creative selves alone created good and evil. The fire of love glows in the name of all virtues, as well as the fire of anger.

Many lands saw Zarathustra, and many peoples: and he found no greater power on earth than the work of the lovers: "good" and "evil" is their name.

Truly, a veritable monster is the power of this praise and blame. Say, who will overcome it for me, my brothers? Say, who will throw chains about the thousand necks of this creature?

A thousand goals have existed up to now,

for a thousand peoples have existed. Only the chains about the thousand necks are still lacking, the One Goal is lacking: for as yet mankind has no goal.

But tell me, my brothers: if mankind is still lacking a goal, is it not lacking—itself?

Thus spoke Zarathustra.

The Antichrist

2.

What is good?—Everything that heightens our feeling of power, our will to power, the power in man itself.

What is bad?—Everything that comes from weakness.

What is happiness?—The feeling that our power is *growing*—that resistance is being overcome.

Not contentment, but rather more *power*; *not* peace at all, but rather war; *not* virtue, but rather excellence [virtue in the renaissance sense: virtù, virtue without sanctimony].

The weak and the misbegotten should go to their destruction: that is the first principle of *our* humanism. And they should be helped along their way.

What is more harmful than any vice?—Active pity for all the misbegotten and the weak—Christianity . . .

3.

Our problem is not with what ought to take the place of man in the sequence of living beings (—man is an end—), but with what type of man should be *cultivated,* striven for, as the higher value, the more worthy of life, as the being most certain of his future.

This higher type has already existed: but as the fortunate exception, the product of chance; never as consciously *desired.* On the contrary, he has been the object of fear, he has been up to now almost *the* most fearsome creature;—and out of this fear the opposite type of man was desired, cultivated, *attained*: the domestic animal, the herd animal, the sick animal man—the Christian.

4.

Mankind does *not* represent a development towards something better, or stronger, or higher, in the sense that people today believe this to be the case. "Progress" is simply a modern idea, that is to say, a false idea. The European of today is far inferior to the renaissance man with respect to his values; a progressive development is absolutely *not* to be confused with advance, heightening, strengthening.

In another sense there have been successful individual cases in the most various parts of the world and in the most various cultures in which in fact a genuine *higher* type presents itself: a type that is, in comparison to mankind at large, a kind of superman. Such exceptional cases of great successes were always possible, and perhaps always will be. And even entire races, tribes, and peoples can at times constitute such a *bull's eye.*

5.

We should not try to whitewash Christianity: it has fought a *deadly war* against this *higher* type of man, it excommunicated all

Nietzsche, *The Antichrist.* Translated by Eugene Kelly, 1980.

the basic instincts of this type, it decocted out of these instincts the concept of evil, the evil man: the strong man as typically depraved, as the "depraved man." Christianity took up the cause of the weak, the low, the misbegotten; it constructed an ideal out of its contradiction with the survival instincts of those strong with life; it even corrupted the reason itself of the most spiritually powerful natures by teaching them to consider the highest values of spirituality as sinful, as deceptive, as *temptations*. The most pitiful example of this is the corruption of Pascal, who believed in the corruption of his reason through original sin, whereas it had been corrupted only by his Christianity!—

6.

A painful, horrifying charade was just played out before my eyes. I drew the curtain away from the *corruption* of man. This word in my mouth is protected, at least, from one suspicion: that it contains a moral condemnation of man. It is—let me insist again—intended as entirely free of sanctimony: so much so that this corruption is found by me to be the strongest where people up to now aspired most consciously toward "virtue," toward "holiness." I understand corruption—you have guessed it already—in the sense of decadence: I maintain that all values that mankind calls its highest values are the values of decadence.

I call an animal, a class, an individual corrupt when it loses its instincts, when it chooses, even *prefers* what is to its own disadvantage. A history of the "higher feelings," the "ideals of mankind"—and it is possible that I will *have to* describe them—would almost furnish us with the explanation of *why* man is so corrupt. Life itself is to me an instinct for growth, for continued existence, for the accumulation of strength, for *power*: where the will to power is lacking, there is decline. I maintain that all the highest values of man *lack* this will—that the values of decline, *nihilistic* values, rule over us under the most holy names.

7.

People call Christianity the religion of *compassion*. Compassion is contrasted to the invigorating emotions, which increase the energy with which we feel ourselves alive: it is a depressive. We lose strength when we feel compassion. When we suffer with others [Mitleiden, com-passion], the loss of strength which suffering produces by itself is increased and multiplies. Suffering itself is communicated to others by means of compassion; under certain circumstances it can produce a total loss of life and vital energy which stands in an absurd disproportion to the quantity of its cause (—the case of the death of the Nazarene). That is the first point, there is another still more important. If one measures compassion according to the strength of the reactions which it usually produces, its life-threatening character appears in a much stronger light. Compassion usually sets itself against the law of evolution, which is the law of *selection*. It helps maintain what is ripe for destruction, it puts up a fight for what has been disenfranchised and condemned by life, it gives to life itself a gloomy and questionable aspect because of the presence of misbegotten forms of life upon the earth, which it helped to survive. People have dared to call compassion a virtue (in any noble morality it is counted as a weakness); others have gone even further, they have made virtue itself of it, made of it the very soil and source of all virtues—only, of course (a fact we must keep always in mind), from the standpoint of a nihilistic philosophy, one that wrote the *denial of life* upon its coat of arms. Schopenhauer was within his rights when he wrote that life is rejected, *made more worthy of rejection*, through compassion. Compassion is the *praxis* of nihilism. Put another way: this depressive and contagious instinct sets itself against those instincts which are directed towards the maintenance and the augmentation of the value of life: it is as much as the *multiplier* of misery as the *preserver* of everything miserable that it functions as the major instrument in the advancement of decadence—compassion converts us to *nothingness*! Only one does not, of course, use the word "nothingness"; one speaks instead of "the next world," or "God," or "the *true* way," or Nirvana, or salvation, or beatitude . . . This innocent rhetoric from the realm of religious-moral animosities immediately appears *much less innocent* when we consider what tendencies are dressing themselves in the cloak of sublime words: tendencies *inimical to life*. Schopenhauer was an enemy of life; *for that reason* compassion became a virtue for him . . . Aristotle realized, as is well known, that compassion is a morbid and dangerous state that one does well to combat occasionally with a purgative: he understood tragedy as a purgative. In the interest of the life instincts one ought in fact to search for a means to strike a blow against such a morbid and dangerous accumulation of compassion, as in the case of Schopenhauer (and unfortunately in all of our collected literary and artistic decadence from St. Petersburg to Paris, from Tolstoy to Wagner): a blow that will make it *explode* . . . Nothing is more unhealthy than Christian pity at the center of our unhealthy modernity. Here to be a physician, to wield the knife without pity . . . that is *our* task, that is our kind of humanism, in this way we are philosophers, we Hyperboreans!—

11.

A word against Kant as a *moralist*. A virtue must be *our* invention, *our* most personal and urgent defense, our most pressing need: in any other fashion it is simply a danger. What is not the basis of life *harms* life: to have a virtue just because of a feeling of respect before the word "virtue" is harmful. "Virtue," "duty," the "good in itself," goodness as an impersonal quality and with universal validity—chimeras in which decline, a terminal impotence of life, Königsberg Christianity, reaches its final expression. Precisely the reverse is offered by the deepest law of preservation and growth: that each person invent *his* virtue, *his* categorical imperative. A people goes to its ruin when it confuses *its* sense of duty with the concept of duty in general. Nothing harms more deeply, more intimately, than all "impersonal" duties, than every sacrifice before the Moloch of abstraction—And that we never suspected that Kant's categorical imperative was *dangerous to life!* . . . It was only the theological instinct that was able to protect it! An action to which we are impelled by the instinct of life has in joy its proof that it is a *right* action: and every nihilist with the entrails of Christian dogma understood joy to be an *objection*. . . . What destroys a man more quickly than to work, think, and feel without an internal necessity, without a deep personal choice, without *joy*? As the automaton of "duty"? This is precisely the *recipe* for decadence, even for idiocy. . . . Kant himself became an idiot.—And this was the contemporary of *Goethe*! This disastrous spider was considered to be *the* German philosopher—even to this day! I would hate to say what I think of the Germans. [. . .] This blundering instinct in everything and anything, *unnaturalness* as instinct, German decadence as philosophy—that is Kant!—

The Gay Science

125.

The madman.—Have you heard of the madman who lit his lantern one bright afternoon, ran into the marketplace, and cried incessantly: I seek God! I seek God! As many people were standing about who did not believe in God, he caused great laughter. Has he gotten lost? said one. Has he run away like a child? said another. Or is he hiding? Is he afraid of us? Has he gone away to sea? Emigrated?—so they all cried out and laughed. The madman leapt among them and ran them through with his stare. "Where is God?" he called, "I will tell you! *We have murdered Him*—you and I. We are all His murderers! But how have we done this? How were we able to drink up the sea? Who gave us the sponge to wipe away the horizon? What did we do when we unchained the earth from its sun? Whither is it moving? Whither are we moving? Away from all suns? Are we rather not continually falling? Falling backwards, sideways, forwards, in all directions? Is there still an above and below? Are we not lost wanderers in an infinite nothingness? Empty space breathes upon us; it has become cold! Is it not always darkest night? Must we not light our lanterns even in the brightest day? Do we hear nothing of the clatter made by the undertakers who are burying God? Do we smell nothing of the divine corpse in decay?—for even gods decay! God is dead! God remains dead! And we have killed him! Where shall we find one to comfort us, we murderers of all murderers? The holiest and most powerful thing that the world has possessed until now has bled to death under our knives—who shall wipe the blood from our hands? With what water shall we cleanse ourselves? What celebrations of atonement, what pious games will we have to invent? Is the act not too great for us? Do we not ourselves have to become gods in order to appear worthy of it? There never was a greater act—and whoever is born after us belongs by reason of this act in a higher historical realm than ever existed throughout history!" The madman fell silent, and gazed at his listeners; they were silent also, and looked strangely upon him. At last he threw his lantern upon the ground, so that it broke in pieces and went out. "I come too soon," he said then, "the time has not yet come. This terrible event is still in the making, and wanders about—the ears of man have not yet heard it. Thunder and lightning need time, the light from the stars needs time, acts of men need time, even after they have been done, to be seen and heard. This act is even farther still from man than the farthest star—and yet *man has done it himself*!" The story goes on that the madman entered many churches that same day and there sang his requiem to God. When he was led out and forced to account for himself, he would say only this: "What are these churches now, if not the sepulchres and mausoleums of God?"

341.

The greatest weight.—What if one day or

Nietzsche, *The Gay Science.* Translated by Eugene Kelly, 1980.

night a demon were to slip into your loneliest of lonelinesses and say to you: "This life that you are now living and have lived, you will once more and endless times more have to live again; and there will be nothing new the next time, but every pain and every joy and every thought and sigh and every incident of your life both great and small must happen again to you, and everything in the same order and with the same consequences—just as also will return this spider and this moonlight between the trees and this moment and I myself. The eternal hourglass of existence will be turned about ever and ever again—and you along with it, bit of dust made of dust!" Would you not throw yourself upon the ground and grind your teeth and curse the demon that spoke to you thus? Or have you once experienced a great moment, one in which you would have answered: "You are a god, and never have I heard a thought more divine!" If that thought took control of you, it would transform you, as you are now, and perhaps reduce you to ashes; to ask yourself the question before each and every event, "do you wish this to happen again, and perhaps an untold number of times?" would place the greatest weight upon your actions! Or how much more you would have to become in your own eyes and in the eyes of life as to *desire* nothing more than this final eternal confirmation and seal?

William James: What Pragmatism Means

Some years ago, being with a camping party in the mountains, I returned from a solitary ramble to find every one engaged in a ferocious metaphysical dispute. The *corpus* of the dispute was a squirrel—a live squirrel supposed to be clinging to one side of a tree-trunk; while over against the tree's opposite side a human being was imagined to stand. This human witness tries to get sight of the squirrel by moving rapidly round the tree, but no matter how fast he goes, the squirrel moves as fast in the opposite direction, and always keeps the tree between himself and the man, so that never a glimpse of him is caught. The resultant metaphysical problem now is this: *Does the man go round the squirrel or not?* He goes round the tree, sure enough, and the squirrel is on the tree; but does he go round the squirrel? In the unlimited leisure of the wilderness, discussion had been worn threadbare. Every one had taken sides, and was obstinate; and the numbers on both sides were even. Each side, when I appeared, therefore appealed to me to make it a majority. Mindful of the scholastic adage that whenever you meet a contradiction you must make a distinction, I immediately sought and found one, as follows: "What party is right," I said, "depends on what you *practically mean* by 'going round' the squirrel. If you mean passing from the north of him to the east, then to the south, then to the west, and then to the north of him again, obviously the man does go round him, for he occupies these successive positions. But if on the contrary you mean being first in front of him, then on the right of him, then behind him, then on his left, and finally in front again, it is quite as obvious that the man fails to go round him, for by the compensating movements the squirrel makes, he keeps his belly turned towards the man all the time, and his back turned away. Make the distinction, and there is no occasion for any further dispute. You are both right and both wrong according as you conceive the verb 'to go round' in one practical fashion or the other."

Although one or two of the hotter disputants called my speech a shuffling evasion, saying they wanted no quibbling or scholastic hair-splitting, but mean just plain honest English "round," the majority seemed to think that the distinction had assuaged the dispute.

I tell this trivial anecdote because it is a peculiarly simple example of what I wish now to speak of as *the pragmatic method.* The pragmatic method is primarily a method of settling metaphysical disputes that otherwise might be interminable. Is the world one or many?—fated or free?—material or spiritual?—here are notions either of which may or may not hold good of the world; and disputes over such notions are unending. The pragmatic method in such cases is to try to interpret each notion by tracing its respective practical consequences. What difference would it practically make to any one if this notion rather than that notion were true? If no practical difference whatever can be traced, then the alternatives mean practically the same thing, and all dispute is idle. Whenever a dispute is serious, we ought to be able to show some practical difference that must follow from one side or the other's being right.

A glance at the history of the idea will show

you still better what pragmatism means. The term is derived from the same Greek word πραγμα, meaning action, from which our words "practice" and "practical" come. It was first introduced into philosophy by Mr. Charles Peirce in 1878. In an article entitled "How to Make Our Ideas Clear," in the *Popular Science Monthly* for January of that year, Mr. Peirce, after pointing out that our beliefs are really rules for action, said that, to develop a thought's meaning, we need only determine what conduct it is fitted to produce: that conduct is for us its sole significance. And the tangible fact at the root of all our thought-distinctions, however subtle, is that there is no one of them so fine as to consist in anything but a possible difference of practice. To attain perfect clearness in our thoughts of an object, then, we need only consider what conceivable effects of a practical kind the object may involve—what sensations we are to expect from it, and what reactions we must prepare. Our conception of these effects, whether immediate or remote, is then for us the whole of our conception of the object, so far as that conception has positive significance at all.

This is the principle of Peirce, the principle of pragmatism. It lay entirely unnoticed by any one for twenty years, until I, in an address before Professor Howison's Philosophical Union at the University of California, brought it forward again and made a special application of it to religion. By that date (1898) the times seemed ripe for its reception. The word "pragmatism" spread, and at present it fairly spots the pages of the philosophic journals. On all hands we find the "pragmatic movement" spoken of, sometimes with respect, sometimes with contumely, seldom with clear understanding. It is evident that the term applies itself conveniently to a number of tendencies that hitherto have lacked a collective name, and that it has "come to stay."

To take in the importance of Peirce's principle, one must get accustomed to applying it to concrete cases. I found a few years ago that Ostwald, the illustrious Leipzig chemist, had been making perfectly distinct use of the principle of pragmatism in his lectures on the philosophy of science, though he had not called it by that name.

"All realities influence our practice," he wrote me, "and that influence is their meaning for us. I am accustomed to put questions to my classes in this way: In what respects would the world be different if this alternative or that were true? If I can find nothing that would become different, then the alternative has no sense."

That is, the rival views mean practically the same thing, and meaning, other than practical, there is for us none. Ostwald in a published lecture gives this example of what he means. Chemists have long wrangled over the inner constitution of certain bodies called "tautomerous." Their properties seemed equally consistent with the notion that an unstable hydrogen atom oscillates inside of them, or that they are unstable mixtures of two bodies. Controversy raged, but never was decided. "It would never have begun," says Ostwald, "if the combatants had asked themselves what particular experimental fact could have been made different by one or the other view being correct. For it would then have appeared that no difference of fact could possibly ensure; and the quarrel was as unreal as if, theorizing in primitive times about the raising of dough by yeast, one party should have invoked a 'brownie,' while another insisted on an 'elf' as the true cause of the phenomenon."

It is astonishing to see how many philosophical disputes collapse into insignificance the moment you subject them to this simple test of tracing a concrete consequence. There can *be* no difference anywhere that doesn't *make* a difference elsewhere—no difference in abstract truth that doesn't express itself in a difference in concrete fact and in conduct consequent upon that fact, imposed on somebody, somehow, somewhere, and somewhen. The whole function of philosophy ought to be to find out what definite difference it will make to you and me, at definite instants of our life, if this world-formula or that world-formula be the true one.

There is absolutely nothing new in the pragmatic method. Socrates was an adept at it. Aristotle used it methodically. Locke, Berkeley, and Hume made momentous contributions to truth by its means. Shadworth Hodgson keeps insisting that realities are only what they are "known as." But these forerunners of pragmatism used it in fragments: they were preluders only. Not until in our time has it generalized itself, become conscious of a universal mission, pretended to a conquering destiny. I believe in that destiny, and I hope I may end by inspiring you with my belief.

Pragmatism represents a perfectly familiar attitude in philosphy, the empiricist attitude, but it represents it, as it seems to me, both in a more radical and in a less objectionable form than it has ever yet assumed. A pragmatist turns his back resolutely and once for all upon a lot of inveterate habits dear to professional philosophers. He turns away from abstraction and insufficiency, from verbal solutions, from bad *a priori* reasons, from fixed principles, closed systems, and pretended absolutes and origins. He turns towards concreteness and adequacy, towards facts, towards action and towards power. That means the empiricist temper regnant and the rationalist temper sincerely given up. It means the open air and possibilities of nature, as against dogma, artificiality, and the pretense of finality in truth.

At the same time it does not stand for any special results. It is a method only. But the general triumph of that method would mean an enormous change in what I called in my last lecture the "temperament" of philosophy. Teachers of the ultra-rationalist type would be frozen out, much as the courtier type is frozen out in republics, as the ultramontane type of priest is frozen out in protestant lands. Science and metaphysics would come much nearer together, would in fact work absolutely hand in hand.

Metaphysics has usually followed a very primitive kind of quest. You know how men have always hankered after unlawful magic, and you know what a great part in magic *words* have always played. If you have his name, or the formula of incantation that binds him, you can control the spirit, genie, afrite, or whatever the power may be. Solomon knew the names of all the spirits, and having their names, he held them subject to his will. So the universe has always appeared to the natural mind as a kind of enigma, of which the key must be sought in the shape of some illuminating or power-bringing word or name. That word names the universe's *principle,* and to possess it is after a fashion to possess the universe itself. "God," "Matter," "Reason," "the Absolute," "Energy," are so many solving names. You can rest when you have them. You are at the end of your metaphysical quest.

But if you follow the pragmatic method, you cannot look on any such word as closing your quest. You must bring out of each word its practical cash-value, set it at work within the stream of your experience. It appears less as a solution, then, than as a program for more work, and more particularly as an indication of the ways in which existing realities may be *changed.*

Theories thus become instruments, not answers to enigmas, in which we can rest. We don't lie back upon them, we move forward, and, on occasion, make nature over again by their aid. Pragmatism unstiffens all our theories, limbers them up and sets each one at work. Being nothing essentially new, it harmonizes with many ancient philosophic tendencies. It agrees with nominalism, for instance, in always appealing to particulars; with utilitarianism in emphasizing practical aspects; with positivism in its disdain for verbal solutions, useless questions and metaphysical abstractions.

All these, you see, are *anti-intellectualist* tendencies. Against rationalism as a pretension and a method pragmatism is fully armed and militant. But, at the outset, at least, it stands for no particular results. It has no dogmas, and no doctrines save its method. As the young Italian pragmatist Papini has well said, it lies in the midst of our theories, like a corridor in a hotel. Innumerable chambers open out of it. In one you may find a man writing an atheistic volume; in the next some one on his knees praying for faith and strength; in a third a chemist investigating a body's properties. In a fourth a system of idealistic metaphysics is being excogitated; in a fifth the impossibility of metaphysics is being shown. But they all own the corridor, and all must pass through it if they want a practicable way of getting into or out of their respective rooms.

No particular results then, so far, but only an attitude of orientation, is what the pragmatic method means. *The attitude of looking away from first things, principles, "categories," supposed necessities; and of looking towards last things, fruits, consequences, facts.*

So much for the pragmatic method! You may say that I have been praising it rather than explaining it to you, but I shall presently explain it abundantly enough by showing how it works on some familiar problems. Meanwhile the word pragmatism has come to be used in a still wider sense, as meaning also a certain *theory of truth.* I mean to give a whole lecture to the statement of that theory, after first paving the way, so I can be very brief now. But brevity is hard to follow, so I ask for your redoubled attention for a quarter of an hour. If much remains obscure, I hope to make it clearer in the later lectures.

One of the most successfully cultivated branches of philosophy in our time is what is called inductive logic, the study of the conditions under which our sciences have evolved. Writers on this subject have begun to show a singular unanimity as to what the laws of nature and elements of fact mean, when formulated by mathematicians, physicists and chemists. When the first mathematical, logical, and natural uniformities, the first *laws,* were discovered, men were so carried away by the clearness, beauty and simplification that resulted, that they believed themselves to have deciphered authentically the eternal thoughts of the Almighty. His mind also thundered and reverberated in syllogisms. He also thought in conic sections, squares and roots and ratios, and geometrized like Euclid. He made Kepler's laws for the planets to follow; he made velocity increase proportionally to the time in falling bodies; he made the laws of the sines for light to obey when refracted; he established the classes, orders, families and genera of plants and animals, and fixed the distances between them. He thought the archetypes of all things, and devised their variations; and when we rediscover any one of these his wondrous institutions, we seize his mind in its very literal intention.

But as the sciences have developed further, the notion has gained ground that most, perhaps all, of our laws are only approximations. The laws themselves, moreover, have grown so numerous that there is no counting them; and so many rival formulations are proposed in all the branches of science that investigators have become accustomed to the notion that no theory is absolutely a transcript of reality, but that any one of them may from some point of view be useful. Their great use is to summarize old facts and to lead to new ones. They are only a man-made language, a conceptual shorthand, as some one calls them, in which we write our reports of nature; and languages, as is well known, tolerate much choice of expression and many dialects.

Thus human arbitrariness has driven divine necessity from scientific logic. If I mention the names of Sigwart, Mach, Ostwald, Pearson, Milhaud, Poincaré, Duhem, Ruyssen, those of you who are students will easily identify the tendency I speak of, and will think of additional names.

Riding now on the front of this wave of scientific logic Messrs. Schiller and Dewey appear with their pragmatistic account of what truth everywhere signifies. Everywhere, these teachers say, "truth" in our ideas and beliefs means the same thing that it means in science. It means, they say, nothing but this, *that ideas (which themselves are but parts of our experience) become true just in so far as they help us to get into satisfactory relation with other parts of our experience,* to summarize them and get about among them by conceptual short-cuts instead of following the interminable succession of particular phenomena. Any idea upon which we can ride, so to speak; any idea that will carry us prosperously from any one part of our experience to any other part, linking things satisfactorily, working securely, simplifying, saving labor; is true for just so much, true in so far forth, true *instrumentally.* This is the "instrumental" view of truth taught so successfully at Chicago, the view that truth in our ideas means their power to "work," promulgated so brilliantly at Oxford.

Messrs. Dewey, Schiller, and their allies, in reaching this general conception of all truth, have only followed the example of geologists, biologists and philologists. In the establishment of these other sciences, the successful stroke was always to take some simple process actually observable in operation—as denudation by weather, say, or variation from parental type, or change of dialect by incorporation of new words and pronunciations—and then to generalize it, making it apply to all times, and produce great results by summating its effects through the ages.

The observable process which Schiller and Dewey particularly singled out for generalization is the familiar one by which any individual settles into *new opinions*. The process here is always the same. The individual has a stock of old opinions already, but he meets a new experience that puts them to a strain. Somebody contradicts them; or in a reflective moment he discovers that they contradict each other; or he hears of facts with which they are incompatible; or desires arise in him which they cease to satisfy. The result is an inward trouble to which his mind till then had been a stranger, and from which he seeks to escape by modifying his previous mass of opinions. He saves as much of it as he can, for in this matter of belief we are all extreme conservatives. So he tries to change first this opinion, and then that (for they resist change very variously), until at last some new idea comes up which he can graft upon the ancient stock with a minimum of disturbance of the latter, some idea that mediates between the stock and the new experience and runs them into one another most felicitously and expediently.

This new idea is then adopted as the true one. It preserves the older stock of truths with a minimum of modification, stretching them just enough to make them admit the novelty, but conceiving that in ways as familiar as the case leaves possible. An *outrée* explanation, violating all our preconceptions, would never pass for a true account of a novelty. We should scratch round industriously till we found something less eccentric. The most violent revolutions in an individual's beliefs leave most of his old order standing. Time and space, cause and effect, nature and history, and one's own biography remain untouched. New truth is always a go-between, a smoother-over of transitions. It marries old opinion to new fact so as ever to show a minimum of jolt, a maximum of continuity. We hold a theory true just in proportion to its success in solving this "problem of maxima and minima." But success in solving this problem is eminently a matter of approximation. We say this theory solves it on the whole more satisfactorily than that theory; but that means more satisfactorily to ourselves, and individuals will emphasize their points of satisfaction differently. To a certain degree, therefore, everything here is plastic.

The point I now urge you to observe particularly is the part played by the older truths. Failure to take account of it is the source of much of the unjust criticism levelled against pragmatism. Their influence is absolutely controlling. Loyalty to them is the first principle—in most cases it is the only principle; for by far the most usual way of handling phenomena so novel that they would make for a serious arrangement of our preconception is to ignore them altogether, or to abuse those who bear witness for them.

You doubtless wish examples of this process of truth's growth, and the only trouble is their superabundance. The simplest case of new truth is of course the mere numerical addition of new kinds of facts, or of new single facts of old kinds, to our experience—an addition that involves no alteration in the old beliefs. Day follows day, and its contents are simply added. The new contents themselves are not true, they simply *come* and *are*. Truth is *What we say about* them, and when we say that they have come, truth is satisfied by the plain additive formula.

But often the day's contents oblige a rearrangement. If I should now utter piercing shrieks and act like a maniac on this platform, it would make many of you revise your ideas as to the probable worth of my philosophy. "Radium" came the other day as part of the day's content, and seemed for a moment to contradict our ideas of the whole order of nature, that order having come to be identified with what is called the conservation of energy. The mere sight of radium paying heat away indefinitely out of its own pocket seemed to violate that conservation. What to think? If the radiations from it were nothing but an escape of unsuspected "potential" energy, preexistent inside of the atoms, the principle of conservation would be saved. The discovery of "helium" as the radiation's outcome, opened a way to this belief. So Ramsay's view is generally held to be true, because, although it extends our old ideas of energy, it causes a minimum of alteration in their nature.

I need not multiply instances. A new opinion counts as "true" just in proportion as it gratifies the individual's desire to assimilate the novel in his experience to his beliefs in stock. It must both lean on old truth and grasp new fact;

and its success (as I said a moment ago) in doing this, is a matter for the individual's appreciation. When old truth grows, then, by new truth's addition, it is for subjective reasons. We are in the process and obey the reasons. The new idea is truest which performs most felicitously its function of satisfying our double urgency. It makes itself true, gets itself classed as true, by the way it works; grafting itself then upon the ancient body of truth, which thus grows much as a tree grows by the activity of a new layer of cambium.

Now Dewey and Schiller proceed to generalize this observation and to apply it to the most ancient parts of truth. They also once were plastic. They also were called true for human reasons. They also mediated between still earlier truths and what in those days were novel observations. Purely objective truth, truth in whose establishment the function of giving human satisfaction in marrying previous parts of experience with newer parts played no rôle whatever, is nowhere to be found. The reasons why we call things true is the reason why they *are* truth, for "to be true" *means* only to perform this marriage-function.

The trail of the human serpent is thus over everything. Truth independent; truth that we *find* merely; truth no longer malleable to human need; truth incorrigible, in a word; such truth exists indeed superabundantly—or is supposed to exist by rationalistically minded thinkers; but then it means only the dead heart of the living tree, and its being there means only that truth also has its paleontology, and its "prescription," and may grow stiff with years of veteran service and petrified in men's regard by sheer antiquity. But how plastic even the oldest truths nevertheless really are has been vividly shown in our day by the transformation of logical and mathematical ideas, a transformation which seems even to be invading physics. The ancient formulas are reinterpreted as special expressions of much wider principles, principles that our ancestors never got a glimpse of in their present shape and formulation.

Mr. Schiller still gives to all this view of truth the name of "Humanism," but, for this doctrine too, the name of pragmatism seems fairly to be in the ascendant, so I will treat it under the name of pragmatism in these lectures.

Such then would be the scope of pragmatism—first, a method; and second, a genetic theory of what is meant by truth. And these two things must be our future topics.

What I have said of the theory of truth will, I am sure, have appeared obscure and unsatisfactory to most of you by reason of its brevity. I shall make amends for that hereafter. In a lecture on "common sense" I shall try to show what I mean by truths grown petrified by antiquity. In another lecture I shall expatiate on the idea that our thoughts become true in proportion as they successfully exert their go-between function. In a third I shall show how hard it is to discriminate subjective from objective factors in Truth's development. You may not follow me wholly in these lectures; and if you do, you may not wholly agree with me. But you will, I know, regard me at least as serious, and treat my effort with respectful consideration.

You will probably be surprised to learn, then, that Messrs. Schiller's and Dewey's theories have suffered a hailstorm of contempt and ridicule. All rationalism has risen against them. In influential quarters Mr. Schiller, in particular, has been treated like an impudent schoolboy who deserves a spanking. I should not mention this but for the fact that it throws so much sidelight upon that rationalistic temper to which I have opposed the temper of pragmatism. Pragmatism is uncomfortable away from facts. Rationalism is comfortable only in the presence of abstractions. This pragmatist talk about truths in the plural, about their utility and satisfactoriness, about the success with which they "work," etc., suggests to the typical intellectualist mind a sort of coarse lame second-rate makeshift article of truth. Such truths are not real truth. Such tests are merely subjective. As against this, objective truth must be something non-utilitarian, haughty, refined, remote, august, exalted. It must be an absolute correspondence of our thoughts with an equally absolute reality. It must be what we *ought* to think unconditionally. The conditioned ways in which we *do* think are so much irrelevance and matter for psychology. Down with psychology, up with logic, in all this question!

See the exquisite contrast of the types of mind! The pragmatist clings to facts and concreteness, observes truth at its work in particular cases, and generalizes. Truth, for him, becomes a class-name for all sorts of definite working-values in experience. For the rationalist it remains a pure abstraction, to the bare name of which we must defer. When the pragmatist undertakes to show in detail just *why* we must defer, the rationalist is unable to recognize the concretes from which his own abstraction is taken. He accuses us of *denying* truth; whereas we have only sought to trace exactly why people follow it and always ought to follow it. Your typical ultra-abstractionist fairly shudders at concreteness: other things equal, he positively prefers the pale and spectral. If the two universes were offered, he would always choose the skinny outline rather than the rich thicket of reality. It is so much purer, clearer, nobler.

I hope that as these lectures go on, the concreteness and closeness to facts of the pragmatism which they advocate may be what approves itself to you as its most satisfactory peculiarity. It only follows here the example of the sister-sciences, interpreting the unobserved by the observed. It brings old and new harmoniously together. It converts the absolutely empty notion of a static relation of "correspondence" (what that may mean we must ask later) between our minds and reality, into that of a rich and active commerce (that any one may follow in detail and understand) between particular thoughts of ours, and the great universe of other experiences in which they play their parts and have their uses.

But enough of this at present. The justification of what I say must be postponed. I wish now to add a word in further explanation of the claim I made at our last meeting, that pragmatism may be a happy harmonizer of empiricist ways of thinking with the more religious demands of human beings.

Men who are strongly of the fact-loving temperament, you may remember me to have said, are liable to be kept at a distance by the small sympathy with facts which that philosophy from the present-day fashion of idealism offers them. It is far too intellectualistic. Old fashioned theism was bad enough, with its notion of God as an exalted monarch, made up of a lot of unintelligible or preposterous "attributes"; but, so long as it held strongly by the argument from design, it kept some touch with concrete realities. Since, however, Darwinism has once for all displaced design from the minds of the "scientific," theism has lost that foothold; and some kind of an immanent or pantheistic deity working *in* things rather than above them is, if any, the kind recommended to our contemporary imagination. Aspirants to a philosophic religion turn, as a rule, more hopefully nowadays towards idealistic pantheism than towards the older dualistic theism, in spite of the fact that the latter still counts able defenders.

But, as I said in my first lecture, the brand of pantheism offered is hard for them to assimilate if they are lovers of facts, or empirically minded. It is the absolutistic brand, spurning the dust and reared upon pure logic. It keeps no connexion whatever with concreteness. Affirming the Absolute Mind, which is its substitute for God, to be the rational presupposition of all particulars of fact, whatever they may be, it remains supremely indifferent to what the particular facts in our world actually are. Be they what they may, the Absolute will father them. Like the sick lion in Esop's fable, all footprints lead into his den, but *nulla vestigia retrorsum.* You cannot redescend into the world of particulars by the Absolute's aid, or deduce any necessary consequences of detail important for your life from your idea of his nature. He gives you indeed the assurance that all is well with *Him,* and for his eternal way of thinking; but thereupon he leaves you to be finitely saved by your own temporal devices.

Far be it from me to deny the majesty of this conception, or its capacity to yield religious comfort to a most respectable class of minds. But from the human point of view, no one can pretend that it doesn't suffer from the faults of remoteness and abstractness. It is eminently a product of what I have ventured to call the rationalistic temper. It disdains empiricism's needs. It substitutes a pallid outline for the real world's richness. It is dapper, it is noble in the bad sense, in the sense in which to be noble is to be inapt for humble service. In this real world of sweat and dirt, it seems to me that when a view of things is "noble," that ought to count as a presumption against its truth, and as a philosophic disqualification. The prince of darkness may be a gentleman, as we are told he is, but whatever the God of earth and heaven is, he can surely be no gentleman. His menial services are needed in the dust of our human trials, even more than his dignity is needed in the empyrean.

Now pragmatism, devoted though she be to facts, has no such materialistic bias as ordinary empiricism labors under. Moreover, she has no objection whatever to the realizing of abstractions, so long as you get about among particulars with their aid and they actually carry you somewhere. Interested in no conclusions but those which our minds and our experiences work out together, she has no *a priori* prejudices against theology. *If theological ideas prove to have a value for concrete life, they will be true, for pragmatism, in the sense of being good for so much. For how much more they are true, will depend entirely on their relations to the other truths that also have to be acknowledged.*

What I said just now about the Absolute, of transcendental idealism, is a case in point. First, I called it majestic and said it yielded religious comfort to a class of minds, and then I accused it of remoteness and sterility. But so far as it affords such comfort, it surely is not sterile; it has that amount of value; it performs a concrete function. As a good pragmatist, I myself ought to call the Absolute true "in so far forth," then; and I unhesitatingly now do so.

But what does *true in so far forth* mean in this case? To answer, we need only apply the pragmatic method. What do believers in the Absolute mean by saying that their belief affords them comfort? They mean that since, in the Absolute finite evil is "overruled" already, we may, therefore, whenever we wish, treat the temporal as if it were potentially the eternal, be sure that we can trust its outcome, and, without sin, dismiss our fear and drop the worry of our finite responsibility. In short, they mean that we have a right ever and anon to take a moral holiday, to let the world wag in its own way, feeling that its issues are in better hands than ours and are none of our business.

The universe is a system of which the individual members may relax their anxieties occasionally, in which the don't-care mood is also right for men, and moral holidays in order—that, if I mistake not, is part, at least, of what the Absolute is "known-as," that is the great difference in our particular experiences which his being true makes, for us, that is his cash-value when he is pragmatically interpreted. Farther than that the ordinary lay-reader in philosophy who thinks favorably of absolute idealism does not venture to sharpen his conceptions. He can use the Absolute for so much, and so much is very precious. He is pained at hearing you speak incredulously of the Absolute, therefore, and disregards your criticisms because they deal with aspects of the conception that he fails to follow.

If the Absolute means this, and means no more than this, who can possibly deny the truth of it? To deny it would be to insist that men should never relax, and that holidays are never in order.

I am well aware how odd it must seem to some of you to hear me say that an idea is "true" so long as to believe it is profitable to our lives. That it is *good,* for as much as it profits, you will gladly admit. If what we do by its aid is good, you will allow the idea itself to be good in so far forth, for we are the better for possessing it. But is it not a strange misuse of the word "truth," you will say, to call ideas also "true" for this reason?

To answer this difficulty fully is impossible at this stage of my account. You touch here upon the very central point of Messrs. Schiller's, Dewey's, and my own doctrine of truth, which I cannot discuss with detail until my sixth lecture. Let me now say only this, that truth is *one species of good,* and not, as is usually supposed, a category distinct from good, and co-ordinate with it. *The true is the name of whatever proves itself to be good in the way of belief, and good, too, for definite, assignable reasons.* Surely you must admit this, that if there were *no* good for life in true ideas, or if the knowledge of them were positively disadvantageous and false ideas the only useful ones, then the current notion that truth is divine and precious, and its pursuit a duty, could never have grown up or become a dogma. In a world like that, our duty would be to *shun* truth, rather. But in this world, just as certain foods are not only agreeable to our taste, but good for our teeth, our stomach, and our tissues; so certain ideas are not only agreeable to think about, or agreeable as supporting other ideas that we are fond of, but they are also helpful in life's practical struggles. If there be any life that it is really better we should lead, and if there be any idea which, if believed in, would help us to lead that life, then it would be really *better for us* to believe in that idea, *unless, indeed, belief in it incidentally clashed with other greater vital benefits.*

"What would be better for us to believe!" This sounds very like a definition of truth. It comes very near to saying "what we *ought* to believe"; and in *that* definition none of you would find any oddity. Ought we ever not to believe what it is *better for us* to believe? And can we then keep the notion of what is better for us, and what is true for us, permanently apart?

Pragmatism says no, and I fully agree with her. Probably you also agree, so far as the abstract statement goes, but with a suspicion that if we practically did believe everything that made for good in our own personal lives, we should be found indulging all kinds of fancies about this world's affairs, and all kinds of sentimental superstitions about a world hereafter. Your suspicion here is undoubtedly well founded, and it is evident that something happens when you pass from the abstract to the concrete that complicates the situation.

I said just now that what is better for us to believe is true *unless the belief incidentally clashes with some other vital benefit.* Now in real life what vital benefits is any particular belief of ours most liable to clash with? What indeed except the vital benefits yielded by *other beliefs* when these prove incompatible with the first ones? In other words, the greatest enemy of any one of our truths may be the rest of our truths. Truths have once for all this desperate instinct of self-preservation and of desire to extinguish whatever contradicts them. My belief in the Absolute, based on the good it does me, must run the gauntlet of all my other beliefs. Grant that it may be true in giving me a moral holiday. Nevertheless, as I conceive it—and let me speak now confidentially, as it were, and merely in my own private person—it clashes with other truths of mine whose benefits I hate to give up on its account. It happens to be associated with a kind of logic of which I am the enemy, I find that it entangles me in metaphysical paradoxes that are inacceptable, etc., etc. But as I have enough trouble in life already without adding the thought of carrying these intellectual inconsistencies, I personally just give up the Absolute. I just *take* my moral holidays; or else as a professional philosopher, I try to justify them by some other principle.

If I could restrict my notion of the Absolute to its bare holiday-giving value, it wouldn't clash with my other truths. But we cannot easily thus restrict our hypotheses. They carry supernumerary features, and these it is that clash so. My disbelief in the Absolute means then disbelief in those other supernumerary features, for I fully believe in the legitimacy of taking moral holidays.

You see by this what I meant when I called pragmatism a mediator and reconciler and said, borrowing the word from Papini, that she "unstiffens" our theories. She has in fact no prejudices whatever, no obstructive dogmas, no rigid canons of what shall count as proof. She is completely genial. She will entertain any hypothesis, she will consider any evidence. It follows that in the religious field she is at a great advantage both over positivistic empiricism, with its anti-theological bias, and over religious rationalism, with its exclusive interest in the remote, the noble, the simple, and the abstract in the way of conception.

In short, she widens the field of search for God. Rationalism sticks to logic and the empyrean. Empiricism sticks to the external senses. Pragmatism is willing to take anything, to follow either logic or the senses and to count the humblest and most personal experiences. She will count mystical experiences if they have practical consequences. She will take a God who lives in the very dirt of private fact—if that should seem a likely place to find him.

Her only test of probable truth is what works best in the way of leading us, what fits every part of life best and combines with the collectivity of experience's demands, nothing being omitted. If theological ideas should do this, if the notion of God, in particular, should prove to do it, how could pragmatism possibly deny God's existence? She could see no meaning in treating as "not true" a notion that was pragmatically so successful. What other kind of truth could there be, for her, than all this agreement with concrete reality?

In my last lecture I shall return again to the relations of pragmatism with religion. But you see already how democratic she is. Her manners are as various and flexible, her resources as rich and endless, and her conclusions as friendly as those of mother nature.

Bertrand Russell: Mysticism and Logic

Metaphysics, or the attempt to conceive the world as a whole by means of thought, has been developed, from the first, by the union and conflict of two very different human impulses, the one urging men towards mysticism, the other urging them towards science. Some men have achieved greatness through one of these impulses alone, others through the other alone: in Hume, for example, the scientific impulse reigns quite unchecked, while in Blake a strong hostility to science co-exists with profound mystic insight. But the greatest men who have been philosophers have felt the need both of science and of mysticism: the attempt to harmonise the two was what made their life, and what always must, for all its arduous uncertainty, make philosophy, to some minds, a greater thing than either science or religion. . . .

Mystical philosophy, in all ages and in all parts of the world, is characterized by certain beliefs. . . .

There is, first, the belief in insight as against discursive analytic knowledge: the belief in a way of wisdom, sudden, penetrating, coercive, which is contrasted with the slow and fallible study of outward appearance by a science relying wholly upon the senses. All who are capable of absorption in an inward passion must have experienced at times the strange feeling of unreality in common objects, the loss of contact with daily things, in which the solidity of the outer world is lost, and the soul seems, in utter loneliness, to bring forth, out of its own depths, the mad dance of fantastic phantoms which have hitherto appeared as independently real and living. This is the negative side of the mystic's initiation: the doubt concerning common knowledge, preparing the way for the reception of what seems a higher wisdom. Many men to whom this negative experience is familiar do not pass beyond it, but for the mystic it is merely the gateway to an ampler world.

The mystic insight begins with the sense of a mystery unveiled, of a hidden wisdom now suddenly become certain beyond the possibility of a doubt. The sense of certainty and revelation comes earlier than any definite belief. The definite beliefs at which mystics arrive are the result of reflection upon the inarticulate experience gained in the moment of insight. Often, beliefs which have no real connection with this moment become subsequently attracted into the central nucleus; thus in addition to the convictions which all mystics share, we find, in many of them, other convictions of a more local and temporary character, which no doubt become amalgamated with what was essentially mystical in virtue of their subjective certainty. We may ignore such inessential accretions, and confine ourselves to the beliefs which all mystics share.

The first and most direct outcome of the moment of illumination is belief in the possibility of a way of knowledge which may be called revelation or insight or intuition, as contrasted with sense, reason, and analysis, which are regarded as blind guides leading to the morass of illusion. Closely connected with this belief is the conception of a Reality behind the world of appearance and utterly different from it. This Reality is regarded with an admiration often amounting to worship; it is felt to be always and everywhere close at hand, thinly veiled by the shows of sense, ready, for the receptive mind, to shine in its glory even through the apparent folly and wickedness of Man. The poet, the artist, and the lover are seekers after that glory: the haunting beauty that they pursue in the faint reflection of its sun. But the mystic lives in the full light of the vision: what others dimly seek he knows, with a knowledge beside which all other knowledge is ignorance.

The second characteristic of mysticism is its belief in unity, and its refusal to admit opposition or division anywhere. We found Heraclitus saying "good and ill are one"; and again he says, "the way up and the way down is one and the same." The same attitude appears in the simultaneous assertion of contradictory propositions, such as: "We step and do not step into the same rivers; we are and are not." The assertion of Parmenides, that reality is one and indivisible, comes from the same impulse towards unity. In Plato, this impulse is less prominent, being held in check by this theory of ideas; but it reappears; so far as his logic permits, in the doctrine of the primacy of the Good.

A third mark of almost all mystical metaphysics is the denial of the reality of Time. This is an outcome of the denial of division; if all is one, the distinction of past and future must be illusory. We have seen this doctrine prominent in Parmenides; and among moderns it is fundamental in the systems of Spinoza and Hegel.

The last of the doctrines of mysticism which we have to consider is its belief that all evil is mere appearance, an illusion produced by the divisions and oppositions of the analytic intellect. Mysticism does not maintain that such things as cruelty, for example, are good, but it denies that they are real: they belong to that lower world of phantoms from which we are to be liberated by the insight of the vision. Sometimes—for example in Hegel, and at least verbally in Spinoza—not only evil, but good also, is regarded as illusory, though nevertheless the emotional attitude towards what is held to be Reality is such as would naturally be associated with the belief that Reality is good. What is, in all cases, ethically characteristic of mysticism is absence of indignation or protest, acceptance with joy, disbelief in the ultimate truth of the division into two hostile camps, the good and the bad. This attitude is a direct outcome of the nature of the mystical experience: with its sense of unity is associated a feeling of infinite peace. Indeed, it may be suspected that the feeling of peace produces, as feelings do in dreams, the whole system of associated beliefs which make up the body of mystic doctrine. But this is a difficult question, and one on which it cannot be hoped that mankind will reach agreement.

Four questions thus arise in considering the truth or falsehood of mysticism, namely:

I. Are there two ways of knowing, which may be called respectively reason and intuition? And if so, is either to be preferred to the other?

II. Is all plurality and division illusory?

III. Is time unreal?

IV. What kind of reality belongs to good and evil?

On all four of these questions, while fully developed mysticism seems to be mistaken, I yet believe that, by sufficient restraint, there is an element of wisdom to be learned from the mystical way of feeling, which does not seem to be attainable in any other manner. If this is the truth, mysticism is to be commended as an attitude towards life, not as a creed about the world. The metaphysical creed, I shall maintain, is a mistaken outcome of the emotion, although this emotion, as colouring and informing all other thoughts and feelings, is the inspirer of whatever is best in Man. Even the cautious and patient investigation of truth by science, which seems the very antithesis of the mystic's swift certainty, may be fostered and nourished by that very spirit of reverence in which mysticism lives and moves.

I. REASON AND INTUITION

Of the reality or unreality of the mystic's world I know nothing. I have no wish to deny it, nor even to declare that the insight which reveals it is not a genuine insight. What I do wish to maintain—and it is here that the scientific attitude becomes imperative—is that insight, untested and unsupported, is an insufficient guarantee of truth, in spite of the fact that much of the most important truth is first suggested by its means. It is common to speak of an opposition betwen instinct and reason; in the eighteenth century, the opposition was drawn in favour of reason, but under the influence of Rousseau and the romantic movement instinct was given the preference, first by those who rebelled against artificial forms of government and thought, and then, as the purely rationalistic defence of traditional theology became increasingly difficult, by all who felt in science a menace to creeds which they associated with a spiritual outlook on life and the world. Bergson, under the name of "intuition," has raised instinct to the position of sole arbiter of metaphysical truth. But in fact the opposition of instinct and reason is mainly illusory. Instinct, intuition, or insight is what first leads to the beliefs which subsequent reason confirms or confutes; but the confirmation, where it is possible, consists, in that last analysis, of agreement with other beliefs no less instinctive. Reason is a harmonising, controlling force rather than a creative one. Even in the most purely logical realm, it is insight that first arrives at what is new.

Where instinct and reason do sometimes conflict is in regard to single beliefs, held instinctively, and held with such determination that no degree of inconsistency with other beliefs leads to their abandonment. Instinct, like all human faculties, is liable to error. Those in whom reason is weak are often unwilling to admit this as regards themselves, though all admit it in regard to others. Where instinct is least liable to error is in practical matters as to which right judgment is a help to survival: friendship and hostility in others, for instance, are often felt with extraordinary discrimination through very careful disguises. But even in such matters a wrong impression may be given by reserve or flattery; and in matters less directly practical, such as philosophy deals with, very strong instinctive beliefs are sometimes wholly mistaken, as we may come to know through their perceived inconsistency with other equally strong beliefs. It is such considerations that necessitate the harmonising mediation of reason, which tests our beliefs by their mutual compatibility, and examines, in doubtful cases, the possible sources of error on the one side and on the other. In this there is no opposition to instinct as a whole, but only to blind reliance upon some one interesting aspect of instinct to the exclusion of other more commonplace but not less truthworthy aspects. It is such one-sidedness, not instinct itself, that reason aims at correcting. . . .

The theoretical understanding of the world, which is the aim of philosophy, is not a matter of great practical importance to animals, or to savages, or even to most civilized men. It is hardly to be supposed, therefore, that the rapid, rough and ready methods of instinct or intuition will find in this field a favourable ground for their application. It is the older kinds of activity, which bring out our kinship with remote generations of animal and semi-human ancestors, that show intuition at its best. In such matters as self-preservation and love, intuition will act sometimes (though not always) with a swiftness and precision which are astonishing to the critical intellect. But philosophy is not one of the pursuits which illustrate our affinity with the past: it is a highly refined, highly civilized pursuit, demanding, for its success, a certain liberation from the life of instinct, and even, at times, a certain aloofness from all mundane hopes and fears. It is not in philosophy, therefore, that we can hope to see intuition at its best. On the contrary, since the true objects of philosophy, and the habit of thought demanded for their apprehension, are strange, unusual, and remote, it is here, more almost than anywhere else, that intellect proves superior to intuition, and that quick unanalysed convictions are least deserving of uncritical acceptance.

In advocating the scientific restraint and balance, as against the self-assertion of a confident reliance upon intuition, we are only urging, in the sphere of knowledge, that largeness of contemplation, that impersonal disinterestedness, and that freedom from practical preoccupations which have been inculcated by all the great religions of the world. Thus our conclusion, however it may conflict with the explicit beliefs of many mystics, is, in essence, not contrary to the spirit which inspires those beliefs, but rather the outcome of this very spirit as applied in the realm of thought.

II. UNITY AND PLURALITY

One of the most convincing aspects of the mystic illumination is the apparent revelation of the oneness of all things, giving rise to pantheism in religion and to monism in philosophy. An elaborate logic, beginning with Parmenides, and culminating in Hegel and his followers, has been gradually developed, to prove that the universe is one indivisible Whole, and that what seem to be its parts, if considered as substantial and self-existing, are mere illusion. The conception of a Reality quite other than the world of appearance, a reality one, indivisible, and unchanging, was introduced into Western philosophy by Parmenides, not, nominally at least, for mystical or religious reasons, but on the basis of a logical argument as to the impossibility of not-being, and most subsequent metaphysical systems are the outcome of this fundamental idea.

The logic used in defence of mysticism seems to be faulty as logic, and open to technical criticisms, which I have explained elsewhere. I shall not here repeat these criticisms, since they are lengthy and difficult, but shall instead attempt an analysis of the state of mind from which mystical logic has arisen.

Belief in a reality quite different from what appears to the senses arises with irresistible force in certain moods, which are the source of most mysticism, and of most metaphysics. While such a mood is dominant, the need of logic is not felt, and accordingly the more thoroughgoing mystics do not employ logic, but appeal directly to the immediate deliverance of their insight. But such fully developed mysticism is rare in the West. When the intensity of emotional conviction subsides, a man who is in the habit of reasoning will search for logical grounds in favour of the belief which he finds in himself. But since the belief already exists, he will be very hospitable to any ground that suggests itself. The paradoxes apparently proved by his logic are really the paradoxes of mysticism, and are the goals which he feels his logic must reach if it is to be in accordance with insight. The resulting logic has rendered most philosophers incapable of giving any account of the world of science and daily life. If they had been anxious to give such an account, they would probably have discovered the errors of their logic; but most of them were less anxious to understand the world of science and daily life than to convict it of unreality in the interests of a super-sensible "real" world. . . .

Such an attitude naturally does not tend to the best results. Everyone knows that to read an author simply in order to refute him is not the way to understand him; and to read the book of Nature with a conviction that it is all illusion is just as unlikely to lead to understanding. If our logic is to find the common world intelligible, it must not be hostile, but must be inspired by a genuine acceptance such as is not usually to be found among metaphysicians.

III. TIME

The unreality of time is a cardinal doctrine of many metaphysical systems, often nominally based, as already by Parmenides, upon logical arguments, but originally derived, at any rate in the founders of new systems, from the certainty which is born in a moment of a mystic insight. . . .

The belief that what is ultimately real must be immutable is a very common one: it gave rise to the metaphysical notion of substance, and finds, even now, a wholly illegitimate satisfaction in such scientific doctrines as the conservation of energy and mass.

It is difficult to disentangle the truth and the error in this view. The arguments for the contention that time is unreal and that the world of sense is illusory must, I think, be regarded as fallacious. Nevertheless there is some sense—easier to feel than to state—in which time is an unimportant and superficial characteristic of reality. Past and future must be acknowledged to be as real as the present, and a certain emancipation from slavery to time is essential to philosophic thought. The importance of time is rather practical than theoretical, rather in relation to our desires than in relation to truth. A truer image of the world, I think, is obtained by picturing things as entering into the stream of time from an eternal world outside, than from a view which regards time as the devouring tyrant of all that is. Both in thought and in feeling, even though time be real, to realise the unimportance of time is the gate of wisdom.

That this is the case may be seen at once by asking ourselves why our feelings towards the past are so different from our feelings towards the future. The reason for this difference is wholly practical; our wishes can affect the future but not the past, the future is to some extent subject to our power, while the past is unalterably fixed. But every future will some day be past: if we see the past truly now, it must, when it was still future, have been just what we now see it to be, and what is now future must be just what we shall see it to be when it has become past. The felt difference of quality between past and future, therefore, is not an intrinsic difference, but only a difference in relation to us; to impartial contemplation, it ceases to exist. And impartiality of contemplation is, in the intellectual sphere, that very same virtue of disinterestedness which, in the sphere of action, appears as justice and unselfishness. Whoever wishes to see the world truly, to rise in thought above the tyranny of practical desires, must learn to overcome the difference of attitude towards past and future, and to survey the whole stream of time in one comprehensive vision.

The kind of way in which, as it seems to me, time ought not to enter into our theoretic philosophical thought, may be illustrated by the philosophy which has become associated with the idea of evolution, and which is exemplified by Nietzsche, pragmatism, and Bergson. This philosophy, on the basis of the development which has led from the lowest forms of life up to man, sees in *progress* the fundamental law of the universe, and thus admits the difference between *earlier* and *later* into the very citadel of its contemplative outlook. With its past and future history of the world, conjectural as it is, I do not wish to quarrel. But I think that, in the intoxication of a quick success, much that is required for a true understanding of the universe has been forgotten. Something of Hellenism, something, too, of Oriental resignation, must be combined with its hurrying Western self-assertion before it can emerge from the ardour of youth into the mature wisdom of manhood. . . .

Life, in this [evolutionist] philosophy, is a continuous stream, in which all divisions are artificial and unreal. Separate things, beginnings and endings, are mere convenient fictions: there is only smooth unbroken transition. The beliefs of to-day may count as true to-day, if they carry us along the stream; but tomorrow they will be false, and must be replaced by new beliefs to meet the new situation. All our thinking consists of convenient fictions, imaginary congealings of the stream; reality flows on in spite of all our fictions, and though it can be lived, it cannot be conceived in thought. Somehow, without explicit statement, the assurance is slipped in that the future, though we cannot foresee it, will be better than the past or the present; the reader is like the child which expects a sweet because it has been told to open his mouth and shut its eyes. Logic, mathematics, physics disappear in this philosophy, because they are too "static"; what is real is an impulse and movement towards a goal which, like the rainbow, recedes as we advance, and makes every place different when it reaches it from what it appeared to be at a distance.

I do not propose to enter upon a technical examination of this philosophy. I wish only to maintain that the motives and interests which inspire it are so exclusively practical, and the problems with which it deals are so special, that it can hardly be regarded as touching any of the questions that, to my mind, constitute genuine philosophy.

The predominant interest of evolutionism is in the question of human destiny, or at least of the destiny of Life. It is more interested in morality and happiness than in knowledge for its own sake. It must be admitted that the same may be said of many other philosophies, and that a desire for the kind of knowledge which philosophy can give is very rare. But if philosophy is to attain truth, it is necessary first and foremost that philosophers should acquire the disinterested intellectual curiosity which characterises the genuine man of science. Knowledge concerning the future—which is the kind of knowledge that must be sought if we are to know about human destiny—is possible within certain narrow limits. It is impossible to say how much the limits may be enlarged with the progress of science. But what is evident is that any proposition about the future belongs by its subject-matter to some particular science, and is to be ascertained, if at all, by the methods of that science. Philosophy is not a short cut to the same kind of results as those of the other sciences: if it is to be a genuine study, it must have a province of its own, and aim at results which the other sciences can neither prove nor disprove.

Evolutionism, in basing itself upon the notion of *progress*, which is change from the worse to the better, allows the notion of time, as it seems to me, to become its tyrant rather than its servant, and thereby loses that impartiality of contemplation which is the source of all that is best in philosophic thought and feeling. Metaphysicians, as we saw, have frequently denied altogether the reality of time. I do not wish to do this; I wish only to preserve the mental outlook which inspired the denial, the attitude which, in thought, regards the past as having the same reality as the present and the same importance as the future. "In so far," says Spinoza, "as the mind conceives a thing according to the dictate of reason, it will be equally affected whether the idea is that of a future, past, or present thing." It is this "conceiving according to the dictate of reason" that I find lacking in the philosophy which is based on evolution.

IV. GOOD AND EVIL

Mysticism maintains that all evil is illusory, and sometimes maintains the same view as regards good, but more often holds that all Reality is good. . . . The possibility of this universal love and joy in all that exists is of supreme importance for the conduct and happiness of life, and gives inestimable value to the mystic emotion, apart from any creeds which may be built upon it. But if we are not to be led into false beliefs, it is necessary to realise exactly *what* the mystic emotion reveals. It reveals a possibility of human nature—a possibility of a nobler, happier, freer life than any that can be otherwise achieved. But it does not reveal anything about the non-human, or about the nature of the universe in general. Good and bad, and even the higher good that mysticism finds everywhere, are the reflections of our own emotions on other things, not part of the substance of things as they are in themselves. And therefore an impartial contemplation, freed from all pre-occupation with Self, will not judge things good or bad, although it is very easily combined with that feeling of universal love which leads the mystic to say that the whole world is good. . . .

I believe . . . that the elimination of ethical considerations from philosophy is both scientifically necessary and—though this may seem a paradox—an ethical advance. Both these contentions must be briefly defended.

The hope of satisfaction to our more human desires—the hope of demonstrating that the world has this or that desirable ethical characteristic—is not one which, so far as I can see, a scientific philosophy can do anything whatever to satisfy. The difference between a good world and a bad one is a difference in the particular characteristics of the particular things that exist in these worlds: it is not a sufficiently abstract difference to come within the province of philosophy. Love and hate, for example, are ethical opposites, but to philosophy they are closely analogous attitudes toward objects. The general form and structure of those attitudes towards objects which constitute mental phenomena is a problem for philosophy, but the difference between love and hate is not a difference of form or structure, and therefore belongs rather to the special science of psychology than to philosophy. Thus the ethical interests which have often inspired philosophers must remain in the background: some kind of ethical interest may inspire the whole study, but none must obtrude in the detail or be expected in the special results which are sought.

If this view seems at first sight disappointing, we may remind ourselves that a similar change has been found necessary in all the other sciences. The physicist or chemist is not now required to prove the ethical importance of his ions or atoms; the biologist is not expected to prove the utility of the plants or animals which he dissects . . . In psychology, the scientific attitude is even more recent and more difficult than in the physical sciences; it is natural to consider that human nature is either good or bad, and to suppose that the difference between good and bad, so all-important in practice, must be important in theory also. It is only during the last century that an ethically neutral psychology has grown up; and here too, ethical neutrality has been essential to scientific success.

In philosophy, hitherto, ethical neutrality has been seldom sought and hardly ever achieved. Men have remembered their wishes, and have judged philosophies in relation to their wishes. Driven from the particular sciences, the belief that the notions of good and evil must afford a key to the understanding of the world has sought a refuge in philosophy. But even from this last refuge, if philosophy is not to remain a set of pleasing dreams, this belief must be driven forth. It is a commonplace that happiness is not best achieved by those who seek it directly; and it would seem that the same is true of the good. In thought, at any rate, those who forget good and evil and seek only to know the facts are more likely to achieve good than those who view the world through the distorting medium of their own desires.

We are thus brought back to our seeming

paradox, that a philosophy which does not seek to impose upon the world its own conceptions of good and evil is not only more likely to achieve truth, but is also the outcome of a higher ethical standpoint than one which, like evolutionism and most traditional systems, is perpetually appraising the universe and seeking to find in it an embodiment of present ideals. In religion, and in every deeply serious view of the world and of human destiny, there is an element of submission, a realisation of the limits of human power, which is somewhat lacking in the modern world, with its quick material successes and its insolent belief in the boundless possibilities of progress. "He that loveth his life shall lose it"; and there is danger lest, through a too confident love of life, life itself should lose much of what gives it its highest worth. The submission which religion inculcates in action is essentially the same in spirit as that which science teaches in thought; and the ethical neutrality by which its victories have been achieved is the outcome of that submission.

The good which it concerns us to remember is the good which it lies in our power to create—the good in our own lives and in our attitude towards the world. Insistence on belief in an external realisation of the good is a form of self-assertion, which, while it cannot secure the external good which it desires, can seriously impair the inward good which lies in our power, and destroy that reverence towards fact which constitutes both what is valuable in humility and what is fruitful in the scientific temper.

Human beings cannot, of course, wholly transcend human nature; something subjective, if only the interest that determines the direction of our attention, must remain in all our thought. But scientific philosophy comes nearer to objectivity than any other human pursuit, and gives us, therefore, the closest constant and the most intimate relation with the outer world that it is possible to achieve. To the primitive mind, everything is either friendly or hostile; but experience has shown that friendliness and hostility are not the conceptions by which the world is to be understood. Scientific philosophy thus represents, though as yet only in a nascent condition, a higher form of thought than any pre-scientific belief or imagination, and, like every approach to self-transcendence, it brings with it a rich reward in increase of scope and breadth and comprehension. Evolutionism, in spite of its appeals to particular scientific facts, fails to be a truly scientific philosophy because of its slavery to time, its ethical preoccupations, and its predominant interest in our mundane concerns and destiny. A truly scientific philosophy will be more humble, more piecemeal, more arduous, offering less glitter of outward mirage to flatter fallacious hopes, but more indifferent to fate, and more capable of accepting the world without the tyrannous imposition of our human and temporary demands.

Jean-Paul Sartre: Existentialism Is a Humanism

Actually, it [Existentialism] is the least scandalous, the most austere of doctrines. It is intended strictly for specialists and philosophers. Yet it can be defined easily. What complicates matters is that there are two kinds of existentialist; first, those who are Christian, among whom I would include Jaspers and Gabriel Marcel, both Catholic; and on the other hand the atheistic existentialists, among whom I class Heidegger, and then the French existentialists and myself. What they have in common is that they think that existence precedes essence, or, if you prefer, that subjectivity must be the starting point.

Just what does that mean? Let us consider some object that is manufactured, for example, a book or a paper-cutter: here is an object which has been made by an artisan whose inspiration came from a concept. He referred to the concept of what a paper-cutter is and likewise to a known method of production, which is part of the concept, something which is, by and large, a routine. Thus, the paper-cutter is at once an object produced in a certain way and, on the other hand, one having a specific use; and one can not postulate a man who produces a paper-cutter but does not know what it is used for. Therefore, let us say that, for the paper-cutter, essence—that is, the ensemble of both the production routines and the properties which enable it to be both produced and defined—precedes existence. Thus, the presence of the paper-cutter or book in front of me is determined. Therefore, we have here a technical view of the world whereby it can be said that production precedes existence.

When we conceive God as the Creator, He is generally thought of as a superior sort of artisan. Whatever doctrine we may be considering, whether one like that of Descartes or that of Leibnitz, we always grant that will more or less follows understanding or, at the very least, accompanies it, and that when God creates He knows exactly what He is creating, Thus, the concept of man in the mind of God is comparable to the concept of paper-cutter in the mind of the manufacturer, and, following certain techniques and a conception, God produces man, just as the artisan, following a definition and a technique, makes a paper-cutter. Thus, the individual man is the realization of a certain concept in the divine intelligence.

In the eighteenth century, the atheism of the *philosophes* discarded the idea of God, but not so much for the notion that essence precedes existence. To a certain extent, this idea is found everywhere; we find it in Diderot, in Voltaire, and even in Kant. Man has a human nature; this human nature, which is the concept of the human, is found in all men, which means that each man is a particular example of a universal concept, man. In Kant, the result of this universality is that the wild-man, the natural man, as well as the bourgeois, are circumscribed by the same definition and have the same basic qualities. Thus, here too the essence of man precedes the historical existence that we find in nature.

Excerpts from "Existentialism Is a Humanism" in *Existentialism and Human Emotions* by Jean-Paul Sartre. Reprinted by permission of the Philosophical Library Inc., New York.

Atheistic existentialism, which I represent, is more coherent. It states that if God does not exist, there is at least one being in whom existence precedes essence, a being who exists before he can be defined by any concept, and that this being is man, or, as Heidegger says, human reality. What is meant here by saying that existence precedes essence? It means that, first of all, man exists, turns up, appears on the scene, and, only afterwards, defines himself. If man, as the existentialist conceives him, is indefinable, it is because at first he is nothing. Only afterward will he be something, and he himself will have made what he will be. Thus, there is no human nature, since there is no God to conceive it. Not only is man what he conceives himself to be, but he is also only what he wills himself to be after this thrust toward existence.

Man is nothing else but what he makes of himself. Such is the first principle of existentialism. It is also what is called subjectivity, the name we are labeled with when charges are brought against us. But what do we mean by this, if not that man has a greater dignity than a stone or table? For we mean that man first exists, that is, that man first of all is the being who hurls himself toward a future and who is conscious of imagining himself as being in the future. Man is at the start a plan which is aware of itself, rather than a patch of moss, a piece of garbage, or a cauliflower; nothing exists prior to this plan; there is nothing in heaven; man will be what he will have planned to be. Not what he will want to be. Because by the word "will" we generally mean a conscious decision, which is subsequent to what we have already made of ourselves. I may want to belong to a political party, write a book, get married; but all that is only a manifestation of an earlier, more spontaneous choice that is called "will." But if existence really does precede essence, man is responsible for what he is. Thus, existentialism's first move is to make every man aware of what he is and to make the full responsibility of his existence rest on him. And when we say that a man is responsible for himself, we do not only mean that he is responsible for his own individuality, but that he is responsible for all men.

The word subjectivism has two meanings, and our opponents play on the two. Subjectivism means, on the one hand, that an individual chooses and makes himself; and, on the other, that it is impossible for man to transcend human subjectivity. The second of these is the essential meaning of existentialism. When we say that man chooses his own self, we mean that every one of us does likewise; but we also mean by that that in making this choice he also chooses all men. In fact, in creating the man that we want to be, there is not a single one of our acts which does not at the same time create an image of man as we think he ought to be. To choose to be this or that is to affirm at the same time the value of what we choose, because we can never choose evil. We always choose the good, and nothing can be good for us without being good for all.

If, on the other hand, existence precedes essence, and if we grant that we exist and fashion our image at one and the same time, the image is valid for everybody and for our whole age. Thus, our responsibility is much greater than we might have supposed, because it involves all mankind. If I am a workingman and choose to join a Christian trade-union rather than be a communist, and if by being a member I want to show that the best thing for man is resignation, that the kingdom of man is not of this world, I am not only involving my own case—I want to be resigned for everyone. As a result, my action has involved all humanity. To take a more individual matter, if I want to marry, to have children; even if this marriage depends solely on my own circumstances or passion or wish, I am involving all humanity in monogamy and not merely myself. Therefore, I am responsible for myself and for everyone else. I am creating a certain image of man of my own choosing. In choosing myself, I choose man. . . .

To give you an example which will enable you to understand forlornness better, I shall cite the case of one of my students who came to see me under the following circumstances: his father was on bad terms with his mother, and, moreover, was inclined to be a collaborationist; his older brother had been killed in the German offensive of 1940, and the young man, with somewhat immature but generous feelings, wanted to avenge him. His mother lived alone with him, very much upset by the half-treason of her husband and the death of her older son; the boy was her only consolation.

The boy was faced with the choice of leaving

for England and joining the Free French Forces—that is, leaving his mother behind—or remaining with his mother and helping her to carry on. He was fully aware that the woman lived only for him and that his going-off—and perhaps his death—would plunge her into despair. He was also aware that every act that he did for his mother's sake was a sure thing, in the sense that it was helping her to carry on, whereas every effort he made toward going off and fighting was an uncertain move which might run aground and prove completely useless; for example, on his way to England he might, while passing through Spain, be detained indefinitely in a Spanish camp; he might reach England or Algiers and be stuck in an office at a desk job. As a result, he was faced with two very different kinds of action: one, concrete, immediate, but concerning only one individual; the other concerned an incomparably vaster group, a national collectivity, but for that very reason was dubious, and might be interrupted en route. And, at the same time, he was wavering between two kinds of ethics. On the one hand, an ethics of sympathy, of personal devotion; on the other, a broader ethics, but one whose efficacy was more dubious. He had to choose between the two.

Who could help him choose? Christian doctrine? No. Christian doctrine says, "Be charitable, love your neighbor, take the more rugged path, etc., etc." But which is the more rugged path? Whom should he love as a brother? The fighting man or his mother? Which does the greater good, the vague act of fighting in a group, or the concrete one of helping a particular human being to go on living? Who can decide *a priori*? Nobody. No book of ethics can tell him. The Kantian ethics says, "Never treat any person as a means, but as an end." Very well, if I stay with my mother, I'll treat her as an end and not as a means; but by virtue of this very fact, I'm running the risk of treating the people around me who are fighting, as means; and, conversely, if I go to join those who are fighting, I'll be treating them as an end, and, by doing that, I run the risk of treating my mother as a means.

If values are vague, and if they are always too broad for the concrete and specific case that we are considering, the only thing left for us is to trust our instincts. That's what this young man tried to do; and when I saw him, he said, "In the end, feeling is what counts. I ought to choose whichever pushes me in one direction. If I feel that I love my mother enough to sacrifice everything else for her—my desire for vengeance, for action, for adventure—then I'll stay with her. If, on the contrary, I feel that my love for my mother isn't enough, I'll leave." . . .

Thus, I think we have answered a number of the charges concerning existentialism. You see that it can not be taken for a philosophy of quietism, since it defines man in terms of action; nor for a pessimistic description of man—there is no doctrine more optimistic, since man's destiny is within himself; nor for an attempt to discourage man from acting, since it tells him that the only hope is in his acting and that action is the only thing that enables a man to live. Consequently, we are dealing here with an ethics of action and involvement.

Nevertheless, on the basis of a few notions like these, we are still charged with immuring man in his private subjectivity. There again we're very much misunderstood. Subjectivity of the individual is indeed our point of departure, and this for strictly philosophic reasons. Not because we are bourgeois, but because we want a doctrine based on truth and not a lot of fine theories, full of hope but with no real basis. There can be no other truth to take off from than this: *I think; therefore, I exist.* There we have the absolute truth of consciousness becoming aware of itself. Every theory which takes man out of the moment in which he becomes aware of himself is, at its very beginning, a theory which confounds truth, for outside the Cartesian *cogito,* all views are only probable, and a doctrine of probability which is not bound to a truth dissolves into thin air. In order to describe the probable, you must have a firm hold on the true. Therefore, before there can be any truth whatsoever, there must be an absolute truth; and this one is simple and easily arrived at; it's on everyone's doorstep; it's a matter of grasping it directly.

Secondly, this theory is the only one which gives man dignity, the only one which does not reduce him to an object. The effect of all materialism is to treat all men, including the one philosophizing, as objects, that is, as an ensemble of determined reactions in no way distinguished from the ensemble of qualities and phenomena which constitute a table or a chair or a stone. We definitely wish to establish the human realm as an ensemble of values distinct from the material realm. But the subjectivity that we have thus arrived at, and which we have claimed to be truth, is not a strict individual subjectivity, for we have demonstrated that one discovers in the *cogito* not only himself, but others as well.

The philosophies of Descartes and Kant to the contrary, through the *I think* we reach our own self in the presence of others, and the others are just as real to us as our own self. Thus, the man who becomes aware of himself through the *cogito* also perceives all others, and he perceives them as the condition of his own existence. He realizes that he can not be anything (in the sense that we say that someone is witty or nasty or jealous) unless others recognize it as such. In order to get any truth about myself, I must have contact with another person. The other is indispensable to my own existence, as well as to my knowledge about myself. This being so, in discovering my inner being I discover the other person at the same time, like a freedom placed in front of me which thinks and wills only for or against me. Hence, let us at once announce the discovery of a world which we shall call intersubjectivity; this is the world in which man decides what he is and what others are.

Besides, if it is impossible to find in every man some universal essence which would be human nature, yet there does exist a universal human condition. It's not by chance that today's thinkers speak more readily of man's condition than of his nature. By condition they mean, more or less definitely, the *a priori* limits which outline man's fundamental situation in the universe. Historical situations vary; a man may be born a slave in a pagan society or a feudal lord or a proletarian. What does not vary is the necessity for him to exist in the world, to be at work there, to be there in the midst of other people, and to be mortal there. The limits are neither subjective nor objective, or, rather, they have an objective and a subjective side. Objective because they are to be found everywhere and are recognizable everywhere; subjective because they are *lived* and are nothing if man does not live them, that is, freely determine his existence with reference to them. And though the configurations may differ, at least none of them are completely strange to me, because they all appear as attempts either to pass beyond these limits or recede from them or deny them or adapt to them. Consequently, every configuration, however individual it may be, has a universal value.

Every configuration, even the Chinese, the Indian, or the Negro, can be understood by a Westerner. "Can be understood" means that by virtue of a situation that he can imagine, a European of 1945 can, in like manner, push himself to his limits and reconstitute within himself the configuration of the Chinese, the Indian, or the African. Every configuration has universality in the sense that every configuration can be understood by every man. This does not at all mean that this configuration defines man forever, but that it can be met with again. There is always a way to understand the idiot, the child, the savage, the foreigner, provided one has the necessary information.

In this sense we may say that there is a universality of man; but it is not given, it is perpetually being made. I build the universal in choosing myself; I build it in understanding the configuration of every other man, whatever age he might have lived in. This absoluteness of choice does not do away with the relativeness of each epoch. At heart, what existentialism shows is the connection between the absolute character of free involvement, by virtue of which every man realizes himself in realizing a type of mankind, an involvement always comprehensible in any age whatsoever and by any person whosoever, and the relativeness of the cultural ensemble which may result from such a choice; it must be stressed that the relativity of Cartesianism and the absolute character of Cartesian involvement go together. In this sense, you may, if you like, say that each of us performs an absolute act in breathing, eating, sleeping, or behaving in any way whatever. There is no difference between being free, like a configuration, like an existence which chooses its essence, and being absolute. There is no difference between being an absolute temporarily localized, that is, localized in history, and being universally comprehensible.

This does not entirely settle the objection to subjectivism. In fact, the objection still takes several forms. First, there is the following: we are told, "So you're able to do anything, no matter what!" This is expressed in various ways. First we are accused of anarchy; then they say, "You're unable to pass judgment on others, because there's no reason to prefer one configuration to another"; finally they tell us, "Everything is arbitrary in this choosing of yours. You take something from one pocket and pretend you're putting it into the other."

These three objections aren't very serious. Take the first objection. "You're able to do anything, no matter what" is not to the point. In one sense choice is possible, but what is not possible is not to choose. I can always choose, but I ought to know that if I do not choose, I am still choosing. Though this may seem purely formal, it is highly important for keeping fantasy and caprice within bounds. If it is true that in facing a situation, for example, one in which, as a person capable of having sexual relations, of having children, I am obliged to choose an attitude, and if I in any way assume responsibility for a choice which, in involving myself, also involves all mankind, this has nothing to do with caprice, even if no *a priori* value determines my choice.

If anybody thinks that he recognizes here Gide's[1] theory of the arbitrary act, he fails to see the enormous difference between this doctrine and Gide's. Gide does not know what a situation is. He acts out of pure caprice. For us, on the contrary, man is in an organized situation in which he himself is involved. Through his choice, he involves all mankind, and he can not avoid making a choice: either he will remain chaste, or he will marry without having children, or he will marry and have children; anyhow, whatever he may do, it is impossible for him not to take full responsibility for the way he handles this problem. Doubtless, he chooses without referring to pre-established values, but it is unfair to accuse him of caprice. Instead, let us say that moral choice is to be compared to the making of a work of art. And before going any further, let it be said at once that we are not dealing here with an aesthetic ethics, because our opponents are so dishonest that they even accuse us of that. The example I've chosen is a comparison only.

Having said that, may I ask whether anyone has ever accused an artist who has painted a picture of not having drawn his inspiration from rules set up *a priori?* Has anyone ever asked, "What painting ought he to make?" It is clearly understood that there is no definite painting to be made, that the artist is engaged in the making of his painting, and that the painting to be made is precisely the painting he will have made. It is clearly understood that there are no *a priori* aesthetic values, but that there are values which appear subsequently in the coherence of the painting, in the correspondence between what the artist intended and the result. Nobody can tell what the painting of tomorrow will be like. Painting can be judged only after it has once been made. What connection does that have with ethics? We are in the same creative situation. We never say that a work of art is arbitrary. When we speak of a canvas of Picasso, we never say that it is arbitrary; we understand quite well that he was making himself what he is at the very time he was painting, that the ensemble of his work is embodied in his life.

The same holds on the ethical plane. What art and ethics have in common is that we have creation and invention in both cases. We can not decide *a priori* what there is to be done. I think that I pointed that out quite sufficiently when I mentioned the case of the student who came to see me, and who might have applied to all the ethical systems, Kantian or otherwise, without getting any sort of guidance. He was obliged to devise his law himself. Never let it be said by us that this man—who, taking affection, individual action, and kind-heartedness toward a specific person as his ethical first principle, chooses to remain with his mother, or who, preferring to make a sacrifice, chooses to go to England—has made an arbitrary choice. Man makes himself. He isn't ready made at the start. In choosing his ethics, he makes himself, and force of circumstances is such that he can not abstain from choosing one. We define man only in relationship to involvement. It is therefore absurd to charge us with arbitrariness of choice.

In the second place, it is said that we are unable to pass judgment on others. In a way this is true, and in another way, false. It is true in this sense, that, whenever a man sanely and sincerely involves himself and chooses his configuration, it is impossible for him to prefer another configuration, regardless of what his own may be in other respects. It is true in this sense, that we do not believe in progress. Progress is betterment. Man is always the same. The situation confronting him varies. Choice always remains a choice in a situation. The problem has not changed since the time one could choose between those for and those against slavery, for example, at the time of the Civil War, and the present time, when one can side with the Maquis Resistance Party, or with the Communists.

But, nevertheless, one can still pass judgment, for, as I have said, one makes a choice in relationship to others. First, one can judge (and this is perhaps not a judgment of value, but a logical judgment) that certain choices are based on error and others on truth. If we have defined man's situation as a free choice, with no excuses and no recourse, every man who takes refuge behind the excuse of his passions, every man who sets up a determinism, is a dishonest man.

The objection may be raised, "But why mayn't he choose himself dishonestly?" I reply that I am not obliged to pass moral judgment on him, but that I do define his dishonesty as an error. One can not help considering the truth of the matter. Dishonesty is obviously a falsehood because it belies the complete freedom of involvement. On the same grounds, I maintain that there is also dishonesty if I choose to state that certain values exist prior to me; it is self-contradictory for me to want them and at the same state that they are imposed on me. Suppose someone says to me, "What if I want to be dishonest?" I'll answer, "There's no reason for you not to be, but I'm saying that that's what you are, and that the strictly coherent attitude is that of honesty."

Besides, I can bring moral judgment to bear. When I declare that freedom in every concrete circumstance can have no other aim than to want itself, if man has once become aware that in his forlornness he imposes values, he can no longer want but one thing, and that is freedom, as the basis of all values. That doesn't mean that he wants it in the abstract. It means simply that the ultimate meaning of the acts of honest men is the quest for freedom as such. A man who belongs to a communist or revolutionary union wants concrete goals; these goals imply an abstract desire for freedom; but this freedom is wanted in something concrete. We want freedom for freedom's sake and in every particular circumstance. And in wanting freedom we discover that it depends entirely on the freedom of others, and that the freedom of others depends on ours. Of course, freedom as the definition of man does not depend on others, but as soon as there is involvement, I am obliged to want others to have freedom at the same time that I want my own freedom. I can take freedom as my goal only if I take that of others as a goal as well. Consequently, when, in all honesty, I've recognized that man is a being in whom existence precedes essence, that he is a free being who, in various circumstances, can want only his freedom, I have at the same time recognized that I can want only the freedom of others.

Therefore, in the name of this will for freedom, which freedom itself implies, I may pass judgment on those who seek to hide from themselves the complete arbitrariness and the complete freedom of their existence. Those who hide their complete freedom from themselves out of a spirit of seriousness or by means of deterministic excuses, I shall call cowards; those who try to show that their existence was necessary, when it is the very contingency of man's appearance on earth, I shall call stinkers. But cowards or stinkers can be judged only from a strictly unbiased point of view.

Therefore though the content of ethics is variable, a certain form of it is universal. Kant says that freedom desires both itself and the freedom of others. Granted. But he believes that the formal and the universal are enough to constitute an ethics. We, on the other hand, think that principles which are too abstract run aground in trying to decide action. Once again, take the case of the student. In the name of what, in the name of what great moral maxim do you think he could have decided, in perfect peace of mind, to abandon his mother or to stay with her? There is no way of judging. The content is always concrete and thereby unforeseeable; there is always the element of invention. The one thing that counts is knowing whether the inventing that has been done, has been done in the name of freedom.

NOTE

1. André Gide, French writer, 1869–1951; Nobel Prize for literature, 1947. He is best known to English readers for *The Immoralist* (trans. 1930) and *The Counterfeiters* (trans. 1927).

Biographical Notes

ANSELM, SAINT (c. 1033–1109). Italian-born Archbishop of Canterbury. Anselm was noted for his vigorous leadership of the Catholic Church in England against the encroachments of secular authorities. His fame as a philosopher derives from his origination of the ontological argument for the existence of God in the *Monologium* (1070). His other works, such as the *Cur Deus Homo?* (1094–98) established his reputation as one of the founders of scholasticism.

ARISTOTLE (384-322 B.C.). Macedonian student of Plato, and teacher of Alexander the Great. After Plato's death, Aristotle's school of philosophy, called the Peripatetic, was founded in an Athenian gymnasium called the Lyceum. His students' lecture notes, which were edited in the first century B.C., bear the titles of works in virtually all areas of intellectual concern, and include the *Physics, Metaphysics,* and *Organon* (treatises on logic), the *Politics,* the *Nichomachean Ethics,* and the *Poetics.*

BERKELEY, GEORGE (1685–1753). British empiricist philosopher, subjective idealist. Berkeley was known for a remarkable humanitarian effort to organize a school for American Indians in Bermuda. He went to Rhode Island in 1728, where he awaited financial support for his undertaking. This support never materialized, and after three years in America, he returned to Ireland to become Bishop of Cloyne. Most of Berkeley's philosophical works were written during his youth. These include the *Treatise Concerning the Principles of*

Human Knowledge (1710), and *Three Dialogues Between Hylas and Philonous* (1713).

DESCARTES, RENE (1596–1650). First great philosopher of the scientific revolution. Descartes is considered today to be the founder of the rationalist tradition in modern philosophy. In his *Meditations* (1641), from which excerpts are included here, Descartes rejected the received philosophy of his day, and sought to give a new foundation to the search for knowledge. His other works include the *Discourse on Method* (1637), and the *Rules for the Direction of the Mind* (1628?).

DIDEROT, DENIS (1713–1784). French Enlightenment thinker, and editor of the *Encyclopedia,* the greatest compendium of knowledge produced up to that date. Diderot, like most of his colleagues, was an opponent of the French monarchy and of the Catholic Church; many of his writings, therefore, are polemical, as is the dialogue included here. Diderot is also known for his plays and novels, including *The Father of the Family,* and *Rameau's Nephew.*

EPICTETUS (c. 50-138 A.D.). Stoic philosopher, born a slave in Phrygia in what is now Turkey. His thought appears in the *Enchiridion,* included here, and in the *Discourses of Epictetus,* both of which were recorded by his disciple Arrian.

HOBBES, THOMAS (1588–1679). English philosopher known for his mechanistic materialism, which he applied to an understanding of human nature and human society. In his *Leviathan* (1651), he argues for a social contract based upon the natural instinct for survival. His other works include *De Cive* (1642) and *De Homine* (1651).

HUME, DAVID (1711–1776). British empiricist philosopher, born in Scotland. Hume's philosophy constitutes both a radical criticism of the rationalist and empiricist traditions of modern Western thought, and, despite Hume's generally skeptical stance, the starting point of a new tradition in philosophy that was carried forward by the Kantian critical philosophy in epistemology, and utilitarianism in ethics. His greatest work is *A Treatise of Human Nature* (1739), and he is also noted for his *Enquiry Concerning Human Understanding* (1759), *Dialogues Concerning Natural Religion* (published posthumously), and the *Enquiry Concerning the Principles of Morals* (1751).

JAMES, WILLIAM (1842–1910). American pragmatist philosopher. James began as a physician and psychologist (*Principles of Psychology,* 1890), later turning to philosophical issues as a writer and lecturer on both technical and popular subjects. His works include *The Will to Believe* (1897), from which one of our selections is taken, *The Varieties of Religious Experience* (1902), and *Pragmatism* (1907). The last-named work is a compilation of popular lectures, similar in style to our second excerpt from James, "What Pragmatism Means."

KANT, IMMANUEL (1724–1804). Considered to be one of the greatest of Western philosophers, Kant was known for the extreme regularity of his daily habits and the careful and systematic design of his philosophical works. He lived all his life in Königsberg in eastern Germany, where he was a professor from 1770 until his death. His three greatest works set down his "critical philosophy," intended as a synthesis of rationalism and empiricism: *The Critique of Pure Reason* (1781), *The Critique of Practical Reason* (1778), and *The Critique of Judgment* (1790). Our selection in Chapter VI is taken from the *Prolegomena to Any Future Metaphysic* (1783), which presents some of the central conclusions of the first Critique. The selection in Chapter IV is from *Fundamental Principles of the Metaphysic of Morals.*

KIERKEGAARD, SØREN (1813–1855). Danish philosopher and theologian, considered today to be the father of existentialism. He explored moral and spiritual stances toward life in such pseudonymous works as *Either/Or* (1843) and *Stages on Life's Way* (1845). His greatest theoretical works are *Philosophical Fragments* (1844) and *Concluding Unscientific Postscript* (1846), both written under pseudonyms. His last works were written under his own name, and constitute a scathing attack upon the Danish Christian church of his day: *Training in Christianity* (1850) and *The Attack upon "Christendom."*

KRISTOL, IRVING (1920–). American editor, author, and teacher; editor of the political quarterly *The Public Interest,* and Henry Luce Professor of Urban Values at New York University. Author of numerous essays on current political questions. Two collections of his essays have been published: *On the Democratic Idea in America* (1972), and *Two Cheers for Capitalism* (1978).

KURTZ, PAUL (1925–). American philosopher and educator, professor of philosophy at the State University of New York at Buffalo. Paul Kurtz has been the leading exponent of the humanist movement in the United States for many years. His works include *A Current Appraisal of the Behavioral Sciences* (1964), *Decision and the Condition of Man* (1965), *The Fullness of Life* (1974), and *Exuberance* (1977).

LOCKE, JOHN (1632–1704). English philosopher; considered to have founded British empiricism with his *Essay Concerning Human Understanding* (1689), in which he attempts to establish a science of the human mind in opposition to that suggested by the work of Descartes. Because of the politics of some of his high-placed friends, he was forced to spend many years abroad, especially in Holland. Chapter V contains selections from his great political work, *Two*

Treatises on Civil Government (1690), which was to influence the authors of the American Constitution. The selection in Chapter VI is taken from the *Essay.*

MARX, KARL (1818–1883). German philosopher and radical activist; one of the founders, along with his lifelong friend Friedrich Engels, of "scientific socialism," and theoretician of Communism. Because of his political views, Marx was forced to live abroad, first in Paris, and then in London, where he died. Marx helped to organize revolutionary political parties, most notably the International Workingmen's Association (1864), for which he and Engels wrote the *Communist Manifesto* (1848). His chief theoretical work is *Das Kapital* (vol. I, 1867), where he explores the economic structures of capitalism.

MILL, JOHN STUART (1806–1873). English philosopher, economist, and one-time member of Parliament. His remarkable education at the hands of his father, the philosopher James Mill, is described in his *Autobiography* (1873). *On Liberty* (1859), from which excerpts are included here, is considered to be the most fundamental statement of the ideals of modern democracy, and his *Utilitarianism* (1863), also represented here, is an original and influential formulation of that ethical theory. An empiricist in philosophy, his *System of Logic* (1843) developed the principles of inductive logic.

MOORE, GEORGE EDWARD (1873–1953). English philosopher, for most of his life professor at Cambridge, where he edited the influential journal *Mind.* His central concern in philosophy was with ethical issues. His *Principia Ethica* (1903), from which our selection is taken, is considered a classic treatise on the subject.

NIETZSCHE, FRIEDRICH (1844–1900). German philosopher and poet. Because of ill health, Nietzsche abandoned a brilliant career as a professor of classical philology. While in private life he composed such works as *Beyond Good and Evil* (1886) and *Thus Spoke Zarathustra* (1883), in which he attacks contemporary society, religion, and morality for its "decadence." Nietzsche was hopelessly insane during the last eleven years of his life. His works were later used by the Nazis to justify their policies of heroic militarism and racial superiority.

PALEY, WILLIAM (1743–1805). English theologian and moralist. Many of his writings are in defense of Christianity, such as *A View of the Evidences of Christianity* (1794) and *Natural Theology* (1802). We include here his celebrated statement of the teleological argument for the existence of God, taken from the later work. His major book on ethics is *Principles of Moral and Political Philosophy* (1790).

PLATO (c. 427–347 B.C.). Greek philosopher. Most of the problems and concerns that make up the core of philosophical studies can be traced back to Plato as their primary source and impulse. Born to an aristocratic Athenian family, Plato came under the influence of Socrates at an early age, and turned from political to intellectual pursuits. The Academy he founded was the first institute of higher learning in the world. Plato's works, excluding the *Letters,* are all in the form of imaginary conversations between his contemporaries and Socrates. These works include *The Republic* (on justice), *Theaetetus* (on knowledge), *Timaeus* (on the cosmos), and the *Apology* (the trial of Socrates).

ROUSSEAU, JEAN-JACQUES (1712–1778). Influential French political philosopher and writer, whose ideas played a decisive role in the French Revolution. Two of his most important works are *Emile* (1762), a penetrating analysis of education, and *The Social Contract* (1762).

RUSSELL, BERTRAND (1872–1970). British philosopher, essayist, and political reformer, perhaps the greatest thinker to have written in English. His most significant work is *Principia Mathematica* (1910–13), written in collaboration with Alfred North Whitehead, in which the attempt is made to demonstrate the logical bases of arithmetic. His other technical works include *Our Knowledge of the External World* (1914) and *Principles of Mathematics* (1903). Our selection is from the collection of essays published under the title of *Mysticism and Logic* (1918).

SARTRE, JEAN-PAUL (1905–1980). French philosopher, novelist, playwright, and essayist. Sartre is considered to be the leading exponent of the philosophical tendency known as existentialism. His chief philosophical work is *Being and Nothingness* (1943); themes developed there were first given expression in the novel *Nausea* (1938), and later in such plays as *The Flies* (1943), *No Exit* (1944), and *The Devil and the Good Lord* (1951). Long an advocate of socialism, Sartre's theoretical work on politics, the *Critique of Dialectical Reason,* appeared in 1960.

SOCRATES (469–399 B.C.). If philosophy could have a patron saint, it would surely be Socrates, whose incessant probing of the minds of men for answers to the questions of how we should live, personifies the philosophical life. He wrote down none of his ideas, for he claimed to know nothing himself. Our knowledge of Socrates is thus derived from the works of men who wrote about him: Plato, Xenophon, and Aristophanes. His central conviction, however, appears to be that virtue is knowledge, a view that denies the relativism of the Sophists, and sends men who would be virtuous on the search for deeper understanding of the nature of things.

STEVENSON, CHARLES (1908–1979). Contemporary ethical theorist associated with the school of emotivism, long a professor at Yale University and the University of Michigan. Stevenson's works include *Ethics and Language* (1944) and *Facts and Values* (1963).

THOMAS AQUINAS, SAINT (1225–1274). Italian philosopher, considered to be the greatest medieval thinker. He went to the University of Paris as a Dominican friar, and later was named a professor of theology there. In his work, the thought of Aristotle is placed at the foundation of a comprehensive Christian philosophy. His greatest writings are in the form of textbooks on theology; they are the *Summa contra gentiles* (1258–1260), and the *Summa theologica* (1267–1273).

WISDOM, ARTHUR JOHN TERRENCE DIBBEN (1904–). English philosopher, longtime lecturer in moral sciences and professor at Cambridge; active in this country at the University of Oregon (1968–1972). Author of *Other Minds* (1952) and *Paradox and Discovery* (1966).